CAUSATION IN
THE LAW

CAUSATION IN THE LAW

BY

H. L. A. HART

AND

TONY HONORÉ

SECOND EDITION

OXFORD · AT THE CLARENDON PRESS

Oxford University Press, Walton Street, Oxford OX2 6DP
Oxford New York Toronto
Delhi Bombay Calcutta Madras Karachi
Petaling Jaya Singapore Hong Kong Tokyo
Nairobi Dar es Salaam Cape Town
Melbourne Auckland
and associated companies in
Beirut Berlin Ibadan Nicosia

Oxford is a trade mark of Oxford University Press

Published in the United States by
Oxford University Press, New York

First published 1959
Reprinted from corrected sheets of the first edition
1962, 1967, 1973, 1978
Second edition 1985
Reprinted 1987

British Library Cataloguing in Publication Data
Hart, H. L. A.
Causation in the law.—2nd ed
1. Causation 2. Law
I. Title II. Honoré, Tony
340'.11 K240
ISBN 0-19-825474-1 Pbk

Library of Congress Cataloging in Publication Data
Hart, H. L. A. (Herbert Lionel Adolphus), 1907–
Causation in the law.
Bibliography: p.
Includes index.
1. Proximate cause (Law) I. Honoré, Tony, 1921–
II. Title.
K940.H37 1984 346.03'2
83–26836 342.632
ISBN 0-19-825474-1 (pbk.)

Printed in Great Britain
at the University Printing House, Oxford
by David Stanford
Printer to the University

CONTENTS

PART I

THE ANALYSIS OF CAUSAL CONCEPTS

ii   CONTENTS

PART II

THE COMMON LAW

CONTENTS iii

LIST OF ABBREVIATIONS

AC	Appeal Cases (UK 1891–)
AcP	*Archiv für die civilistische Praxis* (1829–)
Act. Jur. (SA)	*Acta Juridica* (Cape Town/Amsterdam, 1958–)
AD	Appellate Division Reports (South Africa: 1910–46)
Ad. & E.	Adolphus & Ellis' Reports (KB 1834–40)
Ala.	Alabama Supreme Court Reports (1820–)
Ala. LR	*Alabama Law Review* (1948–)
ALI	American Law Institute
ALJ	*Australian Law Journal* (1927–)
ALJR	Australian Law Journal Reports (1959–)
Allen	Allen's Reports (Superior Court, Massachusetts, 1861–7)
All ER	All England Reports (1936–)
ALR	American Law Reports annotated (1919–)
ALR	Australian Law Reports (1974–)
Am. Dec.	American Decisions (1760–1869)
Am. Rep.	American Reports (1868–87)
Am. St. Rep.	American State Reports (1887–1911)
Ann. Cas.	American Annotated Cases (1911–18)
App. Cas.	Appeal Cases (UK 1876–90)
App. DC	District of Columbia Appeal Cases (1893–)
App. Div.	Appellate Division of the New York Supreme Court (1896–)
Arch. Ph. Dr.	*Archives de philosophie du droit* (1952–)
Arg. LR	Argus Law Reports (Victoria: 1895–)
Ark.	Arkansas Supreme Court Reports (1837–)
ARSP	*Archiv für Rechts- und Sozialphilosophie* (Berlin, 1933/4–)
Atl.	Atlantic Reporter (USA: 1885–)
Aust. LT	*Australian Law Times* (1879–1928)
BAG	*Entscheidungen des Bundesarbeitsgerichts* (1955–)
Barn. KB	Barnadiston's Reports (KB 1726–35)
BCR	British Columbia Law Reports (1860–)
Beav.	Beavan's Reports (Rolls 1836–66)
Bell	Bell's Reports (Crown 1858–60)
BGB	*Bürgerliches Gesetzbuch*
BGHSt	*Entscheidungen des Bundesgerichtshofs in Strafsachen*
BGHZ	*Entscheidungen des Bundesgerichtshofs in Zivilsachen*
Bing	Bingham's Reports (CP 1822–34)
B. & S.	Best & Smith's Reports (KB 1861–5)
BWB	*Burgerlijk Wetboek* (Netherlands)
C.	Cape Provincial Division (South Africa: 1947–)
Cal.	California Supreme Court Reports (1850–)
Calif. LR	*California Law Review* (1912–)
Cal. Rep.	California Reporter (1960–)
Cam. LJ	*Cambridge Law Journal* (1921–)
Camp.	Campbell's Reports (NP 1808–16)
Can. BR	*Canadian Bar Review* (1923–)
Can. CC	Canadian Criminal Cases (1898–)
CAR	Criminal Appeal Reports (CCA 1909–)
Cass.	Cour de cassation (France)
CB	Common Bench Reports (CP 1845–66)

CC	Code civil (France)
CCR	Reports of Cases determined by the Court for Crown Cases Reserved (1865–75)
Ch.	Chancery Reports (Eng. 1891–)
Ch.D.	Chancery Division Reports (1876–90)
C. & K.	Carrington & Kirwan's Reports (NP 1843–50)
CLP	*Current Legal Problems* (London: 1948–)
CLR	Commonwealth Law Reports (Australia: 1903–)
C. & M.	Carrington & Marshman's Reports (NP 1840–2)
Col. LR	*Columbia Law Review* (1901–)
Conn.	Connecticut Supreme Court Reports (1785–)
Cox CC	Cox's Criminal Cases (1843–1940)
CP	Common Pleas Reports (1866–75)
CP	Code pénal (France)
C. & P.	Carrington & Payne (NP 1823–41)
CPD	Cape Provincial Division (South Africa 1911–46)
CPD	Common Pleas Division (1876–80)
Crim. LR	*Criminal Law Review* (England)
Cro. Car.	Croke's Reports (KB 1625–41)
Cro. Jac.	Croke's Reports (KB 1603–25)
D.	*Digesta Iustiniani Augusti* (ed. Th. Mommsen, Berlin, 1877)
Dalloz A.	*Dalloz Analytique* (France)
Dears. & B.	Dearsly & Bell's Reports (Crown 1852–6)
De G., M. & G.	De Gex, M'Naghten & Gordon's Reports (Ch. 1851–7)
Del.	Delaware Reports
DLR	Dominion Law Reports (Canada: 1912–)
East	East's Reports (KB 1801–12)
EDL	Eastern Districts Local Division Reports (South Africa: 1911–46)
Eq.	Reports of Equity Cases (England 1866–75)
ER	The English Reports (Edinburgh 1932)
Ex.	Exchequer Reports (1866–75)
Ex. Div.	Exchequer Division Reports (1875–80)
F.	Federal Reporter (USA: 1880–)
F.	Fraser's Reports (Scottish Session Cases 1899–1908)
F. & F.	Foster & Finlason's Reports (NP 1858–67)
Fla.	Florida Reports
Ga.	Georgia Supreme Court Reports (1805–)
Golt. Arch.	*Goltdammers Archiv* (Germany)
Gratt.	Grattan's Reports (Virginia Supreme Court 1844–80)
Harv. LR	*Harvard Law Review* (1887–)
H. & C.	Hurlstone & Coltman's Reports (Ex. 1862–6)
HEL	W. S. Holdsworth, *History of English Law* (17 vols., 1903–72)
HL	House of Lords Reports (1866–75)
HLC	House of Lords Cases (HL 1847–66)
HRR	*Höchstrichterliche Rechtsprechung*
ICLQ	*International and Comparative Law Quarterly* (1952–)
Idaho	Idaho Supreme Court Reports (1866–)
IECL	*International Encyclopedia of Comparative Law*
Ill.	Illinois Supreme Court Reports (1819–)
ILTR	Irish Law Times Reports (1867–)
Ind.	Indiana Supreme Court Reports (1817–)
Iowa	Iowa Reports (1892–)

Ir. R. *or* IR	Irish Reports
J. Law Econ.	*Journal of Law and Economics* (1958–)
J. Leg. Stud.	*Journal of Legal Studies* (1972–)
Johns. NY	Johnson's Reports (New York 1806–23)
W. Jones	Wm. Jones' Reports (KB 1620–41)
JP	Justice of the Peace Reports (England)
J. Phil.	*Journal of Philosophy* (1904–)
JZ	*Juristenzeitung* (1951–)
Kan.	Kansas Reports (1889–)
KB	King's Bench Reports (England)
Keb.	Keble's Reports (KB 1661–79)
Kel. J.	Kelyng's Reports (KB 1662–9)
Ky	Kentucky Court of Appeals Reports (1785–)
La.	Louisiana Supreme Court Reports (1809–)
La. Ann.	Louisiana Annotated Cases
La. LR	*Louisiana Law Review* (1938–)
L. & C.	Leigh & Cave's Reports (Crown 1861–5)
Lew. C. C.	Lewin's Criminal Cases on the Northern Circuit (1822–38)
LJ	Law Journal Reports (1832–1949)
Ll. LR	Lloyd's List Law Reports (1919–67)
Ll. R.	Lloyd's Reports (1968–)
LQR	*Law Quarterly Review* (England: 1885–)
LRA	Lawyers' Reports Annotated (USA: 1888–1918)
LT	Law Times Reports (England: 1859–1948)
M.	Macpherson's Reports (Scottish Session Cases: 1861–4)
McLean	McLean's Reports (Seventh Circuit 1829–55)
Man. LJ	*Manitoba Law Journal* (1962–)
Mass.	Massachusetts Superior Court Reports (1761–)
Md.	Maryland Court of Appeals Reports (1658–)
Melb. ULR	Melbourne University Law Review
M. & G.	Manning & Grainger's Reports (CP 1840–4)
Mich.	Michigan Supreme Court Reports (1943–)
Mich. LR	*Michigan Law Review* (1902–)
Minn.	Minnesota Supreme Court Reports (1851–)
Minn. LR	*Minnesota Law Review* (1917–)
Miss.	Mississippi Supreme Court Reports (1818–)
Miss. LR	*Missouri Law Review* (1936–)
MLR	*Modern Law Review* (England: 1937–)
Moo. PC	Moore's Reports, Privy Council (PC 1836–62)
Moo. & R.	Moody & Robinson's Reports (NP 1831–44)
MPR	Maritime Provinces Reports (1929–)
M. & S.	Maule & Selwyn's Reports (KB 1813–17)
M. & W.	Meeson & Welsby's Reports (Ex. 1836–47)
Nat. LF	*Natural Law Forum* (1956–)
NC	North Carolina Supreme Court Reports (1778–)
NE	North Eastern Reporter (USA: 1855–)
Neb.	Nebraska Supreme Court Reports (1860–)
Neb. LR	*Nebraska Law Review* (1922–)
New LJ	*New Law Journal* (England: 1966–)
NH	New Hampshire Supreme Court Reports (1802–)
NI	Northern Ireland Reports
NILQ	*Northern Ireland Legal Quarterly* (1936–)
NJ	New Jersey Reports
NJL	New Jersey Law Reports (1790–)

NJW	*Neue Juristische Wochenschrift* (1947–)
NP	Nisi Prius
NPD	Natal Provincial Division Reports (1910–46)
NS	New Series
NSW	New South Wales State Reports (1901–)
NSWLR	New South Wales Law Reports (1971–)
NSWR	New South Wales Reports (1960–70)
NW	North Western Reporter (USA: 1879–)
NWULR	*Northwestern University Law Review* (1952/3–)
NY	New York Supreme Court Reports (1847–)
NY App.	New York Court of Appeals Reports (1847–)
NYS	New York Supplement (1888–)
NZLJ	*New Zealand Law Journal* (1925–)
NZLR	New Zealand Law Reports (1883–)
OGHBZSt	*Entscheidungen des obersten Gerichtshofs für die Britische Zone*
Ohio	Ohio Supreme Court Reports (1821–)
Okla.	Oklahoma Supreme Court Reports (1890–)
Ont. LR	Ontario Law Reports (–1931)
Ont. R.	Ontario Reports (1931–)
Or.	Oregon Supreme Court Reports (1853–)
Osgoode Hall LJ	*Osgoode Hall Law Journal* (1958–)
Ottawa LR	*Ottawa Law Review* (1966–)
OWN	Ontario Weekly Notes (1909–)
Oxf. JLS	*Oxford Journal of Legal Studies* (1981–)
P.	Probate, Divorce and Admiralty Division Reports (1891–)
Pa.	Pennsylvania Supreme Court Reports (1754–)
Pac.	Pacific Reporter (USA: 1883–)
Pa. Super.	Pennsylvania Superior Court Reports (1895–)
PD	Probate, Divorce and Admiralty Division Reports (1876–90)
Peake	Peake's Reports (NP 1790–1812)
Proc. Aristot. Soc.	*Proceeding of the Aristotelian Society*
QB	Queen's Bench Reports (1891–1901, 1952–)
QBD	Queen's Bench Division Reports (1876–90)
QR	Queensland Reports (1973–)
QSR	Queensland State Reports (1902–72)
QWN	Queensland Law Reporter Weekly Notes (1908–)
R.	Rettie's Reports (Scottish Session Cases 1865–99)
RabelsZ	*Rabels Zeitschrift für ausländisches und internazionales Privatrecht*
Rev. trim. dr. civ.	*Revue trimestrielle de droit civil* (France)
RGSt	*Entscheidungen des Reichsgerichts in Strafsachen*
RGZ	*Entscheidungen des Reichsgerichts in Zivilsachen* (Germany)
RI	Rhode Island Supreme Court Reports (1828–)
Riv. it. dir. pen.	*Rivista italiano di diritto penale*
RMG	*Entscheidungen des Reichsmilitärgerichts*
S.	Sentencia del Tribunal Supremo (Spain)
SA	South African Law Reports (1947–)
SALJ	*South African Law Journal*
SASR	South Australian State Reports (1921–)
SC	Session Cases (Scotland)
SchwZSt	*Schweizerische Zeitschrift für Strafrecht* (Bern)

SCR	Supreme Court Reports (Canada: 1970–)
SE	South Eastern Reporter (USA: 1887–)
Seuff.	Seufferts Blätter für Rechtsanwendung
Sirey	Recueil Sirey de Jurisprudence
SLT	Scots Law Times Reports (1893–)
So.	Southern Reporter (USA: 1887–)
SR	Southern Rhodesian Reports
SR (NSW)	State Reports (New South Wales: 1901–)
Stan. LR	*Stanford Law Review* (1948–)
Stark.	Starkie's Reports (NP 1815–22)
StGB	Strafgesetzbuch (Germany)
Str.	Strange's Reports (KB 1716–49)
St. Tr.	*Howell's State Trials* (London, 1828)
SW	South Western Reporter (USA: 1886–)
Tel Aviv St. L.	*Tel Aviv Studies in Law* (1975–)
Tenn.	Tennessee Supreme Court Reports (1791–)
Tenn. LR	*Tennessee Law Review* (1922–)
Tex.	Texas Supreme Court Reports (1840–)
Tex. Civ. App.	Texas Civil Appeals (1876–92)
Tex. Cr. R.	Texas Criminal Reports
Tex. Crim. App.	Texas Criminal Appeals (1876–)
TLR	Times Law Reports (England: 1884–1952)
TPD	Transvaal Provincial Division Reports (1911–46)
TR	Term Reports (KB 1785–1800)
U. Ch. LR	*University of Chicago Law Review* (1933–)
U. Colo. LR	*University of Colorado Law Review* (1962–)
U. Pa. LR	*University of Pennsylvania Law Review* (1852–)
US	United States Supreme Court Reports (1754–)
Utah	Utah Reports (1855–)
U. Toro. LJ	*University of Toronto Law Journal* (1935–)
Va.	Virginia Supreme Court Reports (1790–)
Vanderbilt LR	*Vanderbilt Law Review* (1947–)
VLR	Victoria Law Reports (1875–1956)
VR	Victoria Reports (1957–)
WALR	West Australian Law Reports (1899–)
Wash.	Washington Supreme Court Reports (1854–)
Wash. ULQ	*Washington University Law Quarterly* (1955–)
W. Bl.	William Blackstone's Reports (KB 1746–80)
Willes	Willes' Reports (CP 1737–60)
Wis.	Wisconsin Supreme Court Reports (1842–)
Wis. LR	*Wisconsin Law Review* (1921–)
WLD	Witwatersrand Local Division Reports (South Africa: 1911–46)
WLR	Weekly Law Reports (England: 1953–)
WN	*Weekly Notes* (England)
W. Rob.	W. Robinson's Reports (Ecc. Adm. P. & D. 1838–50)
W. Va.	West Virginia Supreme Court Reports (1864–)
WWR	Western Weekly Reports (Canada: 1911–)
Yale LJ	*Yale Law Journal* (1891–)
Y. & J.	Younge & Jervis's Reports (Ex. 1826–30)
ZgesHR	*Zeitschrift für das gesamte Handelsrecht und Konkursrecht* (1858–)
ZStrW	*Zeitschrift für die gesamte Strafrechtswissenschaft* (Germany)

TABLE OF CASES

PREFACE TO THE SECOND EDITION

1. PRELIMINARY

Causation in the Law was published twenty-four years ago. It has continued to be read and discussed over that period, and the time has now come, we think, when some fruits of that discussion and of subsequent developments can profitably be drawn together in this second edition. The preparation of the new edition has fallen mainly to Honoré;[1] but we have tried to ensure that at least the principal themes continue to represent our shared view, as they did in the original work.

As the introduction to the first edition explained, the book had two main objectives. The first drew on the philosophical currents of the fifties. At that time the analysis of ordinary language was regarded by many as the key to the clarification of conceptual difficulties. In this spirit we argued that the language of ordinary people and of lawyers both revealed and obscured the truth about causal concepts. What it revealed, when studied in conjunction with the decisions of courts and the judgments of ordinary people, confronted with various sets of facts, was that the concept of causation, as we use it in ordinary life, is not a unitary one. There is rather a central concept of physical manipulation or intervention round which cluster a whole group of concepts, which can in a broad sense be termed causal, and which are related in different ways to the central case. Among these related causal notions are those of providing reasons and opportunities for people to act or occasions for events to occur. There are also negative variants of these relationships. But if ordinary language and legal discourse contain clues to the existence of these various notions and to the analogies and distinctions between them, they also have a pathological aspect. For though in everyday life we make a distinction between conditions and causes and, with the help of the distinction, explain puzzling events, control our environment, and assign praise or blame, we are often unable to explain the principles on which we do so. Hence lawyers in particular, when called upon to give an account of the causal principles they apply, often resort to obscure metaphors of 'causal potency', the 'exhaustion' of causes, and the 'breaking of

[1] Who has been able to draw on his discussion of causal problems in tort law in *International Encyclopedia of Comparative Law* (*IECL*), vol. xi, chap. 7, 'Causation and Remoteness of Damage' (1971).

causal chains'. Here our aim was therapeutic. We tried to translate
the bewildering metaphors into factual terms and to dissipate the
sense of mystification which they engender.

Concern with the analysis of ordinary language, which was a
dominant element in the philosophy of the fifties, has since become
absorbed into a wider conception of philosophy, more receptive to
general theory; but this does not show that our use of the methods
of linguistic philosophy was inappropriate for our purpose. As we
pointed out,[2] courts have continually claimed that it is the ordinary
man's conception of cause that is used by the law and enters into
various forms of legal responsibility. Though in legal contexts that
conception has to be refined and modified in various ways, the
clarification of the structure of ordinary causal statements was and
is an indispensable first step towards understanding the use of causal
notions in the law. This edition therefore adopts the standpoint
that the method we chose remains viable and that the analysis we
propounded by the use of it is still, in its main lines, tenable. In the
first five chapters, therefore, which are devoted to the analysis of
causal concepts, we have changed the text very little, though we have
added references to a type of causal relationship (depriving others
of opportunities) whose full importance, especially in legal contexts,
escaped us twenty-four years ago. Criticism has, of course, been
directed against various aspects of our analysis. We deal with three
of these criticisms in section 2 of this Preface.

The second aim of the book was to evaluate the body of legal
theory which may be designated 'causal minimalism'. According to
this, genuine causal issues are of small importance in settling questions of legal responsibility. In most instances they are confined to
the issue whether the harm would have occurred in the absence of
the wrongful conduct, and even this factual-sounding question is
often answered in a way which owes more to considerations of legal
policy than to any genuine attempt to determine the facts of the
case. It is true that courts appear to take seriously, as raising causal
issues, such further questions as whether the defendant's conduct
was the 'proximate cause' of the harm or whether the harm was 'too
remote'. They speak as if these presented issues of fact suitable, in
an appropriate case, for submission to a jury. But the issues in
question are not, according to causal minimalism, really either causal
or factual and to treat them as such is to 'overload'[3] the causal issue.
They are rather issues of legal policy in disguise, better answered by
asking whether, all things considered, the defendant should be held

[2] 1st edn., p. 8.
[3] Leon Green, 'The Causal Relation Issue in Negligence Law', (1961) 60 *Mich. LR*
543, 544.

liable for the harm which ensued, or, on another view, whether the harm was foreseeable, within the risk, or within the scope of the rule violated by the defendant.

The central part of the book, consisting of Chapters VI to XV, was devoted to assembling and analysing material from which these questions could be tackled, particularly as they arise in common law jurisdictions. The answer we suggested was to reject causal minimalism without embracing causal maximalism. We did not, that is to say, argue that questions of responsibility should be settled solely by reference to causal criteria. Something like this has, it is true, since been advocated by Epstein, but we give reasons in section 5 of this Preface for rejecting his theory. What we attempted, rather, was twofold. We sought, first, as Becht and Miller express it,[4] to put a rational and critical foundation under the case law as it stands. We tried to show that decisions in many jurisdictions stretching over both civil and criminal law were consistent with the view that the courts, whether consciously or unconsciously, apply the causal criteria analysed in the first part of our book. But this does not imply that causal connection, established in accordance with these criteria, is either necessary or sufficient for legal responsibility. It is not necessary because there are forms of legal responsibility (e.g. insurance) which do not require the defendant's conduct to be causally connected with the harm. Neither is causal connection in any of its forms always sufficient for liability. There are many reasons for limiting the extent of responsibility other than the absence of causal connection. The relevance of causal connection, as traditionally understood, to legal responsibility, is, indeed, rather complicated. We have tried in section 3 of this Preface to make the connections between it and the determination of legal responsibility clearer than we were able to do in the first edition. In this way we hope to elucidate the assertion that, as we argued in the first edition, causal connection is *often* a necessary element in responsibility and *sometimes* sufficient. In any event, the cases in which causal connection is necessary and sufficient for liability form a paradigm against which the variations can be more clearly understood. That we are responsible for the harm we cause is a principle that makes an immediate appeal to common moral sensibility. The numerous cases in which we are responsible for harm which we did not cause and not responsible for harm which we did cause can reasonably be seen as variants, though variants of great practical, perhaps of growing, importance.

The other aim of the central ten chapters of the book was to argue, in the interests of clarity, that causal issues should be kept separate

4 Becht and Miller, *The Test of Factual Causation in Negligence and Strict Liability Cases*, 153.

from issues of legal policy, and, indeed, that the latter should be carefully distinguished from one another. Some of these policy issues concern the optimum allocation of social risks, some the scope of particular rules of law, some the impact in a given case of the equities as between the parties. Many of our critics would accept this thesis, or the first part of it, only because, as causal minimalists, they would confine causal issues to *sine qua non* or 'cause-in-fact'. We, on the other hand, wish to maintain the distinction even when the causal issues are defined in the broader, traditional way which we tried to elucidate. In this respect our views, particularly in relation to the civil law of negligence, are diametrically opposed to those of Leon Green and his followers. The latter see merit in making no attempt to discriminate between the various limitations on liability and in appealing, instead, to the feel of the judge or jury for the justice of the situation. It may well be that on this issue little more remains to be said, so far as the principle is concerned. The revision of the central chapters has therefore taken the form of detailed additions and amendments. We have added references to several hundred new cases and taken account of some of the recent writing, though of course without any pretension to completeness. In Chapter VI, besides many alterations of detail, the explanation of 'voluntary' conduct has been modified. In Chapter IX, on foreseeability and risk, we have discussed the ripples created by the decision in *The Wagon Mound*. Chapter XIII, on causing harm in criminal law, takes up the impact on causal problems of some modern medical techniques. Some parts of the book have been more extensively rewritten. This is true in particular of Chapter VIII, sections III and IV (additional and alternative causes); of Chapter XI, where the various limitations on contractual liability are now more sharply distinguished from one another than previously; and especially of Chapter XV, on evidence and procedure. Here we have taken account of decisions about the burden of proof which, if carried through, promise or threaten to revolutionize the law of torts. We have also tried to meet the criticism that our analysis was unhelpful to practitioners[5] by setting out our views about the formulation of hypothetical issues, the division of function between judge and jury, and the presentation of causal issues to a jury.

We have no doubt that many of the theoretical principles defended in this second edition of the book will continue to be controversial among both philosophers and lawyers. None the less we believe that the assembly and detailed discussion of cases in the light of those

[5] E. W. Thode, 'The Indefensible Use of the Hypothetical Case to Determine Cause in Fact', (1968) 46 *Tex. LR* 423, 429 n. 24; Green, op. cit., p. 565 (our apparatus too complex to be reliable when use must be made of it by thousands of practitioners and judges).

principles which the book, as now revised, contains, will illuminate the complex issues at stake in this still-developing area of the law.

2. PHILOSOPHICAL CRITICISMS

Our main reason for presenting a second edition of this book is the development of the law on its subject during the twenty-five years since the first edition was published. There has been a mass of case law and much legal writing and we have, as explained, attempted to incorporate references to this both in the footnotes and in additions to the text. But in this edition we have left largely untouched Chapters I-V, where we presented philosophical analyses of causal concepts. This is not because we think that our views are uncontroversial or are all immune from criticism. On the contrary it is clear that on many issues which our analysis raised there is great division among philosophers of standing. But the philosophical literature on the subject which has developed in the last twenty-five years is vast, complex, and much of it highly technical. No consensus is in sight on many issues relevant to our analysis, notwithstanding the publication in 1974 of the late John Mackie's masterly *The Cement of the Universe*, in chapter V of which many of the main criticisms of our analysis are to be found. These include criticisms of our claim that singular causal statements are implicitly general and require for their defence generalizations which assert regular (even if incompletely known) connections between kinds of events, and criticisms of the contrast we draw between singular causal statements and statements that a person acted for a given reason which, we claim, are not implicitly general.

An adequate consideration of the complex arguments on these and other large issues which are to be found in the philosophical literature would require a book of its own and we have therefore decided not to attempt this but to deal in this edition only with those points of criticism which, if well founded, would clearly call for a revision of what we have said in the first edition about particular cases.

Three such points of criticism emerge clearly from Mackie's book. One of these, which we think well founded, is our failure in the first edition to notice that what is cited as the cause of an outcome may be either a whole concrete *event*, or the *fact* that an event was of a certain type or possessed a certain feature causally relevant to the outcome. It is important for the understanding of these alternative ways of referring to causes in legal as in other cases to realize that in citing a concrete event as a cause we may identify it by a description which includes some causally irrelevant feature. Thus, to take the example from our book discussed by Mackie,[6] where a collision at sea was caused by the negligent navigation of a competent but uncertificated ship's officer we may cite as the cause either 'an uncertificated ship's officer navigating' or 'the fact that the ship's officer navigated negligently'.

In our book we considered this and other such cases under the heading 'When conditions *sine qua non* are causally irrelevant'[7] and there committed ourselves to the misleadingly expressed view that the uncertificated officer's navigating was a *sine qua non* of the collision only in an 'incidental, causally irrelevant sense'.[8] In fact, since 'an uncertificated officer's navigating' is a correct identification of the event which caused the collision (though its being an event with those features was causally irrelevant) it was, as Mackie says, *qua* event, both a cause and a *sine qua non* of the collision. What is true but is too obscurely suggested by our phraseology ('merely incidental, causally irrelevant sense of *sine qua non*') is that the concrete event was a *sine qua non* of the collision in a slightly different sense from that in which the fact that the ship's officer navigated negligently was a *sine qua non* of it. The concrete event was a *sine qua non* because it possessed among others a causally relevant feature, though one not mentioned in its description; whereas the fact that the ship's officer navigated negligently specifies only that causally relevant feature.

Attention to the possibility stressed by Mackie of referring to a cause in either of these two ways (roughly as whole concrete events or as facts) serves to clarify the exposition of a number of features of the law, especially of the law relating to negligence, which have puzzled legal writers. We have therefore incorporated in the present edition references to this important point, for which we are indebted to Mackie.[9]

Mackie has also criticized, and as we think rightly, our treatment, as further examples of a 'merely incidental causally irrelevant' condition *sine qua non*, of certain problematical cases where motorists exceeding the speed limit have become involved in accidents. The cases in question are problematical because the only relevance of the excessive speed in these cases is that it brought the motorist to the scene of the accident at the same time that it was reached by the victim, though at the time of the accident the motorist was no longer speeding or the speeding then made no difference to the outcome. We attempted to defend the view taken by some American courts that in such cases the motorist's speeding was causally irrelevant to

[6] *The Cement of the Universe*, pp. 129–30, 266.
[7] 1st edn., p. 109.
[8] Ibid., p. 112.
[9] pp. lviii–lix, 119.

the occurrence of the accident, but we recognize that our grounds for accepting this view, viz. our belief that no general connection could be traced between the motorist's speeding and the occurrence of the accident, was inadequately explained.

We should have said that in the speeding cases it is important that the excessive speed merely serves to secure that the motorist is present at a given place at a time earlier than would have been the case had he not speeded, and that the risk of an accident occurring at that earlier time is no greater than it would have been had he arrived later. As we stated in our general discussion of 'Change in time and place'[10] such cases are analogous to but not identical with those where a causal connection between a wrongful act and ensuing harm is held to be negatived because the harm is brought about through a conjunction of events which is so unlikely as to constitute a coincidence. The difference between such cases of coincidence and the cases of speeding is that in the latter it is irrelevant whether the conjunction of events required to bring about the accident is likely or unlikely. So long as that conjunction was *no more* likely to occur at the time of the accident than it would have been at the later time, the motorist's speeding is not recognized as a cause of the accident. It is on this ground, consistent with the case law discussed below,[11] that the decision of those courts which have held that a motorist's speeding is not the 'proximate cause' of an ensuing accident may best be supported. Indeed, this ground of decision may be implicit in their expressed view that, where there is no loss of control by the driver and an even greater speed would have avoided the accident, the driver's speeding was not a proximate cause.

It is to be observed that Mackie's contrary opinion that a general connection is traceable in such cases between the speeding and the accident depends on his view that if certain kinds of event (voluntary actions, abnormal events, or coincidences) are treated as negativing a sufficient connection for purposes of legal responsibility, this is not a requirement of any *causal* principle, but reflects only pragmatic or policy considerations.

A substantial issue between Mackie's account of causation and ours with a direct bearing on legal cases concerns the possibility, which we recognize but he does not, that in some cases a cause of an event which has happened may be sufficient in the circumstances but not necessary for the occurrence of the effect, so that it is possible for an effect to be causally overdetermined. Mackie allows, as we do, that in most cases a cause will be both necessary and sufficient in the circumstances for the occurrence of the effect; but he insists

[10] 1st edn., p. 157.
[11] pp. 168–70.

that where (as is mostly the case in legal contexts) we are dealing with past sequences, and the effect has actually happened, statements of the form 'X caused Y' entail that X was necessary in the circumstances for Y but not that X was sufficient for Y. He admits[12] that his view conflicts with our readiness to infer from statements of the form 'X caused Y' statements such as 'Y occurred because X did' and 'since X occurred, Y did', and also that future causal statements ('X will cause Y') or statements of the form 'X would cause Y' imply that X will or would be sufficient in the circumstances for Y.

As far as the law is concerned it is important that Mackie's view entails the rejection of the possibility that an event may be causally overdetermined either because two conditions each sufficient though not necessary in the circumstances for its occurrence are present together (additional causes) or because they are so related that if one had not been present the other would have been (alternative causes). Causal overdetermination of both kinds is, however, recognized by the law and examples of it are discussed in our Chapter VIII.[13]

Both Mackie's argument designed to show that a condition which is only sufficient in the circumstances but not necessary cannot be a cause of an event which has happened and his explanation of cases which are taken to be examples of causal overdetermination are, we think, unsatisfactory. It is striking that in a work generally characterized by rigorous argument Mackie should tender in support of his view on this important point only a speculation as to what we should say if we were faced with two partly indeterministic machines each of which, after the insertion of a coin of a given value, produced a bar of chocolate.[14] One of these machines in normal circumstances always produces a bar after a coin of the right value is inserted, but also occasionally, for no discoverable reason, produces a bar spontaneously, i.e. without the previous insertion of a coin. The other machine conversely never produces a bar unless a coin is inserted but may as a matter of pure chance fail to produce one when this is done. In the first machine the insertion of a coin of the right value is a sufficient but not a necessary condition for the appearance of a bar; in the second it is a necessary but not a sufficient condition for its appearance. Mackie's contention is that we would say of a bar produced by the second machine after the insertion of a coin that the insertion of the coin caused its appearance but would not say this of a bar produced by the first machine after the insertion of a coin.

---

12 Mackie, *Cement*, p. 38.
13 Below, pp. 235–53.
14 *Cement*, pp. 40 f.

Mackie's appeal to our intuitions of what we would say in such bizarre conditions is surely controversial. It seems inadequate support for those conclusions and not to have any weight against the strong connection between being a cause and being a sufficient condition which is reflected, as Mackie admits, in many ordinary forms of causal statement and argument. But it is on these slender grounds that he rules out the possibility of causal overdetermination in either of the two forms (additional and alternative) which the law as well as common sense seems to recognize. Thus, in considering a hypothetical case in which a man is shot by a firing squad and two bullets, either of which would have been immediately fatal, enter his heart at once, Mackie simply says that it is natural to reject the statement 'this bullet caused his death' since no detailed story could discriminate between the two candidates for the role of cause.[15] His conclusion is that only the volley of shots as a cluster of events can be taken as the cause, since it is only that which was clearly necessary in the circumstances. But this conclusion seems either to assume that what is sufficient in the circumstances but not necessary for an occurrence cannot be its cause, or to rest on the inadequate support drawn from the imaginary chocolate-machine examples.

To deal with suggested cases of alternative overdetermination Mackie insists that if we make our description of the effect sufficiently fine-grained and specify it not in general broad terms as, for example, 'death' but describe it as 'death as it came about'[16] it can be shown that in all such cases the cause is necessary in the circumstances and not merely sufficient for the effect. Of course, this move tacitly concedes the importance of the fact that an alternative event may be merely sufficient for the occurrence of the effect; for the need to make the move only arises because the alternative event would be sufficient for the effect described in broad terms.

Certainly, as we ourselves explained in Chapter V of the first edition,[17] some cases may be disposed of by showing that, if a sufficiently fine-grained description of the effect is used, what would otherwise appear, because of the existence of an alternative sufficient cause, to have been only sufficient in the circumstances for its occurrence was in fact necessary. Thus, to take one of Mackie's examples, if a man dies of a heart attack but had he not so died he would have died at exactly the same time of a stroke, if the effect is described broadly as 'death' the heart attack will appear only as sufficient in the circumstances for the effect but not necessary, but if the effect is described narrowly 'as it came about', i.e. with all the

15 Ibid., p. 47.
16 Ibid., p. 46.
17 1st edn., p. 118.

symptoms of a heart attack, it will be seen to be necessary.[18] But not all cases of causal overdetermination by alternative sufficient causes will yield to this treatment. If it is true that A caused an explosion by pressing a button but also that, if he had not pressed it, B would have pressed it at the same time with exactly the same result, then A's pressing of the button was only sufficient in the circumstances, not necessary to the result. No finer description or detailed story could discriminate between the explosion 'as it came about' and as it would have come about had B pressed the button instead of A.

This conclusion can be escaped only if the cause of the explosion is made part of its description. If this were legitimate then there would be no need to appeal to the chocolate-machine argument to show that a cause must be necessary and not merely sufficient for the effect, nor would there be a need for any fine-grained examination of the cases. Causal overdetermination would simply be logically impossible. Mackie does not take this line; wisely, we think, because, if it were taken in such cases as our explosion example, the statement that A's pressing the button was necessary in the circumstances for the explosion would be true only if it were equivalent to the uninformative statement 'If A had not pressed the button, there would not have been an explosion produced by A's pressing it'.

However, as far as the law is concerned there are more general objections to the substitution of any fine-grained description of an effect which will show its cause to have been necessary in the circumstances for its occurrence and avoid the conclusion that it was causally overdetermined. For the law is often concerned with causal outcomes only so far as they satisfy a description of a certain level of generality. If in the explosion example A had caused the explosion in order to kill C and had succeeded in this, it could not be plausibly argued that a murder charge against A could only succeed if some fine-grained description of C's death would show that it differed from what it would have been had B not A pressed the button, so that A's pressing the button was necessary for C's death 'as it came about' and not merely sufficient. Accordingly, we think that for the exposition of the law we need the idea that a cause may be merely sufficient for the occurrence of an effect that has happened, and that there are genuine cases of causal overdetermination.

3. LEGAL RESPONSIBILITY AND LEGAL POLICY

Even sympathetic critics of the first edition accused us of distorting the relation of legal policy to causal issues. Street, for example, though he found our analysis of causation 'excellent' remarked that

[18] *Cement*, pp. 44–5.

'the book takes insufficient account of the blending of questions of causality and policy in judicial decisions on remoteness'.[19] Leon Green found our exposition 'chaste, crisp and clear' but demurred at the 'slight attention' we gave to the administrative, economic, moral, and other environmental factors that have conditioned the decisions of courts.[20] Mansfield thought that at times we were so absorbed with causal concepts that we seriously neglected non-causal factors,[21] especially in the 'mechanical' analysis of decisions in criminal law which turned on considerations 'quite different from causal connection'.[22] Fleming considered that our approach made too little allowance for policy, and thereby, quite unintentionally, fostered the naïve belief that decisions in actual cases are controlled by rules to the exclusion of a host of extra-legal factors.[23] To see whether these criticisms are justified we must try to disentangle the various ways in which legal policy influences the determination of questions of legal responsibility.

Since our book was about causation we took causal issues to be of central importance and touched only incidentally on other aspects of legal responsibility. To deal with the above criticisms, however, we need to say something of the different grounds of legal responsibility, the factors which limit responsibility, the formulation of causal issues in litigation, and the incidence of the burden of proof on such issues. For there are at least these four points at which what may broadly be termed 'legal policy' can impinge on the determination of causal issues. These four points of impact need to be distinguished if the criticism is to be kept in focus. What follows, therefore, is an elementary typology of the grounds of legal responsibility and of the subsidiary issues related to it. We set out the various grounds of responsibility in traditional language, in which causal connection is taken to be something more than the relation of causally relevant condition and consequence (often identified with 'but for' causation). Though we appreciate that many of our critics would prefer to use a different terminology, and that some would wish to restate the whole law of responsibility in terms of risk, we do not think that we beg any questions by adhering for the present to customary legal language which is also that of ordinary speech.

(a) Grounds of legal responsibility.

By 'legal responsibility' we mean the liability of a person to be punished, forced to compensate, or otherwise subjected to a sanction

[19] Street, *Torts* (6th edn.), p. 142.
[20] Green, 'The Causal Relation Issue in Negligence Law', (1961) 60 *Mich. LR* 543.
[21] J. H. Mansfield, 'Hart and Honoré: Causation in the Law', (1963-4) 17 *Vanderbilt LR* 487, 489-90.
[22] Ibid., p. 516; cf. p. 518.
[23] J. G. Fleming, 'The Passing of Polemis', (1961) 39 *Can. BR* 489, 509.

by the law. There are many grounds on which responsibility may be
imposed, and others may be invented in the future, but those which
have featured in legal systems up to now can be classified according
to three criteria. The first is the conduct of the person held responsible: is he responsible on account of his conduct, or is he held
responsible irrespective of his conduct? The second is causal connection. When a person is to be held responsible for harm, must it be
shown that his conduct caused the harm? Or is it sufficient that he
occasioned it, e.g. by providing an opportunity for the harm to be
done?[24] Or can he be held responsible in the absence of any such connection? The third is fault. Can a person be held responsible only when
he is shown to have been at fault or can he be held responsible even in
the absence of fault, i.e. on the basis of strict liability? The criss-
crossing of these three considerations yields at least seven possible
grounds, or combined grounds, of legal responsibility, as follows:

(i) *Conduct, causation, and fault must be shown.* The person to
be held responsible (in current usage, which we shall adopt, the
'defendant', whether the proceedings are civil or criminal) must be
shown to have conducted himself in a way which entails fault and
thereby to have caused the harm for which he is to be punished or
made to compensate. Let us take 'fault' to mean the violation of a
standard set by the law compliance with which is within the capacity
of the person subject to it or, at the minimum, of an average person.
Sometimes such violation will be by conduct accompanied by an
intention to cause the harm complained of. At other times an unintentional fault, such as a negligent act, will suffice. Either sort of
fault may involve a positive act or an omission, for example the
negligent omission to perform a duty. The required causal connection between fault and harm is to be assessed according to the
common-sense criteria explained in our book. It is not enough that
it should have 'occasioned' the harm. Thus the required causal
connection is excluded by a 'superseding cause', '*novus actus
interveniens*', etc. This form of liability is found in criminal law, in
tort, and in certain types of contract. An example of the latter is the
failure of a doctor, in breach of contract, to exhibit reasonable
medical skill.

(ii) *Conduct and causation must be shown.* It must be clear that the
defendant's conduct caused the harm but he need not be shown to
have been at fault: he is strictly liable for harm caused by his conduct.
The conduct may as before consist of a positive act or an omission.
It must be shown to have caused the harm complained of on ordinary
causal criteria. The fact that the liability is strict, however, often

[24] On the difference between 'causing' and related notions such as 'occasioning' see
pp. 59-61, 194-204, 374-6.

influences the description of the defendant's conduct and so the ease
with which causal connection can be proved. For example, it is easier
to show that harm was caused by storing or using explosives (which
may entail strict liability under *Rylands* v. *Fletcher* or for ultrahazardous activities) than by storing or using them without due care,
which will amount to negligence and constitute an instance of fault.

(iii) *Conduct occasioning harm and fault must be shown.* The defendant need not be shown to have caused the harm complained of;
it is sufficient that by his conduct he 'occasioned' it.[25] But he must in
addition be shown to have been at fault. An example is the motorist
who leaves his car unlocked with the key in the ignition and who
is, in some states, held liable to a victim run over by a thief who
steals the car and drives it away.[26] The motorist is negligent in thus
facilitating the theft and so is guilty of fault. In addition his conduct
is a causally relevant condition of the harm to the victim. This
relevance can in many cases, as here, be tested by the *sine qua non*
or 'but for' rule. Provided this connection is shown the defendant is
liable even if the harm comes about through the intervention of
something which would ordinarily count as a 'superseding cause',
'*novus actus interveniens*', or an event of '*force majeure*'. The defendant who negligently leaves petrol in a barge is liable when it is
struck by lightning,[27] though that would ordinarily be accounted an
'act of God' or *force majeure*, and would negative causal connection
in the ordinary sense.

(iv) *Conduct occasioning harm must be shown.* The defendant must
have occasioned the harm complained of by his conduct but need
not be shown to have been at fault. For example, a seller of goods is
in breach of contract in not delivering the goods on the agreed date.
This may not be due to any fault on his part. He is strictly liable for
non-delivery, and he may have to bear the risk of the goods perishing
provided that they would not have perished had he delivered them
on time. He is liable for the harm occasioned by his breach of
contract, even if the cause of their perishing is something (e.g. an
unprecedented flood) which would ordinarily count as a 'superseding
cause'.

In this and the preceding type of case it may be said that the
defendant bears the risk of a certain type of harm being occasioned
by his conduct. The term 'risk liability' or 'liability based on risk' is,
however, more naturally applied to cases in which there is strict
liability (see (ii) above) for harm caused by the defendant's conduct,
e.g. by storing explosives on his land. Such conduct, though it entails

[25] Above, n. 24.
[26] Below, pp. 203-4.
[27] Below, p. 201.

a high degree of risk to others, is not forbidden; hence it cannot be said to constitute fault.

(v) *Conduct and fault must be shown.* The defendant is liable for conduct which constitutes fault but the conduct need not be shown to have caused or occasioned harm. This type of liability is commonest in criminal law. An example is the offence of knowingly possessing a dangerous weapon.

(vi) *Conduct alone need be shown.* The defendant is liable for conduct which need not be shown either to constitute fault or to have caused or occasioned harm. An example, again taken from criminal law, is the liability of the seller of adulterated food, who may be convicted though he did not know that the food was adulterated and though nobody was harmed by consuming it.

(vii) *Neither fault nor conduct causing or occasioning harm need be shown.* The liability of the defendant is based on insurance or guarantee. His conduct need not be shown to have caused or occasioned the harm for which he has to pay, and he is not at fault. One who guarantees the payment of another's debt is liable if the debt is not paid no matter what the reason for the non-payment. It is not his duty, but that of the other person, the principal debtor, to pay the debt. One who insures against accident or marine perils or unemployment is liable, again, though he does not himself cause or occasion the accident or shipwreck or loss of employment. That is not to deny that insurance liability may also raise causal issues. It very often does so; but the issues are those which arise when it is necessary to decide, for example, whether a given loss was caused by accident, or by a marine peril, or by something else. Since the risks in insurance policies and schemes are usually broadly defined, it is often relatively easy to prove that the harm is causally connected with the insured risk. Sometimes, as in the case of third-party liability insurance, the issue of causal connection with human conduct will arise at one remove. The insurer will be liable if it is shown that an insured motorist was legally liable for harm to a third party because he caused the harm by his fault. But it is not the conduct of the insurer that is in issue. And certainly insurance can be framed in such a way as to avoid causal issues altogether. For instance, people can be insured against sickness occurring within a certain period. Unemployment insurance comes close to this, though causal issues may arise as to whether the lack of employment was self-inflicted.

It is possible to combine grounds of responsibility into mixed types. Thus, vicarious liability in tort law is a form of liability in which the employer is made liable for providing the employee with an opportunity to inflict harm on others; but it has generally to be shown that the employee himself is at fault (and indeed is legally liable) to the other person for the harm inflicted. Vicarious liability is therefore a combination of (i) and (iv) above. But whatever ground or combination of grounds is selected, the choice will have a bearing on the causal issues which are relevant to responsibility and on how easy or difficult it is to prove the required causal connection, if any. The determination of the ground of responsibility falls within the province of legislators and, in default of clear guidance from them, of judges. Their enactments or decisions therefore determine what type of connection, if any, has to be shown (e.g. 'causing' or only 'occasioning' or neither); whether it must be shown between defendant's conduct or some other event (e.g. accident, marine perils, his employee's fault) and the harm. They also determine how the defendant's conduct is to be described in order to settle whether the required connection exists.

Nothing in our book casts doubts on the importance of these policy decisions. Our analysis of causality only comes into play once a decision has been reached by the legislator or judge that makes causal issues relevant. Furthermore, even in regard to causal issues, the book concentrates mainly on causal connection between a defendant's conduct and the subsequent harm and says little about such issues as they arise in private or social insurance law.

(b) The limits of legal responsibility.

All forms of legal responsibility have a limited scope. Rules of law determine expressly or implicitly what is the harm for which punishment or compensation may be exacted, and how it must be connected with the defendant's conduct in order for responsibility to arise. The definition of a crime normally determines the harm (e.g. death) for which the defendant may be punished. When the ground of responsibility is insurance or guarantee the contract of insurance or guarantee determines its limits. When there is civil responsibility for causing or occasioning harm the outer limit of responsibility is set by the need for the harm to have been caused or occasioned, as the case may be, by the defendant's conduct. But, particularly in civil law, there are other limits set by courts which are not inherent, or at least not obviously inherent, in the definition of the responsibility or in the grounds of responsibility we have listed. The fixing of these is a matter of legal policy. Legal policy therefore comes into play at a second stage, after the initial choice of the ground of responsibility has been made by the legislature or judge. These limits are, in our view, non-causal, and our book argues at length and in detail the case for keeping them separate from the causal limits already mentioned.

How are these non-causal limits settled? The sources on which legislators and judges can draw for this purpose are surprisingly limited. Even taking account of different branches of the law and different legal systems, it hardly seems possible to find more than three notions (together with their species and variants), besides the causal ones, which are employed by courts and theorists for this purpose. Taking all the limiting factors, causal and non-causal, together, this yields five notions, details of which are discussed by Honoré in the chapter on 'Causation and Remoteness of Damage' in the *International Encyclopedia of Comparative Law* (1971).[28] That discussion concerns tort law, but the limiting ideas are of general application. The five ideas are those of necessity, later intervention,[29] probability, the scope of the rule of law in question, and equity. The first two of these count from a common-sense point of view as 'causal', if we take 'occasioning harm' as being in a broad sense a causal relationship. The last three count as non-causal.

The notion of necessity draws attention to the fact that, for all types of responsibility *for harm* ((a) (i) to (a) (iv) above), except that based on insurance or guarantee, the defendant's conduct must at least have occasioned the harm. For that to be the case the conduct must be a causally relevant condition of the harm, i.e. normally a necessary element in a complex of conditions together sufficient to produce it. The relevant sense of 'necessary' is discussed in Chapter V of our book. This requirement can often be tested in a straightforward case by asking whether the harm would have occurred in the absence of the wrongful conduct. The 'but for' or *sine qua non* rule reflects this method of testing the connection; the exceptions testify to the fact that it is not always adequate.

The second limiting idea, that of later intervention, comes into play in cases which fall under (a) (i) and (a) (ii) above, when the defendant's conduct, whether or not it constitutes fault, must be shown to have caused, and not merely to have occasioned the harm. The basic notion is that after the supposed cause there intervenes, as a condition of the upshot, something which shares with the supposed cause those characteristics by which we distinguish causes from conditions, as explained in Chapter II of our book.

In regard to legal responsibility the requirement of causal connection can be most simply expressed in the form that wrongful conduct is not regarded as having caused harm when there has intervened between conduct and harm something (voluntary or abnormal conduct or abnormal event) which is regarded as displacing the original

[28] Vol. xi, chap. 7.
[29] In *IECL*, xi, chap. 7 the term 'explanatory force' was used, but it is perhaps better to regard the notion of intervention as primitive and its role in relation to explanation and the attribution of responsibility as derivative.

conduct both as an explanation of the harm and, when later conduct is in issue, as a focus of responsibility. In such cases the defendant is not regarded as having caused the harm and so is not liable for causing harm, when that is a ground of responsibility. His conduct is thought of simply as part of the circumstances in which some other cause operated. The battery of metaphors found in the law in causal contexts, which at first sight seem so bizarre, are to be explained as reflections of this common-sense idea that where the analogy with manipulation is too remote the conduct cannot be regarded as causing the harm. It is this that underlies the language of direct, efficient, and potent causes on the one hand, and on the other of causes that are exhausted, come to an end, are superseded; of chains that are broken and new causes that intervene. Of course, it must be borne in mind that, though for want of causal connection the grounds of liability listed under (i) and (ii) above are excluded in such cases, the defendant may still be liable under (iii), (iv), or (vii) above for occasioning the harm or as an insurer of it.

Apart from these two limiting notions (necessity, later intervention), which may broadly be treated as causal, there are three non-causal notions which can be used to limit the extent of responsibility. These are the notions of probability, the scope of legal rules, and equity. Before dealing with them individually, it is important to note that they may be and in practice are employed *in addition to* the causal limitations, not in substitution for them. Thus, it is commonly held in the English civil law of negligence that harm is 'too remote' if *either* it was not caused by the wrongful conduct *or* it was in the relevant sense unforeseeable. In the law of contract damages for breach are not recoverable if *either* the breach did not cause the harm claimed *or* that harm was not in the contemplation of the parties at the time of contracting, i.e. was not within the scope of the law of contractual damages. The same is true of the non-causal limitations *inter se*. They too may be and often are employed cumulatively. Thus, an employee cannot sue for injury caused by his employer's breach of statutory duty if *either* that type of injury was not what the statute was intended to guard against *or*, though it was, the employee is morally disentitled to complain of the employer's breach because the employer is in default only because of the employee's own breach of the statute.[30] A claim for breach of contract is ruled out if the harm was *either* outside the contemplation of the parties at the time of contracting *or* came about in a freakishly unforeseeable way. Of course, courts need not have recourse to all these non-causal types of limitation in a particular case. But they

[30] Green, op. cit., p. 545.

are often free to take them into account, and sound legal policy frequently impels them to do so.

Of the three non-causal notions listed probability, in its many varieties, is the most popular both with courts and writers. Particularly in civil law, harm is often held to be irrecoverable if it was not foreseeable, or if the apparent risk of its occurrence was not sufficiently great given the defendant's conduct, or was not sufficiently increased by the defendant's conduct, or if the conduct was not 'adequate' to produce it. We analyse these suggested limitations and the theories which seek to justify them in Chapters IX and XVII of the book. The two other factors, the scope of the legal rule in issue (*Normzweck, Schutzbereich*) and fairness or equity between the parties to the litigation, are more briefly discussed in Chapter X.

This scale of discussion does not reflect our view of the relative importance of these notions from the viewpoint of sound legal policy. On the contrary, sound legal policy seems to us to require that courts should limit liability for harm by carefully fixing the scope of the rule violated and to a lesser extent by paying attention to simple considerations of equity.[31] Very often a particular statutory or common law rule has a quite limited purpose which courts can fix or discover. Even when the rule is intended to protect others against a wide variety of harms there still remain losses which ought properly to be borne by the victim, or which he can be expected to cover by insurance, or for which he can preferably recoup himself from collateral sources, other than the wrongdoer. These losses fall within what the Germans call the victim's own sphere of risk (*Gefahrbereich*).[32] Examples are the danger that one may have to defend oneself on a criminal charge; that one may suffer the economic and psychological side-effects of physical injuries inflicted on others; and other matters which count among the ordinary chances of life which we reckon to meet from our own resources. But even within those interests which it is reasonable for the law to seek to protect there is room for recognition by the courts of degrees of importance. The safety of persons surely ought to have a higher priority than the safety of property. One of the welcome developments of recent years has been the greater awareness which courts have shown of the importance of classifying and grading interests when they are setting the bounds of legal protection. If we do not deal *in extenso* with these matters in the book it is because the subject of the optimum allocation of risks in a society would require, if justice were to be done to the complexities of the problem, one or more full-length studies of its own.

[31] Below, p. 217 n. 58.
[32] e.g. U. Huber, 'Normzwecktheorie und Adäquanztheorie', *JZ* 1969, 677, 683; below, pp. 476–8.

We are certainly less enthusiastic about the use of foreseeability, risk, and the other notions connected with probability as techniques for limiting responsibility. They often tend in practice to function simply as formulae under cover of which common-sense causal notions or those derived from the scope of the rule violated are applied; or simply as pegs on which the judge can hang any decision he likes. They are apt, as we explain in Chapter IX, to mislead the unwary into thinking that the decision is morally justifiable because the same criteria are (apparently) being used both to fix responsibility and to determine its extent. But, while we think that some scepticism is called for in the assessment of these popular notions, that is not to deny that they have a proper use. They may sensibly be used in tort law to *extend* liability to harm of a foreseeable sort which defendant's conduct occasions even though the conduct does not cause the harm. They can be used to exclude liability for freakish sequences of events, especially when the causal processes involved are very different from those that could have been envisaged *ab initio*. But they do not provide the sort of all-purpose tool kit which many courts and writers think they do. Indeed, 'it would be unsound to adopt any theory of causation if by it a court was committed to the view that there is only one ground on which a [tortfeasor's] responsibility can properly be limited. The real function of the theories is rather to emphasize a particular technique of limitation while not rigidly excluding the use of others.'[33] But courts and writers do not always recognize this, and legal rules sometimes prevent their doing so overtly. This leads to a fusion of causal and non-causal issues, and so to a third point of impact between considerations of legal policy and the resolution of causal issues.

(c) The formulation of causal issues in litigation.

It is quite often the case that statutes or common law rules are so framed as to make it difficult for courts to take account of the variety of grounds, explained above, on which responsibility may be limited. For example, the civil law of negligence is often formulated in the following way: the plaintiff must establish that the defendant owed him a duty of care, that he broke that duty, and that the harm suffered by the plaintiff is not too remote a consequence of the breach. In the alternative version popular in America there must be a duty, the defendant must have been negligent, and the negligence must be the proximate cause of the harm complained of. If the law is stated in this way then it becomes difficult for the court to fit in

[33] Honoré, *IECL*, xi, chap. 7-105.

limitations which are based on the scope of the law of negligence, for example that certain types of harm (e.g. mental distress from feelings of guilt) are not meant to be compensated in actions for negligence. Are we to say that, whereas there was a duty not to cause the plaintiff other sorts of harm, there was no duty not to cause him this type of harm? That is a possible analysis, but it implicitly adds to the requirement of breach of duty to the plaintiff a further requirement that the breach of duty must relate to a particular type of harm. In substance this would be a way of saying that the type of harm must be within the scope of the rule violated. But, since this notion does not fit easily into the conventional analysis of tort liability for negligence, courts often tend instead to hold that the harm is 'too remote' or 'not proximate'.

In that way they amalgamate the issue of the scope of the law of negligence with ordinary causal issues. The court or jury must then deal, under the rubric of remoteness or proximity, both with the appropriate scope of the law of negligence and with the question whether on this occasion defendant's breach of duty caused the harm complained of. This amalgamation is undesirable, because the scope issues raise questions of law, and the causal issues questions of fact. The former are more appropriate for the judge to decide, the latter for the jury or trier of fact. Much the same is true of the interplay between limitations based on probability and causal limitations. An English judge has spoken of 'remoteness in the sense of causal connection' (as opposed to foreseeability).[34] It would surely be better, in the interests of clarity, not to use the same rubric to cover both.

When Street, then, speaks of our book taking 'insufficient account of the blending of questions of causality and policy in judicial decisions on remoteness',[35] he may be right in the sense that our account does not accurately reproduce the amalgam which so often obscures decisions or jury directions in common law countries. Our purpose was rather to disentangle causal limitations and in doing so to draw the line between them and policy limitations in the way marked out by common sense, rather than by modern theories which seek to confine causal issues to the question whether defendant has occasioned harm and which use the 'but for' or 'substantial factor' test for the purpose.

Still, there is little doubt that the amalgamation of causal and non-causal issues under headings such as 'remoteness' and 'proximity' does afford a further point at which legal policy can impinge on the decision of causal issues. It encourages habits of thought, much as we may deplore them, which tend to assimilate the different

[34] *Monarch Steamship Co.* v. *Karlshamns Oljefabriker* [1949] AC 196, 225.
[35] *Torts* (6th edn.), p. 142.

limits on responsibility. As part of this process, causal limitations may be seen as just another set of policy limitations, which incorporate some intuitive notion of the reasonable limits of responsibility. Indeed, this mode of thinking has its explicit advocates, in Green and his followers, who go on to argue that, if this amalgamation is to take place, the least specific formula possible should be employed in setting out the issue to be decided. Hence the charm Green finds in the notion of foreseeability (and equally of risk) which is delightfully apt, he avers, to stimulate the sense of judgment.[36] Indeed, it cannot be denied that *if* all the limits of responsibility are to be reduced to a single formula, the emptier the formula the better. But to accept the demand for a single 'neat formula'[37] is surely a *pis aller*. Is it not this monism, rather than attachment to causal notions, that constitutes the juristic theory of the Stone Age which we ought by now to have outgrown? And it is hardly an improvement, as is now fashionable in some southern states of the USA, to substitute a duty-risk analysis for the previous duty-proximate cause analysis.[38] The new formulation is just as impoverished, and just as apt to obscure the genuine issues, as the old one.

(d) The incidence of the burden of proof.

The fourth channel through which legal policy flows into the causal river is that of the incidence of the burden of proof on causal issues. This has become of increasing significance during the last twenty-five years. As will be seen from Chapter XV, the rules of the burden of proof, and of presumptions, can be manipulated so as to make it more or less easy to prove causal connection or in effect to dispense with proof of anything more than a *possible* causal connection between conduct and harm. When this is done, under the doctrine of 'material contribution', 'market share liability', or the like, the effect is that the defendant is made to insure the plaintiff against a defined sort of harm which is known to be of the type that is *often* or *sometimes* causally connected with the defendant's activity, though the connection is not demonstrated in the particular case. The defendant remains theoretically free to disprove causal connection in these cases, but in practice he cannot do so. Hence in effect the ground of responsibility is no longer that of causing harm by one's conduct, with or without fault. Nor is the ground even that of

36 Green, '*The Wagon Mound No. 2*: Foreseeability Revised', (1967) *Utah LR* 197 (foreseeability a 'delightful and useful fiction' which 'serves in every case to call forth a fresh judgment').
37 Green, 'Foreseeability in Negligence Law', (1961) *Col. LR* 1401, 1402.
38 'Duty-Risk Experience in Louisiana Tort Law', (1977) 23 *Loyola LR* 523.

occasioning harm by one's conduct. For though liability may be imposed because the defendant has by his activity (e.g. the sale of dangerous drugs), created the risk of harm of a certain type (e.g. cancer), the plaintiff need not show that defendant's conduct has even occasioned the harm, viz. that the harm would not have occurred without it.

It is true that if the defendant could disprove causal connection he would escape liability; but such disproof is, in certain instances, virtually impossible. How can a defendant manufacturer show that it was not his product that, many years ago, the plaintiff's mother bought and used when she was pregnant, with harmful consequences to the plaintiff?[39] This type of responsibility is close to insurance against the deleterious consequences of an activity in which the defendant engages, perhaps along with many others. The rules about the burden of proof on causal issues can therefore in effect transform a causal ground of liability into a non-causal one. This is no more than a dramatic instance of a familiar phenomenon. For instance, when the doctrine of *res ipsa loquitur* is held to transfer the burden of persuasion in a case of negligence, the effect is often to transform fault liability into strict liability, since the defendant has no way of discharging the burden cast upon him. Again, when a court adopts a presumption that, if a defendant had supplied a safety appliance, the victim would have used it to good effect, it is giving effect to a policy which in practice makes a possible rather than a probable causal connection sufficient for liability. We should be on our guard, therefore, against too readily accepting the apparent ground of responsibility or the ostensible standard of proof at face value. It may be that, when the rules of proof are investigated, what appears to be fault liability will turn out to be strict; or strict liability may hide a species of insurance; or proof of causal connection on a balance of probabilities may resolve into proof of *possible* causal connection.

This completes our brief survey of the main ways in which legislative or judicial policy may enter into the determination of causal issues as they affect legal responsibility. Legal policy determines the ground or grounds on which responsibility is to be imposed in a given case, and so what causal issues, if any, arise. It may, via rules for the discharge of the burden of proof, transform one ground of responsibility into a different one. It may set non-causal as well as causal limits to a given type of responsibility, and it may, by encouraging a 'monistic' formulation of the limits, encourage ways of thinking among lawyers which fail to make clear distinctions between causal and non-causal issues.

But what this shows is just that there is no shortage of ways in which the law, at least in common law countries, can respond to

[39] Below, p. 424.

changing conceptions of social and legal policy. It does not show that causal issues raise questions of legal policy, if by that is meant issues of policy *of the same sort* as those involved in determining the ground of responsibility, the incidence of the burden of proof, the scope of legal rules, and the weight to be given to considerations of equity between the parties. True it is that causal issues become relevant only when legislators or judges decide that they should be. True also that at certain points, for example when the reasonableness of the plaintiff's or a third party's conduct is to be assessed, value judgments influence causal judgments.[40] But causal judgments, though the law may have to systematize them, are not specifically legal. They appeal to a notion which is part of everyday life and which ordinary people, including jurymen, can handle with a minimum of guidance. There is no gain, and much danger, in seeking to assimilate them to policy judgments which are specifically legal, whether they concern particular rules of law or branches of the law or represent aims of the legal system as a whole. The rule that in contract law damages are recoverable only for items within the contemplation of the parties at the time of contracting is a rule which sets limits to the scope of the law of contract. It is based on considerations peculiar to contracting, viz. that there are certain risks which a party to a contract can and should take into account when he enters into a contract, and others which he cannot be expected to take into account. This rule of the scope of the law of contract has little or nothing in common with the rule that, for damages to be recoverable, the breach of contract must have caused or occasioned the harm complained of. Or rather, what it has in common is that it represents a distinct limitation on the extent of contractual liability. There is no case for trying vainly to assimilate the two.

4. SOME LEGAL CRITICISMS

Our book was fairly widely reviewed by lawyers and philosophers[41] and has since been discussed in a number of books and articles.[42] Judgments differed. Some found it a 'difficult book to

40 Below, pp. 156–7.
41 Reviews by H. Battifol, *Arch. Ph. Dr.* (1961), 253; D. C. Bennett (1960–1) 13 *Stan LR* 701; P. Q. R. Boberg (1961) 78 *SALJ* 120; R. Brett (1961–2) 3 *Melb. ULR* 93; R. D. Childres (1960–1) 32 *Miss. LR* 222; L. K. Cooperider (1960) 58 *Mich. LR* 951; J. H. Coutts (1960) 23 *MLR* 708; M. P. Golding, *J. Phil.* 59 (1962), 85; Roger Hancock (1960–1) 6 *Nat. LF* 143; O. Lahtinen (1963) 49 *ARSP* 368; J. H. Mansfield (1963–4) 17 *Vanderbilt LR* 487; F. H. Newark (1960) 76 *LQR* 592; G. D. Nokes (1960) 9 *ICLQ* 353; M. Siniscalco, *Riv. it. dir. pen.* 3 (1962), 501; H. Stoll (1962–3) 27 *RabelsZ* 553; J. C. de Wet (1962) *Act. Jur.* (*SA*) 139; Morton White (1960) 60 *Col. LR* 1058; Glanville Williams 1961 *Cam. LJ* 62.
42 T. L. Beauchamp and A. Rosenberg, *Hume and the Problem of Causation* (New York, 1981), chap. 8; A. C. Becht and F. W. Miller, *The Test of Factual Causation in Negligence and Strict Liability* (St. Louis, 1961), 152–223; R. H. Cole, 'Windfall and

read', lacking in systematic arrangement,[43] and complained that it contained a 'serious amount of confusion and repetitiousness'.[44] To another reviewer its merit was 'the combination of legal scholarship with the sharp tools of philosophic analysis' and he added 'The combination is rare, and this work is a model of how fruitful it can be'.[45] Some authors adopted the substance of our analysis, for example Tunc in France,[46] Heuston in Ireland,[47] McGregor in England,[48] Peczenik in Sweden,[49] Vanquickenborne in Belgium,[50] and van Schellen in Holland.[51] Supporters of a generalized risk theory, such as Leon Green,[52] Fleming,[53] and Glanville Williams,[54] on the other hand, naturally rejected it. Some of the objections raised have been dealt with in the preceding section of the Preface or in the body of the book, but there remain some detailed points which can best be answered here.

Becht and Miller had completed writing their treatise *The Test of Factual Causation in Negligence and Strict Liability* when our book came out but had not published it. In the published version (1961) they added a final section of seventy pages which analyses our work from their point of view.[55] They recognized the merit of our book as a 'reasoned explanation and criticism of the way in which "cause" is used in the administration of the law'[56] but preferred to confine themselves to the 'cause-in-fact' relationship, i.e. to what we term the relationship of causally relevant condition and consequence (see Chapter V below). Like other causal minimalists[57] they regard this

Probability: a Study of "Cause" in Negligence Law', (1964) 52 *Calif. LR* 459, 764; H. Fain, 'Hart and Honoré on Causation in the Law', *Inquiry* 9 (1966) 322; S. Gorovits, 'Causal Judgments and Causal Explanation', *J. Phil.* 62 (1965), 695; L. Green, 'The Causal Relation Issue in Negligence Law', (1961) 60 *Mich. LR* 543; A. Harari, *The Place of Negligence in the Law of Torts* (Sydney, 1962); R. E. Keeton, *Legal Cause in the Law of Torts* (Columbia, 1963); R. H. Leflar, review of Becht and Miller, (1961) 75 *Harv. LR* 1691; J. Mackie, *The Cement of the Universe* (1974), chap. 5; A. Peczenik, *Causes and Damages* (Lund, 1979); M. Vanquickenborne, *De Oorzakelijkheid in het Recht van de Burgerlijke Aansprakelijkheid* (Gent, 1971).

[43] De Wet (above, n. 41), p. 139.
[44] Mansfield (above, n. 41), p. 488.
[45] Hancock (above, n. 41), p. 152.
[46] *Dalloz A.* 1956.2, 354, 357 (commenting on our articles in (1956) 72 *LQR* 58, 260, 398).
[47] Salmond and Heuston on *Torts* (18th edn. 1981), pp. 503-4.
[48] McGregor on *Damages*, pp. 71-2.
[49] Op. cit. (above, n. 42), pp. 186-7.
[50] Op. cit. (above, n. 42), p. 381.
[51] J. van Schellen, *Juridische Causaliteit* (Deventer, 1972).
[52] See above, p. xxxiv n. 3.
[53] 'The Passing of Polemis', (1961) *Can. BR* 489; 509, *Torts* (5th edn.), p. 190 n. 25.
[54] 'Causation in the Law', (1961) *Cam. LJ* 62.
[55] pp. 152-223. Their book was reviewed by L. Green in (1961) 60 *Mich. LR* 543 and W. H. Pedrick in (1964) 58 *NWULR* 853.
[56] Op. cit., p. 155.
[57] Above, p. xxxiv.

as presenting the only genuine issue of fact, but, unlike writers such as Wex Malone,[58] they argue that the existence of this relationship *always* presents a pure question of fact. According to them, whether conduct is a 'cause-in-fact' of subsequent harm is a question that has no policy component, even in doubtful cases. The decision of the judge to submit or refuse to submit the causal issue to the jury is, indeed, influenced by legal policy, but that does not convert the issue, once submitted, into one of value.[59] The philosophical foundation of Becht and Miller's treatment of causal questions is the assumption that in many cases we know, presumably by intuition, that a causal relationship exists even though the concept is indefinable.[60] They do not accept that singular causal statements involve an implicit reference to generalizations, as we do (above, section 2). They draw a distinction, however, between two types of causal relationship, 'simple causes' and 'hypothetical causes'.[61] A positive act is a simple cause of the harm it brings about but an omission, such as the negligent omission to perform a duty, is only a hypothetical cause of harm. In the case of a simple cause it is usually not necessary to test the existence of causal connection by constructing a hypothetical series of events ('parallel series'), but to establish the existence of a hypothetical cause a parallel series is always necessary. The authors further argue that it is a mistake to inquire into the causes of events other than physical events, for example a loss of earnings incurred by one who has suffered physical injury. 'If we look past known injuries to the future and unknown consequences of injuries a host of unanswerable questions could be raised.'[62] But this objection itself makes use of the term 'consequence' in a sense which is unclear. The authors' substantial point seems to be to insist that the assessment of damages ('measure of damages') presents a different issue from that of the extent of liability for physical consequences.[63] We, on the other hand, treat issues such as whether a loss of earnings suffered by the plaintiff is a consequence of the physical injuries inflicted on him by the defendant as turning on whether a certain type of causal relationship (depriving the plaintiff of opportunities to earn) exists between the physical injuries and the loss of earnings and so, indirectly, between the defendant's conduct and the loss of earnings.

[58] 'Ruminations on Cause-in-fact', (1956-7) 9 *Stan. LR* 60; 'Ruminations on *Dixie Drive It Yourself* v. *American Beverage Co.*', (1969-70) 30 *La. LR* 363.
[59] Becht and Miller, op. cit., p. 175.
[60] Ibid., p. 20.
[61] Ibid., pp. 22 f.
[62] Ibid., p. 216.
[63] Ibid., p. 218.

These various theoretical differences lead to some divergences in our interpretations of the cases, but not as many as might be expected. Becht and Miller recognize that, where divergences exist, our treatment is closer to the decisions than is theirs.[64] In particular, we do not treat every 'cause-in-fact' (causally relevant condition) as a cause of the harm in the full sense, whereas they do. Since they do not admit causal relationships other than 'cause-in-fact' they do not accept the distinctions which we draw between different types of causal relationship, such as the initiation of physical sequences, and the provision of reasons or opportunities for action. They conclude that, though there may be mistakes of detail in both books, a partly evaluative theory of causation in the law must look something like ours and a purely factual one like theirs.[65]

We do not think that the distinction between causing harm by positive act and by omission justifies Becht and Miller in speaking of two different types of cause, simple and hypothetical. The basic point to grasp, whether the harm is alleged to have been caused by a positive act or an omission, is that verifying the existence of causal connection involves counterfactual speculation (constructing a 'parallel series') to determine that the act or omission was at least a *sine qua non* of the harm. To understand certain issues, however, raised by them and also by Keeton, we need to grasp two important features of the use of causal notions as a determinant of legal responsibility.

1. When the law makes certain conduct wrongful and imposes civil liability for its harmful consequences, two possibilities must be envisaged. Either (*a*) it must be shown that the wrongful feature of the defendant's conduct is causally connected with the harm, or (*b*) given that the conduct is wrongful it is sufficient that the harm is causally connected with some feature or features of the defendant's conduct other than the wrongful one. In other words, either the occurrence of the harm must (as is normally required) be the consequence of the *fact that the defendant acted wrongfully*, or it is enough that it is the consequence of conduct of the defendant which is indeed wrongful, but not of the fact that renders it wrongful. We can illustrate the distinction from the facts of the *Empire Jamaica*,[66] a case discussed in our book and also by Mackie.[67] An ordinance forbade shipowners to send their ships to sea without a complement of certificated officers. The owners of the *Empire Jamaica* nevertheless did so, and while an experienced but uncertificated man,

64 Becht and Miller, op. cit., pp. 155, 223.
65 Ibid., p. 223.
66 [1955] P. 52. The decision was affirmed on appeal in [1955] 3 All ER 60 (CA) and [1956] 3 All ER 144 (HL), where, however, the causal issue was not prominent.
67 J. Mackie, *The Cement of the Universe* (1980 edn.), 129–30, 266.

Sinon, was officer of the watch, a collision occurred. The extent of the shipowners' liability depended indirectly on whether the breach of the ordinance was the cause of the collision. The answer to this question depended in the first place on the interpretation of the ordinance. Did it mean that a shipowner in breach is liable if a collision occurs in consequence of the fact that the ship was navigated by an uncertificated man? The requisite causal connection might on that interpretation be shown, for example, by proving that the uncertificated man did not possess the competence which is needed to obtain a certificate and that his lack of competence accounted for the collision. Alternatively the law might be construed to mean that, if a shipowner sends a ship to sea without a complement of certificated officers and a collision occurs, the shipowner is liable in full even though the collision is not the consequence of the fact that the navigator was uncertificated. The court assumed that the first interpretation was correct; but there are other contexts in which courts have held the second to be the right approach.[68] The choice between them is clearly a matter of law.[69] The analysis of causal concepts cannot tell us how to choose.

2. As the above example indicates, in most legal contexts the important question is the definition of the situation of fact that must be shown to be causally connected with the harm in order for liability to be imposed. But it is possible, and in many contexts unobjectionable, to cite an *event* rather than a *fact* as the cause of an outcome.[70] An event, when it is cited as the cause, may be identified or described by reference to features which need not be causally connected with the outcome, provided that there are other features of the event which are causally connected with it. Thus, in answering in a non-legal context the question 'What caused the *Empire Jamaica* collision?', it might properly be said that the collision was caused by the navigation of the uncertificated officer Sinon. This event, this particular piece of navigation, might be cited as the cause of the collision, though the fact that Sinon was not certificated was not causally relevant. It would be proper to cite this event as the cause because Sinon's navigation, a feature of the event, *was* causally connected with the collision.

If these two points are borne in mind it is easier to see why Becht and Miller's division of causes into 'simple' and 'hypothetical' is mistaken. The first step in any civil case in which causal connection is in dispute is to interpret the law so as to determine what fact it is that has to be shown to be causally connected with the harm. Once

---

[68] e.g. *Martin* v. *Blackburn* (1942) 38 NE 2d 939; below, pp. 120–1.

[69] Thode, 46 *Tex. LR* 423, 428–9, but there are American cases which make the issue a jury one: W. H. Pedrick, (1978) *Wash. ULQ* 645, 655–6.

[70] Mackie, *Cement*, pp. 248 ff. Cf. above, pp. xxxvii–xxxviii.

this has been done a 'parallel series' must be constructed on the hypothesis that the fact which has to be shown to be so connected was absent. In detail, the appropriate method is as follows:

(i) *When the wrongful feature of defendant's conduct must be shown to be causally connected with the harm.* In this case the parallel series is constructed by asking what the course of events would have been had the defendant acted lawfully. But the notion of 'acting lawfully' needs to be spelled out more fully than it was in our book. What this phrase means is that the defendant must be taken to have acted exactly as he did except that he conformed to the law to the full extent that a lawful and reasonable person would have done, not just minimally. Clearly this requirement is influenced by the fact that it is an aim of the legal system to secure conformity to certain standards of conduct.

Thus, if the wrongful feature of the act consisted in the defendant's omission to perform a legal duty, we must ask what would have happened had he fulfilled his duty. It may, of course, be difficult to answer the question unequivocally, especially if we have to guess what the reaction of the plaintiff or of third parties would have been had the defendant acted lawfully.[71] Again, if the defendant acted unlawfully by performing a lawful act in a forbidden manner, e.g. by driving above the speed limit, we must ask what would have happened had he driven at a reasonable speed. The proper hypothesis is not that he drove marginally within the speed limit, nor that he refrained from driving altogether. Conformity to the law does not require the defendant to refrain from driving but does require him, if the road conditions indicate it, to drive below the maximum permitted speed.

If, again, conduct is forbidden unless some specified condition is fulfilled, e.g. piloting without a certificate, we must ask what would have happened had the defendant had the necessary qualifications to obtain a certificate, not what difference it would have made had he carried a particular piece of paper in his wallet. The object of the law requiring certificates is (we assume) to ensure that pilots are competent, not just to raise revenue.

(ii) *When the wrongful feature of defendant's conduct need not be causally connected with the harm.* Suppose that a law requiring a pilot to have a certificate were interpreted to mean that one who, while piloting without a certificate, causes a collision is liable even if the wrongful aspect of his conduct is causally irrelevant to the occurrence of the collision. In that case a 'parallel series' must be constructed on the hypothesis that the defendant did not do the causally relevant act (here, piloting the ship). One way of expressing

---

[71] Below, pp. 413–18.

the effect of this interpretation is to say that the uncertificated pilot navigates the ship at his risk.

(iii) *When the defendant's conduct need not be wrongful but must be causally connected with the harm.* In certain cases of strict liability (e.g. accumulating explosives on one's land) the defendant's conduct need not be wrongful, since the accumulation is not itself forbidden (we assume) and the defendant has exercised all proper care. Nevertheless he may be liable for any explosion which occurs in consequence of the accumulation. In this sort of case a 'parallel series' is constructed by supposing that the defendant did not do the action for the consequences of which the law imposes liability, i.e. did not accumulate the explosives.

Contrary to the view of Becht and Miller, therefore, a parallel series has to be constructed in all cases in order to test whether defendant's conduct was a causally relevant condition of the harm for which it is sought to hold him liable. The answer to the counterfactual question is usually straightforward in cases of type (ii) and (iii) but often obscure in cases of type (i).

Becht and Miller also criticize us for not providing an account of the 'negligent segment' of a defendant's conduct.[72] This may refer to the fact that, for the reasons given earlier,[73] we treat the question whether the wrongful features of the defendant's conduct must be shown to be causally connected with the harm as a question of law which involves interpreting the rule in question. All that can usefully be said on this problem of interpretation is that courts generally require the wrongful features of the defendant's conduct to be shown to be causally relevant, but sometimes, for special reasons, impose a more stringent liability by treating the causality of other, lawful features of his conduct as sufficient. Becht and Miller are perhaps also puzzled by the fact that, even where the negligent aspect of conduct is causally irrelevant, it may still be proper in a non-legal context to give as the cause the whole event (e.g. 'the driving' rather than 'the negligent driving') and to refer to it by citing features of it which may be causally irrelevant (e.g. 'the driving of the man in the red pullover'). Conversely, it may be in order to refer to an event as the cause by mentioning the negligent aspect of conduct (e.g. 'driving without keeping a proper lookout') even when this is causally irrelevant.

On the larger question whether the 'cause-in-fact' issue is purely one of fact, as Becht and Miller argue,[74] or is a mixed issue of fact and policy, as Wex Malone asserts, we hold an intermediate view.

72 Op. cit., p. 179.
73 Above, pp. lviii–lvix.
74 Above, pp. lvi–lvii.

The mere fact that the answer to the question may be influenced by the incidence of the burden of proof does not make the issue even partly one of policy. If that were so, every decision on a point of fact would be partly one of policy, since the burden of proof on every issue of fact must be placed on one or other party (apart from rare cases of 'neutral onus'). But when there is likely to be little reliable evidence with which to answer a hypothetical question, as is the case in law when we have to ask, for example, how an employee would have reacted had the employer provided safety equipment, the answer is likely to be determined by the presumption of law or fact which the court adopts.[75] In such cases, therefore, the issue of causal relevance is a mixed issue of fact and policy. This is still clearer if it is made virtually impossible for the defendant to rebut the presumption of causal connection, as in the case of market share liability.[76] The rules of proof then virtually substitute a different ground of liability (insurance) for the ostensible one (fault or strict liability). The 'cause-in-fact' issue is almost superseded by a policy decision. But it would be seriously misleading to suggest that the issue of causal relevance is not a factual one in the vast majority of cases, including many run-of-the-mill cases of negligence. The impact of legal policy is that the law, correctly interpreted, defines the conduct which must be shown to be causally relevant to the harm, and, by allocating the burden of proof, determines the result when convincing evidence is likely to be unobtainable.

Keeton's *Legal Cause in the Law of Torts* appeared in 1963. The book vigorously defended the risk theory, though the author was aware of the 'amorphous quality of the concept of risk'[77] and was prepared to allow departures from the theory when it fails to correspond to our intuitions about the limits of responsibility.[78] In the ordinary run of case, however, Keeton argues that the 'risk rule' is equivalent to the rule that requires the 'negligent aspect' of conduct to be a causally relevant condition (cause-in-fact) of the harm. The risk rule is therefore 'a rule of causation in a cause-in-fact sense'.[79] In particular, the following propositions are equivalent to one another:[80]

(i) A negligent actor is legally responsible for that harm, and only that harm, of which the negligent aspect of his conduct is a cause in fact, and

(ii) A negligent actor is legally responsible for the harm, and only the harm, that not only (1) is caused in fact by his conduct but also

75 Below, pp. 413–17.
76 Below, p. 424.
77 Keeton, op. cit., p. 60.
78 Ibid., p. 67.
79 Ibid., p. 13.
80 Ibid., pp. 9–10.

(2) is a result within the scope of the risks by reason of which the actor is found to be negligent.

Keeton's 'negligence' includes what in English law would count as breach of statutory duty. So his point can perhaps be rephrased for English lawyers in the following way: whenever the negligent or unlawful aspect of the defendant's conduct is causally relevant to the harm it is also the case that the harm is of the sort that made it negligent at common law for the defendant to act as he did or of the sort that the statutory duty is intended to guard against. Is this proposition correct?

Certainly, there are instances in which it will be correct. If it is negligent of the defendant to hand a child a loaded gun, and the child drops the gun on his foot and injures it, the injury to the foot is not within the risk (shooting) that made it negligent to hand the child the loaded gun. It is also true that the aspect of the defendant's conduct which made it negligent, the fact that the gun was loaded, was not causally relevant to the injury, since that fact did not significantly increase the gun's weight. If all cases were like this one, therefore, it would be true that, whenever harm is not within the risk that makes conduct negligent, the feature of the conduct that makes it negligent is not causally relevant to the harm. But it is easy to think of contrary examples. The famous case of *Gorris* v. *Scott*,[81] which Keeton discusses,[82] furnishes one. In that case plaintiff's sheep were washed overboard (it was assumed) as a result of the defendant's failure to provide sheep pens, contrary to a statute which required there to be pens of not more than a certain dimension. The statute was aimed at preventing disease, and hence disease was the risk which led to the imposition of the statutory duty. A similar situation would have arisen had it been held that the failure to provide pens was negligent at common law because of the danger of disease. In both cases the harm which occurred by the sheep being washed overboard would have been caused by the failure to provide pens (whether that amounted to negligence at common law or breach of statutory duty) but the harm would not be, in Keeton's terminology, 'within the scope of the risks' by reason of which the defendant was found to be negligent or which led the legislature to impose the statutory duty. A different result is therefore reached according as causal connection or risk is taken to be the criterion of liability.

81 (1874) LR 9 Ex. 125.
82 Op. cit., p. 16.

To overcome the difficulty Keeton points out that the shipowners might have violated the statute not, as they did, by omitting to provide pens altogether, but by providing pens of a larger size than was permissible under the legislation. These larger pens might, like the statutory pens, have had the fortunate effect of preventing the sheep from being washed overboard. Since, therefore, unlawful conduct on the defendant's part could have prevented the loss, his actual unlawful conduct should not be taken to have caused it. But this is a *non sequitur*. It is indeed true that, if I act unlawfully, but harm of a very similar type and extent would have followed from my lawful conduct, there is a case for denying that my unlawful conduct caused[83] the harm. But the mere fact that I could have prevented the harm by resorting to a different sort of unlawful conduct from that which is said to have caused it is not an argument against the existence of causal connection with my actual unlawful conduct. It merely shows that harm may be caused by one form of unlawful conduct though it could have been prevented by another. For a particular form of unlawful conduct to cause harm it must be shown that lawful conduct (i.e. conduct required by law) would not have resulted in that harm. It need not be the case that every other form of unlawful conduct would have caused the same or greater harm. If it is my duty to store your books in a room where the humidity is appropriately low, and instead I leave them outside in the rain, it is no answer to a claim for damages for harm done to the books by the damp that I could have preserved them by placing them outside in a shed where, as it happens, the humidity was equally appropriate to their preservation.

So Keeton fails to show that harm of which the negligent conduct was a causally relevant condition (cause-in-fact) is equivalent in all cases to harm within the risk. The equivalence will hold good when the required precaution can serve only to prevent a particular type of danger (e.g. not loading a gun can serve only to prevent shooting; disinfecting cattle can serve only to prevent disease). For in that case the omission of the precaution will be irrelevant to the prevention of other types of danger and so will not be causally connected with them if they occur. When, on the other hand, a host of dangers lead to the imposition of a duty (e.g. 'do not let a young child wander unaccompanied in the street'), the unlawful conduct, letting the child go unaccompanied, will not be tied to any particular risk and it may easily turn out that such conduct causes harm which is not within any apparent risk. It then becomes a matter of legal policy to decide whether the defendant who is guilty of the unlawful conduct should be liable for all the harm to which his conduct is causally relevant;

[83] Below, pp. 252-3.

or only for harm which is, in addition, also within the apparent risk; or (as an insurer) for harm within the risk irrespective of whether his conduct is causally relevant to it. When such divergences between causal and risk criteria occur, the case cannot be decided except by a determination of the appropriate ground of responsibility, which, as explained in the previous section,[84] depends on the interpretation of the law in question. The general question of whether it is possible to employ risk criteria as a substitute for causal criteria is explored in Chapter IX, section III below.

Peczenik's *Causes and Damages*, published in 1979, adopted much of our analysis. He differed from us, however, in preferring Mackie's view of the fundamental identity of the various causal relations (above, section 3) and in drawing a distinction between 'strong' and 'weak' causes. A weak cause is a relevant and non-redundant member of a set of conditions jointly sufficient to produce the effect. A strong cause is a relevant and non-redundant member of such a set of conditions which is, in addition, in a certain sense necessary to the effect.[85] The sense of 'necessary' required by Peczenik for a strong cause is the third of our senses of the word.[86] The strong cause must be necessary *on the particular occasion* for the production of the harm. Hence, when there are multiple sufficient causes (additional causes) each cause is only a weak cause, in Peczenik's sense, since it is not necessary on the particular occasion to the outcome. There can, however, be grades of strength, since, according to the author, a cause may be treated as strong if, on the particular occasion, the harm would not have occurred in its absence, or probably would not have occurred, or was considerably less likely to have occurred, or might not have occurred.[87] It is a matter of policy what degree of strength is required for a strong cause in a given case, and it is also a matter of legal policy whether in a particular context a wrongful act is required to be a weak or a strong cause of harm.

We agree with Peczenik that there are both strong and weak causal relationships. Generally speaking a weak causal relationship seems to be sufficient for the imposition of legal responsibility. Thus, in the stock example of multiple sufficient causes, when A and B simultaneously but independently shoot C dead, so that it cannot be said that C died of A's shot rather than B's, it seems natural to say that both A and B caused C's death, although the conduct of each is only a 'weak' cause of it. It may be that our inclination to say this is influenced by the fact that, if a strong causal relationship were required in this type of case, neither A nor B could be held responsible

84 Above, p. viii.
85 Peczenik, op. cit., pp. 13–14.
86 Below, pp. 112–13.
87 Peczenik, op. cit., p. 13.

for C's death. This would support Peczenik's view that legal policy determines whether a strong or weak causal relationship is required in a particular type of case. On the other hand, it may be that our inclination to hold that both A and B caused C's death simply reflects the fact that the act of each was sufficient, in the circumstances, to bring about C's death as and when it occurred.

We must, however, distinguish the type of case of which simultaneous shooting furnishes an example from the sort of case in which, given the legal requirements, only a strong relationship is possible. Thus, if the law imposes liability for loss of income consequent upon physical injury, this may be construed as requiring the plaintiff to show that the defendant has deprived him of an opportunity to earn which he would otherwise have had. If so, a strong relationship must be shown to exist between the defendant's conduct and the lost opportunity. This is because the plaintiff cannot be said to have been 'deprived' of earnings which he would not in any event have made, e.g. because of a subsequent depression in the industry in which he worked.[88] It is for the law to determine in such a case whether the plaintiff must show that he has been deprived of an economic opportunity rather than merely suffering a reduction in his physical capacity. But, given that such a deprivation must be shown, there is no further choice to be made on grounds of policy between a strong and a weak causal relationship.

Glanville Williams, a supporter of the risk theory, thought that we had been unlucky in the timing of our book. 'Unfortunately for the authors they have backed a loser in supporting *Re Polemis* and criticizing the foreseeability test and since much of their argument depends on their opinion on this question, their book must now [1961] be accounted largely out of date.'[89] Twenty years later things look rather different. The reviewer's opinion was doubtless influenced by the then recent decision in *The Wagon Mound (No. 1)*,[90] in which the Privy Council held, as explained in Chapter IX, that in the law of negligence recovery must be restricted to foreseeable harm, since the criteria of culpability and compensation are the same.

We had not been concerned, in fact, to make any particular prediction about what doctrine the Privy Council, or other appeal courts, were likely to embrace. We were concerned to argue, rather, that, whatever doctrine they might purport to apply, they were likely in practice to give a large place to common-sense causal criteria, since these are deeply ingrained in the thought of both ordinary people and lawyers. The fate of the *Wagon Mound* decision was to

88 Below, pp. 250-1.
89 G. Williams, 'Causation in the Law', (1961) *Cam. LJ* 61.
90 [1961] AC 388; below, pp. 272-4, 282.

confirm our contention in the most striking way. The idea that the same criteria govern the existence of culpability and the extent of compensation was soon forgotten. The courts never abandoned the traditional principle that existing circumstances, however unexpected, do not negative causal connection. Hence, as we explain in Chapter IX,[91] a tortfeasor continues to take his victim as he finds him. The courts further made it clear that in the civil law of negligence causal connection is a requisite of liability which is *additional* to the foreseeability of the type of harm.[92] In this context causal connection is to be interpreted in more than a *sine qua non* sense. It requires that there should not intervene between the negligent conduct and the harm the sort of factor which we discuss in our book and which counts as a 'superseding cause', '*novus actus interveniens*', or the like. The causal principles relating to existing circumstances and those regarding intervening actions and events therefore remain unaffected by the *Wagon Mound*. All that decision did was to come down on one side of the fence in regard to a question in which decisions have, throughout the twentieth century, regularly gone both ways. When a causal process of a radically different sort from any that could be expected freakishly results in harm, some courts hold that the 'type' of harm is unforeseeable and so irrecoverable, others that the loss should fall on the tortfeasor.[93] It hardly needed the panoply of the Privy Council decision to make the point that there is something to be said for the former solution. To hail the decision as a turning point in the law of 'remoteness' was to mistake a verbal formula, whose deficiencies we had pointed out two years before it was declared orthodox,[94] for a meaningful guide to judicial decision in the ordinary run of negligence cases. If the *Polemis*[95] case would be differently decided today, it would be because the fire was (implausibly) thought to be of this freakish sort.

5. CAUSAL MINIMALISM AND CAUSAL MAXIMALISM

In both this and the first edition of our book much of our argument has been directed against those writers whom we have termed 'causal minimalists'.[96] They are theorists who allot only a minor role to causal issues in determining questions of legal responsibility, and who for the most part hold that the only genuine causal issue is that of *sine qua non* or 'cause in fact'.

91 Below, p. 274 n. 83.
92 Below, pp. 282-3.
93 Below, p. 176 n. 46.
94 1st edn., pp. 224-8; cf. Fleming, *Torts*, p. 196.
95 [1921] 3 KB 560; below, pp. 173-4.
96 Above, p. xxxiv.

In the sixties a new group of theorists joined the ranks of the causal minimalists. These theorists were primarily concerned with the economic analysis of law. The impulse to undertake this form of analysis stemmed from criticisms which were then being directed against the traditional system of tort liability based on fault. In reply to these criticisms a new school of economic theorists, of whom Posner was the chief,[97] began to ask whether the existing rules of tort law could be explained and justified on economic grounds. They came to the conclusion that, by and large, these traditional rules did indeed serve certain rational economic ends.

According to the economic school, these rules serve to maximize wealth,[98] and they do so by minimizing costs. (In an alternative version, it is utility[99] rather than wealth that is maximized, but, since the impact on causal issues is *mutatis mutandis* the same, we shall concentrate on wealth maximization.) The rules of tort law, it is argued, are such that if *A* is proposing to act in a way which will diminish *B*'s resources, whether *A*'s conduct will be treated as tortious will depend on whether, if he refrains from acting in that way, the combined cost to him and to *B* will be less than if he does so act. If *A* has already acted in such a way as to diminish *B*'s resources, he will have to compensate *B* if the combined cost to both of them of *A*'s action and *B*'s loss is greater than if *A* had not so acted. These rules of tort law would, it is true, be unnecessary if it cost nothing for *A* and *B* to bargain with one another about the use of the resources in question. For in that case the party who could best use them to maximize wealth would obtain them by bargaining with the other party. In practice, however, bargaining of this sort may be impossible and will in any case involve transaction costs. Hence the rules of tort law are needed to secure the result which, in a world without transaction costs or other impediments to bargaining about resources, would arise automatically through private treaty.

This analysis applies both to accidental and to intentional harm. In the case of accidental harm the calculation will be as follows. If the cost of the accident is, say, twice that of the cost of avoiding it,

[97] Particularly relevant to tort law are: 'A Theory of Negligence', (1972) 1 *J. Leg. Stud.* 29; 'Strict Liability', (1973) 2 *J. Leg. Stud.* 215; 'The Concept of Corrective Justice in Recent Theories of Tort Law', (1981) 10 *J. Leg. Stud.* 187; 'Epstein's Tort Theory: a Critique', (1979) 8 *J. Leg. Stud.* 457.
[98] In 'Strict Liability' (preceding note) Posner refers to the 'joint value' of the activities of the parties. But what look like moral considerations may indirectly serve the cause of economic efficiency: Posner, *The Economic Analysis of Law* (2nd edn. 1977), 179–91; M. J. Rizzo, 'A Theory of Economic Loss in the Law of Torts', (1982) 11 *J. Leg. Stud.* 281.
[99] e.g. R. H. Coase, 'The Problem of Social Cost', (1960) 3 *J. Law Econ.* 1, 27–8 ('weighing of utilities'); G. Calabresi, 'Some Thought on Risk Distribution and the Law of Tort', (1960–1) 70 *Yale LJ* 499, 534–5.

the party who could have avoided it will be held 'negligent'[1] and so will either be liable to pay compensation to the other party or will fail to recover compensation from him, or both. But if the cost of avoiding the accident is twice that of the accident itself, should it occur, the party who could have avoided it at that greater cost will not be held 'negligent' and will incur no tort liability.

Obviously it will be possible for the law to minimize costs in this way only over a period in which the deterrent or permissive effects of judgments can become known and can influence parties who find themselves in situations similar to those that have been litigated. Nevertheless, there is some reason to think, the economic theorists argue, that their way of approaching tort problems is compatible with the existing law of negligence, at least as it was expounded in the classic judgment of Judge Learned Hand in *U.S.* v. *Carroll Towing Co.*[2] In that case the judge pointed to three variables which, he said, had to be taken into account in deciding whether a defendant had a duty to take the precautions which he was alleged to have neglected. These were: the probability of harm, its likely gravity should it occur, and the burden of adequate precautions.

There seems, therefore, to be at least some judicial support for the view that an important part of the law of tort is concerned with the search for the 'cheaper cost-avoider'. Accidents cannot be prevented without cost and the decision whether to require someone to take measures to prevent them must rest on a comparison of the sum of the costs to both parties of alternative courses of action. Nor need this analysis be confined to cases of accidental harm. If a manufacturer pollutes a river, so that the fish are killed, the cost of stopping the manufacturer polluting the river must be compared with the cost of bringing to a halt the use of the river for fishing and other activities which the pollution prevents. Indeed, in very many cases in which the law of tort is relevant the situation can, on this view, be analysed as one in which a plaintiff and a defendant make incompatible claims on resources. Each seeks to impose costs on the other by using something in a way which the other would prefer to see used differently or by preventing the other from using something in the way he wishes.

This analysis, if accepted, has implications so far as causal issues are concerned. In the first place, if the aim of the law of tort is to maximize wealth and minimize costs, tort liability can be imposed only on a person who has by his conduct reduced wealth or increased costs. His conduct must therefore have been at least a *sine qua non*

<hr>

1 'Negligence' being the legal equivalent of the failure to maximize wealth.
2 (1947) 159 F. 2d 169.

of the increased cost for which he is required to compensate.[3] It must, of course, also be the case that his conduct is a *sine qua non* of the physical or other harm which leads to the increased cost. But it is important in examining the economic theories to bear in mind the distinction between 'harm' in the ordinary sense (e.g. injury and damage to goods) and 'harm' in the economists' sense, which is confined to increased cost and the resultant failure to maximize wealth. (We use the term 'cost' for the latter.) From the point of view of the economic theorists the law is not concerned to avoid harm in the ordinary sense as such, but only those items of harm which cost more than their avoidance would cost. Hence the fact that the defendant's conduct was, according to common-sense causal criteria, a cause of the harm for which compensation is claimed cannot, consistently with the economic theories, govern the decision whether the defendant should be liable to the plaintiff in a tort action. Of course, a judgment on the causal issue is a preliminary to the reaching of a decision on economic grounds. For the economic question can be put in this way: is it better, in the circumstances, for the defendant to have caused the harm he did to the plaintiff, or for him not to have done so? This economic question does not arise unless it is the case that the defendant *has* caused the harm to the plaintiff.

It might well be argued that in this context 'cause' should be interpreted according to common-sense criteria, so that, if on those criteria the harm would not count as caused by the wrongful conduct, no question of tort liability would arise. Suppose, for example, that it is held that *A*'s leaving his car unlocked is *not* the cause of the injury to *B* who is run over when a thief steals the car and drives it away. Should it not then be irrelevant that the combined cost to *A* and *B* had *A* locked the car would have been less than the combined cost of leaving it unlocked?—the costs in question being simply those losses of which the conduct in question is a *sine qua non*.

The economic theorists, however, in practice adopt the view that the only sense of cause relevant to tort liability is that of *sine qua non*. Thus, to cite some vivid examples which recur in the literature, if sparks from a railway engine burn the farmer's crops alongside the railway line, the crops (or, more exactly, the act of the farmer in sowing them) are said to be as much the cause of the spark damage as the engine. If my rabbits eat your lettuces, you and I are, according to Coase, equally 'responsible'.[4] The implication of remarks of this sort is that nothing that would ordinarily count as 're-sponsibility' is relevant to tort liability. The railway which runs the

[3] e.g. Coase, op. cit., p. 11; J. P. Brown, 'Towards an Economic Theory of Liability', (1973) 2 *J. Leg. Stud.* 323, 326; Posner, 8 *J. Leg. Stud.* 459-60.
[4] Op. cit., p. 37.

engines from which the sparks escape and the farmer who plants the crops which the sparks burn are equally the 'cause', and equally 'responsible' for the spark damage, in the sense that the use of the land by each is a *sine qua non* of the economic loss.

But tort liability will not be settled by this or any other causal issue. It will depend simply on which use of the land creates more net wealth after deduction of costs. Will it make for greater wealth for the railway engines to be run without spark absorbers and for some crops to be burned or for spark absorbers to be fitted and the crops to be saved? The answer clearly depends in the main on the relation between the cost of the precaution which would be needed to prevent the escape of the sparks and the value of the crops which would thereby be saved.

The economic theorists are therefore for the most part causal minimalists. Calabresi[5] appears at first sight to be an exception. In an article published in 1975 which attracted a good deal of attention Calabresi disclaimed any intention of analysing the meaning of the term 'cause' but argued that in law its function was always 'to identify those pressure points that are most amenable to the social goals we wish to accomplish'.[6] This remark, in the spirit of Collingwood[7] and F. S. Cohen,[8] suggests that not every *sine qua non* of harm will count as its cause. The cause will rather be that condition which is most easily controllable and which therefore, if prevented, will afford the cheapest way of avoiding the occurrence of the harm.

Though disclaiming concern with 'meaning' Calabresi says that there are three 'concepts of cause' of concern to lawyers.[9] The first is that of 'causal linkage'. When we can predict that the recurrence of an action will lead to an increased chance of harm of a certain type occurring, there is a 'causal link' between actions of this class and harm of this type though in a given case it may not be true that the harm would not have occurred without the action. The second concept is that of 'but for' cause or *sine qua non*. The third is that of 'proximate cause', which Calabresi defines in a 'conclusory' sense. By this he means that a proximate cause of harm is any action to which the legal system assigns responsibility for the harm in whole or in part. Such action is usually but not always 'causally linked' to the harm and a 'but for' cause of it.

Despite the talk of three concepts of cause, Calabresi might well be classed as a causal minimalist. The first notion, that of 'causal

5 G. Calabresi, 'Concerning Cause and the Law of Tort', (1975–6) 43 *U. Ch. LR* 69; cf. *The Cost of Accidents* (1970), p. 6 n. 8.
6 Calabresi, 43 *U. Ch. LR* 105–6.
7 Below, p. 33.
8 Below, p. 300.
9 Calabresi, 43 *U. Ch. LR* 71.

linkage', is really one of probability. Given conduct of a certain class the probability of harm of a given type is greater than it would have been without that conduct. This fact may indeed sometimes point to a causal link between classes of events or individual events, but it may not. Thus, it may be that those who take a certain quack remedy for cancer are more likely to die of cancer than those who do not. But this is not because the taking of the quack remedy causes the deaths. So it is surely misleading for Calabresi to describe his relationship of increased probability as a 'causal link'.

The third notion, that of proximate cause, is used by Calabresi simply as a label for a relationship to which the law attaches responsibility. As he emphasizes, the ground for attaching responsibility may be the furtherance of any one of a number of the goals of tort law. So 'proximate cause', too, has a very weak claim to be treated as 'causal'; it is exclusively, or almost exclusively, designed as a vehicle for policies which are non-causal.

What are these policies? According to Calabresi, they are four in number.[10] The law of tort has two 'compensation goals' and two 'deterrence goals'. The former are the goals of loss-spreading and the redistribution of wealth. The latter are the goals of collective deterrence (e.g. when legislation forbids certain conduct) and of market deterrence (e.g. when the cost to the plaintiff of harm is so great that he is induced to spend a lesser amount on precautions to avoid it). 'Proximate cause' is relevant to all these goals, though Calabresi thinks it is in practice not used much for redistributing wealth. But that is because it can be the vehicle of any policy whatever. It cannot be said that any of the objectives of tort law as Calabresi sees them *requires* there to be a doctrine of proximate cause, except in the sense that they require there to be some rubric under cover of which the policies can be implemented.

So-called 'causal linkage' is not relevant to the compensation objectives but it is, according to Calabresi, to the deterrence objectives. But this, of course, will only be true if the linkage in question really is causal and not merely probabilistic. For it is only when the link is causal that the absence of the conduct to be deterred will make the harmful outcome less likely. Thus, a programme of reducing the incidence of deaths from cancer will not be furthered by forbidding resort to quack remedies, despite the fact that those who resort to quack remedies for cancer are more likely to die from cancer than those who do not.[11]

10 Calabresi, 43 *U. Ch. LR* 73.

11 The prohibition of quack remedies might indirectly lead to a decrease in cancer deaths, if those who would otherwise have resorted to the quack remedies were persuaded by the impossibility of doing so to have proper treatment. Even so, abstention from the quack remedies will not *by itself* have any tendency to decrease deaths from cancer.

The 'but for' relationship is not relevant to the compensation objectives nor to collective deterrence, since collective deterrence can work by forbidding practices known to be risky whether or not in the particular case they issue in harm. On the other hand, 'but for' causation is an essential part of market deterrence, since it is only those who can avoid costs by taking precautions who can be deterred from incurring the costs that could be avoided. 'Market deterrence alone among the tort goals outlined above can explain the virtual universality of the but for test.'[12] This test, says Calabresi, ensures that the injury costs allocated to the cheapest cost-avoider include only those costs which are relevant to the choice between injury and safety.

Calabresi is entitled to credit for having attempted in some detail to show what use a law of tort directed towards the objectives he mentions would make of causal criteria. But, apart from the weaknesses mentioned already, it is doubtful whether the objectives he set out will command general approval. Certainly 'compensation' is an objective of tort law, but it is often understood to mean not just that one who suffers harm should be compensated from some source or other, but that he should be compensated *by the person who caused the harm*. 'Loss spreading' and 'wealth distribution' do not exhaust the notion of compensation as normally understood, if indeed they can be said to form a central part of it at all. Again, 'deterrence' is certainly an aim of tort law, but the point of deterrence would ordinarily be thought to be to avoid injury or damage to goods rather than excessive costs. In the end his theory does not, we think, avoid the weaknesses that afflict the economic theories in general.

It is not surprising, therefore, that the economic theories have provoked a reaction from an opposing group of writers who deny that the aims of the law of tort are confined to maximizing wealth, utility, or some other forward-looking objective, such as loss spreading or the redistribution of wealth. They argue that this branch of the law is concerned to right the injustices done by those who have caused harm to others. They object, in this connection, to the minimalist identification of cause and *sine qua non*. Epstein[13] and others[14] point out that this identification does violence to common-sense judgments of causality. They maintain that causal connection is

12 Calabresi, 43 *U. Ch. LR* 85.
13 'A Theory of Strict Liability', (1973) 2 *J. Leg. Stud.* 151; 'Defenses and Subsequent Pleas in a Scheme of Strict Liability', (1974) 3 *J. Leg. Stud.* 165; 'Intentional Harms', (1975) 4 *J. Leg. Stud.* 391; 'Nuisance Law: Corrective Justice and its Utilitarian Constraints', (1979) 8 *J. Leg. Stud.* 49; 'Causation and Corrective Justice: a Reply to Two Critics', (1979) 8 *J. Leg. Stud.* 477.
14 G. P. Fletcher, 'Fairness and Utility in Tort Theory', (1972) 85 *Harv. LR* 537.

to be understood as ordinary people understand it and that, so understood, it is a moral principle that those who cause harm to others should compensate them for the harm so caused. They advocate what we have termed 'causal maximalism',[15] viz. the doctrine that causing harm is a necessary and sufficient condition of tort liability. They urge that this principle ought to be, and to some extent already is, embodied in tort law. It is true that some qualifications are called for. Thus, considerations of moral responsibility dictate that excuses such as infancy or insanity and justifications such as necessity should be admitted. On the other hand, fault should not be relevant to liability. To allow judges or juries to make decisions turn on the presence or absence of negligence is to entrust too much power to them.

It would seem, therefore, that in Epstein's tort system a plaintiff ought to succeed, subject to certain defences, simply by showing that, on the criteria of ordinary speech, the defendant has caused the harm. For Epstein takes the notion of cause which is appropriate to the law to be that embedded in ordinary speech and refers in that connection to our book.[16] But he does not conclude that causing harm in this sense is sufficient without more. The plaintiff, he argues, must in addition show that the manner of causing harm falls within one of four 'paradigms'. These are: the use of force; fright; the exercise of compulsion; and the creation of a dangerous situation. Only if harm is caused in one of these four ways will it count for purposes of tort liability. If there is a conflict between paradigms (e.g. each party has caused harm to the other, but by a different method), certain paradigms prevail over others. In certain cases liability is to be shared.[17]

The role of the paradigms is puzzling. Epstein says that they are the 'modes of description which best capture the ordinary use of causal language'.[18] But it can hardly be said that ordinary language confines 'causing' to causing by one of these modes. They might at most be described as typical ways in which harm can be caused. Nor do the rankings between paradigms seem to derive from the judgments of ordinary people. Both the paradigms and the rankings seem rather to play something of the part that in ordinary legal systems is played by the classification of conduct as lawful or unlawful.

The theoretical background to Epstein's theory is that the aim of the law of tort is not, as the economic theorists argue, to maximize

---

[15] Above, p. xxxv.

[16] Epstein, 2 *J. Leg. Stud.* 162; 8 *J. Leg. Stud.* 479; cf. J. Borgo, 'Causal Paradigms in Tort Law', (1979) 8 *J. Leg. Stud.* 419, 425.

[17] M. J. Rizzo and F. S. Arnold, 'Causal Apportionment in the Law of Torts: an Economic Theory', 80 *Col. LR* (1980) 1399.

[18] 2 *J. Leg. Stud.* 166.

wealth or utility or spread losses but rather to redress injustices. Causal maximalists see the purpose of the law of tort as being to set right the past rather than to promote a better state of affairs in the future. Citing Aristotle, they appeal to 'corrective justice'. This is a notion which reflects a wish to 'restore' or 'straighten out' a situation that has been disturbed.

Can it be said that Epstein's maximalist theory presents a viable alternative to those of his minimalist opponents? It seems to us that, as against them, he makes two valuable points but, in common with them, overlooks a third. The first matter on which he is surely right is that the law of tort cannot be accounted for solely as an instrument for maximizing future wealth or utility or some other socially desirable end. Backward-looking aims, such as the redress of wrongs, play at least some part in it and will continue to do so in any society in which regard continues to be paid to the moral sensibility of ordinary people. For one of our most widely shared intuitions concerning the redress of wrongs is that we are responsible for the harm we cause by the wrong we do and that we ought in a proper case to pay compensation for it. So far it seems that Epstein is right.

But Epstein's maximalist conclusion that the causing of harm is a necessary and sufficient condition of tort liability does not follow from his premises, even if one of the four paradigms is satisfied. Granted that the law of tort had backward- as well as forward-looking aims, and that the notion that we are responsible for what we bring about is morally one of central importance, that principle does not by itself serve to identify the cases in which injustices have been committed. As Posner has plausibly objected,[19] when Aristotle speaks of corrective justice he presupposes that a *wrong* has been done. He is not saying that any and every causing of harm, or causing of harm within some paradigm, entails a duty to submit to punishment or pay compensation. And it is certainly a feature of most, if not all modern legal systems, that they classify conduct as lawful or unlawful and, *on the basis of that classification*, impose liability for causing harm. In the common law, as in civil law systems, a defendant is normally liable to compensate only if he has acted unlawfully (e.g. is in breach of a duty of care owed to the plaintiff) and has *in addition* caused the plaintiff harm.

There are indeed some areas of tort law in which strict liability is imposed on a defendant who has caused harm by his *lawful* conduct, e.g. by storing explosives on his land, but this form of liability is not the norm. The Epstein theory implies a system of universal strict liability, such that no activity could be pursued except at the cost of paying for the harm, falling within the paradigms, which it generates.

[19] 10 *J. Leg. Stud.* 189–92.

Surely this would rightly be resented as unduly inhibitive? Granted that we might accept an extension of strict liability to cover activities, such as motoring, which seem particularly dangerous, is it not valuable that there should remain many areas of life in which, provided we take due care, we can go about our normal pursuits without having to fear that we shall be liable to pay compensation for any harm we cause? And will not this be true even of harm caused by force, fright, and the other paradigms? If I accidentally jog someone, I do harm by force. If he topples over, frightened by my appearance, I do harm by fright. If I firmly tell my son to study law rather than economics I do harm by compulsion, or something akin to compulsion. Surely the causal criteria of liability to compensate need to be supplemented by others?

Indeed, both the maximalists and the economic theorists have failed to pay sufficient attention to the value that attaches to the exercise of rights even when their exercise causes harm or inconvenience to others. The exercise of a right over any object is apt to cause harm or inflict costs on those who would prefer to use it themselves or to have it used in a different way. Is it not an important consideration that the farmer whose crops are burned by sparks or eaten by rabbits is *entitled* to plant his crops where he pleases? Is it not on this footing that damages are paid by the tortfeasor to the farmer and that the wrongdoer is not merely fined as an incentive to abstain from uneconomic use of land? Are not the farmer's rights respected even when another could make an economically better use of his land, so that he imposes a cost on the other and harms society by failing to maximize wealth? In the case of property rights at least, it can be argued that the property owners who inflict such costs on others by keeping them out of their land do so by force or the threat of force. The law, after all, endorses the use of force to exclude others from one's property. Even if Epstein does not have this type of case in mind when he speaks of the 'paradigm' of force, is there any real difference between this and, say, a violent assault, other than the fact that one is lawful and the other unlawful?

Another objection to Epstein's views has been touched on already. As Borgo points out,[20] Epstein's paradigms, despite what he says of them, do not accurately reproduce common-sense causal judgments. The latter are highly contextual. They focus on those factors which *in a particular situation* appear abnormal or unusual. The paradigms, on the other hand, lay emphasis on the method by which harm is caused, e.g. force. It is no doubt often the case that we are prepared to identify as the cause of an event that condition which involves motion or force. But it is easy to think of contrary examples. If A's

[20] Op. cit., pp. 425, 440.

car collides with *B*'s while *A* is driving his car and *B*'s is stationary, it might be natural, if we knew nothing more, to say that *A* had caused the collision. But suppose it turns out that *A* was driving carefully with his lights on while *B*'s car was parked without lights at night. In that case we might be inclined to cite *B*'s act in leaving his car parked in that way as the cause of the collision. The truth is that the paradigms are too crude and inflexible either to reproduce the judgments of common sense about causes or to replace the conventional classifications of certain types of conduct as unlawful.

The maximalist theory therefore fails to provide a viable alternative to the minimalist one. But Epstein is surely right to point to the 'sheer tenacity of causal language on the one hand and the perverse implications of most causal theorizing on the other'.[21] Though causal maximalism goes too far, we think it is a moral and legal principle of central importance that people are responsible for the harm they cause, where 'cause' is understood not as *sine qua non* but in the sense in which ordinary people understand it. It is true that merely to cause harm is not generally sufficient for liability. Normally, we hold people responsible for causing harm only when they do so by their wrongful or unlawful conduct and when other considerations of policy do not require the limitation of responsibility. But there are exceptional cases, often of strict liability, in which even lawful conduct causing harm carries with it a duty to compensate. Conversely, people are not generally responsible for harm which they did not cause; though, here again, there are important exceptions, such as the vicarious liability of an employer for wrongs committed by his employees in the course of their employment.

That we are responsible, then, for the harm we bring about is a principle that retains a firm hold on our sensibilities. But, asks Posner,[22] does it serve any social or ethical end to make people responsible for the harm they cause?

6. THE RATIONALE OF COMMON-SENSE CAUSAL PRINCIPLES AS A BASIS AND LIMIT OF RESPONSIBILITY

In asking the question 'Why hold people responsible for the harm they cause?' Posner means to refer to our common-sense concept of cause:[23] so in effect he is asking 'Why limit legal responsibility for

---

21 8 *J. Leg. Stud.* 477.
22 2 *J. Leg. Stud.* 218.
23 Posner is replying to Epstein, whose starting-point is the common-sense notions of causation embodied in ordinary language. Though Epstein adds to these a doctrine of paradigms which we do not accept (above, p. lxxiv), this does not affect our reply to Posner's question. For purposes of our rationale of common-sense causal principles as a basis and limit of responsibility, the paradigm doctrine can be treated as a suggested non-causal limitation on responsibility, like fault or *mens rea*.

the outcomes of an individual's conduct to those that are produced without the voluntary interventions of others or abnormal contingencies?' Presumably those who ask this sceptical question would not regard as satisfactory the answer that *moral* responsibility, as manifested in the way we blame people for their conduct and the outcome of their conduct, is limited in this way; and that there are obvious reasons why the law should not here conflict with moral principles. For Posner is presumably after something more fundamental. He means to raise a question about the rationality of such limitations on both moral and legal responsibility for the outcome of conduct.

A first step towards something more fundamental (and one which incidentally has the merit of exhibiting the non-arbitrary character of the distinction between a mere condition *sine qua non* and a cause) is the following. As we note on pp. 28–32 the simplest forms of actions affecting other people and things (e.g. hitting, pushing, breaking, stabbing) are changes in the world which we bring about through our voluntary action without the intervention of others or of abnormal conditions. What we ascribe to ourselves as *our* actions in changing the world and to others as *their* actions in doing so are items of this sort. It is important that in acting on the world and so changing it we take the world as it has been fashioned by prior natural events and prior human actions. Thus, it will very often be the case that one man *A* has by his earlier action created conditions which another, *B*, later exploits; and that *A*'s action is a condition *sine qua non* of what *B* brings about by his.

But this relationship does not lead to the conclusion that *B*'s action is part of *A*'s action. *A*'s action ends where *B*'s action begins; the latter is, despite their *sine qua non* connection, a 'new action', *novus actus*.

This is how actions are individuated in both moral and legal contexts. What applies to simple actions, where the outcome is close in time to the initiation of the action, applies also to those more protracted, less direct sequences where we distinguish the action (e.g. hitting) from its effects (e.g. a black eye). The same limiting principles apply. If, as is likely in the case of a black eye, the effect comes about without the intervention of other voluntary actions or abnormal contingencies, it counts as part of the agent's intervention in the world, caused by him. If, on the other hand, *A* hits someone so that he lies unconscious and *B* (not acting in concert with *A*) takes advantage of his condition to stab him, the stabbing is not part of *A*'s intervention. Even though *A*'s action is sufficient without the intervention of any voluntary action or abnormality to create the condition (unconsciousness of the victim) which *B*'s action exploits,

A does not cause *B*'s action or its outcome; though it is, of course, a *sine qua non* of that outcome.

So the principles limiting what an agent is said to 'cause' are the same as those embodied in our ways of individuating actions—the acts of successive actors. Is this latter not rationale enough for the former?

Of course, as we have explained above (pp. xliii–xlvii), causing harm is only one, though a centrally important and common, ground for responsibility. Other grounds include providing opportunities of specific sorts, especially by the neglect of common precautions, and providing reasons for others to do harm. In such cases the prior actor who provides the opportunity or reason may be liable for the outcome of another's voluntary action. It is true that in such cases the prior act may be a *sine qua non* of the later act, but it will also have additional features which distinguish it from other conditions *sine qua non*. These are analysed in the discussion of such cases in our book (pp. 51–61, 185–203).

But the sceptic may press on in search of a more basic rationale for treating causing harm as a ground of responsibility. He may complain that we have shown no reason why, when legal responsibility (liability to punishment or enforced compensation) is at stake, we should follow the principles by which we individuate successive actions. Why should we regard this as the central form of legal responsibility for outcomes? Why should a legal system bent on minimizing the harm arising from human conduct by its regulation of that conduct pay attention to our ordinary concepts of action? Why should it attend to the way in which we identify separate actions, and so the limits of action? Here, we think, the answer to the sceptic must be sought mainly in the virtues of the distinctive form which the legal control of conduct takes.

It is thinkable that legal control of conduct might take the form of Brave New World conditioning, so that people were never tempted to disobey the law, or of preventive or incapacitating measures, so that people were unable to disobey. In contrast with such forms of control the law of crime and tort, quite apart from sanctions, makes its primary appeal to individuals as intelligent beings who are assumed to have the capacity to control their conduct, and invites them to do so. It defers coercion and punitive measures until it is shown that this primary appeal has broken down, viz. until a crime has been committed or some harm has been done. The latter is the price to be paid for a form of control that invites the subject's obedience and so, by preserving the possibility of disobeying, maximizes freedom within the framework of coercive sanctions.

But what is it reasonable for the law to demand when it makes this primary appeal? Plainly no more than normal individuals can reasonably hope to deliver; that is, first and foremost, that they will not do those things which are sufficient to produce harm without the intervention of others or of abnormal contingencies. It would be quite unreasonable for the law to demand and for any individual to undertake that his action will not be the condition *sine qua non* of another's voluntary action and so of the harm it produces. It will on the other hand be reasonable enough for the law to demand and the subject to undertake, as subsidiary forms of responsibility in a restricted range of cases, liability for providing reasons for others to act or, in defiance of common precautions, providing opportunities for others to do harm.

Sanctions are a secondary matter to what we have called the law's primary appeal. But if by 'holding responsible' we mean holding liable to the sanctions of punishment or enforced compensation, there are good reasons for limiting these to cases where the law's primary appeal has failed; that is, to cases where the individual has done what is sufficient without the intervention of others or of abnormal contingencies to produce the harmful outcome.

Of course this shows only that the central case of responsibility should conform to causal principles and limits; and it makes clear why the *sine qua non* relationship is not enough. Besides the central case there will also be the neighbouring quasi-causal bases of responsibility (providing reasons or opportunities, etc.). But these are subsidiary to the central case, and narrower in their range of application.

It seems, then, that the limits to responsibility set by common-sense causal principles are appropriate to the law as a system designed to minimize harm by an appeal to individuals to control their conduct.

In addition to the foregoing considerations there is, we think, a further argument which could be convincingly put to the sceptic, though we can here do no more than sketch it. The argument is as follows. The idea that individuals are primarily responsible for the harm which their actions are sufficient to produce without the intervention of others or of extraordinary natural events is important, not merely to law and morality, but to the preservation of something else of great moment in human life. This is the individual's sense of himself as a separate person whose character is manifested in such actions. Individuals come to understand themselves as distinct persons, to whatever extent they do, and to acquire a sense of self-respect largely by reflection on those changes in the world about them which their actions are sufficient to bring about without the intervention of others and which are therefore attributable to them separately. This sense of respect for ourselves and others as distinct persons would be much weakened, if not dissolved, if we could not think of ourselves as separate authors of the changes we make in the world. If we had to share the authorship of such changes with numerous prior agents, of whom it could be said that, had they not acted as they did, we should not have been able to bring about the change, we could no longer think of ourselves as separate authors in the way we now do. This would be true even if the responsibility of the prior agents was only a prima facie responsibility, which might be excluded, for example, by the absence of some mental element required by law or morality (e.g. intention). For the allocation and apportionment of responsibility for the changes which human action brings about would in that case be inherently a matter of dispute; there would be nothing that we could unequivocally claim to be *our doing*.

Oxford   H.L.A.H.
May 1983   A.M.H.

PART I

THE ANALYSIS OF CAUSAL CONCEPTS

INTRODUCTION

THIS book has two related main objectives. The first is to identify the sources of the uncertainties and confusions which continue to surround the legal use of causal language in spite of a vast juristic literature dedicated to its clarification. If we believe it is possible to make further progress here, it is because past efforts seem to us not to have gone far enough, and to have left unearthed one major source of trouble. The images and metaphors, the fluid and indeterminate language, upon which both courts and textbook writers (even when most anxious to jettison traditional ideas) still fall back when deciding issues in causal terminology, or explaining such decisions to others, have their roots in certain features of a variety of concepts which permeate the daily non-legal discourse of ordinary men. These features need to be brought to light and described in literal terms; for the assertion often made by the courts, especially in England, that it is the plain man's notions of causation (and not the philosopher's or the scientist's) with which the law is concerned, seems to us to be true. At least it is true that the plain man's causal notions function as a species of basic model in the light of which the courts see the issues before them, and to which they seek analogies, although the issues are often very different in kind and complexity from those that confront the plain man. These notions have very deep roots in all our thinking and in common ideas of when it is just or fair to punish or exact compensation. Hence even lawyers who most wish the law to cut loose from traditional ways of talking about causation concede that at certain points popular conceptions of justice demand attention to them.

It may, of course, well be that when we thoroughly understand the common-sense notions of causation we should no longer wish our thought on any matters, let alone legal judgments of responsibility, to be dominated by them: we may think that they are vague, crude, or anthropomorphic, or all of these: they may be 'the metaphysics of the Stone Age' which should be replaced by modern notions of probability or 'risk'. This is a question to be decided in conjunction with our second main topic, but the delineation of the causal concepts which pervade ordinary thought is an indispensable preliminary. Accordingly, much of the first section of this book is concerned with the examination of a cluster of different but related concepts which are to be seen in the standard use, in and out of the law, of terms like 'cause', 'effect', 'results', 'consequences'. This analysis of common notions would now (at least in England and America) be accounted philosophy, but it is not the philosophical doctrine which the courts have so often and so vehemently repudiated as useless in the elucidation of the lawyer's perplexities concerning causes.

We attempt, in a preliminary chapter, to show precisely why the past philosophical discussions of causation have seemed so irrelevant to the lawyer, and in Chapters II and III to trace the outline of three different concepts latent in ordinary thought from which the causal language of the lawyer and also the historian very frequently draws its force and meaning. The first of these has a claim to be considered the central concept; it is that of a contingency, usually a human intervention, which initiates a series of physical changes, which exemplify general connections between types of event; and its features are best seen in the simplest cases of all where a human being manipulates things in order to bring about intended change. Here the language of 'cause and effect' sits most happily; and in the light of this simple case the complex imagery and metaphors associated with causes can be understood, and, with them, the distinctions drawn in more complex cases between voluntary interventions and abnormal events as 'causes' and other events as 'mere conditions'.

To be distinguished from this central case is the concept of one man by words or deeds providing another with a reason for doing something. Here there is not even an approximation, as there is in the first case, to the model of 'regular sequence' which since Hume has been accepted as the essence of causal connection. This concept is often required for the analysis of the notion of one man's 'causing' or 'making' another act and many other relationships (such as 'inducing' and 'enticing') between human actions.

Thirdly, the idea that the provision of an opportunity, commonly exploited for good or ill, may rank as the cause of the upshot when the opportunity is actually exploited is very important both in law and history. Its main application in the law is where an opportunity is provided for harm by the neglect of a common precaution.

All three types of concept have important negative variants; for there are frequent contexts when the *failure* to initiate or interrupt some physical process; the failure to provide reasons or draw attention to reasons which might influence the conduct of others; and the failure to provide others with opportunities for doing certain things or actively depriving them of such opportunities are thought of in causal terms. Two aspects of this mode of elucidating the subject deserve attention. The study of concepts is not to be identified with, nor should it lead to, the vice known to lawyers as 'conceptualism'. To isolate the main features of the concepts latent in causal language, though it certainly involves the study of the dominant trends of usage, is not to provide a code for the use of that language: still less is it to construct rules from which legal decisions on causal questions can be deduced. The utility of a conceptual investigation of this sort is to increase our understanding and powers of criticism of the framework within which legal thought moves and to permit the clear formulation of constantly recurrent factors which count, though not conclusively, for or against decisions. Further, there is at the present time a special reason for this approach. It is fatally easy and has become increasingly common to make the transition from the exhilarating discovery that complex words like 'cause' cannot be simply defined and have no 'one true meaning' to the mistaken conclusion that they have no meaning worth bothering about at all, but are used as a mere disguise for arbitrary decision or judicial policy. This is a blinding error, and legal language and reasoning will never be understood while it persists. The proper inference from the fact that no common property can be found in all the cases where causal language is used is that some more complex principle or set of principles may guide, though not dictate its use. The pains of unearthing these, though considerable, seldom go unrewarded.

Our second objective, to which our first is a preliminary, is to confront and evaluate a whole trend in legal thought about causation which originated, and has its most powerful advocates, in the United States, but is accepted, at least in principle, by many theorists in many jurisdictions. According to this point of view, which has many variations discussed in Chapters IV and V, causation in the law is less a concept to be analysed than a ghost to be exorcised. Legal rules say that men shall be punished, or shall make compensation, for the harm their wrongful acts have caused or 'proximately caused'; but, according to the theory under discussion, once it has been settled that no harm would have occurred without a wrongful act, there is no further causal question remaining for the courts to discuss. The only question is what limits the courts *ought* to impose on the wrongdoer's liability, and no answer is to be found to this question by thinking about the meaning or meanings of causation. So when, as

so often in a civil case, the question arises, as to the *extent* of a
wrongdoer's liability for harm which would not have occurred without the wrongful act, and even in a criminal case where the question
arises whether some person, without whose action another's death
would not have occurred, is legally responsible for that death, we
must take care not to be deceived, by the language used, as to the
character of these issues. The terminology of legal rules often tempts
courts to consider these issues in the form of questions whether the
harm was the 'consequence' or 'effect' or 'caused by' the wrongful
act, or whether it was 'too remote' or 'insufficiently proximate', or
whether some third party's action, or some extraordinary natural
event was a 'superseding cause'. These questions *look* like questions
of fact to be answered by reference to general principles or definitions
telling us in what the relationship of cause and effect consists, or
what a superseding cause is. All this, according to the newer doctrine,
is illusion: these questions are never questions of fact. They are to
be answered, not by inquiring whether the facts of a particular case
fall under some general definition of causal connection, but only by
inquiring what limit on liability or responsibility is required by 'the
scope', 'the purpose', or 'the policy' of specific legal rules involved
in the particular case. Is it consonant with the character of the
relevant rules to extend the wrongdoer's liability to harm occurring
in the way it did? Do sane principles of punishment require this
person, without whose act another's death would not have occurred,
to be treated as guilty of homicide, having regard to the manner in
which the death occurred?

Efforts to lay down, even for separate branches of the law, or even
for a specific jurisdiction, general rules defining causal connection,
or 'proximate cause', or determining when harm is too 'remote' to
be attributed to antecedent wrongdoing as its consequence, are, on
some variants of this view, all misguided. They are useless because
they are inevitably couched in language so vague as to permit courts
to attach any meaning they wish to them. Worse, they disguise as a
finding of fact, albeit a peculiarly recondite kind of fact, the often
creative function which the courts discharge when they determine in
concrete cases the proper limits or scope of general rules. All such
rules are a deception and a cheat, encouraging a superstition and
blinding us to the nature of an important judicial duty.

Much of the second part of this book is occupied with varieties of
this doctrine and its relation to the actualities of judicial decision.
According to many of its advocates, questions of the proper scope
or purpose or policy of legal rules represent all that there has ever
been in the minds of those who have used the traditional causal
language in the old misleading way in deciding the extent of liability

for wrongdoing. As far back as 1874 this view was put forcibly by
N. St. J. Green: 'Where a court says the damage is remote, it does
not follow naturally, it is not proximate, all they mean and can mean
is that they think that in all the circumstances the plaintiff *should*
not recover.' It is, however, necessary to distinguish the claim that
such questions are all that should be in the minds of courts when
discussing 'proximate cause' from the claim that this is all that
there is or ever has been in their minds. It is one thing to urge the
replacement of causal notions by considerations of legal 'policy',
and another to urge that there is nothing to replace: the first may be
desirable, but the second may be false, and a certain dogmatism and
incoherence in the modern outlook is due to the failure to distinguish
these two questions.

It seems clear, on a balanced view of the trend of decision in many
different areas of the law, that not only the language of courts but
their thought has been dominated by one or other of the group of
causal concepts that enter into the structure of ordinary non-legal
thought expressed in causal terms. Hence it is that, over a great
range of cases where causal connection with harm is made an element
in responsibility, the courts, as we show in Part II of this book, have
sought to apply the notion that an act is the cause of harm if it is an
intervention in the course of affairs which is sufficient to produce
the harm without the co-operation of the voluntary actions of others
or abnormal conjunctions of events. This has led the courts, in
tracing consequences of conduct, to scrutinize the precise manner in
which harm has eventuated from it and to distinguish often in the
cloudy terminology of *novus actus interveniens* and 'superseding
cause' those occurrences which 'break the chain of causation' and
so cut short liability from those which do not. In other types of case,
where the issue is whether one person has caused or induced another
to act in certain ways, they have often, with consistency and clarity,
investigated the different type of question whether the first person's
words or deeds constituted the second person's reason for acting as
he did. In others again they have used the common-sense notion
that accepts the omission of a common precaution against harm as
the cause of the harm when it eventuates.

The causal language used by the courts in determining such issues,
unsatisfactory as it often is, has seldom been a mere disguise for
judgments of policy or expediency or judicial intuitions of what is
just; though since the causal notions latent in ordinary thought, like
all other fundamental concepts, have aspects which are vague and
indeterminate, decisions involving them outside the central area of
simple cases have been powerfully and properly influenced by
judicial conceptions of policy or justice. On the other hand the

principles determining the extent of liability in tort, and especially for negligence and breach of statutory duty, have undergone and are still undergoing rapid transformation. It is now clear that the traditional firm distinction between questions concerning the nature of the duty imposed by legal rule and questions of the *extent* of liability for the breach of the duty is at certain points already quite unreal. This development has certainly complicated the exposition of the place of causal notions in the law of tort and made Chapters VI and VII where we distinguish 'causing harm' from 'occasioning harm', in order to assess the interplay of the new and old ideas, the most difficult to write and also no doubt the most difficult to read. The pattern of this very important development may, however, be shortly summarized here as follows. Where it is clear that the ground for regarding conduct as negligent, or the reason for prohibiting it by rule, is the very fact that it provides an opportunity, commonly exploited by others, for deliberate wrongdoing, it would obviously be senseless to treat their voluntary intervention as a ground for relieving the person who has provided the opportunity for it of the responsibility for the harm which they have done. So much is in accord with ordinary thought, which so often treats the omission of a common precaution against harm as the cause of the harm when it materializes. But the law has gone much further in holding persons responsible for harm, where their breach of a legal rule has provided an opportunity for others to do harm or an occasion for it to occur. Where a legal rule has been violated and harm has occurred which may be regarded as 'within the risk' in the sense that the harm is of a kind which the rule was designed to prevent, the courts may consider it enough that the defendant, by his breach of the rule, has done something without which the harm would not have occurred and so provided an occasion for it. They then hold him responsible for the harm, whatever the way in which it has eventuated from the occasion which he has provided, even if it was by a most unusual intervention or coincidence. A final stage is reached when the courts feel free to ascribe to legal rules in such cases the 'intention' or 'purpose' to prevent *any sort* of harm for which they think it expedient or just to make the defendant pay. This is the vanishing point of ordinary notions of causal connection as an element in responsibility.

The extent to which such 'risk theory' has supplanted older notions of causal connection cannot be determined without a thorough scrutiny of the hydra-headed notions of 'foresight' and 'risk' and these we examine at length in Chapter IX together with certain still perplexing features concerning the 'relativity' of negligence.

Is it possible to see in this developing use of the notion of 'harm within the risk' signs of the long-wished-for general simplification of the problems of 'proximate cause' which vex the law in every field? Our own view is that one form of the risk theory has come to stay in certain branches of the law where it extends liability beyond the point at which the older causal tests would cut it off: but so far as it would confine liability to something short of the extent allowed by causal tests it is not yet admitted into the law nor desirable that it should be. Hence it is a supplement to, not a substitute for, causal notions. There are, however, other reasons why the idea of risk cannot be a general solution or dissolution of causal problems. In much of the criminal law and in many important branches of the civil law causal connection enters into the definition of legal wrongs and must be established to show the *existence* of liability as distinct from its *extent*. Here the risk theory unless qualified by a tacit readmission of causal notions would give absurd and unjust results. We have, however, in Chapter XIII given extended consideration to the admirably clear and succinct proposals of the American Law Institute's Model Penal Code, which redefine the causal relation between act and harm required for criminal responsibility in terms of the three elements of condition *sine qua non*, *mens rea*, and risk. Partly because of the light it throws on the possibilities and limitations of the risk theory, we have studied in our final chapters the 'adequacy' theories of causation of Continental law; and we have traced the use and development of this and other theories, especially in German law. Here in a different idiom and in the shadow of a different philosophical tradition jurists have striven towards a general simplification of this tangled topic very similar to that now urged by American writers.

Other chapters of the book include a study of certain causal problems in the law of contract where the central notion of 'causing economic loss' requires a special analysis as a negative variant of the idea of providing opportunities: for to cause such loss is often to *fail* to provide some stipulated opportunity for gain. We have also confronted in Chapter XV certain problems of evidence in relation to causal questions in the law. This is virgin soil except for Wigmore's footsteps. In Chapter VIII on Concurrent Causes, where we consider causal problems mainly in relation to contributory negligence, we have also examined in some detail the anomalies, legal and logical, generated by those cases where two sufficient causes are either present together or in succession on the same occasion, or where one counteracts or renders impossible the normal operation of the other. Both lawyers and philosophers may draw a moral from this curious aspect of things; for here in a sense causal concepts break down and there are reasons for both affirming and denying causal connection. Here, as in other cases where principles point in contrary directions, decision in particular cases involves choosing between them. In the exercise of this choice it is necessary, though not enough, that we should be clear as to the character of the complexities.

I

PHILOSOPHICAL PRELIMINARIES

I. PARTICULAR AND GENERAL

BOTH the historian and the lawyer frequently assert that one particular event was the 'effect' or 'the consequence' or 'the result' of
another or of some human action; or that one event or human
action 'caused' or was 'the cause of' another event: somewhat less
frequently they assert that one person 'caused' another to do something or 'made' him do it. In such language, a variety of related
concepts are deployed which have bred many problems, and practitioners of both disciplines have given divergent accounts of its meaning. Philosophers, whose discussions of causation, protracted over
centuries, have certainly contributed something to the understanding
of causation in the natural sciences, till very recently have contributed little to further understanding here: lawyers, indeed, have
seen this and said very clearly that the issues which philosophers
discuss fail to illumine the specific aspects of causation which trouble
them. So they have rejected philosophical theories usually with the
insistence that the lawyer's causal problems are not 'scientific in-
quests'[1] but are to be determined 'on common-sense principles'.[2]
Similar dissatisfaction with what the philosopher has hitherto
tendered as an analysis of the meaning of causation is often expressed
by saying that this analysis, though doubtless adequate for the
scientist's causal notions, distorts what the historian does, or
attempts to do, in identifying the causes of particular events.[3]

Why has philosophy been thought irrelevant here while relevant
to science? What similarity between law and history, and which of
the many differences between these two and science account for this?
Among many factors an important one is this. The lawyer and the
historian are both primarily concerned to make causal statements
about *particulars*, to establish that on some particular occasion some

---

[1] *Weld-Blundell* v. *Stephens* [1920] AC 956, 986, *per* Lord Sumner.

[2] *Hogan* v. *Bentinck Collieries* [1949] 1 All ER 588; *Leyland Shipping Co.* v. *Norwich
Union Fire Insurance Society* [1918] AC 350, 363, *per* Lord Dunedin: 'I think the case
turns on a pure question of fact to be determined by common-sense principles. What
is the cause of the loss?'; *Haber* v. *Walker* [1963] VR 339, 357-8 ('concepts relating
to causation are latent in ordinary thought').

[3] See, P. Nowell Smith, 'Are Historical Events Unique?', *Proceedings of the
Aristotelian Society*, 57 (1957), 107. W. Dray, *Laws and Explanation in History*
(Oxford, 1957).

particular occurrence was the effect or consequence of some other particular occurrence. The causal statements characteristic of these disciplines are of the form 'This man's death on this date was caused by this blow.' Their characteristic concern with causation is not to discover connections between types of events, and so not to *formulate* laws or generalizations, but is often to *apply* generalizations, which are already known or accepted as true and even platitudinous, to particular concrete cases. In this and other respects the causal statements of the lawyer and the historian are like the causal statements most frequent in ordinary life: they are singular statements identifying in complex situations certain particular events as causes, effects, or consequences of other particular events. Such singular causal statements have their own special problems and it is these that most trouble the lawyer and historian. By contrast, in the experimental sciences, by which so much of the philosophical discussion of causation has been influenced, the focus of attention is the discovery of generalizations and the construction of theories. What is typically asserted here is a connection between kinds of events, and particular causal statements, made in the tidy controlled setting of the laboratory, have *only* the derivative interest of instances and present no special difficulties.

Since Hume, European philosophy has been dominated by the doctrine that the generalization or laws which it is the prime business of the experimental sciences to discover, constitute the very essence of the notion of causation. Hence even singular causal statements which appear to be confined to the connection between two particular occurrences are in fact covertly general; their causal character is derivative and lies *wholly* in the fact that the particular events with which they are concerned exemplify some generalization asserting that kinds or classes of events are invariably connected. So the very distinction between mere *post hoc* (*A*'s blow was followed by *B*'s death) and *propter hoc* (*A*'s blow caused *B*'s death) lies just in the fact that the latter, but not the former, depends upon and implies the truth of one or more general propositions relating directly or indirectly events of these two kinds. This analysis of the very notion of cause in terms of generalizations or laws asserting invariable connection between kinds of events seemed to dissolve many of the perplexities and obscurities which had so long attended it, and which had made men think that, in using causal language, they were committed to belief in the existence of unobservable 'forces', or 'powers' which some events had to 'produce' others, or to mysterious relationships which constituted the causal connection between particular events. All this was condemned by the philosophical analysis of cause as so much confusion, and was attributed to neglect of the simple fact that every singular causal statement was an instance of one or more general propositions asserting invariable sequence, and that causal connection consisted solely in this. The Humean analysis certainly swept away much lumber. Above all it offered to the scientist a more or less adequate account of those aspects of causation with which he is concerned: it freed him from the need to worry about the old obscure notions of unobservable powers and forces, for it told him, in effect, that there was nothing in these notions, or in the idea of cause itself, over and above the generalizations and laws which it was his business to discover. There are, however, other difficulties connected with causation not touched by this analysis. They are felt by those who, like the historian and the lawyer, are not primarily concerned to discover laws or generalizations, but often apply known or accepted generalizations to particular cases; they are difficulties peculiar to singular causal statements. The most notorious of these difficulties is this: when generalizations are used to identify the cause of a particular event on a particular occasion, the question arises whether something should be said to be the cause of something else, or only its 'occasion', 'a mere condition', or 'part of the circumstances' in which the cause operated. This is an inseparable feature of the historian's and the lawyer's and the plain man's use of causal notions. Plainly, the distinction has little to do with the generalizations which may be required to establish any singular causal statement, but very much to do with the particular context and purpose for which a particular causal inquiry is made and answered.

In most cases where a fire has broken out the lawyer, the historian, and the plain man would refuse to say that the cause of the fire was the presence of oxygen, though no fire would have occurred without it: they would reserve the title of cause for something of the order of a short-circuit, the dropping of a lighted cigarette, or lightning. Yet there are contexts where it would be natural to say that the presence of the oxygen was the cause of the fire. We have only to consider a factory where delicate manufacturing processes are carried on, requiring the exclusion of oxygen, to make it perfectly sensible to identify as the cause of a fire the presence of oxygen introduced by someone's mistake. The general laws which we may need to demonstrate causal connection in these two cases of fire will not tell us that in one case oxygen can be sensibly cited as the cause and in the other not. Yet in making this distinction it is plain that our choice, though responsive to the varying context of the particular occasions, is not arbitrary or haphazard. The question is, 'What sort of principles guide our thoughts?' Legal theorists have often written as if only the lawyer, in manipulating the concept of cause, was faced with such a task of selection, and with the need to draw a distinction between causes and mere conditions or circumstances. They have often said this under the influence of a somewhat inaccurate version of John Stuart Mill's doctrine which we later consider, and have insisted that, apart from legal rules, or the special requirements of legal 'policy', or conceptions of justice, every factor necessary for the occurrence of an event is equally entitled to be called 'the cause'. Yet this is not the case: neither the plain man, nor the historian, uses the expression 'cause', or any related expression, in this way. For the contrast of cause with mere conditions is an inseparable feature of all causal thinking, and constitutes as much of the meaning of causal expressions as the implicit reference to generalizations does.

A related difficulty, also peculiar to the application of causal notions to particular cases, is the following. If we are puzzled by someone's sudden death and ask for the cause there seem to be natural limits forbidding us to give in answer, on the one hand events which are too near in time to the death, and on the other events which are too remote in time. If a man has been shot by another it would usually be stupid or inappropriate, though not false, to give as the cause of his death the fact that his blood-cells were deprived of oxygen, and equally inappropriate to give the manufacturer's action in selling the gun to the killer's father from whom the killer had inherited it. What considerations control the normal refusal to cite or accept the first answer or to carry things back as far as the second? Again it seems clear the choice is not arbitrary here, but has to do with the context of the inquiry, who asks the question and why.

Much the same is true if we consider causal statements as pressing connections forwards, not backwards, in time. The historian, the lawyer, and the plain man are often concerned to work out consequences in this way and so to deploy, in identifying the consequences of some particular event, not one but several generalizations concerning the regular course of events. In doing this there are some cases where it seems natural to pursue connections 'through' a sequence of independent events: A lights a fire in the open, a mild breeze gets up and the fire spreads and consumes the adjoining house. Here the breeze was independent of the man's action in lighting the fire, but in the terms of the law's favourite though perhaps most misleading metaphor, it does not 'break the chain of causation'. It would be correct and natural to say that A's action was the cause of the destruction of the house. But if a man shoots at his wife intending to kill her, and she takes refuge in her parents' house where she is injured by a falling tile, though we may believe, on the strength of various general propositions, that if the man had not shot at his wife she would not have been injured (just as we may believe also, on the strength of general propositions, that if *A* had not lit the fire the house would not have been destroyed), this would not justify the assertion that the man had caused his wife's injury either in a legal context or in any other. It is obvious that, when we pursue causal connection in particular cases through a series of events, we have to take account, not only of generalizations which may inform us what sorts of events are necessary or sufficient conditions of the occurrence of others, but also of considerations of a quite different order, concerning the way in which generalizations may be combined and applied in particular cases. Again, this is not a peculiarity of the legal use of causal notions, but a feature of their use in all branches of thought where particular causal statements are made.

The character of the distinction between causes and conditions, and the principles imposing limits on the pressing of causal connections backwards or forwards in time, are the source of most of the difficulties in understanding the causal concepts with which the lawyer works, and they have received very little attention in the traditional philosophical discussions of cause. Perhaps a shift in philosophical method is really necessary before these problems could be seen to be as central as they are to our understanding of causation. They come into view only when the philosopher is prepared to forgo, at least temporarily, larger questions concerning the 'status' or 'validity' or the 'necessity' of the idea of causation, and to examine and chart in some detail the actual use made in given disciplines or in ordinary discourse of the key expressions like 'cause', 'consequence', and 'effects'. Such things emerge only when we observe the way in which a shifting context affects the force and meaning of these expressions.

II. HUME AND MILL

If we now turn back to Hume, the source of most contemporary philosophical thought about causation, we can see in detail why his discussion of the subject has appeared so remote from anything that troubles the lawyer. Throughout, notwithstanding the penetrating originality of his emphasis on vital distinctions neglected by previous philosophy, his treatment is on a level of generality which is *au-dessus de la mêlée* of the lawyer and the historian. The topic is scarcely considered from the point of view of those who, as they do, accept from common sense its broad generalizations or from science various causal laws, and then find problems of application when these are used to discover the cause of a particular event, or to work out the consequences of some earlier particular event. Instead, two very large general problems occupied Hume's attention: the first concerns the truth and character of the principle that every event has a cause, and the second concerns the notion of necessary connection between a cause and its effect. The first of these became the central problem for Kant and for most Continental philosophy and plainly hardly touches the lawyer: for, since in the main he is concerned to identify particular causes with the aid of established causal laws or accepted generalizations, he finds his problems in the very task of this application to concrete cases. He can afford not to be worried by the philosophical question whether there are some events which happen without cause, or whether the status of the general principle that every event has a cause is that of an empirical generalization of a peculiar sort of 'a necessary truth' or, as Hume concludes, is a belief not founded on any argument either 'demonstrative or intuitive', and is devoid of any 'absolute or metaphysical necessity'.[4] Even on the broadest interpretation of legal philosophy, the truth and status of the belief in universal causation seems a problem which may be safely left outside it, except perhaps when the moral foundations of criminal responsibility are under scrutiny, and the spectre of the 'free will' problem arises.

Hume's second problem, the analysis of the belief that when two particular events are related as cause and effect the cause *necessarily* has the effect it does, and that a cause has 'power' or 'efficacy' or 'produces' its effect, comes nearer, though not very near, to the problems of the lawyer. His great philosophical invention was to show that the 'necessity' (the 'must happen'), felt to be an essential part of causal connection, was neither some 'mysterious bond' linking particular causes and effects, nor some occult property inherent in the cause, and was different from the kind of necessity which is traceable by deductive reasoning only between propositions. In order to understand causality, Hume insisted that we must attend to two things: first that we make causal statements only after experience of the 'constant conjunction' or 'regular sequence' of pairs of events in nature, and secondly that, after experience of several instances of events regularly conjoined, we feel 'a determination of the mind to pass from one object to its usual attendant'. This feeling we transfer to objects. Whenever we speak of events as causing their effects we suppose 'necessity and power' to lie in objects, though we cannot find them when we look for them; in fact necessity is not to be found

---

[4] Hume, *Treatise of Human Nature*, Book I, Part III, chap. 14 (Selby-Bigge edn., p. 172).

in nature. 'It belongs entirely to the soul which considers the union of two or more objects in all past instances.'[5]

This doctrine has descended through Mill to the modern world, but in a somewhat altered form: it has changed its psychological form for a logical one. Hume's insistence that constant conjunction or regular sequence between events is the essence of the notion of causation is represented by the doctrine that every singular causal statement implies, by its very meaning, a general proposition asserting a universal connection between kinds of events; to make such a singular causal statement is therefore to claim that the events which it relates are instances of such a universal connection between types of events. The psychological analysis of the idea of necessary connection between cause and effect has undergone a more drastic change: it is generally accepted that, though Hume was right in insisting that necessity does not 'lie in objects', not all events which follow each other in invariable sequence are causally related, and not every general proposition asserting such sequence between kinds of events is ranked as a 'causal law'. Those that are, are distinguished not by the 'feeling' which they engender in the mind, but more by the place they occupy in a set of related general propositions, or within a scientific theory, or by the fact that they are used, as many other generalizations are not, to justify inferences, not merely as to what has happened or will happen, but 'counterfactual' inferences as to what *would* have been the case if some actual event, which in fact happened, had not happened.[6]

Again, little of this makes contact with the lawyer's special problems about causal connection. The doctrine that, whenever we make a singular causal statement asserting that two particular events are causally connected, we are logically committed to one or more general propositions asserting a universal connection between kinds of events, is not one that is ever stressed in legal writings on causation. The reasons for this are complex: partly it is, as we shall see later, that something far less rigid than a universal generalization constitutes the general element in most causal statements, and partly that the generalizations which are needed to defend particular causal statements are, for the most part, truisms derived from common experience. They concern the effects of impacts, blows, gross mechanical movements, and are often so deeply embedded in our whole outlook on nature that we scarcely think of them as separate elements in causal statements. Apart from this, however, the lawyer approaches the general element inherent in causal statements in a

---

[5] Ibid., p. 166.
[6] See R. B. Braithwaite, *The Nature of Scientific Explanation* (Cambridge, 1953), chap. 13.

different way, which disguises it: when it is suggested that *A* is the cause of *B* he is apt to ask as the first question, would *B* have happened without *A*? And though in fact, in order to answer this question, we have, as some legal writers have seen, to use our general knowledge of the course of nature, it looks as if this general knowledge were just part of the *evidence* that a particular event was the cause of another, and not constitutive of the very meaning of the particular causal statement. This indirect recognition of the general character of causal statements for the most part serves the lawyer well enough: there are, however, a number of problems for the elucidation of which a recognition of the essential generality of the central type of causal statements is required.

Apart from the lack of contact between the main issues discussed by Hume and the lawyer's peculiar problems, Hume's terminology is almost perfectly designed to conceal their existence. This is so in three respects, and it is significant that Mill, who was the first among philosophers to touch on problems like the lawyer's, differs from Hume on all of them. The first is this. Hume is throughout content to refer to particular causes as 'events' or 'objects'; and these terms are appropriate enough in the kind of examples which he uses of the impact of one billiard ball on another, and of sounds caused by the vibration of strings and similar occurrences. Yet in the causal statements which permeate history, law, and ordinary discourse, the category of what is spoken of as causes is not restricted in this way to 'events' or 'objects'. It includes persistent states as well as events, and not only positive happenings but the failure of events to happen, or the failure or omission of human beings to act. Besides the examples used by Hume we need, for a proper perspective, to bear in mind diverse ranges of singular causal statements such as 'The icy condition of the road was the cause of the accident', 'The signalman's failure to pull the lever was the cause of the accident', 'Lack of rain was the cause of the failure of the crop.' Mill, in his discussion of the common notion of cause, insists on this feature of it, and offers an account intended to set at rest the misgivings of those who are reluctant to accept anything but an active 'force' as the cause of an occurrence. He shows that this is not the way we talk or think, and that there is no reason why we should confine the category of causes in this way.

Secondly, Hume, and most of the philosophers who accept the analysis of causation in terms of uniform sequence, take far too simple a view of what it is that is found to recur in the regular sequence of nature. Hume, perhaps misled by his terminology of events, so often speaks as if it were pairs of single events that are related in this way; whereas Mill correctly insists that 'it is seldom if ever between a consequent and the single antecedent that this invariable sequence subsists. It is usually between a consequent and the sum of several antecedents, the concurrence of all of them being requisite to produce, that is to be certain of being followed by the consequent.'[7] Mill's recognition of this complexity leads not to an abandonment of Hume's doctrine but to a restatement of it which at any rate permits us to see how the typical causal problems of the lawyer arise. We often speak of a single event as the cause of an occurrence, yet we never find that whenever a single event of one kind occurs it is 'invariably' followed by some occurrence of another kind. Uniform sequences in nature, if they exist, are not thus simple: our causal generalizations inform us only that an occurrence of a given kind regularly follows when a complex set of conditions is satisfied. So when we identify single events as causes it appears that we choose one element from such a set, although each of the members of the set is equally required for the production of the effect. We identify the dropping of a lighted cigarette in a waste-paper basket as the cause of a fire, but in fact this leads to fire only if certain other conditions are satisfied: if there is oxygen in the air, combustible material in the waste-paper basket, and so on. A bent rail is identified as the cause of a railway accident, but this leads to such accidents only in conjunction with a number of other factors: the vehicles moving over the rails must be of a certain construction and weight and must move at a certain minimum speed. As far as their general and uniform connection with the effect is concerned, each of the members of the complex set of conditions from which the cause is selected is in the same position: each is required to complete the set; each is equally necessary *and in this sense* 'equivalent'.

This analysis lays bare a problem scarcely mentioned before in the history of philosophy:[8] are there any principles governing the selection we apparently make of one of a complex set of conditions as the cause? Is it arbitrary, irrational, the mere survival, perhaps, of metaphysical beliefs in the superior 'potency' possessed by some events?

Mill's answer to this question is not clear-cut. Hume, who had noticed that we often distinguish the cause from the occasion of an occurrence (though he never connects this, as Mill so illuminatingly does, with the complexity of the elements that appear in regular sequence in nature), said quite clearly that we must reject the distinction of cause and condition or occasion as due to 'prejudice and

---

7 Mill, *System of Logic*, Book III, chap. v, s. 3.
8 Bentham was aware of this problem. See his *Theory of Fictions*, Part I: I: B: 9 (cf. Ogden edn., 1932, pp. 39–48).

popular errors which have very much prevail'd in philosophy'. 'All causes are of the same kind.' 'If constant conjunction be implied in what we call an occasion 'tis a real cause.'[9] Mill does not take this short way with a distinction which he sees to be deeply rooted in common sense. His doctrine is that the cause 'philosophically speaking is the sum total of the conditions' of an event and 'we have philosophically speaking no right to give the name of cause to one of them exclusively of the others'.[10] He even speaks of the 'incorrectness' of doing this and of the 'incompleteness' of statements of causes which do not introduce mention of all of the conditions required to complete the set on which the effect invariably follows. Yet he does not think the selection we make, in identifying one event or condition as the cause, always arbitrary or without a rationale or due to bad metaphysics. After remarking that 'Nothing can better show the absence of any scientific ground for the distinction between the cause of a phenomenon and its conditions, than the capricious manner in which we select from among the conditions that which we choose to denominate the cause',[11] he proceeds to connect this variable selection with 'the purpose of our immediate discourse', and in his footnotes[12] to speak of 'the occasions' when in the 'accuracy of common discourse' we are led to speak of some one condition of a phenomenon as its cause. His view is that in the application of 'the common notion of a cause' a number of different considerations control this selection: in the text he stresses the condition immediately preceding the effect, 'the one condition the fulfilment of which completes the tale', which is often regarded as the cause; though we must not think 'that this or any other rule is always adhered to'.[13] In his footnotes, where he gives greater attention to detail, he connects the distinction primarily with the contrast between what a person inquiring into the cause of something already knows at the outset, and what he may require to be informed of as previously unknown to him. In our next chapter we consider in some detail how the selection from a set of conditions inherent 'in the common notion of a cause' is made. We show that the knowledge initially possessed by the inquirer is not as important as Mill thinks in guiding this selection, but is itself a subordinate aspect of a more general principle. It is, however, clear that Mill has here opened up a new aspect of causation, and moreover in attempting to clarify it uses a method which deserves notice. Instead of a frontal attack on the question,

9 Hume, op. cit., p. 171.
10 Mill, loc. cit.
11 Loc. cit.
12 Ibid., footnotes.
13 Ibid.

'What is a cause?' or 'What is causation?' Mill pursues his inquiries in an altered and more fruitful form. He asks, in effect, under what conditions and for what purposes is a single event spoken of as a cause. This shift in the form of inquiry is more important than it may appear at first sight. It leaves open the possibility that the common notion of causation may have features which vary from context to context, that there may be different types of causal inquiry, and that there may not be a single concept of causation but rather a cluster of related concepts. We shall see later that this is in fact the case, and that to bring these features to light we need to present our inquiry in this more flexible form.

The third respect in which Mill differs from Hume, and in so doing approaches much nearer the causal concepts of the lawyer and common sense, relates to what has come to be known since Mill as the doctrine of the plurality of causes. Hume and many other philosophers had written as if a cause must not only be *sufficient* for the occurrence of an effect, but also necessary: X is only the cause of Y if X is always followed by Y, and also Y never occurs unless X has occurred. Mill, by contrast, presents the notion of a cause in terms of sufficient conditions though, as we have seen, he stresses the complexity of these conditions: we find not a single condition sufficient to produce an effect, but a set of conditions which are together sufficient. 'The cause is then philosophically speaking the sum total of the conditions positive and negative taken together; the whole of the contingencies of every description which being realized the consequence invariably follows.'[14] He then insists that for an event of a given kind there need not be just one such set of jointly sufficient conditions, but there may be several independent causes of an event of the same kind. Sometimes it may be produced by one cause and sometimes by another. 'Many causes may produce mechanical motion: many causes may produce some kind of sensation: many causes may produce death.'[15] Thus Mill insists both on the complexity and the plurality of causes. It is worth noting that these are quite independent ideas: for it is especially easy for lawyers to confuse them since the phrase 'multiple causation' is often used in legal writing to describe the not uncommon situation when each of two wrongful acts which are *together* sufficient to produce some particular harm on a given occasion is said, though each of them would be *insufficient* without the other, to be '*a* cause', for legal purposes, of that harm. This admission of multiple causation shows only that sometimes more than one event is selected from a single

14 Op. cit., Book I, chap. v, s. 3.
15 Op. cit., Book III, chap. x, s. 1.

set of jointly sufficient conditions and each is dignified with the title of a 'cause' of the harm happening on a single occasion. It has nothing to do with the doctrine of plural causes according to which there may be several sets of independent conditions sufficient for the production of a certain *type* of event which may thus have different causes on different occasions.

Many philosophers have found the doctrine of plural causes un-intelligible, and have insisted that 'strictly' or 'scientifically' it cannot be that an event of a given kind is sometimes produced by one cause and sometimes by another, and they have accordingly ruled this out by defining the cause of an event as a condition or set of conditions which is both necessary and sufficient for its occurrence. They have argued that only the vagueness or looseness of our ordinary vocabulary makes it appear that the same event may have different sufficient causes: very often science has shown an unsuspected common element in causes hitherto taken to be independent or, more often, that the effects which we take at a common-sense level to be instances of the same kind of event with different causes are really instances of similar but different kinds of events which are classed together, in spite of their difference, for the rough practical purposes of everyday life under such headings as 'harm', 'injury', or 'death'. On this view apparent plurality of causes is due to our failure or inability to analyse the effects with the same particularity as the causes. Whether this belief in the 'ultimate' disappearance of the plurality of causes is philosophically well founded or not, it is clear that the lawyer, the historian, and the plain man accept the doctrine that an event of a given kind may be produced by different causes. They are perfectly prepared to treat, for example, death, as caused sometimes by poisoning, sometimes by starvation, and sometimes by shooting, or heat as the effect of friction, or of chemical change; and are unconcerned with the possibility that at some level of analysis, finer than that required for their purposes, common elements may be found in apparently independent causes; or differences may be found in what they treat as the 'same' effects, as has indeed been found to be the case in the last example. Of course, it is usually assumed that only one of several independent sufficient causes will be found to be present on a single occasion where we inquire for the cause of some event, but sometimes this assumption breaks down; and the presence on the same occasion of two causes, each of which is sufficient for the production of what is classed as the same harm, breeds certain puzzles for the law which we later discuss.

The philosophical discussion of cause did not of course come to an end with Mill, but he is one of the few philosophers to whom legal writers constantly refer[16] in explaining the idea of causation. He certainly deserves this tribute for he was the first to make clear at least how one question which often puzzles the lawyer arises out of the notion of causation. Yet there are aspects of 'the common notion of a cause' which Mill very much over-simplifies, and some which he neglects altogether, and these include matters very important for the understanding of causation in the law. These we shall discuss in some detail in the next chapter, and merely draw attention to them here as reasons for regarding Mill's analysis as incomplete.

The general account of causation which emerges from Mill's doctrine is distinguished by emphasis on four points. First, for Mill (as for Hume and most contemporary philosophers) the central notion of the concept of causation is that of invariable sequence of events in nature, with its corollary that to assert that one event is the cause of another is indirectly to assert that events of the one kind are invariably followed by events of the other. If challenged, particular causal statements must therefore be defended by proof of the relevant generalization asserting such invariable sequence.

Secondly, Mill shows that if we consider carefully the causal sequences to be found in nature we find, not that single events are followed by others, but the antecedents of such invariable sequences are complex sets of conditions which may include not only events but persistent states and negative conditions.

Thirdly, Mill distinguishes a 'philosophical' or 'scientific' notion of cause from 'the common notion'. According to the former only the whole set of conditions jointly sufficient for the production of the effect is the cause, whereas it is characteristic of the latter that one of these is 'selected' or 'singled out' as the cause, though it is in fact related to the effect in precisely the same way as the other

16 But very often the doctrine of 'the equivalence of conditions' attributed to Mill is wrongly identified by legal writers with the view that everything which is a *sine qua non* or necessary condition of some event has an equal right to be treated as the cause of that event. From this develops the view, stressed by legal writers, that, as far as the facts go, any event, however remote in the past, 'but for' which a given event would not have happened, is as much the cause of the later event as any other. This ignores Mill's definition of cause in terms of *sufficient* conditions (not *necessary* conditions) and his insistence on invariable sequence as the essential element in causation, with its consequence that the assertion, that one event is the cause of another, implies a generalization asserting that events of one kind are invariably followed by events of another. Hence there is no support in Mill for the following statement typical of many found in legal discussions of causation. 'Everybody is now in accord that logically there is no escape from the doctrine of the equivalence of conditions according to which a defendant's conduct must be held to have caused damage if, but for that conduct, however remotely connected with it, it would not have occurred ... and that everything which ensues is to the bitter end its consequence' (Lawson, *Negligence in the Civil Law*, p. 53). See also Prosser, *Selected Topics on the Law of Tort*, p. 228.

Certain ambiguities in the notion of a 'necessary condition' may have led to this misinterpretation of Mill's doctrine. These are discussed in Chap. V.

constituents of the set. This selection is made on principles which vary with the context and purpose of the particular causal statement.

Fourthly, Mill insists that there may be several independent sets of sufficient conditions for an event of a given type and so, both according to the philosophical (or scientific) and the common notion of cause, the same event may have different causes on different occasions.

III. DEFECTS OF MILL'S ANALYSIS

In Mill's analysis, if it is regarded as an account of common-sense notions of causation, there are certain large defects. The first is that the unqualified definition of cause in terms of invariable sequence does not correspond to the way in which causal notions are in fact used. It is true that there is a general element implied in a centrally important type of singular causal statement made by the plain man, the lawyer, and the historian (at least where what is said to be caused is an event other than a human action). This is true in the sense that if such particular causal statements are challenged statements of what generally happens must certainly be marshalled in order to show that what has occurred was a case of *propter hoc* and not merely *post hoc*. But these generalizations are not statements, as Mill's doctrine requires they should be, identifying sets of conditions invariably followed by events of a given kind. This sets a standard unrealistically high, indeed impossible to achieve, and a singular causal statement is not regarded as unjustified simply because generalizations of this order cannot be produced for its defence. As we show later[17] the relevant generalizations involved in common-sense causal statements are necessarily of a broader, less specific and often quite platitudinous type, and the way in which they are brought to the defence of singular causal statements is less simple than Mill suggests. Mill's doctrine in fact presents an idealized model of one centrally important type of causal concept. It is useful and clarifying for the exposition of certain features of ordinary causal statements but seriously misleading as to others.

A second more fundamental objection is that there are ranges of cases where the lawyer, the historian, and the ordinary man use the language of 'cause' and 'consequence' to designate certain relationships between human actions. For the analysis of this use of causal language a different model from that presented by Mill is required. The lawyer has frequently occasion to assert that one man caused another to do something; and it is often said with less

17 Chap. II, s. III.

formality, that one man 'made' another do something. These specific causal expressions are appropriate where one man exercises coercion, for example, by threats or authority over another, but the language of 'consequence' is used in a wider range of cases, as when we say that one man did something in consequence of another's advice or promise of reward or false statement. The central common notion in these various relationships between persons (which we term 'interpersonal transactions') is that the first person's words or actions constituted the reason or part of the reason why the second acted as he did. Of this notion we offer an analysis in Chapter II. Its most important feature is that the statement that a person acted for a given reason does not require for its defence generalizations asserting connections between types of events. When we assert that one person acted as he did because of another's threats our point is that this was his conscious reason, and an honest account from him of his deliberations would settle the question of its truth or falsity. It is no part of the meaning of such a statement that if the same circumstances recurred he would do the same again. A person may have reasons for his actions and yet not act consistently.

Hence if we are to understand the causal language of common discourse we must free ourselves from Mill's model and recognize (among others) two main types of causal statement. Statements that a physical event was caused by another such event or by a human action often approximate to Mill's account; but statements of interpersonal transactions involve the notion of a person's reason for acting and have no such dependence on general connections between events as the first type of statement. It is, however, true that behind such simple forms of statement as 'X caused Y's death' either one or a combination of both these causal concepts may lie: it may be that X simply shot Y or it may be that he made a soldier under his command shoot him. Besides this complexity there are, as we show in the discussion of the law, cases where causal language is used to indicate relationships different from either of these two main types but with important affinities to them.

Lastly, Mill, perhaps because, like his predecessors, he has principally in mind the scientist's concern with causation and his discovery of causal laws used in the explanation of occurrences, does not carry his examination of the different types of context in which causal statements are made very far. As his examples show, he is always thinking of a context where we ask for the cause of something because we are *puzzled* and do not understand how something has happened, and so ask for the cause because we want an *explanation*. We are presented with some contingency (a railway accident or someone's sudden death) which we find puzzling: we do not know why or how it happened. Here the inquiry into the cause brings to light previously unknown factors (e.g. in the railway accident a rail was bent or the driver fainted); when these are established the accident will be explained since we see then how the new fact that has been learnt 'made the difference' between the accident occurring and normal functioning. The existence of a bent rail, together with the factors relating to the weight and speed of the train, account for its running off the lines.

We may call such contexts where causal statements are made 'explanatory' contexts, and of course they typify a vast class of common-sense causal statements. Yet in order to see the lawyer's problems for what they are, another type of context in which causal questions are asked and answered must be distinguished. When the issue is whether someone is to be blamed or punished or made to compensate others for harm which has occurred, we may indeed, at a preliminary stage of our investigation, not understand how the harm came about, and at this stage an inquiry for the cause of some harm is still a search for an explanation. Sometimes such preliminary causal inquiries in a law court, designed to establish how or why something happened, are difficult and the plaintiff may fail to discharge the onus of showing how his injuries happened. Yet such searches for explanation are not the source of the lawyer's main perplexities: these arise when, after it is clearly understood how some harm happened, the courts have, because of the form of legal rules, to determine whether such harm can be attributed to the defendant's action as its consequence, or whether he can properly be said to have caused it. These may be called attributive inquiries. When such questions are difficult the difficulties are of a different character from those that prompt explanatory inquiries. They are generated less by ignorance of fact than by the vagueness or indeterminacy of the very concept of causal connection which we are endeavouring to apply in a particular case. Typically what precipitates these difficulties is that, among the conditions required to account for the harm which has occurred, there is found in addition to the defendant's action a factor (usually a human action or some striking natural phenomenon) which itself has some of the characteristics by which common sense distinguishes causes from mere conditions; so that there seems as much reason to attribute the harm to this third factor as to the defendant's action. Most contemporary writers on causation in the law would contend that such questions should be looked upon wholly as questions of 'policy' calling for a decision as to what ought to be done in the particular case in which they arise. They would claim that such questions raise no issue of fact and have nothing in common with explanatory inquiries, which are 'genuinely factual' questions. Whether or not this point of view over-simplifies or distorts the character of attributive causal statements, and exaggerates or obscures the difference between these and explanatory statements, it is clear that they have special features which require elucidation.

II

CAUSATION AND COMMON SENSE

I. THE VARIETY OF CAUSAL CONCEPTS

THE courts, as we have seen, often insist that the causal questions which they have to face must be determined on common-sense principles. Textbook writers often echo this, but sometimes with the warning that it is impossible to characterize any principles on which common sense proceeds.[1] This seems a counsel of despair which we should hesitate to accept. Whatever difficulties attend the notion of causation, we do after all succeed in communicating with each other satisfactorily over a great area of discourse where we use this notion; we manage to agree in our judgments about particular cases of causation in a very large number of cases. The position surely cannot be therefore as desperate as such writers claim. We must not think of a common-sense notion as necessarily a matter of mere impression, or so intuitive that it cannot be further elucidated, at least in its application to standard cases, however vague a penumbra may surround it. Common sense is not a matter of inexplicable or arbitrary assertions, and the causal notions which it employs, though flexible and complex and subtly influenced by context, can be shown to rest, at least in part, on statable principles; though the ordinary man who uses them may not, without assistance, be able to make them explicit. Here we are faced with a not uncommon phenomenon which prompts the search for definitions and has stimulated much that is valuable in philosophical inquiry. The ordinary man has a quite adequate mastery of various concepts within the field of their day-to-day use, but, along with this practical mastery goes a need for the explicit statement and clarification of the principles involved in the use of these concepts.

It is, on the other hand, true that many difficulties present themselves when we start to examine the common use of causal language in order to identify the 'common-sense principles' which courts profess to apply. We must expect both ambiguity and vagueness as well

[1] See Prosser, *Torts*, p. 240, speaking of the requirement that a cause must be a 'substantial factor', says, 'It is neither possible nor desirable to reduce it to any lower terms.' Street similarly warns us, at the conclusion of his examination of the place of causation in the law of tort, that 'cause must be regarded in a popular sense' and the final question is very often one to be settled by the common man's judgment, but does not define or characterize any principles (*The Law of Torts*, 1st edn., p. 149).

as variations which can be explained as more or less systematic adaptations of a common notion to contexts of different kinds. These facts make it impossible to do more than select for study *standard* examples of the way in which causal expressions are constantly used in ordinary life; and even then to focus attention only on certain characteristic features which have a bearing on those aspects of causation which most perplex the lawyers. As with every other empirical notion we can hope only to find a core of relatively well-settled common usage amid much that is fluctuating, optional, idiosyncratic, and vague: but the study of this core, as in other cases, may be enough to shed light on at least the darkest corners. A conceptual investigation is served by the delineation of the main trends of usage, not by the compilation of a dictionary.

There is, however, in this case a special initial difficulty. Preoccupation with the familiar pair of terms 'cause and effect' may make us think that there is a *single* concept of 'causation' awaiting our inspection and that the huge range of other causal expressions, 'consequence', 'result', 'caused by', 'due to', 'lead to', 'made', etc., are mere stylistic variants. Sometimes indeed expressions of this group may be substituted without alteration of meaning. It matters little, for example, whether we say that a fire was *caused by* a short circuit, or was *due to* it or that a short circuit *led* to the fire. Yet very often this substitution cannot be made without change of meaning or gross incongruity of expression. The use of the term 'effect' is in fact fairly definitely confined to cases where the antecedent is literally a *change* or *activity* of some sort (as distinct from a persistent state or negative condition), and where the event spoken of as the effect is a change brought about in a or person continuing thing. Thus, though the icy condition of the road, or a failure to signal, may be the cause of an accident, this is not spoken of as the 'effect' of these causes. Again, though we say of a person fined for driving a car at an excessive speed that this was the *consequence* of his speeding it is not the effect of it. The expression 'the effect of speeding' calls to mind (because its standard use is to refer to them) such things as the heating of the engine, or the nervous fatigue of the driver. 'Effects' as distinct from 'consequences' are usually 'on' something, brought about as the terminus of a series of changes which may or may not be deliberately initiated by human agents but involve no deliberate intervention by others. 'Consequences' has a much wider application, though it cannot always be used where 'effects' is appropriate, since it is not normally used of the terminus of a very short series of physical or physico-chemical changes. Hence the incongruity in speaking of, for example, the melting of wax in a flame as the consequence of heating it: it is its effect. 'Results' has also special implications and so a characteristic sphere of application different from either of the other two expressions. It is typically used of what emerges as the culminating phase or outcome of a process which is complex and consciously designed. So we speak of the 'result' of a game, a trial, or an experiment. Here no substitution of 'effect' or 'consequence' could be made without change of meaning. The prisoner's acquittal is the *result* of a trial, its *effect* on the public may be one of astonishment and the eventual change in the law may be one of its *consequences*. It is clear that 'cause and effect' have caught too much of the limelight of philosophical attention; for they are in fact not as frequently used as this has led us to think.

These few examples of what can be done to draw out differences between various causal expressions perhaps suffice to show that there is not a single concept of causation but a group or family of concepts. These are united not by a set of common features but by points of resemblance, some of them tenuous. Of this group the correlatives 'cause and effect' mark off one member which is of fundamental importance in practical life and for that reason, if no other, has a claim to be considered the central notion, by comparison and contrast with which the other related notions can be best characterized and understood. In this chapter we shall first exhibit certain salient features of the central notion and, secondly, show how analogies with these characterize the common-sense identification of causes in a wider field and the way in which the contrast between the cause and mere circumstances or conditions is drawn there. We shall then examine the cases where the language of 'cause' and 'consequence' is also used to refer to the interpersonal transactions mentioned in Chapter I and to certain other relationships even more distantly related to the central notion of 'cause and effect'.

II. CAUSE AND EFFECT: THE CENTRAL NOTION

Human beings have learnt, by making appropriate movements of their bodies, to bring about desired alterations in objects, animate or inanimate, or in their environment, and to express these simple achievements by transitive verbs like push, pull, bend, twist, break, injure. The process involved here consists of an initial immediate bodily manipulation of the thing affected and often takes little time. Men have, however, learnt to extend the range of their actions and have discovered that by doing these relatively simple actions they can, in favourable circumstances, bring about secondary changes, not only in the objects actually manipulated, but in other objects. Here the process initiated by bodily movements and manipulation may be protracted in space or time, may be difficult to accomplish and involve a series of changes, sometimes of noticeably different kinds. Here we use the correlative terms 'cause' and 'effect' rather than simple transitive verbs: the effect is the desired secondary change and the cause is our action in bringing about the primary change in the things manipulated or those primary changes themselves. So we cause one thing to move by striking it with another, glass to break by throwing stones, injuries by blows, things to get hot by putting them on fires. Here the notions of cause and effect come together with the notion of means to ends and of producing one thing by doing another. Cases of this exceedingly simple type are not only those where the expressions cause and effect have their most obvious application; they are also paradigms for the understanding of the causal language used of very different types of case. This is so for two reasons: first some important point of resemblance, or at least analogy, with these simple cases is traceable in the wider range to which causal language is extended; and, secondly, expressions which have a literal use in the simple cases have come to be used in a metaphorical and sometimes baffling way in cases far outside their scope. It is therefore important to consider certain prominent features of these simple cases which affect the general use of causal language in this way.

Human action in the simple cases, where we produce some desired effect by the manipulation of an object in our environment, is an interference in the natural course of events which *makes a difference* in the way these develop. In an almost literal sense, such an interference by human action is an intervention or intrusion of one kind of thing upon another distinct kind of thing. Common experience teaches us that, left to themselves, the things we manipulate, since they have a 'nature' or characteristic way of behaving, would persist in states or exhibit changes different from those which we have learnt to bring about in them by our manipulation. The notion, that a cause is essentially something which interferes with or intervenes in the course of events which would normally take place, is central to the common-sense concept of cause, and at least as essential as the notions of invariable or constant sequence so much stressed by Mill and Hume. Analogies with the interference by human beings with the natural course of events in part control, even in cases where there is literally no human intervention, what is to be identified as the cause of some occurrence; the cause, though not a literal intervention, is a *difference* from the normal course which accounts for the difference in the outcome.

In these basic cases involving human manipulation the cause is not only an intervention but one which characteristically involves movement of things; for when we bring about changes in things by manipulating them or other things, the first stages of this process consist of movements of our own body or parts of it, and consequently movements of things or parts of the things which we manipulate. Very often these initiating movements are accompanied by experiences characteristically associated with the exertion of pressure or force. The prominent part played in the simple cases by movement is responsible for two related ways of speaking about causes. First, it has bred a whole host of metaphors: causes quite outside the range of the simple cases we are considering are spoken of as 'forces' 'being active', 'operating', 'coming to rest', having 'power' or 'potency', 'active force', even when it is clearly realized that what is thus spoken of does not consist of movement or of anything like it. We find, for example, courts using such expressions freely: even the question whether the sale of a gun to a child was the cause of some injury has been discussed in the form of the inquiry as to whether or not the sale was an 'active force' that had 'come to rest' when the child's mother took the gun from him.[2] Conversely, preoccupation with the basic simple cases, where causes literally are movements, is the undiagnosed source of the difficulties which some theorists have experienced in seeing how a 'static condition' or a 'negative condition' or an omission could be the cause of anything. Mill in his footnotes argued against just such an objection, but the analogies with a thing which is active or moves have darkened and continue to darken[3] many a discussion of causation.[4] The position here is a

[2] *Henningsen* v. *Markowitz* (1928) 132 Misc. 547, 230 NYS 313.

[3] Becht and Miller, *The Test of Factual Causation in Negligence and Strict Liability* (1961), 22-3, 216 argue that omissions can only be 'hypothetical causes' while positive acts can be 'simple causes'. Consistently with this emphasis on physical motion, they hold that only physical effects such as injuries can be caused; it is therefore a 'mistake' to inquire into the cause of, for example, loss of earnings. Above, p. lvii.

[4] See *Rocca* v. *Stanley Jones & Co.* (1914) 7 BWCC 101, where a doctor's failure to attend to an injured workman and not the original injury was treated as the cause of the subsequent disability; but as late as 1944 du Parcq LJ said: 'Where . . . injury is left to take the course which nature . . . prescribes it might be that, were the point free from authority, the last state . . . could only be attributed to the original injury': *Rothwell* v. *Caverswall Stone Company* [1944] 2 All ER 350, 356. Sceptical doubts about 'negative' causes are still voiced. See comment on *Rothwell*'s case in (1945) 61 *LQR* 6: 'The negligence was negative, for it consisted in not treating the injured man . . . we should have thought it clear that mere failure to act could not be said to cause an incapacity', and comment to the same effect on *Hogan* v. *Bentinck West Collieries Ltd.* in (1948) 64 *LQR* 162.

In French law there is strict liability under s. 1384 of the civil code for 'acts' of a thing which the defendant has in his control. At first there was a tendency to hold that a thing 'acted' only when it moved. Later decisions concentrate on whether the thing was in the position or state which one would normally expect. If so, it has not 'acted', otherwise it may have. Thus it has been decided that the owner of a stationary vehicle left unlighted at night is liable to a person who suffers injury from driving into it on the ground that, in the absence of rebutting evidence, there is no ground for supposing that the stationary vehicle played a purely 'passive' part. It must therefore be presumed to be the 'generating' cause of the accident. Civ. 20.3.1933, *Sirey* 1933.1.257; Civ. 19.2.1941, *Sirey* 1941.1.49; Civ. 5.3.1947, *Dalloz* 1947 J.296. There is a full discussion in H. and L. Mazeaud and A. Tunc, *Traité de la responsabilité civile* (2nd edn. 1958), ii. 194-284.

curious, though not unfamiliar one when the terminology used in a given type of case is extended to cases which are only partly analogous. On the one hand it is perfectly common and intelligible in ordinary life to speak of static conditions or negative events as causes: there is no convenient substitute for statements that the lack of rain was the cause of the failure of the corn crop, the icy condition of the road was the cause of the accident, the failure of the signalman to pull the lever was the cause of the train smash. On the other hand the theorist, when he attempts to analyse the notion of a cause, is haunted by the sense that since these ways of speaking diverge from the paradigm where a cause is an event or force, they must be somehow improper. The corrective is to see that in spite of differences between these cases and the simple paradigms, the very real analogies are enough to justify the extension of causal language to them.

In these simple cases, where we speak of a deliberate human intervention or the primary changes initiated by it as the cause of an occurrence, we rely upon general knowledge and commit ourselves to a general proposition of some kind; but this is something very different from causal 'laws' or general propositions asserting invariable sequence which Mill regarded as essential to causal connection. When we assert that A's blow made B's nose bleed or A's exposure of the wax to the flame caused it to melt, the general knowledge used here is knowledge of the familiar way to produce, by manipulating things, certain types of change which do not normally occur without our intervention. If formulated they are broadly framed generalizations, more like recipes,[5] in which we assert that doing one thing will 'under normal conditions' produce another, than statements of 'invariable sequence' between a complex set of specified conditions and an event of the given kind. Mill's description of common sense 'selecting' the cause from such a set of conditions is a *suggestio falsi* so far as these simple causal statements are concerned; for, though we may gradually come to know more and more of the conditions required for our interventions to be successful, we do not 'select' from them the one we treat as the cause. Our intervention is regarded as the cause from the start before we learn more than a few of the other necessary conditions. We simply continue to call it the cause when we know more.

It is, moreover, a marked feature of these simple causal statements that we do not regard them as asserted unjustifiably or without warrant in a particular case if the person who makes of them cannot specify any considerable number of the further required conditions.

5 For this aspect of causation see D. Gasking, 'Causation as Recipes', *Mind*, 64 (1955), 479.

It is perfectly legitimate to say that A's blow caused B's nose to bleed and to feel confidence in the truth of his statement, though we could not formulate or would have very little confidence in a generalization purporting to specify conditions under which blows are invariably followed by bleeding from the nose. Yet even at this simple level where the cause is our own deliberate intervention, *propter hoc* is recognized to be different from *post hoc*. It is *possible* that just at the moment A struck, B independently ruptured a blood-vessel; experience may alert us to such possibilities, and science teach us how to recognize them. Yet this would be a remarkable coincidence and there is a presumption, normally fulfilled but rebuttable, that when we deliberately intervene in nature to bring about effects which in fact supervene, no other explanation of their occurrence is to be found. Hence to make this type of causal statement is justified if there is no ground for believing this normally fulfilled presumption not to hold good. It is, however, a feature of this, as of other types of empirical statement, that exceptionally they are not vindicated in the result and have to be withdrawn. But this does not mean that in asserting these causal statements we claim that they are instances of some general proposition asserting invariable sequence. We shall see later that even with causal statements of a more sophisticated kind somewhat similar qualifications must be put on the 'invariable sequence' doctrine.

III. CAUSATION AND EXPLANATION

The use of the word 'cause' in ordinary life extends far beyond the relatively simple cases where 'effects' are deliberately produced by human actions: it is also generally used whenever an *explanation* is sought of an occurrence by which we are puzzled because we do not understand why it has occurred. Causal statements made in answer to such requests for an explanation were distinguished at the end of Chapter I from attributive causal statements where the perplexities are of a different kind and may exist even though we need no explanation of what has occurred. In this section we shall be concerned only with explanatory causal statements and with one feature of them: the distinction between cause and mere conditions to which common sense adheres in face of the demonstration that cause and conditions are 'equally necessary' if the effect is to follow. In attempting to characterize the ways in which this distinction is drawn in typical contexts, we shall *provisionally* adopt Mill's account of the generalizations involved in singular causal statements and we shall *provisionally* speak as if it were true that what common sense distinguishes as the cause is one of a set of conditions believed to be *invariably* followed by the effect. We do this because the serious qualifications to be made in this account of the generality of causal statements can only be made clear if the principal ways of distinguishing the cause from other equally necessary conditions are well understood. The two questions 'How are causes distinguished from mere conditions?' and 'What sorts of generalizations are involved in singular causal statements?' are more intimately connected than has been thought.

The line between cause and mere condition[6] is in fact drawn by common sense on principles which vary in a subtle and complex way, both with the type of causal question at issue and the circumstances in which causal questions arise. Any general account of these principles is therefore always in danger of over-simplifying them. Some philosophers have succumbed to this temptation. Collingwood, who notices much that Hume and Mill neglected, treats the question 'What is the cause of an event?' as if it were always equivalent to 'How can we produce or prevent this?' On his view the cause is always the event or state of things by producing or preventing which we can produce or prevent the effect. This is to identify all cases with the fundamental type of case considered above; whereas in fact often only *analogies* with the fundamental type can be found. Such a view would make it improper to speak of knowing, for example, the cause of cancer if we could not use our knowledge to prevent it.[7] Perhaps the only general observation of value is that in distinguishing between causes and conditions two contrasts are of prime importance. These are the contrasts between what is abnormal and what is normal in relation to any given thing or subject-matter, and between a free deliberate human action and all other conditions. The notions in this pair of contrasts lie at the root of most of the metaphors which cluster round the notion of a cause and must be used in any literal discussion of the facts which they obscure. We shall now consider separately how these contrasts serve to distinguish causes from mere conditions in explanatory inquiries.

A. *Abnormal and normal conditions*

(i) In the sciences causes are often sought to explain not *particular* occurrences but *types* of occurrence which usually or normally happen: the processes of continuous growth, the tides, planetary

---

[6] Modern philosophical discussions of the distinction drawn by common sense between cause and conditions include C. J. Holloway, *Language and Intelligence*, pp. 68 ff.; P. Gardiner, *The Nature of Historical Explanation*, pp. 5-12, 99-111; G. J. Warnock, 'Every Event has a Cause', in *Logic and Language*, series ii, pp. 95, 103-4; R. G. Collingwood, *An Essay on Metaphysics* (1940), pp. 296-7.

[7] Collingwood accepted this corollary of his own doctrine (op. cit., p. 300).

motions, senile decay. In ordinary life, by contrast, the particular causal question is most often inspired by the wish for an explanation of a *particular* contingency the occurrence of which is puzzling because it is a departure from the normal, ordinary, or reasonably expected course of events: some accident, catastrophe, disaster, or other deviation from the usual course of events. With this in mind it is possible to see at once why certain types of conditions are classified as mere conditions and would be rejected as causes. In the case of a building destroyed by fire 'mere conditions' will be factors such as the oxygen in the air, the presence of combustible material, or the dryness of the building. In a railway accident they will be such factors as the normal speed and load and weight of the train and the routine stopping or acceleration. These factors are, of course, just those which are present alike both in the case where such accidents occur and in the normal cases where they do not; and it is this consideration that leads us to reject them as the cause of the accident, even though it is true that without them the accident would not have occurred. It is plain, of course, that to cite factors which are present both in the case of disaster and of normal functioning would explain nothing: such factors do not 'make the difference' between disaster and normal functioning, as the bent rail or the dropping of a lighted cigarette do. Mill's suggestion that the mere conditions are those which the inquirer is already aware of at the outset of the inquiry touches only a subordinate aspect of this more fundamental distinction between what is normal and abnormal for a given subject-matter. Very often but not always Mill's criterion and this more fundamental one coincide: in most cases a person who is told that there has been a railway accident in which lives have been lost, or that a house has been burnt down, and who is moved by this to ask what was the cause of the accident or the fire, would know of or assume the existence of many factors. These are treated as mere conditions because they are present both in the case of the disaster and of normal functioning. Very often some of such mere conditions, like the presence of oxygen in the air, will not only be a normal feature of the thing or place concerned, but will be a pervasive omnipresent feature of the human environment: other mere conditions, such as the weight and speed of the train, will not be universal features of our environment, but normal features of the thing in question. So in many cases the existence of such factors will very often be taken for granted by anyone who inquires into the cause. Yet this is not always so: we are very often quite ignorant of factors which science may show us as common to the cases both of disaster and normal functioning; yet when we learn of these we still classify them as mere conditions. The dropping of a lighted cigarette remains the cause of a fire even when we learn from science, what we may not have initially known, that the presence of oxygen is among the conditions required for its occurrence.

This, then, is the character of one principal distinction between normal and abnormal conditions: normal conditions (and hence in causal inquiries mere conditions) are those conditions which are present as part of the usual state or mode of operation of the thing under inquiry: some of such usual conditions will also be familiar, pervasive features of the environment: and many of them will not only be present alike in the case of disaster and of normal functioning, but will be generally known to be present by those who make causal inquiries. The analogy here with the fundamental case of the deliberate production of effects is plain. What is abnormal in this way 'makes the difference' between the accident and things going on as usual. It is easy, therefore, to think of such causes as 'intervening' or to use the metaphor of 'intruding' into an existing state of affairs. Yet we should be aware of the metaphor and be prepared to explicate it in terms of factors abnormal in this sense.

(ii) What is normal and what is abnormal is, however, relative to the context of any given inquiry in two different ways, and it is important to see precisely what this relativity is. Otherwise we may surrender prematurely to the temptation to say that the distinction between causes and mere conditions, which depends upon it, is arbitrary or subjective. If a fire breaks out in a laboratory or in a factory, where special precautions are taken to exclude oxygen during part of an experiment or manufacturing process, since the success of this depends on safety from fire, there would be no absurdity at all in *such* a case in saying that the presence of oxygen was the cause of the fire. The exclusion of oxygen in such a case, and not its presence, is part of the normal functioning of the laboratory or factory, and hence a mere condition; so the presence of oxygen in such a case is not a feature common (as the relative dryness of the building is) both to the disaster and normal functioning. It is therefore in such a case treated as 'making the difference' and so as the cause of the disaster.

There is, however, a different type of relativity to context: in one and the same case (not in different cases as in the oxygen example) the distinction between cause and conditions may be drawn in different ways. The cause of a great famine in India may be identified by the Indian peasant as the drought, but the World Food authority may identify the Indian government's failure to build up reserves as the cause and the drought as a mere condition. A woman married to a man who suffers from an ulcerated condition of the stomach might identify eating parsnips as the cause of his indigestion: a doctor might identify the ulcerated condition of his stomach as the cause and the meal as a mere occasion. It is cases of this sort that have led writers, notably Collingwood, to insist that the identification of a cause among other 'mere' conditions is always dictated by practical interest; and to attribute the relativity of the distinction to the varying means at the disposal of different people to produce results. But though this motive is often present in the identification of the cause it seems clear that it has not the great scope which Collingwood suggests. The willingness of common sense to classify a factor as the cause does not seem to depend directly upon ability to use it or interfere with it as a method of control. The discovery of the cause of cancer would still be the discovery of the cause, even if it were useless for the cure or avoidance of the disease; drought is the cause of failure of the crops and so of famine, lightning the cause of a fire for those who can do nothing about them and even if no one can. Indeed, when we do learn to establish techniques for controlling these things we may cease to look upon them as the cause and shift to speaking of the failure to use the established technique (in the case of famine and drought, food reserves and catchment areas), as the cause.

The relevance of controllability is often in fact quite indirect; it is usually a subordinate aspect of the principal criterion for 'mere conditions', viz. the normal or usual: for the factors which we cannot control may persist and, however unwelcome, become known and accepted as the normal course of things, as the standing conditions or environment of our lives to which we adjust ourselves more or less well. When things go wrong and we then ask for the cause, we ask this on the assumption that the environment persists unchanged, and something has 'made the difference' between what normally happens in it and what has happened in it on this occasion. So the wife of the man with the ulcerated stomach, who looks upon the parsnips as the cause of his indigestion, in asking what has given him indigestion is in fact asking: 'What has given this man in his condition indigestion when usually he gets by without it?' The doctor who gives the man's ulcerated condition as the cause approaches the case with a wider outlook and a different set of assumptions;[8] but they are different not because the disease in question is something that can be controlled or cured, but because he is professionally concerned only with a restricted type of abnormalities, i.e. diseases or deviations from the standard physical condition of human beings. His question (in contrast with the wife's) is: 'What gave *this* man

[8] And the doctor himself may identify the cause either as the ulcer or as the failure to take a drug which cures it according to whether his attention is directed towards diagnosis or therapy.

CAUSATION AND COMMON SENSE

indigestion when other men do not get it?'; for him what the man ate (controllable though it is) is a mere occasion—part of the normal conditions of most men's lives. So though *often* what cannot be controlled may be accepted or assumed to be the normal standing condition of some thing or subject-matter, it is *this* assumption, not just the inability to control, that leads to its classification as a mere condition; just as it is the abnormality rather than the controllability of some factor which leads to its classification as the cause. What very often brings 'controllability' and cause together is the fact that our motive in looking for the abnormality which 'makes the difference' is most often the wish to control it and, through it, its sequel.[9]

Although, as explained, the distinction between cause and condition may be drawn in different ways in one and the same case according to the context, there is a sense in which these distinctions themselves can be ranged according to the breadth of the perspective from which they are made. Thus, it is natural and correct, according to the context, to speak of the eating of the parsnips, the ulcerated condition of the man's stomach, and his failure to take a prescribed drug as the cause of his indigestion on a given occasion. But the second of these judgments is made from a broader perspective than the first and the third than the second. The second, unlike the first, focuses on a persistent pathological condition rather than an isolated meal, and the third, unlike the second, takes account of the possibility of curing or alleviating even such long-term pathological conditions.

(iii) Though what is treated as normal represents in many ways our practical interests and our attitude to nature, it would be wrong to identify as the normal and so always as part of the 'mere conditions' of events the ordinary course of nature unaffected by human intervention. This is an over-simplification, because what is taken as normal for the purpose of the distinction between cause and mere conditions is very often an artefact of human habit, custom, or convention. This is so because men have discovered that nature is not only sometimes harmful *if* we intervene, but is also sometimes harmful *unless* we intervene, and have developed customary techniques, procedures, and routines to counteract such harm. These have become a second 'nature' and so a second 'norm'. The effect of drought is regularly counteracted by governmental precautions in conserving water or food; disease is neutralized by inoculation; rain by the use of umbrellas. When such man-made normal conditions are established, deviation from them will be regarded as exceptional and so rank as the cause of harm. It is obvious that in such cases

---

[9] Mackie, *Cement*, chap. 2 and pp. 118–19 adopts our account and expresses it in the form that 'different fields may be chosen for causal accounts of the same event'.

38   THE ANALYSIS OF CAUSAL CONCEPTS

what is selected as the cause from the total set of conditions will
often be an omission which coincides with what is reprehensible by
established standards of behaviour and may be inhibited by punishment. But this does not justify the conclusion which some have
drawn that it is so selected merely because it is reprehensible.[10]

(iv) A deviation from such man-made norms will very often be an
omission, i.e. a failure to act in some way expected or required by
the norm. Much of the difficulty found in admitting that an omission
could be the cause of an occurrence is due to preoccupation with
those cases where human manipulation or alteration of the environment is the cause. The terminology of 'active force' is influential
here; yet there are other sources of perplexity. One source is confusion about negative statements: we easily think of omissions as
'negative events' and these in turn as 'simply nothing'. The corrective
here is to realize that negative statements like 'he did not pull the
signal' are ways of describing the world, just as affirmative statements are, but they describe it by *contrast* not by *comparison* as
affirmative statements do. 'He pulled the signal' *compares* this case
with the standard situation which we describe this way: 'He did not
pull the signal' *contrasts* this case with the standard situation but it
describes the world, a real state of affairs, not just 'nothing'.[11] The
most respectable objection to treating omissions as causes may perhaps be best expressed as follows. A gardener whose duty it is to
water the flowers fails to do so and in consequence they die. It can
be said that it is impossible to treat the gardener's omission here as
the cause unless we are prepared to say that the 'failure' on the part
of everybody else to water the flowers was equally the cause, and in
ordinary life we do not do this. This can, however, be explained
consistently with the analysis we have given of the distinction between cause and mere conditions. The 'failure' on the part of persons
other than the gardener to water the flowers would, accordingly, be
a normal though negative condition and, just because such negative
conditions are normal, no mention of them would usually be made.
The gardener's failure to water the flowers, however, stands on a
different footing. It is not merely a breach of duty on his part, but
also a deviation from a system or routine. It is, however, true that
in such cases there is a coincidence of a deviation from a usual
routine with a reprehensible dereliction from duty.

[10] Or 'a useful point at which public pressure can be placed', see F. S. Cohen, 'Field
Theory and Judicial Logic', (1950) 59 *Yale LJ* 238, 251–6. Cf. Calabresi, 'Concerning
Cause and the Law of Torts', (1975) 43 *U. Ch. LR* 105–6; P. J. Kelley, 'Causation
and Justice: a Comment', (1978) *Wash. ULQ* 635, 638 (alleging an 'ambiguity' in our
notion of the 'normal course of events').
[11] Cf. *State* v. *O'Brien* (1867) 32 NJL 169 (failure to adjust a switch the cause of
death).

(v) It is natural but mistaken to think of the mere conditions of an event as always existing contemporaneously with what is identified as the cause of that event; perhaps this is due to the natural metaphors of a 'background' or a 'medium' for the 'operation' of causes which we use when we refer to mere conditions. But it is vital to appreciate that what are contrasted with the cause as mere conditions always include some events or conditions subsequent in time to the cause. Conditions are *mere* conditions as distinct from causes because they are normal and not because they are contemporaneous with the cause. Thus if X lights a fire in the open and, shortly after, a normal gentle breeze gets up and the fire spreads to Y's property, X's action is the cause of the harm, though without the subsequent breeze no harm would have occurred; the bare fact that the breeze was subsequent to X's action (and also causally independent of it) does not destroy its status as a mere condition or make it a 'superseding' cause. To achieve the latter status, a subsequent occurrence must at least have some characteristic by which common sense usually distinguishes causes from mere conditions.

(vi) We have said that the distinctions so far considered between normal and abnormal conditions depend upon the fact that in ordinary life the request for a causal explanation is most often prompted by the occurrence of something unusual, of accidents, catastrophes, deviations from the normal. We must now consider a different ground, altogether neglected by Mill, for refusing the title of cause to certain conditions though they are as much required as it for the production of the effect. We do not call these either 'cause' or 'mere conditions' on or in which the cause 'operates': in fact the only way to describe them is by saying that they are merely parts of the process by which the 'effect' is always produced, or mere detail of the manner in which it is produced. Take, for example, a case where one man shoots another and kills him. Here we should treat the shooting, not the later deprivation of his blood-cells of oxygen, as the explanation and the cause of his death, although it is perfectly true that we could predict the man's death from knowledge of the latter more certainly than we could from knowledge of the earlier part of the process. Plainly, in passing over these in the search for the explanation of the man's death, we are passing over a whole set of sufficient conditions, not merely distinguishing one member of a set from other mere conditions, though we do that when we reach the shooting and identify *it*, not its attendant 'conditions', as the cause. One (but only one) important motive for rejecting the later conditions as the causal explanation in such common-sense inquiries is the fact that in such cases we are not looking for the cause of 'death', but for the cause of death *under circumstances which call for an explanation*. We want to know why Smith died when he did; we do not want to be told what is always the case whenever death occurs. The former is typical of the common-sense interest in causal inquiries ('Why did this happen when normally it would not?'); the second is typical of the experimental sciences ('What are the general conditions of death?'), though of course the applied sciences like medicine approximate to the former type.

So here the title of cause is refused to such later stages of the process, not because they are normal conditions, which they are not; but because they are common to all cases of a very general kind. It is the particularity of our interest in a given man's death at a given time that leads us to reject the latest phases of the process as the cause: these do not explain *this* man's death *now*. The basis of this discrimination can be made to appear, if we state in detail precisely what the puzzle is which the inquiry into the cause is to solve. Very little pressure is needed to allow that by 'What was the cause of death?' in such cases is meant 'What caused this man's death at this time?'

These considerations constitute one reason why common sense, far from rejecting the idea that an omission may be the cause of something, insists on regarding it as such. In circumstances where the cause of the flowers' dying is said to be the gardener's failure to water them the only alternative to citing this omission as the cause would be to cite the later physical conditions which led to their death. But to cite these would not satisfy the special interest in the particular case: it would show what *always* happens when flowers die, why *flowers* die: whereas an explanation is wanted not of that, but of the death of *these* flowers when normally *they* would have lived: what made *this* difference was the gardener's omission—an abnormal failure of a normal condition.

There is, however, a second distinct motive for refusing the title of cause to events which are later phases in processes initiated by abnormal events or interventions. These later phases only come to light *after* we have identified through common experience abnormal occurrences or human interventions of certain broadly described kinds ('shooting', 'blows', etc.),which bring about disturbances of or deviations from the normal course of things. Our knowledge of these later phases of the process is therefore a more precise, but *secondary* knowledge (often supplied by science) of what is regarded as mere ancillary detail which accompanies the cause; it is regarded as a mere further specification of the cause itself. Knowledge of these stages of the process between what has been identified already as the cause, and its effect, is thus a mere refinement of our primary knowledge. The initial disturbance of the normal condition of the thing affected

is the cause: these are merely the details of the way it develops. To
cite these later phases of the process as the cause would be pointless
in any explanatory inquiry; for we only know of them as the usual
or necessary accompaniments of the abnormal occurrence or human
intervention, which has been already recognized as 'making the difference' between the normal course of events and what has in fact
occurred, and so as explaining the latter. The details of the process
have in themselves no explanatory force.

B. *Voluntary action*

(i) Often when we look for the explanation of some particular
occurrence a human action will be found among the set of conditions
required to produce it, and will be identified as the cause. Sometimes
the action will be a deliberate voluntary action intended to bring
about what in fact has occurred: sometimes it will be an action which
by the standards of ordinary life is considered not a voluntary one
or not wholly voluntary. In common speech, and in much legal
usage, a human action is said not to be voluntary or not fully
voluntary if some one or more of a quite varied range of circumstances are present: if it is done 'unintentionally' (i.e. by mistake
or by accident); or 'involuntarily' (i.e. where normal muscular control is absent); 'unconsciously', or under various types of pressure
exerted by other human beings (coercion or duress); or even under
the pressure of legal or moral obligation, or as a choice of the lesser
of two evils, which is often expressed by saying that the agent 'had
no choice' or 'no real choice'. Of course the terms 'voluntary' and
'not voluntary' are not always used in this way; sometimes an action
done under coercion is spoken of as voluntary: we say (though in
Latin) *coactus voluit*.[12]

In many cases a human action which (in this relatively narrow but
common sense of voluntary) is not wholly voluntary may be
identified as the cause of some occurrence simply on the score of its
abnormality in relation to the thing or subject-matter affected, on
the principles already discussed: for it is plain that such an action
may be as much a disturbance of or interference with the normal
course of things, or a deviation from some normal man-made routine, as the most deliberate voluntary intervention. What we call

[12] This use of 'voluntary' and 'not voluntary' depends, no doubt, on a conception
of a human agent as being most free when he is placed in circumstances which give
him a fair opportunity to exercise normal mental and physical powers and he does
exercise them without pressure from others. As Aristotle (*Nic. Eth.* III. i. 2–19) first
pointed out, human actions may be 'not voluntary' for many irreducibly different
reasons of which he identified two: coercion and mistake (βία, ἄγνοια). This wide
notion of what is not voluntary or fully voluntary and its reflection in legal usage is
discussed further in Chap. VI.

'accidents' are often, though not always, occurrences of an untoward or surprising character which have as their explanation, and so as their cause, a human action which is done unintentionally or involuntarily. Someone may discharge a gun by an involuntary movement or pull the trigger in the mistaken belief that it is not loaded; if another person's death is the upshot these actions of a non-voluntary character are the explanation of the disaster and the cause of it. Such cases, although involving human action, fall under the principles for distinguishing causes from mere conditions already discussed.

Yet a voluntary human action intended to bring about what in fact happens, and in the manner in which it happens, has a special place in causal inquiries; not so much because this, if present among a set of conditions required for the production of the effect, is often treated as the cause (though this is true), but because, when the question is how far back a cause shall be traced through a number of intervening causes, such a voluntary action is often regarded both as a limit and also as still the cause even though other later abnormal occurrences have provisionally been recognized as causes. We shall illustrate these two different points in the next two sections. They both concern the extent to which it is true that the cause of a cause is itself regarded as the cause of the ultimate effect.

(ii) If unusual quantities of arsenic are found in a dead man's body, this is up to a point an explanation of his death and so the cause of it: but we usually press for a further and more satisfying explanation and may find that someone deliberately put arsenic in the victim's food. This is a fuller explanation in terms of human agency; and of course we speak of the poisoner's action as the cause of the death; though we do not withdraw the title of cause from the presence of arsenic in the body—this is now thought of as an ancillary, the 'mere way' in which the poisoner produced the effect. Once we have reached this point, however, we have something which has a special *finality* at the level of common sense: for though we may look for and find an explanation of why the poisoner did what he did in terms of motives like greed or revenge, we do not regard his motive or speak of it as the cause of the *death* into which we are inquiring, even if we do (as is perhaps rare) call the poisoner's motive the 'cause' of his action. The causal explanation of the particular occurrence is brought to a stop when the death has been explained by the deliberate act, in the sense that none of the antecedents of that deliberate act will count as the cause of death. This is not to say that causal inquiries may not be pursued further. We may, for example, discover that someone provided a reason or opportunity for the poisoner to do the deed, e.g. by persuading him not to hesitate or by supplying an appropriate dose of poison. In that case a causal relationship *of some sort*[13] may indeed be established between the conduct of the person who supplies the advice or means and the death of the victim. The latter can properly be described as a consequence of the persuasion or the provision of poison. But the fact that what is here unearthed is not the central type of causal relationship but something more tenuous is marked by the fact that we would not happily say that the accomplice had either 'caused' the death or 'caused' the poisoner to kill. We do not therefore trace the *central type* of causal inquiry *through* a deliberate act.

(iii) Conversely we do very often trace the cause through other causes to reach a deliberate act. It is to be noted that, despite what is commonly said by philosophers, causal relationships are not always 'transitive': a cause of a cause is not *always* treated as the cause of the 'effect', even when the cause of the cause is something more naturally thought of as a cause than a man's motive is. Thus the cause of a fire may be lightning, but it would be rare to cite the cause of the lightning (the state of electric charges in the atmosphere) as the cause of the fire; similarly the cause of the motor accident may be the icy condition of the road, but it would be odd to cite the cold as the cause of the accident. By contrast, we do not hesitate to trace the cause back through even very abnormal occurrences if the sequence is deliberately produced by some human agent: if I take advantage of the exceptional cold and plan the car accident accordingly by flooding the road with water my action is the cause of what happened. Like the poisoner's arsenic, the icy condition of the road is now regarded as a mere means by which the effect is produced. The analogy of the simple cases discussed in section I is obviously very close here: the deliberate act 'reduces' the intermediate abnormalities to the status of mere 'means' and the law recognizes somewhat similar principles in its adage that 'intended consequences cannot be too remote'. It is, however, true that the causal relationship is sometimes transitive in other cases: notably when there is some other ground for thinking of the intermediate causes as analogous to 'means' by which the earlier cause produces its effects. This will be so when it is *well known* that a given event is likely, by leading to the intermediate cause, to lead to the 'effect'. Thus, when we discover that a short circuit was the cause of the fire and later learn that the cause of the short circuit was the decay of the insulating material, the latter would naturally be cited as an explanation or 'fuller explanation' of the fire.[14]

13 For an analysis of these relationships see below, pp. 51-9.

14 There are other principles at work accounting for the transitivity of the causal relation where the cause of a cause is a deliberate act and the upshot is contrived. Such an act excludes the notion of a *coincidence*: which is also excluded if (as in the short-circuit example) the intermediate event is, because of its appreciable likelihood, thought of as analogous to the means by which the first event commonly produces its effects.

44   THE ANALYSIS OF CAUSAL CONCEPTS

A deliberate human act is therefore most often a barrier and a
goal in tracing back causes in such inquiries: it is often something
through which we do not trace the cause of a later event and something *to* which we do trace the cause through intervening causes of
other kinds. In these respects a human action which is not voluntary
is on a par with other abnormal occurrences: sometimes but not
always we trace causes through them, and sometimes but not always
we trace effects to them through other causes.

IV. CAUSAL GENERALIZATIONS

What kinds of generalization are involved in ordinary singular
causal statements? How are these defended from the objection that
the alleged cause did not cause but was merely followed by the effect?
So far we have provisionally assumed that Mill's account of this
is substantially correct: that the primary meaning of causation is
'invariable and unconditional sequence'[15] of classes of complex
events or conditions; and hence that when we identify a single event
as a cause of an event we 'select' it from a set known or believed to
be 'invariably and unconditionally' followed by an event of that
kind. Plainly this account must be qualified, for it is obvious that,
though singular causal statements are frequently made not only with
confidence but with a confidence not judged improper, very little
confidence would either be felt or judged proper in any generalization
of this exceptionless kind. In what relevant generalization of 'invariable and unconditional sequence' would or should we feel the same
confidence as we do in the singular causal statement that the kettle
boiled because it had been put on the fire? Precisely what qualifications are needed to represent the normal standards of everyday
life is a question of some difficulty. It is tempting to say that the
generalizations involved in ordinary causal statements merely assert
that in *most cases* events of one kind are and will be followed by
events of the other; we need merely scale down Mill's 'invariably' to
'in the great majority of cases'. The truth unfortunately is not thus
simple.[16]

The type of generalization in fact involved in singular causal statements will best be seen if we consider various ways in which Mill's
theory is defective as an account of 'the common notion of a cause'.
There is first the general objection that Mill's standard of 'invariable

15 We have written hitherto as if Mill had merely said 'invariable' (as he often
does). We have done this both for brevity and because the difference between this
and 'invariable and unconditional' has not been important: but it needs attention
here.
16 Though this too simple view was previously taken by the authors: see 'Causation
in the Law', (1956) 72 *LQR* 58, 71.

and unconditional sequence' cannot be met. Even the scientist can only discover uniformities which he has evidence for believing will hold good over a far wider range of conditions than any that can be discovered by common sense: he does not assert or have grounds for asserting that they will hold good under 'all possible conditions' (unconditionally) or 'always' (invariably). This is in fact an absurdity both in practice and principle. To meet such a standard there would have to be evidence that 'everything' (*all* other things, events, or states) apart from the set of conditions specified in the generalization was irrelevant, so that the specified conditions would be unconditionally and invariably sufficient.[17] Neither in practice nor in principle is this possible. Even when some persistent feature of the universe is known and identified (e.g. the motion of the planets) it may be impossible to tell whether, if this were to change, any given causal generalization would be affected and so whether a full statement of the generalization should include it; and of course there must be many such persistent features still unidentified, as cosmic background radiation was till recently. Apart from these practical difficulties, the supposition that there are in the 'universe' a finite number of things or events or states, which in principle could be examined and found relevant or irrelevant, is chimerical; the 'universe' is not a box with a finite number of objects in it, each describable in a finite number of ways.

More important than these general objections is the fact that Mill's view that we 'select' or 'single out' the cause from a complex set of conditions previously identified, and that these are known or believed to be invariably followed by the effect, is misleading. It radically misrepresents the character of those actual situations (in and outside law courts) where we ask and succeed in obtaining a satisfactory answer to questions about the cause of some particular past occurrence. For there is in fact no 'selection' or 'singling out' of the cause from a set of jointly sufficient conditions: what is true is that, after causes have been identified, we come in the course of later experience to learn more detail both about the conditions (i.e. other factors without which they would not be followed by their effects) and about the process of change between cause and effect. So we identify a 'blow' as the cause of a child's injury, for example, a broken leg, without knowing or caring what conditions must also be satisfied, if a blow of just that force is always to be followed by such an injury. When we learn later that the blow would be sufficient only if the bone structure was, as in the child's case, of less than a

17 It would not be enough if those conditions not included in the generalization always in fact coexisted with those included, for then the specified conditions would merely be 'invariably' followed by the effect but not 'unconditionally'.

certain thickness, nothing is added to our confidence in the initial statement that this blow caused the injury, though we would have been grateful for this information had we been attempting to predict the outcome of the blow.

Mill's account in fact suggests—and this is its main defect—that, in order to answer the question 'What was the cause of this occurrence?' we should ideally be able to *predict* with certainty that it would happen, from detailed and precise knowledge of antecedent conditions. It is, however, vital to see that logically the demands of the situation in which we ask for the cause of what has happened, and that in which we are concerned to predict, are very different. In the first case it is an *inquest* that we are conducting. The 'effect' has happened: it is a particular puzzling or unusual occurrence, or divergence from the standard state or performance of something with whose ordinary states or modes of functioning we are familiar; and when we look for the cause of this we are looking for something, usually earlier in time, which is abnormal or an interference in the sense that it is not present when things are as usual. Such abnormalities or interferences we recognize and describe in broad general terms (as 'blows', 'storms', 'heat') which sit loosely to their instances, since they cover a wide range of different occurrences, and we are indifferent to their detailed specification. In identifying some such occurrence, thus broadly described, as the cause of what has happened we must be satisfied that its connection with the effect is itself unproblematic, not in need of explanation. It is in ordinary life enough for this purpose if we know: first, that contingencies of these broadly described kinds ('blows', 'injuries') commonly go together as a familiar feature of experience the statement of which might often be quite platitudinous; and, secondly, if cases where these general connections do not hold can be distinguished from the case before us. In all but the simplest cases the causal connection will be 'indirect', i.e. will have to be traced through a number of successive stages which exemplify a number of different familiar general connections. The statement that a slate falling from a house-top caused the bruises of a passenger in an open car on whom it fell rests, for common sense, on a set of both mechanical and physiological platitudes.

In effect, in the typical case with which the law is concerned, when we ask for the cause, we are asking that some abnormal lapse from routine (some accident, injury, or loss) be rendered intelligible by being exhibited as an instance of certain other normalities, namely, those general connections which characterize experience and are formulated in broad and general terms. It is therefore not a defect, but an essential feature of the generalizations used in establishing that some thing was the cause of another, that these should remain formulated in broad terms capable of covering not only the particular case before us (and any exactly like it) but many similar cases differing from it in detail. If the particular case cannot be connected in this way by a broad generalization with a multiplicity of past cases, the minimum explanatory force, which discovery of the cause must have, will be lacking. The abnormality will not have been shown to be some variety of the usual or familiar.

This concern, in giving the cause of a particular occurrence, to link the case in question with others that have happened is not present when we are attempting to predict. What we want then is *certainty*, not explanatory force, and a generalization which is as near Mill's prescription as possible will serve us best, even if it is so specific and complex as to apply only to this case. This is a warning: it shows that acceptance of the theory that the only respectable support for a singular causal statement is a Mill-like generalization would drive us into an *impasse*. In our asymptotic approach to the inappropriate ideal of 'invariable sequence' we should have to treat a multiplicity of cases, which at present fall under a single unifying generalization, as instances of separate generalizations, specially adapted to the quantitative and qualitative differences of different cases. These separate generalizations, with their application only to cases falling under such highly specific descriptions, could not possibly guide us to or be our warrant for asserting any singular causal statement; for this must have the link with other cases provided by broad generalizations such as those of common experience. Only when highly specific generalizations are deductions from a single wider theory do these form part of the ground for singular causal statements. In such cases the theory has a unifying and explanatory force comparable to those of the loosely framed generalizations of common sense. This is notably the case when the cause of mechanical failures or the breakdown of scientifically constructed devices, for example, an electrical circuit, are identified by reference to deductions from the theory on which they are constructed.

These considerations explain why it is that we do not regard a singular causal statement, made on the strength of the rough rubrics of common experience, for example, that the cause of a particular fire was the dropping of a lighted cigarette, as strengthened when we learn from science that without the presence of oxygen the fire would not have occurred. Of course this would have to be mentioned if we were really concerned to exhibit the case as an instance of a generalization specifying the conditions in the present case which would be invariably followed by fire. Yet when we come to learn such further necessary conditions we do not treat our past statement of the cause, though made in ignorance of them, as one made without proper justification which has luckily turned out to be correct. The knowledge of the further conditions helps us to understand the causal process involved, and so *why* lighted cigarettes so often cause fires, but adds nothing to our identification of the lighted cigarette as the cause of the fire on this occasion. For the same reason, there is nothing absurd in combining with the assertion that this was the cause of the fire a refusal to formulate or assent to any given generalization specifying conditions of invariable sequence, though we do not and could not deny the formal claim of (unspecified) *ceteris paribus*, i.e. that there are some factors in the present case which, if they recurred, would always be followed by fire.

At this point, however, a caution is necessary. We must not conclude, from the fact that the generalizations we use in identifying the cause of a particular event are broadly formulated, that it is sufficient to defend a singular causal statement by a simple appeal to 'high probabilities', i.e. generalizations to the effect that the alleged cause is and will be followed by the effect in 'the great majority' of cases. We may be tempted into this belief by a very common form of general causal statement such as 'A short circuit very frequently causes fire' or 'A bent rail will very probably cause an accident'. These may suggest that singular causal statements state merely that a given case is one of the majority or large number of cases to which such statements refer, and are established by simple appeal to these statements of high probabilities. Yet, that this is not so is perhaps evident from the fact that causal statements of this form also include statements such as 'Diphtheria now very *rarely* causes death'. These causal apophthegms (as they might be called) merely indicate what on particular occasions (numerous in the case of short circuits, few in the case of diphtheria) have been found to be the causes of the events to which they refer; but they are *not* the generalizations used on these particular occasions to establish the cause. They could be paraphrased to read, 'It has been very often or on rare occasions found that X was the cause of Y.' So too general statements (not including the word 'cause') of high probability of sequence, though relevant to establish causal statements, are not sufficient support for them *per se*. The statement that on this occasion X was the cause of Y differs from the conjunctive statement that X was followed by Y on this occasion and X's are followed by Y's in the great majority of cases. The statement that the dropping of the lighted cigarette caused the fire asserts more than that fire followed in this case and there was a high probability that this would be so. The crucial difference is that, if we assert that X was followed by Y in a given case and Y's are highly probable given X's, we are *not* committed to explaining the cases where X's have not been followed by Y's nor to showing that the given case differs from them. On the other hand, if it is asserted that X was the cause of Y, something must be done to anticipate and answer the objection 'Yes: X was here followed by Y as in the majority of cases, but was it the cause in this case?'

This requirement means that counter-examples or exceptions to the generalizations used in support of particular causal statements must be distinguished from the case in hand; till this is done a rival causal explanation must still be sought. Of course the applied sciences represent a vast storehouse of counter-examples with which common-sense judgments about the causes of accidents, injuries, and losses, which typically come before law courts, must be reconciled; and scientific accounts of the fine detail of different causal processes often determine a choice between rival causal explanations. Very often, however, a description in non-scientific terms of the successive stages of, for example, an accident will show that these stages are linked by firm if platitudinous generalizations; and, though there may be many cases where the same injury would not have resulted from the same initiating occurrence, a simple description of the stages would reveal differences. Though a falling tile may rarely kill a passer-by, we may in a particular case easily trace the connection from fall to impact, and from impact to injury, because there is nothing to suggest that any counter-examples to the simple rough generalizations implicitly used are relevant here. Of course, in the face of Cartesian doubt we could marshal scientific theories and measurements of forces and velocities to prove the point, but this would be sensible only if there were a rival explanation to disprove.

Let us use the expression 'causal principles' as a compendious term both for the generalizations by which singular causal statements are defended, and the manner in which they are brought to bear on particular cases. It can be said then that, when it is asserted that something is the cause of a particular occurrence, the case must be shown (if necessary by a description of its component stages) to exemplify generalizations broad enough to cover a variety of different cases; secondly, the case must be distinguishable from counter-examples or cases outside the known limits of any generalization used. There is also a third requirement of particular importance in the law. Though it is true in all cases that the factor we designate as the cause would not be followed by the effect without the co-operation of many others, if we find, on attempting to trace by stages a causal connection, that these factors include voluntary interferences, or independent abnormal contingencies, this brings into question our right to designate the earlier factor as *the* cause; for this expression is used of something which, with the co-operation only of factors that rank as mere conditions and not themselves as causes, is sufficient to 'produce' the effect. The fact that a fire would not have spread to a neighbouring house without the normal breeze does not inhibit us in treating the lighting of it as the cause of the disaster; it would be different if someone deliberately fanned the embers or, just as they were dying out, a leaking petrol tin fell from the back of a jeep. This displacement of one event from the position of 'the cause' by other events, which have also the characteristics by which common sense distinguishes causes from mere conditions, is of crucial importance, as we show in the next chapter, when causal connection is the basis of the attribution of responsibility.[18]

There are also intermediate cases where it is natural to speak of each of two contingencies as *a* cause and of neither as *the* cause. This is so where both are abnormal to a degree sufficient to preclude their classification as 'mere conditions' but their abnormality is not of that extreme or coincidental character required for the contingency in question to be regarded as the sole cause.

This account of causal principles, though applicable to the type of case with which the law is usually concerned, does not cover every sort of singular causal statement. As we have said,[19] an account of the way in which deductions from scientific theories are used in the identification of the causes of failures of machines or other artefacts would show that something more nearly approaching Mill's ideal formed part of the reasoning. Indeed, any really comprehensive account of the general element implicit in singular causal statements would show that this varied with different types of subject-matter.

Finally, it is to be noted that the account in this section of causal principles is not directly applicable to those cases, especially numerous and important in the law, where an *omission* or failure to act is identified as the cause of some (usually untoward) event. Someone's failure to wrap up is commonly and intelligibly taken to be the cause of his catching cold, and driving in the dark without lights to be the cause of an accident. The background to this use of causal language is that the natural course of events or human activities has been found to be generally harmful and we have learnt from experience how to counteract the harm by certain procedures. Accordingly the generalizations on which such identifications of omissions as causes of harm rest relate primarily to the adequacy, under standard conditions, of the omitted precautions. Then causal principles require that the conditions of the case in hand should be shown not to differ from the standard case; for example, that the

[18] See, however, above, p. 43 and n. 14, for certain cases where causes are traced backwards through other intermediate causes.
[19] Above, p. 47.

temperature was not so low as to make protective clothing useless, or that the victim of the accident was not so drunk as to be incapable of seeing a lighted car. Our concern here is to show that the omitted precaution *would* have averted the harm, not that when it is omitted harm always results. This form of causal reasoning has certain features of importance in the law which we consider further in Chapter V.

V. INTERPERSONAL TRANSACTIONS: REASONS AND CAUSES

So far[20] our analysis has been concerned with cases where some event, other than human action, is said to be the effect, result, or consequence of some other event or of some human act or omission. We have not considered cases where one human being is said, either by words or deeds, to cause another to act, nor the important and very varied field of cases where one human action is said to be done 'in consequence of', 'because of', or 'as the result of' another, as, for example, where one man induces another to do something. We have reserved this topic for separate treatment because we have here a set of principles different, in certain ways, from those involved in the central type of causation of physical events and occurrences other than human actions. In this field of relationship between two human actions we have to deal with the concept of *reasons* for action rather than *causes* of events; yet there are many transitional cases for, while the contrast between these concepts is important, it shades off in many directions.

The range of notions under examination in this section is exemplified in the standard use of such expressions as 'He made me do it', 'He persuaded me to do it', 'He induced me to do it', 'I did it because he ordered me to do it', 'I did it because he offered me a reward', 'I did it because he threatened to hit me', 'I did it on his advice'. We shall call these cases 'interpersonal transactions'. There are indeed many differences within this group of notions, but also important common features: of these the most important is that such relationships between two persons' actions, though often and intelligibly called causal connection, especially by legal writers,[21] do

20 But see above, pp. 42-3.
21 Street, *The Law of Torts*, 6th edn. p. 340: 'There has been much discussion of what has been thought to be a significant distinction between advice and persuasion but the problem . . . presents just the same difficulties on the facts as other problems of causation in torts.' Prosser (*Torts*, pp. 934-5) says that in order to be held liable for interference with a contract, defendant must be shown to have caused the interference, but proposes the same test of 'material and substantial' contribution as for physical sequences.

not depend upon 'regular connection' or sequence as the causal relations between physical events do. Hence the assertion that one person, for example, induced another to act is not 'covertly' general even in the modified sense discussed in section IV.[22] Generalizations have a place here but a less central one.

It would be somewhat unnatural in the informal discourse of ordinary life to describe any of this range of cases by saying that one person *caused* another to act; and in some cases this description would be positively misleading. 'He caused me to act' would be merely unnatural (and 'He made me do it' natural) in those cases where one person is induced to act by threats, coercion, the exercise of authority, or false statements; it would be positively misleading in those cases where one person merely advised, or tempted, or requested another to act, or procured his action by offering a reward. The special factors which are entailed by the expressions 'causing' another to act or 'making' him do something are that the first person should intend the second to do the act in question, and should use means of persuasion or inducement (e.g. threats) which render it not wholly voluntary.

There is a temptation to assimilate the relationships between human actions here under discussion to those exhibited in ordinary cases of causal connection, and so to think of cases where one person induces another to act, and cases where the impact of one body on another causes it to move, as different examples of the same causal relationship, differing only because, in the first case, the terms related are human actions involving psychological and mental factors; whereas in the second, more familiar case the terms related are merely physical events. Hypnosis and many cases of the infliction of nervous shock *are* cases where the difference from familiar cases of causation consists simply in the fact that psychological elements are involved; they do not involve the *radical* differences which separate 'He induced me to do it' from 'His blow caused the victim's death'. The temptation to ignore the more radical differences between these two types of relationship has many roots; there are important similarities as well as differences, which are sometimes expressed by saying that a reason for action is just a cause 'looked at from the inside'. Many important causal idioms are appropriate for the description both of such relationships between human actions and ordinary causal sequences; when one person induces another to act we correctly say that the latter acted 'because of', or 'as the result of', what the first person said or did, and these expressions are often apt to describe the effect of the impact of one body on another. Further, an important and characteristic use of such statements as

---

[22] Above, p. 44.

'*X* induced *Y* to steal' is to provide an explanation as an answer to the question 'Why did *Y* steal?' So, just like ordinary causal statements, discovery of the relationship between two actions may have an explanatory force. Moreover, these relationships constitute an important element in different sorts of legal and moral responsibility, criminal or civil liability; and special *exemptions* from these forms of liability often depend, for example, on whether one person coerced or induced someone into doing some action. Hence references to such relationships between two human actions appear scattered throughout every branch of most legal systems.

Four common features demand attention in the various relationships of this type: (i) in all of them the second actor knows of and understands the significance of what the first actor has said or done; (ii) the first actor's words or deeds are at least part of the second actor's reasons for acting; (iii) the second actor forms the intention to do the act in question only after the first actor's intervention; (iv) except in the case where the first actor has merely advised the second act, he intends the second actor to do the act in question.

1. In all the cases under discussion one essential requirement, if such a relationship is to exist, is that words spoken or actions done by one person must have been known to the second person, and in the case of words they must not only have been known[23] but understood. They do not 'affect' the second person merely as so much noise, for he recognizes their meaning. One person can only be 'induced' to act by another if he knows and understands what that other has said. In this sense the relationship between the two actions in such cases is 'through the mind' of the second person. Precisely what the second person's mental attitude to the action or words of the first person must be, depends on what form of relationship is said to exist. In the case of deceit and false pretences it is necessary that he should have understood and also believed what was said to him; in the case of threats or bribes he must not merely know of and understand what is said to him, but at least think there is some chance that what is threatened or offered will be forthcoming. Even in the case of certain gross forms of persuasion where non-rational means are used to incite another to act, it must at least be the case that any words used, for example, in inflammatory speeches, should be understood, and to the extent that the incitement consists of

---

[23] One person *knowing, understanding*, and in some cases *believing* what another has said is essential where the act of the first person consists in his saying something. This is one necessary stage to be distinguished from the further stage where the second person acts *because* of what he has understood or believed. Even if the first stage is (as some analysts of the notion of communication hold) a causal connection of the familiar kind, the second is not.

non-rational stimuli (shrieks, groans, gestures) the second person must at least be aware of them. These last cases where, as we say, the first person 'works on' the feelings of the second come very close to cases of ordinary causal connection.

2. In nearly all these cases the first actor's words or deeds constitute at least part of the second actor's *reasons* for doing the act in question; and in all cases but those of disinterested advice and the grosser forms of incitement by non-rational means, the reason is of a special kind; for it entails that the first actor should by his words or deeds have done something to render some course of action more *eligible* in the eyes of the second actor than it would otherwise have been. This element is most obvious in the cases where one person induces another to act by bribes, threats or offers of reward. Here the second actor is led to believe that, if he acts as required, he will obtain, through the agency of the first actor, something he wants or escape something he dislikes. In this way the action in question is rendered more eligible: he has an extra reason for doing the action, in addition to any reason he might have had independently of the first actor. So it is often said that the first act has 'provided a motive' for doing the second act, and this expression is only misleading to the extent that it conceals the fact that normally in such cases the second actor will have had a pre-existing wish to seek, for example, material benefits or to avoid pain, in conjunction with which the first actor's offers or threats constitute a reason for acting. In some cases, however, there need not be a pre-existing disposition of this sort, since the first actor may both arouse the second's desires or cupidity and also make offers to satisfy it contingently on his doing some action.

Where inducement takes the form of false statements the action is rendered more eligible in the eyes of the second actor simply because he is led to believe that he will gain in a way which he had not thought of; but, unless the false statement takes the form of a prediction by the first actor of his own future conduct or a statement of his own intentions, the benefits which the second actor is led to expect are independent of the agency of the first actor. This is one of the main ways in which inducement by false statement differs from inducement by threats or offers of reward.

Mere advice differs from inducement in that the role of the first person is primarily that of drawing the attention of the second to reasons for or against doing some action. This is to advise another *upon* or *about* some contemplated action. Mere advice may be a ground of legal liability, as for instance when a solicitor or doctor negligently gives a client or patient the wrong information, on which the latter acts; in this type of case there may also be liability for

CAUSATION AND COMMON SENSE

failing to provide correct information. To advise another *to do* an action, of course, goes beyond this discussion of the pros and cons. In saying 'I advise you to do this' the speaker personally commends the action, and his doing this may of itself render it eligible in the eyes of someone who trusts or respects him. Hence, if the advice is taken, the mere giving of the advice may be the second person's reason for acting; in other cases the merits of the action which have emerged in the course of the discussion may also have weighed with him in deciding to do it.

3. Whenever it is appropriate to say that one person has acted in consequence of what another has done or said (whether this constitutes inducement or merely advice), it must be the case that the person so acting should have made up his mind to act only after the first actor's intervention by words or deeds. If before this intervention the second actor had already intended to do the act in question, all such relationships are excluded; for in such cases the intervention could not be the second actor's reason for deciding to do what he did, though it may be his reason for persisting in a resolution already formed rather than changing his mind.

It is often said that if the first actor's words or deeds are to be accepted as the second actor's reasons for doing what he did, the first must be a condition *sine qua non* of the second, i.e. it must be true that he would not have acted in the way he did, had the first actor not said or done what he did. Even if this is true (and in certain contexts legal and non-legal statements of an actor's reasons seem not to have this implication) it is wrong to conclude that, if this relationship between two actions is to subsist, the first person's words or deeds must have the general connection with the act of the second which is characteristic of causal relationships between physical events. The statement that one person did something because, for example, another threatened him, carries no implication or covert assertion that if the circumstances were repeated the same action would follow; nor does such a statement require for its defence, as ordinary singular causal statements do, a generalization of the kind discussed in section iv.[24] This is most obvious if we consider not a third person's statements about the case where someone has done something because of another's threats, but the threatened person's own statement that he acted because of those threats. It would be absurd to call upon him to show that there really was this connection between the threats and his action, by showing that generally he or other persons complied when threats were made. This general statement might be quite untrue and yet his statement of his reasons might be true: the assertion that he acted because of the threats

[24] Above, p. 44.

carries no implication that, given similar circumstances, he would act again in this way or that, in similar circumstances, he or other persons have always acted in that way. By contrast, if he had said that a blow had caused a bruise, where no statement of *reasons* for acting is involved, evidence of what experience has shown to be generally the case would be required to show that this was a case of *propter hoc* not *post hoc*.

The question, whether or not a given person acted on a given occasion for a given reason, is primarily a question as to the way in which the agent reaches his decision to do the act in question: whether the thought of a given reason weighed with him as he made up his mind, and whether or not in doing the action he consciously adapted the manner of its execution accordingly. These are questions primarily about the agent's experience in contemplating, deciding upon and carrying out the action in question, and for this reason the agent's own declarations about his reasons have a special primacy or importance. This is recognized in the law as well as in ordinary life. If asked to make sure, in giving evidence, that his reasons for acting were as he claims, an honest witness will not be expected to produce generalizations, but to attempt to reconstruct the deliberative situation or his 'state of mind' at the time.

Of course generalizations about the way in which either the person in question or other persons respond, e.g. to threats, or by what reasons they are or are not actuated, have an important place in such cases. They may be used as *evidence* that a person in saying he acted from a certain reason was not speaking the truth (or was forgetful), because it was 'out of character' for him, or is rare for anyone to act for such a reason. Such generalizations are built up from knowledge of many individual cases where we have found that a person acted (or did not act) from a given reason, and we now use them in a new case to confirm or throw doubt on the agent's statement that he did act for this reason. But the instances out of which such generalizations are constructed were themselves cases where it was found that an individual had a certain reason for action, and this was known independently of such generalizations. On the other hand, a singular càusal statement asserting that one physical event was the cause of another depends on generalizations in a different way: here the latter are not merely *evidence* that in the particular case the events are causally related; they are *part* of what is meant by causal connection; and the instances from which these causal generalizations are constructed were not already recognized *apart* from such generalizations as cases of causal connection but only as cases of succession between events.

The matter is, however, complicated by one point. Though there is no implication of uniform sequence in asserting that a person acted for a given reason, what we recognize as a possible reason is not independent of how in a general very broad sense most people act. If a person said he left the room 'because Caesar died in 44 BC' we should not understand him. Roughly speaking, we recognize as a reason for action (and therefore as a given person's reason on a particular occasion) something which is relevant to the promotion of some purpose known to be pursued by human beings and so renders an action eligible by human beings as we know them. The concept of reasons therefore *presupposes* that, in general, human beings respond to certain situations in such ways as fleeing from danger, or conforming with social rules or conventions, etc. Yet this presupposition of broad similarity in human behaviour, without which we could not have the concept of a reason for action, does not mean that, when on a particular occasion we assert that a person acted for a particular reason (e.g. to avoid threatened danger), we are committed to any assertion that, if the circumstances were repeated, the same action would follow: it may be that neither he nor anyone else would act so again in such circumstances. All that is required is that, if the case is to be one of a person acting for a reason, we must understand how it promoted some objective analogous at least in some way to those which human beings are known to pursue by action.

In some of the relationships considered here the intermediate act may be fully voluntary. This will be the case, for example, if the first actor has done no more than advise the second actor or offer him a reward for acting; whereas in cases where the first actor resorts to threats or gives orders which the second is under some duty to obey the second action is less than fully voluntary. It is this second class of case that would be expressed by saying that the first actor 'caused' the second to act or 'made him act' as he did. A more detailed analysis of the use in criminal law of the expression 'causing something to be done' is given in Chapter XIV.

Mixed and borderline cases

Between the interpersonal transactions so far examined and ordinary cases of natural causation, where one physical event is caused by another, or by a single human intervention, there are two major points of contrast. First, all cases of interpersonal transaction involve the notion of one person intentionally providing another with a reason for doing something, and so rendering it eligible in his eyes. Secondly these cases are logically independent of generalizations even of the modified kind suggested in section IV[25] as a substitute, in

---

[25] Above, p. 44.

58   THE ANALYSIS OF CAUSAL CONCEPTS

cases of the causation of physical events, for Mill's 'invariable and unconditional sequence'. It is, however, clear that there are many forms of causal language which may be used indifferently for cases of either type, and also that there are mixed or borderline cases having some of the features of both types.

Thus 'causing another to do something' or 'making him do it' does not always refer to an interpersonal transaction in which one person induces another to act by threats or the use of his authority: it may take a form very similar to the causal manipulation of things even though it in some way involves the mind. Hypnotism is one such case; where post-hypnotic suggestion is successful the subject is caused to act or move but not given reasons for acting. If the causal connection is challenged in such cases it would require defence by generalizations, tracing general connections between similar stimuli and behaviour, as do statements that one physical event was the cause of another. More important are cases which are like interpersonal transactions, in that an honest account of conscious experience and not an appeal to generalizations best verifies them, and yet do not involve the provision of a reason in the sense of rendering action more eligible. Thus, if one person, by suddenly appearing, startles another so that he jumps or runs away in fright, the sudden appearance would correctly be said to have made the second person behave as he did; and the latter's statement that this was so would neither be a conclusion from any generalization nor require defence by one. Yet though the sudden appearance of the first person would be properly mentioned in answer to the question, 'Why did you jump?' as well as to the question 'What made you jump?' it is not a reason for jumping in the same sense of reason as that involved in our interpersonal transactions. It does not show the action to be eligible or to be one that furthered any purpose or objective; in this non-purposive aspect these cases resemble causal connection between two physical events.[26] In the law there are many examples of this borderline type of causal concept. Perhaps the most important is the case of provocation, though its characteristics are masked by the rule that, unless a person with a reasonable degree of self-control[27] would have lost self-control under the same circumstances, the fact that a person accused of murder was provoked by his victim's words or deeds will not avail him. It is, however, an integral part of the idea of provocation that one person arouses another's passions and *makes* him lose normal self-control; this is indeed spoken of as the 'effect';[28] yet, that this connection exists in

[26] See the discussion of such cases (called 'mental causation') by G. E. M. Anscombe in *Intention* (Oxford, 1957), ss. 9–12.
[27] *D.P.P.* v. *Camplin* [1978] AC 705; New Zealand Crimes Act 1961, s. 169 (2).
[28] Homicide Act, 1957, s. 3.

any particular case is a matter that in principle could be conclusively settled by a description of the agent's state of mind without any appeal to generalizations.

VI. OPPORTUNITIES

It remains to notice a class of relationships between the actions of two persons which have analogies with interpersonal transactions; when harm arises from them they are important in the law and are often assimilated by it to simpler cases of causation. The central notion in these relationships is that of one person providing another not with a reason, but with an oppportunity for doing something or with the means or information which he requires in order to do it. The first person does something, often unintentionally, which renders the second person's action possible or at least easier. A man who carelessly leaves unlocked the doors of a house, entrusted to him by a friend, has provided the thief with an opportunity to enter and steal the spoons though he has not caused him to steal or made him steal. Of course, providing such an opportunity is an omission to take a common precaution against a common danger, and hence the causal language used in other cases of omission, where harm ensues without the deliberate intervention of others, is easily extended to this case. It would be natural to say that the loss was the consequence of the failure to lock up the house; the careless friend might be held morally and legally bound to compensate the owner for the loss just as for loss 'directly' caused, for example, by carelessly starting a fire. The line between causing harm by initiating a sequence of physical events, and by creating opportunities for others to do harm, though it is conceptually distinct, is often neglected for practical purposes, as we show in our discussion of the law of tort.[29]

Conversely, there are cases where causal language is used, both in the law and outside it, which require for their analysis the notion of depriving a person of or failing to provide him with the opportunity or the means of doing something. In the law this is frequently involved in situations where one person is said to have caused another economic loss; for certain forms of loss may be caused either by the destruction of another person's goods or bodily facilities which he is entitled to exploit for gain or by a failure to provide another with goods or services to which he is entitled, and which would normally be exploited or used for economic gain. So a failure to deliver to a manufacturer on time a piece of machinery which he has ordered, may, like the destruction of his existing machinery, be held the cause

29 Below, pp. 133-4, 186.

of the loss of those profits which would have been made by its use. A parallel case in history is one where the failure of a government to send a general reinforcements or an untimely recall of part of his troops is held to have been the cause of a defeat.

These relationships where one person provides or fails to provide another with or deprives another of the opportunity or the means for some action differ from interpersonal transactions; these are not cases where one person does or says something with the intention that it should appear to the other as a reason for doing something. On the other hand, they are not elucidated by Mill's analysis of causation even with the modifications described in section IV.[30] It would seem that their essential features are the two following. First, when causal language is used of the provision or failure to provide another with an opportunity, it is implied that this is a deviation from a standard practice or expected procedure; the notions of what is unusual and what is reprehensible by accepted standards both influence the use of causal language in such cases. Hence the case of a householder whose prudential storing of firewood in the cellar gave a pyromaniac his opportunity to burn it down would be distinguished from that of the careless friend who left the house unlocked: the fire would not be naturally described as a consequence of the storing of the wood though the loss of the spoons was a consequence of leaving the house unlocked. This feature of deviation from standard or expected practice need not, however, be present when the relation in question is that of depriving a person of opportunities, e.g. by the destruction of equipment, rather than that of providing or failing to provide them. Secondly, though generalizations are required for the defence of these statements, they are not related to them in the way in which the generalizations required for the defence of a statement that one physical event caused another are related to it. For the generalizations required to show, for example, that the failure to deliver the machinery or to send reinforcements was the cause respectively of the loss and defeat, would show that the machinery or troops were essential if the profit was to be made or the battle won, and that, had they been available, they could, in standard conditions, have been exploited in such a way as to achieve success. It need not, however, be the case that when they are available they are invariably so exploited. Despite their availability, other factors (strikes, bad generalship) may obstruct success. The rest of the demonstration would consist in showing that there was nothing in the circumstances of the particular case to differentiate it from the standard case, e.g. that the workers were not on strike or the general manifestly incompetent. The structure of such argument is mainly

[30] Above, p. 44.

hypothetical; it is designed to show what would have happened had the opportunity been provided rather than that the failure to provide it always has such an outcome. This contrasts with the use of those generalizations which in the last resort have to be deployed to show, perhaps stage by stage, the causal connection between two physical events such as the falling of a tile and the injury to a passer-by.

III

CAUSATION AND RESPONSIBILITY

I. RESPONSIBILITY IN LAW AND MORALS

WE have so far traced the outline of a variety of causal concepts the diversity of which is to be seen in such familiar examples of the use of causal language as the following: 'The explosion of gas caused the building to collapse', 'He made him hand over his money by threatening to shoot', 'The consequence of leaving the car unlocked was that it was stolen', 'The strike was the cause of the drop in profits.'

The main structure of these different forms of causal connection is plain enough, and there are many situations constantly recurring in ordinary life to which they have a clear application; yet it is also true that like many other fundamental notions these have aspects which are vague or indeterminate; they involve the weighing of matters of degree, or the plausibility of hypothetical speculations, for which no exact criteria can be laid down. Hence their application, outside the safe area of simple examples, calls for judgment and is something over which judgments often differ. Even the type of case which is most familiar, and most nearly approximates to Mill's model for 'cause and effect', where causal connection between a physical event and some earlier initiating event or human action is traced through a series of physical events, involves an implicit judgment on such imprecise issues as the *normal* condition of the thing concerned and the *abnormality* of what is identified as the cause. Very often, in particular where an omission to take common precautions is asserted to be the cause of some disaster, a speculation as to what *would have* happened had the precaution been taken is involved. Though arguments one way or another over such hypothetical issues may certainly be rational and have more or less 'weight', there is a sense in which they cannot be conclusive. When such areas of dispute are reached, the decision whether to describe the facts of a case in the terms of some given form of causal connection will be influenced very much by factors connected with the context and purpose of making the causal statement.

Hitherto we have discussed only one principal purpose for which causal language is used: i.e. when an explanation is sought or pro-vided of some puzzling or unusual occurrence. But as well as this explanatory context, in which we are concerned with what *has* happened, there are many others. Our deliberations about our own conduct often take the form of an inquiry as to the future consequences of alternative actions; here causal connections are *ex hypothesi* bounded by the horizon of the foreseeable. But even if we confine ourselves to causal statements about the past there are still different contexts and purposes to be discriminated. Thus it would be wrong to think of the historian as using causal notions only when he is explaining. The movement of his thought is not always from the later problematic event to something earlier which explains it and in using causal language he is not always engaged in diagnosis. His thought very often takes the contrary direction; for in addition to providing explanations (answers to the question 'why?') he is also concerned to trace the outcome, the results, or the consequences of the human actions and omissions which are his usual starting-points, though he may also work out the 'effects' of natural events. So he will discuss the consequences of a king's policy or the effects of the Black Death. This is so because the narrative of history is scarcely ever a narrative of brute sequence, but is an account of the roles played by certain factors and especially by human agents. History is written to satisfy not only the need for explanation, but also the desire to identify and assess contributions made by historical figures to changes of importance; to triumphs and disasters, and to human happiness or suffering. This assessment involves tracing 'consequences', 'effects', or 'results', and these are more frequently referred to than 'causes' which has a primarily diagnostic or explanatory ring. In one sense of 'responsibility' the historian determines the responsibility of human beings for certain types of change; and sometimes he does this with an eye to praising or blaming or passing other forms of moral judgment. But this need not be so; the historian, though concerned to trace the consequences of human action, need not be a moralist.

In the moral judgments of ordinary life, we have occasion to blame people because they have caused harm to others, and also, if less frequently, to insist that morally they are bound to compensate those to whom they have caused harm. These are the moral analogues of more precise legal conceptions; for, in all legal systems, liability to be punished or to make compensation frequently depends on whether actions (or omissions) have caused harm. Moral blame is not of course confined to such cases of causing harm. We blame a man who cheats or lies or breaks promises, even if no one has suffered in the particular case: this has its legal counterpart in the punishment of abortive attempts to commit crimes, and of offences constituted by the unlawful possession of certain kinds of weapons, drugs, or materials, for example, for counterfeiting currency. When the occurrence of harm is an essential part of the ground for blame the connection of the person blamed with the harm may take any of the forms of causal connection we have examined. His action may have initiated a series of physical events dependent on each other and culminating in injury to persons or property, as in wounding and killing. These simple forms are the paradigms for the lawyer's talk of harm 'directly' caused. But we blame people also for harm which arises from or is the consequence of their neglect of common precautions; we do this even if harm would not have come about without the intervention of another human being deliberately exploiting the opportunities provided by neglect. The main legal analogue here is liability for 'negligence'. The wish of many lawyers to talk in this branch of the law of harm being 'within the risk of' rather than 'caused by' the negligent conduct manifests appreciation of the fact that a different form of relationship is involved in saying that harm is the consequence, on the one hand, of an explosion and, on the other, of a failure to lock the door by which a thief has entered. Again, we blame people for the harm which we say is the consequence of their influence over others, either exerted by non-rational means or in one of the ways we have designated 'interpersonal transactions'. To such grounds for responsibility there correspond many important legal conceptions: the instigation of crimes ('commanding' or 'procuring') constitutes an important ground of criminal responsibility and the concepts of enticement and of inducement (by threats or misrepresentation) are an element in many civil wrongs as well as in criminal offences.

The law, however, especially in matters of compensation, goes far beyond these causal grounds for responsibility in such doctrines as the vicarious responsibility of a master for his servant's civil wrongs and that of the responsibility of an occupier of property for injuries suffered by passers-by from defects of which the occupier had no knowledge and which he had no opportunity to repair. There is a recognition, perhaps diminishing, of this non-causal ground of responsibility outside the law; responsibility is sometimes admitted by one person or group of persons, even if no precaution has been neglected by them, for harm done by persons related to them in a special way, either by family ties or as members of the same social or political association. Responsibility may be simply 'placed' by moral opinion on one person for what others do. The simplest case of such vicarious moral responsibility is that of a parent for damage done by a child; its more complex (and more debatable) form is the moral responsibility of one generation of a nation to make compensation for their predecessors' wrong, such as the Germans admitted in payment of compensation to Israel.

At this point it is necessary to issue a caveat about the meaning of the expression 'responsible' if only to avoid prejudicing a question about the character of *legal* determinations of causal connection with which we shall be much concerned in later chapters. Usually in discussion of the law and occasionally in morals, to say that someone is responsible for some harm means that in accordance with legal rules or moral principles it is at least permissible, if not mandatory, to blame or punish or exact compensation from him. In this use[1] the expression 'responsible for' does not refer to a factual connection between the person held responsible and the harm but simply to his liability under the rules to be blamed, punished, or made to pay. The expressions 'answerable for' or 'liable for' are practically synonymous with 'responsible for' in *this* use, in which there is no implication that the person held responsible actually *did* or *caused* the harm. In this sense a master is (in English law) responsible for the damage done by his servants acting within the scope of their authority and a parent (in French and German law) for that done by his children; it is in this sense that a guarantor or surety is responsible for the debts or the good behaviour of other persons and an insurer for losses sustained by the insured. Very often, however, especially in discussion of morals, to say that someone is responsible for some harm is to assert (*inter alia*) that he *did* the harm or *caused* it, though such a statement is perhaps rarely confined to this for it usually also carries with it the implication that it is at least permissible to blame or punish him. This double use of the expression no doubt arises from the important fact that doing or causing harm constitutes not only the most usual but the primary type of ground for holding persons responsible in the first sense. We still speak of inanimate or natural causes such as storms, floods, germs, or the failure of electricity supply as 'responsible for' disasters; this mode of expression, now taken only to mean that they caused the disasters, no doubt originated in the belief that all that happens is the work of spirits when it is not that of men. Its survival in the modern world is perhaps some testimony to the primacy of causal connection as an element in responsibility and to the intimate connection between the two notions.

We shall consider later an apparent paradox which interprets in a different way the relationship between cause and responsibility. Much modern thought on causation in the law rests on the contention that the statement that someone has caused harm either

[1] Cf. *OED sub tit.* Responsible: Answerable, accountable (*to* another *for* something); liable to be called to account: 'being responsible to the King for what might happen to us', 1662; Hart, 'Varieties of Responsibility' (1967) 83 *LQR* 346, reprinted with additions as 'Responsibility and Retribution' in Hart, *Punishment and Responsibility* (Oxford, 1968), chap. IX.

means no more than that the harm would not have happened without ('but for') his action or where (as in normal legal usage and in all ordinary speech), it apparently means more than this, it is a disguised way of asserting the 'normative' judgment that he is responsible in the first sense, i.e. that it is proper or just to blame or punish him or make him pay. On this view to say that a person caused harm is not really, though ostensibly it is, to give a *ground* or *reason* for holding him responsible in the first sense; for we are only in a position to say that he has caused harm when we have decided that he is responsible. Pending consideration of the theories of legal causation which exploit this point of view we shall use the expression 'responsible for' only in the first of the two ways explained, i.e. without any implication as to the type of factual connection between the person held responsible and the harm; and we shall provisionally, though without prejudicing the issue, treat statements that a person caused harm as one sort of non-tautologous ground or reason for saying that he is responsible in this sense.

If we may provisionally take what in ordinary life we say and do at its face value, it seems that there coexist in ordinary thought, apart from the law though mirrored in it, several different types of connection between a person's action and eventual harm which render him responsible for it; and in both law and morals the various forms of causal connection between act or omission and harm are the most obvious and least disputable reasons for holding anyone responsible. Yet, in order to understand the extent to which the causal notions of ordinary thought are used in the law, we must bear in mind the many factors which must differentiate moral from legal responsibility in spite of their partial correspondence. The law is not only not bound to follow the moral patterns of attribution of responsibility but, even when it does, it must take into account, in a way which the private moral judgment need not and does not, the general social consequences which are attached to its judgments of responsibility; for they are of a gravity quite different from those attached to moral censure. The use of the legal sanctions of imprisonment, or enforced monetary compensation against individuals, has such formidable repercussions on the general life of society that the fact that individuals have a type of connection with harm which is adequate for moral censure or claims for compensation is only *one* of the factors which the law must consider, in defining the kinds of connection between actions and harm for which it will hold individuals legally responsible. Always to follow the private moral judgment here would be far too expensive for the law: not only in the crude sense that it would entail a vast machinery of courts and officials, but in the more important sense that it would inhibit or discourage too many other valuable activities of society. To limit the *types* of harm which the law will recognize is not enough; even if the types of harm are limited it would still be too much for any society to punish or exact compensation from individuals whenever their connection with harm of such types would justify moral censure. Conversely, social needs may require that compensation should be paid and even (though less obviously) that punishment be inflicted where no such connection between the person held responsible and the harm exists.

So causing harm of a legally recognized sort or being connected with such harm in any of the ways that justify moral blame, though vitally important and perhaps basic in a legal system, is not and should not be either always necessary or always sufficient for legal responsibility. All legal systems in response either to tradition or to social needs both extend responsibility and cut it off in ways which diverge from the simpler principles of moral blame. In England a man is not guilty of murder if the victim of his attack does not die within a year and day. In New York a person who negligently starts a fire is liable to pay only for the first of several houses which it destroys.[2] These limitations imposed by legal policy are prima facie distinguishable from limitations due to the frequent requirement of legal rules that responsibility be limited to harm caused by wrongdoing. Yet a whole school of thought maintains that this distinction does not exist or is not worth drawing.

Apart from this, morality can properly leave certain things vague into which a legal system must attempt to import some degree of precision. Outside the law nothing requires us, when we find the case too complex or too strange, to say whether any and, if so, which of the morally significant types of connection between a person's action and harm exists; we can simply say the case is too difficult for us to pass judgment, at least where moral condemnation of others is concerned. No doubt we evade less easily our questions about our own connection with harm, and the great novelists have often described, sometimes in language very like the lawyers, how the conscience may be still tortured by uncertainties as to the *character* of a part in the production of harm, even when all the facts are known.[3]

2 The rule is defended on the ground that, most houseowners being insured, it promotes efficient loss distribution: Harper and James, *Torts*, s. 20.6 n. 1.
3 See the following passage from *The Golden Bowl* by Henry James. (Mrs Assingham, whose uncertain self-accusation is described here, had, on the eve of the Prince's marriage, encouraged him to resume an old friendship with Charlotte Stant. The relationship which developed came to threaten the marriage with disaster.) 'She had stood for the previous hour in a merciless glare, beaten upon, stared out of countenance, it fairly seemed to her, by intimations of her mistake. For what she was most immediately feeling was that she had in the past been active for these people to ends that were now bearing fruit and that might yet bear a greater crop. She but

The fact that there is no precise system of punishments or rewards for common sense to administer, and so there are no 'forms of action' or 'pleadings' to define precise heads of responsibility for harm, means that the principles which guide common-sense attributions of responsibility give precise answers only in relatively simple types of case.

II. TRACING CONSEQUENCES

'To consequences no limit can be set': 'Every event which would not have happened if an earlier event had not happened is the consequence of that earlier event.' These two propositions are not equivalent in meaning and are not equally or in the same way at variance with ordinary thought. They have, however, both been urged sometimes in the same breath by the legal theorist[4] and the philosopher: they are indeed sometimes said by lawyers to be 'the philosophical doctrine' of causation. It is perhaps not difficult even for the layman to accept the first proposition as a truth about certain physical events; an explosion may cause a flash of light which will be propagated as far as the outer nebulae; its effects or consequences continue indefinitely. It is, however, a different matter to accept the view that whenever a man is murdered with a gun his death was the consequence of (still less an 'effect' of or 'caused by') the manufacture of the bullet. The first tells a perhaps unfamiliar tale about unfamiliar events; the second introduces an unfamiliar, though, of course, a possible way of speaking about familiar events. It is not that this unrestricted use of 'consequence' is unintelligible or never found; it is indeed used to refer to bizarre or fortuitous connections or coincidences: but the point is that the various causal notions employed for the purposes of explanation, attribution of responsibility, or the assessment of contributions to the course of history carry with them implicit limits which are similar in these different employments.

brooded at first in her corner of the carriage: it was like burying her exposed face, a face too helplessly exposed in the cool lap of the common indifference . . . a world mercifully unconscious and unreproachful. It wouldn't like the world she had just left know sooner or later what she had done or would know it only if the final consequence should be some quite overwhelming publicity. . . . The sense of seeing was strong in her, but she clutched at the comfort of not being sure of what she saw. Not to know what it would represent on a longer view was a help in turn to not making out that her hands were embrued; since if she had stood in the position of a producing cause she should surely be less vague about what she had produced. This, further, in its way, was a step toward reflecting that when one's connection with any matter was too indirect to be traced, it might be described also as too slight to be deplored' (*The Golden Bowl*, Book 3, chap. 3). We are much indebted to Dame Mary Warnock for this quotation.

4 Lawson, *Negligence in the Civil Law*, p. 53.

It is, then, the second proposition, defining consequence in terms of 'necessary condition', with which theorists are really concerned. This proposition is the corollary of the view that, if we look into the past of any given event, there is an infinite number of events, each of which is a necessary condition of the given event and so, as much as any other, is its cause. This is the 'cone'[5] of causation, so called because, since any event has a number of simultaneous conditions, the series fans out as we go back in time. The justification, indeed only partial, for calling this 'the philosophical doctrine' of causation is that it resembles Mill's doctrine that 'we have no right to give the name of cause to one of the conditions exclusive of the others of them'. It differs from Mill's view in taking the essence of causation to be 'necessary condition' and not 'the sum total'[6] of the sufficient conditions of an event.

Legal theorists have developed this account of cause and consequence to show what is 'factual', 'objective', or 'scientific' in these notions: this they call 'cause in fact' and it is usually stressed as a preliminary to the doctrine that any more restricted application of these terms in the law represents nothing in the facts or in the meaning of causation, but expresses fluctuating legal policy or sentiments of what is just or convenient. Moral philosophers have insisted in somewhat similar terms that the consequences of human action are 'infinite': this they have urged as an objection against the Utilitarian doctrine that the rightness of a morally right action depends on whether its consequences are better than those of any alternative action in the circumstances. 'We should have to trace as far as possible the consequences not only for the persons affected directly but also for those indirectly affected and to these no limit can be set.'[7] Hence, so the argument runs, we cannot either inductively establish the Utilitarian doctrine that right acts are 'optimific' or use it in particular cases to discover what is right. Yet, however vulnerable at other points Utilitarianism may be as an account of moral judgment, this objection seems to rest on a mistake as to the sense of 'consequence'. The Utilitarian assertion that the rightness of an action depends on its consequences is not the same as the assertion that it depends on all those later occurrences which would not have happened had the action not been done, to which indeed 'no limit can be set'. It is important to see that the issue here is not the linguistic one whether the word 'consequence' would be understood if used in this way. The point is that, though we could, we do not think in this way in tracing connections between human actions and

---

[5] Glanville Williams, *Joint Torts and Contributory Negligence*, p. 239.
[6] Mill, Book III, chap. v, s. 2.
[7] Ross, *The Right and the Good*, p. 36.

events. Instead, whenever we are concerned with such connections, whether for the purpose of explaining a puzzling occurrence, assessing responsibility, or giving an intelligible historical narrative, we employ a set of concepts restricting in various ways what counts as a consequence. These restrictions colour *all* our thinking in causal terms; when we find them in the law we are not finding something invented by or peculiar to the law, though of course it is for the law to say when and how far it will use them and, where they are vague, to supplement them.

No short account can be given of the limits thus placed on 'consequences' because these limits vary, intelligibly, with the variety of causal connection asserted. Thus we may be tempted by the generalization that consequences must always be something intended or foreseen or at least foreseeable with ordinary care: but counter-examples spring up from many types of context where causal statements are made. If smoking is shown to cause lung cancer this discovery will permit us to describe past as well as future cases of cancer as the effect or consequence of smoking even though no one foresaw or had reasonable grounds to suspect this in the past. What is common and commonly appreciated and hence foreseeable certainly controls the scope of consequences in certain varieties of causal statement but not in all. Again the voluntary intervention of a second person very often constitutes the limit. If a guest sits down at a table laid with knife and fork and plunges the knife into his hostess's breast, her death is not in any context other than a contrived one[8] thought of as caused by, or the effect or result of the waiter's action in laying the table; nor would it be linked with this action as its consequence for any of the purposes, explanatory or attributive, for which we employ causal notions. Yet as we have seen there are many other types of case where a voluntary action or the harm it does are naturally treated to the consequence of to some prior neglect of precaution. Finally, we may think that a simple answer is already supplied by Hume and Mill's doctrine that causal connection rests on general laws asserting regular connection; yet, even in the type of case to which this important doctrine applies, reference to it alone will not solve our problem. For we often trace a causal connection between an antecedent and a consequent which themselves very rarely go together: we do this when the case can be broken down into intermediate stages, which themselves exemplify different generalizations, as when we find that the fall of a tile was the cause of someone's death, rare though this be. Here our problem

---

[8] e.g. if the guest was suspected of being a compulsive stabber and the waiter had therefore been told to lay only a plastic knife in his place.

reappears in the form of the question: When can generalizations be combined in this way?

We shall examine first the central type of case where the problem is of this last-mentioned form. Here the gist of the causal connection lies in the general connection with each other of the successive stages; and is not dependent on the special notions of one person providing another with reasons or exceptional opportunities for actions. This form of causal connection may exist between actions and events, and between purely physical events, and it is in such cases that the words 'cause' and 'causing' used of the antecedent action or event have their most obvious application. It is convenient to refer to cases of the first type where the consequence is harm as cases of 'causing harm', and to refer to cases where harm is the consequence of one person providing another with reasons or opportunities for doing harm as cases of 'inducing' or 'occasioning' harmful acts.[9] In cases of the first type a voluntary act, or a conjunction of events amounting to a coincidence, operates as a limit in the sense that events subsequent to these are not attributed to the antecedent action or event as its consequence even though they would not have happened without it. Often such a limiting action or coincidence is thought of and described as 'intervening': and lawyers speak of them as 'superseding' or 'extraneous' causes 'breaking the chain of causation'. To see what these metaphors rest on (and in part obscure) and how such factors operate as a limit we shall consider the detail of three simple cases.

(i) A forest fire breaks out, and later investigation shows that shortly before the outbreak A had flung away a lighted cigarette into the bracken at the edge of the forest, the bracken caught fire, a light breeze got up, and fanned the flames in the direction of the forest. If, on discovering these facts, we hesitate before saying that A's action caused the forest fire this would be to consider the alternative hypothesis that in spite of appearances the fire only succeeded A's action in point of time, that the bracken flickered out harmlessly and the forest fire was caused by something else. To dispose of this it may be necessary to examine in further detail the process of events between the ignition of the bracken and the outbreak of fire in the forest and to show that these exemplified certain types of continuous change. If this is shown, there is no longer any room for doubt: A's action *was* the cause of the fire, whether he intended it or not. This seems and is the simplest of cases. Yet it is important to notice that even in applying our general knowledge to a case as simple as this,

9 See Chaps. VI, VII, XII, XIII, where we distinguish these different relationships in the law.

indeed in regarding it as simple, we make an implicit use of a distinction between types of factor which constitute a limit in tracing consequences and those which we regard as mere circumstances 'through' which we trace them. For the breeze which sprang up after *A* dropped the cigarette, and without which the fire would not have spread to the forest, was not only subsequent to his action but entirely independent of it: it was, however, a common recurrent feature of the environment, and, as such, it is thought of not as an 'intervening' force but as merely part of the circumstances in which the cause 'operates'. The decision so to regard it is implicitly taken when we combine our knowledge of the successive stages of the process and assert the connection.

It is easy here to be misled by the natural metaphor of a causal 'chain', which may lead us to think that the causal process consists of a series of single events each of which is dependent upon (would not have occurred without) its predecessor in the 'chain' and so is dependent upon the initiating action or event. In truth in any causal process we have at each phase not single events but complex sets of conditions, and among these conditions are some which are not only subsequent to, but independent of the initiating action or event. Some of these independent conditions, such as the evening breeze in the example chosen, we classify as mere conditions in or on which the cause operates; others we speak of as 'interventions' or 'causes'. To decide how such independent elements shall be classified is also to decide how we shall combine our knowledge of the different general connections which the successive stages exemplify, and it is important to see that nothing *in* this knowledge itself can resolve this point. We may have to go to science for the relevant general knowledge before we can assert with proper confidence that *A*'s action did cause the fire, but science, though it tells us that an air current was required, is silent on the difference between a current in the form of an evening breeze and one produced by someone who deliberately fanned the flames as they were flickering out in the bracken. Yet an air current in this deliberately induced form is not a 'condition' or 'mere circumstance' through which we can trace the consequence; its presence would force us to revise the assertion that *A* caused the fire. Conversely if science helped us to identify as a necessary factor in producing the fire some condition or element of which we had previously been totally ignorant, e.g. the persistence of oxygen, this would leave our original judgment undisturbed if this factor were a common or pervasive feature of the environment or of the thing in question. There is thus indeed an important sense in which it is true that the distinction between cause and conditions is not a 'scientific' one. It is not determined by laws or generalizations concerning connections between events.

When we have assembled all our knowledge of the factors involved in the fire, the residual question which we then confront (the attributive question) may be typified as follows: Here is A's action, here is the fire: can the fire be attributed to A's action as its consequence given that there is also this third factor (the breeze or B's intervention) without which the fire would not have happened? It is plain that, both in raising questions of this kind and in answering them, ordinary thought is powerfully influenced by the analogy between the straightforward cases of causal attribution (where the elements required for the production of harm in addition to the initiating action are all 'normal' conditions) and even simpler cases of responsibility which we do not ordinarily describe in causal language at all but by the simple transitive verbs of action. These are the cases of the direct manipulation of objects involving changes in them or their position: cases where we say 'He pushed it', 'He broke it', 'He bent it'. The cases which we do confidently describe in causal language ('The fire was caused by his carelessness', 'He caused a fire') are cases where no other human action or abnormal occurrence is required for the production of the effect, but only normal conditions. Such cases appear as mere long-range or less direct versions or extensions of the most obvious and fundamental case of all for the attribution of responsibility: the case where we can simply say 'He did it'. Conversely in attaching importance to thus causing harm as a distinct ground of responsibility and in taking certain kinds of factor (whether human interventions or abnormal occurrences), without which the initiating action would not have led to harm, to preclude the description of the case in simple causal terms, common sense is affected by the fact that here, because of the manner in which the harm eventuates, the outcome cannot be represented as a mere extension of the initiating action; the analogy with the fundamental case for responsibility ('He did it') has broken down.

When we understand the power exerted over our ordinary thought by the conception that causing harm is a mere extension of the primary case of doing harm, the interrelated metaphors which seem natural to lawyers and laymen, in describing various aspects of causal connection, fall into place and we can discuss their factual basis. The persistent notion that some kinds of event required in addition to the initiating action for the production of harm 'break the chain of causation' is intelligible, if we remember that though such events actually *complete* the *explanation* of the harm (and so *make* rather than *break* the causal explanation) they do, unlike mere normal conditions, break the *analogy* with cases of simple actions. The same analogy accounts for the description of these factors as

74   THE ANALYSIS OF CAUSAL CONCEPTS

'new actions' (*novus actus*) or 'new causes', 'superseding', 'extraneous', 'intervening forces': and for the description of the initiating action when 'the chain of causation' is broken as 'no longer operative', 'having worn out', *functus officio*.[10] So too when the 'chain' is held not to be 'broken' the initiating action is said to be still 'potent',[11] 'continuing', 'contributing', 'operative', and the mere conditions held insufficient to break the chain are 'part of the background',[12] 'circumstances in which the cause operates',[13] 'the stage set', 'part of the history'.

(ii) *A* throws a lighted cigarette into the bracken which catches fire. Just as the flames are about to flicker out, *B*, who is not acting in concert with *A*, deliberately pours petrol on them. The fire spreads and burns down the forest. *A*'s action, whether or not he intended the forest fire, was not the cause of the fire: *B*'s was.

The voluntary intervention of a second human agent, as in this case, is a paradigm among those factors which preclude the assimilation in causal judgments of the first agent's connection with the eventual harm to the case of simple direct manipulation. Such an intervention displaces the prior action's title to be called the cause and, in the persistent metaphors found in the law, it 'reduces' the earlier action and its immediate effects to the level of 'mere circumstances' or 'part of the history'. *B* in this case was not an 'instrument' through which *A* worked or a victim of the circumstances *A* has created. He has, on the contrary, freely exploited the circumstances and brought about the fire without the co-operation of any further agent or any chance coincidence. Compared with this the claim of *A*'s action to be ranked the cause of the fire fails. That this and not the moral appraisal of the two actions is the point of comparison seems clear. If *A* and *B* both intended to set the forest on fire, and this destruction is accepted as something wrong or wicked, their moral wickedness, judged by the criterion of intention, is the same. Yet the causal judgment differentiates between them. If their moral guilt is judged by the outcome, this judgment though it would differentiate between them cannot be the source of the causal judgment; for it presupposes it. The difference just is that *B* has caused the harm and *A* has not. Again, if we appraise these actions as good or bad from different points of view, this leaves the causal judgments unchanged. *A* may be a soldier of one side anxious to burn down the enemy's hide-out: *B* may be an enemy soldier who has decided that his side is too iniquitous to defend. Whatever is the

10 *Davies* v. *Swan Motor Co.* [1947] 2 KB 291, 318.
11 *Minister of Pensions* v. *Chennell* [1947] KB 250, 256. Lord Wright (1950), 13 *MLR* 3.
12 *Norris* v. *William Moss & Son Ltd.* [1954] 1 WLR 46, 351.
13 *Minister of Pensions* v. *Chennell* [1947] KB 250, 256.

moral judgment passed on these actions by different speakers it would remain true that *A* had not caused the fire and *B* had.

There are, as we have said, situations in which a voluntary action would not be thought of as an intervention precluding causal connection in this way. These are the cases discussed further below where an opportunity commonly exploited for harmful actions is negligently provided, or one person intentionally provides another with the means, the opportunity, or a certain type of reason for wrongdoing. Except in such cases a voluntary intervention is a limit past which consequences are not traced. By contrast, actions which in any of a variety of different ways are less than fully voluntary are assimilated to the means by which or the circumstances in which the earlier action brings about the consequences. Such actions are not the outcome of an informed choice made without pressure from others, and the different ways in which human action may fall short in this respect range from defective muscular control, through lack of consciousness or knowledge, to the vaguer notions of duress and of predicaments, created by the first agent for the second, in which there is no 'fair' choice.

In considering examples of such actions and their bearing on causal judgments there are three dangers to avoid. It would be folly to think that in tracing connections through such actions instead of regarding them, like voluntary interventions, as a limit, ordinary thought has clearly separated out their non-voluntary aspect from others by which they are often accompanied. Thus even in the crude case where *A* lets off a gun (intentionally or not) and startles *B*, so that he makes an involuntary movement of his arm which breaks a glass, the commonness of such a reaction as much as its compulsive character may influence the judgment that *A*'s action was the cause of the damage.

Secondly we must not impute to ordinary thought all the fine discriminations that could be made and in fact are to be found in a legal system, or an equal willingness to supply answers to complex questions in causal terms. Where there is no precise system of punishment, compensation or reward to administer, ordinary men will not often have faced such questions as whether the injuries suffered by a motorist who collides with another in swerving to avoid a child are consequences attributable to the neglect of the child's parents in allowing it to wander on to the road. Such questions courts have to answer and in such cases common judgments provide only a general, though still an important indication of what are the relevant factors.

Thirdly, though very frequently non-voluntary actions are assimilated to mere conditions or means by which the first agent brings about the consequences, the assimilation is never quite complete.

This is manifested by the general avoidance of many causal locutions which are appropriate when the consequences are traced (as in the first case) through purely physical events. Thus even in the case in which the second agent's role is hardly an 'action' at all, e.g. where *A* hits *B*, who staggers against a glass window and breaks it, we should say that *A*'s blow made *B* stagger and break the glass, rather than that *A*'s blow caused the glass to break, though in any explanatory or attributive context the case would be *summarized* by saying that *A*'s action was the cause of the *damage*.

In the last two cases where *B*'s movements are involuntary in the sense that they are not part of any action which he chose or intended to do, their connection with *A*'s action would be described by saying that *A*'s blow *made B* stagger or *caused* him to stagger or that the noise of *A*'s shot *made* him jump or *caused* him to jump. This would be true, whether *A* intended or expected *B* to react in this way or not, and the naturalness of treating *A*'s action as the cause of the ultimate damage is due to the causal character of this part of the process involving *B*'s action. The same is, however, true where *B*'s actions are not involuntary movements but *A* is considered to have made or caused *B* to do them by less crude means. This is the case if, for example, *A* uses threats or exploits his authority over *B* to make *B* do something, e.g. knock down a door. At least where *A*'s threats are of serious harm, or *B*'s act was unquestionably within *A*'s authority to order, he too has made or forced or (in formal quasi-legal parlance) 'caused' *B* to act.

Outside the area of such cases, where *B*'s will would be said either not to be involved at all, or to be overborne by *A*, are cases where *A*'s act creates a predicament for *B narrowing* the area of choice so that he has either to inflict some harm on himself or others, or sacrifice some important interest or duty. Such cases resemble coercion in that *A* narrows the area of *B*'s choice but differ from it in that this predicament need not be intentionally created. *A* sets a house on fire (intentionally or unintentionally): *B* to save himself has to jump from a height involving certain injury, or to save a child rushes in and is seriously burned. Here, of course, *B*'s movements are not involuntary; the 'necessity' of his action is here of a different order. His action is the outcome of a choice between two evils forced on him by *A*'s action. In such cases, when *B*'s injuries are thought of as the consequence of the fire, the implicit judgment is made that his action was the lesser of two evils and in this sense a 'reasonable' one which he was obliged to make to avoid the greater evil. This is often paradoxically, though understandably, described by saying that here the agent 'had no choice' but to do what he did. Such judgments involve a comparison of the importance of the respective

interests sacrificed and preserved, and the final assertion that A's
action was the cause of the injuries rests on evaluations about which
men may differ.

Finally, the ground for treating some harm which would not have
occurred without B's action as the consequence of A's action may
be that B acted in ignorance of or under a mistake as to some feature
of the situation created by A. Poisoning offers perhaps the simplest
example of the bearing on causal judgments of actions which are
less than voluntary in this Aristotelian sense. If A intending B's
death deliberately poisons B's food and B, knowing this, deliberately
takes the poison and dies, A has not, unless he coerced B into eating
the poisoned food, caused B's death: if, however, B does not know
the food to be poisoned, eats it, and dies, A has caused his death,
even if he put the poison in unwittingly. Of course only the roughest
judgments are passed in causal terms in such cases outside law
courts, where fine degrees of 'appreciation' or 'reckless shutting of
the eyes' may have to be discriminated from 'full knowledge'. Yet,
rough as these are, they indicate clearly enough the controlling principles.

Though in the foregoing cases A's initiating action might often be
described as 'the cause' of the ultimate harm, this linguistic fact is
of subordinate importance to the fact that, for whatever purpose,
explanatory, descriptive, or evaluative, consequences of an action
are traced, discriminations are made (except in the cases discussed
later) between free voluntary interventions and less than voluntary
reactions to the first action or the circumstances created by it.

(iii) The analogy with single simple actions which guides the
tracing of consequences may be broken by certain kinds of conjunctions of physical events. A hits B who falls to the ground stunned
and bruised by the blow; at that moment a tree crashes to the ground
and kills B. A has certainly caused B's bruises but not his death: for
though the fall of the tree was, like the evening breeze in our earlier
example, independent of and subsequent to the initiating action, it
would be differentiated from the breeze in any description in causal
terms of the connection of B's death with A's action. It is to be
noticed that this is not a matter which turns on the intention with
which A struck B. Even if A hit B inadvertently or accidentally his
blow would still be the cause of B's bruises: he would have caused
them, though unintentionally. Conversely even if A had intended his
blow to kill, this would have been an attempt to kill but still not the
cause of B's death, unless A knew that the tree was about to fall just
at that moment. On this legal and ordinary judgments would be
found to agree; and most legal systems would distinguish for the

purposes of punishment[14] an attempt with a fatal upshot, issuing by such chance or anomalous events, from 'causing death'—the terms in which the offences of murder and manslaughter are usually defined. Similarly the causal description of the case does not turn on the moral appraisal of A's action or the wish to punish it. A may be a robber and a murderer and B a saint guarding the place A hoped to plunder. Or B may be a murderer and A a hero who has forced his way into B's retreat. In both cases the causal judgment is the same. A had caused the minor injuries but not B's death, though he tried to kill him. A may indeed be praised or blamed but not for causing B's death. However intimate the connection between responsibility and causation, it does not determine causal judgments in this simple way. Nor does the causal judgment turn on a refusal to attribute grave consequences to actions which normally have less serious results. Had A's blow killed B outright and the tree, falling on his body, merely smashed his watch we should still treat the coincidental character of the fall of the tree as determining the form of causal statement. We should then recognize A's blow as the cause of B's death but not the breaking of the watch.

The connection between A's action and B's death in the first case would naturally be described in the language of *coincidence*. 'It was a coincidence: it just happened that, at the very moment when A knocked B down, a tree crashed at the very place where he fell and killed him.' The common legal metaphor would describe the fall of the tree as an 'extraneous' cause. This, however, is dangerously misleading, as an analysis of the notion of coincidence will show. It suggests merely an event which is subsequent to and independent of some other contingency, and of course the fall of the tree has both these features in relation to A's blow. Yet in these respects the fall of the tree does not differ from the evening breeze in the earlier case where we found no difficulty in tracing causal connection.[15] The full elucidation of the notion of a coincidence is a complex matter for, though it is very important as a limit in tracing consequences, causal questions are not the only ones to which the notion is relevant. The following are its most general characteristics. We speak of a coincidence whenever the conjunction of two or more events in certain spatial or temporal relations (1) is very unlikely by ordinary standards and (2) is for some reason significant or important, provided (3) that they occur without human contrivance and (4) are independent of each other. It is therefore a coincidence if two persons known to each other in London meet without design in Paris on their way to separate independently chosen destinations; or if two persons living in different places independently decide to write a book on the same subject. The first is a coincidence of time and place ('It just happened that we were at the same place at the same time'), and the second a coincidence of time only ('It just happened that they both decided to write on the subject at the same time').

Use of this general notion is made in the special case when the conjunction of two or more events occurs in temporal and/or spatial relationships which are significant, because, as our general knowledge of causal processes shows, this conjunction is required for the production of some given further event. In the language of Mill's idealized model, they form a necessary part of a complex set of jointly sufficient conditions. In the present case the fall of the tree just as *B* was struck down within its range satisfies the four criteria for a coincidence which we have enumerated. First, though neither event was of a very rare or exceptional kind, their conjunction would be rated very unlikely judged by the standards of ordinary experience. Secondly, this conjunction was causally significant for it was a necessary part of the process terminating in *B*'s death. Thirdly, this conjunction was not consciously designed by *A*; had he known of the impending fall of the tree and hit *B* with the intention that he should fall within its range *B*'s death would not have been the result of any coincidence. *A* would certainly have caused it. The common-sense principle that a contrived conjunction cannot be a coincidence is the element of truth in the legal maxim (too broadly stated even for legal purposes) that an intended consequence cannot be too 'remote'. Fourthly, each member of the conjunction in this case was independent of the other; whereas if *B* had fallen against the tree with an impact sufficient to bring it down on him, this sequence of physical events, though freakish in its way, would not be a coincidence and in most contexts of ordinary life, as in the law, the course of events would be summarized by saying that in this case, unlike that of the coincidence, *A*'s act was the cause of *B*'s death, since each stage is the effect of the preceding stage. Thus, the blow forced the victim against the tree, the effect of this was to make the tree fall and the fall of the tree killed the victim.

One further criterion in addition to these four must be satisfied if a conjunction of events is to rank as a coincidence and as a limit when the consequences of the action are traced. This further criterion again shows the strength of the influence which the analogy with the case of the simple manipulation of things exerts over thought in causal terms. An abnormal *condition* existing at the time of a human intervention is distinguished both by ordinary thought and, with a striking consistency, by most legal systems[16] from an abnormal event or conjunction of events subsequent to that intervention; the former, unlike the latter, are not ranked as coincidences or 'extraneous' causes when the consequences of the intervention come to be traced. Thus A innocently gives B a tap over the head of a normally quite harmless character, but because B is then suffering from some rare disease the tap has, as we say, 'fatal results'. In this case A has caused B's death though unintentionally. The scope of the principle which thus distinguishes contemporaneous abnormal conditions from subsequent events is unclear; but at least where a human being initiates some physical change in a thing, animal, or person, abnormal physical states of the object affected, existing at the time, are ranked as part of the circumstances in which the cause 'operates'. In the familiar controlling imagery these are part of 'the stage already set' before the 'intervention'.[17]

Judgments about coincidences, though we often agree in making them, depend in two related ways on issues incapable of precise formulation. One of these is patent, the other latent but equally important. Just how unlikely must a conjunction be to rank as a coincidence, and in the light of what knowledge is likelihood to be assessed? The only answer is: 'very unlikely in the light of the knowledge available to ordinary men'. It is, of course, the indeterminacies of such standards, implicit in causal judgments, that make them inveterately disputable, and call for the exercise of discretion or choice by courts. The second and latent indeterminacy of these judgments depends on the fact that the things or events to which they relate do not have pinned to them some uniquely correct description always to be used in assessing likelihood. It is an important pervasive feature of all our empirical judgments that there is a constant possibility of more or less specific description of any event or thing with which they are concerned. The tree might be described not simply as a 'tree' but as a 'rotten tree' or as a 'fir tree' or a 'tree sixty feet tall'. So too its fall might be described not as a 'fall' but as a fall of a specified distance at a specified velocity. The likelihood of conjunctions framed in these different terms would be differently assessed. The criteria of appropriate description like the standard of likelihood are supplied by consideration of common knowledge. Even if the scientist knew the tree to be rotten and could have predicted its fall with accuracy, this would not change the judgment that its fall at the time when B was struck down within its range was a coincidence; nor would it make the description 'rotten tree'

16 Below, pp. 172, 342.
17 Below, p. 172.

appropriate for the assessment of the chances involved in this judgment. There are other controls over the choice of description derived from the degree of specificity of our interests in the final outcome of the causal process. We are concerned with the fall of an object sufficient to cause 'death' by impact and the precise force or direction which may account for the detail of the wounds is irrelevant here.

Opportunities and Reasons

Opportunities. The discrimination of voluntary interventions as a limit is no longer made when the case, owing to the commonness or appreciable risk of such harmful intervention, can be brought within the scope of the notion of providing an opportunity, known to be commonly exploited for doing harm. Here the limiting principles are different. When *A* leaves the house unlocked the range of consequences to be attributed to this neglect, as in any other case where precautions are omitted, depends primarily on the way in which such opportunities are commonly exploited. An alternative formulation of this idea is that a subsequent intervention would fall within the scope of consequences if the likelihood of its occurring is one of the reasons for holding *A*'s omission to be negligent.

It is on these lines that we would distinguish between the entry of a thief and of a murderer; the opportunity provided is believed to be sufficiently commonly exploited by thieves to make it usual and often morally or legally obligatory not to provide it. Here, in attributing consequences to prior actions, causal judgments are directly controlled by the notion of the risk created by them. Neglect of such precautions is both unusual and reprehensible. For these reasons it would be hard to separate the two ways in which such neglect deviates from the 'norm'. Despite this, no simple identification can be made of the notion of responsibility with the causal connection which is a ground for it. This is so because the provision of an opportunity commonly taken by others is ranked as the cause of the outcome independently of the wish to praise or blame. The causal judgment may be made simply to assess a contribution to some outcome. Thus, whether we think well or ill of the use made of railways, we would still claim that the greater mobility of the population in the nineteenth century was a consequence of their introduction.

It is obvious that the question whether any given intervention is a sufficiently common exploitation of the opportunity provided to come within the risk is again a matter on which judgments may differ, though they often agree. The courts, and perhaps ordinary thought also, often describe those that are sufficiently common as 'natural' consequences of the neglect. They have in these terms discriminated the entry of a thief from the entry of a man who burnt the house down, and refused to treat the destruction of the house as a 'natural' consequence of the neglect.[18]

We discuss later in Chapter IX the argument that this easily intelligible concept of 'harm within the risk', overriding as it does the distinctions between voluntary interventions and others, should be used as the general test for determining what subsequent harm should be attributed for legal purposes to prior action. The merits of this proposal to refashion the law along these simple lines are perhaps considerable, yet consequences of actions are in fact often traced both in the law and apart from it in other ways which depend on the discrimination of voluntary interventions from others. We distinguish, after all, as differing though related grounds of responsibility, causing harm by one's own action and providing opportunities for others to do harm, where the guiding analogy with the simple manipulation of things, which underlies causal thought, is less close. When, as in the examples discussed above, we trace consequences through the non-voluntary interventions of others our concern is to show that certain stages of the process have a certain type of connection with the preceding stages, and not, as when the notion of risk is applied, to show that the ultimate outcome is connected in some general way with the initiating action. Thus, when A's shot makes B start and break a glass it is the causal relationship described by the expression 'made B start' that we have in mind and not the likelihood that on hearing a shot someone may break a glass. Causal connection may be traced in such cases though the initiating action and the final outcome are not contingencies that commonly go together.

Apart from these conceptual reasons for distinguishing these related grounds for responsibility, it is clear that both in the law, as we show in Chapter VI, and apart from it we constantly treat harm as caused by a person's action though it does not fall 'within the risk'. If, when B broke the glass in the example given above, a splinter flew into C's eye, blinding him, A's action is indeed the cause of C's injury though we may not always blame him for so unusual a consequence.

Reasons. In certain varieties of interpersonal transactions, unlike the case of coercion, the second action is quite voluntary. A may not threaten B but may bribe or advise or persuade him to do something. Here, A does not 'cause' or 'make' B do anything: the strongest words we should use are perhaps that he 'induced' or 'procured' B's act. Yet the law and moral principles alike may treat one person as

18 *Bellows* v. *Worcester Storage Co.* (1937) 297 Mass. 188, 7 NE 2d 588.

responsible for the harm which another free agent has done 'in consequence' of the advice or the inducements which the first has offered. In such cases the limits concern the range of those actions done by *B* which are to rank as the consequence of *A*'s words or deeds. In general this question depends on *A*'s intentions or on the 'plan of action' he puts before *B*. If *A* advises or bribes *B* to break in and steal from an empty house and *B* does so, he acts in consequence of *A*'s advice or bribe. If he deliberately burns down the house this would not be treated as the consequence of *A*'s bribe or advice, legally or otherwise, though it may in some sense be true that the burning would not have taken place without the advice or bribe. Nice questions may arise, which the courts have to settle, where *B* diverges from the detail of the plan of action put before him by *A*.

IV

CAUSATION IN LEGAL THEORY

I. THE VARIETY OF CAUSAL QUESTIONS

THE most important modern literature on causation in the law is concerned almost exclusively with the extent of liability for the tort of negligence.[1] Causal questions, however, appear in every branch of the law and there is a variety of ways, even in a single branch, in which legal rules make causal connection an element in responsibility. It is important to bear this in mind in considering the account given in this chapter of modern criticisms of the traditional approach to questions of causation, and in this section, as a reminder of the ubiquity and diversity of these questions, we make a very brief survey of their place in the law.

The most frequent type of causal question which courts face is whether a human action or omission caused some specific harm; but even this one form of question may be relevant to legal responsibility in different ways. In criminal law this question usually has to be answered because criminal offences are often defined in simple terms as acts causing specific harms: in such cases a causal connection between some action of the accused and the specified harm must be shown in order to establish the *existence* of liability, i.e. that a particular offence has been committed and that the accused is liable to punishment. So on a charge of murder or manslaughter it must be shown that the act of the accused caused death: once this is shown no further question has to be determined as to what range of further harm his offence has caused, though some attention may be paid to this in sentencing. In other types of case it is necessary to show causal connection between action and harm in order to determine the *extent* of liability; and in others still it will be necessary, in order to determine both the existence and the extent of liability. In

---

[1] Preoccupation with causation in negligence often tends to shut out consideration of the topic in relation to other torts. Thus Wright (*Cases on the Law of Torts*) included 'Causation and Remoteness' in the chapter on Negligence, and did not deal separately with causation elsewhere, though the arrangement has been changed in Wright and Linden, *Canadian Tort Law* (7th edn. 1980). Similarly the *Restatement of Torts* (*Second*) gives the whole of chapter 16 to 'The Causal Relation Necessary to Responsibility for Negligence' but contains only short scattered references to causation in other torts (e.g. ss. 279, 280, 465). McCormick, *Damages*, deals with 'proximate cause' in the part on Torts, but has no separate treatment of causation in contract.

contract, for example, it may often suffice to establish the existence of liability simply to show that the defendant failed to deliver goods on the stipulated day, and this usually raises no causal question; but some of the most perplexing causal questions arise in determining, in such cases, how much loss the defendant's failure to deliver has caused to the plaintiff. On the other hand, even in the law of contract the very existence of liability, as distinguished from the extent of recoverable damages, may depend on the truth of a causal statement. This is most obvious in contracts of indemnity or insurance, for example, against the negligence of others: the insured may have to show that loss was 'proximately' caused by the particular type of 'peril' covered by the policy.

In tort causal questions are usually relevant both to the existence of liability and to its extent. In certain cases where damage need not be proved and no special damage is claimed, as in libel, the only causal question may be whether or not the defendant caused the publication of the libel. In negligence there is an unsettled doctrinal dispute as to whether this tort is established without proof of damage once the defendant is shown to have failed to take due care to avoid harm to the plaintiff. If this view were correct the only causal question in negligence would be that concerning the extent of the damage caused by the failure to take care.[2]

Though in most branches of the law, where liability and the extent of liability depend on proof of causal connection between an action or omission and harm, the action or omission is that of the person sought to be made responsible, this is not always so. In tort, where liability is vicarious, the relevant causal connection is that between the servant's action or omission and the harm, and in no sense of causation is it necessary to establish any causal connection between the master's conduct and the harm. There is of course also a vast range of statutory enactments where the causal connection to be shown is between harm and the action of a human being who is not a party to legal proceedings. Examples may be seen in the schemes for compensation for harm or loss 'caused by the discharge of any missile . . . by the enemy'[3] or 'occurring . . . as a direct result of action taken by the enemy'.[4]

Further, it is not always the case that the causal connection upon which liability depends is a causal connection between a human being's action (or omission) and harm. In tort where liability is strict,

[2] The Germans have invented useful expressions distinguishing the part played by causation in respect of the existence of liability and its extent. They speak of the former as *haftungbegründende Kausalität* and of the latter as *haftungausfüllende Kausalität*—Enneccerus-Lehmann, *Lehrbuch des bürgerlichen Rechts*, ii. 60.
[3] Personal Injuries (Emergency Provisions) Act, 1939, s. 8.
[4] War Damage Act, 1943, s. 2 (1(*a*)).

as in cases falling under the principle of *Rylands* v. *Fletcher*, once it
is proved that the defendant has accumulated a noxious substance
on his land, he is liable if *it* escapes and causes harm, whether or
not he could have prevented this escape. Causal questions of difficulty may arise as to whether a plaintiff's injuries were caused by
the escape or some subsequent intervention of a third party or
whether the escape itself was caused by an act of a stranger or an
'act of God'. The same is true of liability of the occupiers of premises
for damage to wayfarers caused by the defective state of the premises
abutting on the highway: the occupier is liable if harm is caused, for
example, by a fall of bricks on a passer-by, even if he had only just
acquired the property and had no possible opportunity of preventing
the fall. Other examples of cases where the causal connection to be
established is between some natural occurrence and harm, and not
between some human action and harm, are to be found in many
statutory schemes for compensation for industrial injuries or war
injuries, and in contracts of insurance. A ship may be insured against
loss caused by 'marine perils' but not warlike operations.[5]

It is also pertinent that though in the vast majority of cases the
causal connection with which the law is concerned is that between
harm or *loss* and some other contingency, this is not always the case;
it may be necessary in some cases to show that a benefit has been
caused by some act or omission. This is so because in certain cases a
defendant may seek to rely in reduction of damages on a benefit
which has accrued to the plaintiff: it is therefore sometimes material
to determine whether such a benefit as, for example, the payment of
an indemnity under an insurance contract or of a pension is the
consequence of a defendant's wrongful act or of some act of the
plaintiff or a third person.[6]

The terminology used by the law to refer to causal connection is
very various. The expression 'proximate cause' is most commonly
used in the formulation of common law rules and also appears in
statutes.[7] It is a remnant of the maxim 'In jure non remota causa
sed proxima spectatur', and by most lawyers the parent maxim is
regarded as acceptable solely for its negative force as a reminder
that, to demonstrate causal connection between events for legal

[5] *The Matiana* [1921] AC 104; *Yorkshire Dale S.S. Co.* v. *Minister of War Transport*
[1942] AC 691.
[6] See *Payne* v. *Railway Executive* [1952] 1 KB 26, where the plaintiff was injured
by the defendant's negligence and invalided out of the Royal Navy with a pension.
The pension was held not to be deductible from the amount of the damages since it
was the consequence not of the tort but of the Navy service.
[7] e.g. The Marine Insurance Act, 1900, s. 58(1), provides that 'subject to the
provisions of this Act and unless the policy otherwise provides the insurer is liable
for any loss proximately caused by any peril insured against but subject as aforesaid
he is not liable for any loss not proximately caused by a peril insured against'.

purposes, it is not enough to show that one was a necessary condition (cause in fact) of the other. So far as the maxim suggests that proximity in space or time is the criterion or chief criterion which differentiates the causal connection which is legally significant from that which is not, it is usually agreed to be misleading.[8]

The expression 'cause' alone does, however, very frequently occur both in statutes and in the traditional formulation of common law rules, though the word 'effect' is comparatively rare. Besides this pair of expressions there are in common use, both in statutory and judicial language, such expressions as 'due to', 'owing to', 'result',[9] 'attributable to',[10] 'the consequence of', 'caused by'.[11] For some purposes it is important to distinguish between these various expressions,[12] though their similarity on many vital points justifies grouping them together as examples of causal terminology. But it is specially necessary to bear in mind two variants of causal terminology since very different considerations will apply to them. Sometimes liability or its extent depends on the proof that a wrongful action, or some other contingency, was *the* cause of harm: this may be so even where common sense, left to itself, might wish to describe the situation by saying that there were several causes of the harm so each was only *a* cause. Yet, even in the black and white Anglo-American system, it is very often sufficient for the plaintiff to show that the defendant's action or omission was *a* cause of his injuries, and he will succeed, even though no damage would have occurred but for a third party's negligence, which itself might be regarded as *a* cause or a concurrent cause. Further, in cases where apportionment is allowed (as under the present English rules for contributory negligence) this is on the footing that neither party's negligence was *the* cause of harm but that each was *a* cause.

[8] The same may be said of Bacon's much-quoted accompaniment to this maxim 'It were infinite for the law to judge the causes of causes and their impressions one of another; therefore it contenteth itself with the immediate cause' (*Maxims of the Law*, Reg. I). It is probable that the 'cause of causes' meant for Bacon a chain of events each of which would on *ordinary criteria* be regarded as a *cause* of its successor and not merely as a necessary *condition* of it. It is to be noted that some contemporaries are prepared to defend the expression 'not proximate' as best conveying the contention of the plain man that though one event may be a necessary condition of another the connection between them may be too freakish, extraordinary, or accidental to serve as a basis for legal responsibility. See Prosser, 'Palsgraf Revisited' (*Selected Topics in the Law of Tort*, p. 191). The suggestion is that no further analysis of his commonsense feeling for what is 'proximate' can be given.

[9] Workmen's Compensation Act, 1925, s. 9(1) ('where incapacity for work results from the injury'). Cf. Sales of Goods Act, 1979, s. 51(2) ('loss directly and naturally resulting in the ordinary course of events').

[10] Royal Warrant for Pensions.

[11] Personal Injuries (Emergency Provision) Act, 1939, s. 1.

[12] In *Commonwealth* v. *Butler* (1958) 102 CLR 465, 480 Windeyer J. says that the formulation (statutory in that case) 'Did the death result from the injury?' is preferable to 'Did the injury cause the death?' when the latter invites the reply that the injury was a 'contributing factor'.

The second type of causal expression requiring separate attention is used to refer to certain of the interpersonal transactions already discussed. Under many legal rules, both statutory and common law, it is necessary, in order to establish liability, to show that one person has caused another person *to act* in a certain way, or has caused something *to be done* by another person.[13] Thus, under the Road Traffic Act, 1930, s. 35(1), it is an offence to cause or permit any person to use a motor vehicle not insured against third party risks. Apart from statute there are many species of criminal and civil liability which depend on proof that one person has caused another to do something. A man may, for example, undertake that he will cause certain actions to be done or be liable for such actions as he should cause or procure to be done by others. Moreover, as already mentioned, the familiar concepts of inducing and procuring other persons to act in certain ways are commonly regarded by legal writers as special cases of one person causing another person to act in certain ways. And similar, though not identical, notions are involved in the analysis of the common concepts of causing harm by deceit or obtaining by false pretences.

II. THE TRADITIONAL APPROACH

Much contemporary writing on causation in the law is a literature of revolt against an older conception of the character of those issues which courts discuss and decide in causal terminology so often with an accompanying cloud of metaphors. Though agreed that they are in revolt, modern writers often differ in their estimate of the vitality of the old tradition: some speak as if it were already dead and gone and the 'real' issues lurking behind the causal terminology had at last been recognized not only by the theorists but also by the courts; others are convinced that there is an old misconception of these issues which is still alive and to be combated. 'Modern cases have substituted the test of responsibility or fault for that of causation.'[14] 'What is important is to free the law from the encrusted precedents on "proximate causation" offering a principle that will permit both courts and juries to begin afresh in facing problems of this kind'.[15] The extent to which 'modern cases' have in various branches of the law overcome 'encrusted precedents' and traditional ways of thinking about causation is a question we discuss in later chapters of this

13 See Chaps. VII and XIII below for the place of this notion in civil and criminal responsibility.
14 A. L. Goodhart, 'Notes of an Address on Special Problems of the Law of Torts', p. 11, reprinted in (1955) 71 *LQR* 402 at p. 413.
15 American Law Institute Draft Penal Code (1956), Tentative Draft 4, p. 135.

book; here we are concerned to characterize in general terms first, the traditional conception—or misconception—of the causal questions faced by courts, and, secondly, the main varieties of modern criticism and modern substitutes for the old approach. The contrast between old and new in its strongest form may be understood from the following example. In the State of New York it is and has since 1866 been the law that, if a fire negligently started spreads to buildings, damages may be recovered only in respect of the first of the buildings affected.[16] It is not difficult to understand what might lead a court to restrict liability in this way: such a restriction may suit the needs of a crowded urban economy where, if fires are started, very many buildings are likely to burn, and where it is possible and relatively easy to insure against fire. Without a restriction of this kind business enterprise may be crippled by the enforced payment of gigantic sums in compensation or may be deterred from operating by the prospect of such burdens. Such a restriction may also be inspired by simpler less utilitarian conceptions of what is just: the negligence that starts a fire is a common incident in urban life, and not a sufficiently grave moral offence to warrant the transfer of the whole of vast losses from where they fall to the shoulders of the negligent.

Whatever their motivation and however respectable it is, such rules limiting liability seem at first sight, both to the non-legal and to the conventional legal eye, to have nothing whatever to do with causation. They are rules limiting the extent of liability simply out of consideration of what is expedient or just or both: they represent a particular *policy* which a particular legal system has adopted in a particular branch of the law, and there is nothing surprising in the fact that other jurisdictions do not recognize the same restrictions.

Hence when a court, applying these rules, rejects the claim of the owner of the second house destroyed by the spread of the fire, it seems to act on principles very different in kind from those that lead it to reject the claim of the owner of the first house because it transpired that just as the fire was flickering out a third party deliberately poured paraffin on the embers. The natural though possibly naïve description of these two different cases would be that, though the damage in the first case was caused by the defendant's negligence, the legal rules only allowed compensation for part of the damage so caused; whereas in the second case, though the damage would not have occurred without the defendant's negligence, it was not caused by it. In the first case, according to the traditional way of regarding such matters, the claim was rejected because the court had answered adversely to the plaintiff a general question of law,

---

16 *Ryan* v. *New York Central R. Co.* (1866) 35 NY 210, 91 Am. Dec. 9.

viz. 'May damages be recovered for the destruction of a house caused by a fire negligently started if it is not the first affected?' In the second it is rejected because the court answers adversely to the plaintiff a particular question of fact 'Was the destruction of the house caused by the negligent act of the defendant?'

The traditional conception of questions of causation at least purported to take seriously the differences between these two ways of rejecting a plaintiff's claim: it distinguished limitations on liability, imposed because courts think them expedient or just or because they hold certain kinds of harm to be outside the 'scope' of a statute, from particular findings that loss was or was not 'proximately caused' by the defendant's act, made in applying a general principle that compensation will be given only for harm 'proximately' caused. By contrast the modern approach insists on the identity in character of these two sorts of determinations. Such limitations as the New York fire rules are now[17] discussed in most American textbooks on tort under the same heading of 'proximate cause' as cases where defendants have been held not to be responsible for loss because their negligent conduct would not have resulted in harm without, for example, the deliberate intervention of a third party or some extraordinary event.

This identification, under the heading of 'proximate cause', of what for conventional thought are quite different principles defining the extent of liability is felt by many modern writers to be a major clarification, and it is almost always accompanied by the insistence that the only factual element in the question whether a defendant's act is for legal purposes the cause of harm is whether or not the harm would have happened without the act. This factual component is variously termed 'cause in fact', 'material cause', *conditio sine qua non*, and is the sole point of contact with what causation means apart from the law. All the remaining components are questions of the law's policy, to be found in the court's conception of what limitations are just and expedient or in accord with the rationale or 'purpose' of legal rules. 'What we do mean by the word "proximate" is that because of convenience, of public policy, of a rough sense of justice, the law arbitrarily declines to trace a series of events beyond a certain point. This is not logic. It is practical politics.'[18]

[17] Prosser, Wade, and Schwartz, *Cases and Materials on Torts* (6th edn. 1976), chap. VI; below, p. 106.
[18] *Palsgraf* v. *Long Island R.R. Co.* (1928) 248 NY 339, 162 NE 99, *per* Andrews J. There are a variety of ways in which this cardinal feature of the modern outlook is expressed. The two main forms are (1) that the questions of causal connection which courts decide are not purely questions of fact but a blend of fact and policy, for they include both the genuine question of fact whether the alleged cause was a *sine qua non* of the loss and also a non-factual question masquerading under such names as proximate or legal cause; (2) that the question of causation is purely a question of

The contrast between old and new may be pointed in another way. It is, of course, open to a legal system to choose whether in any given area of the law to recognize causing harm as one element in responsibility. Traditional and modern views would agree that *this* choice (whatever causing harm may mean) is a matter of policy. The traditional view differs from the modern in holding that once this choice has been made then particular questions arising in particular cases as to whether a defendant's act was the cause of harm are not themselves questions of policy but questions of fact, and this is not confined to the question of whether the defendant's act was a *sine qua non* of the harm. The distinction between questions of law and policy and questions of fact is, of course, not a perspicuous one; but the traditional insistence that questions of causation are questions of fact did not merely mean that so long as there were juries they should answer them; and it never precluded superior courts from reviewing decisions on 'proximate' cause or 'remoteness'.

The traditional contention meant that the criteria for deciding such questions were not inventions of the law but were to be found outside the law in what was assumed, rightly or wrongly, to be part of the ordinary man's stock of general notions. Hence the insistence that these questions were questions of fact often went together with the insistence that the criteria for deciding them were to be drawn from common sense. 'I think the case turns on a pure question of fact to be determined by common-sense principles. What is the cause of the loss?'[19]

Not even in its most conceptualist period was it possible, even for English law, to ignore the fact that common sense, when asked to say whether a particular act was the cause of some harm in the bewilderingly complex or freakish combination of circumstances which often confront the courts, might not be prepared to give any

fact, but that decisions do not turn simply on causation but on a combination of causation and responsibility (see *McLean* v. *Bell* (1932) 147 LT 262, p. 264). Common to both these formulations is the thesis that the only factual part of causal questions is whether or not the alleged cause was a *sine qua non* of what has occurred. In general there is agreement that the 'but for' test ('Would the harm have occurred but for the defendant's act?') is an adequate criterion for the presence of the 'cause in fact relation'. On the other hand not all modern writers identify the factual component in 'legal cause' with a condition *sine qua non*. Some like Leon Green consider that it is best described as the requirement that to be a legal cause a factor must be 'substantial' or 'appreciable' and that these terms though 'factual' cannot be further analysed: other writers accept this only when the 'but for' test yields undesirable results as in certain cases of 'multiple causation'. Finally, recent writers contend that even the question of 'cause-in-fact' is largely one of policy (see below p. 102). The notion of a condition *sine qua non* and its various forms are discussed in Chap. V.

[19] *Leyland Shipping Co.* v. *Norwich Union Fire Insurance Society* [1918] AC 350, 363, *per* Lord Dunedin.

answer to a question in that form. The plain man's principles are worked out for plain cases and there must always be ranges of cases in which they fail to determine a conclusive or unique answer. But indeterminacy of common notions, when applied to circumstances outside a range recurrent and familiar in everyday life, has never yet deterred English law from treating questions which involve them as questions of fact, and distinguishing them from general questions of expediency, justice, or social policy. This is in part because it is considered that though such notions have a large and debatable penumbra of vagueness, there is also a central core of commonly agreed meaning where no doubts are felt about their application to particular cases. There will always, for example, be innumerable clear cases where we can say that a man's negligent action in starting a fire did in fact cause the destruction of three houses however just or expedient it may be to limit the liability to the first. This remains true, even if there are borderline cases where owing to the character of the intervening events we may hesitate or disagree. More important, however, is the conviction that use can be and is still made of common-sense notions even when the debatable borderline questions are reached: for decisions here may be controlled not simply by considerations of what would be just, or expedient, or on the whole best, as they would be if the matter were at large, but also by considerations of how like or unlike the standard clear case the present debatable case is. The process of decision is in part a search for analogies with and differences from standard cases which lends to decisions a character and a predictability sufficient to distinguish them from 'arbitrary' determinations of policy.

In this respect the conception that there are common-sense principles of causation in the law is similar to the conventional view of the law's use of other highly general notions such as those of temporal or spatial location or of the notion of an 'attempt'. For the law the question of where or when something happened or whether a person attempted or merely prepared to do something is a question to be decided according to common-sense principles; yet it would be absurd to pretend that common-sense principles, subtle and flexible though they are, in accordance with which events are spatially or temporally located, would be always adequate to answer the type of question that may perplex the lawyer. Common-sense principles could not yield an answer to the type of question concerning the place where a contract was made which arises in the conflict of laws; in ordinary life, we do not have to locate the making of contracts with an eye to the distinction between the place where the offeree spoke (over the telephone) words of acceptance and the place where the offeror heard them. For similar reasons common-sense principles

would provide no answer to the question where one man killed
another, when a distinction has to be drawn between the place where
the trigger was pulled and the place where the victim was hit, which
is so vital a distinction for the law when a jurisdictional border
separates the two.[20] Before an answer can be given to such questions
as these, common-sense criteria have to be supplemented by legal
principles or considerations of what is best or just. It is true that a
decision is made between alternatives which are necessarily left open
by common-sense principles; yet these define the limits within which
such questions have to be answered and are the source of analogies
by reference to which decisions are controlled and often predictably
made.

A legal system may mark more or less strongly and in various ways
the distinction between the limits on liability imposed by principles of
causation and those imposed by special principles of policy like the
New York fire rules. The distinction may be preserved simply by
judicial habits of speech, or by the use of a special technical apparatus
for classifying these two kinds of questions under different heads.
Judges may simply choose not to refer in causal language to rules
limiting liability out of considerations of policy or convenience such
as the common law rule that no one can be convicted of murder or
manslaughter if his victim does not die within a year and a day of
the fatal blow. Or, in rejecting claims, judges may make explicit that
their ground in doing so is their view of what is just or convenient
or of the intended scope or purpose of a statutory rule. When a
plaintiff claiming compensation for loss of sheep, washed overboard
in a rough sea for want of the sheep-pens prescribed by statute, is
told that his claim fails because the loss which 'we assume to have
been caused by' the defendant's breach of statutory duty is 'of such
a nature as was not contemplated at all by the statute', that 'there
was no purpose direct or indirect to protect against such damage . . .
the Act is directed against the possibility of sheep or cattle being
exposed to disease . . . ',[21] this marks off questions of the policy and
scope of legal rules as different from questions of causation.

Further, in the law of negligence the requirement that the plaintiff
must show not only that the defendant's careless action has caused

[20] As to contracts, see *Entores Ltd.* v. *Miles Far East Corporation* [1955] 2 QB 327.
See also *State* v. *Hall*, where the accused stood on the North Carolina side of the
state line and shot into Tennessee, 114 NC 909, 19 SE 602 (1894); cited in W. W.
Cook, *The Logical and Legal Basis of the Conflict of Laws*, p. 12. Similar problems
defeating common-sense principles arise for the law over the temporal location of
events. *X* digs on his own ground and much later the surface of his neighbour's land
falls in. When, for the purpose of the Limitation Acts, did *X* infringe his neighbour's
right to support? Was it when he excavated his own land or when his neighbour's
land fell in? (*Darley Main Colliery* v. *Mitchell* (1886) 11 App. Cas. 127.)
[21] *Gorris* v. *Scott* (1874) LR 9 Ex. 125, 130, *per* Kelly CB.

the harm but that the defendant was under 'a duty of care' has served (among the confusions it may also have perpetrated) to provide a special rubric for limitations on liability imposed out of consideration of legal policy, and to distinguish these from questions of causation. Hence contemporary objectors to the traditional doctrine very often urge that this apparatus is actually misleading, that the three questions whether the defendant was under a duty of care, whether he was in a legal sense guilty of negligence to the plaintiff, and whether his action was the proximate cause of the plaintiff's injury are really one and the same.[22]

The chief factors which make for or against preservation of the distinction between causal limitations and general policy limitations on liability are perhaps the following. The authoritative text of legal rules in the case of statutes or codes, or the accepted formulations of common law rules may provide in bold terms that individuals are to be responsible for the harm their actions cause. 'Tout fait quelconque de l'homme qui cause à autrui un dommage oblige celui par la faute duquel il est arrivé à le réparer.'[23] 'A person who causes the death of another by an unlawful act amounting to a misdemeanour is guilty of manslaughter.' 'A person acting negligently is responsible for all harm to another of which his negligence is the proximate cause.' These simple formulae in which causing harm is made not merely a necessary but a sufficient ground of liability are unrealistic; in the course of applying them courts find that there are limitations required by consideration of what is just, or what is in practice workable. It may be felt wrong to treat a man as guilty of manslaughter who causes another's death by dressing up as a ghost and frightening him, even though this is a misdemeanour, or to impose the burden of compensation for vast losses on someone who has caused them by an act which is negligent only because some relatively minor harm was its likely or foreseeable outcome. If in such cases the courts wish to do justice, and yet not openly to flout the authority of rules stated in bald causal terms, one expedient is to take such matters into account under the heading of causation and to extend this term to cover the limitations of policy thought desirable. This was in fact done by the judge in *Ryan*'s case in formulating the New York fire rules in terms of proximate cause. Inevitably if this is done the colour flows back: questions of policy are called questions of 'proximate cause' and questions of proximate cause cease to be distinguished from questions of policy.

22 Morris, 'Duty, Negligence and Causation', (1952) 101 *U. Pa. LR* 189; and, more tentatively, Denning LJ in *Roe* v. *Minister of Health* [1954] 2 QB 66, 86: 'Instead of asking three questions I should have thought that in many cases it would be simpler and better to ask the one question: "is the consequence within the risk?"'
23 Code civil, art. 1382.

III. MODERN CRITICISM

In breach of a statute forbidding the sale to an infant under the age of 16 of dangerous weapons, the defendant sold an air rifle and ammunition to a boy of 13. The boy's mother told the boy to return the weapon to the defendant and get a refund: on the defendant's refusal to take the rifle back, the boy's mother took it from the boy and hid it. Six months later the boy found it and allowed a playmate to use it, who shot and accidentally wounded the plaintiff, destroying the sight of one eye.[24]

Was the defendant's violation of the statute the proximate cause of the plaintiff's injury?

The defendant, in breach of statutory duty, failed to keep a crossing in proper repair. The plaintiff was lawfully travelling upon the highway and assisted the driver of a truck to pull a car out of a mud hole on the crossing. He knelt down to tie one end of the rope to the axle of the truck, while the owner was tying the other end to the car. When the plaintiff, who had a wooden leg, after giving the truck driver a signal to start, stepped from between the two vehicles, he put his leg into the mud hole. He caught hold of the back end of the truck expecting to be pulled out of the hole, but as he did this the slack in the rope became entwined round his sound leg and broke it at the ankle.[25]

Was the defendant's violation of the statute the proximate cause of the plaintiff's injury?

A ship, insured against loss caused by marine perils other than such losses as were the consequence of warlike operations, was engaged, during wartime, in a convoy from Scotland to Norway. Under the convoy orders she pursued a zigzag course and dimmed her lights. She met an unexpected tide and was driven on to the rocks several miles off course in a fog.[26]

Was the loss caused by an excepted peril?

The accused brutally assaulted and raped the deceased who thereafter swallowed 6 tablets of bichloride of mercury. She died either from this poison or from the poison and the wounds inflicted by the accused.[27]

Did the accused cause her death?

[24] *Henningsen* v. *Markowitz* (1928) 132 Misc. 547, 230 NYS 313.
[25] *Hines* v. *Morrow* (1921) 236 SW 183 (Texas Civil Appeals).
[26] *Yorkshire Dale S.S. Co.* v. *Minister of War Transport* [1942] AC 691.
[27] *Stephenson* v. *State* (1932) 205 Ind. 141, 179 NE 633.

A man was stabbed in his stomach during a fight, receiving a severe wound perforating the gut. There was evidence that he was taken to hospital and there, as a protection against infection, was given two doses of an antibiotic, although, after the first dose, there were symptoms that he was intolerant of this drug. As a result of this and other mistaken treatment, he developed pneumonia and died, though the stab wound was healed at the time of his death.[28]

Was there an issue for the jury whether the accused caused his death?

These cases, extraordinary enough in their own ways, are examples of questions presented in causal terms which courts have to face fairly frequently and somehow to answer. Much of the criticism of the traditional conception of proximate cause as raising issues distinct from legal policy, might be expressed as the complaint that this conception threw no light on the way in which these questions should be answered in cases such as these. If it is true that questions of causation are 'pure questions of fact to be determined by common-sense principles',[29] what are these principles and how do they apply to cases as complex as these? The most powerful among many different reasons for breaking with the old approach to proximate cause is that this demand has always remained unsatisfied.

There have, of course, been formulations enough: but the 'rules of causation' which writers adhering to the older tradition have laboured to provide have never performed the task for which they were designed. 'The positive programs suggested in some of their explorations in the world of fiction or fancy, completely unrelated to the ways in which practical men think, are to me entirely incredible.'[30] The objections to most 'rules for the determination of proximate cause' were either that they were couched in metaphors for which no literal translation was provided, or that they succeeded in conveying a meaning only by making oblique or covert references to the very considerations of legal policy, justice, or expediency which, according to the modern outlook, represent the real issues behind the causal terminology.

Generally speaking, the more rigid the rules, the more they exploited the traditional metaphors attached to the notion of causation. The rules, for example, formulated by Beale[31] were presented

28 *R.* v. *Jordan* (1957) 40 Cr. App. R. 152.
29 *Leyland Shipping Company* v. *The Norwich Union Fire Insurance Society* [1918] AC 350, 363, *per* Lord Dunedin.
30 Gregory, 'Proximate Cause in Negligence. A Retreat from "Rationalization" ', (1938) 6 *U. Chicago LR* 36, 58.
31 'The Proximate Consequences of an Act', (1920) 33 *Harvard LR* 633.

in a terminology of mechanical 'forces'; and if cases are examined in which a perplexed judge made valiant efforts to apply these rules, it is impossible not to sympathize with the wish to cut loose from the tradition which gave such rules birth. Their main effect was to render obscure the language of the court's decision without affording it any guidance. This can be observed in *Henningsen* v. *Markowitz*,[32] the first of the above five examples: here the judge endeavoured to apply Beale's formula which he found had been 'frequently cited' as a concise statement of a governing rule: '*where the defendant's active force has come to rest in a position of apparent safety the court will follow it no longer; if some new force later combines with this condition to create harm the result is remote from the defendant's act.*' This led the judge to use a fantastic terminology of 'forces' throughout his opinion. The defendant's wrongdoing was described as a 'force which the defendant set in motion', and the mother's intervention as 'an ineffectual check' which 'did not bring this force to rest', because it 'continued operative and capable of producing damage without the necessity of any other new force combining therewith'. That these phrases were all empty of guidance for the court was neatly demonstrated by the fact that the judge was able to find that the surrender by the boy of the gun to his mother and her retention of it for six months, did not mean that the case fell within the scope of the quoted rule. This conclusion was reached simply by the assertion that 'the active force did not in legal contemplation come to rest'; and so the 'chain of causation' between the defendant's wrongdoing and the plaintiff's injury was not 'broken'.

Even when they were not pernicious in this particular way, general rules for determining proximate cause very often contained explicit or implicit references to principles of legal policy; their appearance of defining proximate cause in factual, policy-neutral terms was little more than a sham, since they only asserted, in effect, that to be the proximate cause of harm something must be *in law* its cause. The vicious circle in such formulations was not usually as short as this, but it was vicious none the less. Rules were formulated in terms of factors which were 'substantial' or 'efficient', and factors negativing causal connection were described as 'intervening forces', but to each of these quoted expressions the words 'in law' had to be added; and this threw the problem back on to the tribunals which the rules were intended to guide. Even the definition of supervening or intervening forces or of the harm that was too remote in terms of what could not be reasonably 'foreseen' was by some critics found, on analysis, to be open to similar objections. This was not so much because of a

[32] (1928) 230 NYS 313.

doubt about what was reasonable, but because the harm or intervening factor could always be made to appear 'foreseeable' if described in one way, and not 'foreseeable' if described in another, and there seemed to be no authoritative guide as to the manner in which the facts were to be described. If in *R.* v. *Jordan*, the fifth case quoted above, we choose to describe the treatment in the hospital as mistaken treatment, this might be reasonably foreseen; if we describe it in very great detail it could not, and until the description is settled the criterion of what could reasonably be foreseen cannot be applied.[33]

This type of criticism of the old approach of course accorded well and indeed was part of the general scepticism as to the possibility of framing rules which developed into the 'Realist' movement of the 1930s; and Leon Green, who, more perhaps than any single writer, provided the dynamic for the new approach to the problems of causation, linked his views on the particular topic of causation to a quite general theory of the illusory character of legal rules and a general demonstration of the futility of the attempt to make 'word schemes' do in advance what can only be done by the exercise of judgment in particular cases. At the best 'rules will carry [judges] into the neighbourhood of a problem and then [they] must get off and walk'.[34]

The objection that rules for the determination of proximate cause *cannot* be found was usually united with a second distinguishable objection that, even if general rules defining common-sense principles of causation could be found, it would be undesirable to make legal responsibility depend upon them; for being general they could not be responsive to the special needs of different branches of the law. This objection took many forms. Sometimes, as with Green, it was simply the conviction that the most rational and socially satisfying thing we can do to secure rational decision is to institute tribunals and prescribe processes for passing judgment, and then leave questions as to the limits of liability when wrong has been done to the judgment of such tribunals in particular cases. 'The sweep of judgment quickly passes beyond the reach of any rules that can be framed. And, what is more, the judicial process ought to be left free of hampering restraints in fixing limits of protection in the particular cases.'[35]

The view that, even if general criteria for determining proximate causation could be found, they should be eliminated in favour of

[33] See for criticisms of this character Morris, 'On the Teaching of Legal Cause', (1939) 39 *Col. LR* 1087, 1102 and especially 'Proximate Cause in Minnesota', (1950) 34 *Minn. LR* 185.
[34] Leon Green, *Judge and Jury*, p. 214.
[35] Ibid., p. 222.

something else more responsive to the special needs of the law, was also advanced by critics not committed to Green's general scepticism of the possibility or desirability of rules. To many, for example, the claim that responsibility in areas of law so different in character and objective as the criminal law and tort, should be linked to common principles of causation, seemed a barren piece of conceptualism ignoring the obvious truth that the grounds of policy which must govern the scope of limits of liability in these two different spheres were different.[36] To such critics the use in determining responsibility of general principles of causation, assuming that such could be found, as compared with principles worked out for the special branch of the law under consideration, would inevitably focus attention on irrelevances and divert it from considerations which should rationally be controlling in the given field. If, as in the case of *Stephenson* v. *State*, the fourth of the above examples, a tribunal is satisfied that it has before it on a charge of murder a criminal who wilfully inflicted grave injury, without which death would not have occurred, what rational considerations force us to attend to the precise manner in which death came about? Why should the issue of responsibility, where the criminal's intention is clear, depend on the character of intervening events? If we try to fit such cases into general framework of causal principles we may lose sight of the elements relevant to the retributive and deterrent objectives of punishment. So it was said that in a case such as *Stephenson*'s we must not 'overlook the fact that the court was dealing with a defendant of unexampled viciousness. It was not so much a question of whether or not the defendant's force had continued to operate harmfully until death occurred, or whether or not it had come to rest in a position of apparent safety; the question was whether it was socially advantageous to give legal effect to the relation between the defendant's acts and the death.'[37]

The point of such writers[38] was not merely that courts, when faced with borderline cases, should be, as perhaps they always are, influenced by consideration for the objectives to be secured by punishment in deciding them; but that in classifying the act as homicide these policy issues, rather than 'the more or less fortuitous course of events subsequent to the act',[39] should be the controlling factors. 'As the seriousness of the defendant's act increases, not only in the danger to life which it creates but also in the viciousness of the intent

[36] See Wechsler and Michael, 'A Rationale of the Law of Homicide', (1937) 37 *Col. LR* 724.
[37] These are quotations from an extended comment on the case of *Stephenson* v. *State*, loc. cit., by 'G.C.T.' in (1933) 31 *Mich. LR* 659, 681.
[38] Their views are critically considered in detail in Chaps. XII and XIV below.
[39] G.C.T., 31 *Mich. LR* 663.

with which it is committed, the legal eye follows its consequences farther and farther.'[40] Similarly in tort and especially in cases of negligence, the effort to apply doctrines of 'superseding cause' and *novus actus interveniens*, even if clear criteria for their identification could be found, was felt to be mistaken, for the effort to apply them leads to an undue, irrational preoccupation with the precise character of intervening events, whereas judicial attention should be concentrated on the broader and more intelligible issue as to whether the reasons for treating the initial action as tortious or negligent included the prospect or 'risk' that harm would eventuate from it of the kind which in fact occurred.

Besides urging that responsibility should not depend on 'the fortuitous course of subsequent events', many critics considered that the factors upon which doctrines of *novus actus interveniens* or rules for the determination of proximate cause laid stress, were often of quite subordinate importance. In particular, the significance attached in many formulations to the question whether or not a deliberate human act had intervened, and the treatment of this as negativing in most cases causal connection between a defendant's action and eventual harm, seemed to many critics a mere survival from a bygone age and not warranted by any reasonable social policy that should now inspire the law. 'Contemporaries do not stress freewill as their grandparents did and cases of that sort no longer constitute a class to which only one result is appropriate.'[41]

A third main objection to the old approach was the confusion which critics felt to be latent in the very notion that 'proximate cause' *could* be an issue of fact. Until we have found out whether the harm would or would not have occurred but for the defendant's act, there is indeed some matter of fact about which we are still ignorant and something which we still do not understand about the case. To remove our ignorance and to complete our understanding, we require evidence to show that the defendant's action was 'material' in just this way, and sometimes we may have to go to science to find an answer. Such questions as this are, according to most critics, in an obvious sense factual, and there are objective criteria in no way connected with the law's policies or its aims for answering these questions: we are in the area when we can talk of fact and evidence and proof. When this stage is passed and the question of proximate cause arises we face an utterly different kind of question; since 'a legal cause problem raises the question of what legal results attach to events which are already understood from every other

---

40 G.C.T., 31 *Mich. LR* 675-6.
41 Morris, 'On the Teaching of Legal Cause', (1939) 39 *Col. LR* 1087, 1106.

pertinent point of view'.[42] How can any approach to the question of causation be sound which fails to stress the radical difference between these two types of question?

This criticism seemed to many reinforced by patient study of the cases where on identical facts courts had arrived at divergent conclusions on the issue of proximate cause. A driver of a train of petrol cars negligently collides with an obstruction on the line: the cars overturn and the spilled petrol ignites and pours into a river. It is carried downstream for a mile and then sets fire to dry grass: the fire spreads across the fields and burns the plaintiff's house a mile away. In New Jersey[43] the plaintiff recovered on the footing that the driver's negligence was the 'proximate cause' of his injury, and on almost identical facts in Pennsylvania[44] the plaintiff failed because the damage was 'too remote'. Parallels of this sort were always at hand as an objection to those who claimed that legal determinations of proximate cause, apart from the issue whether the harm would have occurred without the harmful act, rested on agreed factual and objective criteria.

Indeed matters have gone farther than this: some later writers, impressed, as logicians always have been, by the fact that singular hypothetical statements of the form 'If X which in fact happened had not happened, Y would not have happened' (contrary-to-the-fact conditionals) are not verifiable or falsifiable in any straightforward way, have claimed that even the determination whether the harm would have happened without the defendant's act cannot be regarded as a factual or policy-neutral question.[45] How can a court *know* that if the defendants had equipped their vessel with proper lifesaving devices the deceased who was drowned would not have drowned, and so reach the conclusion, as a matter of fact, that the culpable failure to provide the equipment was a necessary condition (cause in fact) of the harm? How can a question about facts which concededly never existed be a question of fact? Examination of decided cases has convinced some critics that the prime determinants of such questions are not factual estimates of probabilities but findings that defendant's action was wrongful, and the kind of harm which came about was of the very kind which the rule it violated was designed to prevent. The further claim that not only is this all that courts in fact often do consider in determining the factual-looking question 'Would this harm have occurred but for the defendant's wrongful act?', but all that it should consider represents

---

42 Ibid., 1094.
43 *Kuhn* v. *Jewitt* (1880) 32 NJ Eq. 647.
44 *Hoag* v. *Lake Shore and Michigan S.R. Co.* (1877) 85 Pa. 293, 27 Am. Rep. 653. See for comment on these cases Morris, 39 *Col. LR* 1090-1.
45 E. W. Thode, 'The Indefensible Use of the Hypothetical Case to Determine Cause in Fact', (1968) 46 *Tex. LR* 423.

an uncompromising form of the programme for eliminating causation from the law as an element in responsibility.[46]

A still more radical version of this programme has recently been
advanced. If it is impracticable to ascertain the cause of the injury
to plaintiff, e.g. because she contracts cancer from a drug administered to her mother during pregnancy but cannot show which
manufacturer of the drug sold it to her mother, she may sue any
manufacturer who had a substantial share of the market for the drug
at the time. Such a manufacturer will be liable in proportion to his
market share,[47] his liability being a form of strict products liability.
It remains open to the manufacturer, but in practice impossible, to
show that his product did not cause the harm. He is treated as a
member of a class of persons engaged in a dangerous activity, who
are required collectively to compensate those harmed by their
activities. Collective responsibility is substituted in effect for responsibility based on causation.

Distinct, but tending in the same direction, is the view of those
writers who argue that if a plaintiff can show a chance (e.g. a 40 per
cent chance) that a precaution which defendant ought to have taken
would have averted the harm of which he complains, he should be
entitled to recover the appropriate percentage of the harm suffered.[48]
According to this view the creation of a risk of harm which in fact
accrues should entail a limited responsibility even though it cannot
be proved that the risk-creating conduct caused the harm.

The claim that the issues presented in the terminology of causation
either are 'really' or should be decided by reference to legal policy
is, of course, not only a large but a vague claim. It is necessary to
consider what is meant by 'policy', for there are many important
differences dividing those who use this word to characterize their
common opposition to the old traditional approach. One common
feature of importance does, however, run through all the variants:
this is the insistence that where the existence or the extent of liability
for the violation of statute is in issue, a range of problems, which
appear insoluble if considered in causal terms, are relatively easily
solved if viewed as questions concerning the scope or purpose of the
statute, or the nature of the interests it was designed to protect.

[46] See Wex S. Malone, 'Cause in Fact', (1956) 9 *Stanford LR* 60 for an elaborate
discussion of the policy issues concealed in determinations of the 'but for' questions
and for the view that a strict insistence on 'but for' causality may often defeat the
deterrent purpose of legislative or common law rules. Malone's views are criticized
by Becht and Miller, *The Test of Factual Causation in Negligence and Strict Liability
Cases* (1961), pp. 2–9.
[47] Below, pp. 424.
[48] Below, p. 417, and cf. *McGhee* v. *National Coal Board* [1972] 3 All ER 1008
(HL), below, p. 410; Klemme, 'The Enterprise Liability Theory of Torts', (1976) 47
U. Colo. LR 153.

Whatever difficulties surround the notion of legislative intent and its discovery, there is often at any rate a clear answer to be obtained in these terms. A defendant, driving a car, exceeds the statutory speed limit and arrives at a point on the road just in time to knock down and injure a small child, who has dashed in front of his vehicle which he is at that point driving carefully and at a proper speed. Courts in such cases should not ask, as they have done,[49] whether there was a causal relation between the speeding and the accident but dispose of the case on the grounds, which few would dispute, that the hazards peculiar to speed which the statute was designed to suppress were such things as loss of control, and that the instant case fell clearly outside these.

In Germany writers who have welcomed the 'policy approach' do so explicitly on the ground that gnawing problems posed in causal terms drop away if we substitute for them the questions: What is the purpose or function of the statutory rule providing protection (*Sinn und Zweck des Schadenersatzes*)? Is this harm within the protection intended by the violated rule (*Schutzzweck der Norm*)?[50] These questions give intelligible and intelligent answers, whereas the old questions, familiar in German jurisprudence, whether there was a 'relationship of adequate causation' between act and harm, give answers which often are neither. A bus company admits passengers in excess of the maximum imposed for the safety of the vehicle, and a pickpocket, taking advantage of the crush, steals a passenger's property. The reason why in such cases there is no liability is to be found by asking what the purpose or scope of the statute is.

However, once the point is passed where consideration of legislative intent, or the needs or purposes of statutory rules gives a clear specific answer, modern critics, in spite of their agreement that questions of proximate cause are questons of legal policy, divide. The most important division is between those who admit neither the possibility nor desirability of finding general policies for the determination of the limits of responsibility, and those who on the contrary think that this is at least desirable and in some cases possible.

For writers of the first school 'policy' is just a name for an immense variety of considerations which do weigh and should weigh with courts considering the question of the existence or extent of responsibility. No exhaustive enumeration can be given of such factors and no general principles can be laid down as to how a balance should be struck between them. Policy, on this interpretation, is

---

[49] *Draxton* v. *Katzmarek* (1938) 280 NW 288 (Minn.), discussed further below, pp. 122, 168-70.
[50] E. von Caemmerer, *Das Problem des Kausalzusammenhangs im Privatrecht*.

atomized: the courts must focus attention on the precise way in which harm has eventuated in a particular case, and then ask and answer, in a more or less intuitive fashion, whether or not on these particular facts a defendant should be held responsible. The court's function is to pass judgments acceptable to society for their time and place on these matters, and general policies can never take the place of judgment.[51] Edgerton says, 'It neither is nor should be possible to extract rules which cover the subject (of legal cause) and are definite enough to solve cases. . . . The solution . . . depends upon a balancing of considerations which tend to show that it is or is not reasonable or just to treat the act as the cause of the harm . . . these considerations are indefinite in number and in value and incommensurable.'[52]

The most radical exponent of this atomized form of policy, Leon Green, like most other advocates of policy, divides the traditional question of causation into two elements, one of fact and the other of legal policy, but differs from them in refusing to identify the factual element with the notion of *sine qua non* to be answered by the application of the 'but for' test. His reason is in part that there are certain exceptional cases where two independent wrongdoers each did something sufficient to lead to the harm and in such cases the application of the 'but for' test would lead to the undesirable conclusion that neither was responsible. His main reason, however, is that he thinks it impossible for a court or jury to determine or speculate profitably as to what *might* have happened but did not. Accordingly the question of fact is best described in the terminology of 'substantial', 'material', or 'appreciable' factor. This language, in his view, provides a formula for submission to the jury of a question of fact which 'cannot be reduced to any lower terms; it has no multiples'.[53] The remaining question of policy is one for the court, not the jury, and is always the question whether the interest of plaintiff is one protected by the law and whether it is protected against the particular hazard in question.[54] The reference to 'hazard' does not import that the event which occurred must have been likely or foreseeable in advance, for Green rejects the notion that foreseeability is of much assistance in determining questions of responsibility for harm.[55]

Green, in effect, refuses to distinguish between the question whether the defendant owed a duty in the circumstances of the case

[51] Green, *Judge and Jury*, chaps. i and vi.
[52] 'Legal Cause', (1924) 72 *U. Pa. LR* 211.
[53] Green, *Rationale of Proximate Cause*, p. 137. Presumably 'multiples' should be 'factors'; cf. *Judge and Jury*, pp. 190 ff.
[54] *Rationale of Proximate Cause*, p. 3.
[55] Op. cit., pp. 88, 120.

or, in particular, whether he owed a duty to the plaintiff, and the question of proximate cause,[56] i.e. whether a third factor negatives causal connection between the wrongful act and the harm. He treats them equally as questions of policy and does not think that any broad distinctions can be drawn between the types of policy involved in answering the two questions. Hence, in Green's view, the court must always ask, upon the detailed facts of a particular case, whether the plaintiff's interest is protected. A good example is to be found in his treatment of the extraordinary Texas case of *Hines* v. *Morrow*,[57] one of the cases described on p. 95 above. In that case the plaintiff succeeded despite the defence that the consequence could not be foreseen and was not 'proximate'. Green comments, 'This was not the issue. The only problem was whether this risk fell within the radius of the rule which the plaintiff relied upon, i.e. the defendant's duty to keep the crossing in proper repair, and which admittedly had been violated by the defendant. A recovery was allowed, but had the issue of negligence itself been a contestable one, the result would probably have been different.'[58]

Other critics of the traditional doctrine are less eager to rely as heavily as Green and Edgerton do upon the intuitive judgments of court or jury, and at least hope that the policy which is to take the place of the bad old rules of 'proximate cause' may be framed in terms sufficiently general to guide particular decisions and to frame questions suitable for submission to the jury as questions of fact. Hence many writers on tort combine the view that the limitations of proximate cause are limitations of policy, and not 'really' questions of causation at all, with the attempt to frame general principles limiting the extent of liability in terms of what is 'foreseeable', 'within the risk', or 'within the hazard' created by tortious conduct. These, it is felt, are consonant with the general purposes of the law of tort and the classification of types of conduct as negligent or otherwise tortious. Such a broad conception of policy is best seen in Prosser's admirable works on tort. He subscribes to the general modern distinction between the policy issue of 'proximate cause' and the question of 'cause in fact', which with some exceptions he identifies with the question whether harm would have occurred 'but for' the wrongful act. 'Proximate cause is the limitation which the courts have been compelled to place, as a practical necessity, upon the actor's responsibility for the consequences of his conduct. The limitation is sometimes one of causation but more often is one of the

---

56 Except so far as this is done, in certain cases of coincidence, under the vague heading of 'substantial factor'. See below, Chap. X, where Green's treatment of specific cases is examined.

57 (1921) 236 SW 183 (Texas Civil Appeals).

58 Op. cit., p. 22.

various considerations of policy which have nothing to do with causation. The tendency of the courts to state these considerations in terms of causation often obscures the real issues involved.'[59] It seems clear, however, that Prosser recognized, at least by implication, two different sorts of policy in the law of negligence, one of which he dealt with under 'Duty'[60] and 'Interests Protected':[61] this included the problem whether a plaintiff could recover if no danger to him could reasonably be foreseen but danger to others was foreseeable; and whether recovery was allowed for mental disturbance, fright, or shock. The other sort of policy was discussed under the heading 'proximate cause'[62] and his view seemed to be that there may be separate rules of policy applicable to the cases which are usually treated by the courts as raising causal questions. The principles of policy which he applied to these last questions were relatively broad. One of these is that a reasonably foreseeable intervening cause will not ordinarily relieve an actor of responsibility;[63] whereas, if an unforeseeable and abnormal intervening cause produces an unforeseeable result, the actor will ordinarily be relieved of responsibility.[64] This is an attempt to formulate policy in a broad, general way which makes the decision in particular cases to a considerable extent one of fact. Indeed, Prosser closes his chapter on causation by quoting the dictum that 'Proximate cause is ordinarily a question of fact for the jury, to be solved by the exercise of good common sense in the consideration of the evidence of each particular case.'[65]

[59] Prosser, *Torts*, 1st edn., p. 310, s. 45. In the fourth edition Prosser says that the limitation is 'sometimes, though *rather infrequently*, one of the facts of causation. *More often* it is purely one of policy': op. cit., p. 237 (our italics). How, one wonders, can we recognize those rare 'proximate cause' cases which do not involve policy? How would they be decided?

[60] 1st edn., s. 36.

[61] 1st edn., s. 37.

[62] Smith and Prosser's *Cases and Materials on Torts* does not, however, make this distinction. Chap ix, 'Proximate Cause', includes the material on 'Bodily injury resulting from Shock' and 'Prenatal injuries' which in the textbook come under 'Duty' and 'Interests protected', *Torts*, 4th edn., ss. 54, 55. The *Restatement of Torts*, having made this distinction in the original edition, has now adopted the view that 'a completely accurate analysis of the hazard element in negligence would require the material on superseding cause in [the chapter on the causal relation necessary to responsibility for negligence] to be placed in [the section dealing with whether actor's conduct is negligent with respect to a protected interest].' In deference to past judicial practice, however, the discussion of 'superseding causes' is left in the part on causation. *Restatement*, 1948 supplement, p. 651, comment (*ee*).

[63] 4th edn., p. 272.

[64] 4th edn., p. 280.

[65] Op. cit., p. 282, s. 50: *Healy* v. *Hoy* (1911) 115 Minn. 321, 132 NW 208. Varieties of 'Risk' or 'Foresight' theories of (or substitutes for) proximate cause are considered in detail in Chap. IX below. Writers in England adopting similar views usually eschew the word 'policy' and instead claim that questions of proximate causation are questions of 'responsibility'. See Goodhart, op. cit., p. 1 above.

American writers on proximate cause in criminal law have similarly sought to substitute for the traditional doctrine and its 'encrusted precedents' general principles of a type specially relevant to the purposes of punishment. These are intended for use when legal rules make causing harm an element in criminal responsibility. Some writers have only adumbrated these principles in general terms or insisted that in substance they are already at work behind the jargon of proximate cause in the existing law. One comprehensive and systematic attempt to state such principles has been made in the tentative drafts of the American Law Institute's Model Penal Code.[66] Here the issue of causation (apart from the cause-in-fact or 'but for' relationship) is made to turn generally on the question whether harm was within 'the contemplation' of the accused or 'within the risk' of which he was or should have been aware, according as the mental element required for conviction is that of knowingly or recklessly or negligently causing harm.[67]

It remains finally to record the varying optimism with which different modern writers view the search for rational principles of social policy to guide courts in the determination of cases of proximate cause. Some of those concerned with tort and the criminal law consider that there is only a small residue of cases where either deeply ingrained legal ideas, or popular conceptions of what is just, demand liability for harm resulting from a wrongful act even though it is not in any straightforward sense 'within the risk', 'hazard', or other general notion used in the formulation of such principles of policy; and that similarly there is only a small residue of cases where there is a demand, too strong to be resisted, that there should *not* be liability for harm even though the harm resulting from a wrongful act was 'within the risk' if the manner in which it actually occurred was too 'remote' or 'accidental'.[68] To deal with these marginal issues most writers admit special principles or a direct appeal to the jury's sense of what is just. Such questions are felt, though important, to be on the periphery of a generally successful substitution of intelligible criteria, based on social policy, for the irrelevant or meaningless distinctions characterizing the old tradition.

By contrast other authors sound a more sombre note. 'Though text writers have often said that problems of the scope of liability are at bottom problems of policy they throw virtually no light on how these problems can best be solved to serve society. Only in the

---

[66] See also Hall, *Principles of Criminal Law*, chap. 9, and (1933) 31 *Mich. LR* 659.

[67] Discussed in detail below, Chap. XIV, s. II. See also Wechsler and Michael, 'A Rationale of the Law of Homicide', (1937) 37 *Col. LR* 701.

[68] See for such exceptions ALI Model Penal Code: Draft 1962 (Comment on s. 2.03), and Fleming James and Perry, 'Legal Cause', (1951) 60 *Yale LJ* 761 and below, pp. 394 ff.

108   THE ANALYSIS OF CAUSAL CONCEPTS

cases in which extended liability is disastrously severe, or is likely to inundate the courts in a flood of litigation, have the courts used policy arguments to justify limitations of liability.'[69] This author, who is more sceptical than others of criteria constructed out of the ideas of 'foresight', 'risk', or 'hazard', concludes that while the issue of cases of proximate cause may often be affected by 'prejudices and assumed social values' it seems unlikely 'that a rational program of social betterment can be served by their solution or furnish guidance to the proper solutions'.[70] This scepticism of the new does not, how-ever, entail restored faith in the old, but rather the recognition that here we must learn to live among uncertainties, mitigated by the not inconsiderable measure of predictability which in fact will be found in the decisions on proximate cause of any single jurisdiction. The task of the jurist is not to search for general policies but rather to reveal the true character of the issues wrapped up in the blurred notions of causation, and the strategy and procedure involved in their presentation to courts. 'Here instruction ends with a feeling of satisfaction because the student has not been misled and a feeling of sorrow because we were born before the man who can formulate useful general tests of legal cause.'[71]

69 Morris, 'Duty, Negligence and Causation', (1952) 101 *U. Pa. LR* 189, 222.
70 Op. cit., p. 222.
71 Morris, 'The Teaching of Legal Cause', (1939) 39 *Col. LR* 1087.

V

CAUSATION AND *SINE QUA NON*

I. NECESSARY CONDITIONS

T wo indisputable advances towards simplicity and clarity in dealing with causal questions in the law are due to the modern criticism of the traditional approach. The first of these is the beneficially increased emphasis on the important point that very often consideration of the purpose of a legal rule will show that certain kinds of harm alleged to have been caused by a breach of the rule are altogether outside its scope, since it is obvious that the rule is not concerned to give protection against that sort of harm. When this is so it will be unnecessary to investigate the often obscure question whether, in the appropriate sense of 'cause' or 'consequence', the injuries were caused by or the consequence of the breach. If a statute designed for the protection of forests forbids the felling of trees, there is no need to debate the question whether the death of a person killed by the fall of a tree felled illegally, though with every care for life, was caused by this breach of the statute: it will be enough to say that it was not within its scope. So, too, if a passenger in a car driven in excess of the speed limit is struck by lightning in a storm, which he would not have encountered had the car not been driven at that speed, his claim for compensation may properly be rejected on the simple ground that the rule forbidding speeding was never intended for the protection of persons from injuries of this sort.

Scholastic discussions may often thus be intelligibly avoided. There is, however, a limit to such ways of escape from causal problems. Even if it is obvious or agreed that only injuries arising through contact with speeding cars are within the scope of the rule forbidding speeding, this leaves many causal questions undetermined. How much of the harm arising after the accident, either through steps taken on the spot or through later medical mistreatment, disablement, or loss of financial opportunities, is a consequence of the initial wrongdoing? These are problems of 'ulterior harm'. Or again, in what *way* must the accident eventuate from speeding to be attributable to it as its consequence? Would it still be so if the speed accounted for the accident only in conjunction with the intervention of some third party or suicidal behaviour of the injured person? These are problems of the manner of upshot. The 'purposes' discoverable in modern legal rules can never be so detailed or specific as to provide answers to most of such questions: they must either be resolved by general principles of limitation guiding the decisions of courts or left to their discretion.

The second major advance secured by modern criticism we shall call the bifurcation of causal questions. The single question typically confronted by courts: 'Was this harm (*Y*) the consequence of this act or omission (*X*)?' is divided into two questions. *First*: 'Would *Y* have occurred if *X* had not occurred?' *Second*: 'Is there any principle which precludes the treatment of *Y* as the consequence of *X* for legal purposes?' The utility and clarifying force of this bifurcation of causal questions also has its limitations which we consider later in this chapter, but, in a wide range of cases, it has solid merits. It is usually insisted upon by modern writers as something obviously required by the doctrine ascribed (though as we have seen inaccurately) to Mill that 'objectively' or 'scientifically' or 'in fact' every one of the infinite number of prior conditions of which it is true that if it had not occurred some given event would not have occurred is equally the cause of that event. According to the legal interpretation of this doctrine anyone who asks for the cause of an event faces an *embarras de choix* of literally cosmic proportions. From this predicament the inquirer can be rescued only by 'arbitrary' practical principles of selection or limitation supplied by the law. Consistently with this theoretical background, the first half of the bifurcated question is said to be concerned with a question of fact and the second half with questions of law or legal policy. So when a negative answer is forthcoming to the question 'Would *Y* have occurred if *X* had not?' *X* is referred to not merely as a 'necessary condition' or *sine qua non* of *Y* but as its 'cause in fact' or 'material cause'.

The bifurcation of causal questions has, however, real merits which are independent of this theoretical background and of the vocabulary thus chosen to emphasize the conviction that the only element in causation which is 'factual' or independent of legal policy or rule is the relation of *sine qua non*. These merits are real, because even if it is the case that some principles of selection and limitation used by the law in answering the second half of the bifurcated question are not *inventions* of the law but mirror principles characterizing ordinary non-legal thought, none the less the central and most common form of causal relation has two different aspects which correspond roughly with the two halves of the bifurcated question. The first is that a cause is *in some sense* necessary for the production of the consequence: the second is that the cause of an event is in some way distinguishable from other factors which are, in the same sense, necessary.

These two aspects of causation, even if they cannot be crudely opposed as 'factual' and 'non-factual', are of a very different character. They occasion different kinds of doubts and difficulties, and different kinds of criteria are used in their resolution. The necessity of the cause for the production of the consequence means that, in making causal statements, we must consult our knowledge of the general course of events. Under what sorts of conditions do things of this sort happen? Does this kind of thing happen without that kind of thing? The second aspect forces us to consider less definite issues and very often matters of degree. Although principles distinguishing between causes and mere conditions, or between factors which 'break the chain' of causation and those which do not, are to be found in ordinary thought apart from the law, their application often raises disputable questions of classification: Was this a coincidence? How likely was it? Was this a voluntary informed intervention? Had he a fair choice in the circumstances? In these questions the issue is not so much: 'Did X happen?' but rather 'Is what happened sufficiently like the standard case of an X to be classified with it for legal purposes?'

In this chapter we shall be concerned wholly with the first aspect of causation and so with the first half of the bifurcated question. Why is it usually right to ask as the initial question: 'Would Y have occurred if X had not occurred?' In what way may this approach be misleading or inappropriate? Is every condition *sine qua non* a causally relevant factor and vice versa?

The notion of a condition *sine qua non* may best be clarified if we recall those parts of Mill's analysis of 'the common notion of a cause' which survive the criticisms made of it in Chapter III. The central idea of his analysis is that the cause of an event is a special member of a complex set of conditions which are sufficient to produce that event in the sense that the set is 'invariably and unconditionally' followed by it. Each of the members of this set (whether distinguished by common sense as 'the cause' or classified by it as a 'mere condition') is necessary to complete the set thus linked by regular sequence to the consequent. In this doctrine as an account of ordinary thought we found three defects. First there are types of causal relation between human actions (e.g. interpersonal transactions and provision of opportunities) which require a different analysis. Secondly, even in the common cases of causation to which the main features of Mill's doctrine are applicable, the generalizations implied in singular causal statements are not statements of 'unconditional and invariable sequence' and the sense in which the cause is sufficient to produce its consequence cannot be defined in this strict way. The generalizations involved are statements of general connection between broadly described types of event which are brought to bear on particular cases distinguished from counter-examples in the manner described in Chapter III. Thirdly, 'the cause' is not 'selected' from a set of jointly sufficient conditions previously identified, but we have come, through experience of counter-examples or with the aid of scientific theory, to identify certain conditions without which our broadly formulated generalizations fail but with which they hold good.

If we remember and allow for these defects, Mill's conception of the cause as a special member of a set of jointly sufficient conditions is a clarifying one, for it enables us to allot to their place in causal thinking the notions of 'sufficient condition', 'necessary condition', and 'condition *sine qua non*'. This analysis reproduces, while ex- aggerating its precision, the ordinary thought that the cause is something which is *sufficient* to bring about the consequence in conjunction with other 'mere conditions' even if only a few of these last can be specified. Two further parts of Mill's thought, also co- inciding with ordinary thought, explain the different sense in which the cause is *necessary*: he subscribes to the belief that every event has a cause, and his doctrine of the plurality of causes reproduces the common belief that an event of a given kind may have different independent kinds of cause though normally only one of these is present on any given occasion. These three points taken together yield three different ways, hidden by the general expression 'neces- sary', in which a cause may be said to be a necessary condition of the consequence.

1. A condition may be necessary just in the sense that it is one of a set of conditions jointly sufficient for the production of the consequence: it is necessary because it is required to complete this set. If we consider the simple case where a man's action in throwing a lighted cigarette into the waste-paper basket would be treated both by common sense and the law as the cause of the fire, it is plain that the man's action is required to complete such a set of conditions jointly sufficient to produce the fire.

2. A condition may be necessary in a stronger sense, viz. that we may know that it is a necessary member of *every* set of sufficient conditions of a given type of occurrence. Thus we know that the presence of oxygen is in this sense a necessary condition of fire: no fire can occur without it and, though we believe that there are many alternative sets of sufficient conditions for fire, in all of them oxygen figures as a necessary constituent.

3. A condition which is necessary in the first of these ways may still not be necessary in a third sense, required in a *sine qua non*, for

it may not be necessary *on the particular occasion*[1] for the occurrence of the event. This is so because the normal assumption that on any given occasion only one sufficient cause is present may break down: two men may shoot and simultaneously lodge a bullet in their victim's brain or they may simultaneously approach escaping gas with a lighted candle. But if, as we ordinarily assume, for every such event there is present on any given occasion one and only one independent set of conditions sufficient to produce it, then every member of this set will be necessary on that occasion for the occurrence of the event and hence a condition *sine qua non* of it. Of every such condition it is true both that it is required to complete the conditions sufficient to produce the event, and that the event would not have occurred without it.

A condition which is necessary in the first of the above three ways is a *causally relevant factor* whether it is ranked as 'the cause' (like the man's action in throwing away the cigarette) or as a 'mere' condition like the presence of oxygen. In ordinary cases, where only one sufficient cause is present, a causally relevant factor will also be a condition *sine qua non* and so the question 'Would *Y* have happened if *X* had not?' will generally serve to bring a causally relevant factor to light. It is this fact that accounts for the prominence in law of the negative *sine qua non* test, of which a simple example is the following: a negligent omission to patrol a warehouse in which whisky is stored is not causally connected with the theft of the whisky if the latter was stolen before the patrolman was due to make his visit.[2] This rough test for causal relevance has, however, important limitations, for the ideas of causal relevance and condition *sine qua non* are not the same: and the law is in general only concerned with the latter so far as it is an indication of the former. In abnormal cases where more than one sufficient cause is present, the test will yield misleading answers.

These limitations on the utility of the *sine qua non* test, resulting from the fact that not every causally relevant factor is a condition

1 Philosophers may find the description of a condition as 'necessary on a particular occasion' paradoxical since the idea of necessity is connected with that of 'laws' or at least generalizations. The explanation of the paradox here is that if the doctrine of the plurality of causes is combined with the principle that every event must have a sufficient cause, the statement that a cause was 'necessary on a given occasion' when only one is present is a simple application of the 'law' that no event happens without one of a *disjunction* of sufficient causes.
2 *British Road Services v. Crutchley* [1968] 1 All ER 811 (HL); cf. *Rouleau v. Blotner* (1931) 84 NH 539, 152 Atl. 916 (plaintiff would not have seen signal had it been given); *Waugh v. Suburban Club Ginger Ale* (1948) 167 F. 2d 758; *Technical Chemical v. Jacobs* (1972) 480 SW 2d 602; *Stacy v. Knickerbocker Ice Co.* (1893) 84 Wis. 614, 54 NW 1091 (required wooden fence would have been 'gossamer before those powerful horses, frantic with fright'); *Baker v. Herman Mutual* (1962) 117 NW 2d 725 (Wis.); Honoré, *IECL*, xi, chap. 7-106 to 7-118.

sine qua non, are discussed in detail later. Here, however, we concentrate attention on the converse, more elusive, fact that not every condition *sine qua non* is a causally relevant factor. This is the case because the expression 'condition *sine qua non*' is ambiguous or at least unspecific: and the form of statement '*Y* would not have happened if *X* had not' may be true when the connection between *X* and *Y* has nothing to do with any form of causal connection even in the broadest sense of 'causal'. Such a *sine qua non* connection between *X* and *Y* may exist simply in virtue of the meaning of expressions used to describe events: or it may exist simply because the same unique action or event may be an instance of two different characteristics one only of which is a causally relevant factor. In neither case will the connection exemplify any form of empirical general connection between events of different kinds. These two types of causally irrelevant *sine qua non* connection (which we distinguish as *analytic* and *incidental* connection) have occasioned some perplexities in the law which we examine in the next section.

II. WHEN CONDITIONS *SINE QUA NON* ARE CAUSALLY IRRELEVANT

(*a*) *Analytic connection.* Whenever descriptions of actions or events are logically connected it is possible to construct out of them sentences of the form 'If *X* had not happened *Y* would not have happened' which are *necessarily* true. They do not convey factual information about the connection between different events, though in some cases it may be difficult to distinguish such necessarily true statements from factual statements that if one event had not happened another event would not have happened. In simple cases the merely linguistic or logical character of the connection is obvious. 'If she had never married she would not have been a widow.' Such a remark would have a function as a *reminder* that it would not be correct to say that she was a widow if she had never been married: we might make such a remark either in teaching the meaning of words or in pointing out the inconsistency of someone who had asserted at different stages in an argument that the same woman had never been married and was a widow.[3] Plainly, this is a condition *sine qua non* which it would be absurd to list among that infinite

---

[3] The status of such statements as analytic or factual will depend on the varying sense in which the constituent phrases are intended. 'This moment will never return' *may* mean 'Experiences like these will never return.' Similarly, 'If he had not had his purse on him he would not have dropped it' may mean 'If he had not taken his purse he would not have lost it.' In this case they are factual and, if true, not necessarily so. But taken in a stricter sense they are necessarily true, and convey no factual information.

series of necessary conditions from which, according to modern juristic theory, we have to select the 'proximate cause'. Equally plainly, we do not need legal rules or legal policies to enable us to rule out such *logically* necessary conditions, nor is there anything 'arbitrary' in rejecting them. They are ruled out because a causal connection is some form of connection between logically distinct items. Whatever else may be disputed in Hume and Mill's doctrine, this solid contention remains. Yet, in portraying the lawyer's causal problems legal writers or even courts have spoken as if even this sort of condition *sine qua non* ranked among the 'causes in fact' between which the lawyer has to select. If a man is knocked down and injured by a vehicle the fact that he is a man, human, and has a body, is something which is logically entailed by the description of the event with which we start and whose cause we may seek. Yet occasionally the courts have disregarded this fact.

Cause and effect find their beginning and end in the limitless and un-knowable. . . . Hence arbitrary limits have been set and such qualifying words as 'proximate' and 'natural' have come into use as setting the limits beyond which the courts will not look in the attempt to trace the connection between a given cause and a given effect. A plaintiff comes into court alleging, as an effect, some injury that has been done to his person or property. He shows that antecedent to the injury a wrongful act of another person occurred and that if the wrongful act had not occurred the injury complained of would not (as human probabilities go) have occurred. . . . We then say in common speech that the wrong was a cause of the injury. But to make such a standard (that if the cause had not existed the effect would not have occurred) the basis of legal responsibility would soon prove unsatisfactory: for a *reductio ad absurdum* may be promptly established by calling to mind that if the injured person had never been born, the injury would not have happened.[4]

The excuse (though not the justification) for this confusion of ana-lytic with factual connection is that, when we assert of a particular man referred to by either a pronoun or proper name that he was injured ('Smith (or he) was injured'), we do not actually *state* but *presuppose* the truth of the statement ('He is a man') which entails that he was born.

(b) *Incidental connection.*[5] We have already had occasion to notice as an important feature of causal and indeed all empirical statements the constant possibility of more or less specific or detailed description

---

4 *Atlantic Coast Line Railway Company* v. *Daniels* (1911) 8 Ga. App. 775, 70 SE 203.
5 See Preface, pp. xxxviii–xxxix, where it is conceded that what is treated here as a causally irrelevant condition *sine qua non* is in fact causally relevant but only in the indirect sense that it may be used to identify the concrete event which possesses a causally relevant feature.

of the particular actions, events, or things to which they refer. There is no uniquely correct principle of classification of anything we can discriminate: any particular may be an instance of an indefinite number of general characteristics.

This fact breeds another causally irrelevant use of the expression 'condition *sine qua non*' and of statements of the form 'If *X* had not happened *Y* would not have happened.' If a man shoots at another and kills him his action, described as 'shooting', is a causally relevant factor in the victim's death and, if no other independent sufficient cause of death was present, it was also a condition *sine qua non* of it. We could if necessary establish the causal relevance of the shooting by showing how, stage by stage, the case exemplified familiar generalizations concerning connections between types of event: shooting in such circumstances constitutes a set of conditions with a traceable general connection with death. We may, however, describe the act of shooting in fuller detail: we may add that he shot with his right hand, wearing a black glove, in fine weather, on a Sunday. It is plain that these further features are, unlike the shooting, not causally relevant factors in the man's death though in some way connected with it. They have not even the causal relevance of factors which would be ranked not as 'the cause' but only as 'mere conditions' like the fact that the cartridge was charged with explosive: for that too has a traceable general connection with the death as well as being a condition *sine qua non* on this occasion. It is required along with the shooting to make up a set of conditions the connection of which with the death exemplifies general connections between events. All that is secured by citing the further features, 'wearing a black glove', 'in fine weather', 'on a Sunday', etc., possessed by this particular act of shooting, is a description so detailed that it is unlikely to apply to any other case of shooting. Sometimes to supply such detail would have a point. There may, for example, be a question, if the man has fired a number of shots, as to which one has killed the victim, and the best way to *identify* it uniquely may be to cite features which as a group are likely to apply to it alone. These identifying features are only incidentally connected with the man's death yet, because his death was caused by this one unique case of shooting identified by these other features, it is possible to say 'If he had not fired while wearing a black glove or in fine weather or on a Sunday the other would not have been killed.' Of course, to assert this is to say no more than that this particular act of shooting, uniquely identified in this way, caused the death. Understood in any other way the statement would be false. But since such assertions have the form of statements of conditions *sine qua non* it is tempting to argue, as some legal writers have, that 'factually' or 'objectively' there is no difference in point of causal connection with the death between such incidental features and the man's act described as 'shooting': if we do discriminate between them it must be because legal principles or policies guide the selection of the cause from an infinite number of equally necessary conditions *sine qua non.*

The courts, however, have often sensed a difference between those characteristics of a single act which are causally related to some outcome, and those which are not, but simply serve to specify further, or individuate this act; though they have not made very clear what this difference is. The recognition of it is important in legal systems which, like our own, contain both rules making certain kinds of action defined in specific ways illegal and also general principles providing that compensation is to be paid for harm caused by illegal action: it is also important when the criminal law distinguishes, as the English law of manslaughter does, between harm caused by an illegal act and the same harm caused by an act which is not illegal. In such cases it often happens that a defendant has caused certain harm by some act of his but those aspects of the act which are wrongful have no causal connection with it: one and the same act may have wrongful but causally irrelevant features and also features which are causally relevant but not wrongful.

In such cases a variety of different issues are intertwined with the causal question which consideration of the following type of problem, familiar to lawyers, may help to elucidate: A statute requires drivers of motor vehicles to obtain a driving licence and makes driving without a licence a punishable offence. *D*, an unlicensed driver, without negligence, knocks down and injures *P*. Is this wrongful act on *D*'s part in breach of the statute the cause of *P*'s injuries? In all such cases two preliminary issues must be faced, since a decision on one of them may make it unnecessary to decide any causal question, and a decision on the other may make the difference between causal connection and incidental connection of no importance in the particular case. First: Is *any* harm of this *sort*, however caused, within the scope of this statute and so of the general principle that compensation is payable for harm caused by illegal acts, or was the statute designed only for revenue purposes?

If this point is disposed of and it is conceded that protection from physical injury is within the scope of the statute forbidding driving without a licence, the second preliminary question arises. This concerns the meaning of the statement that the plaintiff's injuries were the consequence of *the defendant's illegal act or breach of the statute* which is the basis of the claim. Do these words here italicized mean that a causal connection must be shown between the plaintiff's injuries and all those features of the defendant's act which made it

wrongful? Or is it enough to show in such a case that the defendant
did by his action (driving without a licence) infringe the statute, and
in the course of so doing did an act which in fact caused the plaintiff's
injury, even though the only respect in which it was wrongful (that
it was done without a licence) was causally irrelevant?

If this second point is disposed of by a decision that a causal
connection must be shown between the plaintiff's injuries and all
those aspects of the defendant's conduct which made it wrongful,
most lawyers and laymen would perhaps express the view that in
this case the absence of the licence was causally irrelevant and would
defend it by saying that, had the defendant had a licence,[6] but all
other conditions remained the same, the plaintiff would still have
suffered the same injuries. They might even put the point by saying
that the fact that the defendant drove without a licence simply specified further the particular circumstances of the particular case, and
it 'just happened' that, while so driving, he knocked down the
plaintiff. So to argue would be to use implicitly as a criterion of
causal connection a common-sense approximation to Mill's model:
a cause must be a necessary element in some set of conditions connected generally with an outcome of this sort, and not merely connected with this particular outcome as a feature happening to
characterize the particular action which was the cause.

The courts have not used the conception of the scope or purpose
of legal rules to avoid this causal question as frequently as might be
expected, and they have often construed legal rules in a manner
which forces them to distinguish the case where all the features of
the wrongful act are causally relevant from the case where they are
not. 'The causal relation must be shown to exist between that aspect
of a defendant's conduct which is wrongful and the injury.'[7] Modern
writers may regret this attitude,[8] but it is firmly marked. Until it is
abandoned it remains true that preliminary attention must be given,
when causal questions arise, to the precise description of the wrongful act whose consequences are in question. In the case of statutory
liability the correct description or definition of the wrongful act will
usually not be difficult, but in cases of negligence it may be. This
preliminary point arose in *Thurogood* v. *Van den Bergh & Jurgens
Ltd.*[9] In that case a proper description of the defendant's wrongful

---

[6] i.e. had he undergone the procedure needed to acquire a licence, for instance by
passing a driving examination, not had he possessed an official document in his
wallet. Below, pp. 411-12.

[7] Fleming James and Perry, op. cit., 60 *Yale LJ* 761, 789.

[8] Leon Green, 'The Causal Relation Issue in Negligence Law', (1961) 60 *Mich. LR*
543, 547 says that 'the attempt to link the victim's injury to the absence of a driver's
licence would be impossible as well as uncalled for', since 'negligence' cannot cause
harm, only 'conduct', viz. movement.

[9] [1951] 2 KB 537.

act was found to be 'setting in motion on the floor of the factory a fan without a guard', Lord Asquith saying that 'the negligence lies in this triple and indivisible complex'.[10] It would obviously be necessary to settle the appropriate description of the wrongful act before embarking on such causal inquiries as whether a workman who caught a chill in consequence of the draught from the fan could truly say that his chill was caused by the defendant's wrongful act.[11]

The branch of the law which most often precipitates questions of this kind is that where a statute requires a person to obtain some licence or certificate of fitness before engaging on a given activity. In the *Empire Jamaica*,[12] owners of a vessel, in breach of a Hong Kong ordinance, sent a ship to sea without duly certificated officers. The master, though uncertificated, was a perfectly competent man of long experience, but the ship was in fact involved in a collision when he was the officer of the watch and guilty of negligent navigation. The question then arose whether there was any causal connection between the owners' breach of the Hong Kong ordinance and the collision. The judgment of Willmer J. shows how important it may be to distinguish the merely incidental, causally irrelevant sense of *sine qua non*.

This involves the question whether they (the owners) have satisfied me that this breach on their part of the Hong Kong ordinance had no causal connection with the collision. That it was a cause in the sense of it being a *causa sine qua non* there can be no doubt because we know that Sinon, the uncertificated officer, was in fact the officer of the watch at the time that the collision happened, and the officer in respect of whose negligent navigation the plaintiffs have already admitted their liability. But that to my mind does not conclude the matter. The plaintiffs have given evidence . . . that Sinon, although uncertificated, was a perfectly competent man. . . . The only matter relied upon by the defendants is the fact that Sinon had not a certificate. . . . In this case the evidence as to the competence of Sinon is all one way. Having regard to that evidence it appears to me to be quite impossible to say that there was any causal connection between the fact of his not having a certificate and the fact of his negligent navigation which led to this collision.[13]

On the judge's findings in this case that the non-possession of a certificate was in no way evidence of incompetence, the owners'

[10] Ibid., p. 551.
[11] See the discussion of the problem by Goodhart, 'The Imaginary Necktie and the Rule *in re Polemis*', (1958) 62 *LQR* 514. Note, however, the important distinction between citing as the cause an *event* which may be identified by some causally irrelevant feature and citing as the cause the fact that a certain causally relevant feature was present: Mackie, *Cement*, pp. 129-30, 248 ff., 266; Preface above, pp. xxxvii-xxxviii.
[12] [1955] P. 52.
[13] Ibid., [1955] P. 57, 58; Mackie, *Cement* (1980 edn.), 129-30.

breach of the Hong Kong ordinance in taking on an uncertificated master was plainly a *sine qua non* of the negligent navigation only in the incidental sense discussed: it was merely a further detail of the case without any form of general connection with the other elements.

In many jurisdictions decisions on statutes requiring driving licences are to the effect that the failure to obtain a licence may be causally irrelevant to an accident, and the fact that the failure is a *sine qua non* in an incidental sense is not enough for liability. Thus in *Mandell* v. *Dodge, Freedman Poultry Co.*[14] the plaintiff, driving without a licence in breach of statute, was injured in collision with the defendant's truck. In this case the statute provided that absence of a licence was '*prima facie* evidence of unfitness to operate a motor vehicle'. On appeal the majority of the court held that the plaintiff's failure to obtain a licence was irrelevant, unless unfitness to drive was in fact in part a cause of the accident. In other American jurisdictions a correct distinction is drawn between the case where failure to comply with a statute requiring licence or registration is 'an effective contributing cause' or, on the other hand, 'merely an attendant circumstance'.[15]

It is, however, quite clear that many jurisdictions attach to failure to obtain a licence or certificate required by statute a legal effect which disregards these principles of causal connection. Methods of interpretation are used which in effect avoid the causal question. Thus, in some jurisdictions failure to obtain a driving licence or register a car entails the legal consequence that the driver is treated as a trespasser on the high-road and so cannot recover for injuries unless intentionally or recklessly caused.[16] Other jurisdictions may make civil liability for injuries in a motor accident depend simply on the driver's lack of a licence. They in effect lay down that an unlicensed driver is liable for harm caused by the fact that he was driving even if it is not caused by the fact that he was driving without a licence.[17] This is a perfectly intelligible rule of law, but it is confusing in the extreme for such results to be reached by the assertion that the lack of an operator's licence is 'causal in the strictest

[14] (1946) 94 NH 1, 45 A. 2d 577, 163 ALR 1370.

[15] *Dean* v. *Leonard* (1949) 323 Mass. 606, 83 NE 2d 443. Becht and Miller, *The Test of Factual Causation*, p. 196 rightly draw attention to the fact that often there is no independent evidence whether the unlicensed driver, etc., was in fact driving carelessly. It then becomes crucial from a legal point of view to decide whether the absence of a licence can be treated *per se* as evidence of want of skill and so of causal connection with the harm. A decision on this point cannot be determined by ordinary causal criteria. It must depend on legal policy, legislative or judicial.

[16] *Koonovsky* v. *Quellette* (1917) 226 Mass. 474, 116 NE 243; *Bridges* v. *Hart* (1939) 302 Mass. 239, 18 NE 2d 1020.

[17] See Preface above, pp. lviii–lix.

sense'.[18] Some courts, in considering statutory enactments, may go further and reach the conclusion that it is not necessary to show a causal connection between the defendant's act and the plaintiff's injuries, but make the defendant, if he is in breach of the law, an insurer of injuries which fall within a certain category. Thus where a statute provided that anyone injured by an intoxicated person might sue the person who had caused the intoxication by selling or giving the liquor, an Illinois court held that a plaintiff might recover when attacked by an intoxicated person, although the attack was not due to the intoxication.[19]

Speed

The fact that one event may be a condition *sine qua non* of another and yet not causally connected with it has been recognized by the courts, though without a clear formulation of the distinction, in certain types of case where it is argued that a motorist's wrongful action in exceeding the speed limit was the cause of the plaintiff's injuries suffered in an accident on the road. There are of course many types of case where driving at an excessive speed may quite properly be said to be the cause or a cause of an accident: it may, for example, lead through easily traceable stages to the driver losing control and this in its turn to the collision; or the speed may account for the great violence of the impact and this in turn for the plaintiff's injuries or the damage to his vehicle. In such cases not only is it true that if the driver had not speeded the accident would not have happened, but the sequence of events, traceable stage by stage, exemplifies general connections between kinds of events, statable in broad generalizations, holding good for other instances at other times and places, even though we cannot exhaustively specify all the limits within which they do so. In such cases the defendant's action, as an instance of speeding while driving a car, is both wrongful and causally connected with the outcome as a necessary element in a set of conditions generally connected through intermediate stages with it.

The problematic cases are those where the driver, having speeded earlier, either was not speeding at the time of the accident or his speeding at the time of the accident was admittedly irrelevant. In

[18] *Johnson* v. *Boston & Maine R. Co.* (1928) 83 NH 350, 364, 143 A. 516, 523, 61 ALR 178.
[19] *Martin* v. *Blackburn* (1942) 312 Ill. App. 549, 38 NE 2d 939. The cases also reveal many other techniques for avoiding consideration of the causal question. Thus in some jurisdictions the principle of *versari in re illicita* is applied. See *Danluk* v. *Birkner* (1946) Or. 427; (1946) 3 DLR 172, where a plaintiff, keeping a disorderly house, was injured in trying to escape from it during a police raid, owing to the disrepair of premises for which the defendant was responsible. It was held by an application of this principle that he was not entitled to sue the defendant in these circumstances.

such cases it has been argued that the earlier speeding was a cause of the accident, since had he not speeded he would not have arrived at the scene of the accident at the time when he did, and so there would have been no accident. Many writers have urged that such claims should be rejected on the simple and reasonable ground that the purpose of rules against speeding is to protect persons from injuries arising in certain familiar ways which would normally be regarded as the risks attendant on speeding. This is why speeding is made illegal by statute or classed as negligent. This sensible way of dealing with the matter makes consideration of the causal question unnecessary. The writers who urge this approach usually also insist that in such cases speeding was a cause of the accident.

The American courts have not, however, treated the problem in the way urged by such writers, but have said in such cases that though the accident would not have happened without the earlier speeding this was not causally connected with the accident. They have sometimes added, as a reason for this, that had the defendant gone faster still there would have been no accident.[20] This, as it stands, is not a very clear or cogent argument, since the same observation could be equally well made in cases where speeding led to the driver's loss of control and was plainly connected causally with the accident. It does, however, suggest that the reason for the American courts' decisions in such cases is their view that a factor, which is merely sufficient to secure the presence of a person or thing at a given place at a time different from what it would otherwise have been, is not to be treated as causally connected with the ensuing accident, unless the risk of the accident occurring at that different time was greater.[21]

III. WHEN CAUSALLY RELEVANT FACTORS ARE NOT CONDITIONS *SINE QUA NON*

1. *Additional causes*

Nearly all modern writers who use the notion of a condition *sine qua non* to elucidate the legal conception of a cause and hold it to be the sole 'factual' component in causal relations qualify this doctrine at certain points. They do so in a way which tacitly acknowledges the central importance of the notion of a set of conditions which is

---

20 *Draxton* v. *Katzmarek* (1938) 280 NW 288 (Minn.).

21 As Windeyer J. said in *Faulkner* v. *Keffalinos* (1971) 45 ALJR 80, 86: 'But for the first accident plaintiff might still have been employed by the appellants and therefore not have been where he was when the second accident happened: but lawyers must eschew this kind of but for or *sine qua non* reasoning about cause and consequence.' In cases of delay in breach of contract, however, a *sine qua non* relationship is sometimes sufficient for liability; below, pp. 321-4.

sufficient to produce a given event in the sense that its connection with that event, traceable through successive stages, exemplifies certain generalizations, broad though these may be. These qualifications are brought in to deal with certain anomalous situations, where there are good reasons both for saying that some given event was caused by some action and also that it would still have happened without this action: here the question 'Would *Y* have happened if *X* had not?' is a misleading test of causal connection. These anomalies breed problems for the law which we examine in detail in a later chapter together with a variety of solutions. Here we shall draw attention to their general structure and state the issues they raise in a terminology which we think is clearer than that current in legal writings.

We have already touched on one variety of these causal anomalies. This is the case where two causes, each of them sufficient to bring about the same harm, are present on the same occasion. A defendant starts a fire which, before it destroys property, joins a fire started by another. Each would have been sufficient to have burnt the property.[22] Two men may simultaneously fire and lodge a bullet in their victim's brain, or may simultaneously approach an escaping gas with a lighted candle.[23] In these cases the normal assumption that on any given occasion only one set of sufficient conditions of a given contingency is present has broken down. With it goes the possibility of treating either of the two 'causes' as a necessary condition in the third of the three senses analysed above: we cannot say that either was necessary on this occasion and so a condition *sine qua non*, because the other cause would have sufficed to produce it.

This difficulty is met by writers in different ways. Professor Glanville Williams concedes that here the definition of 'cause in fact' in terms of *sine qua non* must be supplemented with a provision that a condition may rank as a cause in fact if it either is a *sine qua non*, or would have been a *sine qua non* had no other conditions sufficient to produce the effect been present. Prosser, to deal with this and certain other difficulties, qualifies the statement that a 'cause in fact' is to be identified with a *sine qua non*. For him cause in fact is a 'substantial factor' and *'ordinarily* [a defendant's act or omission] will be a substantial factor if the result would not have occurred without it'.[24] He offers no definition of the expression 'substantial factor': indeed he says it is a phrase 'sufficiently intelligible to the layman to furnish an adequate guide in instructions to the jury and it is neither

[22] *Anderson* v. *Minneapolis St. P. & S. St. M.R. Co.* (1920) 179 NW 45 (Minn.). These and other cases are discussed in greater detail at pp. 236 ff. below.
[23] See the discussion of this hypothetical case by Glanville Williams, (1954) 17 *MLR* 66.
[24] Prosser, op. cit., p. 321.

possible nor desirable to reduce it to lower terms'.[25] But he makes quite plain that the defendant's act or omission would be a 'substantial factor' if it was one of two causes concurring to bring about an event and either of them operating alone would have been sufficient to cause the identical result. This is of course to bring into the analysis of 'cause in fact' the notion of a set of sufficient conditions. The difficulty in such cases can be simply stated. Two sufficient causes of an event of a given kind are present and, however finegrained or precise we make our description of the event, we can find nothing which shows that it was the outcome of the causal process initiated by the one rather than the other. It is perfectly intelligible that in these circumstances a legal system should treat each as the cause rather than neither, as the *sine qua non* test would require. Little, however, seems to be gained by describing, even to a jury, such cases in terms of the admittedly indefinable idea of a 'substantial factor'.

There are, however, variants of such anomalies, where a more precise description of the event whose cause is sought will discriminate between different causal processes. *A* gives *B* a fatal dose of poison but before it takes effect *C* shoots and kills him: *A* starts a fire which is about to burn down *B*'s house when a flood, bursting through a dam broken by *C*, extinguishes the fire and sweeps away the house. In these cases two causes each sufficient according to our general knowledge to produce the 'harm', if this is described in the usual broad categories ('death', 'destruction of the house'), are present in succession, and the second counteracts the first which otherwise would have produced the 'same harm'. The processes initiated by the second are connected with the outcome in a way which exemplifies general causal connections known to us; yet because of the presence of the first we cannot say the 'harm' would not have happened without it. Legal systems tend to dispose of such cases on the basis that causal connection is made out when the supposed cause both determines the mode of death or destruction and shortens life or accelerates the damage.[26] From this point of view *C* is correctly said to have caused *B*'s death and the destruction of *B*'s house. That *C*'s act was also a *sine qua non* of these harms is true only if the causal process by which the harm came about is treated as part of its description ('death by shooting', 'destruction by flooding'). But we reach this result only by first deploying the more fundamental notion of sufficient conditions and so identifying the causal process which culminated in the harm.

A second variant of these problems arises from what may be

25 Prosser, op. cit., p. 324.
26 Below, pp. 237 f.

termed alternative causes. *A* kills *B*, yet it may be clear that had he not done so *C* would have killed him, perhaps at the same time and in the same way; or *A* wrongly puts *B*'s goods where they are destroyed by fire but, had he not done so, another fire would have destroyed them. In these cases if the *sine qua non* question: 'Would *Y* have happened if *X* had not?' is broadly phrased in terms of 'death' or 'destruction', *A* would escape this test for causal connection, and at least in the criminal case this would be an absurd result. Again we may save the test by refining the description of the event, but we only have a reason for substituting such a finer description because the alternative cause would be sufficient to produce the effect more broadly described. Different legal systems, from the Roman to our own, have been vexed by these anomalies which in a sense represent the breakdown of our ordinary causal concepts: puzzles more extreme than those which the law has yet had to face may be constructed as salutary reminders of how much is taken for granted in the ordinary case.[27]

2. *Reasons and opportunities*

The various anomalies of additional causation may arise when one of the two actual or putative causes which generate the difficulty is related to the consequence by one of the types of interpersonal transaction examined in Chapter III.

It may be that when a person is made to do something harmful by another's threats or false statements, another independent cause sufficient to produce the 'same' harm was either present at the same time or connected with it as an alternative cause. *A* may force *B* by threats to set fire to a house at the same time as *C* starts a fire, or just before a flood descends on it. These cases raise no different issues from those already discussed. What is problematic is the place of the notion of condition *sine qua non* within the sphere of 'interpersonal transactions' and 'reasons for action' itself. Does the statement that *X* made *Y* do something by threats or induced him to do it by bribes or false statements imply that *Y* would not have done what he did if *X* had not threatened or bribed or misled him?

If we are to accept the statement that *Y* did something *because* of *X*'s threats, etc., we require to be satisfied that *Y* had not already decided or intended to do the action before considering *X*'s words, and that these were regarded by him at least as part of a sufficient reason for deciding to act in this way.[28] We may be satisfied of this either by indirect evidence or, if we think *Y* honest, by his statements

---

[27] See below, pp. 248-52.
[28] Unless *X*'s threat was taken by *Y* as a reason for persevering in a decision, already formed, to do the action rather than changing his mind: see below, p. 193.

reconstructing the past deliberative situation and the way he reached his decision. In the usual case of this kind the threats, false statements, or bribes may be *Y*'s only reason for doing what he did. Yet there seems nothing intrinsically absurd in the statement that a person who decided to do something for two independent reasons, both present to his mind, would also have done the same thing for either of these reasons alone. A man may kill another both because he has been ordered to by his superior officer and because he wishes to revenge himself for a private wrong: or he may be ordered to hand over his purse by two persons threatening to shoot. In such cases of compresent reasons it is possible to believe that one alone would have sufficed. No doubt both the assessment of our reasons for past action, and the hypothetical statement that we would have acted for one alone, are not easy to confirm or falsify with other evidence;[29] yet in some cases a person's conduct on other occasions and his character may make this sufficiently clear. Parallels to the cases of alternative causes are easy to construct in this sphere. One man may kill another because he was ordered to do so and be sure that had he not been told to do so he would have killed him on his own initiative.

Such possibilities make the *sine qua non* test misleading within the sphere of interpersonal transactions as a test whether or not a person was in fact induced or made to act in a certain way by another. It is of course open to the law to refuse to attach legal significance to interpersonal transactions such as threats or bribes or false statements unless these were 'the sole reasons' for action: if so, an admission that the same action would have been done for some other reason (whether actually present to the mind at the time of action or not) may be fatal to claims based on the existence of such connections. Here the law is not finally settled;[30] but it is settled that a misstatement, even if only one of a number of individually insufficient reasons, may, with the rest, be an inducement in law.[31]

The relevance of the notion of condition *sine qua non* is very much the same in cases where some loss is due to one person having provided another with an opportunity to do harm. *A* carelessly leaves the door of *B*'s house unlocked: a thief enters and steals the spoons. Where there is legal liability for the consequences or (as the law often terms it) the 'natural' consequences of such neglect, such a case would fall within their scope: the thief did in fact exploit an opportunity commonly exploited in this way and the failure to lock the door was the omission of a common precaution against just

[29] For the legal problems see below, pp. 411–18.
[30] Below, p. 193.
[31] Below, p. 193 n. 44.

such harm. It seems irrelevant, in assessing the consequences of the neglect, that it may be clear that the thief would have broken in anyhow, or that another opportunity noticed but not exploited by the thief was provided by someone else's neglect in leaving a ladder under an open window. If these facts are relevant at all, it is conceivable that they might (like the fact that the house with all its contents was destroyed by fire just after the theft) be considered in assessing in monetary terms the value to *B* of the lost spoons, but not in determining whether the loss of the spoons was 'due to' or 'the consequence of' the neglect.

3. *Omissions generally*

The careless provision of opportunities for others to do harm is one kind of omission to take precautions against harm. In other cases the distinction between the usually irrelevant question whether there was another or an alternative cause or opportunity to do the same harm, and the relevant question whether the neglected precaution was causally related to the harm, may be less obvious. It is easy to overlook this ambiguity lurking behind an affirmative answer to the *sine qua non* form of question 'Would this harm have happened without this neglect?'

Thus where the omitted precaution consists, as it does in vast areas of factory law, in a failure to supply safeguards or equipment to be used by workers, it is always relevant to show that, in a given case where these safeguards were not provided, they would not have been used if provided or, if used, would not have been sufficient to avert the harm, as they are in the standard case. Proof in *this* case that a workman would not have used the equipment or that it would have been ineffective as a guard against *this* fire would show that the omission was not causally connected with the harm.[32] By contrast, proof that the workman would have suffered the same injury on the same day through a fire in his home on returning there would show only an alternative cause; yet here as in the other case it could be said that the neglect was not a condition *sine qua non* of the 'harm', unless we refine our description of the harm in the light of the conclusion (reached independently of the *sine qua non* test) that the neglect was causally connected with the burns received in this particular way. Similar considerations apply to omissions of precautions of a simpler sort. A man's failure to take an umbrella may in many different contexts be rightly said to be the cause of his getting wet; this is still so even if it is clear that, had he not turned back, because he was drenched by the rain, he would have been caught and soaked by the tide: it would not be so if the rainstorm was so great that an umbrella would have been useless.

Finally, we may note that the problems of additional causation also arise in regard to omissions when each of two or more conditions needs to be fulfilled in order that a beneficial consequence may follow. In such very common cases the omission of any one condition is fatal to the beneficial outcome. Thus, suppose that two switches need to be turned off in order to avert a fire, and that X has a duty to turn off one, Y the other. If neither does so and a fire which would have been averted had they both performed their duty breaks out, both X and Y can argue that his omission was not a *sine qua non* of the destruction done by the fire. Suppose, again, that a house can be built and profitably sold only if X delivers bricks and Y mortar. If both X and Y default in delivery so that the projected house cannot be built and sold each can argue, again, that his default is not a *sine qua non* of the loss of profit on the sale of the house, since the default of the other was sufficient to preclude it. Despite this, lawyers and ordinary people would agree in saying, in these cases of concurrent failure to intervene in a physical process or to provide opportunities for gain, that the omission of each is causally relevant to the ensuing harm and that each could in a proper case be held responsible for it.[33] Nor are these rare or isolated cases. It is a pervasive feature of human existence that goods such as life, health, the security of property, and the manufacture of products depend for their continuance or achievement on the simultaneous fulfilment of many different conditions, each necessary to the good which it is sought to preserve or achieve. Given this feature of human life and activity, the fact that the *sine qua non* test fails to account for our causal judgments in such cases of concurrent omission is by no means a minor deficiency.

IV. GENERAL IMPORTANCE OF CONDITION *SINE QUA NON*

A general moral may be drawn from the examination in this chapter of cases where a condition *sine qua non* is not a causally relevant factor and the converse cases where a causally relevant factor is not a condition *sine qua non*. Plainly, to be a condition *sine qua non* of some event on some given occasion and to be causally connected with it are not the same thing. The general utility in legal cases of the question 'Would this harm have happened without this

[33] The view implied here that both omissions, being members of a set of jointly sufficient conditions of the harm, can be treated as a cause of the harm, is rejected by Mackie, *Cement*, pp. 43–7, 120–1, above, pp. 11–14.

event, act, or omission?' as a test of causal connection does not
spring from the fact that a condition *sine qua non* is the fundamental
element in the notion of causation or its sole factual component; for
this is not the case. We must distinguish between the mistaken claim
that all that is *meant* by 'cause' (apart from the contribution of legal
rules or policy) is condition *sine qua non*, and the general principle
that no event happens without a cause. The utility of the *sine qua
non* test depends on a combination of one form of this principle, viz.
no harm occurs unless some one of the varieties of causal connection
we have distinguished exists to be traced between it and some earlier
action, omission, or event, with the assumption (normally but not
invariably fulfilled) that the various complications of additional
causation are not present. Hence, if we allow for these complications,
and are careful to distinguish the merely analytic or incidental forms
of condition *sine qua non* then we may treat a factor that attracts a
negative answer to the test question 'Would Y have happened if X
had not?' as likely to be causally relevant in some one of the ways
we have distinguished. It may be a necessary element in some set of
conditions generally connected with the harm: or it may have operated
as someone's reason for doing something harmful: or it may have
constituted an opportunity for doing the harm or a denial of a
safeguard against harm or of an opportunity for gain. Often the law
will not need to distinguish between the various types of causal
connection which thus hide behind the apparently simple idea of
condition *sine qua non*: but a full understanding of the difficulties
which so often beset the law in dealing with causal questions often
depends, as we show in Part II of this book, on distinguishing
between them.

PART II

THE COMMON LAW[1]

INTRODUCTION

In the next nine chapters the reader will find a discussion of causation in the law of tort[2] and contract[3] and in criminal law.[4] Its main themes run counter to some of the modern criticism of which an account was given in Chapter IV. It is, we think, quite true that no code of causal principles[5] is to be found which will determine the answers to all problems of proximate cause and relieve the courts of the burden of discretion or creative choice; but an impartial consideration of the way in which courts have decided these cases does not confirm the modern view that in using the language of causation they have merely given effect to their conceptions of justice, expediency, or chosen policy. Over a great area of the law they have, in using causal language, sought to apply a group of causal notions embedded in common sense; and these notions have very much the structure discussed in Part I. So on our view the modern way with problems of proximate cause is too short a way: there is more to be said about the actual practice of courts than the blend of *sine qua non* and policy to which such problems are now customarily reduced.

Accordingly parts of the following chapters are designed to establish that courts have often applied, in their determinations of causal questions, a central concept in which great emphasis is laid on

[1] Reference has, however, been made to South African, French, German, and Scottish decisions in certain places.
[2] Chaps. VI–X.
[3] Chap. XI.
[4] Chaps. XII–XIV.
[5] The best-known attempt to lay down rigid rules for determining causal connection is Beale, 'The Proximate Consequences of an Act', (1920) 33 *Harv. LR* 633: above, pp. 96–7. Beale's rules are expressed metaphorically in the language of mechanics. A more flexible set of rules was proposed by Carpenter, 'Workable Rules for Determining Proximate Cause', (1932) 20 *Calif. LR* 229–59, 396–419, 471–539 (the rules are summarized on p. 472). According to Levitt, (1922) 21 *Mich. LR* 34, 36, 'the rules connected with proximate cause are like the rules of mathematics or any exact science which depends upon the observation of physical phenomena and the determination of causal connection between such phenomena'.

voluntary action or abnormal and coincidental events as negativing causal connection. We also show that the courts have often meant by causal connection certain varieties of interpersonal transactions such as inducement and, to an increasing extent, the provision of opportunities commonly exploited for harm.

The extent to which courts have consciously avowed these principles has certainly varied. Sometimes they have explicitly addressed their minds to causal problems and in doing so have appealed to the notions of 'voluntary' and 'abnormal' or similar notions to solve them. Sometimes they have addressed their minds to causal problems but have offered solutions couched in obscure, metaphorical language which, on examination, is found to reflect the causal distinctions of common sense. Sometimes, again, the courts have used non-causal language, for instance the terminology of foreseeability, but in such a way that the decision does not really follow from the criterion referred to but would follow if common-sense causal distinctions were applied. Indeed, what is true of nature is true of causation: *expelles furca, tamen usque recurret.*[6]

Naturally, the cases on which this exposition is based are only a selection from the common law decisions, which could not be read in a single lifetime. There are many decisions, in which causal language is employed by the court, which do not fit the common-sense causal scheme. But the fact that our exposition is selective does not make it arbitrary, for it covers many cases and represents a doctrine traditionally accepted by many courts.

Modern criticism is, however, only in part to be viewed as a statement of what courts actually do or have done in using causal language.

It is more important perhaps as a set of claims that we should replace obscure concepts for determining the extent of liability by rational considerations of expediency, justice, or policy. These range from large-scale general principles such as foresight and risk to the atomistic or case-by-case intuitions favoured by Leon Green.

We have endeavoured in relation to both tort[7] and crime[8] to assess the character and merits of some of the more systematic substitutes for old ideas. This has led us into a fairly large scale examination of the concept of foresight and of the basis of criminal responsibility.

Throughout we would ask the reader to bear in mind and avoid a potent source of confusion which has much entangled the issue. In Anglo-American law causal connection is very generally required as a ground of liability and is sometimes, at least in conjunction with

6 Horace, *Ep.* 1. 10. 24.
7 Chaps. IX-X.
8 Chap. XIV.

wrongful conduct and the appropriate mental element, sufficient. Thus, an act done with intent to kill which causes death generally amounts to murder. But there is nothing to compel a legal system to accept a causal connection with harm as either necessary or sufficient for liability. A system may, where it seems just to do so, introduce special principles of 'policy' or scope rules to enlarge or cut short liability independently of causal connection.[9] An example is the rule that damages for breach of contract must have been foreseeable at the time of contracting. But, however pervasive such rules may be in different branches of the law, there is reason to keep them distinct from genuinely causal limitations on the extent of liability. Causal limitations are to a great degree the same in tort, contract, and criminal law. They raise questions of fact which are conveniently submitted to the judgment of a jury or other trier of fact. Scope limitations, on the other hand, vary from branch to branch of the law and, indeed, within the various branches, according as the legal policy relating to the particular subject-matter requires. The issues they raise are questions of law relating to legislative intent or to the appropriate scope of common law rules devised by judges. It is, we believe, specially important to bear in mind the difference between these types of limitation when, because of the way in which the law is formulated (e.g. in terms of 'remoteness of damage' or 'proximate cause'), advocates or judges are forced to treat them under the same head. Forensic necessity may indeed make bedfellows of 'causal' and 'scope of rule' limitations. When it does so the judge or jury, if they are to limit responsibility at all, must purport to do so on the ground that the harm is 'too remote' or 'not proximate', whether the reason which really weighs with them is that the harm was not caused by the wrongful conduct of defendant or that the scope of the rule he violated does not extend to compensating for that type of harm. But the theorist, who is concerned to understand rather than to manipulate the principles of legal responsibility, must keep them separate.

Consistently with this point of view, we have departed at certain points from the traditional expositions of the subject. In Chapters VI to VIII we have expounded causal connection in the law of tort and have not treated the law of negligence as a separate topic, because it seems to us that, so far as issues of causation are concerned, the same principles apply here as elsewhere. Conversely, though we here deal with tort, contract, and crime separately, this is not because we believe that causation has a different meaning in these branches of the law but in order to assess the modern claims that, in a rational system, different policy substitutes for proximate cause should be adopted in these different branches.

[9] See Preface, pp. xlix–li.

VI

THE LAW OF TORT: CAUSING HARM

In this chapter we are concerned to inquire how far in the law of tort,[1] when causal connection between a wrongful act and harm is an element in responsibility, the decisions of the courts have been controlled by the principle that this connection is negatived if the factors required, in addition to the wrongful act, for the production of the harm include a voluntary human action or an abnormal occurrence.[1a] Our conclusion is that this principle has been applied over a very wide area of the law of tort, sufficient perhaps to enable us to speak of a traditional doctrine.

There is, however, an initial complexity, which has led us to divide the discussion of tort between the present chapter and the next, in which we contrast 'inducing' and 'providing opportunities for' or 'occasioning' harm with the notion of 'causing' harm. In the law of civil negligence and breach of statutory duty it has increasingly come to be recognized that it is sometimes enough for liability negligently to create opportunities or conditions under which others can voluntarily do harm or extraordinary events cause it. In these branches of the law what common sense would distinguish as 'causing harm' and 'enabling others (or other things) to do harm' are both adequate grounds for responsibility. They are usually not distinguished as different relationships between act and harm, but referred to under the same terminology of 'proximate cause', 'consequence', or 'natural and probable consequence'. We, however, have distinguished these bases of liability, since our concern is to assess the interplay between common-sense notions of causation, having a reality apart from the law, and legal policy. It may well be that the extension of liability from a basis of causing harm to include cases of providing opportunities for harm represents a response to felt needs. Though the existence of this form of liability does not mean that questions of proximate cause are just questions of legal policy in any of the forms portrayed in Chapter IV, it represents a partial approach to that form of policy theory, examined in detail in Chapter IX, which in the law of negligence would *impose* liability if the harm is 'within the hazard' created by the wrongful act or because of which the act

---

1 There are a few references to cases in contract or statutory compensation schemes where the principles involved do not differ materially from those of the law of tort.
1a Cf. Tunc, *Dalloz A.* 1956.2. 354, 357 (*éventualité, liberté humaine*).

is considered negligent; but it does not entail acceptance of that aspect of the 'risk theory' which would *limit* recovery to the harm 'within the risk'.

Form of question and terminology

The type of problem we consider, stated in the traditional causal language, involves three terms. In its simplest form the question is whether certain harm is the consequence of a certain wrongful act *given the presence of a third factor*,[2] e.g. whether the death in hospital of a person negligently run down by defendant is the consequence of defendant's negligent act, given some third factor such as that deceased was an alcoholic and *delirium tremens* flared up after the accident;[3] that he contracted scarlet fever from the attending physician;[4] that a surgeon was negligent in performing an operation on him[5] or, mistaking him for another patient, operated on the wrong side;[6] or, taking pity on his sufferings, deliberately killed him;[7] or that on the way to hospital he was struck by a falling tile. In all these instances we assume that the wrongful act and the third factor were each a necessary condition of the harm, but in each instance a causal problem is raised by the presence of the third factor: the law must decide whether or not the third factor negatives causal connection.

In a more general form the problem may be stated as follows: given a prior contingency, which is usually a tort, breach of contract, or breach of statute, but may also be a state of affairs or event designated by the law, such as 'the discharge of any missile . . . by the enemy';[8] given a subsequent contingency, which is usually some harm but also may be a benefit; and given a third factor, which may be the act or omission of a human being, the act of an animal, or a natural event or state of affairs, does the third factor negative causal connection between the prior and subsequent contingencies? Since 'prior contingency' and 'subsequent contingency' are rather clumsy expressions we often use 'wrongful act' and 'harm' instead but it should be remembered that these substitutes are really too narrow.

The question whether the third factor negatives causal connection between the wrongful act and the harm may be put in the form: 'Is

---

2 Sometimes called *nova causa* or *novus actus* (*interveniens* or *antecedens*). Salmond and Heuston, *Torts*, p. 516. The use of these expressions does not, however, clarify the problem. For similar formulations to ours see Tunc, note on Paris 18.4.1955, *Dalloz A.* 1956.2. 357; Vanquickenborne, *De Oorzakelijkheid in het Recht van de Burgerlijke Aansprakelijkheid* (Gent, 1971), p. 381; McGregor, *Damages* (1980), chap. 6, especially para. 101; Luntz, Hambly, and Hayes, 2. 1. 06; *Haber* v. *Walker* [1963] VR 339, 357-8.
3 *McCahill* v. *New York Transportation Co.* [1911] 201 NY 221, 94 NE 616, 48 LRA (NS) 13.   4 *Bush* v. *Commonwealth* (1880) 78 Ky. 268.
5 *Restatement of Torts*, s. 457, illustration 1; *Thompson* v. *Fox* (1937) 326 Pa. 209, 192 Atl. 107, 112 ALR 550.
6 *Purchase* v. *Seelye* (1918) 231 Mass. 434, 121 NE 413, 8 ALR 503.
7 Cf. *Restatement*, s. 457, illustrations 4, 5.
8 Personal Injuries (Emergency Provisions) Act, 1939, s. 8(1).

the harm a consequence of the wrongful act?' In legal discourse it is also often put in the form: 'Is the wrongful act the cause (or a cause[9]) of the harm?'[10] The latter formulation may be a source of confu- sion because it involves a use of 'cause' inconsistent with the common-sense explanatory use of that notion.[11] For instance, the Saskatchewan Motor Vehicle Insurance Act provides that 'every person is hereby insured . . . against loss resulting from bodily injuries sustained by him . . . provided that such bodily injuries are suffered as a result of driving, riding in or on, or operating a moving motor vehicle in Saskatchewan'.[12] Clearly it is not an explanation of a road accident to say that someone was driving a motor vehicle in Saskatchewan. Hence to ask 'Was driving the cause of the accident?' appears artificial;[13] it invites the retort that the driver's negligence or the state of the roads was the cause. To ask 'Was the accident the consequence (or result)[14] of driving?' is more natural. It is not the case, therefore, that when some harm is attributed to an act or event as its consequence this act or event will always be described as the cause of the harm.[15] For this reason we prefer the 'consequence' form: 'Was the harm the consequence[16] of the wrongful act?' to the 'cause' form: 'Was the wrongful act the cause of the harm?'

Factors negativing causal connection

We now consider how far the law recognizes voluntary human action and abnormal occurrences as factors negativing causal con- nection. We do so under separate heads because in many cases an abnormal contingency which is held to negative causal connection

9 'A cause' is usually the better formulation. *Gantt* v. *Sissell* (1954) 263 SW 2d 916 (Ark.); *Godwin* v. *Johnson Cotton Co.* (1953) 238 NC 627, 78 SE 2d 772; *Continental Southern Lines* v. *Klaas* (1953) 65 So. 2d 76.
10 e.g. *Minister of Pensions* v. *Chennell* [1947] KB 250, 252, *per* Denning J. 'The best way is to start with the injury and inquire what are the causes of it.' This formulation is perhaps more appropriate to an explanatory inquiry.
11 For the distinction between the use of 'cause' in explanatory and attributive contexts see pp. 32–44, above.
12 Saskatchewan Motor Vehicle Insurance Act, 1947, s. 16(1). Cf. Road Traffic Act, 1930, s. 22, by which an accident must in certain circumstances be reported if it occurs 'owing to the presence of a motor vehicle on a road'. *Quelch* v. *Phipps* [1955] 2 QB 107. Code civil art. 1384. Colin-Capitant-Julliot, *Droit civil français*, ii. 272.
13 But as explained in the Preface, pp. xxxvii–xxxviii, an event identified otherwise than by reference to its causally relevant features may be cited as the cause in contexts where a full explanation is not called for.
14 There may be important differences, which we do not here consider, between 'results' and 'consequences'. 'Effect' would be quite out of place. See pp. 359–60 below.
15 In *R.* v. *Storey* Blair J. said, 'I confess I cannot understand how death can be a consequence of negligence if the negligence was not the cause.' [1931] NZLR 417, 468. There may indeed be a strict correlation in the case of negligence, for a negligent act is abnormal and so usually a cause in an explanatory context.
16 Blair J. in *R.* v. *Storey*, above, mentions but does not explain a distinction between 'the consequence' and 'a consequence'.

is itself causally independent[17] of the wrongful act, i.e. it would have occurred irrespective of the occurrence of the wrongful act, whereas a voluntary act which negatives connection will always be found to be in some sense dependent on it, e.g. it will be motivated by the fact that the wrongful act has occurred or by the belief that it may occur. It will be done in response to or in anticipation of some untoward situation.

Voluntary conduct[18] therefore demands separate treatment, though it should be noticed that a human act which is not wholly voluntary may nevertheless be held to negative causal connection on the distinct score of its abnormality, and that therefore human acts often have to be considered in relation to both principles. Some lawyers have been led by the special importance of voluntary human acts to describe them, in defiance of the literal truth, as 'irresistible'. It has been said that one who deals in a dangerous substance is not responsible when 'the proximate cause of the accident' is the 'conscious act of another volition' for 'against such conscious act of volition no precaution can really avail'.[19] In the case from which the citation is taken the defendant's negligent installation of a defective gas boiler was admittedly a necessary condition of the harm,[20] so that Lord Dunedin's reason must be taken as a metaphorical reflection of the special status of voluntary acts. The truth may be that precautions against such acts are specially difficult, since a man who is bent on harm will usually find some way of doing it.

The same description has been applied to so-called 'acts of God'[21] but we treat them under the heading not of voluntary acts but of abnormal contingencies.[22]

I. VOLUNTARY HUMAN CONDUCT

The general principle of the traditional doctrine is that *the free, deliberate and informed act or omission of a human being, intended to exploit the situation created by defendant, negatives causal connection.*[23] Here are a few simple illustrations:

17 Cf. *Restatement of Torts*, s. 441, comment *c*. There are some exceptions to this. Below, pp. 181–5.

18 We use the word 'voluntary' in a very narrow sense, for which see pp. 41, 137–8, and we use the word 'conduct' to include both acts and omissions.

19 *Dominion Natural Gas Co.* v. *Collins* [1909] AC 640, 646–7, *per* Lord Dunedin. Cf. Mackie, op. cit., p. 108 (voluntary agent would readily find a substitute for the condition which he exploits). Though this may often be the case it is by no means invariably true; the only wallet which the thief finds to steal may be that of the pedestrian whom the driver has knocked unconscious.

20 For which they were held responsible since the intervening act was not such a 'conscious act of volition' as to negative causal connection.

21 'An irresistible and unsearchable Providence nullifying all human effort': *GWR* v. *Owners of S.S. Mostyn* [1928] AC 57, 105, *per* Lord Blanesburgh. *Greenock Corporation* v. *Caledonian Rly.* [1917] AC 556.

22 Below, pp. 163–4.

23 In the first edition we added that the act, to be voluntary, must be 'intended to

A defendant who negligently allowed a pit to remain in a road was not liable to the plaintiff, a sheriff, when an escaping prisoner threw the sheriff into the pit:[24] the decision is otherwise if the intervening actor pushed plaintiff in accidentally[25] or negligently.[26] Defendant negligently left open an unguarded lift shaft; he was not liable to plaintiff when a lad, impersonating the lift operator and knowing the lift was not there, invited plaintiff to step into it, which he did, suffering injuries.[27] When defendants, partners, wrongfully left a cellarway unguarded they were not jointly responsible for injury to plaintiff sustained when one of them deliberately pushed him into the way. Plaintiff's remedy was for assault against the partner who pushed him.[28] When defendant wrongfully instituted proceedings against plaintiff he was not responsible for the injury to plaintiff when a policeman, transporting him after his arrest, wrongfully shot him.[29] When defendant wrongfully had plaintiff's goods seized he was not responsible for the subsequent conversion of the goods by the legal custodian.[30] When defendant wrongfully renewed a drug prescription he was not liable for the death of decedent who deliberately committed suicide by taking an overdose.[31] When plaintiff was injured by defendant's fault in Australia he was not entitled to charge defendant with the cost of returning to England to be with his family during convalescence. To do so was his own choice, not something medically necessary.[32]

Four preliminary points about this principle may be noted: (i) the narrow sense of 'voluntary' already discussed and here adopted;[33] (ii) that the principle extends to omissions; (iii) that voluntary conduct negatives causal connection not only with loss but with gain; (iv)

---

produce the consequence which is in fact produced'. This was a mistake. It is clear that the intervening act can be voluntary in the full sense though it is not intended to produce the harm that in fact ensues. For example, if defendant negligently causes a car crash and the person intervening is injured while trying to rob the unconscious victim, his intervention is voluntary. He was not acting in pursuance of any duty; on the other hand, he did not intend to injure himself. The intention of the intervening actor is, however, relevant in the sense that he must intend to exploit the situation created by the defendant, i.e. to treat it as providing the opportunity or occasion for a certain course of conduct. A prime example of this is the case where the intervening actor exploits the situation by bringing about some intended consequence.

24 *Alexander* v. *Town of New Castle* (1888) 17 NE 200 (Ind.).
25 Prosser, Wade, and Schwartz, *Cases*, p. 338.
26 *Village of Carterville* v. *Cook* (1889) 129 Ill. 152, 22 NE 14, 16 Am. St. Rep. 248.
27 *Cole* v. *German Savings & Loan Society* (1903) 124 F. 113; cf. *Scholes* v. *North London R. Co.* (1870) 21 LT 835.
28 *Miller* v. *Bahmmuller* (1908) 108 NYS 924.
29 *RGZ* 106 (1922), 14 (Germany).
30 Civ. 22.2.1944, *Dalloz A.* 1944.57 (France).
31 *Runyon* v. *Reid* (1973) 510 P. 2d 943, 58 ALR 3d 814.
32 *Carnsew* v. *Bruhn* [1966] SASR 397.
33 Above, p. 41.

that the principle is elastic and the voluntary nature of an act to some extent a matter of degree.

(i) 'Voluntary' is often used in a wider sense than we give to it,[34] but it is also used in the law as we use it here. Of acts of self-preservation De Grey CJ said that they were not the acts of 'free agents' but done 'under a compulsive necessity'.[35] Wright J. spoke of fright rendering an act 'involuntary'.[36] Of the repetition of a slander by a person not subject to defendant's control Tindal CJ said that it was the 'voluntary act of a free agent',[37] thus using the expression 'voluntary' to exclude such control. In ordinary speech we recognize that even a social obligation restricts our freedom, so that if I have accepted an invitation to dine with you I am 'not free' to dine with anyone else. So too in the law. 'The emergency caused by a collision may be such as to compel any normal person to take a particular course of action, in the sense of affording such strong motives for that particular action that every reasonable person would be induced by them so to act.'[38]

As we explained earlier[39] our use of 'voluntary' and 'not voluntary'[40] depends on a conception of a human agent as being most free when he is placed in circumstances which give him a fair opportunity to exercise normal mental and physical powers and he does exercise them without pressure from others.

In a very general sense, the various circumstances which render conduct less than fully voluntary correspond with the factors which diminish moral and legal responsibility, but it would be quite wrong to *identify* non-voluntary conduct with the absence of moral or legal responsibility. Every merely negligent act is non-voluntary in our sense, since by hypothesis the actor did not intend to exploit the situation, but an actor is often morally or legally responsible for negligence.[41]

(ii) *Omissions.* Human conduct can be described alternatively in terms of acts or omissions. 'A medical man who diagnoses a case of measles as a case of scarlet fever may be said to have omitted to make a correct diagnosis; he may equally well be said to have made

---

[34] e.g. *S.S. Singleton Abbey* v. *S.S. Paludina* [1927] AC 16, 26, 32: 'an act of volition, not automatic, reflex or without consciousness of what he was doing'.
[35] *Scott* v. *Shepherd* (1773) 2 W. Bl. 892, 900, 96 ER 525, 529.
[36] *Wilkinson* v. *Downton* [1897] 2 QB 57, 61.
[37] *Ward* v. *Weeks* (1830) 7 Bing. 211, 215, 131 ER 81, 83.
[38] *The San Onofre* [1922] P. 243, 254, *per* Atkin LJ.
[39] Above, p. 41.
[40] In English it is sometimes artificial to speak of defects of knowledge rendering conduct non-voluntary; but in the absence of recognized words to express what Aristotle had in mind 'voluntary' and 'non-voluntary' have been chosen as the closest in meaning. There is some support in legal usage for regarding acts done in ignorance or by mistake as less than fully voluntary. Below, pp. 149–51.
[41] See further below, pp. 152–3.

an incorrect diagnosis.'[42] Sometimes it is more appropriate to describe the conduct as an omission; if there is a legal duty to do an act, and the subject has not done it, the legally relevant description will be in terms of an omission to perform the act in question. But the description of conduct as an omission may not imply any bodily movements by the person whose conduct is in question: e.g. if the description is: 'The defendant failed to inspect the electrical wiring.' Consequently those courts and writers who are impressed by 'setting in motion' as a prime instance of causation, and who further conclude that we can only set things in motion by ourselves making movements, find it difficult to understand how an omission to act can negative causal connection.[43]

It is now thought, at least in England, that there is no special difficulty about omissions. This is particularly clear if the omission is the plaintiff's. For instance, in *Sachs* v. *Miklos*,[44] defendant, with whom plaintiff had left his furniture for storage during the war, wrote asking plaintiff to remove his goods but received no reply. Defendant then sold the furniture, the value of which continued to rise. The Court of Appeal decided that if plaintiff received the letter and omitted to take steps to collect his furniture, any loss due to the subsequent rise in value did not 'flow from' defendant's act of conversion.

When the omission is by a third party[45] the objectors have the support of section 452 of the *Restatement of Torts* which states that 'Failure of a third person to perform a duty owing to another to protect him from harm threatened by the actor's negligent conduct is not a superseding cause of the other's harm.' But the trend of decisions in England is against any such rigid rule.[46] In truth, no rational distinction can be drawn between the causal status of acts and omissions,[47] but there is room, in relation to both, for a distinction between conduct which is deliberate or, still more, intended to exploit the situation, and conduct which is culpably inadvertent.[48]

---

[42] *Harnett* v. *Bond* [1924] 2 KB 517, 541, *per* Bankes LJ.
[43] *Rothwell* v. *Caverswall Stone Co.* [1944] 2 All ER 350, 354, 364; (1945) 61 *LQR* 7. Above, p. 30 nn. 3, 4. On this difficulty see Honoré, *IECL*, xi. 7-25 to 7-31.
[44] [1948] 2 KB 23.
[45] Cf. omission by defendant: *Grant* v. *National Coal Board* [1956] AC 649, 659.
[46] *Pope* v. *St. Helen's Theatre* [1947] KB 30. For America see *Goar* v. *Village of Stephen* (1923) 157 Minn. 228, 196 NW 171; *Shupe* v. *Antelope County* (1953) 157 Neb. 374, 59 NW 2d 710; the majority of American decisions continue to apply s. 452 but, so far as can be judged, in no case was the subsequent omission intended to exploit the situation created by the negligent conduct. *Parks* v. *Starks* (1955) 342 Mich. 443, 70 NW 2d 805.
[47] *Harnett* v. *Bond* [1924] 2 KB 517; *Canadian Pacific Ry.* v. *Kelvin Shipping Co.* (1927) 138 LT 369, 374.
[48] This was possibly the substantial point that the authors of s. 452 wished to make. Lapse of time is important only as evidence that the peril has been discovered. *Grant* v. *National Coal Board* [1956] AC 649, 659, 667.

Although an omission may feature as a cause in an explanatory context and may negative causal connection in an attributive context, we shall notice in Chapter XIII that sometimes the verb 'to cause', and some other transitive verbs which incorporate the same notion, cannot appropriately be used when the relevant aspect of the conduct in question is an omission. In such contexts it is more correct to speak of 'permitting' or 'not preventing' something than of 'causing' it; but it is a mistake to introduce this distinction when the question is not how the defendant's conduct should be described but whether certain harm is the consequence of it. In *East Suffolk Catchment Board* v. *Kent*[49] defendants exercised statutory powers to repair a breach in a wall but did the work so carelessly that plaintiff's marshland remained flooded for 164 days instead of the 14 days in which it could have been cleared. The House of Lords by a majority rejected plaintiff's claim for the damage caused by the extra 150 days' flooding of his land. Lord Simon, one of the majority, said that the damage done by flooding was not 'due to the exercise of the appellant's statutory powers at all. It was due to the forces of nature which the appellant, albeit unskilfully, was endeavouring to counteract.'[50] The substance behind this view is merely that it would be inappropriate to say that defendants had *caused* the 150 days' flooding; they had permitted the flooding to continue, or not abated it. But this is no reason for denying in an attributive context that the damage was the consequence of defendant's carelessness, or even that defendant's failure to do the work properly was *the cause* of the flooding lasting so long; on this point Lord Atkin's dissenting judgment is more convincing[51] (he says the continued harm was 'caused by' their act). The real question in this case was not causal connection but whether defendant had a duty to abate the flooding of plaintiff's land or merely not to make it worse. The argument is not explicitly concerned with whether an omission can constitute 'causing' but Lord Simon's views plainly derive from the conviction that it could not. The same was assumed in *Dutton* v. *Bognor Regis U.D.C.*,[52] where defendants in the exercise of powers under a by-law, carelessly passed as being secure the foundations of the house later bought by plaintiff. The court held that defendants were liable for the subsidence of the house. One ground for the decision was that, in contrast with the *East Suffolk* case, the harm was probably the result of the surveyor's carelessness. But, as explained, so far as causal connection is concerned the only distinction is that the surveyor's incompetence caused the subsidence by failing to bring to

49 [1941] AC 74.
50 [1941] AC 74, 85.
51 [1941] AC 74, 93.
52 [1972] 1 QB 373 (CA).

light information which would probably have prevented it, while the catchment board's incompetence failed to prevent only the *continuation* of the flooding.

(iii) *Deduction of gain.* As already explained a defendant cannot set off gain accruing to plaintiff unless it accrues in consequence of his wrongful act; and where the immediate source of the gain is an indemnity, compensation, or gift[53] from a third person the rule is that it cannot be taken into consideration if the third person acted voluntarily.[54]

(iv) *Matters of degree.* To some extent what is voluntary conduct is a matter of degree. This may be illustrated with reference to conduct which shows a reckless disregard of the possibility of the harm which in fact occurs. The prime case of voluntary conduct would be conduct which is intended to exploit a situation created by defendant. A straightforward instance of this would be an act done with the intention of inflicting some injury. But in the law of contributory negligence it is generally held that plaintiff's or defendant's recklessness also negatives causal connection and therefore, under a system of apportionment, excludes apportionment.[55]

On the other hand, recent English decisions on breach of statutory duty tend, with considerable hesitation,[56] to hold that the recklessness of plaintiff or deceased in exposing himself to a danger which he fully appreciates does not negative causal connection but merely leads to reduced damages.[57] This illustrates the flexibility of the causal principle involved and the influence on judicial decision of the policy underlying legislation such as the Factories Act.[58] On the

[53] *Peacock* v. *Amusement & Equipment Co. Ltd.* [1954] 2 QB 347; *Redpath* v. *Belfast & County Down R. Co.* [1947] NI 167; *Rawlinson* v. *Babcock* [1966] 1 WLR 481; *Hay* v. *Hughes* [1975] QB 790 (CA).

[54] *Liffen* v. *Watson* [1940] 1 KB 556; *Klingman* v. *Lowell*, 1913 WLD 186; *Myers* v. *Hoffman* [1956] 1 DLR 2d 272; *Francis* v. *Brackstone* [1955] SASR 270; *National Insurance* v. *Espagne* (1961) 105 CLR 569, 580, 597-8 (intention of donor important); *Mockridge* v. *Watson* [1960] VR 405; *Papowski* v. *Commonwealth* [1958] SASR 293. *Contra: van Heerden* v. *African Guarantee Indemnity Co.*, 1951 (3) SA 730 (C). It is debatable whether a voluntary payment by the tortfeasor should be taken to reduce his liability: *Jenner* v. *West* [1959] 2 All ER 115 (yes) but *Boarelli* v. *Flanagan* (1973) 36 DLR 3d 4, 14, (no, if it can be regarded as the payment by an employer to his employee of part of the latter's wage).

[55] *Restatement of Torts*, s. 482; *Harvey* v. *Road Haulage Executive* [1952] 1 KB 120, 126; *Anglo-Newfoundland Development Co.* v. *Pacific Steam Navigation Co.* [1924] AC 406; *Kasanovich* v. *George* (1943) 348 Pa. 199, 34 Atl. 2d 523 ('wanton misconduct').

[56] In *Stapley* v. *Gypsum Mines* [1953] AC 663, causal connection was affirmed by a majority of three judges to two in the House of Lords; the judges of the Court of Appeal wished to deny it.

In *Williams* v. *Sykes & Harrison Ltd.* [1955] 1 WLR 1180; [1955] 3 All ER 225 the Court of Appeal affirmed causal connection but Singleton LJ would have denied it but for the authority of the *Stapley* case. Ibid., p. 1188.

[57] *Stapley* v. *Gypsum Mines* [1953] AC 663; *National Coal Board* v. *England* [1954] AC 403; *Williams* v. *Sykes & Harrison* [1955] 1 WLR 1180. *Contra: Norris* v. *Moss*, [1954] 1 WLR 346, [1954] 1 All ER 324. Below, p. 199.

[58] *Carr* v. *Mercantile Produce Co.* [1949] 2 KB 601, 608, *per* Stable J.

other hand, the fact that the principle involved is not to be swept aside by policy is shown by the hesitations of the judges who have considered these cases and by the fact that it has never been suggested that a workman who injures himself by deliberately thrusting his hand into dangerous and unguarded machinery can recover for breach of statutory duty.[59]

Again, the degree of appreciation of circumstances needed before an act can count as 'informed' offers some scope for judicial discretion. When someone deliberately sets fire to a substance but without fully appreciating the extent of its inflammability, it is a matter of degree whether his appreciation makes his act so voluntary as to negative causal connection.[60]

Finally, what is voluntary sometimes involves the notion of a 'fair choice', and this in turn depends in part on what conduct is regarded from a moral or legal point of view as reasonable in the circumstances: this raises questions of legal policy.[61]

Non-voluntary Conduct

We now consider in turn the various circumstances which will prevent conduct being considered voluntary. These include many heterogeneous factors which it is possible to group in various ways, such as lack of control, lack of knowledge, and pressure exerted by others. The most obvious application of 'not voluntary' is to a physical movement imparted to the actor's body against his will by some other person or thing. Here we can hardly speak of an act at all. When, however, the actor exercises a choice, his act is in one sense free, but if the choice is made under pressure from a prior wrongful act, or is not a fair choice because the alternative is serious harm, or may be said not to be a 'real' choice because the alternative is neglecting a duty, the decision to avoid the pressure, harm, or breach of duty is not treated as free either in ordinary life or in the law. How grave the alternative must be to justify our speaking of conduct as not free involves important questions of legal policy.

Physical compulsion. When defendant seized plaintiff and swung him round till he was dizzy and ultimately struck his head against a

---

[59] *Rushton* v. *Turner* [1959] 3 All ER 517 (plaintiff's act in deliberately inserting his hand into the moving groove of the fibre-crushing machine was the 'effective cause' of the accident to his fingers). The treatment of such reckless conduct as voluntary is no doubt an extension of the idea that a voluntary act must be intended to exploit a situation created by defendant.

[60] *Philco Radio* v. *Spurling* [1949] 2 All ER 882; 65 TLR 757. *Watson* v. *Kentucky & Indiana Bridge & R. Co.* (1910) 137 Ky. 619, 126 SW 146. *Walker Inc.* v. *Burgdorf* (1951) 244 SW 2d 506 (Tex.).

[61] Below, pp. 156-7.

hook plaintiff's movements did not negative causal connection.[62] The case in which the person moving is physically propelled by defendant must be contrasted with one in which he voluntarily moves to a given place.[63] *Concussion, shock, fright, dizziness, hypnosis.* Not unlike physical compulsion are cases where a defendant concusses, shocks, dazes, or hypnotizes some person who in that condition acts to his own injury or that of another. We should hesitate to call the movement of a person who has lost consciousness an act. Defendant's servant left a lift unattended with the door open and plaintiff's children started it up while her back was turned; on seeing this plaintiff fainted and fell into the elevator shaft. She recovered damages despite the argument that her fright was the 'proximate cause' of her injuries.[64] So with a person who, without losing consciousness, suffers a shock; the difficult legal problem is, on the traditional view, not whether the shock negatives causal connection but whether the scope of the legal rule enjoining due care extends to harm caused in this way.[65]

The movement of someone who is merely stunned or dazed might count as an act but does not negative causal connection. When plaster from defendant's ceiling fell on plaintiff's head and she then ran forward and fell down a flight of stairs, sustaining further injuries, it was held that she could recover for all her injuries since her 'dazed mental condition was the direct result of the blow on her head. The fall down the stairs was the direct result of the dazed mental condition.'[66] On the other hand when plaintiff had been injured by defendant's wrongful act and three years later, after suffering periodic dizzy spells, fell from the kitchen sink on which she had climbed to check a leak in a pipe, she did not recover for her consequent injuries.[67] The court said that the injuries were caused by her 'voluntary and independent' action,[68] but, since she did not intend to exploit the situation, her conduct was perhaps more analogous to an act of contributory negligence.[69]

Though authority has not been traced, it seems certain that an 'act' performed in a hypnotic trance or under a psychological compulsion

[62] *Ricker* v. *Freeman* (1870) 50 NH 420, 9 Am. Rep. 267.
[63] *R.* v. *Storey* [1931] NZLR 417. See below, p. 326.
[64] *Cohn* v. *Ansonia Realty Co.* (1914) 162 App. Div. 791, 148 NYS 39.
[65] Above, pp. 89–94.
[66] *Wisotsky* v. *Frankel* (1917) 165 NYS 243, 244. Accord: *Hall* v. *Coble Dairies Inc.* (1951) 234 NC 206, 67 SE 2d 63, 29 ALR 2d 682; *Eli Witt Cigar & Tobacco Co.* v. *Matatics* (1951) 55 So. 2d 549 (Fla.); *Hill* v. *Associated Transport* (1962) 354 Mass. 55, 185 NE 2d 642; *Slatter* v. *British Railways* [1966] 2 Ll. LR 395.
[67] *Snow* v. *New York N.H. & H.R. Co.* (1904) 70 NE 205 (Mass.).
[68] Ibid., p. 206.
[69] See below, p. 206.

implanted during a hypnotic trance would not negative causal connection.

Self-preservation. An intervening act is regarded as unfree if the actor had literally a choice but not a fair choice, the alternative being a risk of death or serious injury to himself. The most obvious example is the resort by plaintiff, injured by defendant's wrong, to medical treatment which involves him in expense or aggravates his injury. But it applies equally when plaintiff takes a risk in order to avoid the initial injury. 'It is sufficient [to make defendant liable] if [plaintiff] was placed by the misconduct of the defendant in such a situation as obliged him to adopt the alternative of a dangerous leap, or to remain at certain peril.'[70]

This applies primarily to acts reasonably done in order to save the life of the actor or to avert serious injury. The act is often that of plaintiff, as when defendant sold liquor to plaintiff's alcoholic husband, who then attacked her, so that plaintiff shot her husband in self-defence.[71] But it may equally be that of a third party, as when a third party, to save himself from injury, threw defendant's squib across a market-house so that it ultimately struck plaintiff in the eye, [72] or when fellow passengers of plaintiff, in an effort to escape from apparent danger, pushed her off a horse car negligently driven by defendants' servant.[73]

It matters not that the act is done, after initial damage has been sustained, with a view to averting further loss. In the *City of Lincoln*[74] defendants' negligence caused the loss of the compass, charts, and log of plaintiff's ship. Her captain steered for a port of safety as best he could but grounded the ship. The grounding was held the consequence of the original collision. In *Lauritzen* v. *Barstead*[75] owing to defendant's drunken steering plaintiff, his passenger, was stranded in cold weather and set off to find help. When rescued thirty-six hours later he was suffering from frost-bite and his feet had to be amputated. It was held that the amputation was the consequence of defendant's negligence.

In criminal law it has been held that an act done by a woman to preserve her chastity does not negative causal connection.[76] No civil

[70] *Jones* v. *Boyce* [1816] 1 Stark. 493, 495, 171 ER 540, 541. *Latham* v. *Johnson* [1913] 1 KB 398, 413; *De Alba* v. *Freehold Investment Co.* (1895) 21 VLR 204; *Winnipeg Electric Railway* v. *Canadian Northern Railway* (1920) 59 SCR 352.
[71] *Kiriluk* v. *Cohn* (1959) 148 NE 2d 607 (Ill.): noted (1958-9) 11 *Ala. LR* 369.
[72] *Scott* v. *Shepherd* (1773) 2 W. Bl. 892, 96 ER 525.
[73] *Washington & Georgetown R. Co.* v. *Hickey* (1897) 166 US 521.
[74] (1889) 15 PD 15. Cf. *The Metagama* (1927) 138 LT 369; *The Oropesa* [1943] P. 32; *The Gertor* (1894) 70 LT 703; *Nesting & Madsen* v. *Dalton* (1952) 5 WWR (NS) 419. Proper medical treatment: *Bloor* v. *Liverpool Derricking Co.* [1936] 3 All ER 399, 402; *Adelaide Chemical Co.* v. *Carlyle* (1940), 64 CLR 514.
[75] (1965) 53 DLR 2d (Alta.).
[76] *People* v. *Goodman* (1943) 44 NYS 2d 715. Below, pp. 330-1.

law decision has been traced on this point or on an act done to avert embarrassment. The problem would arise if *A* threatened to rape *B*, who shot at *A* and accidentally wounded *C*, who sues *A* for damages. If the actor unreasonably supposes himself to be in peril, he is not 'forced' to act in self-preservation and his conduct is therefore voluntary and negatives causal connection. In *Venter* v. *Smit*[77] defendant unlawfully loosed one of the traces of a cart and horses. Plaintiff, a stout woman, dismounted from the cart and suffered a rupture. Defendant was held not liable for the damage because 'she was in no immediate danger at the time'.[78]

If the actor reasonably supposes that he is in peril but does not adopt the best means of avoiding it his act does not negative causal connection unless it is reckless or so grossly negligent as to do so on the score of abnormality.[79] If plaintiff's act is in question, something less than this will amount to contributory negligence[80] but the mere failure to adopt what turns out to have been the best course of action does not in itself even amount to contributory negligence.[81]

When a train started to move without warning and the next stop was eighty miles away it was held that the jury might find that a person who jumped off could recover for injuries suffered as a result, though he was not in danger of injury had he remained on the train.[82]

Preservation of property. Threatened injury to property will sometimes have the same effect, but there is, on the traditional view, a distinction between the causal problem involved and the policy question whether a plaintiff acting to save property as opposed to life should be protected. In an American case plaintiff's intestate discovered a fire lit through defendant's negligence and, to prevent it spreading to her house, raked some dry leaves towards the fire. However, her clothes caught fire and she suffered burns from which she died. Recovery was allowed on the ground that despite her intervention defendant's negligence was the 'proximate cause' of the death.[83]

[77] 1927 CPD 30.
[78] Ibid., p. 34 *per* Watermeyer J. For another reason see p. 158 below.
[79] *Clark* v. *Du Pont de Nemours Powder Co.* (1915) 146 Pac. 320 (Kan.); *Robinson* v. *Butler* (1948) 226 Minn. 491, 33 NW 2d 821.
[80] *Holomis* v. *Dubuc* (1975) 56 DLR 3d 351 (BC).
[81] *Tuttle* v. *Atlantic City R. Co.* (1901) 49 Atl. 450 (NJ); *The Bywell Castle* (1879) 4 PD 219.
[82] *Caterson* v. *Commissioner of Railways* (1973) 128 CLR 99. The conduct here may also be thought of as instinctive; below, pp. 148–9.
[83] *Illinois Central R. Co.* v. *Siler* (1907) 229 Ill. 390, 82 NE 362. Cf. *Hyett* v. *G.W.R.* [1948] 1 KB 345; *Steel* v. *Glasgow Iron & Steel Co.* [1944] SC 237; *Re Guardian Casualty Co.* (1938) 253 App. Div. 360, 2 NYS 2d 232; *Hutterly* v. *Imperial Oil Co.* [1956] 3 DLR 719; *The Guildford* [1956] P. 364; *Compania Naviera Maropan* v. *Bowaters Lloyd Pulp Mills* [1955] 2 QB 68; *The Gertor* (1894) 70 LT 703; *Collins* v. *Middle Level Commissioners* (1869) LR 4 CP 279; *Scholes* v. *North London R. Co.* (1870) 21 LT 835, 836; *St. Louis–San Francisco R. Co.* v. *Ginn* (1953) 264 P. 2d 351

On the other hand it was held that no action lay when defendant
negligently started a fire which threatened plaintiff's building and
she wrenched her shoulder in getting buckets of water to put the fire
out.[84] In nearly all these cases the court adduces the foreseeability
of the intervening act as the reason for the decision, saying that in
the first case the raking of the leaves was 'one of the intervening
causes which the appellant with reasonable diligence might have
foreseen' while in the second case defendant 'had no reason to
anticipate' that plaintiff would hurt herself through the method
adopted in extinguishing the fire. The reasons for rejecting this approach are fully explained in Chapter IX.[85] It would be simpler to
ask whether plaintiff was acting reasonably to protect his property
and allow recovery if he is injured in consequence of such an act.
We do not expect a person to abandon valuable property if there is
a chance to save it; but 'expect' here refers not merely to what is
likely but to what is thought of as a fair choice.

Safeguarding other rights or privileges. An act done to preserve a
right will similarly not count as free, the actor not being presented
with a fair choice. In one case a ketch sank through defendant's
negligence and obstructed a river and a wharf of which plaintiffs were
licensees. Plaintiffs paid to have the ketch removed and recovered the
cost of doing so from defendants on the ground that they were acting
in protection of their rights.[86] Of course, if the right is of trifling
importance the intervention may not be justified.

Safeguarding interests. The defence of an interest not amounting
to a recognized legal right may have the same effect. For example,
in *Holden* v. *Bostock*[87] defendants in breach of contract supplied
plaintiffs, brewers, with sugar containing arsenic. It was held the
'natural consequence' of this that plaintiffs advertised a change of
brewing materials and the cost of doing so was recovered from
defendants.

A special case of this occurs when the third factor is the institution
of criminal proceedings. When defendant bank wrongfully failed to
honour a cheque drawn by plaintiff and presented by another bank

(Okla.); *Curtis* v. *Shell Pipe Line* (1954) 265 P. 2d 488 (Okla.). If plaintiff who seeks
to preserve his property is also at fault, the damages may, in a jurisdiction which
admits apportionment, be apportioned: *Miraflores (Owners)* v. *George Livanos
(Owners)* [1967] 1 AC 826.

[84] *Whitman* v. *Mobile & O.R. Co.* (1927) 217 Ala. 70, 114 So. 912; (1927–8) 26
Mich. LR 832. Cf. *Seale* v. *Gulf, Colorado & S.F.R. Co.* (1886) 65 Tex. 274; *Malcolm*
v. *Dickson* [1951] SC 542, 549, 554 ('coldly and voluntarily').

[85] pp. 262–7.

[86] *Dee Conservancy Board* v. *McConnell* [1928] 2 KB 159. Cf. *Clayards* v. *Dethick*
(1848) 12 QB 439, 116 ER 932; *Clark* v. *Chambers* (1878) 3 QBD 327; *Halestrap* v.
Gregory (1895) 1 QB 561.

[87] (1902) 18 TLR 317.

it was held that their failure was the 'proximate cause' of plaintiff's arrest at the instance of the other bank on a charge of obtaining money by false pretences.[88] The arrest was described as the 'natural and probable consequence' of defendant's wrong. It would be more illuminating to point out that the bank was acting reasonably, since it had an interest in the enforcement of the law.

Legal obligations. In everyday life we regard even social obligation as limiting our freedom.[89] The law adopts the view that the performance of a legal obligation, where choice is conceived as not wholly free because of the pressure of duty, does not as such negative causal connection. Hence, in a proper case, a purchaser of goods may recover from the seller damages paid to a subpurchaser owing to the seller's breach of contract.[90] Here, as usual, a warning is needed against confusing the causal question with the different question of precedent and policy, whether the recovery of damages for breach of contract is limited to items within the contemplation of the parties at the time of contracting.

A similar view prevails in tort. A striking example of an act done in pursuance of a legal obligation is to be found in *Estes* v. *Brewster Cigar Co.*[91] in which after a quarrel defendant pursued plaintiff in the street shouting 'Thief! Robber!' A policeman, hearing this, shot plaintiff, who was held entitled to recover provided that the policeman had acted reasonably in pursuance of his duty to prevent the escape of a suspected felon.

A similar view was reached on the interpretation of a war injury statute.[92] When a house was damaged by the blast of a bomb and a workman repairing it under a contract was injured by the collapse of a floor the injury was held to be 'caused by' the impact of the bomb.[93]

Moral obligations. In jurisdictions which have given protection to rescuers it has been held to be immaterial whether the rescuer acts under a legal duty or from a sense of moral obligation and whether or not he acts on impulse,[94] even if, in the absence of such a duty, his

88 *Collins* v. *City National Bank & Trust Co.* (1944) 131 Conn. 167, 38 Atl. 2d 582. Cf. *Mouse* v. *Central Savings Co.* (1929) 120 Ohio St. 599, 167 NE 868.
89 Above, p. 138.
90 *Grébert-Borgnis* v. *Nugent* (1885) 15 QBD 85.   91 (1930) 287 Pac. 36.
92 Personal Injuries (Emergency Provisions) Act, 1939.
93 *Taylor* v. *Sims* [1942] 2 All ER 375, 167 LT 414, 58 TLR 339. Cf. *Dickson* v. *Commissioner for Railways* (1922) 30 CLR 579; *National Theatres* v. *Macdonalds Consolidated* [1940] 1 WWR 168.
94 *Haynes* v. *Harwood* [1935] 1 KB 146, 158-9, *per* Greer LJ; *Morgan* v. *Aylen* [1942] 1 All ER 489; *Wagner* v. *International Ry. Co.* (1921) 232 NY 176, 133 NE 437, 19 ALR 1; *D'Urso* v. *Sanson* [1939] 4 All ER 26; *Brown* v. *Ross* (1956) 345 Mich. 54, 75 NW 2d 68; *Parks* v. *Starks* (1955) 342 Mich. 443, 70 NW 2d 805; *Williams* v. *Chick* (1967) 373 F. 2d 330; *Britt* v. *Mangum* (1964) 261 NC 250, 134 SE 2d 235; *Schmartz* v. *Harper* (1961) 22 Conn. Sup. 308, 171 Atl. 2d 89 (property); *Richardson*

conduct might be described as 'unreasonably brave'.[95] If, however, a person attempts a rescue when not under an obligation legal or moral to do so his act will negative causal connection.[96]

The recognition of moral obligation as relevant to causal problems is not confined to rescue cases. In *The Oropesa*[97] the master and engineer of the *Manchester Regiment* set out in a boat after a collision for which the *Oropesa* was partly to blame in order to persuade the master of the *Oropesa* to signal for help. The engineer was drowned when the boat overturned. The act of setting out in the boat was held not to negative causal connection between the collision and the drowning. The court said: 'To break the chain of causation it must be shown that there is something which I will call ultroneous, something unwarrantable, a new cause which disturbs the sequence of events, something which can be described as either unreasonable or extraneous or extrinsic.'[98] It would have been simpler to say that the acts were done partly for self-preservation and partly in pursuance of what was at least a moral duty to save the lives of those on board.

Unreflective acts. Without being unfree in the sense explained above an act may be instinctive or unreflective. The actor has a choice, but his act is unconsidered. Human acts of this sort approximate to the behaviour of animals.

A purely automatic reaction is not deliberate, as when a person struck by another instinctively pushes him away.[99] But the reaction may equally well spring from a psychological impulse, as when a wife, seeing her husband in peril, clutches him to pull him from danger.[1] 'If what she did was done instinctively and was in the circumstances a natural and proper thing to do, I think she is entitled to recover.'[2] The movement of one who, startled by a sudden noise, stumbles and clutches a rail[3] or who, when a truck tyre comes

v. *U.S.* (1965) 248 F. Supp. 99; *Harrison* v. *British Railways* [1981] 3 All ER 679 (contributory negligence of rescuer). It should make no difference that the rescuer is injured while hurrying to give or get help: *Corothers* v. *Slobodian* (1975) 51 DLR 3d 1; *contra Crossley* v. *Rawlinson* [1981] 3 All ER 674.

[95] *Baker* v. *Hopkins* [1959] 3 All ER 225 (CA).

[96] *Cutler* v. *United Dairies (London) Ltd.* [1933] 2 KB 297, was expressly decided by Scrutton LJ on the ground that plaintiff had no duty to attempt the rescue. Ibid., p. 304. Cf. *The San Onofre* [1922] p. 243; *Malcolm* v. *Dickson* [1951] SC 542, 553, 556; *Macdonald* v. *Macbrayne* [1915] SC 716; Tunc, note on Paris 18.4.1955, *Dalloz A.* 1956.2. 354, 357 (person seeking to loot car rather than to rescue trapped passengers cannot recover).

[97] *The Oropesa* [1943] P. 32. [98] Ibid., p. 39, *per* Lord Wright.

[99] *Ricker* v. *Freeman* (1870) 50 NH 420, 9 Am. Rep. 267, above, p. 143, in which the injury was immediately occasioned by the act of a third party who instinctively threw plaintiff against a hook.

[1] *Brandon* v. *Osborne, Garrett & Co.* [1924] 1 KB 548; *Malleys Ltd.* v. *Rogers* (1955) 55 SR (NSW) 390; *Mill & Co.* v. *Public Trustee* [1945] NZLR 347. *Contra* when there is time for reflection: *Brine & Brine* v. *Dubbin* [1933] 2 WWR 25; but probably there was a moral duty to act in this case.

[2] Ibid., p. 552, *per* Swift J. [3] *Slatter* v. *British Railways* [1966] 2 Ll. LR 395.

through the front door, jumps out of bed and slips on a rug[4] is not treated as a voluntary action negativing causal connection.

When defendant's conduct causes panic an act done under the influence of panic or extreme fear will not negative causal connection unless the reaction is wholly abnormal. When defendant, a pilot, negligently dived at a plane in which a student was at the controls and the student, terrified, 'froze' at the controls so that a crash occurred in which plaintiff was injured, the injury was held the consequence of defendant's negligence.[5]

Analogous, but further removed from the purely instinctive, are acts done under provocation. In *Wise* v. *Dunning*[6] the Catholics of Liverpool reacted to the Protestant preacher's insulting speeches by committing breaches of the peace. Though illegal, this retaliation was regarded as 'natural', and the disturbances being the consequence of the inflammatory speeches, there were sufficient grounds for binding the preacher over.[7]

The doctrine of alternative danger, or of the agony of the moment, as applied in the law of contributory negligence, depends on the acts in question not being fully deliberate when circumstances do not permit time for adequate reflection.[8] Many acts that fall within this doctrine are also done with a view to self-preservation.[9]

Mistake, accident, and negligence. These familiar defects in human conduct are of course closely related and mistake may be found in combination with either of the other two. In the case of mistake the agent is ignorant of some relevant circumstance and in the case of accident and negligence some consequence, not expected nor desired, accrues from his movements. In both cases, therefore, it cannot be said that the agent intended to exploit the situation created by the wrongdoer.

(i) *Mistake.* An act done without knowledge or appreciation of the circumstances does not negative causal connection. For instance, the act of a consumer who uses a product without knowing that it is defective will not bar an action against a negligent manufacturer,[10]

4 *Hill* v. *Associated Transport* (1962) 345 Mass. 55, 185 NE 2d 642.
5 *Rich* v. *Finley* (1949) 325 Mass. 99, 89 NE 2d 213, 12 ALR 2d 669. Cf. *Christianson* v. *Chicago St. P.M. & O.R. Co.* (1896) 69 NW 640 (Minn.); *Schofield* v. *Roche & McTavish* [1938] 4 DLR 802.
6 [1902] 1 KB 167. A criminal case.
7 A French court decided that when a man's wife assaulted his mistress the provocation offered by the mistress should go to reduce her damages since the assault was in part the consequence of her provocation. Abbeville 22.12.1936, Gaz. Tri. 4.2.1937.
8 *The Bywell Castle* (1879) 4 PD 219. Salmond and Heuston, *Torts*, p. 487. The principle operates to prevent a failure to adopt the best course of action from being treated as contributory negligence. *A fortiori* such an act does not negative causal connection.
9 Above, pp. 144-5.
10 *Donoghue* v. *Stevenson* [1932] AC 562; *Grant* v. *Australian Knitting Mills* [1936] AC 85.

150   THE COMMON LAW

whilst the consumer's knowledge of the defect will bar recovery at any rate if he is not compelled to use the thing in any case.[11] 'The principle of *Donoghue*'s case can only be applied where the defect is hidden and unknown to the consumer, otherwise the directness of cause and effect is absent: the man who consumes or uses a thing which he knows to be noxious cannot complain in respect of whatever mischief follows, because it follows from his own conscious volition in choosing to incur the risk or certainty of mischance.'[12]

Appreciation implies something more than mere correct sense perception. An actor may well see and not understand. This was the case in *Philco Radio Ltd.* v. *Spurling Ltd.*[13] where the court held that a typist's act in setting fire to film scrap with her cigarette was not such a 'conscious act of another volition'[14] as to relieve defendants of liability for their negligent delivery of the scrap. Two members of the court decided the case on the footing that she set fire to the scrap accidentally, the third on the footing that even if she did so intentionally she did not appreciate its high inflammability.[15]

Appreciation is a matter of degree, and it is not surprising to find divergent decisions. When defendant negligently caused petrol to flow in the street and one Duerr, according to a witness, said 'Let us go and set the damn thing on fire' and then struck a match causing an explosion in which plaintiff, a bystander, was injured, the court held that Duerr's act negatived causal connection if it was 'malicious and done for the purpose of causing the explosion'.[16] In another case, it was held that the act of a man who said, 'You know that water and gasoline will not burn', and then deliberately threw a lighted match into a mixture of the two, did not negative causal connection.[17] In a third case when watered petrol was allowed to escape and an unidentified negro said, 'I wonder if this stuff is gasoline or water' and threw a match in it, causing the destruction of plaintiff's car, recovery was disallowed but there was another factor besides the negro's act which was alleged to negative causal

---

[11] *Farr* v. *Butters* [1932] 2 KB 606; *Denny* v. *Supplies & Transport Co.* [1950] 2 KB 374.

[12] *Grant* v. *Australian Knitting Mills* [1936] AC 85, 105. The doctrine that a negligent manufacturer is relieved of liability if discovery of the defect by intermediate inspection is probable (*Kubach* v. *Hollands* [1937] 3 All ER 907; *Buckner* v. *Ashby* [1941] 1 KB 321; *Holmes* v. *Ashford* [1950] 2 All ER 76; *Eccles* v. *Cross and M'Ilwham* [1938] SC 697) cannot be regarded as resting on causal principles: *Ford Motor Co.* v. *Matthews* (1974) 291 So. 2d 169; *Boeing Airplane* v. *Brown* (1961) 291 F. 2d 310; *Clay* v. *Crump* [1963] 3 All ER 687; *Taylor* v. *Rover* [1966] 2 All ER 181.

[13] [1949] 2 All ER 882, 65 TLR 757.

[14] *Dominion Natural Gas Co.* v. *Collins* [1909] AC 640, 646.

[15] *Philco Radio* v. *Spurling* [1949] 2 All ER 882, 885, 887, 889.

[16] *Watson* v. *Kentucky & Indiana Bridge & R. Co.* (1910) 137 Ky. 619, 126 SW 146.

[17] *Walker Inc.* v. *Burgdorf* (1951) 244 SW 2d 506 (Tex.).

connection.[18] With these borderline cases may be contrasted a simple example. When the third factor was the act of one who in ignorance of the presence of petrol threw away a match, thereby causing damage, this did not negative causal connection, and defendant was held liable.[19]

(ii) *Accident.* This term describes the situation in which a consequence that is neither expected nor desired accrues from the agent's movements. The relevance of the notion to that of free and voluntary conduct is as follows. When the agent is not acting freely, for example because he is performing a duty or protecting his own interests, and in the course of this he accidentally does harm, his conduct does not negative causal connection. His conduct counts as unfree whether or not it is performed with success and accuracy. But if his conduct is voluntary, for example if he chooses to try to steal from a pedestrian rendered unconscious by defendant's negligence, and in doing so he accidentally injures himself or another, his conduct will negative causal connection between defendant's negligence and the accidental harm. This is because the decision to exploit the situation by stealing from the pedestrian has intervened. This free decision negatives causal connection even though, in executing it, the thief has brought about a consequence which he did not intend.

A simple example of the first type of accident in which the agent is not acting freely is the following. When defendant obstructed a pavement and deceased, to avoid the obstruction, walked in the street, and was there struck by a passing car and killed, it was held a question for the jury whether the death was the consequence of the wrongful obstruction.[20] When defendant wrongfully injured plaintiff and fifteen months later she suffered a miscarriage, it was held that this might be found to have been caused by the original injury,[21] pregnancy in these circumstances being assimilated to accidental conduct. When defendant's servants, having imbibed several drinks of whisky, ran a hand car at an excessive speed and plaintiff at the back of the car in front fell on the track and was run over, it was held that plaintiff could recover for his injuries if he had accidentally

---

[18] *Spence* v. *American Oil Co.* (1938) 197 SE 468, 118 ALR 1120 (Va.). The other factor was the fact that plaintiff discovered that defendants had served him with watered petrol and ordered a garage to drain it.

[19] *Gibson Oil Co.* v. *Sherry* (1927) 291 SW 66 (Ark.).

[20] *O'Neill* v. *City of Port Jervis* (1930) 253 NY 423, 171 NE 694. Cf. *Canadian Pacific Railway* v. *Kelvin Shipping Co.* (1927) 138 LT 369; *The City of Lincoln* (1889) 15 PD 15; *Clayards* v. *Dethick* (1848) 12 QB 439, 116 ER 932; *Pietersburg Municipality* v. *Rautenbach* 1917 TPD 252; *Prosser* v. *Levy* [1955] 3 All ER 577, [1955] 1 WLR 1225; *Macdonald* v. *Macbrayne* [1915] SC 716; *Fishlock* v. *Plummer* [1950] SASR 176.

[21] *Sullivan* v. *Old Colony St. Ry. Co.* (1908) 197 Mass. 512, 83 NE 1091, 125 Am. St. Rep. 378. 'The perpetuation of the human race cannot be termed a voluntary act but it rests upon instincts and desires which are fundamentally imperative': p. 380.

lost his hold on the lever handle of the car on which he was travelling.[22]
Of course the result would have been different if he had deliberately
thrown himself on the track not in order to avoid danger but as a
lark; for in that case he would have been acting freely. In none of
these cases was the intervening act intended to exploit the dangerous
situation, nor was it even negligent.

(iii) *Negligence.* The expression 'accident' perhaps strictly applies
to those cases where the agent does not anticipate the consequences
and the consequences are not what would reasonably be expected in
the circumstances. A negligent act is unintentional but not accidental, for such act would reasonably be expected, in the circumstances, to lead to harm.

In general the negligent act of a third party who is attempting to
deal with a dangerous situation created by defendant is not held to
negative causal connection[23] unless it does so on the score of its
gross abnormality.[24] Some cases have, however, applied the now
discredited principle that the last wrongdoer is alone responsible[25]
and Lord Sumner, adopting a very wide notion of voluntary conduct,
held, in a decision which has been generally criticized, that even
accidental conduct might relieve the original wrongdoer of responsibility.[26] When, on the other hand, the decision of the third
party to intervene was voluntary, and he does so in a negligent
manner, the resulting harm will not be treated as the consequence
of the original wrongdoing. For example, if defendant wrongfully
started a fire and, just as it was petering out, the third party decided
to stoke the embers, but did so negligently, with the result that
plaintiff's house was burned down, the destruction of the house will
not be treated as the consequence of defendant's wrongdoing. It
might be different if the third party was a fireman who tried to put
out the fire in order to prevent its spreading, but did so ineptly, with
the result that instead it spread.

Though, as has been said, a merely negligent act done by a third
party in pursuance of his duty or in defence of his interests does not
in general relieve the first wrongdoer of responsibility it is otherwise
with reckless acts. As was mentioned earlier, the law, especially
in the sphere of contributory negligence, has sometimes tended to

---

[22] *Christianson* v. *Chicago St. P.M. & O.R. Co.* (1896) 69 NW 640 (Minn.).
[23] *Shearer* v. *Harland & Wolff* [1947] NI 102; *Martin* v. *McNamara Construction Co.* [1955] 3 DLR 51; *Engelhart* v. *Farrant* [1897] 1 QB 240; *Burrows* v. *March Gas Co.* (1870) LR 5 Ex. 67; (1872) LR 7 Ex. 96; *Philco Radio* v. *Spurling* [1949] 2 All ER 882; *Pelle* v. *Bersea* [1936] 4 DLR 517; *Adams* v. *Parrish* (1920) 225 SW 467 (Ky.); *Teasdale* v. *Beacon Oil Co.* (1929) 164 NE 612 (Mass.); *Rouse* v. *Squires* [1973] QB 88; *Lucas* v. *Juneau* (1955) 127 F. Supp. 730 (Ala.); *State* v. *Weinstein* (1965) 398 SW 41 (Mo).   [24] Below, pp. 183-4.
[25] *Brown* v. *Walton & Berkenshaw & Brown* [1943] 2 DLR 437. Below, pp. 219 ff.
[26] *S.S. Singleton Abbey* v. *S.S. Paludina* [1927] AC 16, 28.

assimilate a reckless disregard of consequences to an intentional courting of them.[27] When a bomb was dropped at 9.10 p.m. and the railway authorities, knowing that the track circuit was broken and communication with the next town interrupted, ordered the engine driver to proceed at caution and he was killed when the engine fell into the crater, his death was held not to be 'caused by' the impact of the bomb.[28] The decision has been criticized,[29] but it may be argued that the order to proceed at caution amounted to recklessness and not merely to negligence on the part of the railway. When a workman sawed a shell which he knew came from an enemy aeroplane and it turned out to be charged and exploded, injuring him, it was held that his conduct was 'doing a deliberate act in which the origination of the shell was only part of the history'.[30] His conduct might well have been described as reckless. In another case a man picked up an object, really a bomb, which looked to him like a piece of piping and put it in his pocket; next evening he took it out in the company of friends and examined it while holding a lighted cigarette. An explosion occurred in which he suffered wounds. It was held that these were caused by the impact of an enemy bomb, although his act might amount to negligence or serious misconduct.[31] Here the statutory scheme provided for a reduction of benefit in the event of such misconduct, but even had this not been expressly provided, it seems clear that a distinction would be drawn between recklessness which would negative causal connection and mere negligence which would not.

The negligent conduct of plaintiff in seeking to avoid the danger created by defendant or its consequences will not in general negative causal connection between defendant's act and plaintiff's harm but may bar recovery or lead to reduced damages because of the doctrines of contributory negligence and avoidable consequences.[32]

Acts of persons under a disability. These generally suffer from one or more of the defects listed above. The acts of young children are often unreflective or misinformed and it is familiar that such acts do

[27] Above, pp. 141–2; below, pp. 213–18.
[28] *Greenfield* v. *L.N.E.R.* [1945] KB 89; *McLaughlin* v. *Mine Safety Appliance* (1962) 181 NE 2d 430 (use of unwrapped heating blocks by foreman who knew they should be wrapped); *Taylor* v. *Rover* [1966] 2 All ER 181 (continued use of chisel known to be dangerous).
[29] By Denning J. in *Minister of Pensions* v. *Chennell* [1947] KB 250, 256.
[30] *Smith* v. *Davey Paxman & Co.* [1943] 1 All ER 286. There were 'a series of fortuitous interventions by curious boys or men acting for their own purposes': p. 288.
[31] *Minister of Pensions* v. *Williams* [1947] 1 KB 875.
[32] *Jones* v. *Watney, Combe, Reid & Co.* (1912) 28 TLR 399; *Glover* v. *L.S.W.R. Co.* (1867) LR 3 QB 25 (plaintiff left glasses in railway carriage 'either voluntarily or negligently').

not normally negative causal connection,[33] while the act of an older child, capable of appreciating what he is doing, may have that effect.[34] Thus when a boy picked up an incendiary bomb and took it home and later took it to a public thoroughfare and tampered with it, with the result that it exploded and injured a schoolgirl, her injury was held to be caused by the impact of the bomb.[35] But when defendant left his shotgun in an accessible position in the garage and his thirteen-year-old son fetched it, loaded it, and injured plaintiff's son, this was held a 'conscious act of volition' which negatived causal connection between defendant's alleged negligence and the harm.[36]

There are a number of American decisions on the legal position when defendant sells a rifle or ammunition to a child in breach of statute and the child or another child in using the arms injures plaintiff. On the whole the decisions hold that the experiments of children, however mischievous, do not negative causal connection, but the conduct of parents presents some difficulties. The distinction drawn is that if a parent discovers his child's possession of the arms and attempts to keep them from the child but is unsuccessful, his conduct does not negative causal connection,[37] but if the parent permits the child to play with them recovery is not allowed.[38] This may be supported, from a common-sense causal point of view, on the ground that the parent's conduct in deliberately permitting his child to play with dangerous weapons is reckless, whereas his unsuccessful efforts to hide or remove them are at most negligent.

Young children are not, however, the only class whose acts are frequently defective in one or more ways. Drunkards and the physically or mentally ill are other such classes. In one American case a man became ill on defendant's train but the employee in charge of the rail depot allowed him to leave while in a 'mentally irresponsible' condition. He wandered for several hours and was then run over by a train five miles from the depot.[39] His dependants recovered for

33 *Lynch* v. *Nurdin* (1841) 1 Ad. & E. 29, 113 ER 1041; *Haynes* v. *Harwood* [1935] 1 KB 146; *Yachuk* v. *Oliver Blais Co. Ltd.* [1949] AC 386; *Henningsen* v. *Markowitz* (1928) 230 NYS 313, 132 Misc. 547; *Booth* v. *St. Catharines* [1948] 4 DLR 686; *Glasgow Corporation* v. *Taylor* [1922] 1 AC 44; *Latham* v. *Johnson* [1913] 1 KB 398, 413; *Thompson* v. *Bankstown Corporation* (1953) 87 CLR 619; *Dixon* v. *Bell* (1816), 5 M. & S. 198, 105 ER 1023; *Sullivan* v. *Creed* [1904] 2 Ir. R. (KB) 317.
34 *Cole* v. *German American Savings & Loan Society* (1903) 124 F. 113; *Wessels* v. *Ten Oever*, 1938 TPD 26. Though a child is old enough to be guilty of negligence its negligence may not relieve defendant of responsibility. *Hatfield* v. *Pearson* [1956] 1 DLR 2d 745.
35 *Minister of Pensions* v. *Chennell* [1947] KB 250; Mathieson, 'The Detonator Case', (1961) NZLR 261, 297.
36 *Wessels* v. *Ten Oever*, 1938 TPD 26.
37 *Henningsen* v. *Markowitz* (1928) 132 Misc. 547, 230 NYS 313.
38 *Pittsburg Reduction Co.* v. *Horton* (1908) 113 SW 647 (Ark.); *Carter* v. *Towne* (1870) 103 Mass. 507; *Calkins* v. *Albi* (1967) 431 P. 2d 17, 19–20 (jury question when mother left cherry bomb where child could find it).
39 *Atchison, Topeka & Santa Fe Ry.* v. *Parry* (1903) 73 Pac. 105 (Kan.).

the employee's negligence. In another, a highway collision occurred through the negligence of defendant, whereby a third party was trapped in his car and injured. Plaintiff, seeing the collision, went to help and, finding a pistol on the floor, handed it to the injured man, who, in a state of delirium through the shock of the accident, fired at plaintiff and wounded him. For this plaintiff recovered from defendant.[40]

Cases of suicide by insane persons raise some difficult problems. An act intended to exploit the situation created by defendant, by treating it as providing the occasion for doing what the actor independently wants to do, usually negatives causal connection.[41] On the other hand, an act done without a full appreciation of the circumstances does not. Courts have some rope to play with here, and while many have held that an act of suicide negatives connection unless it is the result of an uncontrollable impulse, or is accomplished in delirium or frenzy,[42] others have allowed recovery if the suicide took place during a depression caused by insanity,[43] mental instability, or acute anxiety neurosis,[44] or when the victim was deprived by pain and depression of his normal judgment,[45] since the latter are now recognized as 'things which in fact would dethrone the power of volition of the injured man'.[46]

In an interesting case the South Carolina court considered whether the act of a drug addict negatived causal connection.[47] A statute forbade the sale of barbiturates without a medical prescription and required labels to be placed on the box of capsules. Defendant sold the deceased barbiturate capsules in breach of the statute; he continued to purchase them and became an addict and, while under the influence of drugs or moroseness caused by drugs, committed suicide. The demurrer argued that the drug habit 'was a direct consequence of his own voluntary act in taking the barbiturate capsules'; this seems correct, since the court inferred that at least after the first purchase deceased knew the nature of the drug. The court found for

---

[40] *Lynch* v. *Fisher* (1947) 34 So. 2d 513 (La.).

[41] *Runyon* v. *Reid* (1973) 510 P. 2d 943, 58 ALR 3d 814; *Swanie* v. *Lo* (1980) 105 DLR 3d 451 (suicide fourteen months after injury to right hip 'unforeseeable').

[42] *Daniels* v. *New York, N.H. & H.R. Ry. Co.* (1903) 67 NE 424 (Mass.); *Arnsow* v. *Red Top Cab Co.* (1930) 292 Pac. 436 (Wash.); *Fuller* v. *Preis* (1974) 363 NYS 2d 568 (post-convulsive psychosis); *Tucson Rapid Transit* v. *Tocci* (1966) 414 P. 2d 179, 185 (Ariz.); *Orcutt* v. *Spokane City* (1961) 364 P. 2d 1102 (Wash.).

[43] *Malone* v. *Cayzer, Irvine & Co.* [1908] SC 479; *Marriott* v. *Maltby Main Colliery Co.* (1920) 37 TLR 123; *Murdoch* v. *British Israel Federation* [1942] NZLR 600; *Haber* v. *Walker* [1963] VR 339, 358–9; *Cauverien* v. *de Metz* (1959) 188 NYS 2d 627 (suicide allegedly caused by owner's distress at the wrongful conversion of his diamond).

[44] *Cavanagh* v. *London Transport Executive, The Times* 23.10.1956; *Pigney* v. *Pointer's Transport Services* [1957] 1 WLR 1121.

[45] *Graver Tank Co.* v. *Industrial Commission* (1965) 399 P. 2d 664.

[46] *Dixon* v. *Sutton Heath Colliery Co.* (1930) 23 BWCC 135, 140, *per* Slesser LJ.

[47] *Scott* v. *Greenville Pharmacy* (1948) 212 SC 485, 48 SE 2d 324.

defendant but on the unsatisfactory ground that 'it might be that defendant should reasonably have foreseen that deceased would become a drug addict but not that he would kill himself'.

The intervening acts of drunken persons are not usually regarded as negativing the responsibility of a wrongdoer.[48]

Before we leave this general discussion of voluntary action as a factor negativing causal connection between tortious conduct and harm we must consider an objection to describing the action of a person who takes steps to prevent loss threatened by defendant's wrongful conduct as 'not voluntary'. It may be said that this account of the various cases considered above conceals, in pseudo-factual terms, the real factors to which courts attach importance in deciding whether harm is too remote, viz. whether the act done in defence of the threatened interests is adjudged a *reasonable* step for the party in question to take. This judgment, it is argued, must be one of policy, for it involves weighing the value of the interests threatened against the magnitude and likelihood of the harm involved in trying to protect them. The criteria used in settling whether the interests threatened were sufficiently important to justify the risk involved in their defence are the values believed to be currently set on them by society, not those which the party acting himself sets on them. On this view the root question is one of policy: ought the law to protect, at defendant's expense, a party so acting?

Courts often have to decide the relative importance of alternative interests. In *Clark* v. *Gay*[49] recovery of the full value of a house was reduced when defendant pursued one of plaintiff's servants into plaintiff's house and killed him in the presence of the family, who refused to live in the house any longer. It is unreasonable to give up a house rather than live in a place where a murder has been committed. On the other hand it may be reasonable not to insist on one's strict legal rights to the damage of one's commercial reputation.[50]

The facts to which the objection draws attention are important but not inconsistent with the description of these cases in terms of voluntary action. When we take a step reluctantly, as the lesser of two evils, this is one way in which, for common sense and the law, our act is something less than fully voluntary: in extreme cases we would even say 'I had no choice, or no real choice, but to do what I did' and it is just in such contexts that the law speaks of 'necessary

[48] *Pearson* v. *Vintners* [1939] 2 DLR 198.
[49] (1901) 38 SE 81 (Ga.). Cf. cases on unreasonable refusal of medical treatment. *Warncken* v. *Moreland* [1909] 1 KB 184; *Cant* v. *Fife Coal Co.* [1921] SC (HL) 15; *Fyfe* v. *Fife Coal Co.* [1927] SC (HL) 103; *Steele* v. *Robert George* [1942] AC 497. *Matters* v. *Baker* [1951] SASR 91. Below, pp. 359–62.
[50] *Finlay* v. *N. V. Kwik Hoo Tong* [1929] 1 KB 400. See cases above, pp. 145–6. Law Reform (Personal Injuries) Act, 1948, s. 2(4); *Block* v. *Martin* [1951] 4 DLR 121.

consequences'. This is indeed a point at which the concept of a fully voluntary action incorporates judgments of value. A man who, to save his life, hands over his purse to a highwayman and one who, for the same reason, hands over strategic plans to the enemy are treated differently because the value of the interest sacrificed is different. In the first case one would readily say that the man was 'bound', 'obliged', or 'forced' to act as he did, but not in the second. We have here a meeting-place between the notion of a predicament which justifies the action taken and that of pressure which makes it not fully voluntary.

Hence there is little objection to saying that judgments in these cases of what is 'reasonable' are judgments of policy, provided it is remembered that it is not just any conception of policy that is relevant. We are not here committed to a general inquiry 'Would it be a good thing for plaintiff to recover?' but to a specific one 'Did the value of the interest threatened justify the risk the actor took?'[51] We have ourselves chosen the terminology of 'not voluntary' because we believe this stresses the fact that the person acting is placed by defendant in a predicament which limits his area of choice by rendering one alternative less eligible and presents an analogy with other cases of non-voluntary conduct (duress, psychological or physical constraint) where the courts clearly think of the conduct as not fully free.

In the case of duress, though the person threatened is literally able to choose whether to act as instructed or suffer the threatened harm, so that a choice exists, he is no longer free in that he must do or suffer one or the other; whereas before the threat he could avoid both acting as required and suffering the harm threatened. Hence he is *forced to choose*. The same is true when he acts to defend a threatened interest.

A further criticism of the terminology of voluntary action in this context is that it obscures the distinction between the reasonableness of plaintiff's conduct and that of a third party's conduct, which surely raise very different issues. This is true, but the use of the language of 'voluntary' does not commit a court to deciding cases in the same way whether plaintiff has been injured in defending his own interests or has been injured through a third person's attempt to protect himself. A court may reasonably hold that conduct which falls short of negativing causal connection between the tortious act and the harm nevertheless amounts to contributory negligence and so bars plaintiff, in whole or in part, though he would not be barred

---

[51] Justified: *The Guildford* [1956] P. 364; *The City of Lincoln* (1889) 15 PD 15; *Sayers* v. *Harlow U.D.C.* [1958] 1 WLR 623. Not justified: *The Bruxellesville* [1908] P. 312.

if the conduct were that of a third party. The objection would only have force if thus to elucidate, by reference to common-sense causal notions, the distinctions employed by the law entailed a refusal to admit any other criterion of responsibility than the existence of causal connection between act and harm.

'*Natural and probable*'. It is often said of a reaction which is not wholly voluntary that it is the 'natural consequence' or the 'natural and probable consequence' of defendant's act. In this context the description of the reaction as 'natural' means that it is in accordance with human nature, not abnormal, while 'probable' must be taken as meaning 'not unlikely'. This formula, though not necessarily misleading if properly understood, is inadequate. A reaction which is both natural and probable may negative causal connection. For a man who has suffered a serious injury owing to defendant's negligence it may be natural to decide to take a holiday, and it may be probable that he will do so, but it does not follow that he can charge the tortfeasor with the cost of it.

So much for our survey of the circumstances which render conduct less than voluntary. We now attend briefly to more complicated instances of voluntary conduct and to analogous notions.

Opportunities taken. An act may be voluntary in one respect but not in another. In *The Carslogie*[52] the ship of that name negligently damaged the *Heimgar*, which was temporarily repaired so as to be seaworthy but needed further long-term repairs. While crossing the Atlantic she sustained serious damage in a winter storm (not the consequence of the original damage) and had to put into dry dock for thirty days. While there she took the opportunity of having the long-term repairs done concurrently during ten of the days. She recovered from the owners of the *Carslogie* the cost of the long-term repairs but not the loss of hire for the ten days. The repairs she was compelled to have done to save the ship, but she voluntarily, though sensibly, chose to have them done at a period which involved no extra loss of earning time.[53]

Clearly a plaintiff wrongfully injured by defendant cannot charge him with a decision, however sensible, to have an independent operation performed[54] earlier than it would otherwise have been. On the other hand, if defendant's wrong makes it necessary to accelerate

---

[52] *Carslogie S.S. Co.* v. *Norwegian Government* [1952] AC 292. Cf. *Venter* v. *Smit*, 1927 CPD 30 (above, p. 145) where on one view of the facts, even if plaintiff was obliged to dismount from the cart she was not forced to do so without assistance: 'The damage was not caused because she got off the cart, but because she got off without assistance, and it was her own deliberate choice to do so.' Ibid., p. 35.

[53] [1952] AC 292, 306.

[54] *Hoyt* v. *Independent Asphalt Paving Co.* (1909) 101 Pac. 367 (Wash.); *Cutler* v. *Vauxhall Motors* [1971] 1 QB 418 (CA); *Zumeris* v. *Testa* [1972] VR 839, 843.

an operation which would, or would probably, have had to be performed sooner or later, plaintiff should be entitled to something for loss of the chance that the operation might not have proved necessary and for the acceleration of his loss of earnings.[55] The difficult decision in *Hogan* v. *Bentinck West Hartley Collieries*[56] may have been influenced by the view that the operation unwisely performed by the surgeon was intended not merely to remedy the fracture suffered by the workman in the course of employment but also the congenital false thumb from which he suffered. In that case the workman fractured his false thumb at work; the fracture did not heal and a surgeon decided to amputate both the false thumb and the top joint of the ordinary thumb. The operation was unsuccessful and the workman could only do light work after it. The surgeon said he had decided to amputate because of the fracture, not because of the congenital disability; other doctors testified that the amputation was 'for the congenital deformity'. The House of Lords decided by three to two not to disturb a finding of fact by the arbitrator that the ultimate disability did not 'result' from the original fracture.

Routine and independent discretion. Sometimes the conduct which is alleged to negative causal connection is not so much an act as a decision, e.g. to renew a licence or detain a patient under the Mental Deficiency Acts. Here we cannot simply say that such a decision negatives causal connection if all the relevant facts are known to the person deciding but not if he is mistaken about some such fact, for an element of discretion enters into a decision and it is not merely a matter of applying a finding of fact. The distinction applied here is not that between voluntary and non-voluntary acts or omissions but between routine and the independent exercise of a discretion.

Thus in *Harnett* v. *Bond*[57] plaintiff visited Dr Bond who rang up the manager of a licensed house for insane persons and suggested that plaintiff should be sent for. This was done and plaintiff, who was in fact sane, was detained for nearly nine years. During the nine years there were numerous investigations and decisions as to plaintiff's detention by medical men, Commissioners, Visitors, and members of visiting committees. Whether the detention was the consequence of Dr Bond's act depended on whether these were mere matters of routine, as the trial judge thought, or were independent discretionary decisions. The Court of Appeal decided that a number

---

[55] *Meaney* v. *Grantham* [1958] SASR 190; *Savini* v. *Australian Terazzo & Concrete* [1959] VR 811, 823; *Tickner* v. *Glen Line* [1958] 1 Ll. LR 468, 470-1; cf. *Zumeris* v. *Testa* [1972] VR 839, 843-4; Luntz, Hambly, and Hayes, 2. 6. 09; *contra Cutler* v. *Vauxhall Motors* [1971] 1 QB 418, preceding note.

[56] [1949] 1 All ER 588; cf. *People* v. *Stewart* (1976) 358 NE 2d 487 (victim of stab wound died of unrelated hernia operation).

[57] [1924] 2 KB 517. Cf. *Thompson* v. *Schmidt* (1891) 8 TLR 120 (CA).

of independent decisions to detain plaintiff had intervened between Dr Bond's act and plaintiff's final release.[58] 'It is true that the return to [the licensed house] followed and was rendered possible by the action of Dr. Bond, but it cannot in my opinion be said to be directly caused by it. It was the duty of Dr. Adam to form his own opinion about the proper course to pursue and over him Dr. Bond had no control.'[59] 'When there comes in the chain the act of a person who is bound by law to decide a matter judicially and independently, the consequences of his decision are too remote from the original wrong which gave him a chance of deciding.'[60]

Sometimes it has been sought to apply this principle to a judicial decision which follows automatically upon a finding of fact. Thus, it is said that murder cannot be committed by perjury because the cause of death of a person convicted on a capital charge is the court's acceptance of the evidence.[61] This seems unconvincing, for neither verdict nor sentence is discretionary. When, however, the court exercises a discretion there is some analogy in common sense for the view that its decision negatives causal connection. The rule that a defendant who has plaintiff wrongfully arrested is not liable, in an action for false imprisonment, for his further detention if a court remands plaintiff in custody, may be perhaps regarded as causal.[62]

Earned benefits.[63] This is perhaps an appropriate place to mention a causal principle which presents some analogies with the notion that voluntary conduct negatives causal connection. The principle is that, if a benefit is earned by a person's own efforts, these efforts count as the cause of the benefit to the exclusion of other factors. This principle is found in tort, contract and criminal law.[64] In tort its main application is that a benefit accruing to plaintiff on the occasion of a tortfeasor's wrongful act is not deductible from the damages payable by defendant, if plaintiff's own efforts have secured him the benefit.

The prime example is when plaintiff has taken out private insurance, for example accident insurance, against the harm he later suffers.[65] The victim pays the premiums and should be entitled to

[58] Affirmed and new trial ordered by the House of Lords: [1925] AC 669.
[59] [1924] 2 KB 517, 552, *per* Warrington LJ.
[60] [1924] 2 KB 517, 565, *per* Scrutton LJ.
[61] Kenny, *Outlines of Criminal Law* (19th edn. 1966), pp. 136-7.
[62] *Morgan* v. *Hughes* (1788) 2 TR 225, 231, 100 ER 123, 126; *Lock* v. *Ashton* (1848) 12 QB 871, 116 ER 1097; *Austin* v. *Dowling* (1870) LR 5 CP 534.
[63] The subject forms part of the topic of collateral benefits in tort law, on which see Fleming, *Torts*, pp. 224 f. and *IECL*, xi, ch. 11. It involves intricate issues of social policy which, however, leave a place for the causal principle to which we draw attention.
[64] Below, pp. 338-40.
[65] *Bradburn* v. *G.W.R.* (1874) LR 10 Ex. 1; *McKenzie* v. *S.A. Taxicab Co.* [1910] WLD 232.

retain the insurance moneys without losing any part of his claim against the tortfeasor. When the benefit is an incident of employment or service opinions are more divided. When an employer pays wages though the employee is unable to work owing to injury this is seen not as a gain earned by the employee (though in a sense he has earned the wages) but as diminishing his loss of earnings.[66] But when a pension is paid by the employer this has, after some vacillation,[67] been treated as a benefit earned by the employee through his service. Thus, in *Payne* v. *Railway Executive*[68] plaintiff was injured by defendant's negligence and invalided out of the Royal Navy, which awarded him a disability pension. The amount of the pension was held not deductible from the damages awarded to him, since it was the consequence not of the tort, but of his service in the Navy. Cohen LJ said that the naval service was the '*causa causans*' of the receipt of the pension, the injury a mere '*causa sine qua non*'.[69] In *Parry* v. *Cleaver*[70] the House of Lords held that a pension, whether discretionary or not, and whether contributory or not, is the 'fruit, through insurance, of all the money which was set aside in the past in respect of his past work'.[71] So far as social security benefits are concerned, these are generally paid for in part by the contributions of the insured; so that consistency would indicate that they should be treated as earned in part only. This is indeed the solution adopted by statute in England, by which half of certain social security benefits for a limited period are to be deducted from the damages which would otherwise be awarded for personal injury.[72] But in actions for wrongful dismissal the analogy of private insurance and private benevolence has been rejected, so that unemployment or supplementary benefit must be deducted from wages lost up to an amount not exceeding the employee's net gain following on the dismissal.[72a] In actions under the Fatal Accidents Acts 1846–1959[73] the cause of action is so framed that the dependants recover the amount of the injury 'resulting from the death' of the decedent, so that any gains which resulted to them from the death of the bread-winner, for instance under his will, went to reduce the injury

---

[66] *Graham* v. *Baker* (1961) 106 CLR 340; *Parry* v. *Cleaver* [1970] AC 1.
[67] *Browning* v. *War Office* [1963] 1 QB 750.
[68] [1952] 1 KB 26.
[69] Ibid., p. 36.
[70] [1970] AC 1.
[71] [1970] AC 1, 16 *per* Lord Reid. According to *Daish* v. *Wauton* [1972] 1 All ER 25 (CA) National Health facilities are either a gift or akin to the fruits of insurance.
[72] Social Security (Consequential Provisions) Act 1975, Sched. 2, para. 8; Law Reform (Personal Injuries) Act 1948, s. 2.
[72a] *Parsons* v. *BNM Laboratories* [1964] 1 QB 95; *Westwood* v. *Secretary of State for Employment* [1984] 1 All ER 874 (HL).
[73] Fatal Accidents Act 1846, s. 2.

suffered;[74] though it was of course only the acceleration, if any, of benefits under a will or life insurance policy that counted as gains.[75] In England[76] and many other jurisdictions[77] statute, however, now excludes the deduction of insurance moneys and pensions in such cases. Though there are many variations in detail, the distinction between earned and unearned benefits retains great importance and clearly reflects a sentiment that it would be unjust to deprive a plaintiff of a benefit the availability of which he has himself brought about.

The analogy between the present principle and that concerning voluntary interventions lies in the fact that the person whose act is held to be the cause of the benefit intentionally brings it about by his own act that he is entitled, should occasion arise, to receive the benefit. A voluntary intervening actor intentionally brings about certain harm. But there are striking differences between the two principles. The earning of the benefit takes place before the wrongful act which it supplants as the cause of its ultimate receipt; and the benefit need not be voluntarily earned in order to be treated as the cause. A person making compulsory insurance contributions or conscripted into service would be entitled to claim that he had earned his pension.

II. ABNORMALITY

It is important to remember the general form of the causal questions with which we are concerned: 'Is certain harm the consequence of a certain wrongful act given the presence of a third factor?' We now consider a second group of factors which, on the traditional view, negative causal connection, which we group under the rubric 'abnormality'. Here it is convenient to deal separately with physical states or events, animal behaviour, and human conduct, though to a considerable extent the same principles apply to all three.

Physical States and Events

The basic principle is that normal physical events, even subsequent to the wrongful act, do not relieve a wrongdoer of responsibility[78]

---

[74] *Baker* v. *Dalgleish S.S. Co.* [1922] 1 KB 361; *Davies* v. *Powell Duffryn Collieries* [1942] AC 601.

[75] *Heatley* v. *Steel Co. of Wales* [1953] 1 WLR 405 (CA); *Taylor* v. *O'Connor* [1971] AC 115; *Willis* v. *Commonwealth* (1946) 73 CLR 105, 110.

[76] Fatal Accidents Act 1959, s. 2(1).

[77] Fleming, *Torts*, pp. 657–8.

[78] *Commissioner of Railways* v. *Stewart* (1936) 56 CLR 520; *The George & Richard* (1871) 24 LT 717; *Smith* v. *L.S.W.R.* (1870) LR 6 CP 14; *Romney Marsh* v. *Trinity House* (1870) LR 5 Ex. 204; (1872) LR 7 Ex. 247; *Clifford* v. *Denver S.P. & P.R. Co.* (1886) 12 Pac. 219.

but that an abnormal[79] conjunction of events (in this case the wrongful act and the third factor) negatives causal connection, provided
that the conjunction is not designed by human agency. The third
factor must, however, be an event later in time than the prior contingency. Abnormal circumstances of the thing or person affected,
existing at the time of the prior contingency, do not negative causal
connection. The third factor must also be causally independent of
the prior contingency. We take these points in turn.

(i) *Abnormal conjunction of events.* Since the third factor, to negative causal connection, must come later than the original wrongful
act, we may call it an 'intervening event'.[80] Intervening events which
have this effect may be divided into two classes: acts of God, which
are extraordinary whatever the context, and events which need not
be extraordinary in themselves, but are extraordinary in conjunction
with the wrongful act or some admitted consequence of it and so
constitute a coincidence.

The distinction is merely a matter of degree, since even acts of
God cannot be considered completely in isolation from the context
in which they occur. The fall of a heavy meteorite would in a sense
be 'absolutely' abnormal but this merely means from the point of
view of all human experience of the surface of the globe. In *Greenock
Corporation* v. *Caledonian Railway*[81] the question was whether a
rainfall unprecedented in Greenock[82] amounted to *damnum fatale*.
Such rain would certainly have been abnormal in Timbuctoo and
subnormal in Assam, but had to be considered in the context of the
place where it rained. The special feature of acts of God is that,
given the context, they occur very rarely, whereas an event which
constitutes one member of a coincidence may be of a sort that occurs
frequently.

An act of God, in the sense of an event whose occurrence at the
place in question is extraordinary, has often been held to negative
causal connection. Thus in *Toledo & Ohio Central R. Co.* v. *Kibler
& Co.*[83] when a railway negligently delayed a shipment of goods

---

[79] For present purposes it does not matter if 'unforeseeable' is substituted for
'abnormal'. 'Unforeseeable' is the word more commonly used by lawyers. The possible confusions involved in its use are discussed below, pp. 262-7. Cf. Prosser, *Torts*,
p. 272.

[80] Prosser, *Torts*, s. 44; Fleming, p. 203.

[81] [1917] AC 556. It did not because the House of Lords held either that the rainfall,
though unprecedented at Greenock, was not extraordinary for Scotland or that,
though extraordinary, the defendants should have taken precautions against it. Ibid.,
pp. 574, 580.

[82] Ibid., p. 577. The rainfall in other parts of Scotland was regarded as relevant to
what was likely to happen in Greenock.

[83] (1918) 119 NE 733 (Ohio).

which, during the delay, was destroyed by an unprecedented flood, the railway was relieved of liability since the Federal rule as to carriers requires causal connection between the delay and the destruction and not merely that the delay should have been a *sine qua non*.[84] An extraordinary rainfall[85] or frost[86] has been held to relieve from liability under the *Rylands* v. *Fletcher* rule for the escape of a potentially dangerous thing in those jurisdictions which consider the cause of the escape relevant to liability, and the intervention of unpredictable floods relieves a negligent defendant from further liability.[87] Of course, the intervention of an act of God will not be regarded as relevant by a jurisdiction which bases liability on non-causal grounds, in the sense of requiring only that the wrongful act should be a *sine qua non* of the harm.[88]

Coincidence.[89] The idea of a coincidence enters into questions of causation because events, not in themselves extraordinary or unlikely to occur at some place or during some sufficiently long interval of time, are often taken to 'break the chain of causation' if they occur, contrary to general expectation, in certain specific spatial or temporal relations to other events. In order, therefore, to characterize the events which negative causal connection it is not enough to discuss the foreseeability or likelihood of single intervening events. It is most often the occurrence of an event during the short period occupied by another that creates doubt.

Causal questions are not the only ones to which the idea of a coincidence is relevant and the general notion of coincidence is characterized in Chapter III.[90] Its special application to causal questions of the legal type is this: a conjunction of events may be causally significant because their occurrence in some spatial or temporal relationship is necessary for the production of some harm which has occurred. Take the frequently discussed case of a man who through defendant's negligence is run over and suffers injuries. He is taken

---

[84] For a fuller discussion of the divergent decisions in different jurisdictions on carrier's liability see below, pp. 321-4.

[85] *Nichols* v. *Marsland* (1876) LR 2 Ex. Div. 1; *Bratton* v. *Rudnick* (1933) 186 NE 669 (Mass.); *Golden* v. *Amory* (1952) 109 NE 2d 131 (Mass.).

[86] *Murphy* v. *Gillum* (1898) 73 Mo. App. 487.

[87] Prosser, p. 282. *Strobeck* v. *Bren* (1904) 101 NW 795 (Minn.); *Gerber* v. *McCall* (1953) 175 Kan. 433, 264 Pac. 2d 490. Distinguish *Kimble* v. *Mackintosh Hemphill Co.* (1948) 359 Pa. 461, 59 Atl. 2d 68. *Contra: McIntyre* v. *Comox Logging Co.* [1924] 2 WWR 118, 33 BCR 504 (high wind).

[88] *Restatement of Torts*, ss. 510, 522: but note the caveats, which leave it open whether an unforeseeable intervening act intended to cause the harm which in fact occurs excludes liability for the acts of wild or dangerous animals or for ultrahazardous activities.

[89] 'The occurrence was more in the nature of an extraordinary coincidence or conjunction of circumstances.' *Lyons* v. *Georgia Power Co.* (1949) 51 SE 2d 459, 462.

[90] pp. 78-81.

to hospital but on the way is struck by a falling tree and killed.[91] We say intuitively that this is a coincidence, that defendant caused the injuries but not the death. The criteria implicitly used in such a judgment are those specified in Chapter III: the passing of the victim under the tree and the fall of the tree just as he passed are both necessary, though independent, components of the cause of his death. Their conjunction was causally significant, it was not consciously contrived and by ordinary standards it was very unlikely that, in an interval of time so short as that during which the victim passed under the tree, the tree would fall on him.

It is plain that like the cognate ideas of what is 'foreseeable', 'probable', or 'within the risk' the idea of coincidence is essentially a function of limited knowledge of the events concerned. This fact introduces some of the problems which writers who are critical of the use in the law of the idea of foresight have expressed by saying that anything is foreseeable if described in one way and unforeseeable if described in another. Thus it may be said that, in the example given, it is only so long as we choose to describe the events in general terms, e.g. as a *tree* falling, that we think it very unlikely that it should have fallen just as the deceased passed under it. Given sufficient information about the age of the particular tree, the state of its roots, the wind, and so forth, we could describe it more specifically as a 'rotting tree' or speak of the victim's 'passing under a tree just on the point of falling' and on those facts it could have been predicted with certainty that it would fall at the crucial time.

This objection is mistaken. It ignores the fact that all statements of what is 'likely', 'probable', or 'foreseeable' are relative to admittedly limited knowledge, and in the absence of special circumstances (e.g. that an expert on trees is speaking) this means the limited knowledge ordinarily available to the ordinary man. To say that a conjunction of events is a coincidence is not to say that it was unpredictable or improbable given 'full' information, but that it was so, given such knowledge of the conditions at the time and place concerned as the ordinary person might be expected to possess.

Reference to 'ordinary knowledge', what is 'commonly known', and the 'ordinary person' is vague. It will permit any tribunal a

[91] Cf. *Hogan* v. *Bentinck Collieries* [1949] 1 All ER 588, 601, *per* Lord MacDermott: 'If [the workman injured in the course of his employment] gets burned because the hospital he has entered goes on fire, or if he is maimed because the ambulance taking him, say, from hospital to a convalescent home is involved in a street accident, I would not regard' the incapacity as the result of the original injury. Cf. p. 604. But in *Lucas* v. *Juneau* (1955) 127 F. Supp. 730 (Alaska) defendant who negligently injured plaintiff was held liable when the latter was being moved from hospital in Alaska to Seattle and the ambulance-driver had an epileptic fit, so that plaintiff was further injured. The court held that the risk of negligent transportation, like that of negligent medical treatment, should rest on defendant. Cf. *State* v. *Weinstein* (1965) 398 SW 2d 41 (Mo.).

certain leeway in applying such notions; yet the principles are determinate enough not to be a simple verbal cloak for a court's uncontrolled discretion or policy. They will certainly serve to distinguish from the case of the falling tree the case (not a coincidence) where after a fire is negligently lit the evening breeze drives the flames towards the house which they destroy. If we vary the tree case and suppose that it were commonly known that the route to hospital was specially exposed to violent winds or that it lay through an avenue commonly known to be dangerous, this would be some ground for saying that the fall of the tree just as the victim passed was not so very unlikely, though still perhaps unlikely enough.

The fact that there is no uniquely correct way of describing the events (e.g. as a 'tree falling' rather than a 'rotten tree falling' or vice versa) does not, however, in fact present the difficulties which some theorists have found. It will in general be enough to take the description of the events which would ordinarily be given by someone who (without any special knowledge of the area or its condition) could appreciate that they played a necessary part in causing the victim's death. He would speak of a 'tree' or, perhaps, a 'heavy tree' falling and of the 'victim passing under it', and our task is to assess the likelihood, on the basis of common knowledge and experience, of these happening together at that time and place.

It is true—and this is all that is of value in the theorist's warning of the possibilities of alternative descriptions of events—that when we attempt to assess the likelihood of events described in the ordinary way we must make some careful discriminations. We must bear in mind that we are looking for evidence relevant to the fall of a tree which caused death in a certain way and must not allow the way in which the events are described to mislead us into admitting irrelevant evidence or rejecting what is relevant. Thus the fact that trees were known to fall frequently in the area would not show the fall of our tree to be likely if the trees which fell frequently were tender saplings peculiarly likely to be uprooted in a storm. Conversely, the fact that objects other than trees frequently fell in the area during a storm, e.g. lamp-posts, chimney pots, or roofing material, would certainly be relevant unless it were known that their fall was, like that of meteors, determined by factors different from those determining the fall of trees heavy enough to kill the victim.

Many examples of the common-sense notion of coincidence may be found in the cases.[92] In *Central of Georgia R. Co.* v. *Price*[93] plaintiff was, through defendant's negligence, carried beyond her destination.

[92] Drawn without distinction from examples of coincidences where the third factor is either an intervening physical event or human conduct, since the same principles are applicable. Below, pp. 181–3.
[93] (1898) 32 SE 77 (Ga.).

The railway arranged for her to spend the night at a hotel. The hotel proprietor handed her a lamp which exploded during the night, injuring her. The court held that she could not recover from the railway for her injury because their wrong was not the 'proximate cause' of it. The case has also been explained on the ground that the railway's negligence was not a 'substantial factor'[94] in producing the injury.[95] This seems to be merely a metaphorical way of saying that the explosion of the lamp was a coincidence. The chances of a lamp exploding during the course of a single night selected at random are very small.

Two cases on the obstruction of the highway form an illuminating contrast. When defendant wrongfully obstructed the pavement so that pedestrians had to walk into the road in order to pass, it was held that a father might recover for the death of his daughter killed by a passing car while she was walking in the road.[96] When defendants wrongfully obstructed a highway and directed the deceased to take a detour which passed close to a landing ground and deceased was struck by an aeroplane trying to land there was no recovery.[97] The chances of being hit by a car if one has to walk in the middle of the road are quite considerable; those of being hit by a plane are very slight, even if one passes close to a landing ground.

In *Carslogie S.S. Co.* v. *Royal Norwegian Government*[98] a ship was damaged by appellant's negligence and after temporary repairs had been effected so as to make her seaworthy, was further damaged in a winter storm while crossing the Atlantic to have permanent repairs. The storm damage was held not to be a consequence of the original negligence.

When a collision deprives a vessel of one of her chains, so that she is less able to withstand a gale, it has been held a consequence of this that a gale drives her on the rocks.[99] So, when a ship is in breach of contract excluded from a dock and, remaining outside the gates, grounds at the turn of the tide and breaks her back, the harm is a consequence of the breach if the act of remaining outside the gates is neither voluntary nor the fault of the damaged ship.[1] It might be otherwise if while in that position she was involved in a collision

---

[94] Jeremiah Smith (1911) 25 *Harv. LR* 103, 223, 303, 310. Harvard, *Selected Essays on Torts*, pp. 649, 711.

[95] Green, *Rationale of Proximate Cause*, p. 137.

[96] *O'Neill* v. *City of Port Jervis* (1930) 253 NY 423, 171 NE 694. Cf. *H.M.S. London* [1914] P. 72; *Johnson* v. *City of Rockford* (1962) 182 NE 2d 240 (Ill.).

[97] *Doss* v. *Town of Big Stone Gap* (1926) 134 SE 563 (Va.).

[98] [1952] AC 292. Cf. *Powell* v. *Salisbury* (1828) 2 Y. & J. 391, 148 ER 970; *Dallas R. & Terminal Co.* v. *Hendrix* (1953) 261 SW 2d 610 (Tex.).

[99] *The Despatch* (1860) 14 Moo. PC 83, 15 ER 237. Cf. *The City of Lincoln* (1889) 15 PD 15.

[1] *Wilson* v. *Newport Dock Co.* (1866) LR 1 Ex. 177.

through the fault of another ship.[2] The distinction appears to turn on the small chance that a ship will be involved in a collision during a period of a few hours at the gates of a dock.

Again, when a cab driver was negligent in failing to sound his horn and give right of way to plaintiff, a pedestrian, the injury to plaintiff from the cab door, which flew open without fault on the driver's part as he passed, was not treated as the consequence of his negligence.[3] The chances against the door flying open just at that instant must have been very great.

Degree of likelihood. There remains in all cases of this type the question *how* unlikely a conjunction of events must be to negative causal connection. Obviously this is not susceptible of mathematical expression. It has been said that an intervening event does not negative causal connection if it is 'not highly unlikely';[4] perhaps it is impossible to state any more precise criterion than 'very unlikely' for those conjunctions which are inconsistent with causal connection.

In theory the chances of an intervening event occurring might be decided by statistics, but in practice we make use of rough notions of the likelihood of defined events and so can decide from a common-sense point of view whether a given intervening event is a coincidence even though, as we have seen, it is rather a complicated matter to give a theoretical explanation of the reasoning involved.

Change in time and place. We consider under this heading a group of cases which it would be wrong to describe as cases of coincidence but which share an important feature with the latter. A natural comment on a case where the causal connection is negatived because of the coincidental character of intervening events, such as our example of the falling tree, is that defendant's wrongful act did not substantially increase the risk of the victim being hit by a tree: it was so unlikely to happen when it did that it might 'equally well have happened' to him when pursuing his ordinary avocation. Now in certain cases which we cannot describe as coincidences, just this comment can also be made, because the chances that harm would occur were the same, even if very great, both in the position in which defendant put plaintiff by his wrongful act and in the position in which plaintiff would have been had defendant acted rightly.

In some of these cases defendant's conduct or its admitted consequence merely changes the place of some person or thing or changes the time at which some person or thing arrives at a given place; and an intervening event occurring at the altered place or time is also a necessary condition of harm. Here harm is not treated as the

---

2 *Wilson* v. *Newport Dock Co.* (1866) LR 1 Ex. 187, *per* Martin B.
3 *Canada* v. *Royce* (1953) 257 P. 2d 624 (Or.).
4 Prosser, *Torts*, p. 276. Above, pp. 78–9.

consequence of defendant's conduct unless the chances of the occurrence of the intervening event were greater at the altered place or time than at the place or time at which the person or thing would otherwise have been present.

This type of case falls conveniently into three classes: (i) defendant moves a person or thing from one place to another, where the intervening event occurs; (ii) defendant delays a person or thing so that instead of arriving at a certain time he or it arrives at a later time, when the intervening event occurs; (iii) defendant accelerates a person or thing so that instead of arriving at a certain time he or it arrives at an earlier time, when the intervening event occurs.

We now illustrate these three classes of case in which defendant displaces, delays, or accelerates the person or thing which then suffers injury. It should be borne in mind that a given instance may exemplify both a conjunction which is coincidental because very unlikely and one which is made no more likely by defendant's wrong.

(a) When plaintiff's negligence consisted in moving unnecessarily from the west to the east end of a platform, where he was struck by a falling wall, one ground for his not being barred was the fact that the wall was no more likely to fall at one end than at the other.[5] But when defendant forced deceased from the pavement out into the road where she was run over recovery was allowed.[6] Here, in addition to the fact that it was not unlikely that she would be run over in the road, it was also more likely than if she had remained on the pavement.

(b) When, through breach of defendant's contract to provide a seaworthy ship, a cargo due to arrive in July 1939 was seriously delayed, it was held that the cost of transhipping the cargo upon the outbreak of the war was a consequence of the breach of contract, the chances of war breaking out being greater at the actual time of arrival than when the ship should have arrived.[7] On the other hand when defendants in breach of contract delayed goods which, on arrival in port, were placed under an embargo the chances of which were not increased by the delay,[8] or delayed a ship which before arrival was sunk by a submarine, the loss was held not recoverable.[9]

---

[5] Smithwick v. Hall & Upson Co. (1890) 59 Conn. 261. See below, p. 208. Cf. Dallas v. Diegal (1945) 41 Atl. 2d 161 (Md.) (parking on wrong side of street). Schultz v. Brogan (1947) 29 NW 2d 719, 251 Wis. 390; Coray v. South Pacific Co. (1947) 185 Pac. 2d 963 (Utah).

[6] O'Neill v. City of Port Jervis (1930) 253 NY 423, 171 NE 694. Above, p. 167.

[7] Monarch S.S. Co. v. A/B Karlshamns Oljefabriker [1949] AC 196.

[8] The Malcolm Baxter Jr. (1927) 28 Ll. LR 290; (1928) 31 Ll. LR 200; 277 US 323.

[9] Associated Portland Cement Manufacturers (1900) Ltd. v. Houlder Bros. & Co. (1917) 86 LJ (KB) 1495.

(c) In *Berry* v. *Borough of Sugar Notch*[10] plaintiff drove his tram faster than the permissible speed. Defendants had negligently allowed a chestnut tree to remain at the side of the tram lines. As the tram passed the tree during a violent storm it fell and crushed the roof of the tram, injuring plaintiff. In holding that plaintiff was not barred by contributory negligence, the court said his speed was not a contributory cause of the accident. 'That his speed brought him to the place of the accident at the moment of the accident was the merest chance, and a thing which no foresight could have predicted. The same thing might as readily have happened to a car running slowly, or it might have been that a high speed alone would have carried him beyond the tree to a place of safety.' It was further held that, though the speed might have contributed to the *extent* of plaintiff's injury, the evidence did not suffice for the court to take account of the possibility. Here all that plaintiff had done was to pass the dangerous spot earlier than he should have done; as the storm was raging at both times there was no evidence that plaintiff's act, from the standpoint of an observer without special knowledge, increased the chances of his being hit.

(ii) *Designed conjunctions:* '*Intended consequences can never be too remote.*' This is the appropriate context to discuss this sweeping maxim,[11] which, as it stands, is too widely stated. It is certainly possible for an intended contingency to be too remote in one sense, for it may not be, on common-sense principles, the consequence of the wrongful act in question, although it would not have occurred without it. Suppose that the accused, intending to kill his victim, poisoned his food and the victim, while on the way to hospital for treatment was struck by a falling tree and died, the accused would not presumably be convicted of murder, although he intended the victim's death and it would not have occurred but for his act.[12] Similar principles apply in tort.

The truth obscurely expressed in the maxim is that an extraordinary conjunction of events, if intended or designed, does not negative causal connection. The real application of the maxim, therefore, is to prevent an abnormal event or what would otherwise be a coincidence from negativing causal connection. If defendant lights a fire knowing, through a reliable weather forecast, that an hour later a hurricane will pass through the district, the hurricane, however

[10] *Berry* v. *Borough of Sugar Notch* (1899) 43 Atl. 240 (Pa.). Cf. *Draxton* v. *Katzmarek* (1938) 280 NW 288 (Minn.); *Balfe* v. *Kramer* (1936) 249 App. Div. 746, 291 NYS 842. Above, pp. 121–2.

[11] Salmond, *Torts*, p. 505. Winfield, *Torts* (6th edn.), p. 86. The *Restatement of Torts* admits an exception to the maxim where 'the harm results from an outside force the risk of which is not increased by the defendant's act': s. 435A.

[12] Contrast *People* v. *Fowler* (1918) 174 Pac. 892 (Cal.).

abnormal, will not negative causal connection between the defendant's act and the damage resulting from the conjunction of the hurricane and the fire.[13] If he binds his victim and leaves him on the pavement at a place where he has reason to suppose a heavy tree will fall half an hour later, the victim's death from the fall of the tree is no coincidence. The same applies to human interventions, whether or not they would have occurred independently of the wrongful act. If accused persuades his victim to sleep in a house to which he knows a third party will set fire that night, he is presumably guilty of murder if the victim dies in the fire. If defendant wrongfully ejects plaintiff from his bar, knowing that prospective assailants are waiting outside, and plaintiff is injured by the assailants, defendant may be liable for the injuries.[14]

If, however, the wrongdoer is not reasonably certain that the intervening event will take place, the maxim concerning intended consequences will not apply. Suppose the accused compels his victim to travel on an aircraft, hoping but having no reason to believe that it will crash; if it does crash owing to bad weather and the victim is killed, the accused has certainly increased the chances of the victim being killed compared with what they would have been had he remained on the ground. But presumably he is not guilty of murder because he has not caused the death: it would still remain a coincidence that the plane on which he placed his victim crashed. Only when an intervening event is certain or highly probable and the agent knows this, is it appropriate to apply the maxim that the consequences intended by the wrongdoer cannot be too 'remote'.

The maxim in question thus used exhibits a negative aspect of the notion of a coincidence: for a coincidence is always contrasted with what is brought about by an agent intentionally exploiting or working upon a known environment or set of conditions. The maxim therefore emphasizes the overriding importance of voluntary and informed human action in matters of causation: but its importance here is not, as it was in the cases mentioned earlier in the chapter, that it negatives causal connection between two other contingencies but that it excludes the classification of an abnormal conjunction of events as a coincidence. Hence its role here is to counter the suggestion that there is no causal connection between two contingencies.

Where, however, the gist of the alleged causal connection is that defendant coerced or deceived another into acting in a certain way, this connection would be established if he intended him to act in that way, however unusual such action might be. If defendant

[13] *Chesapeake & O.R. Co.* v. *Wix & Sons* (1937) 4 Cir., 87 F. 2d 257 (weather forecast of storm).
[14] *Yashar* v. *Yakovac* (1944) 48 NYS 2d 128.

threatens to call a strike of the employees of a butcher's customer to force the latter to withdraw his custom from the butcher, his intention disposes of the suggestion that the customer's conduct, in complying with his demand, was abnormal or unnatural so as to negative causal connection between the threat and the loss of custom.[15] The maxim about intended consequences is sometimes loosely used to refer to a different point. When courts on grounds of policy limit the recoverable harm (e.g. to that which is foreseeable or within the contemplation of the parties to a contract) they will often not apply these limitations to a defendant who intended to do harm.[16]

(iii) *Coexisting circumstances and intervening events.* If a contingency is, on account of its abnormality, to negative causal connection it must be an *event* and one later in time than, or possibly simultaneous with, the wrongful act. But a *state of the person or thing affected* existing at the time of the wrongful act (a 'circumstance'), however abnormal, does not negative causal connection.

The distinction between an existing state of affairs and an intervening event may be criticized as irrational but it clearly has roots in common sense, which regards a cause as 'intervening' in the course of events at a given time and the state of affairs then existing as the 'setting of the stage' before the actor comes on the scene. Suppose plaintiff is run over through defendant's negligence. If on the way to hospital he is hit by a falling tree, that is a coincidence. If, just previously to being run over, he was hit by a tree and severely injured, that is a circumstance existing at the time of the running over and will not negative causal connection between the running over and the victim's death, even if the victim would not have died from the running down but for the previous blow from the tree.[17] If the offending car and the tree strike the victim simultaneously we should be inclined, perhaps, to treat this as a coincidence also, though we know of no decision on the point.[18] It is, in a sense, as much a coincidence that the victim had been struck by a tree just before he was run over as that he was struck afterwards, but the order in which the two events happen is of crucial importance in determining the consequences of the wrongful act.

The principle that abnormal circumstances existing at the time of the wrongful act do not negative causal connection is well established

---

[15] *Quinn* v. *Leathem* [1901] AC 495. It is in this context that Lord Lindley said, 'The intention to injure the plaintiff . . . disposes of any question as to remoteness of damage.' Ibid., p. 537; *Jones* v. *Fabbi* (1973) 37 DLR 3d 27.

[16] *Doyle* v. *Olby* [1969] 2 QB 158; below, p. 304 n. 47.

[17] *State* v. *Scates* (1858) 50 NC 409; *State* v. *Angelina* (1913) 73 W. Va. 146, 80 SE 141. Below, p. 242.

[18] There are decisions on the concurrence of two simultaneous causes each *sufficient* without the other to cause the harm. *Anderson* v. *Minneapolis, St. P. & S. St. M. R. Co.* (1920) 146 Minn. 430, 179 NW 45. See below, pp. 237-8. But this does not settle the question where the concurrence of both is *necessary* to cause the harm.

as regards physical illnesses or susceptibilities of the victim such as alcoholism,[19] pregnancy,[20] a heart condition,[21] osteoarthritis,[22] tuberculosis active[23] or dormant,[24] or the proverbial eggshell skull.[25] The tortfeasor takes his victim as he finds him. Thus, when the victim was especially susceptible to creosote poisoning, this did not relieve a negligent defendant who had produced the poisoning from which plaintiff died.[26] It is immaterial that defendant does not know of and could not reasonably discover the abnormal circumstance. The law is the same if plaintiff's susceptibility is nervous or emotional,[27] though such susceptibility is often relevant to the issue of culpability.[28] Whether a religious belief or nervous hesitation which dissuades the victim from undergoing a surgical operation,[29] using contraceptives,[30] or taking a blood transfusion[31] is to be treated as an exceptional peculiarity which the tortfeasor takes as he finds or as a reasoned attitude the sacrifice of which may, according to the circumstances, be unreasonable to expect, is controversial. Since religious convictions can be modified or abandoned, the latter approach seems preferable. If it is adopted, then the decision whether the refusal of treatment, etc., is unreasonable and so such as to negative causal connection with the harm which the treatment could have averted involves deciding issues of policy about the relative importance of different values (e.g. conscience and the preservation of human life).

How far the principle extends beyond physical and emotional susceptibilities of the victim has not been much explored by the courts. However, it has been held that damages are not reduced because a plaintiff is wearing spectacles and the injury is thereby

19 *McCahill* v. *New York Transportation Co.* (1911) 201 NY 221, 94 NE 616. Cf. *Cork* v. *Kirby Maclean* [1952] 2 TLR 217; [1952] 2 All ER 402 (epilepsy).
20 *Dulieu* v. *White* [1901] 2 KB 669, 679. Cf. *McDonald* v. *Smellie* (1903) 5 Fraser 955 (SC).
21 *Love* v. *Port of London Authority* [1959] 2 Ll. LR 541.
22 *Watts* v. *Rake* (1960) 108 CLR 158.
23 *Offensend* v. *Atlantic Refining Co.* (1936) 322 Pa. 399, 185 Atl. 745.
24 *Champlin Refining Co.* v. *Thomas* (1937) 93 F. 2d 133.
25 *Dulieu* v. *White & Sons* [1901] 2 KB 669, 679; Luntz, Hambly, and Hayes, 2.2.10. *Wilson* v. *Birt*, 1963 (2) SA 508 (D) is a case where plaintiff's injuries were made worse by a thin skull.
26 *Louisville & N.R. Co.* v. *Wright* (1919) 210 SW 184 (Ky.). Cf. *Richards* v. *Baker* [1943] SASR 245, 250; *Koehler* v. *Waukesha Milk Co.* (1926) 208 NW 901 (Wis.).
27 *Pigney* v. *Pointer's Transport Services* [1957] 1 WLR 1121, 1124; *Alexander* v. *Knight* (1962) 197 Pa. Sup. 799, 177 Atl. 2d 142; *Mount Isa Mines* v. *Pusey* (1970) 125 CLR 383; *Steinhauser* v. *Hertz Corp.* (1970) 421 F. 2d 1169, 1172–3; *Malcolm* v. *Broadhurst* [1970] 3 All ER 508, 511 ('eggshell personality') and cases below, p. 274 n. 83.
28 *Nova Mink* v. *T.C.A.* [1951] 2 DLR 241, 264; *Bourhill* v. *Young* [1943] AC 92, 110.
29 *Marcroft* v. *Scruttons* [1954] 1 Ll. LR 395; *Glavonjic* v. *Foster* [1979] VR 536.
30 *Walker & Flynn* v. *Princeton Motors* [1960] SR (NSW) 488.
31 *Boyd* v. *S.G.I.O.* [1978] QR 195.

increased.[32] It might be contributory negligence in a plaintiff to carry something abnormal in his clothing but this would not, it is submitted, negative causal connection between the wrongful act and an increased injury to himself or another.

It appears that the abnormal physical condition of the inanimate object affected does not negative causal connection. In *Re Polemis*[33] defendants' servants negligently allowed a heavy plank to fall into the hold of a ship. There was, unknown to them, petrol vapour in the hold of the ship and the ship caught fire, apparently because the plank in falling ignited a spark and set fire to the vapour. The owners' claim for the consequent destruction of the ship succeeded. The ground of the decision was that it was immaterial that defendants could not reasonably have foreseen the destruction of the ship at the time of their negligent act, since the loss was the 'direct' consequence of it. Although the decision has been overruled[34] and the reasoning is clearly inadequate, it seems that, if a similar case were to fall for decision now, it would be held that in principle a tortfeasor takes his victim's property, like his person, as he finds it, but subject to the policy limitation that he is not liable for a series of chemical reactions when only mechanical effects were to be expected, since these count as different 'types' of harm.[35]

In the *Palsgraf*[36] case the majority of the New York Court of Appeals took the view that the decision turned not on the question of causal connection between the negligent jostling of the passenger and the explosion which threw the platform scales against the victim, which was clear enough, but on the scope of the law of negligence. This, on common-sense causal principles, appears correct.

The principle that an existing circumstance though abnormal will not negative causal connection has been extended by a natural analogy to include the victim's unusual susceptibility through his relation to other objects. Thus in *Dillon* v. *Twin State Gas & Electric Co.*[37] the deceased was, on one hypothesis, negligently electrocuted

[32] *Bernstein* v. *Western Union Tel. Co.* (1940) 174 Misc. 74, 18 NYS 2d 856; cf. *Wieland* v. *Cyril Lord* [1969] 3 All ER 1006 (defendant's negligence made it more awkward for plaintiff to use bifocal spectacles, so that she fell downstairs).

[33] *Re Polemis & Furness, Withy & Co.* [1921] 3 KB 560. There is a good discussion of this famous case in M. Davies, 'The Road from Morocco: *Polemis* from *Donoghue* to No-Fault', (1982) 45 *MLR* 534. Cf. *R.* v. *Storey* [1931] NZLR 417 (defective brakes of car).

[34] *The Wagon Mound (No. 1)* [1961] AC 388.

[35] Below, p. 269.

[36] *Palsgraf* v. *Long Island R. Co.* (1928) 248 NY 339, 162 NE 99, 59 ALR 1253. Of five judges who considered the matter in the Appellate Division (intermediate court of appeal) three thought causal connection made out, while two considered that the act of the mysterious passenger in carrying a parcel of explosives was an 'independent intervening cause'. In the Court of Appeals itself the four dissenting judges thought causal connection made out.

[37] (1932) 85 NH 449, 163 Atl.111. Cf. *Hill* v. *New River Co.* (1868) 9 B. & S. 303.

by defendants as he was falling to death or certain injury. This, it was held, would not negative causal connection between the negligence and the death, though it would lead to a reduction or extinction of damages on the footing that deceased's life and earning capacity had little or no value when he was electrocuted.

Similarly it is settled law that the owners of a ship damaged through defendant's negligence can recover damages on the basis of the actual contract or charter on which she is engaged.[38] This appears to be the case even if the contract contains onerous clauses which make the owners exceptionally vulnerable to delay.[39]

The decision of the House of Lords in *The Liesbosch*[40] does, of course, appear to conflict with a general principle that abnormal circumstances existing at the time of the wrongful act will not negative causal connection: but the refusal to award damages for loss which would not have occurred but for the plaintiff's exceptional 'impecuniosity' may be supported without recourse to the view that there was no sufficient causal connection between the wrongful sinking of the plaintiff's dredger and the loss involved in hiring an expensive replacement. For the law clearly is often reluctant, as a matter of general policy, to take steps to extricate parties from predicaments into which they would not have fallen but for lack of means.

This is evident in the law of frustration of contract[41] where inability to pay has never been accepted as a ground of discharge, and traces of the principle are found as early as Pothier.[42] On the other hand in an action for breach of contract, in which causal connection between breach and harm is certainly an essential to be proved, damages which would not have occurred had the plaintiff not been financially

---

[38] *The Argentino* (1888) 13 PD 191; (1889) 14 AC 519; *The Kate* [1899] P. 165; *The Racine* [1906] P. 273; *The Philadelphia* [1917] P. 101; *The Llanover* [1947] P. 80. But cf. *The Soya* [1956] 2 All ER 393.

[39] *The Edison* [1931] P. 230. There is nothing in the decision on appeal in this case ([1933] AC 449) to cast doubt on this point.

[40] *The Liesbosch Dredger* v. *Edison (Owners)* [1933] A C 449; *Alberta Carriers* v. *Vollan* (1977) 81 DLR 3d 672. Cf *Duce* v. *Rourke* [1951] 1 WWR (NS) 305 (full discussion of the cases by Egbert J.). If plaintiff was not specially impecunious but, owing to defendant's negligence, his business loses money and is sold by a mortgagee, he can recover for the consequent capital loss: *Taupo Borough Council* v. *Birnie* [1978] 2 NZLR 397 (defendant flooded plaintiff's hotel, so that customers stayed away and borrowed money could not be repaid); cf. *Martindale* v. *Duncan* [1973] 1 WLR 574 (CA); *Dodd Properties* v. *Canterbury C.C.* [1980] 1 All ER 928 (CA); *Fox* v. *Wood* (1981) 35 ALR 607.

[41] McElroy, *Impossibility of Performance*, pp. 7–8.

[42] *Traité des Obligations*, s. 167. The vendor sold a farmer a diseased cow which infected the rest of his cattle, so that the farmer could not run his farm or pay his debts and his goods were sold cheap by his creditors. Pothier thinks the loss of earnings through failure to cultivate the farm is recoverable, the loss through the sale in execution not, even if the vendor was fraudulent. Cf. *Domine* v. *Grimsdall* (1937) 156 LT 456, 461, *per* Atkinson J.

embarrassed are recoverable if in the contemplation of the parties.[43] It seems superfluous, therefore, to have recourse to a special 'legal' use of 'cause' in order to explain why a plaintiff does not usually recover for a loss which he would not have suffered but for his impecuniosity.[44]

It is true that, when the explanation of an accident is sought, circumstances such as alcoholism, impecuniosity, the existence of petrol vapour or concealed explosives may well be cited, if not as *the* cause, at least as *a* cause concurrently with a wrongful act. Yet this fact does not mean that such abnormal circumstances must be taken to negative causal connection between the wrongful act and the harm in attributive enquiries. The susceptibility or precarious situation of plaintiff or his property is, however, rightly taken into account when damages are assessed,[45] since the defendant has injured a victim whose prospects of future life, activity, and earning power were, even before he was affected by defendant's conduct, lower than normal.

(iv) *Causal independence.* If a subsequent physical event would not have occurred but for the wrongful act it does not negative causal connection. If I knock down the first of a row of skittles and each skittle knocks down the next, until the last skittle sets off an explosion, the fall of the intervening skittles does not, of course, negative causal connection between my act and the explosion, because they would not have fallen but for my act.

Thus, in many cases the occurrence of a mechanical freak has been held not to negative responsibility. In *Bunting v. Hogsett*[46] defendant ran an engine over a track which crossed a railway at two places. His engineer drove negligently at the approach to one crossing and collided with a train. Just before the collision he shut off steam. The jar of the collision reopened the throttle and the engine

---

[43] *Muhammad Issa El Sheikh Ahmad v. Ali* [1947] AC 414; *Trans Trust v. Danubian Trading*, [1952] 2 QB 297.

[44] *The Liesbosch* [1933] AC 449, 460. Cf. *Palsgraf v. Long Island R. Co.* (above) *per* Andrews J. dissenting: 'The law arbitrarily declines to trace a series of events beyond a certain point.' 59 ALR 1253, 1261.

[45] *Dillon v. Twin State Gas & Electric Co.* (1932) 85 NH 449, 163 Atl. 111; below, p. 180 n. 61.

[46] (1891) 21 Atl. 31, 23 Am. St. Rep. 192 (Pa.). Cf. *Hill v. Winsor* (1875) 118 Mass. 251; *Gilbertson v. Richardson* (1848) 5 CB 502, 136 ER 974; *Honan v. McLean* [1953] 3 DLR 193; *Harris v. Mobbs* (1878) 3 Ex. D. 268; *Christianson v. Chicago R. Co.* (1896) 67 Minn. 94, 69 NW 640; *Dellwo v. Pearson* (1961) 107 NW 2d 859 (Minn.), 97 ALR 2d 866; *Petition of Kinsman Transit Co.* (1964) 338 F. 2d 708; *Castellan v. Electric Power Transmission* (1967) 69 SR (NSW) 159; *Millard v. Serck Tubes* [1969] 1 WLR 211; *Chavers v. Blossman* (1950) 45 So. 2d 398 (La.). *Contra: Roberts v. De Stephano* (1951) 190 F. 2d 55 (plaintiff out of range); *Chase v. Washington Power Co.* (1941) 111 Pac. 2d 872 (Idaho: hawks completing electric circuit); *Barrett v. Hardie & Thompson* [1924] NZLR 228; *Radigan v. Halloran* (1963) 196 Atl. 2d 160 (RI); *Morris v. Fraser* (1966) 55 DLR 2d 93; *Hoag v. Lake Shore & M.S.R. Co.* (1877) 85 Pa. 293, 27 Am. Rep. 653.

ran backwards and struck the train a second time at the other crossing, injuring plaintiff. Here the reversal of the engine, being itself the consequence of defendant's servant's act, though a 'freak', did not prevent plaintiff's injury being the consequence of the original negligence, although but for its connection with defendant's act the freak reversal of the engine might have been regarded as an extraordinary intervening event and so as negativing causal connection between the defendant's negligence and the plaintiff's injury. The same has been held of a freakish sequence of events which included unexpected psychological reactions.[47]

Similarly in *Sundquist* v. *Madison Railways Co.*[48] plaintiff, a passenger in an automobile which was struck owing to the negligent driving of defendants' streetcar, thereupon became hysterical. Two months later, when travelling in another vehicle, she heard the bell of a streetcar ring and again became hysterical and fainted, suffering paralysis in consequence. The paralysis was held the consequence of the original negligence. Plaintiff's hysteria did not negative causal connection because it was the consequence of defendant's negligence.

A more commonplace illustration is the fact that, when decedent contracts a disease owing to lowered vitality, this does not prevent his consequent death from being treated as the consequence of defendant's wrong if the lowered vitality is itself the consequence of that wrong;[49] similarly if the original negligence causes a disability which in turn results in a further accident.[50] But if the further accident is not caused but merely aggravated by the disability, e.g. if the original negligence causes the loss of an eye and the victim later independently loses his other eye, the original wrongdoer is liable only for the additional loss attributable to the fact that the victim was already disabled at the time of the further accident.[51] If the later accident would not have occurred but for the disability, but plaintiff's

[47] *Rasmussen* v. *Benson* (1938) 135 Neb. 232, 280 NW 890 (sale of poisoned feed led to collapse of business and death from heart strain).
[48] (1928) 221 NW 392 (Wis.). Cf. *Comstock* v. *Wilson* (1931) 257 NY 231, 177 NE 431; *Ominsky* v. *Weinhagen* (1911) 129 NW 845 (Minn.); *Ferrera* v. *Galluchio* (1958) 152 NE 2d 249, 176 NYS 2d 996.
[49] *Wallace* v. *Ludwig* (1935) 292 Mass. 251, 198 NE 159; cf. *People* v. *Kane* (1915) 213 NY 260, 107 NE 655.
[50] *Fishlock* v. *Plummer* [1950] SASR 176; *Jacques* v. *Matthews* [1961] SASR 205; *Boss* v. *Simpson Eastern* [1969] 2 DLR 3d 114; *Wieland* v. *Cyril Lord* [1969] 3 All ER 1006; *Eichstadt* v. *Underwood* (1960) 337 SW 2d 684; *Pyne* v. *Wilkenfeld* (1981) 26 SASR 441; E. Vance, 'Liability for Subsequent Injuries', (1963) 42 *Tex. LR* 86. Whether the second injury results from the first is a 'question of fact' (*Lindeman* v. *Colvin* (1946) 74 CLR 313, 317; *Neall* v. *Watson* (1960–1) 34 ALJR 364; *Commonwealth* v. *Butler* (1959) 102 CLR 465) in determining which it may be relevant whether the injury is one which could just as well have occurred without the disability: *McKiernan* v. *Manhire* (1977) 17 SASR 571.
[51] *Fishlock* v. *Plummer* [1950] SASR 176, 181; Luntz, Hambly, and Hayes, 2. 5. 04.

negligence contributed to its occurrence, damages should be reduced, in a jurisdiction which admits apportionment, to take account of this.[52] When the wrongful conduct is alleged to have caused a psychological condition such as compensation neurosis, which prevents plaintiff working until he receives compensation, it is clear that, if the accident in fact caused the neurosis, plaintiff will be entitled to damages for loss of earnings until he is able to resume work. It is often difficult to decide between this hypothesis and the possibility that plaintiff is malingering and has freely chosen not to work, in which case causal connection with the loss of earnings is negatived.[53] Similarly, if defendant injures plaintiff and thereby causes him or her a disfigurement,[54] or makes him or her more irritable,[55] and this in turn leads to the breakup of plaintiff's marriage, the disfigurement or irritability does not of itself negative causal connection with the loss resulting from the breakup, since it was caused by defendant's wrong. Whether the resulting loss is recoverable from defendant depends, in our view, on whether the domestic situation is so changed by the injury that a spouse cannot reasonably be expected any longer to tolerate it. This will not often be the case, and, if it is not, the loss consequent on the breakup of the marriage should be attributed to the voluntary decision of the spouse who has not been injured. The mere fact that the reaction of the non-injured spouse was foreseeable in the sense of 'not unlikely' should not be sufficient for the imposition of liability.[56]

'*Direct consequences*'. It may be asked: What is the relation between the principles so far expounded and the notion of 'direct consequences' which was used by the Court of Appeal in the *Polemis*[56a] case but has since been discredited in England, though it retains an important place in the law of France and some other countries?[57]

'Direct' has not been judicially defined but it might either mean 'coming in time immediately after the wrongful act' or, as Prosser

[52] *The Calliope* [1970] P. 172; *Jacques* v. *Matthews* [1961] SASR 205.
[53] *O'Donnell* v. *Reichard* [1975] VR 916; *James* v. *Woodall Duckham* [1969] 2 All ER 794 (CA); Bass and Wright, 'An Objective Study of the Whiplash Victim and Compensation Syndrome', (1974–5) 6 *Man. LJ* 333; D. B. Williams, 'Compensationitis: Real *v.* Imaginary', (1977) 127 *New LJ* 757.
[54] Cf. *Lampert* v. *Eastern National Omnibus* [1954] 2 All ER 719.
[55] *Hird* v. *Gibson* [1974] QR 14.
[56] *Contra*, apparently, *Jones* v. *Jones*, *The Times* 29.6.1984.
[56a] *Re Polemis* [1921] 3 KB 560, 570, *per* Bankes LJ; 576, *per* Scrutton LJ. Cf. *Morrison S.S. Co.* v. *Greystoke Castle (Cargo Owners)* [1947] AC 265, 295–6; *The Carslogie* [1952] AC 292. In *Patten* v. *Silberschein* [1936] 3 WWR 169 (subsequent theft of wallet) and *Pigney* v. *Pointer's Transport Services* [1957] 1 WLR 1121 (subsequent suicide) an extraordinarily wide interpretation was given to the notion of 'direct' consequences. Such cases should be decided in the light of their particular facts. On the principles set out in this chapter the first decision is incorrect, the second probably correct but near the borderline.
[57] Honoré, *IECL*, xi, chap. 7-71 to 7-73.

says, following 'in sequence from the effect of the defendant's act
upon conditions existing and forces already in operation at the time,
without the intervention of any external forces which come into
active operation later'.[58] If the first meaning is adopted 'direct' is
seen to be an obscure way of referring to the fact that, if harm occurs
very shortly after the wrongful act, it is unlikely that any event will
have occurred which would constitute a coincidence and so negative
causal connection. This will not always be so for the victim might
be negligently run over by defendant and immediately afterwards
struck by a falling tree.

The second suggested sense of 'direct' merely shifts the problem
one stage farther back, for we can only apply it if we know what is
to count as a 'force coming into active operation later'. But this is
only a metaphorical way of referring to the distinction between
normal and abnormal intervening events, as Prosser himself recognizes when he goes on to say 'No new external factor of *significance*
intervenes.'[59] So 'direct' is no help in solving causal problems until it
is replaced by some more literal expression.

*Criticism of the principle that coexisting circumstances do not nega-
tive causal connection.* The principle here discussed is accepted even
by many modern theorists who are anxious to substitute more
rational policies for the 'obscurities' of proximate cause.[60] But it
certainly results in responsibility being extended in unexpected ways,
and this has led to much criticism, perhaps more on the Continent
than in common law countries. It is not easy to justify a set of
principles which makes a defendant responsible for *X*'s death if he
negligently runs *X* over and kills him because *X* has already, unknown to defendant, been seriously injured, but relieves him of
responsibility if he runs him over and *X* is killed in a further accident
on the way to hospital. Surely it should not make a difference
whether *X* was injured just before or just after defendant's act. The
defence of the principle is that it is rooted in common-sense ideas
of human action and causation, which picture human beings as
intervening on a stage already set. The action consists in the difference made to the scene, and ends when a new actor appears or an
abnormal event disturbs the ordinary course of things. This way

[58] *Torts*, pp. 263-4. There is a careful survey of judicial interpretations of 'direct'
by Egbert J. in *Duce* v. *Rourke* [1951] 1 WWR (NS) 305. Cf. *British Celanese* v. *Hunt*
[1969] 2 All ER 1252.
[59] *Torts*, p. 264. Our italics. Cf. McLaughlin, (1925-6) 39 *Harv. LR* 149, 165:
'Eating bacteria is so foreseeable that it would not be an isolating force.' As we
pointed out earlier mere conditions always include some events later in time than the
putative cause. Above, pp. 71-2.
[60] Prosser, p. 261. 'There is almost universal agreement upon liability beyond the
risk for quite unforeseeable consequences when they follow an impact upon the
person of the plaintiff.'

of looking at human action makes natural a distinction between coexisting circumstances which do not limit responsibility and subsequent events, which may.

A related but distinct point is that this common-sense distinction does not discriminate between normal and abnormal coexisting circumstances. It seems unjust that a defendant should pay full damages when an abnormal susceptibility of plaintiff, of which he did not know, has contributed to the harm. The solution for this is not to abandon common-sense causal principles, but to allow for the reduction of damages in the light of plaintiff's or decedent's abnormal susceptibility. In practice, courts in common law countries do take account of the pre-existing injury, predisposition, or predicament of the victim in assessing damages, whenever the evidence enables them to do so.[61] For example, when defendant has caused the victim's death but the victim would in any case have died shortly afterwards the damages may be nominal or even nil.[62] It has been argued that a distinction should be drawn between a pre-existing condition which in its natural progression would have affected the victim and one which required an external trigger such as the defendant's conduct to set it off.[63] But this distinction appears unsound.[64] At most, it may be said that the chance of an external trigger is sometimes slight, so that the reduction of damages on its account will not be great. Though the defendant has the burden of adducing evidence of the possibility of harm triggered by a later event,[65] he need not show that there was more than an even chance of its occurrence.[66]

There may also be circumstances in which it will amount to contributory negligence on the part of the victim to expose himself

[61] *Batchelor* v. *Polder* [1961] 1 Ll. LR 247; *Cutler* v. *Vauxhall Motors* [1971] 1 QB 418 (CA); *Zumeris* v. *Testa* [1972] VR 839; *Watts* v. *Rake* (1960) 108 CLR 158; *Hole* v. *Hocking* [1962] SASR 128; *Muoio* v. *MacGillivray* [1962] QR 554; *Wilson* v. *Peisley* (1975) 7 ALR 571 (there must be 'real possibility' that plaintiff would anyway have been affected); *McCoy* v. *Watson* (1976) 13 SASR 506 (alcoholism); *Smith* v. *Maximovitch* (1968) 68 DLR 244 (bad teeth); *Smith* v. *Leech Brain* [1962] 2 QB 405; *Taylor* v. *Scott* [1966] 1 NSWR 454; *General Motors-Holden* v. *Moularas* (1964) 111 CLR 234 but *contra* when the condition was very unlikely to have affected plaintiff: *Enge* v. *Piers* (1973) 41 DLR 3d 623; *Dahl* v. *Grice* [1981] VR 513, 525.

[62] *Kerry* v. *England* [1898] AC 742; *Dillon* v. *Twin State Gas & Electric Co.* (1932) 163 Atl. 111; *Von Hartman* v. *Kirk* [1961] VLR 544.

[63] *Marcroft* v. *Scruttons* [1954] 1 Ll. LR 395, 401; *Owen* v. *Reid* [1968] 3 NSWR 88; U. Wagner, 'Successive Causes and the Quantum of Damages in Personal Injury Cases', (1972) 10 *Osgoode Hall LJ* 369, 374-7.

[64] *Australian Aluminium* v. *Goulding* [1964-5] NSWR 1718; Luntz, Hambly, and Hayes, 2. 2. 08.

[65] *Davidson* v. *Howe* (1977) 14 ALR 482.

[66] J. H. King, Jun., 'Causation, Valuation and Chance in Personal Injury Torts Involving Pre-existing Conditions and Future Consequences', (1981) 90 *Yale LJ* 1353; *contra Corrie* v. *Gilbert* [1965] SCR 457.

unnecessarily to danger while suffering from a particular susceptibility.[67] The existence of the susceptibility itself, however, is not normally treated as amountng to fault, even if, as in the case of alcoholism, the conduct of the victim has conduced to it.[68]

Animal Behaviour

In this section and the following one entitled 'Non-voluntary but Abnormal Human Conduct' we are only concerned to bring out certain points where the principles worked out for physical events do not apply and we therefore treat the subject very shortly.

It is necessary in causal inquiries to distinguish two sorts of animal behaviour. What an animal does may either be independent of the wrongful act and its admitted consequences, or, in a sense, dependent on it, i.e. the animal would not have done what it did but for the wrongful act. This distinction between dependent and independent behaviour may be simply illustrated as follows.

Suppose plaintiff is wrongfully imprisoned by defendant in a field where there is a bull. Plaintiff might be injured by the bull either because, just at that moment, the bull happened to see its mate on the other side of the field and charged in that direction, knocking plaintiff down on the way, or because the bull saw plaintiff and attacked him. In the first case the bull would have moved as it did independently of plaintiff's presence. In the second the bull's conduct is a reaction to plaintiff's presence, itself a consequence of the wrongful act of defendant and hence we describe it, in the language appropriate to human responses or reactions, as an 'attack'.

Independent behaviour. Here the same criteria apply as were outlined above in the case of physical events. The animal behaviour, if it is to negative causal connection, must, in conjunction with the prior contingency, form an abnormal or 'very unlikely' sequence of events; it must not be designed; it must be subsequent to the wrongful act. For instance it was a coincidence, when defendant ran a train at an excessive speed, that a cow kicked a man so that he fell under the train[69] or, when defendant collected water from his gutters in a wooden box, that a rat gnawed a hole in the box.[70]

Dependent behaviour. When the animal behaviour is a response to the prior contingency or its admitted consequences, the question

67 *Murphy* v. *McCarthy* (1974) 9 SASR 424. Cf. J. Nguyen Thank Nha, 'L'influence des prédispositions de la victime sur l'obligation à réparation du défendeur à l'action en responsabilité', (1976) 74 *Rev. trim. dr. civ.* 1.
68 *Murphy* v. *McCarthy* (1974) 9 SASR 424.
69 *Schreiner* v. *G.N.R. Co.* (1902) 86 Minn. 245, 90 NW 400.
70 *Carstairs* v. *Taylor* (1871) LR 6 Ex. 217. Cf. *Gilman* v. *Noyes* (1876) 57 NH 627 (jury question whether presence of bears which devoured sheep sufficiently extraordinary).

whether such behaviour negatives causal connection depends not on the abnormality of the conjunction of events but on whether the behaviour is in accordance with the 'nature' of an animal of the kind in question.[71] If not, the animal's behaviour, though dependent in the sense explained, negatives causal connection. This notion of what is natural is strongly influenced by what is usual for the species or individual, but it depends also on human notions of the behaviour which is proper for the animal. Hence the use of the notions of a 'vicious' or 'well-behaved' animal. The concept of 'natural behaviour' is partly but not wholly factual.

Thus it has been held natural for a cow, on regaining consciousness after being stunned through defendant's negligence,[72] to attack a woman but not for a horse to kick a child in the absence of evidence of provocation[73] or for a peaceable cow to kick a man who fell, through defendant's negligence, on a barn floor.[74] Special characteristics of the particular animal may be used as evidence in establishing what its 'nature' is and whether or not its behaviour on a particular occasion is in accordance with its nature. Thus it has been held to be in the nature of a rather restless though not vicious pony, when left unattended for half an hour, to put its feet on the pavement, knock a lady down, and paw her with its feet.[75]

Non-voluntary but Abnormal Human Conduct

Here again a similar distinction must be drawn between dependent and independent conduct. So far as independent conduct is concerned the same principles apply as in the case of physical states or events and independent animal behaviour. Thus an abnormal circumstance existing at the time of the wrongful act does not negative causal connection between the act and the harm, even if it is itself the consequence of some prior non-voluntary human conduct.[76] Similarly a coincidence negatives causal connection even if it

---

71 *Searle* v. *Wallbank* [1947] AC 341, 360; *Cox* v. *Burbidge* (1863) 13 CB (NS) 430, 143 ER 171; *Aldham* v. *United Dairies* [1940] 1 KB 507; *Wormald* v. *Cole* [1954] 1 QB 614, 627, 632. *Contra*: for cattle trespass, *Wormald* v. *Cole* [1954] 1 QB 614, 625. The plaintiff in *Wormald* v. *Cole* could not now succeed since in England the Animals Act 1971, ss. 1(1)(c) and 4, excludes recovery for personal injuries suffered through cattle trespass; but the causal principle is unaffected.

72 *Brown* v. *Travelers Indemnity Co.* (1947) 28 NW 2d 306, 251 Wis. 188. Cf. *Sneesby* v. *Lancs. & Yorks. R. Co.* (1875) 1 QBD 42; *Hill* v. *New River Co.* (1868) 9 B. & S. 303; *Halestrap* v. *Gregory* [1895] 1 QB 561; *Isham* v. *Dow's Estate* (1898) 70 Vt. 588, 41 Atl. 585.

73 *Cox* v. *Burbidge* (1863) 13 CBNS 430. There was no proof of *scienter* in this case. Cf. *Lathall* v. *Joyce* [1939] 3 All ER 854.

74 *Funkhauser* v. *Goodrich* (1949) 210 Pac. 2d 487 (Or.).

75 *Aldham* v. *United Dairies* [1940] 1 KB 507. Cf. *Harris* v. *Mobbs* (1878) 3 Ex. D. 268.

76 *Hill* v. *New River Co.* (1868) 9 B. & S. 303.

is constituted by a conjunction of the defendant's wrongful act and the non-voluntary conduct of a third party.[77] This is perhaps the best explanation of the difficult case of *Woods* v. *Duncan*,[78] where, though the painters negligently obstructed the test-cock of the submarine's torpedo tube, Lt. Woods's use of it without knowledge of the obstruction, for an unusual purpose for which it was not intended, together with the unexplained opening of the bow-cap, was a double coincidence relieving them of liability.[79]

Dependent conduct. If the non-voluntary human conduct is a response or reaction to defendant's wrongful act or some admitted consequence of that act, it cannot be termed a coincidence, for the wrongful act will in such cases have provided a motive or opportunity for the intervention. Nevertheless it will negative causal connection if 'not in accordance with human nature'. But here, in contrast with animal behaviour, it is not usual for the courts to take 'natural' as meaning 'natural given the idiosyncrasies of the individual'. In relation to human conduct, still more than to animal behaviour, the notion of what is 'natural' is strongly influenced by moral and legal standards of proper conduct, though weight is also given to the fact that certain conduct is usual or ordinary for a human being.

An illustration of the mixed character of the question involved here is to be found in *Lynch* v. *Knight*,[80] where the question was whether a husband's act in sending his wife back to her parents was the natural consequence of his believing a false accusation that his wife was a liar and had 'nearly' been seduced before her marriage. The wife's slander action failed for reasons unconnected with causation, but the majority of the House of Lords[81] regarded the husband's reaction as not being 'natural', because either attributable to his own idiosyncrasies[82] or at any rate not reasonable[83] or lawful, whereas a similar reaction to an accusation of adultery against his wife would have been 'natural'; but Lord Wensleydale, stressing the factual element in the notion of 'natural' behaviour, was of opinion that to make the words actionable the consequences must be such as 'taking human nature as it is, with its infirmities, and having regard to the

[77] Above, pp. 164-8.
[78] [1946] AC 401.
[79] 'But what in the present case is decisive is the extraordinary combination of circumstances which produced the disaster.' Lord Simon, ibid., p. 421. 'From the common sense or any other point of view the cause of the accident was . . . what might be termed the double event, viz. the opening of the door when the bow-cap was open.' Lord Russell of Killowen at p. 426.
[80] (1861) 9 HLC 577, 11 ER 854.
[81] Lords Campbell and Cranworth.
[82] Ibid., p. 592, *per* Lord Campbell.
[83] On unreasonable refusal to undergo treatment by an injured workman see pp. 359-61. *McAuley* v. *London Transport* [1957] 2 Ll. LR 500.

relationship of the parties concerned, might fairly and reasonably have been anticipated and feared would follow from the speaking the words, not what would reasonably follow or what we might think ought to follow'.[84]

Gross negligence. Whereas ordinary negligence on the part of an intervening actor is not usually held to exclude a tortfeasor's responsibility,[85] gross or extraordinary negligence is held to do so.[86]

Thus, a mistake in treatment by a doctor is usually held to negative causal connection if it is extravagant from the point of view of medical practice or hospital routine,[87] though run-of-the-mill medical negligence does not.[88] In *Purchase* v. *Seelye*[89] plaintiff, injured through a railroad's negligence, was operated on by defendant on the wrong side. Asked to explain this defendant said: 'I took you for another patient of mine that had a hernia on the left side.' The court held that a release given to the railway did not bar the action against defendant because his mistake was so extravagant that the unauthorized operation could not count as the consequence of the railway's wrong. But a non-negligent medical mistake[90] or one which, though negligent, might ordinarily be made, does not relieve the original wrongdoer,[91] for 'the liability to mistakes in curing is incident to a broken arm'.[92] Negligent mistakes in repairing property,

---

[84] *Lynch* v. *Knight* (1861) 9 HLC 577, 600; *Jones* v. *Jones* (*The Times* 29.6.1984: 'foreseeable' that brain damage to husband would lead to break-up of marriage).

[85] Above, p. 152.

[86] *Restatement of Torts*, s. 447(c). *Giles* v. *Consolidated Freightways* (1952) 244 Pac. 2d 248, 250. *Pilvelis* v. *Plains Township* (1940) 140 Pa. Super. 561, 14 Atl. 2d 557; *Hand* v. *Best Motor Accessories* (1962) 34 DLR 2d 282; *Bradford* v. *Kanellos* (1974) 40 DLR 3d 578 (hysterical conduct of customer when fire broke out in restaurant owing to defendant's negligence); *Priestly* v. *Gilbert* [1972] 3 Ont. R. 501. Below, p. 217.

[87] *Restatement of Torts*, s. 447(c); *Martin* v. *Isbard* (1946) 48 WALR 52 ('inexcusably bad medical advice').

[88] *Moore* v. *A.G.C. Insurances* [1968] SASR 389; cf. *Lawrie* v. *Meggitt* (1974) 11 SASR 5; *Murphy* v. *McCarthy* (1974) 9 SASR 424.

[89] (1918) 231 Mass. 434, 121 NE 413 8 ALR 503. Cf. *Piedmont Hospital* v. *Truitt* (1933) 172 SE 237 (Ga.); *Mercer* v. *Gray* [1941] 3 DLR 564; *Martin* v. *Isbard* (1947) 48 WALR 52. For a non-medical mistake see *Medved* v. *Doolittle* (1945) 19 NW 2d 788 (Minn.): 'extraordinary and culpable negligence', p. 791.

[90] *Watson* v. *Grant* (1970) 72 WWR 665 (two unnecessary operations advised without negligence!).

[91] *Restatement*, s. 457, illustration 1. *Thompson* v. *Fox* (1937) 326 Pa. 209, 192 Atl. 107, 112 ALR 550; *McAvoy* v. *Roberts & Mander Stove Co.* (1953) 98 Atl. 2d 231, 173 Pa. Super. 516; *Gray* v. *Boston Elevated R. Co.* (1913) 102 NE 71 (Mass.); *Thompson* v. *Toorenburgh* (1972) 29 DLR 3d 608 (BC); *Mercer* v. *Gray* [1941] 3 DLR 564.

[92] *Pullman Palace Car Co.* v. *Bluhm* (1884) 109 Ill. 20, 25. Lord MacDermott, dissenting, would have excluded liability 'in regard to acts of surgical negligence of such an exceptional kind that what has been done cannot fairly be related to an endeavour to cure or reduce the infirmity—as, e.g., where a workman loses a sound limb because the surgeon takes him for somebody else' *Hogan* v. *Bentinck Collieries* [1949] 1 All ER 588, 601. For medical mistakes in criminal law see below, pp. 352–62.

on the other hand, are often treated as negativing causal connection.[93] This may reflect a tendency of courts, on grounds of legal policy, to give more weight to the protection of persons than of property.

It will be evident from this short survey of animal and human behaviour that the notion of what is natural or unnatural for a man or animal to do has some affinity with the contrast between what is normal and abnormal, but depends on a blend of factual and normative ideas.

[93] *Exner Sand & Gravel* v. *Petterson Lighterage* (1959) 258 F. 2d. 1; Keeton, *Legal Cause* (1963), p. 71 n. 83.

VII

THE LAW OF TORT: INDUCING WRONGFUL ACTS, OCCASIONING HARM

CAUSING harm by one's own act, inducing another to do harm, providing opportunities for others to do harm, are grounds for responsibility sufficiently similar to justify the use by legal writers of the expression 'causal connection' to refer to them all.[1] Yet if we are to understand the development and evaluate the use of causal notions in the law of tort it is important to see how the idea of causing harm by one's own act (of which a blow inflicting bodily injury is a plain example) differs from the idea of inducing another to do harm, from the other variants of interpersonal transactions, and from the provision of opportunities, the logical structure of which was considered at the end of Chapter II.[2]

Accordingly in this chapter we first study the place in the law of tort of such notions as 'inducing', 'enticing', and 'intimidating' and the dividing lines drawn by courts between these and merely 'advising' or 'facilitating' another's action. Secondly we consider a segment of the law of negligence and certain types of breach of statutory duty where liability is based on the fact that the party in default has provided an opportunity or occasion for other persons to do harm or for natural phenomena of an extraordinary or coincidental character to cause it. This ground of liability has analogies both with the standard case of causing harm by one's own act and with interpersonal transactions.[3] The main feature that unifies 'inducing wrongful acts' and 'occasioning harm' is that these two types of 'causal connection' (to use the expression in the wide sense commonly found in legal writings) are not negatived by the factors that negative the simpler type of causal connection studied in Chapter VI: for both the forms of causal connection between wrongdoer's action and eventual harm studied in this chapter may be traced through an intervening voluntary action and the second form may also be traced through an intervening coincidence. Once the existence of liability is established in one of these ways, however, its extent is generally limited by the factors (voluntary human conduct, abnormality) described in that chapter.

1 Above, p. 62.
2 Above, p. 51.
3 Above, p. 59.

It is important in this connection to observe the growing tendency of some courts, especially in America, to use as the criterion of the extent of responsibility the question whether defendant's wrongful act provided an opportunity or occasion for harm of the sort which may reasonably be regarded as within the scope of the rule he has violated, and not to concern themselves with the manner in which in the particular case the harm arose. This tendency, if continued, will reduce the importance of the classifications made in Chapter VI of facts which do or do not negative causal connection, so far as the initial establishment of liability is concerned. It will to that extent work in favour of the risk theory studied in Chapter IX. In so far, however, as the risk theory is applied to the extent of liability and the solution of the problem of ulterior harm, it confers on the courts so wide a discretion in judging what forms of harm are within the scope of the legal rule violated that the criteria used will in practice resemble that blend of condition *sine qua non* and 'legal policy' or 'sense of justice' advocated by the theorists whose views are studied in Chapters IV and X.

I. INDUCING WRONGFUL ACTS

Conspiracy, interference with contractual relations, intimidation, enticement, and deceit are the principal torts where a relationship between two persons of the sort here called 'interpersonal trans-actions'[4] constitutes an essential element in liability, though other torts may be committed by means of such transactions.[5] We discuss these five torts separately in order to identify the precise form of the required relationship. The reader should bear in mind, together with the general characteristics of this family of notions, the following distinctions specially relevant to these five torts. The courts in general distinguish between advice, which is not sufficient for liability, and a variety of relationships which go beyond mere advice and constitute some form of coercion or inducement. The distinction underlying the decisions (and sometimes expressly recognized in them) is similar to that noted in Chapter II.[6] One who merely advises another may do no more than draw attention to facts which show how eligible or desirable a given course of action is; whereas one who induces, and *a fortiori* one who makes or causes another to act, does something, if only by his words, to make a given course of action more eligible

[4] Generally described above, pp. 51–9.
[5] *Guille* v. *Swan* (1822) 19 Johns. NY 381, 10 Am. Dec. 234; *Fabbri* v. *Morris* [1947] 1 All ER 315 (attracting crowds); *Carney* v. *de Wees* (1949) 136 Conn. 256, 70 Atl. 2d 142 (provoking another driver to drive carelessly, so injuring plaintiff).
[6] pp. 54–5.

or desirable in the eyes of the other than it would otherwise have been, or seem more eligible or desirable than it really is.

Inducement may take various forms, depending on what is said or done to make the action in question more eligible or make it seem so. If threats or actual violence are used, or if the influence of a person in authority is exercised, we speak of 'coercion' and of the person influenced as 'made' or 'caused' to do what he does. Sometimes the influence takes one of many forms of 'inducement' short of coercion. Bribes or rewards may be offered, false statements may be made, or a person may go beyond mere advice by adding insistent requests, making emotional appeals, or by exploiting a 'personal influence' which depends on some existing relationship of affection or respect between the parties.

Courts in discussing these cases use, not always consistently, a varied vocabulary. Sometimes, as with 'induce' and 'procure' or with 'advise' and 'counsel', we have to do with mere stylistic variants. But the main distinction between advice which is not sufficient for liability, and coercion or inducement in its various forms, is clear, though in the tort of interference with contractual relations the further distinction between merely 'facilitating' and 'inducing' a breach of contract may also be important.

Conspiracy. The generally accepted view is that if defendants coerce a third party into acting to plaintiff's harm they have used unlawful means and are guilty of a wrong independent of conspiracy.[7] If they merely induce the third party so to act, by persuasion or giving instructions,[8] they will be liable for conspiracy if the other elements of the tort are present, such as wrongful intention. If they merely warn the third party of the consequences of not acting to plaintiff's detriment, they are not liable for conspiracy.

Allen v. *Flood*[9] conveniently illustrates these points. Allen, a delegate of the ironworkers union, told Halkett and Edmunds, officials of the Iron Company, that unless Flood and Taylor were discharged the members of the union would knock off or be called out on strike. Halkett then lawfully discharged Flood and Taylor. Different judicial views of Allen's conduct were taken. Lord James said that Allen only communicated information to Halkett about what the ironworkers had already decided to do: he did not *induce* them to discharge Flood and Taylor, but merely *warned* them what would

[7] Viz., intimidation. *Tarleton* v. *McGawley* (1793) Peake 270, 170 ER 153; *Garret* v. *Taylor* (1620) Cro. Jac. 567, 79 ER 485; *Allen* v. *Flood* [1898] AC 1, 74, 173.

[8] *Crofter Harris Tweed Co.* v. *Veitch* [1942] AC 435, 440, *per* Lord Simon. There is no inducement if the third party's act is not intended by defendant. *Barber* v. *Lesiter* (1859) 7 CB (NS) 175, 141 ER 782.

[9] [1898] AC 1.

happen.[10] The jury found that Allen *induced* the company to discharge plaintiffs and most of the judges agree with this, though Lord Macnaghten draws a distinction between *procuring* and *inducing* their discharge and says that, since Allen merely stated the truth, he did not *procure* the discharge but at most, in a certain sense, *induced* it,[11] Lord Halsbury, on the other hand, held that Allen *coerced* or *intimidated* Halkett into dismissing the men. His language is strongly causal. The company was within its rights in effecting the dismissal but 'does that affect the question of the responsibility of the person who caused them so to act by the means he used? . . . the question is, what was the cause of their thus exercising their legal right?'[12]

In *Quinn* v. *Leathem*[13] there was again a division of opinion about the character of defendants' act. They were trade unionists who told Munce, the chief customer of plaintiff, a butcher, that unless he stopped dealing with plaintiff they would have no alternative but to call out his (Munce's) employees on strike. Lord Brampton took the view that, in contrast with *Allen* v. *Flood*, defendants were here *coercing* Munce.[14] The jury found that defendants wrongfully *induced* Munce not to deal with plaintiff,[15] which was sufficient to make them liable for conspiracy.

Interference with contractual rights. It is generally thought that, to be liable for this tort, defendant must have *induced*[16] the third party to break his contract with plaintiff. This is contrasted with merely communicating information or giving advice, meaning by the latter 'a mere statement of, or drawing the attention of the party addressed to the state of facts as they were'.[17] The distinction between creating new reasons and drawing attention to existing ones has been criticized[18] but seems to be generally followed. In *Camden Nominees* v. *Forcey*[19] one of plaintiff's tenants, Miss Forcey, *requested* the other tenants not to pay the rent. This was held by Simonds J. to be more

---

[10] *Per* Lord James at p. 178. Cf. Lord Watson at p. 99, Lord Herschell at pp. 115, 130, Lord Shand at p. 161.
[11] p. 149.
[12] p. 74.
[13] [1901] AC 495.
[14] p. 526. Cf. Lord Lindley at p. 538; Lord Halsbury at p. 507.
[15] Ibid., pp. 535-6.
[16] 'Bring about or procure or induce a breach.' *Thomson* v. *Deakin* [1952] Ch. 646, 702, *per* Morris LJ 'Persuading with effect', *Winsmore* v. *Greenbank* (1745) Willes 577, 583; 125 ER 1330, 1332.
[17] *Thomson* v. *Deakin* [1952] Ch. 646, 686, *per* Evershed MR; *Wooley* v. *Dunford* (1972) 3 SASR 243, 290; *Northern Drivers Union* v. *Kawau Island Ferries* [1974] 2 NZLR 617, 622. What is ostensibly the communication of information may in some circumstances amount to persuasion: *Stratford* v. *Lindley* [1965] AC 269, 333, 342; *Torquay Hotel* v. *Cousins* [1969] 2 Ch. 106; *Northern Drivers* v. *Kawau Ferries*, above, at p. 623.
[18] Fleming, *Torts*, 679, arguing that artful advice may be equally effective.
[19] [1940] Ch. 352.

than mere advice and he rejected her explanation that the idea of
not paying rent was 'generated' at the meeting of the tenants apart
from her influence.[20] Again in *South Wales Miners' Federation* v.
Glamorgan Coal Co.[21] Lord Lindley held that the trade unionists
were responsible because 'the so-called *advice* here was much more
than *counsel*: it was accompanied by orders to stop, which could not
have been disobeyed with impunity. A refusal to stop work as
ordered would have been regarded as disloyal to the federation.'[22]

It seems that to avoid liability advice must be disinterested and
unaccompanied by pressure. When an insurance company *requested*
plaintiff's employers to discharge him because of his unsatisfactory
physical condition, the request, it was held, would support an
action.[23] On the other hand, if the distinction between inducement
and advice is taken seriously, defendant should not be liable merely
because he knows that by making a contract with him the third party
is breaking a contract with plaintiff. If the initiative comes from the
third party defendant has not *induced* a breach but merely *facilitated*
it. In *Wilkinson* v. *Powe*[24] Powe, who was running a creamery business, wrote a letter to farmers who, as he knew, were under contract
to have their milk delivered exclusively by Wilkinson's trucks, stating
that after June he would only buy milk delivered in his own (Powe's)
trucks but 'we are hopeful that you will continue to sell us your
milk'. He added that his (Powe's) trucks would call if the farmers
wanted them. It was held that this was 'active solicitation' of a
breach of contract, since the initiative came from Powe's side. On
the other hand, in *Wahl* v. *Strous*[25] defendant settled a claim with a
third party, knowing that the third party had given an irrevocable
power of attorney to plaintiff to settle the same claim. His interference with the contract conferring the power on plaintiff was held
not actionable, perhaps because the third party had independently
decided to break it.

In one case concerning the breach of covenants against the resale
of cars Roxburgh J. took the view that mere *facilitation* of a breach
of contract, without inducement, is enough to support an action.[26]
He thought that 'any active step taken by a defendant having knowledge of a covenant by which he facilitates a breach of that covenant

20 [1940] Ch. 360.
21 [1905] AC 239.
22 Ibid., p. 254. But Lords Halsbury, James, and Lindley all say that it is unnecessary to decide when, if ever, the giving of mere advice may entail liability for
interference with contractual rights: pp. 245, 249, 254.
23 *Harris* v. *Traders & General Insurance Co.* (1935) 82 SW 2d 750 (Tex. Civ. App.).
24 (1942) 300 Mich. 275, 1 NW 2d 539.
25 (1942) 344 Pa. 402, 25 Atl. 2d 820.
26 *British Motor Trade Association* v. *Salvadori* [1949] Ch. 556; cf. *Sefton* v.
Topham's [1964] 1 WLR 1408.

is enough.'[27] He was, however, prepared on the facts before him to find *inducement* in that, even if the motor dealers offered cars to the purchasers in breach of their (the dealers') covenants they did this conditionally on a price being promised by the purchaser and the promise of the price was itself an inducement to sell.[28] But the weight of American authority seems to be that

acceptance of an offered bargain is not in itself inducement of the breach of a prior inconsistent contract, and it is not enough that the defendant has done no more than enter into one with knowledge of the other, although he may be liable if he has taken an active part in holding forth an incentive, such as the offer of a better price or better terms . . . the mere statement of existing facts or assembling of information in such a way that the party persuaded recognises them as a reason for breaking the contract is not enough, as long as the defendant creates no added reason and exerts no other influence or pressure by his conduct.[29]

The elements to be proved are therefore that defendant's conduct was at least one factor which influenced the third party to make up his mind to break his contract and that his conduct went beyond disinterested advice or warning.

Intimidation. A similar distinction between threats and warnings is material in the tort of intimidation. For a union official merely to inform an employer that employees will or may strike is not intimidation.[30] Some statements made in the course of industrial disputes may amount to neither threats nor warnings, but to proposals for changes in the terms of employment.[31]

Enticement. One view is that, in order to succeed in an action for the enticement of a spouse, now abolished in England,[32] plaintiff must show that the spouse's 'will was overborne', viz. that through defendant's conduct she did what she would not voluntarily have done.[33] This was stated by the Court of Appeal in *Place* v. *Searle*[34] to be incorrect; hence, though the wife was a strong-willed woman, it was possible for her to be enticed.

The commonly accepted view is that defendants must be shown to have *induced* or *procured* the departure. Again it seems that mere disinterested advice would not be actionable. In *Smith* v. *Kaye*[35] the wife's sister and sister-in-law visited her and said 'Edith, do you

27 Ibid., p. 565.
28 p. 566.
29 Prosser, p. 934.
30 *Allen* v. *Flood* [1898] AC 1, 130; *Conway* v. *Wade* [1909] AC 506, 510, 514; *Santen* v. *Busnach* (1913) 29 TLR 214 (CA).
31 *Morgan* v. *Fry* [1968] 2 QB 710, 731–2.
32 Law Reform (Miscellaneous Provisions) Act 1970, s. 5.
33 *Sanderson* v. *Hudson*, The Times 29.1.1923, *per* Darling J.
34 [1932] 2 KB 497.
35 (1904) 20 TLR 261.

realise what you have done? [viz. marry the family coachman] How can you exist in such surroundings? You will break the heart of your father and mother. We have come to take you home.'[36] Edith went without saying goodbye to her husband, who was awarded damages for enticement. Defendants appealed to the wife's emotions and thereby showed that, even if what they tendered was advice, they were not indifferent whether it was accepted. In *Place* v. *Searle*[37] persuasion, inducement, or incitement was again contrasted with mere advice. In deciding into which category defendant's conduct fell it was necessary to look at the whole history of the relations between the wife and defendant, not merely at the words 'Come on, Gwen, we will go', which he addressed to her immediately before she left.

It has been suggested that, if the wife asks for advice, defendant, in answering her inquiry, cannot be held to have enticed her. But the fact that a person asks for advice shows that she has not yet made up her mind and, if the answer influences her to leave, the person giving it should be held to have enticed her unless the advice was disinterested.

Deceit and injurious falsehood. Here the main problem is not that of distinguishing advice from inducement, but stems from a difference of legal opinion as to the part which a false statement must play if the case is to rank as one of inducement. To found an action in tort for deceit or injurious falsehood it must be shown that plaintiff was induced to act on the false statement; this is not the same as the requirement that the false statement should have been likely to induce belief and consequent action, and might be satisfied whatever the probabilities. In *Shrewsbury* v. *Blount*[38] plaintiff in an action of deceit was found not to have relied on a prospectus and scrip certificates containing false statements though it would have been reasonable for him to have done so. In *Smith* v. *Chadwick*[39] plaintiff in a similar action admitted that he had not relied on a statement on the front page of a prospectus that a certain person was a director of the company, though an ordinary business man would have been influenced by it. In each case the inducement was not made out. The requirement that a misrepresentation must be of such a nature that 'its tendency or its natural and probable result is to induce the representee to enter into the contract or transaction which in fact he

36 (1904) 20 TLR 262.
37 [1932] 2 KB 497.
38 (1841) 2 M. & G. 475, 133 ER 836.
39 (1884) 9 AC 187, 189 ('inducing cause'). Cf. *Horsfall* v. *Thomas* (1862) 1 H. & C. 90, 99 (purchaser who had not examined gun could not claim that sale was induced by fraudulent concealment of its defects); *Harvey's Investment Trust* v. *Oranjegezicht Citrus Estates*, 1958 (1) SA 479 (AD).

did enter into'[40] is not part of the meaning of 'inducement' but an additional requirement of the law.

It is an interesting question whether inducement can be shown if the party induced would have entered into the contract or acted as he did irrespective of the false statement. There are certainly a number of dicta in the cases and by writers to the effect that the statement must be a *sine qua non* of the act.[41] On the other hand Sir W. M. James VC said, 'I do not think a court of equity is in the habit of considering that a falsehood is not to be looked at because, if the truth had been told, the same thing might have resulted.'[42] Probably the opposing views can be reconciled in the following way. If the representee has already made up his mind to act before the representation is made, the latter cannot be said to have induced him to act, and in this sense the representation must be a *sine qua non* of the representee's decision. Even in this case, however, there may be liability based on the representation having induced the representee to persevere in a decision already reached.[43]

But it is certainly possible for a person to act for two reasons each of which would have been separately sufficient to determine his conduct. If one of these is defendant's false representation it would seem sensible to hold defendant responsible, though the representee would have acted as he did in any case. Suppose that the representee would always be prepared to lend £5 either to an Old Etonian or to a soccer international. Defendant states (falsely) that he is a soccer international and (truly) that he is an Old Etonian, and the representee lends him £5. A court might well decide that both the false and the true representation induced the payment. On the other hand Sir W. M. James's dictum might be interpreted as confined to the law of evidence: the law will not readily presume that the representee would have acted as he did in any case.

It has been held in English law that the representation need only furnish *a* reason for the representee's act in order to found liability;[44] it need not be the 'main' or 'substantial' inducement. In South Africa a different conclusion was reached by Watermeyer J. in *Perlman* v. *Zoutendyk*.[45] Some of plaintiff's money was lent by his father's executor, partly on the strength of a valuation negligently made by defendant. The executor's mind was influenced by the fact that the matter was urgent, that plaintiff had bound himself to lend money

40 Spencer Bower, *Actionable Misrepresentation*, p. 136.
41 De Wet, *Estoppel by Representation*, p. 37.
42 Re *Imperial Mercantile Credit Association* (1869) LR 9 Eq. 223, 226 n. Cf. *Reynell* v. *Spyre* (1852) 1 De G. M. & G. 660, 708, 42 ER 710, 728.
43 *Australian Steel & Mining Corp.* v. *Corben* [1974] 2 NSWLR 202, 209 *per* Hutley JA, citing the first edition of this book.
44 *Edgington* v. *Fitzmaurice* (1884) 29 Ch. D. 459, 485.
45 1934 CPD 328.

to the borrower, that the money lent would ultimately come to plaintiff, and that plaintiff would benefit by obtaining legal work from the borrower. The executor was also mistaken about the identity and extent of the land offered as security. The court held that defendant's valuation was 'only one of a number of causes and of the others [the executor's] misconception as to the identity and extent of the security offered was equally important as his misconception of the value of the security offered'.[46] Liability was here denied because the representation did not provide the sole or substantial reason for the representee's act.

Sometimes it may be difficult for a representee, however honest, to say whether one statement among a large number, e.g. in a prospectus, induced him to part with money. In *Macleay* v. *Tait*[47] Lord Halsbury took the view that in such a case 'if the prospectus is calculated to induce people to take shares, and they do take shares, the prospectus, tainted with falsehood as it is, has acted as a whole, and people cannot be expected to analyse their own mental sensations so minutely as to be able to explain what particular statement had induced them to become subscribers'. This states a rule of evidence, that the court will presume that the false statement was one factor influencing the representee, but here as so often the line between questions of evidence and of substantive law is blurred.

Similar issues arise in anti-discrimination law. In America it has been decided under the Civil Rights Act 1964, Title VII, that where the discriminatory motive played a 'substantial part' in the employer's decision not to renew the employment, the latter must nevertheless be given the opportunity to show that, for other reputable reasons, he would not have rehired the employee in any event.[48] This should be seen as a case where liability is denied despite the existence of a causal relation between the improper motive and the decision. Since it is difficult to eradicate prejudices, there may be reasons of policy for protecting employers in this way.[49]

II. OCCASIONING HARM

There are a number of situations in the law of negligence and breach of statutory duty (and indeed in the law of contract) where a defendant is liable for providing or not removing the opportunity

---

[46] *Perlman* v. *Zoutendyk*, 1934 CPD 328, 337.
[47] [1906] AC 24, 26.
[48] *Mt. Healthy City School* v. *Doyle* (1977) 429 US 274.
[49] M. S. Brodin, 'The Standard of Causation in the Mixed-motive Title VII Action: a Social Policy Perspective', (1982) *Col. LR* 292 (arguing that the decision allows strict requirements of causation borrowed from tort law and increasingly set aside in that area, to defeat the policy of equal treatment); T. A. Eaton, 'Causation in Constitutional Torts', (1981–2) 67 *Iowa LR* 443.

for another to do harm or for a natural event to cause it. The 'causal connection' between a defendant's act and the harm may be succinctly described by saying that he has 'occasioned' it.

The use of this notion in the law is an extension of the general idea, common in non-legal thought, that the neglect of a precaution ordinarily taken against harm is the cause of that harm when it comes about. Causal language is often used to express this idea, even when the neglect consists in the provision of an opportunity to do harm which is both commonly exploited by wrongdoers and of which a wrongdoer takes advantage in the particular instance. Modern developments in the law of tort have extended this notion in many different ways.

We deal first with the notion of providing an opportunity for a human act. The common element in such cases is that defendant may be liable despite the fact that the human act is fully voluntary. But, within this category, different forms of responsibility are found. In the simplest class of case, defendant has a duty to guard against the very sort of intervention which occurs; the point of imposing the duty is precisely to prevent such acts. A banker must lock up his client's securities just because they may be stolen; if an ordinance prescribes that car owners who park their cars on the highway must lock them, its purpose may be solely to prevent the theft of the cars.

Secondly, there are cases in which it is impossible to say that the *only* point of the precaution prescribed is to guard against voluntary human intervention, but it is arguable that such interventions are *part* of what the lawmaker intended to guard against. Take a statute imposing on factory occupiers the duty to fence dangerous machinery. Primarily, no doubt, such a statute is aimed at the risk that workmen will accidentally come into contact with the machinery, but it is arguable that the point of fencing is also in part to guard against negligent or even reckless conduct.[50]

Thirdly, courts may take the view that the point of the statute or rule of common law is to guard against not interventions of a given sort, but ultimate harm of a certain sort, however occurring. It might be argued that the purpose of a machinery-fencing statute was to prevent bodies or clothing being caught in the machinery however this occurred, e.g. even if one workman deliberately pushed another into the unguarded machine, the precise manner of the upshot, on this view, being irrelevant.

Fourthly, a defendant may be held responsible even when it is clear both that the rule violated was not originally adopted in order

---

[50] *Veseley* v. *Sager* (1971) 486 P. 2d 151 (sale of liquor to drunken motorist whose driving later killed plaintiff's husband); *contra Parsons* v. *Jow* (1971) 480 P. 2d 396 (Wyo.) (proximate cause of death at common law is consumption of liquor, not sale).

to prevent the provision of opportunities for deliberately doing harm and that such deliberate wrongdoing is so rare an accompaniment of the violation of the rule that to say that it was the 'purpose' of the rule to prevent it would really be a disguised way of asserting the court's view of what on the whole was fair or just. Suppose defendant drives negligently and runs down a pedestrian, who is knocked unconscious and while in that condition suffers the loss of his watch, stolen by a passer-by. Clearly the rule requiring motorists to drive carefully was not intended to prevent the theft of pedestrians' belongings.[51] Nevertheless, some courts have taken the view that defendant should be responsible in such circumstances, and this might be supported in two ways. One may either say that a defendant who has knocked down a pedestrian has a supplementary duty, at a second stage, to protect him against theft while he is incapable of doing so himself; or that defendant has by a wrongful act exposed the pedestrian to a chance of loss which ought in fairness to be borne by the party at fault. The first reason would bring the case within the first class, where defendant's duty, though at a second stage, is to guard against the very sort of intervention which occurs, but the second involves a different ground of responsibility.

It may seem that the existence of these various forms of responsibility for providing opportunities for others to do harm renders pointless the description in Chapter VI of the traditional doctrine that voluntary human conduct negatives causal connection between a wrongful act and subsequent harm. It is true that, to a lawyer, it would be mere verbalism to speak in this way if every time that, on the traditional principles, a defendant should be relieved of responsibility by a voluntary intervention, he was nevertheless held responsible for the intervention on the new principle that he had provided an opportunity for the intervener to do harm. The law might acknowledge a general principle that, whenever the harmful conduct of another is reasonably foreseeable, it is our duty to take precautions against it or that, if anyone by a wrongful act exposes another to the risk that a third person will deliberately inflict harm on him, he is responsible for the harm which the third person inflicts. If it did so, it would no longer be helpful to describe the law with reference to the common-sense notions expounded in Chapter VI. But, up to now, no legal system has gone as far as this,[52] though there has certainly been a tendency to apply the newer principles

---

[51] Of course it may often be difficult to say what the 'point' of a rule is; but in the example given at least it is clear that danger of theft is not one of the common consequences of negligent driving which led to the adoption of the rule.

[52] *Ely Brewery Co.* v. *Pontypridd U.D.C.* (1903) 68 JP 3; *Carlisle & Cumberland Banking Co.* v. *Bragg* [1911] 1 KB 489; *McDowall* v. *Great Western R. Co.* [1903] 2 KB 331, 338.

partially and in limited spheres. This may reflect the general movement of society away from the principle that, where wrong is deliberately done, only the wrongdoer is responsible. It is possible, though not easy to believe, that the law will ultimately reach the point at which providing others with opportunities to do harm will be as general a ground of liability as causing harm is now.

We now illustrate the different classes of case considered above and draw attention to their restricted scope. An example of the first sort, in which defendant's duty is to guard against the very type of intervention that occurs, is *Stansbie* v. *Troman*,[53] where defendant, a painter, was held liable for the loss of goods stolen by a thief who entered when, in breach of contract, defendant had left the house where he was employed without locking the front door. When defendant railway company offered a girl of eighteen the alternative of being carried far beyond her destination, or being put down, so that on her way home near nightfall she would pass 'a spot which is physically so situated as to lend itself to perpetration of a criminal assault, and which is infested by worthless, irresponsible and questionable characters known as tramps and hoboes', it was held that defendants would be responsible if she were raped on the way home.[54] When defendants, in breach of their contract to recommend a 'good stockbroker', recommended an outside stockbroker to plaintiff, they were responsible when the outside broker converted the money sent to him by plaintiff for investment.[55] In the law of estoppel it must be shown that the detriment to the representee was the consequence of the representation by the principal, which is often to the effect that an agent, who in fact exceeds his authority and acts fraudulently, was authorized to enter into a transaction with the representee.[56]

[53] [1948] 2 KB 48. *Stansbie* v. *Troman* was a case of breach of contract, but it serves as an illustration. Cf. *Davies* v. *Liverpool Corporation* [1949] 2 All ER 175; *Brauer* v. *New York Central R. Co.* (1918) 91 NJL 190, 103 Atl. 166; *Morse* v. *Homer's Inc.* (1936) 295 Mass. 606, 4 NE 2d 625; *Marshall* v. *Caledonian R.* (1899) 1 Rettie 1060; *Geall* v. *Dominion Creosoting Co.* (1917) 39 DLR 242; *Toronto Hydro-Electric Commission* v. *Toronto R. Co.* (1919) 48 DLR 103; *Martin* v. *Stanborough* (1924) 41 TLR 1; *Mtati* v. *Minister of Justice*, 1958 (1) SA 221 (AD); *Steele* v. *Belfast Corporation* [1920] 2 IR 125; *Rawson* v. *Mass. Operating Co.* (1952) 105 NE 2d 220 (Mass.); *Sylvester* v. *New Hospital of Minneapolis* (1952) 53 NW 2d 17 (Minn.); *Winn* v. *Holmes* (1956) 299 Pac. 2d 994; *Howard* v. *Zaney Bar* (1952) 85 Atl. 2d 401 (Pa.) (no liability on the facts); *Hosie* v. *Arbroath F.C.* [1978] SLT 122; *Evans* v. *Glasgow Council* [1978] SLT 18; *Hewson* v. *Red Deer* (1975) 73 DLR 3d 168 (Alberta); *Schuster* v. *City of New York* (1958) 154 NE 534, 180 NYS 2d 265 (police informer allegedly shot because police published his identity without providing protection); *Tarasoff* v. *Regents of California* (1976) 551 P. 2d 334 (psychiatrist failed to warn victim of patient's intention to kill her).
[54] *Hines* v. *Garrett* (1921) 131 Va. 125, 108 SE 690. Cf. *McLeod* v. *Grant County School District* (1953) 255 Pac. 2d 360, 42 Wash. 2d 316.
[55] *De la Bere* v. *Pearson Ld.* [1908] 1 KB 280. A case in contract.
[56] *Scholfield* v. *Londesborough* [1896] AC 514.

In order that a duty to guard against such interventions should
exist in tort law, it has been said in a leading English decision that
the intervention must not merely be a foreseeable possibility but
something very likely to happen.[57] If, however, it was likely to happen, the fact that the conduct was tortious or criminal rather than
innocent does not preclude the existence of a duty to prevent it.
Hence, if borstal boys escaped from custody and damaged a yacht,
and defendants had negligently allowed them to escape, they were
liable for the damage to the yacht.[58] Again, a dealer who lent licence
plates to a buyer, knowing that the buyer could not drive a car, was
held liable for a death caused by the buyer's negligent driving.[59]

An example of the second group of cases is provided by an incident
in Papua New Guinea, where defendant, who by his negligent driving
ran over a child, was held responsible for the reaction of the angry
villagers who in revenge killed a passenger in the car.[60] Breach of
statutory duty provides other instances, in which the duty is imposed
partly with a view to guarding against the type of act that has
occurred; and so, in the light of the policy of the statute, the court
concludes that even a reckless act does not negative causal connection. This is the best explanation of the difficult case of *Stapley* v.
Gypsum Mines[61] where, after Dale had failed to bring down a dangerous stope in the mine, Stapley, his fellow employee, knowing of the
danger, returned to work under the stope and was killed when it
collapsed.[62]

Of course, a duty to guard against another's voluntary intervention is not usually imposed unless such intervention is a common
response to the situation which would be created if defendant did
not take precautions. In a South African case[63] a postmaster employed by plaintiffs carelessly and in breach of regulations left the
office stamp unlocked and allowed a friend to work in the office on
Sunday. The friend was, unknown to him, in possession of some

57 *Home Office* v. *Dorset Yacht Co.* [1970] AC 1004, 1030.
58 Ibid. 1004; cf. *Smith* v. *Lewis* (1945) 70 CLR 256, 261.
59 *Toole* v. *Morris-Webb Motor Co.* (1938) 180 So. 431 (La.); contrast *Estes* v.
Gibson (1953) 257 SW 2d 604, 36 ALR 2d 729 (Ky.).
60 *Government of Papua New Guinea* v. *Moini* (1979) 53 ALJ 19; cf. *Bullock* v.
Tamiani Trail Tours (1959) 266 F. 2d 326 (bus-driver in Florida tells police that black
Jamaican is travelling in white section of bus, so that white bystander overhears and
assaults Jamaican).
61 [1953] AC 663. The employers were held liable for Dale's act both at common
law and as a breach of statutory duty. Below, pp. 215–16.
62 Cf. *Williams* v. *Sykes & Harrison* [1955] 1 WLR 1180; *Hodkinson* v. *Wallwork &
Co.* [1955] 1 WLR 1195.
63 *Union Government* v. *National Bank of South Africa*, 1921 AD 121. Cf. *Cobb* v.
G.W.R Co. [1893] 1 QB 459; [1894] AC 419; *Wheeler* v. *Morris* (1915) 84 LJKB 1435;
113 LT 644; *Ruoff* v. *Long* [1916] 1 KB 148. But see *Liberty National Life Insurance
Co.* v. *Weldon* (1957) 100 So. 2d 696.

THE LAW OF TORT: INDUCING WRONGFUL ACTS, ETC. 199

stolen postal orders which he stamped and initialled and put into circulation. The post office paid the defendant bank the value of the orders in ignorance of the fraud but later reclaimed the money. It was held that, even if the postmaster had been negligent, plaintiffs were not estopped from denying the validity of the postal orders, since it was extraordinary that the friend whom the postmaster had known for twenty-five years should have the stolen postal orders in his possession and should use the stamp to help commit a forgery. The postmaster was not bound to guard against such an unlikely possibility.

It is not every statute or common law rule that is interpreted as imposing a duty to guard against voluntary interventions. Though a general tendency to extend liability in this way is evident it is by no means uniform. To select a modern example: in *Norris* v. *Moss & Sons*,[64] plaintiff, who was employed by defendants to erect a scaffold, knew that the scaffold, contrary to the requirements of a statute, was leaning out of the vertical. He attempted to correct the fault in an entirely unsuitable way but fell and suffered injuries. In an action for breach of statutory duty he failed to recover damages, though the breach of statute was proved and his injuries would not have occurred but for it.[65]

Even, however, where the reason for holding defendants' act wrongful would appear to common sense to be the likelihood of human intervention occurring, the law does not always impose a duty to guard against such interventions, though no doubt it normally does no. As Scrutton LJ rhetorically exclaimed:[66] 'Perhaps the House of Lords will some day explain why, if a cheque is negligently filled up, it is a direct effect of the negligence that some one finding the cheque should commit forgery:[67] while if some one negligently leaves a libellous letter about, it is not a direct effect of the negligence that the finder should show the letter to the person libelled.'[68] The question put can only be answered by saying that the law imposes a duty on one signing a cheque to take precautions against forgery, but does not make one who negligently publishes a libel responsible for its repetition. It is misleading to suggest that the distinction lies in the fact that in the one case the forgery is the 'effect' of the negligence and in the other the repetition not the 'effect' of the negligence. In neither case is 'effect' the appropriate word to describe

64 [1954] 1 All ER 324; [1954] 1 WLR 346.
65 Cf. *Carter* v. *Towne* (1870) 103 Mass. 507; *McKinnon* v. *de Groseilliers* [1946] OWN 110; *Schmidt* v. *U.S.* (1950) 179 F. 2d 724.
66 [1921] 3 KB 560, 577.
67 *London Joint Stock Bank* v. *Macmillan* [1918] AC 777. Cf. *Barker* v. *Sterne* (1854) 9 Ex. 684, 156 ER 293.
68 *Weld-Blundell* v. *Stephens* [1920] AC 956. Cf. *Cobb* v. *G.W.R. Co.* [1894] AC 419; *Baxendale* v. *Bennett* (1878) 3 QBD 525.

the intervening act; in each defendant has merely provided another with an opportunity for doing mischief.

The third class of case, where courts have held that the point of the rule is to prevent harm of a certain sort, however occurring, is somewhat rare but perhaps of growing importance. An example is *Mozer* v. *Semenza*,[69] where defendants did not make their hotel sufficiently fireproof and plaintiffs were injured because an arsonist set fire to the hotel. Defendants were held responsible since 'it is not important whether the fire started in one way or another'.[70] The fourth class of case, when there is liability even though it could not be plausibly argued that the point of the rule was to guard against the harm of the sort that has occurred, may be illustrated by the example of one who negligently renders another unconscious or incapable. Has he a duty to guard against the theft of the other's goods? In *Brauer* v. *New York Central & H.R.R. Co.*[71] the New Jersey Court held that, when defendants' train collided with plaintiff's wagon and horses, stunning him, and empty barrels and a keg of cider which he was carrying were stolen by persons unknown, defendants were responsible for the theft. The court pointed out that 'there were two railroad detectives on the freight train to protect the property it was carrying against thieves but they did nothing to protect the plaintiff's property'. On the other hand the Alberta court came to a different conclusion when defendant negligently injured plaintiff and tools were stolen from plaintiff's car while he was being removed to hospital.[72] The court stated that the theft 'was the consequence of some conscious intervening independent act, for which the defendant was in no wise responsible'. This is correct, but the real problem is whether defendant had a duty to guard against such an act or ought to bear the risk of it. For answering such questions it seems that there are no general criteria. In practice there are few examples of this form of liability.

Physical events. If we now consider cases in which defendant has created an opportunity not for human intervention but for a natural phenomenon to cause harm, they may be grouped into similar classes.

Thus, defendant's duty may be to guard against an abnormal event, just as it may be to guard against the voluntary conduct of a human being or the act of an animal. When defendants wrongfully

---

69 (1965) 177 So. 2d 880, and see below, p. 256, in connection with the risk theory.
70 *Mozer* v. *Semenza* (1965) 177 So. 2d 880, 883.
71 (1918) 91 NJL 190, 103 Atl. 166. *Accord: Patten* v. *Silberschein* (1936) 3 WWR 169; 51 BCR 133. Cf. *Lampert* v. *Eastern National Omnibus Co.* [1954] 2 All ER 719, 720.
72 *Duce* v. *Rourke* [1951] 1 WWR 305 (NS); *Scholes* v. *North London R. Co.* (1870) 21 LT 835.

evicted plaintiff from a ranch where he had shelter for his cattle, and the cattle were lost in the exposed ranch to which plaintiff had to move them, the court held that it was a jury question whether the loss was 'proximately caused' by the eviction, even if the storms were 'unforeseeable', since shelter is particularly designed for severe storms.[73] Though so severe a storm was unlikely, the court formed the view that there was a duty to provide against it. In other cases a defendant has been held liable for harm, despite the intervention of a coincidence, if the ultimate harm is of the sort the likelihood of which is the reason for treating the act as negligent, the actual manner of its occurrence being treated as irrelevant, often on the theory that the manner, as opposed to the type of consequence need not be foreseeable. This may be seen from the American case of *Johnson* v. *Kosmos Portland Cement Co.*[74] where defendants negligently allowed inflammable vapour to remain in the bottom of a barge. The vapour was ignited by a flash of lightning and caused considerable damage. The trial court found that, though defendant was negligent, the explosion was not the 'natural and probable consequence' of the negligence. But on appeal defendants were held liable for the damage despite the lightning which, on causal principles, might well have been regarded as an act of God or coincidence, since the chances of lightning occurring during the period when the vapour was exposed were very small.

Again, in *Gibson* v. *Garcia*[75] the Californian court had to consider a claim by plaintiff who was standing on the pavement near a wooden pole maintained by defendant corporation. The pole was alleged to be rotten and this was known to defendant. A car negligently driven by Garcia struck the pole which fell upon plaintiff and injured her. The corporation argued that Garcia's unforeseeable intervening act, as a matter of law, prevented the injury from being the 'proximate consequence' of their neglect, but the court refused to sustain the demurrer.

The judgment cites many instances in which a similar decision has been reached. Defendant negligently allows a structure to obstruct the highway; plaintiff's horse, frightened by the raising of an umbrella, runs into it.[76] Defendant negligently starts his carriage across

73 *Diamond Cattle Co.* v. *Clark* (1937) 74 P. 2d 857, 116 ALR 912 (Wyo.). Cf. *Carlton* v. *A. & P. Corrugated Box Corp.* (1950) 72 Atl. 2d 290, 364 Pa. 216.
74 (1933) 64 F. 2d 193 (6 Cir.). Contrast *Lyons* v. *Georgia Power Co.* (1949) 78 Ga. App. 445, 51 SE 2d 459.
75 (1950) 69 Cal. App. 2d 681, 216 Pac. 2d 119.
76 *McDowell* v. *Village of Preston* (1908) 104 Minn. 263, 116 NW 470. Cf. *Carroll* v. *Central Counties Gas Co.* (1925) 74 Cal. App. 303, 240 Pac. 53 (negligently kept gas pipe struck by car falling from bridge: foreseeability immaterial). *Contra: Elliott* v. *Allegheny County Light Co.* (1903) 204 Pa. 568, 54 Atl. 278 (plaintiff slipped from ladder and clutched defendant's negligently uninsulated electric wire, suffering burns).

a railway crossing when a train is approaching, but the gates of the crossing are unexpectedly lowered when the carriage is across the tracks, so that plaintiff is pushed from the carriage by passengers trying to escape and injured.[77] In each case plaintiff recovers.

The principle applied in these cases runs parallel to that which we have considered in relation to voluntary conduct. The defendant has provided an occasion for harm of a defined sort. But such harm may be brought about by a conjunction of the defendant's negligent act with third factors of different sorts: some of these may be usual, and not such as would on ordinary causal principles negative causal connection; others may be extraordinary, or such that their conjunction with the defendant's act would constitute a coincidence, and so would on ordinary principles negative causal connection between the defendant's act and that harm.

The exposure of inflammable vapour may commonly be followed by fire, yet some of the ways in which it is ignited may be usual (e.g. the dropping of a lighted cigarette), others very rare (e.g. lightning). Where the law refuses, as it often does, to distinguish the latter class from the former and to treat the exceptional or coincidental form of ignition as negativing responsibility it is, quite reasonably, departing from ordinary causal principles as much as in the cases where it does not recognize a third party's voluntary act as negativing causal connection.

There is certain symmetry about the two groups of cases in the law of negligence where liability is based not on 'causing' but rather on 'occasioning' the harm. What this shows, perhaps, is that the law of negligence is not based on a single principle of responsibility but on several. This being so, there cannot be a unified 'theory' of causal connection in the tort of negligence, because in some contexts it will be necessary to show that defendant's act caused the harm in the strict sense, in others that it occasioned it. There is, however, something to be said for regarding 'causing' as the central relation, which normally must be satisfied, and 'occasioning' as subsidiary. This is because, roughly speaking, there is a general rule that persons must not cause harm by negligent acts but no such rule about occasioning harm.

These conclusions are reinforced if we survey the law of torts as a whole. Inducing others to act is really only analogous to the causing of physical events and the same rules do not always apply to both relations. Liability in tort is sometimes quite independent of causal connection between defendant's acts and the harm, but even when something resembling causal connection is required, we now see that there are a variety of relations appropriate to different torts or

[77] *Washington & Georgetown R. Co.* v. *Hickey* (1897) 166 US 521.

different relations within a tort. The common-sense principles described in Chapter VI still constitute the standard or central case, and
the development of the idea of occasioning harm which the courts
find to be within the purpose or scope of the rule violated, though
important, is not likely to transform the position.

*Limitation of responsibility in cases of inducing wrongful acts and
occasioning harm.* When defendant is liable on the above grounds it
does not follow that his responsibility is unlimited and extends to
all harm of which his act was a necessary condition.[78] If defendant
negligently leaves plaintiff's house unlocked and a thief enters and
steals a box of matches, defendant is responsible for the value of the
box; but what if the thief sets fire to the house with matches? Or if
he steals a sum of money with which he buys and sells heroin, with
harmful effects on those who buy it? Is defendant responsible for
the destruction of the house or the illness of the heroin addicts?
Clearly not, for in each case there has intervened an independent
decision on the part of the thief.

An independent decision here means a voluntary act other than
one which defendant had a duty to guard against. If defendant had
a duty to guard only against theft, the thief's decision to commit
arson or engage in the drug traffic is an independent decision. In this
context it will therefore be correct to say that a voluntary act which
is not reasonably foreseeable, in the sense explained in Chapter IX,
negatives responsibility. But difficult questions may arise in regard
to the scope of defendant's duty to guard against the voluntary
action of others. When a statute or ordinance[79] forbids a motorist
to leave a car unattended with an ignition key in the switch, this
may be designed simply to guard against theft, with the consequent
calls on police time[80] and, perhaps, the danger that thieves may take
risks in driving in an effort to make a get-away.[81] But the prohibition
may also be seen as a measure intended to protect the public against
the high accident-rate that prevails among drivers of stolen cars,[82]
so that the negligent motorist is made to bear the risk of this type of

---

[78] Cf. *Bellows* v. *Worcester Storage Co.* (1937) 297 Mass. 188, 7 NE 2d 588 (not a
'normal' or 'foreseeable' result).

[79] There can also be a common law liability for leaving the ignition key in the car
in a 'skid row' area where theft is specially likely (*Hergenrether* v. *East* (1964) 61 Cal.
2d 440, 393 P. 2d 164 and see (1972) 45 ALR 3d 787) or for doing so after dark
(*Mellish* v. *Cooney* (1962) 183 Atl. 2d 753 (Conn.)).

[80] *Richards* v. *Stanley* (1954) 43 Cal. 2d 60, 271 P. 2d 23; *Meihost* v. *Meihost* (1966)
139 NW 2d 116 (Wis.).

[81] *Ostergard* v. *Frisch* (1948) 77 NE 2d 537 (Ill.); *Ney* v. *Yellow Cab Co.* (1954) 117
NE 2d 74 (Ill.).

[82] *Davis* v. *Thornton* (1970) 180 NW 2d 11; C. J. Peck, 'Liability for Harm Caused
by Stolen Automobiles', (1969) *Wis. LR* 909.

accident, even if it would not ordinarily be regarded as the consequence of his negligence.[83]

For the rest the ordinary causal principles apply. If defendant's
wrong was a failure to guard against a voluntary act, he is responsible for the consequences of that act as ascertained on ordinary
principles. If his wrong was the provision of an occasion for harm
which comes about by an intervening coincidence, he is responsible
for the consequences of that harm, ascertained in the same way. If
he is liable for having induced another to do harm to plaintiff,
his responsibility extends to the consequences of the other's act,
ascertained on common-sense causal principles.

As we shall see in Chapter IX, the risk theory might be described
as a generalization from certain types of case discussed in section II
of this chapter. It is, however, because such cases are still peripheral,
as compared with the central area of decision where voluntary acts
and coincidental occurrences negative liability, that the risk theory
neither tells us what the law in general means by causal connection
as an element in liability nor provides a substitute for it.

[83] *Ross* v. *Hartman* (1943) 78 App. DC 217, 139 F. 2d 14 (though using the language
of 'proximate cause').

VIII

CONCURRENT CAUSES AND CONTRIBUTORY NEGLIGENCE

THE present chapter is complementary to Chapter VI. In Chapter VI we discussed the principles on which a third factor might be held, on the traditional view, to negative causal connection between a wrongful act and some harm of which the wrongful act was a necessary condition. In this chapter we deal with the other possibility, viz. that such a third factor may not negative causal connection but be treated as a concurrent cause. For when the law is faced with two or more wrongful acts or other factors which have some of the characteristics by which causes are distinguished from mere conditions it may regard them as concurrent causes instead of holding that one of them negatives causal connection between the other and the harm suffered.

These cases fall into three groups: in the first both wrongful acts are necessary conditions of the harm. In the second, one act is not a necessary condition of the harm since there is some other independent wrongful act sufficient to produce the harm[1] (additional causation). In the third, even if defendant had complied with the law, either this or another event, which would then have happened, would have produced similar harm (alternative causation). The first group may be termed cases of contributory causation, since here each wrongful act may be said to have contributed to the harm. Of this the main examples occur in the law of joint and concurrent tortfeasors[2] and contributory negligence.[3] Thus in this chapter 'concurrent' is a generic term and covers three distinct types of case, 'contributory', 'additional', and 'alternative' causes. A second topic in this chapter is the working out in terms of compensation of the situation when there are two or more concurrent causes.

(i) The general principle is that in the case of contributory causes each wrongdoer is responsible for the whole damage. As an instance we may take *Grant* v. *Sun Shipping Co.*[4] Plaintiff, a stevedore, was injured because ship repairers left the cover of a hatch off and

[1] This means, of course, sufficient in conjunction with other conditions which were present.
[2] On the distinction between these see Glanville Williams, *Joint Torts and Contributory Negligence*, p. 1.
[3] Similar problems may arise as regards concurrent breaches of contract or trust but these are not prominent enough in practice to justify special mention.
[4] [1948] AC 549.

removed the lights at the side of it and the shipowners, during the lunch interval, failed to inspect the deck and so discover the absence of the hatch cover and lights. It was held that both ship repairers and ship builders were liable in full for the injuries suffered by plaintiff in falling down the hatch. 'I regard it as a well settled principle that when separate and independent acts of negligence on the part of two or more persons have directly contributed to cause injury and damage to another, the person injured may recover damages from any one of the wrongdoers or from all of them.'[5]

When one of the contributory causes is plaintiff's own negligence the general common law principle is that he is not entitled to recover, though this is modified in many jurisdictions by statute. An instance of plaintiff's contributory negligence came before the House of Lords in *The Boy Andrew*.[6] *The Boy Andrew* and the *St Rognvald* were proceeding in a narrow channel on parallel courses when the *St Rognvald* attempted to overtake *The Boy Andrew*. As the *St Rognvald*'s stern came abreast of the stern of *The Boy Andrew* the latter unexpectedly swerved to starboard and the *St Rognvald* was unable to avoid colliding with it. *The Boy Andrew* sank with all hands. It was held that the *St Rognvald* was negligent in attempting to overtake as she did and that *The Boy Andrew* was also negligent in swerving without warning, and that the negligence of both contributed to the sinking of *The Boy Andrew*.

(ii) An instance of additional causation[7] occurs if one accused person stabs the deceased with a knife while another simultaneously fractures his skull with a rock, the act of either being sufficient to cause death.[8] Again, if two fires, for one of which defendant is responsible, combine to burn plaintiff's property, while for the other fire some other person is responsible, we have an instance of additional causation, provided that each fire would have been sufficient to cause the damage which occurred.[9]

Cases may occur which raise special problems because, while resembling those of additional causation, they differ in that one cause neutralizes or counteracts the other. Thus, if one accused person pushes deceased from the top of the Empire State Building and then a second shoots him as he passes the 49th floor, it is the act of the second which causes the death, though but for his intervention the victim would have died as a result of the act of the first accused;

---

[5] *Grant* v. *Sun Shipping Co.*, above, at p. 563, *per* Lord du Parcq. See also *The Koursk* [1924] p. 140, 161; *Hartley* v. *Mayoh* [1954] 1 WLR 355.
[6] *Boy Andrew* v. *St. Rognvald* [1948] AC 140.
[7] Also termed 'over-determination' or 'multiple sufficient causation'. The latter phrase is adopted in Honoré, *IECL*, xi, chap. 7-130 to 7-140.
[8] *Wilson* v. *State* (1893) 24 SW 409 (Texas).
[9] *Anderson* v. *Minneapolis Ry.* (1920) 146 Minn. 430, 179 NW 45.

the intervention of the second neutralizes that of the first, since it prevents the causal process initiated by the first act from being completed.[10] Another variant of additional causation is exhibited by cases such as the following: Defendant $D1$ negligently collides with X: as a result X's leg has to be amputated and he loses the earnings which he would otherwise have made. Shortly afterwards, $D2$ also negligently collides with X so that X's other leg has to be amputated, and the negligence of $D2$ would have been sufficient in the absence of $D1$'s negligence to cause the same loss of earnings.[11] Here both wrongful acts are of a kind sufficient to produce the harm (loss of earnings): they occur in succession but, unlike the last case, the second did not neutralize or counteract the first. The problem arises because if the second act is held to have caused the harm, it must have caused harm already done, while if the first has caused the loss of earnings, it has done so in spite of the fact it has not deprived him of any opportunity which he could have enjoyed.

(iii) Different from all the foregoing are cases of hypothetical alternative causation.[12] Suppose that plaintiff suffers a loss of business because defendant's repairs improperly obstruct the point of access to plaintiff's premises, but that reasonable repairs, which defendant was entitled to carry out, would equally have obstructed the access to his premises. To take another example, suppose that Dr X negligently prescribes the wrong treatment for a certain patient and thereby causes harm; but, had he not prescribed this treatment, the patient would have consulted Dr Y, who would have prescribed it, with similar consequences.[13] The above themes may be varied by supposing a natural event instead of a second wrongful act contributory, additional, or alternative to the first.

I. CONTRIBUTORY CAUSES

In dealing with contributory causes we take cases of contributory negligence[14] as typical and consider joint and concurrent torts only incidentally. Plaintiff's negligence is of legal significance only if

---

[10] Hall, *Principles of Criminal Law*, 1st edn., p. 262.

[11] *McAllister* v. *Pennsylvania R. Co.* (1936) 324 Pa. 65, 187 Atl. 415; *Baker* v. *Willoughby* [1970] AC 467; below, pp. 247–8.

[12] Honoré, *IECL*, xi, chap. 7-126 to 7-129.

[13] Cf. Glanville Williams, *Joint Torts*, pp. 373–4.

[14] Similar considerations apply to the defence of 'misuse' in products liability cases: *General Motors* v. *Hopkins* (1977) 548 SW 2d 344, 350 (Tex.) ('in many cases the question is solely one of causation'), though the rules of law as to the extent to which misuse bars or reduces plaintiff's claim naturally vary from jurisdiction to jurisdiction as they do for contributory negligence.

causally connected with the harm. Thus, to take a simple example, plaintiff's drunkenness did not amount to contributory negligence when he would have been run over by defendant even if sober.[15] But this requirement is sometimes obscured by the ambiguity of the phrase 'contributory negligence' which may mean merely the failure of plaintiff to take reasonable care for his own safety, or may mean such a failure which contributes to plaintiff's injury.[16] We adopt the second sense and use 'negligence' for the first. Thus, the *Restatement* says 'Contributory negligence is conduct on the part of the plaintiff which falls below the standard to which he should conform for his own protection and which is a legally contributing cause, co-operating with the negligence of the defendant in bringing about the plaintiff's harm.'[17]

When is plaintiff's negligence a 'legally contributing cause'? Here there are two views both of which find some support in the cases and divide the writers. The difference between them is one aspect of the general question whether the extent of liability for a negligent act is confined to the harm 'within the risk', i.e. harm, the likelihood of which is among the reasons for holding the act to be negligent,[18] or whether it includes all harm which it was sufficient to produce without the intervention of those factors (abnormal events, coincidences, voluntary human acts) which are held to negative causal connection. We have already considered in Chapter VII certain cases where liability in tort is based on the consideration that the eventual harm is 'within the risk', despite the fact that intervening events have the characteristics usually taken to negative causal connection. In Chapter IX we consider the respective merits of these two approaches in the law of negligence generally. In relation to the present topic of contributory negligence the difference manifests itself in the following way: According to the risk theory it is important to inquire into what precisely plaintiff's negligence consisted of, in order to discover what kinds of harm are within the risk. When this is known, the negligent act will amount to contributory negligence (in the words of the *Restatement* a 'legally contributing cause') if the harm which occurred was of one of these kinds and would not have occurred without plaintiff's act. According to the other theory, the precise description of plaintiff's act has a different importance, for his negligent act will only be taken to be a contributory cause if *all*

15 *Woods* v. *Davidson* [1930] NI 61 (HL).
16 In *Sigurdson* v. *British Columbia E.R. Co.* [1953] AC 291, the jury were asked the single question whether the plaintiff was guilty of negligence contributing to the injury, instead of the double question 'was he negligent?' and 'did his negligence contribute to the injury?'
17 *Restatement of Torts*, s. 463; *Caswell* v. *Powell Duffryn Collieries* [1940] AC 152, 165, *per* Lord Atkin; Street, *Torts*, p. 161.
18 *Restatement*, s. 468; Glanville Williams, op. cit., p. 366.

the features of the conduct which made it negligent were causally relevant, i.e. necessary elements for the production of the harm. If this is the case plaintiff's act will be a contributory cause provided that no factor negativing causal connection intervened between it and the harm.

In a number of cases where plaintiff's negligence has been held not to amount to a contributory cause the decisions can be accounted for equally well on either theory and it cannot be said that the court's language clearly adopts one rather than the other.[19]

Thus, in *Smithwick* v. *Hall & Upson Co.*[20] plaintiff was instructed by his foreman not to stand at the east end of a platform where there was no guard rail and which was slippery because of ice. He nevertheless used the platform and, while he was there, part of the wall above him which, through defendant's negligence, was in bad repair, fell on him. It was held that he might recover for his injuries despite his negligence in standing on the platform. On the risk theory the justification for the decision would be that what made plaintiff's conduct negligent was the risk of slipping, not the risk of being injured by falling bricks. On the strictly causal theory the respect in which plaintiff's conduct was negligent was that he stood on an *icy* platform, i.e. one on which he might slip, but this was causally irrelevant since the injuries he suffered would have been the same whether the platform was slippery or dry. Another reason for the decision was that the risk of the wall falling would have been equally great had he stood at the dry end of the platform.[21]

Again, in *Hudson* v. *Lehigh Valley Railroad*[22] plaintiff, approaching a railway crossing, failed to stop, look, and listen as required by the law of Pennsylvania. He proceeded across on his bicycle and, as he did so, the gate of the crossing was negligently lowered and struck him on the head. The court held that plaintiff could recover despite his negligence. On the risk theory, which the court adopted, this decision might be supported on the ground that the danger of being injured by the gate was not one of the risks

---

[19] *Kinderavich* v. *Palmer* (1940) 127 Conn. 85, 15 Atl. 2d 83, is perhaps a case which would have been decided differently on the strict causal theory. Plaintiff was negligent in crossing the railway track in the path of the westbound train which struck him unconscious and hurled him on the other track where twelve minutes later he was struck by the eastbound train: the court held plaintiff not as a matter of law negligent in relation to the further injuries; cf. *Moor* v. *Nolan* (1960) 94 I LTR 153.

[20] (1896) 59 Conn. 261.

[21] Cf. *New York L.E. & W.R. Co.* v. *Ball* (1891) 53 NLJ 283, 21 Atl. 1052; Eldredge, *Modern Tort Problems*, p. 22; *Gent-Diver* v. *Neville* [1953] QSR 1; *Marshall* v. *Batchelor* (1949) 51 WALR 68; *Schilling* v. *Stockel* (1965) 133 NW 2d 335 (Wis.) (plaintiff negligent to allow arm to protrude from car but damages not reduced when box from truck on other side of street freakishly struck it); above pp. 169–70.

[22] (1913), 54 Pa. Super 107.

which made it negligent not to stop, look, and listen. Alternatively, it might be said that even had plaintiff looked, he would not have seen the gate being lowered, so that failure to look, which is an essential part of the description of his conduct in its negligent aspect, was causally irrelevant to the injuries he received.[23] If plaintiff negligently sits upon an unsafe wall and the driver of a car, not keeping a proper lookout, runs into the wall and knocks it down, so that plaintiff is injured, it has been questioned whether plaintiff would be guilty of negligence contributing to the accident.[24] The answer might depend on whether plaintiff would have suffered the same injuries had he been sitting on a safe wall. If so he would not be guilty of negligence contributing to the injuries, the respect in which his conduct was negligent being causally irrelevant. But it might also be said that it was the risk of falling off the wall, not of being struck, that made his act negligent.

Some cases, however, do appear to reject altogether the principle that the wrongful or negligent features of plaintiff's conduct must have been a necessary element in producing the harm. Thus, some American cases on driving without a licence or on Sunday or otherwise infringing statutory prohibitions lay down that if plaintiff suffers injury while acting in breach of statute he cannot recover from a negligent defendant.[25] Certain of these cases have made use of causal language and have put the decision on the ground that plaintiff's act is causally connected with the harm. Thus, in *Johnson* v. *Boston & Maine R.*[26] plaintiff was an unlicensed driver who collided with defendant's train on a level crossing. It was held that he could not recover despite defendant's negligence and despite the fact that he himself had taken all reasonable care. 'Plaintiff's act of operating a car was causal in the strictest sense. It was not his mere presence on the highway but his operation of the car, which brought him into the collision.' Thus the court appeared to hold that there was a causal connection between plaintiff's unlicensed driving and the harm, even though plaintiff would not have driven more skilfully had he possessed a licence. On a common-sense view this would not be so.[27]

---

23 Glanville Williams, *Joint Torts*, p. 368; Eldredge, *Modern Tort Problems*, p. 20.
24 *Jones* v. *Livox Quarries* [1952] 2 QB 608, 612, *per* Singleton LJ.
25 Above, pp. 120–1.
26 (1928) 83 NH 350, 143 Atl. 516, 61 ALR 1178. Cf. *Dean* v. *Leonard* (1949) 323 Mass. 606, 83 NE 2d 443, where it is denied that, if it is pleaded that a party to a collision is driving an illegally registered car, the violation of the law is, *as a matter of law*, a proximate cause of the collision.
27 Though it would be proper in many contexts to cite as the cause the event identified by a causally irrelevant feature such as the lack of a licence: above, Preface pp. 9–10 and Mackie, *Cement*, pp. 248 f.

The cases to the contrary,[28] which perhaps predominate at the present day, emphasize this by requiring that the want of a licence, etc., should be 'factually causal in whole or in part'.[29] The breach of statute will not be 'factually causal' if compliance with the law, other circumstances remaining unchanged, would have produced the same harm. Decisions of the *Johnson* sort, in effect, go beyond the risk theory and treat a statute-breaker as an outlaw or trespasser on the highway whose conduct disentitles him to the law's protection whether it is causally connected with the harm or not. Sometimes, without going to these lengths, the statute expressly dispenses with proof of causal connection, as when one injured by an intoxicated person is given an action against the person causing the intoxication; it is immaterial whether the injury was inflicted in consequence of the intoxication provided that it was inflicted by an intoxicated person.[30]

Though there are cases which can be explained on either theory, the language of the courts, especially when it is suggested that defendant's action was of a character such as to prevent plaintiff's negligence ranking as a contributory cause, has not been that of the risk theory. In general courts seem to have investigated the character of the acts intervening between plaintiff's negligence and the harm, not in order to assess whether the risk of these occurring was one of the grounds for holding plaintiff's conduct negligent, but in order to determine whether such an intervening act could rank as the sole cause or, in the terminology we have used, negative causal connection between plaintiff's act and the harm.[31] In the following pages we consider such cases in detail and also the related topic of the doctrine of the last clear chance or last opportunity. They show that the basis of decision has very often been that defendant's voluntary or reckless act is, as such, sufficient to negative causal connection between plaintiff's negligent act and the harm. It is more difficult to say whether the courts have also used the notion that an abnormal or coincidental event intervening between plaintiff's act and the harm might prevent the former ranking as contributory to the harm because here the line between a coincidence and what was within the

---

[28] *Mandell* v. *Dodge-Freedman Poultry Co.* (1946) 94 NH 1, 45 Atl. 2d 577, 163 ALR 1370 (driving licence); *Cirsosky* v. *Smathers* (1924) 128 SC 358, 122 SE 864 (driving licence); *Powers* v. *Standard Oil Co.* (1923) 98 NJL 730, 119 Atl. 273 (parking offence); *Weeks* v. *McNulty* (1898) 101 Tenn. 495, 48 SW 809, 70 Am. St. Rep. 693 (failure to provide fire escape); *People's Service Drug Stores* v. *Somerville* (1931) 161 Md. 662, 158 Atl. 12, 80 ALR 449 (failure to label poison).

[29] *Mandell* v. *Dodge-Freedman Poultry Co.* (1946) 163 ALR 1370, 1373, *per* Page J.

[30] *Martin* v. *Blackburn* (1942) 312 Ill. App. 549, 38 NE 2d 939, 942. Above, p. 121.

[31] *The Volute* [1922] 1 AC 129, 144–5; *Jones* v. *Livox Quarries* [1952] 2 QB 608, 616.

212   THE COMMON LAW

risk is very slender. In *Jones* v. *Livox Quarries*³² Denning LJ made
it clear that he did not accept the risk theory, but Singleton LJ
thought that plaintiff had 'exposed himself to the particular danger
which came upon him'.³³ In that case plaintiff rode on the tow-bar
of a lorry and, while in that position, was struck by a vehicle,
negligently driven, from behind. Plaintiff's conduct was negligent
mainly because of the danger that he would fall off while the lorry
was moving. It was not clear that the possibility of his being struck
by another vehicle was one of the reasons for holding his conduct
negligent. Denning LJ was prepared to hold that, even if this possibility was not foreseeable, plaintiff's negligence was none the less a
contributory cause of his injury on the analogy of the principle in
Re Polemis,³⁴ since overruled.

A subsidiary point mentioned by Denning LJ in that case illustrates the slender line dividing the risk theory from the principle that
a coincidence negatives causal connection. He said that he would
not have been prepared to hold plaintiff's negligence contributory
had he been hit in the eye by a shot fired by a negligent sportsman.³⁵
On the risk theory it might be said that the chance of being thus hit
in the eye was not one of the risks which made it negligent to ride
on the tow-bar, while on the causal theory it might be argued that
the intervening act of the sportsman was so highly unlikely as to
negative causal connection between plaintiff's negligence and the
harm. The theories would lead to different conclusions only when
what happened was, on the one hand, not sufficiently likely to be
within the risk and, on the other, not so highly improbable as to
amount to a coincidence. So far as the initial or immediate harm is
concerned, such cases will of course be rare.

The cases which cannot, in view of the court's language, be accounted for on the risk theory are primarily those where courts
have considered whether or not the voluntary character of an act
intervening between plaintiff's negligence and the harm prevents
plaintiff's conduct ranking as contributory negligence. Here the principles used seem very much those explained in Chapter VI. The main
case to be considered is that of a fully voluntary act by defendant,
intended to exploit the situation brought abut by plaintiff's negligence; but a third party may also voluntarily intervene or plaintiff
may intentionally or recklessly bring about his own injury, in which

³² [1952] 2 QB 608, 616.
³³ Ibid., p. 614.
³⁴ [1921] 3 KB 560. A different result was reached in Minnesota when plaintiff's
negligence consisted in riding on the hood of a moving truck which was involved in a
collision with defendant's car, thereby causing injuries to plaintiff. *Guile* v. *Greenberg*
(1934) 192 Minn. 548, 257 NW 649 (plaintiff's negligence did not contribute to the
collision though it may have aggravated his injuries).
³⁵ [1952] 2 QB 608, 616, 618.

case his act ranks as a voluntary intervention. Occasionally the conduct of both plaintiff and defendant has those characteristics which would lead it to be regarded as fully voluntary in the sense explained in Chapter VI.

(i) *Defendant's voluntary act.* This is generally held to negative causal connection both at common law and under a system of apportionment. At common law the leading case is *Davies* v. *Mann*.[36] Plaintiff hobbled the forefeet of his donkey and left him at the side of the highway where he was run over and killed by defendant's wagon and horses, coming downhill rather fast. It was held that the jury might properly find for plaintiff, despite his negligence in hobbling the donkey, if that was not the 'immediate cause of the injury'. The court clearly had in mind a voluntary and intentional act by defendant, for Parke B. said: 'Were this not so, a man might justify the driving over goods left on a public highway, or even over a man lying asleep there, or the purposely running against a carriage going on the wrong side of the road.'[37]

The principle was later extended to reckless conduct by defendant causing injury to plaintiff. In *Anglo-Newfoundland Development Co.* v. *Pacific S.N. Co.*[38] the *Bogota* negligently blocked the fairway of the Clyde but the *Alconda*, knowing this, nevertheless attempted to pass in the narrow space left and, in so doing, collided with and sank the *Bogota*'s tug. It was held that the negligence of the *Alconda* was the sole cause of the loss, and apportionment under the Maritime Conventions Act was therefore excluded. Lord Atkinson said: 'The cause of the collision was, therefore, in my view, the reckless and dangerous action of the *Alconda*, in steaming upstream at the rate and in the way she did in utter disregard of the warning she had received.'[39] Lord Shaw said that the *Alconda* came up the river 'to all intents and purposes regardless of the obstruction altogether' and, if a defendant were not held solely responsible in such circumstances, 'it would always be open to a person negligently and recklessly approaching and failing to avoid a known danger to plead that the reckless encountering of the danger was contributed to by the fact that there was a danger to be encountered'.[40]

This was a case under an apportionment statute but a similar conclusion has been reached in American jurisdictions without an apportionment statute. The *Restatement* says that, subject to one exception, 'a plaintiff's contributory negligence does not bar recovery for harm caused by the defendant's reckless disregard for the

36 (1842) 10 M. & W. 546, 152 ER 588.
37 *Davies* v. *Mann* (1842) 10 M. & W. 546, 549, 152 ER 588, 589.
38 [1924] AC 406.
39 *Anglo-Newfoundland D.C.* v. *Pacific S.N. Co.* [1924] AC 406, 418.
40 [1924] AC 406, 419, 420.

214   THE COMMON LAW

plaintiff's safety'.[41] Thus in *Kasanovich* v. *George*[42] deceased was
negligently walking about 18 inches from a tramline when he was
struck from behind by a tram and killed. The tram driver had had
an unobstructed view of deceased for 200 feet but, according to one
witness, did not brake or sound his gong and approached at a rate
of 30 to 35 m.p.h. The Pennsylvania court held that, if this was
believed, it was a question for the jury whether the tram driver's
conduct showed a wanton disregard for decedent's safety, in which
case recovery should be allowed despite the common law rule of
contributory negligence. Stern J. said: 'It must be understood, of
course, that wanton misconduct is something different from negligence however gross—different not merely in degree but in kind,
and evincing a different state of mind on the part of the tortfeasor.'
Phrases such as 'wilful negligence' or 'wanton misconduct'[43] have
been used to describe the conduct which negatives causal connection
between plaintiff's negligence and his injury. To this Eldredge has
objected that this involves 'an insouciant disregard of the meaning
of words and the fact that "wilful" connotes intentional conduct
while "negligent" connotes unintentional conduct'.[44] This is a ter-
minological point. 'Wilful negligence' would be objectionable as a
phrase if it meant that the person guilty of it both intended and did
not intend *the harm*: but in this context its meaning is that, without
intending the harm, the person knowingly or intentionally (hence
wilfully) neglected to take precautions against harm or did what was
likely to cause harm. The term 'reckless',[45] adopted by the *Restatement*, best expresses this idea.[46] Recklessness is essentially flying
in the face of an apprehended risk, indifferent as to its outcome.

In one case the Privy Council seemed to suggest that an act of
defendant which was neither intentional nor reckless might negative
causal connection between plaintiff's contributory negligence and
his injuries. In *Sigurdson* v. *British Columbia Electric Railway Co.*[47]
plaintiff wished to cross a street and negligently allowed his car to
be hemmed in across a tram line. Defendants' tram collided with his
car and injured him. The tramdriver gave evidence that he did not
notice plaintiff's car until he was 75 feet away. He then applied his

41 *Restatement of Torts*, s. 482(1).
42 (1943) 348 Pa. 199, 34 Atl. 2d 523.
43 *Kasanovich* v. *George* (1943) 34 Atl. 2d 523, 525; Prosser, Wade, and Schwartz,
Cases, p. 600.
44 *Modern Tort Problems*, p. 165. This is said in a discussion of the liability of
occupiers to trespassers.
45 *Harvey* v. *Road Haulage Executive* [1952] 1 KB 120, 126.
46 *Restatement of Torts*, s. 482. But the definition of 'reckless disregard of safety'
in s. 500 appears to confuse recklessness with gross negligence; the latter does not
imply knowledge or apprehension of risks, and merely means the failure to conform
to a very low standard of care.
47 [1953] AC 291.

brakes, but too late. The Privy Council upheld a finding of the jury that plaintiff was not guilty of negligence contributing to the accident. One reason given was that it is not a principle of law that apportionment is excluded when defendant knows of the danger in which plaintiff has put himself, but admitted when 'by his *negligence or deliberate act*[48] he has disabled himself from knowing of it'. Ordinary principles would require a distinction to be drawn between deliberately disabling oneself from knowing of a dangerous situation, which would be evidence of a reckless disregard of danger, and merely negligently doing so. Strictly speaking the point did not arise on the facts of the case since the trial judge's direction to the jury was that 'once [defendant] saw and realised the [plaintiff] was in trouble . . . if he had paid no attention and ran him over the Company would be [wholly] liable'.[49]

(ii) *Plaintiff's voluntary act.* Plaintiff's voluntary conduct may negative causal connection between defendant's wrongful act and plaintiff's harm. Thus, if defendant drove at an excessive speed and plaintiff, in order to commit suicide, threw himself under the wheels of defendant's car but suffered injury short of death, plaintiff, even under a system of apportionment, would presumably be totally barred from recovery. Plaintiff's recklessness may be exemplified by *Porter Co.* v. *Irving Oil Co.*,[50] where defendants negligently piped gasoline instead of oil into plaintiff's tug. Plaintiff's engineer, McLeod, discovered this and attempted to drain the oil in an unreasonable and imprudent way, so that an explosion occurred. Plaintiff's action for damages failed on the ground that 'the chain of causation was broken by the deliberate, conscious and subsequent negligence of McLeod and this negligence of McLeod was the sole cause of the damage complained of'.[51] Here the conduct of plaintiff's employee might properly be described as reckless.

Whether reckless conduct is to be classed as 'voluntary' for purposes of negativing causal connection is a matter on which the courts have a certain latitude. The recent tendency of English courts in cases of breach of statutory duty has been to deny that recklessness on plaintiff's part negatives causal connection with his injuries. In *Stapley* v. *Gypsum Mines*[52] Stapley and Dale were fellow workers of equal status in a gypsum mine. They were instructed to bring down a drummy or hollow stope before continuing work but failed to do

---

[48] Ibid., p. 302. Our italics.
[49] *Sigurdson* v. *British Columbia E.R. Co.* [1953] AC 291, 301.
[50] [1954] 3 DLR 295; *Norris* v. *Moss* [1954] 1 WLR 346; [1954] 1 All ER 324; *Elliott* v. *Philadelphia Transportation Co.* (1947) 53 Atl. 2d 81, 356 Pa. 643.
[51] Above, p. 213.
[52] [1953] AC 663.

so. This amounted to common law negligence and breach of statutory duty on the part of both. Thereafter Stapley returned to work under the drummy roof and was killed when the roof collapsed. The House of Lords held by a majority of three to two, reversing the unanimous judgment of the Court of Appeal, that the claim of Stapley's widow was not wholly barred by his contributory negligence, since Stapley's death was in part a consequence of Dale's wrong. Many will feel that the conduct of Stapley showed such a reckless disregard for his own safety that the view of the minority in the House of Lords is to be preferred.[53] However, it is arguable that, although Stapley's act was voluntary defendants should be liable on the basis, not that their servant caused harm in the strict sense, but that he provided an opportunity for it. This conclusion may be reached in the light of the policy of the Factories Acts which are intended 'not merely to protect the careful, the vigilant and the conscientious workman, but, human nature being what it is, also the careless, the indolent, the inadvertent, the weary and perhaps in some cases the disobedient'.[54] In later cases when plaintiff was reckless a similar view to that in the *Stapley* case has been taken.[55]

In a common law case Denning LJ supported the view that plaintiff's recklessness bars his action. In *Harvey* v. *Road Haulage Executive*[56] defendants left their lorry lying athwart a bypass on a foggy morning. A motor-cyclist approached the lorry from the rear at an excessive speed and saw it a short time before the collision but was unable to avoid it. The Court of Appeal held that there should be an apportionment, plaintiff not being solely responsible. Denning LJ said: 'No valid distinction can be drawn between negligence after seeing the danger and negligence in not seeing it. The only valid distinction in these cases is between conduct which is purposeful or reckless and conduct which is merely negligent.'[57]

When plaintiff's action fails because the harm is the consequence of his voluntary conduct, whether intentional or reckless, it is perhaps strictly speaking incorrect to say that he is barred by his contributory negligence since in such cases his conduct is not *merely* contributory but is described, from a common-sense point of view

---

[53] Lords Asquith and Porter. To these may be added the extrajudicial opinion of Lord Wright: [1955] *Cam. LJ* 163, 171. There is another point mentioned in the judgments in this case, viz. that even if Dale did not *cause* Stapley to return he *encouraged* him to do so. Ibid., p. 679. Above, pp. 51 ff.
[54] *Carr* v. *Mercantile Produce Co.* [1949] 2 KB 601, 608.
[55] *Williams* v. *Sykes & Harrison* [1955] 1 WLR 1180; *Hodkinson* v. *Wallwork & Co.* [1955] 1 WLR 1195; *I.C.I.* v. *Shatwell* [1965] AC 656 (one shotfirer's disregard of his statutory duty was an encouragement to the other to act foolishly).
[56] [1952] 1 KB 120.
[57] Ibid., p. 126.

and also in law, as the 'sole cause'[58] or *the* cause[59] of the harm. The 'defence' is then simply that plaintiff has not proved causal connection between defendant's act and the harm. Often this state of affairs may coincide with one where the defence of voluntary assumption of risk is available. Thus, in *Cutler* v. *United Dairies* [60] defendant's servant negligently allowed a horse to bolt into a field. Plaintiff, who lived nearby but had no experience of horses, went into the field to help hold the horse but was injured in attempting to do so. It was held that he could not recover, both because his interference when there was no moral or legal duty to interfere was a free act[61] (so on traditional principles negativing causal connection between the defendant's negligence and his injuries) and because he had 'voluntarily' assumed the risk of such injury.[62]

(iii) *Third party's voluntary act.* Similarly a wrongdoer is not liable if the subsequent act of another tortfeasor, being voluntary, negatives causal connection between the act of the former and the harm. When defendant wrongfully left a depression in the street and a drunken driver drove into the depression and lost control of his car, so that it travelled 180 feet and struck another depression and then hit a cyclist, defendant's negligence was held not to be the 'legal cause' of the harm.[63] Clearly the driver's conduct was so reckless that it could fairly be accounted a voluntary intervention.

(iv) *Voluntary acts of both plaintiff and defendant.* Sometimes, though rarely, the acts of both plaintiff and defendant exhibit those characteristics which mark them off as fully voluntary and which ordinarily are held to negative causal connection. Thus, both plaintiff and defendant may have acted recklessly. From the point of view of determining whether the act of each is causally connected with the harm these cases present the difficulty of competing analogies. On the one hand it may be argued that since the acts of both parties have these negativing characteristics 'neither can be selected as that

[58] *Norris* v. *Moss & Sons Ltd.* [1954] 1 All ER 324, 326; *Horne* v. *Lec Refrigeration* [1965] 2 All ER 898; *Rushton* v. *Turner* [1959] 3 All ER 517; contrast *Leach* v. *Standard Telephones* [1966] 2 All ER 523. Distinguish the non-causal doctrine that when defendant employer is held to have broken his statutory duty only because plaintiff's breach is imputed to him, plaintiff cannot recover for the resultant injury: *Ginty* v. *Belmont Supplies* [1959] 1 All ER 414. The basis of this rule is the moral injustice of allowing such a claim: *Boyle* v. *Kodak* [1969] 2 All ER 439, 440, 446 (HL).
[59] *Anglo-Newfoundland D.C.* v. *Pacific S.N. Co.* [1924] AC 406, 417.
[60] [1933] 2 KB 297.
[61] Expressly so decided by Scrutton LJ at p. 304. But as he did not intend to injure himself and was not reckless his conduct was not 'voluntary' in our sense.
[62] Cf. *Torrance* v. *Ilford U.D.C.* (1909) 73 JP 225; Street, *Torts*, p. 167.
[63] *Pilvelis* v. *Plains Township* (1940) 140 Pa. Super. 561, 14 Atl. 2d, 557. Cf. *Medved* v. *Doolittle* (1945) 220 Minn. 352, 19 NW 2d 788; *Geisen* v. *Luce* (1932) 185 Minn. 479, 242 NW 8. Above, p. 184.

which is the proximate cause and hence the law must leave both where it finds them'.[64]

But it may equally well be argued that when both parties deliberately contrive to bring about or recklessly disregard the risk of harm which ensues, the acts of both possess those features which ordinarily lead us to treat the agent as the sole cause of the harm and hence each should be responsible for the whole harm.

One apparently easy way out of the difficulty is to sidestep the causal problem and say that plaintiff is barred by his voluntary assumption of the risk of harm, whether he intended it or was merely reckless. This will solve many cases, but does not deal with the situations where assumption of risk is irrelevant, viz. in criminal law, in civil law where statutes exclude the defence, and in cases where one person is injured by the reckless acts of two others not acting in concert. Suppose two motorists, A and B, each drive at a great speed along the centre of a straight highway; each is prepared to have a collision rather than give way, and a head-on crash ensues, in which C, a passenger in A's car, and D, a passenger in B's, are killed. It seems obvious that both drivers should be responsible, civilly and criminally, for the death of both passengers. This result may be justified on the following reasoning: though the general principle is that two voluntary actions cannot be regarded as concurrent causes, this does not hold when each agent knows that the dangerous act of the other is either certain or highly probable.[65] On this footing A's and B's acts are concurrent causes of the deaths of C and D. Hence A and B may properly be held guilty of the manslaughter of C and D and be made to pay damages to C's and D's dependants. If, however, A and B sue one another then, according to the *Restatement*, they will fail because each, knowing of the other's reckless misconduct and the danger involved therein, has recklessly exposed himself thereto.[66] This is clear enough if the defence of voluntary assumption of risk is available, but if it is not it would seem reasonable to apportion the damages; this, at any rate, would seem to follow from the reasoning we have suggested, which treats the act of each as a constituent of the cause of the harm.

In *Stern* v. *Podbrey*[67] plaintiff and others during a strike locked arms and barred the exit to defendant's business. Defendant, a director of the firm, after giving a warning, slowly drove a truck towards the picketers but they stood firm and plaintiff was injured.

[64] *Hinkle* v. *Minneapolis, Anoka & Cuyuna Range R. Co.* (1925) 162 Minn. 112, 202 NW 340, 41 ALR 1377, 1378. Cf. *Nichols* v. *Bresnahan* (1948) 212 SW 2d 570, 357 Mo. 1126; *Rice* v. *Schiller* (1951) 241 SW 2d 330.
[65] Cf. above, pp. 170-1.
[66] *Restatement of Torts*, s. 482 (2).
[67] 1947 (1) SA 350 (C).

She failed to recover since, even if defendant was negligent,[68] her injuries were regarded as caused by her own conduct in deliberately and intentionally exposing herself to a risk of which she knew. Such cases, like those of additional causation discussed later, are anomalous and no single set of principles will neatly account for them. The most that can be done is to exhibit analogies with the central cases to which causal principles apply.

The last clear chance rule

It is now necessary to distinguish the common-sense principle, by which the voluntary act of plaintiff or defendant negatives causal connection between the act of one party and the harm to the other, from a rule which has been adopted in many jurisdictions where there is no machinery for apportionment of damages, viz. that if both parties are negligent but one[69] of them had the last clear chance or last opportunity of avoiding the harm and failed to take it, he is regarded as solely responsible for the harm. We give some extended consideration to this doctrine because it is still applied in many common law jurisdictions, and because the fact that it is often mistakenly presented as an application of causal principles is a source of perennial confusion, and has obscured the nature of the causal principles which are in fact applied in the law of tort.

This rule or doctrine is often traced to the decision in *Davies* v. *Mann*[70] and is stated as if it were a principle or at least a 'test' of causal connection; it is often said that the act of the party who failed to take the last clear chance of avoiding the harm is the 'proximate cause' or 'the cause' of the harm. Thus the House of Lords held that a jury should be asked, in a case of contributory negligence, whose negligence substantially caused the injury and should find for plaintiff if defendant's negligence had done so.[71] It is important to realize that the last clear chance doctrine, though often masquerading as an application of common-sense principles of causation, is in fact a distortion of them; for the notion of failing to take the last clear chance of avoiding harm to the plaintiff is very different from the notion of causing the harm to the plaintiff by a fully voluntary act. In the great majority of cases where the doctrine is applied, the acts of plaintiff and defendant are each, from a common-sense point of view, a cause of the harm to plaintiff, though,

---

[68] The court found that defendant's act was a reasonable exercise of his right of free passage in the circumstances. Ibid., p. 363, *per* Herbstein J.
[69] The rule may operate against plaintiff. *Campbell* v. *Kelly* [1945] NI 70.
[70] (1842) 10 M. & W. 546. Above, p. 213.
[71] *Swadling* v. *Cooper* [1931] AC 1.

as we shall see, courts often speak as if it were possible to identify one, consistently with the judgment of the ordinary man, as *the* cause.

The chief differences between a last clear chance and a voluntary action concern the nature of the opportunity and sequence of plaintiff's and defendant's acts.

(i) *Nature of the failure to take the opportunity.* A simple case of such failure is when 'defendant knows of the plaintiff's situation' in negligently subjecting himself to a risk of harm and 'realises the helpless peril involved therein' and thereafter 'is negligent in failing to utilize with reasonable care and competence his then existing ability to avoid harming plaintiff'.[72] It is important to realize that such failure is not equivalent to any intentional exploitation of plaintiff's situation or to recklessness. At first sight it might look as if the defendant's failure was always fully voluntary, for he must *know* of the plaintiff's situation and *realize* his peril, but his subsequent failure to avoid the harm may well be, and in the overwhelming majority of cases is, merely negligent and not either intentional or reckless. Usually, when fast moving vehicles are concerned, defendant's failure consists in not making the appropriate movements on the spur of the moment and very seldom in an intentional exploitation of plaintiff's situation or in a conscious disregard of the danger to him. In such cases defendant's negligence, though it may involve a knowledge and appreciation of plaintiff's predicament, is not fully voluntary.[73] The elements of reflection, intention and disregard of danger are usually lacking. Thus in *M'Lean* v. *Bell*[74] plaintiff, a pedestrian, was negligent in crossing the street without looking and the defendant, a motorist, travelling fast, did not see her until he was within half a length of the car from her; he then collided with and injured her. It was held a question for the jury whether 'assuming her to be negligent in that sense [viz. in failing to take reasonable care for her own safety] the defender could yet, by the exercise of reasonable care, have avoided striking her'.[75] Here defendant knew of plaintiff's predicament before he struck her, but his act could not rank as fully voluntary, since he did not intend to exploit her predicament nor was he reckless whether he harmed her.

Again, appreciation of plaintiff's predicament at a particular moment does not entail knowledge of what he will do in the future. Especially in traffic accidents, both parties are usually moving and the avoidance of a collision depends in part on anticipation of what the other party is likely to do. Hence in a last clear chance case

72 *Restatement of Torts*, s. 479 (*b*) (i).
73 Above, pp. 41-4, 136-8.
74 (1932) 48 TLR 467.
75 *M'Lean* v. *Bell* (1932) 48 TLR 467, 468.

even the element of appreciation, which is essential to make the defendant's conduct fully voluntary or reckless, may be partly lacking. In *Long* v. *Toronto R. Co.*[76] deceased was crossing the road absorbed in his thoughts and inattentive to his surroundings; defendant's tram driver became aware of this but failed to pull up in time to avoid killing him. The court held that the tram driver's negligence was the *causa proxima* of the death. Here the driver in a sense appreciated deceased's predicament but this did not entail that he knew what deceased would do next, viz. that he had that degree of appreciation essential if his conduct was to be fully voluntary or reckless. When someone is not paying attention to what he is doing his movements are notoriously difficult to predict.

A further difference between the last clear chance rule and the principle that an intervening fully voluntary or reckless act negatives causal connection is that the rule has not been confined to cases where defendant appreciates plaintiff's peril so that his conduct is 'informed'. Instead it has been applied when he 'knows of the plaintiff's situation and *has reason to realize* the peril involved therein'[77] or 'would discover the plaintiff's situation . . . if he were to exercise the vigilance which it is then his duty to the plaintiff to exercise'.[78] Here defendant does not know of or appreciate plaintiff's negligence but he is nevertheless held to have had the last opportunity of avoiding the harm. It becomes more than ever apparent that having the last clear chance does not involve that appreciation of the situation or disregard of the dangers it presents which is one of the elements needed to make conduct fully voluntary or reckless.

In *British Columbia Electric Railway* v. *Loach*[79] the Privy Council extended the notion of a constructive last opportunity to a situation where defendant, through his antecedent negligence, has no chance of avoiding the harm to plaintiff after he learns of plaintiff's predicament. Hence the administrator of Sands, a passenger in a cart, recovered for his death, despite the negligence of Sands in not keeping a lookout at the approach to a level crossing, and the fact that defendant railway's driver was unable to avoid the cart after seeing it because the brake had not been properly adjusted beforehand. Lord Sumner said the railway were responsible because 'whether Sands got in the way of the car with or without negligence on his part, the appellants could and ought to have avoided the consequences of that negligence and failed to do so, not by any combination of negligence on the part of Sands with their own, but solely by the

76 (1914) 20 DLR 369.
77 *Restatement of Torts*, s. 479 (*b*). Our italics.
78 Ibid.
79 [1916] 1 AC 719.

negligence of their servants in sending out the car with a brake whose inefficiency operated to cause the collision at the last moment'.[80]

From this and the preceding examples it seems clear that in jurisdictions where there is no apportionment and no rule of comparative negligence, so that the courts must bar plaintiff for the slightest negligence, unless they can make out the act of defendant to have been the sole cause of the harm, courts often say that defendant's act is the sole cause although it would not ordinarily be reckoned so. Since from a common-sense point of view the phrase 'sole cause' or '*the* cause' is most appropriately applied to voluntary human conduct of which harm is the consequence, the courts attempt to assimilate his conduct to fully voluntary conduct by stressing the knowledge and appreciation which he possessed of the situation, or, where he did not possess this, drawing attention to the fact that he ought to have had such knowledge or appreciation.

Courts have also assimilated the last clear chance rule to common-sense causal principles by treating a person who neglects to take the last opportunity of avoiding harm as guilty of gross or extraordinary negligence, and hence of a reaction to danger so unreasonable as to negative causal connection between prior conduct and subsequent harm. But the rule is not really apt for this purpose; later negligence need not be greater negligence. A closer analogy to causal principles is afforded by the comparative negligence rule adopted in some American jurisdictions. But though there are such analogies, several writers have perceived that the last clear chance rule is not an application of any common-sense principle of causation.[81]

(ii) *Sequence in time.* The last opportunity rule involves the notion that when the one party is no longer in a position to do anything to avoid the harm and when the other knows of his predicament, his negligence 'is exhausted', 'wears out', or 'comes to an end' so that he starts with a clean slate and may recover if *thereafter* the other party alone is negligent. Thus in the *Loach* case Lord Sumner said: 'The consequences of the deceased's contributory negligence continued, it is true, but after he had looked, there was no more negligence, for there was nothing to be done.'[82] In *Davies* v. *Swan Motor Co.*[83] Denning LJ stated the last opportunity rule in the form: 'If the defendant actually saw that a dangerous state of affairs had been created by the negligence of the plaintiff and the defendant, thereafter, by the exercise of reasonable care, could have avoided doing

80 *British Columbia Electric R. Co. Ltd.* v. *Loach* [1916] 1 AC 719, 728. The word 'solely' is very strange in this context.
81 e.g. Glanville Williams, *Joint Torts*, p. 236, correctly distinguishes the rule from 'remoteness of damage'.
82 *British Columbia E.R. Co.* v. *Loach* [1916] 1 AC 719, 724.
83 [1949] 2 KB 291.

any damage, then he is solely liable if he failed to exercise that care' and commented: 'As a proposition of law, it can only be supported by saying that negligence in creating a dangerous obstruction ceases as soon as the driver of the oncoming vehicle sees it.'[84] Denning LJ did not accept that there was or ever had been any such rule.

There are very great difficulties involved in the use in such contexts of the notion of negligence 'ceasing'. 'Cease' might be taken literally to refer to the cessation of bodily movements. A man engaged in a continuing or repetitive activity such as driving or hammering ceases it when he stops driving or hammering. If he is negligently driving too fast or his hammering amounts to a nuisance his negligence or nuisance also ceases in this sense when he stops driving too fast or hammering too loud.

Sometimes, though a man's act is quickly finished, his negligence or wrongdoing may be said to continue because those conditions, the creation of which was wrongful or negligent, continue. If he obstructs the highway by parking his car at right angles to the line of traffic, the initial bodily movements are merely those needed to put the car in this position and thereafter the relevant act has, in the most literal sense, ceased; but the obstruction, which is the consequence of his act and the creation of which was unlawful, remains. So, in an elliptical way, we may say that his unlawful conduct has not ceased.

Neither of these is the sense of 'ceasing' required by the language of the cases. 'Ceasing' is there used metaphorically and means either that at a certain moment it was too late for one of the parties to counteract his own negligent or wrongful conduct, or that on common-sense causal principles the conduct of the other party was *the* cause of the harm. The first interpretation leads to allowing recovery when it is too late for one party to retrieve the situation but not too late for the other, and the latter negligently fails to retrieve it. While there is something to be said for this as a means of making the party whose conduct has been in some way less meritorious pay for the damage, it does not seem to turn on any ordinary causal principle. Only if the party with the last opportunity could *easily* have avoided the harm by taking *elementary* precautions could we justifiably say that his failure to take them was so grossly negligent as to negative causal connection between the conduct of the disabled party and the subsequent harm. In cases of constructive last chance it is moreover a mere fiction that at a particular instant one party could and the other could not put matters right.

The metaphor may be interpreted in the second way with the help of the notion that one party's negligence 'ceases' when the other

[84] Ibid., p. 323.

becomes aware of it in time to take evasive action. But other difficulties arise, for if plaintiff's negligence 'ceases' when the defendant becomes aware of it, then defendant's negligence must presumably also 'cease' if plaintiff becomes aware of it. An accident might then happen in which both parties had been negligent but their negligence had ceased, so that presumably neither would be responsible even under a system of apportionment. This would be a very strange conclusion, but, if it is not drawn, some explanation must be given of why the 'ceasing' occurs in the one case and not in the other. It is of course one of the defects of the last clear chance rule that even if defendant has an opportunity of avoiding the consequences of plaintiff's negligence, plaintiff may well have a simultaneous opportunity of avoiding the consequences of defendant's negligence and, if 'constructive' opportunities are to be counted also, there will be few examples of contributory negligence in which there are not also concurrent opportunities of avoiding the harm. But in any case a party's negligence does not in any real sense 'cease' just because the other party becomes aware of it. If plaintiff's negligence consists in leaving an obstruction in the road 'there is a continuing negligence, which continues after the oncoming driver sees it'.[85] This is to adopt one of the elliptical meanings of 'continue': the negligence is said to continue because the condition wrongfully created continues. If plaintiff's negligence consists in not keeping a proper lookout the fact that defendant realizes this does not entail that plaintiff thereafter *does* keep a proper lookout. One metaphorical meaning of 'cease' is that one party has no further opportunity of avoiding the harm. In the *Loach*[86] case once the cart on which Sands was a passenger was close to the rails Sands could no longer do anything to avoid the collision. It 'ceases' to be negligent not to keep a proper lookout once there is no longer any point in doing so. But this is not true in all cases in which the last clear chance rule is applied. In the *Long*[87] case, for example, Long could (in a certain sense) at any moment up to the last have looked to see if a tram was approaching and, seeing it, have avoided being killed. When plaintiff's movements have ceased at a certain moment it is difficult to see what causal significance this has, since though his movements cease their consequences may, even on Lord Sumner's view, continue and it ought surely to be the latter which are significant from a causal point of view. There is no principle of causation that conduct is only the cause of harm if it continues at the moment of the harm, or, more generally, that a cause must be contemporaneous or nearly contemporaneous with its consequence; for though some philosophers

---

85 *Davies* v. *Swan Motor Co.* [1949] 2 KB 291, 323, *per* Denning LJ.
86 [1916] 1 AC 719.
87 *Long* v. *Toronto R. Co.* (1914) 20 DLR 369. Above, p. 221.

have in the past been led to advocate some such paradoxical view, the common sense of the matter is that a cause often precedes its consequence.

The last clear chance rule is neither a principle nor even a 'test'[88] of causation, in the sense of being evidence strongly pointing to the conduct of the party having the last chance as the sole cause of the harm. At least in its constructive forms, it is compatible with the absence of all the elements which go to make one party's conduct fully voluntary, or grossly abnormal or unreasonable. It is, indeed, merely an inept way of giving effect to a sensible policy, that if the law forbids apportionment it is nevertheless rational to allow a plaintiff to recover if his conduct was less dangerous than that of defendant. The rule is sufficiently obscure to allow the application of the notion of comparative negligence[89] or, better, comparative danger, without express mention of it. There is much point in Holdsworth's comment[90] that plaintiff recovered in the *Loach*[91] case not on any causal ground but because deceased was less negligent than defendants (or better, that his conduct was less dangerous than theirs). 'It is really a most amazing picture, which could be the work of no one but lawyers',[92] says Prosser. Some may think that it is an insult to the man in the street to pretend that the last clear chance rule is an application of *any* common-sense principle.

II. HOW RESPONSIBILITY IS ALLOCATED WHEN THERE ARE CONTRIBUTORY CAUSES

We must here consider three possible classes of case: (i) when the harm is divisible; (ii) when the harm is not divisible but the law provides for apportionment; (iii) when the harm is not divisible and the law does not provide for apportionment.

(i) *Divisible harm.*[93] Harm may be 'divisible' in two ways. First, it may consist in damaged things separately identifiable or measurable by number, quantity, weight, length, etc., so many items. Here the total harm is either plainly divisible into separate items or has extensive magnitude. When this is so, some identified part of the harm may be found to have been caused by one act alone and such part is then termed 'severable'. Twenty bales of wool are destroyed in an accident in which both plaintiff and defendant were negligent; ten

[88] *Davies* v. *Swan Motor Co.* [1949] 2 KB 291, 323 *per* Denning LJ.
[89] Prosser, Selected Topics on the Law of Torts, chap. 1.
[90] *HEL* viii. 462. Aquarius (1945), 62 *SALJ* 126, 140. *Contra: Alford* v. *Magee* (1952) 85 CLR 437, 465.
[91] [1916] 1 AC 719.
[92] *Selected Topics*, p. 14.
[93] Honoré, *IECL*, xi, chap. 7-113.

would have been lost if defendant alone had been negligent. Secondly, the total harm may be an 'intensive magnitude', e.g. we speak of
more or less pain, suffering, or disturbance of plaintiff's comfort and
enjoyment of land, but since there are no units of measurement we
cannot say by exactly how much a particular factor has increased
the pain, etc., suffered. We know, however, that less harm of a
particular sort would have been suffered in the absence of a particular act, and despite the lack of units of measurement, the law
sometimes assigns responsibility for different amounts of pain, etc.,
to different causes and so treats even an intensive magnitude as
divisible.

A variant of the first type of severability is the situation where
different parties by contributing quantifiable items create a state of
affairs which immediately causes the harm, as when A and B each
pile a ton of rubbish against C's wall which, in consequence of the
total pressure, collapses. Here, though the harm is not severable, its
cause is.

Severance of harm which has extensive magnitude presents no
great difficulties, provided the evidence permits us to distinguish the
units of harm which are assignable to their respective causes. But if
defendant's contribution to the harm or the state of affairs which
immediately caused the harm was insignificant he is held not liable
on the principle *de minimis non curat lex*. In *Baltimore & O.R. Co.
v. Sulphur Spring Independent School District* [94] violent rain so raised
the level of water dammed by an embankment that it swept away
plaintiff's school-house. It was held a misdirection to tell the jury to
hold for plaintiff if defendant's negligence in obstructing certain
culverts had 'in any degree' caused the loss. The fact that defendants
had somewhat obstructed three culverts was immaterial when 120
culverts would have been needed to carry off the volume of water.
When defendants intermittently exposed their employee to dust during the course of a month and a previous employer had exposed him
to similar dust for twelve years, it was held that defendant was not
liable for the disease so caused.[95] Indeed, it is in this type of case
that the terminology of 'substantial' or 'material' factor has its most
literal application. The difficult cases are those in which the evidence
is obscure[96] or the harm to be attributed to different factors has
intensive magnitude. Thus, where one wrong has been done a second
may obliterate the evidence of the wrong done by the first wrongdoer, as where one man is run over twice in quick succession; or it

[94] (1880) 96 Pa. 65.
[95] *Golden* v. *Lerch Bros* (1938) 203 Minn, 211, 281 NW 249.
[96] *Nitro-Phosphate Co.* v. *London and St. Katherine Docks* (1878) 9 Ch. D. 503
(flood 3 inches above height of bank which defendants ought to have built: damage
done by this extra flooding to be deducted, if ascertainable).

may be uncertain what part of injuries actually suffered would have been suffered in the absence of one contributing factor. These are problems of evidence. Secondly, even if these difficulties are surmounted, there will be, e.g. in cases of personal injury, other problems, more properly called those of 'severance', in the assessment of the amounts contributed by separate factors to an intensive magnitude like pain.

For instance, in *Smithwick* v. *Hall & Upson*, the facts of which have been given above,[97] it was argued that plaintiff's standing at an unguarded part of the platform considerably aggravated his injuries when he fell off the platform, since had he stood where there was a rail he would have been able to save himself slipping, even if struck by the falling bricks. Hence defendants asserted that one part of his injuries was the consequence of defendants' negligence and another the consequence of the combined negligence of themselves and plaintiff, so that he should be barred as to the latter.[98] The court admitted that if plaintiff's act increased his injuries this would go to reduce damages but decided that on the facts the plaintiff's conduct had not aggravated his injuries. On the other hand in *O'Keefe* v. *Kansas City Western R. Co.*[99] it was held that plaintiff's damages must be reduced where his injuries from a fall were increased by his prior intoxication (amounting to contributory negligence) though this did not contribute to his fall.[1] In *Mahoney* v. *Beatman*,[2] the facts of which are given on p. 296, the Connecticut appeal court allowed plaintiff to recover full damages where his negligence in driving too fast had contributed to his colliding with a stone wall though not to his original impact with defendant's car. But this decision, though ostensibly based on the view that the defendant's conduct was a 'substantial factor' in producing the total harm, can only be justified as an application of the notion of comparative danger.[3] The decision of the trial court and the dissent of Maltbie J. seem amply justified on purely causal grounds. The trial court concluded that plaintiff was barred by his negligence from recovering more than the 200 dollars 'nominal damages' attributable to the initial impact.

The prime difficulty in most of these cases is simply one of evidence.[4] It may not be possible to distinguish what injuries occurred as a result of the first of successive wrongs. When the problem of evidence is surmounted little difficulty is felt in making a rough and

97 p. 208.
98 (1896) 59 Conn. 261, 21 Am. St. Rep. 104, 109.
99 (1912) 87 Kan. 322, 124 Pac. 416.
1 Cf. *Wright* v. *Illinois & Mississipi Tel. Co.* (1866) 20 Iowa 195.
2 (1929) 110 Conn. 184, 147 Atl. 762.
3 Above, p. 225.
4 Honoré, *IECL*, xi, chap. 7-114.

ready division of intensive magnitudes like pain and suffering, or the number of days' repairs attributable to successive collisions. When the evidence shows that defendant has independently caused some of the total harm but it is impossible or very difficult to decide how much, different courts adopt different approaches. In *McAllister* v. *Pennsylvania R.R. Co.*[5] plaintiff was twice injured, once in October in her right leg, and once in the following March in her left leg. Defendant was responsible for the first but not the second injury. The medical witnesses were unable to distinguish the disabilities attributable to each accident. The trial judge charged the jury to apportion to defendant some part of plaintiff's pain, suffering, and disability in accordance with 'reasonableness and common sense' and this direction was upheld on appeal. On the other hand in *Deutsch* v. *Connecticut Co.*[6] deceased was, through his own negligence, struck by a trolley and when lying on the track was further injured by the negligence of defendant's motorman in reversing a tram. The court upheld a directed verdict for defendant since it was a matter of speculation what injury deceased had already suffered before the tram struck him. But in *Micelli* v. *Hirsch*[7] where the victim was injured successively by two negligently driven vehicles, each defendant was held liable for the whole damage. In such cases the first wrongdoer may be liable for the harm done by the second on the grounds that the second wrong did not negative causal connection between the first wrong and the harm suffered in the second accident.[8]

In these three cases it was clear that some part of the physical injuries suffered was caused by one only of two or more independent acts, but what part was not precisely known. The matter turns on the onus of proof. Must plaintiff prove what part of the harm is attributable to defendant's acts or must defendant prove what part of the total is not his responsibility?

It is absurd that a defendant who has clearly done some harm should escape altogether and it is submitted that, if there is no evidence how much of the total is caused by his act, the onus of proof should be transferred to defendant, who would thus be liable for the whole harm unless he can prove what part of it was caused by someone else.[9] Thus, when plaintiff is injured by one defendant's

---

[5] (1936) 324 Pa. 65, 187 Atl. 415; *Loui* v. *Oakley* (1968) 438 P. 2d 393, 397 (rough or, in default, equal apportionment); *Dingle* v. *Associated Newspapers* [1961] 2 QB 162, 189–90 (libels in newspapers with separate readership).

[6] (1923), 98 Conn. 482, 119 Atl. 891. *Huddell* v. *Levin* (1976) 537 F. 2d 726; *Tucker Oil* v. *Matthews* (1938) 119 SW 2d 616. Cf. for criminal law *State* v. *Rounds* (1932) 160 Atl. 249.

[7] (1948) 52 Ohio L. Abs. 426, 83 NE 2d 240.

[8] *Adams* v. *Parrish* (1920) 189 Ky. 628, 225 SW 467; above, pp. 152-3.

[9] *Chrysler Corp.* v. *Todurovich* (1978) 580 P. 2d 1123 (Wyo.) (holding that the injuries, sustained in a single accident, are not 'divisible').

negligent driving and his injuries are aggravated by the fact that his car, manufactured by a second defendant, is not equipped to withstand crashes ('uncrashworthy'), he should recover against the manufacturer to the extent of the aggravation, if this can be ascertained,[10] but, if not, to the full extent of his injuries.[11]

In nuisance, where the harm is often severable, the courts sometimes draw a plausible distinction between cases where defendant's act would have amounted to a wrong to plaintiff independently of the acts of others, and cases where it would not.

If it is clear that defendant's act by itself would have amounted to a wrong to plaintiff, as when several defendants pollute a stream, one view is that the onus should be on defendant to show how much is attributable to him and in the absence of proof the trier of fact should be allowed to make a reasonable guess:[12] but this is not universally accepted.[13] It is assumed, of course, that the various contributors are not acting in concert[14] for, if they are, each will be liable for the acts of the other on the ground of authorization or common purpose. When defendant's act would not independently have amounted to a wrong to plaintiff, the cases exhibit a variety of views. One proposed rule, canvassed in nuisance cases concerning smoke, noise, etc., is that even if defendant has thus contributed to harm which as a whole involves an infringement of plaintiff's rights, he should not be held guilty of a crime[15] or made liable to pay damages. Sometimes, despite this, an injunction is granted in such cases,[16] for it may well be right for this purpose to adopt the rule that a defendant who has made a 'material' or 'significant' contribution to a divisible total of harm should be forbidden to continue to do so.[17] At the other extreme is the view that, even if defendant's contribution would not independently amount to a wrong, he is liable to pay for the whole harm.[18] A compromise view is that he is liable for part only of the harm.[19]

[10] *Huddell* v. *Levin* (1976) 537 F. 2d 726.

[11] *Chrysler Corp.* v. *Todurovich* (1978) 580 P. 2d 1123.

[12] *City of Oakland* v. *Pacific Gas & Elec. Co.* (1941) 47 Cal. App. 2d 444, 118 Pac. 2d 328; *Finnegan* v. *Royal Realty Co.* (1950) 35 Cal. 2d 409, 433, 218 Pac. 2d 17, 32.

[13] *Farley* v. *Crystal Coal & Coke Co.* (1920) 85 W. Va. 595, 102 SE 265, 9 ALR 933; *Slater* v. *Pacific American Oil Co.* (1931) 212 Cal. 648, 300 Pac. 31.

[14] On the difference between concerted and independent action see *Farley* v. *Crystal Coal & Coke Co.* (1920) 85 W. Va. 585, 102 SE 265, 9 ALR 933; *Moses* v. *Town of Morganton* (1926) 192 NC 102, 133 SE 421. In *Arneil* v. *Paterson* [1931] AC 560, the House of Lords held two dog-owners each liable for the whole harm done to the pursuer's sheep under the Dogs Act, 1906, on the ground that the dogs were 'acting together' or that 'each was the cause' of what happened. Ibid., pp. 564, 565. Cf. *Stephens* v. *Schadler* (1919) 182 Ky. 833, 207 SW 714.

[15] *Gay* v. *State* (1891) 90 Tenn. 645, 18 So. 260.

[16] *Warren* v. *Parkhurst* (1904) 45 Misc. 466, 92 NYS 725.

[17] *Duke of Buccleuch* v. *Cowan* (1866) 5 Macpherson 214 (Scot.).

[18] *Town of Sentinel* v. *Riley* (1935) 171 Okl. 533, 43 P. 2d 742.

[19] *Johnson* v. *Dundas* [1945] Ont. R. 670.

THE COMMON LAW

Separate from these and perhaps more compatible with purely causal criteria is the view that defendant is liable if *in the existing circumstances* his contribution makes the difference between infringement and non-infringement of the plaintiff's rights or aggravates an existing infringement. Hence to make half the amount of noise which would be an actionable nuisance to plaintiff is itself actionable if another independent person is simultaneously making the other half, especially if this is known to defendant.[20]

In conclusion two special cases of harm divisible into items may be mentioned. The rule of avoidable consequences[21] lays down that if plaintiff, after he has suffered an invasion of his rights, fails to take reasonable care to avoid further harmful consequences to himself, he is barred from recovering for the further harm which he negligently fails to avert, e.g. if after suffering an injury through defendant's negligence he fails to obtain proper medical care, with consequent aggravation of the injury.[22] By a similar rule, plaintiff's failure to mitigate damages may to that extent reduce his claim.[23] Plaintiff's conduct may amount to a voluntary[24] causing of the further damage, as when defendant in breach of contract furnished inferior seed and plaintiff, knowing of the defect, nevertheless planted the seed; here his voluntary conduct is on common-sense principles the 'sole' cause of his obtaining an inferior crop[25] (good seed being obtainable elsewhere). Again plaintiff's conduct may amount to so unreasonable a reaction to the injury inflicted on him as, on ordinary causal principles, to negative causal connection with the original wrong. It may, however, neither be fully voluntary nor unreasonable but merely a contributory cause of the further loss, as when defendant negligently set fire to the plaintiff's fence and plaintiff, knowing of this, did not take reasonable care to prevent his cattle escaping.[26] The legal effect is the same, viz. that plaintiff cannot recover at all for the further harm, when contributory negligence is a complete bar; but under a system of apportionment it is conceivable that the further loss might be apportioned.[27]

Physical events. When the harm is divisible and part is the consequence of an extraordinary natural event alone, while the rest is the consequence both of defendant's wrong and of the natural event,

---

20 *Lambton* v. *Mellish* [1894] 3 Ch. 163.
21 Prosser, *Torts*, p. 422.
22 *Wingrove* v. *Home Land Co.* (1938) 120 W. Va. 100, 196 SE 563, 116 ALR 1197; McCormick, *Damages*, chap. 5.
23 *British Westinghouse Electric Co.* v. *Underground Electric R. Co.* [1912] AC 673, 689.
24 McCormick, *Damages*, p. 131.
25 *Wavra* v. *Karr* (1919) 142 Minn. 248, 172 NW 118.
26 *Wisconsin* v. *Arkansas Lumber Co.* v. *Scott* (1925) 167 Ark. 84, 267 SW 780.
27 Williams, op. cit., pp. 292-4. This is certainly the rational solution.

the rational solution is that the harm should be severed and defendant held responsible only for part.[28] Thus if defendant has so negligently constructed his dam that some flooding of plaintiff's property would take place during an ordinary rainfall, but in fact an unprecedented storm (an act of God) occurs and more extensive flooding takes place, plaintiff should recover only for the flooding which an ordinary rainfall would have helped to cause.[29] *Elder v. Lykens Valley Coal Co.*[30] may appear to the contrary. There defendants wrongfully deposited culm in a river. An extraordinary flood carried it to plaintiff's land: but ordinary rains would have done so more gradually. The court held defendants liable for the whole harm; but the reasons given are that the flood merely accelerated the descent of the culm and that severance would be impracticable. The view taken in the *Restatement*[31] that even if the extraordinary natural event increases the total harm (and does not merely accelerate it) defendant is liable for the whole, represents a failure to apply common-sense principles of causation in a context where they are appropriate.

Part lawful, part unlawful. Similar considerations apply when some harm to plaintiff would have been caused even had defendant acted lawfully, but the extent of it has been increased by his wrongful act. In *Jenkins v. Pennsylvania R. Co.*[32] plaintiff suffered a nuisance to his enjoyment of his house through odours and smoke from defendant's railway. Part of the smoke would have been necessarily emitted even if defendant's locomotives had been carefully operated, while part was attributable to their carelessness. The court held that a substantial recovery should be allowed, and left the jury to make the best estimate it could of the portion of the total harm caused by defendant's want of care.

(ii) *When the harm is not divisible but the law allows apportionment.* Although the word 'apportionment' is often used to comprise the instances dealt with in (i) above[33] it is useful to distinguish 'severance' from 'apportionment' and to reserve the latter term for a division of the money compensation payable for a loss which cannot be separated into separate items or magnitudes, extensive or intensive, attributable to different causes for which different persons are

[28] Prosser, p. 318. Contrast the case where the extraordinary character of the natural event (a storm) makes no difference to the consequence. *O'Connor v. Chicago M. & St. P.R. Co.* (1916) 163 Wis. 653, 158 NW 343.
[29] *Radburn v. Fir Tree Lumber Co.* (1915) 83 Wash. 643, 145 Pac. 632.
[30] (1893) 157 Pa. 490, 27 Atl. 545, 37 Am. St. Rep. 742.
[31] *Restatement of Torts*, s. 450.
[32] (1902) 67 NJL 331, 51 Atl. 704; *Workman v. G.N.R. Co.* (1863) 32 LJQB 279. *Contra: Inland Power & Light Co. v. Grieger* (1937) 91 F. 2d 811, 112 ALR 1075 (whole recovery allowed).
[33] Prosser, *Torts*, s. 52.

responsible. Thus if two persons wrongfully fail to repair their walls which simultaneously collapse together on plaintiff's property,[34] the harm is not divisible. We cannot treat a fraction of it as attributable to each wall separately. Again, if a slander or libel is separately published by or repeated by several, the resultant loss of reputation is an indivisible item of harm for which all of those legally responsible should be liable in full unless it can be shown that publication by one of them had no effect on the opinions held about plaintiff.[35]

Legislation increasingly provides for apportionment of compensation when harm is the consequence of the conduct of two or more legally responsible persons. In England provision has been made for this both in cases of joint tortfeasors and for contributory negligence. The English legislation allows a tortfeasor who is liable for damage to recover from another tortfeasor liable for the same damage such amount 'as may be found by the court to be just and equitable having regard to the extent of' that tortfeasor's 'responsibility for the damage',[36] and a plaintiff guilty of contributory negligence to recover damages subject to a reduction 'to such extent as the court thinks just and equitable having regard to the claimant's share in the responsibility for the damage'.[37] This makes apportionment turn on the 'extent' or 'share' of responsibility of the parties. The Canadian and American[38] legislation more often enjoins apportionment according to the 'degree' of fault[39] or negligence[40] or both.[41]

In *Smith* v. *Bray*[42] Hilbery J said that under the English tortfeasors statute the damages should be apportioned on the basis of causation not fault. This would seem to call for an assessment of the 'degree'[43] of causation attributable to each party and the 'causative potency'[44] of the conduct of each party. On the other hand Glanville Williams has maintained, in reference to the same statute, that the word 'responsibility' 'refers more naturally to the degree of fault or

---

[34] *Johnson* v. *Chapman and Hutchinson* (1897) 43 W. Va. 639, 28 SE 744. Cf. *Blanton* v. *Sisters of Charity* (1948) 82 Ohio App. 20, 79 NE 2d 688.

[35] *Dingle* v. *Associated Newspapers* [1961] 1 All ER 897, 916 (CA).

[36] Law Reform (Married Women and Tortfeasors) Act, 1935, s. 6(2).

[37] Law Reform (Contributory Negligence) Act, 1945, s. 1.

[38] At least thirty-five states of the US have adopted comparative negligence laws, some by judicial decision. See Wade, Crawford, and Ryder, (1974) 41 *Tenn. LR* 423; J. J. Phillips, 'Reflections on Factual Causation', (1978) *Wash. ULQ* 661, 665.

[39] British Columbia Contributory Negligence Act, ss. 2, 5; Saskatchewan Contributory Negligence Act, 1944, ss. 2, 3: Glanville Williams, *Joint Torts*, app. 2; American Uniform Contribution among Tortfeasors Act, s. 2(4); Williams, op. cit., app. 3; South African Apportionment of Damages Act, 1956, s. 1(1).

[40] Manitoba Tortfeasors and Contributory Negligence Act, s. 4(1).

[41] Ontario RSO, 1937, c. 115, ss. 2(1), 3.

[42] (1939) 56 TLR 200.

[43] *Davies* v. *Swan Motor Co. Ltd.* [1949] 2 KB 291, 326, *per* Denning LJ.

[44] Ibid.

blame'.[45] An intermediate view has been expressed by Denning LJ in regard to the English contributory negligence statute, viz. that 'the amount of reduction does not depend solely on the degree of causation . . . [it] involves a consideration, not only of the causative potency of a particular factor but also of its blameworthiness'.[46] Another view is that responsibility depends on the actor's degree of departure from the standard of care of the reasonable man.[47]

Can a meaning be attached to 'degrees of causation'? There are some indications in ordinary speech that it can.[48] An event is often, outside the law, said to be caused partly by one factor and partly by another, or more by one thing than another, or mostly by a particular factor. 'His failure in the examination was due more to his not working than to the difficulty of the papers.' 'The main [chief, principal] cause of [factor in] his success as a miler was his assiduous training.' These are examples taken from explanatory contexts but perhaps they can be adapted for attributive contexts also. The underlying notion, no doubt a very rough one, in the selection of one cause as more 'important', 'effective', or 'potent' than another is its greater tendency in normal circumstances, and not merely in the particular case, to be followed by harmful (or beneficial) consequences. Long experience teaches us that, with persons of a certain ability, those who work hard normally pass even difficult examinations while those who idle often fail fairly easy ones. Those who have moderate athletic ability and train hard are more often successful than those who have greater ability but neglect their training. This involves an assessment of the chances of harm, in normal circumstances, given a particular act and also of the probable gravity of the harm if it occurs. How the gravity of harm is to be measured is fortunately not a causal problem, but, assuming that common sense provides ways of making the assessment, it is easy to see that 'degrees' of causation can be given a factual, though inescapably vague, interpretation in terms of the more or less dangerous character of particular factors.[49] If, then, 'degrees' of responsibility are to be interpreted in causal terms the most rational basis for apportionment becomes the relatively dangerous character of the acts of the various tortfeasors or of plaintiff and defendant.

45 Op. cit., p. 157.
46 *Davies* v. *Swan Motor Co.* [1949] 2 KB 291, 326.
47 Payne, 'Reduction of Damages for Contributory Negligence', (1955) 18 *MLR* 344, 354. *Pennington* v. *Norris* (1956) 30 ALJ 242, 244 (HC).
48 So far as functional relationships can be regarded as causal there is no doubt that causes can be quantified: Mackie, *Cement of the Universe*, p. 129 n. 23.
49 *Clay* v. *Crump* [1963] 3 All ER 687 (collapsing wall: principal cause failure of architect, second in importance that of demolition contractor, third that of building contractor).

234 THE COMMON LAW

However, it is not clear that an apportionment based on fault, as required by most Canadian and American statutes, will lead to different results from one based on causation, as roughly outlined above; for the chance of harmful consequences and the probable seriousness of the consequences are relevant to the determination of fault, or at least of negligence.[50] Such phrases as 'the degree in which the claimant was at fault *in relation* to the damage' appear to let in a consideration not merely of the degree in which the act was negligent, etc., but of the degree in which the negligent act caused the harm. Hence the 'degree' of negligence or fault may be determined in much the same way as the relatively dangerous character of the various acts, though certain additional matters may perhaps be considered under 'degree' of fault or negligence. Thus it has been said that fault or culpability depends on the mental attitude of the actor, the chance of the harm and the magnitude of the possible harm.[51] The mental attitude of the actor would not make his act more or less dangerous; so no doubt mental attitude is a non-causal element in fault. Also, the moral culpability of the act may perhaps be taken into account under the notion of 'degree of fault'. If a young child is drowned and a suit is brought against X for negligence in maintaining his pond and against Y, a childminder, for failing in breach of her duty to try to rescue the child when she could easily have done so, it may be that, in an apportionment under a tortfeasor's statute the fact that, though both X and Y were guilty of mere negligence, Y's act is more morally reprehensible than X's should be taken into account. We need not consider by what tests degrees of moral reprehensibility are established.

Since 'fault' is one element relevant to responsibility, it would seem that all these considerations can properly be regarded under the English apportionment legislation, which refers, as has been mentioned, to 'degree' or 'share' of responsibility.

(iii) *When the harm is not divisible and the law does not provide for apportionment.* In this situation there would appear to be only two rational alternatives: either to abide by the original common law rule that plaintiff is altogether barred by his contributory negligence or to adopt a rule that a plaintiff can recover if he is less at fault or less negligent than defendant in relation to the harm. Here again the main criterion of greater or less fault will be the relatively dangerous character of plaintiff's and defendant's acts. If the issue were confined to this alone, it would be possible to regard 'relative danger' as a more literal interpretation of the usual metaphors, e.g. that

[50] *United States* v. *Carroll Towing Co.* (1947) 159 F. 2d 169, 173. Below, p. 263.
[51] Aquarius, 'Causation and Legal Responsibility', (1941) 58 *SALJ* 232, 261.

plaintiff can recover if defendant's negligence is 'predominant' or 'more substantial'.

When joint or several tortfeasors have contributed to the same harm the obvious rule is that each should be liable for the whole harm. 'If each contributed to the injury, that is enough to bind both.'[52] This is of course subject to the rule against double recovery and the procedural requirements of joinder.

III. ADDITIONAL CAUSES[53]

In this section we deal with additional causes,[54] i.e. with cases in which there are present on a given occasion two or more factors each sufficient with other normal conditions to bring about certain harm. The two factors must be independent in the sense that neither is a necessary condition of the occurrence of the other.

In our view, as explained in Chapter V,[55] when each factor is sufficient, with other normal conditions, to bring about the harm as and when it occurs, each is properly described as a cause of the harm.[56] Thus, when two persons A and B simultaneously shoot at C, each shot being sufficient to kill him, both A and B are criminally and civilly liable for C's death.[57] This is because each shot is sufficient, in conjunction with other normal conditions, to bring about C's death as it occurred (viz. by shooting) at the moment when it occurred. As Glanville Williams says:[58]

It may also happen in a particular case that [the consequence] is produced by the simultaneous operation of [two conditions], i.e. by two independent causes such that either of them would have been adequate to produce [the consequence]. If [one] was an act committed by one defendant and [the other] an act committed by another defendant, the rule is that both defendants are liable as concurrent tortfeasors, even though the harm would have happened equally if one or other of the defendants had not acted.

Thus, when plaintiff took two drugs, each sufficient to damage his retina, and defendant was responsible for failing to warn of the

---

52 *Corey* v. *Havener* (1902) 182 Mass. 250.

53 Also termed 'multiple sufficient causes' (e.g. Peczenik, *Causes and Damages*, p. 15; Honoré, *IECL*, xi, chap. 7-130 to 7-139) or cases of causal overdetermination (L. E. Loeb, 'Causal Theories and Causal Overdetermination', *J. Phil.* 71 (1974) 525; Mackie, *Cement*, pp. 73-4, 164-5).

54 To save repetition we draw examples from both civil and criminal law.

55 Above, pp. 123-5 ff.

56 Mackie, *Cement*, p. 47, however, argues that neither factor can be said to have caused the harm when 'even a detailed causal story fails to discriminate between the rival candidates for the role of cause' and that in such cases it is only the 'cluster of events' (viz. both shots) that we 'can confidently take as causing these effects'. But this seems simply to be an application of his general doctrine that a cause must always be 'necessary in the circumstances' for the alleged effect.

57 *Restatement of Torts*, s. 432 (2).

58 *Joint Torts*, p. 240 n. 11.

danger of one of them, it was held that he could be held liable for the whole damage.[59] Again, when defendant wrongfully damaged the propeller of plaintiff's ship and inspection revealed other faults rendering the ship unseaworthy and requiring the same repairs to be done it was held that defendant could be held responsible for the whole amount of the repairs.[60] According to Learned Hand J., 'the single tortfeasor cannot be allowed to escape through the meshes of a logical net. He is a wrongdoer. Let him unravel the casuistries resulting from his wrong.' This suggests that the problem is one of evidence and that, given enough information, we could discover which wrongdoer had caused which part of the harm. But, as the judge himself recognized,[61] in this type of case the defendant cannot discharge this onus no matter how detailed and accurate the information available.

It seems self-evident that a similar rule should apply as regards concurrent omissions, each sufficient to produce the harm. If a mason and a carpenter both fail to do their part of the work on a building, so that it cannot be completed by the due date, and the building-owner loses an expected profit, each would be liable for the lost profit provided it was in their contemplation at the time of contracting. So, when a supplier of webbing delayed in delivering it to an overall manufacturer, and the latter incurred contractual penalties on the main contract, the jury was entitled to hold the webbing supplier liable to indemnify the overall manufacturer for the penalties paid, the failure to deliver the webbing being a 'substantial factor' in causing the loss and 'sufficient in itself to have delayed' the fulfilment of the main contract, despite the existence of other 'contributory' causes of the default on the main contract.[62] Neither the terminology of 'contributory causes' nor that of 'substantial factor' is really appropriate in such situations when one of the causes is sufficient without the other, which is also sufficient, to produce the loss complained of; but the decision is clearly correct.

So far we have assumed that both acts or defaults are wrongful. There is perhaps more room for doubt if only one of them is wrongful. In this case, also, according to the *Restatement of Torts*,[63] the wrongdoer will be liable for the harm suffered. 'If two forces are actively operating, one because of the actor's negligence, the other not because of any misconduct on his part, and each of itself is

59 *Basko* v. *Sterling Drug Co.* (1969) 416 F. 2d 417.
60 *Navigazione Libera* v. *Newtown Creek* (1938) 98 F. 2d 694.
61 Ibid.
62 *Krauss* v. *Greenbarg* (1943) 137 F. 2d 569.
63 *Restatement of Torts*, s. 432.

sufficient to bring about harm to another, the actor's negligence may be held by the jury to be a substantial factor[64] in bringing it about.'

If one of the acts in question is that of plaintiff himself, it would seem that he should recover nothing against the defendant who has provided the additional cause. Thus, if plaintiff and defendant each simultaneously and independently approach a gas-filled room with a lighted candle and, as they enter it together, an explosion occurs in which plaintiff is severely injured, plaintiff should recover nothing since his own act was sufficient independently of defendant's act to produce his own injuries.[65] This is distinguishable from a case in which the acts of plaintiff and defendant are not sufficient without the other but each contributes to produce the harm to plaintiff, so that apportionment is appropriate.

Additional complications are introduced when there is an interaction between the acts of two parties, each normally sufficient to produce the harm. In some of these cases the act of one agent reinforces or produces a greater volume of some harmful physical condition, as when two defendants each negligently set a fire and the two fires combine (combinatory cause). In other cases the act of one agent neutralizes that of the other, as when one defendant negligently sets a fire and the other negligently causes a flood which quenches the fire but destroys the property threatened (neutralizing cause). In a third sort of case the second act neither reinforces nor neutralizes the first but it may lead to a revised estimate of the loss caused by the first: for this the Germans have invented the term 'overtaking cause' (*überholende Ursache*). An example occurs when a professional boxer who has lost a leg owing to *A*'s negligence, and so cannot earn prize money, loses his other leg owing to *B*'s negligence before judgment is given in his action against *A*.

(i) *Additional combinatory cause.* When the acts of the two parties, each sufficient to produce the harm, reinforce one another it would appear that either may be held responsible for the whole consequent harm. Thus in *Anderson* v. *Minneapolis, St. P. & S. St. M.R. Co.*[66] a forest fire which was started by defendant's negligence swept over a large part of Northern Minnesota and merged with another fire of uncertain origin, the combined fires burning plaintiff's property. The trial court refused to instruct the jury that they should find for defendant if the second fire was sufficient in itself to destroy plaintiff's

[64] Note that this is a different use of 'substantial' from that discussed above in connection with apportionment in case of contributory causes. Writers have used 'substantial' here because the contention that the act must be a necessary condition of the harm breaks down in these anomalous cases of additional cause. See above, pp. 123–4, and below, p. 238.
[65] Cf. G. Williams, (1954) 17 *MLR* 66, 71.
[66] (1920) 146 Minn. 430, 179 NW 45.

property. This direction was upheld on appeal. The reasoning of the Minnesota court was that a defendant is liable if his act would have been sufficient independently of the act of the other party or of natural agency, provided that his act was in fact a 'substantial' or 'material' element in causing plaintiff's harm. Hence the court, though in general accepting the view that a defendant is liable if his act is generally sufficient to produce the harm, appears to be saying that when the acts of two parties combine, defendant is not liable if his conduct, though sufficient in normal circumstances to produce the harm, has made an insignificant contribution to the combined fire. It would no doubt be difficult to convince a jury or trier of fact that a defendant's fire combined these characteristics; but, if it did, defendant ought surely to be liable for the burning of plaintiff's property, since his conduct was sufficient to result in its being burned and in fact contributed to the outcome. Whether the damages payable should be reduced because the property would in any case have been burned by the other fire is debatable. The operation of the other fire is hardly to be treated as an existing susceptibility of plaintiff's property, which had already reduced its value, so that defendant could be held responsible only for further reducing its value. For plaintiff's property was not affected by the other fire *before* defendant's fire burned it, but at the same time. Nor, on the other hand, is the case like that of an 'overtaking cause', such as a flood which would have overwhelmed plaintiff's property the next day, and which, for a reason to be explained shortly, should not excuse defendant from paying the full value of the property. The case is intermediate between the two, and is closely analogous to that discussed in a *Digest* text,[67] which holds that no economic loss is inflicted by a person who destroys a neighbour's property to prevent a fire spreading to his own, when the neighbour's property would in any case have been destroyed by the fire in question.

In the earlier case of *Cook* v. *Minneapolis St. P. & S. St. M.R. Co.*[68] the Wisconsin court held that, where defendant had negligently set a fire which combined with a fire of unknown origin to destroy plaintiff's property, defendant was relieved of liability because the fire of unknown origin was an intervening event which prevented defendant's negligence being the proximate cause of the ultimate harm. This conclusion was at once challenged by writers and the Wisconsin court took the first opportunity of limiting its effects by holding that it did not apply when the other fire was attributable to human agency. The court further held that when the origin of the other fire was unexplained it might be presumed to be of human

[67] D 43. 24. 7. 4.
[68] (1898) 98 Wis. 624, 74 NW 561, 67 Am. St. Rep. 830.

origin.[69] The view that a defendant who sets a fire sufficient in normal circumstances to burn property is not liable for the destruction so caused if the fire is joined by another similar fire before reaching the property may therefore now be regarded as discredited even, probably, so far as the combination of a negligent act and a natural event is concerned.

(ii) *Additional neutralizing cause.* If the act of one party neutralizes that of the other, it would seem clear on ordinary principles that the party whose subsequent act has neutralized the first act has alone caused the harm, though the first actor may be liable on other grounds, e.g. for an attempt. Thus, *A* negligently sets a fire which would have been sufficient to destroy *C*'s house but, before the fire reaches *C*'s house, it is quenched by the waters which *B* has negligently allowed to escape from a dam; the waters from the dam are sufficient to destroy *C*'s house and in fact do so. *B* should be held responsible for the destruction of the house while *A* should escape civil liability. If in a criminal case both *A* and *B* intentionally cause the fire and flood respectively with a view to destroying *C*'s house, *A* would be guilty of attempted arson while *B* would be guilty of maliciously damaging the house. If *A* acts intentionally and *B* merely negligently, *A* is guilty of a criminal attempt but not of a civil wrong while *B* is liable civilly but not (in Anglo-American law) criminally. If *A* acts negligently and *B* intentionally *B* alone is civilly and criminally liable.

In some cases no harm would occur but for two human actions each sufficient in ordinary circumstances to produce it and yet neither can be said to be its cause, since they each neutralize or render impossible the normal operation of the other. Such cases cannot be simply described by reference to the concept of 'human intervention causing harm' for this requires less paradoxical circumstances for its application. McLaughlin's hypothetical case illustrates the inadequacy of the terminology of 'causing harm' for the description of such cases and the consequent difficulties of applying a rule of law defining such crimes as murder in causal terms where these anomalies are present. The facts of McLaughlin's case are as follows: 'Suppose *A* is entering a desert. *B* secretly puts a fatal dose of poison in *A*'s water keg. *A* takes the keg into the desert where *C* steals it, thinking that it contains pure water. *A* dies of thirst. Who killed him?'[70]

The circumstances which make it impossible to give a satisfactory answer to this question in the terms of either *B* or *C* or both causing

---

[69] *Kingston* v. *Chicago & N.W.R. Co.* (1927) 191 Wis. 610, 211 NW 913.
[70] (1925–6) 39 *Harv. LR* 149, 155 n. 25. McLaughlin supposes that *B* empties the water keg and fills it with salt: the substitution of poison makes the difficulties clearer.

A's death are these: *C* by stealing the keg neutralized *B*'s action so that it did not have its normal consequence in *A*'s death from poisoning. On the other hand the situation created by *B* was such that it is not possible to describe *C*'s later action as causing *A*'s death. The notion of causing death is not as logically simple as might seem. Since everyone dies, 'causing death' involves the notion of shortening the span of life which the victim might normally expect[71] and not merely determining the manner of dying: otherwise the concepts of 'causing death' and 'prolonging life' (i.e. enabling one to live to old age) would be indistinguishable. The notion of causing death is not of course confined to crude cases where the actor initiates changes in the victim's body by introducing some foreign element or by manipulating it; it also extends to cases where the actor shortens the victim's life by depriving him of something needed by his organism for survival. Hence we speak of starving people to death or causing them to die of thirst. But the extension of causal terminology to these latter cases presupposes that the victim had or would, but for the actor's intervention, have had access to the necessary food or drink, and in our imaginary case this presupposition is falsified owing to the intervention of the first malefactor.

Accordingly *C* cannot be said to have caused *A*'s death; he has in fact removed one cause and secured that another cause (thirst) takes effect later. The same is true whenever anyone rescues another from death. Consequently had *C* been a well-intentioned doctor intervening to stop *A* dying of poison, the natural comment would be that he had not deprived *A* of any of the essentials of life, and had incidentally prolonged it slightly, though *as a result of his action A died of thirst instead of poison*. The words italicized are applicable to *C*'s action in the imagined case; and a legal system might indeed say that, if a malefactor does such an action (determining the mode of death) with the intention of shortening, not prolonging life, or in order to secure a more painful death, this is enough to constitute murder.[72] It might also be held in civil law that if *B* acted negligently he is responsible for *A*'s death, since the relation of his conduct to that event is closely analogous to a causal one.[73] But the damages

[71] But one who prolongs another's life, given the particular predicament in which the latter finds himself, might be held to have caused his death. Thus, if *A* poisons *B* so that *B* is too ill to sail on a voyage and *B* dies of the poison a day after the ship is lost with all on board, it would be natural to say that *A* had caused *B*'s death; and nothing would turn on whether the death occurred before or after or at the same time as the loss of the ship. Here *A* initiates a causal process which is completed in the usual way at about the same time as the victim would in the special circumstances have died but before the expiry of the usual life span of a person of that age and health.

[72] To do this would be, on grounds of policy, to impose on a wicked defendant responsibility for homicide though he had not caused the victim's death.

[73] Becht and Miller, p. 210.

payable would be minimal in view of the fact that *A* was doomed. Furthermore, the law might, though less plausibly, say that *B* is responsible because an act done with the intention of shortening life, which would normally be sufficient to kill and which only fails because of the substitution of another cause of death, should be treated as murder. Otherwise it would seem that, though *B* and *C* were both guilty of attempting to kill *A*, one by introducing a harmful substance into his body and the other by depriving him of an element necessary to life, their mutual frustration of each other's plan precludes us from saying that either caused *A*'s death.[74]

The difference between this case and the one mentioned earlier in which the flood neutralized the fire and destroyed the house resides in the fact that the flood initiated a series of physical changes culminating in the destruction of the house, whereas in the water keg case *C* by stealing the keg neither initiated a series of physical changes in *A*'s body nor deprived him of any of the essentials of life.

Some of the difficulties present in the imaginary case may arise in practice, since a causal process initiated by one wrongdoer which would normally terminate in a harmful way may be counteracted by a second wrongdoer who substitutes another cause sufficient to produce similar harm. An example is when *A* 'mortally' wounds *C* but, before *C* dies of *A*'s wound, *B* intentionally kills him.

Here it is important to notice the different senses of the word 'mortal', of which three may be distinguished: (i) the word may simply refer to a type of injurious occurrence (a wound, blow, or dose) which is sufficient to cause the death of a person of average constitution under normal circumstances: here there is no necessary reference to any particular case. Thus we speak in general terms of so many grains of arsenic as a 'mortal dose'; (ii) a wound inflicted on a particular occasion may be called mortal if, given the circumstances including the constitution of the victim and likelihood of medical

---

[74] According to Mackie, *Cement*, pp. 45–6, *C* caused the traveller's death because he caused it to be the case that he died of thirst, and because the event which was *C*'s death was also his death of thirst. The causal chain leading to that event, argues Mackie, was (removal of keg)–lack of water–thirst–death. But, granted that *C* has substituted one 'causal chain' leading to death from thirst, for another leading to death from poisoning, is this enough to justify the conclusion that *C* has caused *A*'s death? Here *C* has deprived *A* of something lethal, viz. of poisoned water, which does not sustain life. That cannot in itself amount to killing *A*. It is true that *C* has not thereby ensured *A*'s survival, because in the special circumstances there was no supply of water available other than the poisoned one. But that circumstance was not brought about by *C*'s conduct. All *C* has done is to determine from which of two conditions, poison or lack of water, a man who was doomed to die from one or the other should in fact die. That is, we think, not enough to justify the conclusion that *C* caused *A*'s death. It would, of course, be different if *C* had deprived *A* of a chance of living, e.g. because the poison might not have turned out to be lethal.

assistance, it is highly probable that it will cause his death;[75] (iii) a wound inflicted on a particular occasion may be said to be mortal if in fact it causes the victim's death even though it was not mortal in either of the two preceding senses, e.g. a mere scratch which the victim neglected. The most difficult problems are generated if A, in the example above, has mortally wounded C in the second sense when B intervenes.

Where there is no connection between A's and B's acts except that A made it possible for B to kill either himself or another (C), B is taken to have caused the harm to the exclusion of A. On the other hand if the second act was not a voluntary one and its non-voluntary characteristics were produced by the first, as when the first act drives the victim mad and he then commits suicide, clearly the death may be treated as the consequence of the first act, although the second act substituted a different causal process. If the second act is voluntary but the reason for its commission is the state of affairs created by the first, as when the victim, though quite sane, commits suicide because of the pain caused by the first act, legal opinion is divided as to the responsibility of the first actor.

In *State* v. *Scates*[76] accused admitted having caused burns to a child but did not admit that he had given the child a blow on the head. The child died and the medical witnesses thought that the burning was the primary cause of death but that the blow might have hastened it. The appellate court held that, if the blow might have been the *independent* act of another and have hastened the death, accused could not be found guilty of homicide merely because he was responsible for the burning. 'If one man inflicts a mortal wound, by which the victim is lingering, and then a second kills the deceased by an independent act, we cannot imagine how the first can be said to have killed him without involving the absurdity of saying that the deceased was killed twice.'

In civil law too it appears that this view is generally accepted. Thus in *Dillon* v. *Twin State Gas & Electric Co.*[77] defendant negligently maintained electric wires carrying current over a bridge. Deceased was playing on the bridge and, losing his balance, fell and instinctively took hold of one of the wires to save himself. He was electrocuted. The court held that defendants might be held liable for wrongfully causing his death but that damages should be assessed upon the basis that deceased would, if not electrocuted, either certainly have fallen to his death or at least have suffered serious injury.

---

[75] It is in this sense that we use 'mortal' unless we indicate otherwise. A fourth sense is propounded by Beadle J. in *R.* v. *Mubila*, 1956 (1) SA 31, 33 (SR): 'an intrinsically dangerous wound from which the injured person is likely to die if he receives no medical attention'.
[76] (1858) 50 NC 409.
[77] (1932) 85 NH 449, 163 Atl. 111.

Hence the court appears to have decided that defendants could be held to have caused death even if the deceased was certain to die within a very short time. Again, in Roman law some of the most prominent jurists took this view. Ulpian, quoting Celsus, says[78] that if one man mortally wounds a slave and another later kills him, the first is not held liable under the *lex Aquilia* for killing but only for wounding. Marcellus approves this view.[79] In another passage Ulpian says[80] that if a slave is mortally wounded and afterwards his death is accelerated by the collapse of a building or shipwreck, no action can be brought for killing but only for wounding. He, however, gives a reason which suggests that the matter is really one of evidence, the later calamity preventing it from being certainly established whether the original blow would have killed the deceased, which seems inconsistent with the description of the first wound as 'mortal'.[81]

Hall[82] propounds a case in which the accused throws the victim from the top of the Empire State Building and a second person acting independently shoots the victim as he passes the 49th floor. Here again, the second act is independent of the first except in the sense that the first actor provided the opportunity for the second to shoot, and it seems clear that the second agent alone has caused death though no doubt the first is guilty of attempted murder.

When the first actor provides not merely the opportunity but also the reason for the second's act not all courts adopt the same solution. In *State* v. *Angelina*[83] accused inflicted a mortal wound upon deceased who a minute or two later shot himself and twenty minutes later died. It was held that, if the act of deceased: was that of an independent responsible agent in no way causally connected with the first act, the 'proximate cause' of the homicide was the act of the deceased. Here the court disregards the fact that the first action was the reason for the suicide.

On the other hand, in *People* v. *Lewis*[84] defendant and deceased were brothers-in-law, and defendant, after a quarrel with deceased, shot him in the abdomen inflicting a mortal wound. Deceased was stunned and his strength soon failed him. Within a few minutes, when no one else was present but a boy of nine, deceased procured a knife, cut his throat and died almost immediately. Had he not

[78] *D.* 9. 2. 11. 3.
[79] Ibid.
[80] *D.* 9. 2. 15. 1.
[81] Perhaps the first sense of 'mortal' is intended: above, pp. 241–2.
[82] *Principles of Criminal Law*, 1st edn., p. 262.
[83] (1913) 73 W. Va. 146, 80 SE 141; *State* v. *Wood* (1881) 53 Vt. 560.
[84] (1899) 124 Cal. 551, 57 P. 470; *Payne* v. *Commonwealth* (1935) 255 Ky. 533, 541, 75 SW 2d 14, 19; *Henderson* v. *State* (1913) 65 So. 721 (Ala.); *State* v. *Payne* (1935) 75 SW 2d 19.

done so he would have died within an hour. The court held that though it was 'impossible to determine whether deceased was induced to cut his throat through pain produced by the wound or from remorse or a desire to shield his brother-in-law', nevertheless defendant was guilty of manslaughter. The reason given in the opinion is the unsatisfactory one that when death occurred the original wound was still 'contributing' to it: 'Drop by drop his life current welled out from both wounds and at the very instant of death the gunshot wound was contributing to the event.' On this basis, even if the throat-cutting had been the act of a third person, defendant would still have been guilty of manslaughter. Only by identifying causation literally with the setting in motion of a physical process which has not come to an end can the cause be said still to be contributing to the event.[85] But one might justify the decision on the ground that the first act provided a reason for the second and was not merely the occasion on which another cause intervened.

There is a tendency in some opinions to hold the second actor responsible upon similar facts, even though his act has not accelerated the consequence. Thus it is asserted in some American cases that, when one defendant has given the victim a mortal wound, another who subsequently wounds him may be held responsible for homicide although the later wound is not shown to have 'contributed to' or 'hastened' death except in a 'minor way'.[86] This leaves open the question what is meant by a 'minor way'. A better ground for decision would be that the law presumes, in the absence of clear evidence, which usually will not be obtainable, that the second actor has accelerated death, even if only by a short interval. Of course this may, if the parties were not acting in concert, lead to the acquittal of the first party or his conviction for an attempt only, and this may be thought morally unsatisfactory when the evidence of acceleration is unclear; for it is often felt that, in the absence of such evidence, the case is like the simultaneous shooting of one person by two assassins acting independently. A more satisfactory approach may perhaps be found in a view of Schreiner JA. In *R*. v. *Mgxwiti*[87] the learned judge considered the position if 'the appellant joined in an obviously murderous attack upon the deceased at a time when she was still alive, though possibly mortally injured'.[88] He there considers the view of Moorman that, where accused has assaulted a person who is already mortally injured, the persons who struck the blows subsequent to the fatal blow are to be treated as having in effect

[85] A similar problem concerning the giving of improper medical treatment to a person mortally wounded is discussed below, pp. 360–2.

[86] *Bennett* v. *Commonwealth* (1912) 100 Ky. 604, 150 SW 806, 808.

[87] 1954 (1) SA 370 (AD).

[88] *R*. v. *Mgxwiti*, 1954 (1) SA 370, 381.

struck a corpse.[89] This view Schreiner JA rejects since 'at least if the later blow accelerates the death by even the briefest period of time he who dealt the blow is responsible for the death'.[90] His solution of the moral injustice of exempting the first assailant from full responsibility is to reject the causal criterion of liability and to hold that, since it would be unjust to allow one of the parties to escape or to make his liability turn upon matters of which accurate evidence is unlikely to be available, recourse should be had to the notion of ratification, i.e. that 'whoever joins in a murderous assault upon a person must be taken to have ratified the infliction of any injuries which have already been inflicted, whether or not in the result these turn out to be fatal either individually or taken together'.

That the difficulty of these cases was felt by the Roman jurists is shown by the view attributed to Julian in the *Digest*.[91] He holds that when a slave is mortally wounded by *A*, then instituted heir, then struck by *B* so that he dies, an action for wrongful death can also be brought against *A* because 'the *lex Aquilia* applies not only to those who have wounded a slave as so to deprive him of life immediately but also to those who have wounded him so that he is certain to lose his life'. Hence both parties may, in Julian's view, be held responsible upon such facts. The distinction between their acts is relevant only to the measure of damages. Hence Julian appears to take a different view from that attributed to Celsus and Ulpian.[92]

(iii) *Additional 'overtaking' cause*.[93] A so-called overtaking cause (which we shall with greater propriety call an 'overtaken' cause) is one which is in a sense frustrated by another sufficient cause so that it does not affect the victim at all or not to the extent that it normally would. Thus, if the victim suffers from a disease which would in due course produce blindness (the overtaken cause), the operation of this disease may be 'frustrated' by the act of a wrongdoer who negligently blinds plaintiff in a car accident before the disease has run its course. Ought this disease to be taken into account in assessing damages for the blinding? Again, a flood which would destroy plaintiff's property on Tuesday may be 'overtaken' by a fire negligently set by defendant which destroys the property on Monday, so that the overtaken cause, the flood, does not have the effect it normally would. Should the damages payable by defendant be reduced because of the doom which awaited the property from the flood?

In attempting to answer these questions, where the problem is to put an economic value on the assets or opportunities of which

---

[89] *Verhandelingen over de Misdaden*, 2.1.23.
[90] *R. v. Mgxwiti*, 1954(1) SA 370, 382.
[91] *D.* 9. 2. 51. pr.
[92] Above, p. 243.
[93] Honoré, *IECL*, xi, chap. 7-130, 7-135 to 7-138; Wagner, 'Successive Causes and the Quantum of Damages in Personal Injury Cases', (1972) 10 *Osgoode Hall LJ* 369.

defendant has deprived plaintiff, it is important to bear in mind the distinction between capital assets and income-producing assets. A house is a capital asset. If A's fire had not destroyed it on Monday its owner might in theory have sold it before Tuesday's flood swept it away.[94] On the other hand the human body is an income-producing asset. It cannot be sold, but can be used, by the exercise of skill, to earn money over a period of time.[95] If a person is negligently injured by A in January so that his earning capacity is permanently reduced and he is then independently disabled by B in February, so that, even apart from A's act, he would have suffered a similar reduction in earning power, he would ordinarily be said to have lost as a result of A's act only what he could have earned during the intervening month. His bodily skill is not something, like a house, of which he could have realized the full value during that month.

With this general point in mind we may turn to the legal difficulties. Suppose a person is run over twice in succession by independent wrongdoers, the second accident being quite independent of the first, and on each occasion loses a limb. The loss of either limb is sufficient to prevent him earning his living again: hence, if the case against the first actor is decided after the second accident, the court is faced with the problem of assessing what loss of earnings has been caused by the first act. The difficulties are generated by the fact that, to assess the loss of future earnings, the court must estimate the course of events subsequent to the infliction of physical injuries; and two different approaches to such problems are possible. The first rests on the argument that, if one looks at the matter immediately after the first wrongful act, the wrongdoer would be said to have deprived the victim of his earnings for the rest of his life. This estimate presupposes that normally a person lives out his life without suffering the loss of a limb. The second approach estimates the loss by reference to any relevant events known to have happened, even though subsequent to the infliction of the injury and however improbable. It may be argued that the estimation of future loss by reference to probabilities is a mere *pis aller* and the court should therefore take account of any fact that is known by the time the case is to be decided, however antecedently improbable.[96] Against this apparently rational consideration is the fact that, if the first wrongdoer is exonerated by the second act, no one will be responsible, because at the time when the second wrongdoer intervened it was already certain that plaintiff would not be able to earn in future, and

94 *Burmah Oil* v. *Lord Advocate* [1965] AC 75 (destruction of oil installations which would later have fallen into Japanese hands: clearly the value was much reduced: see pp. 113, 163).
95 *Faulkner* v. *Keffalinos* (1970) 45 *ALJ* 80, 85.
96 *Williamson* v. *Thornycroft* [1940] 2 KB 658. *The Kingsway* [1918] P. 344, 362.

hence the second wrongdoer cannot be said to have caused any loss of earnings though he has certainly caused the loss of a leg. The decisions suggest that a distinction is to be drawn between the case where both acts are wrongful and where only the first is. If both are wrongful the victim recovers the whole of his loss from the first wrongdoer. This is because, though he has not deprived plaintiff of any gain that he could have made after the date of the second wrong, he is nevertheless held liable for that later loss on the ground that he is taken to guarantee plaintiff against any reduction, on account of later wrongful acts, in the extent of the remedy he might normally have expected. This was the solution adopted by the House of Lords in *Baker* v. *Willoughby*.[97] In that case plaintiff suffered a permanent injury to his leg as a result of *A*'s negligent driving. Three years later he was shot in the same leg in a hold-up by *B*, and the leg had to be amputated. Plaintiff was held entitled to recover against *A* for loss of earnings and amenities even for the period after the second injury. The reasoning of the House is not satisfactory, because plaintiff was said to have suffered a 'devaluation' at the time of the first injury[98] (as if he were a slave) and the first injury was wrongly said to be a 'concurrent cause'[99] of the loss of earnings after the time of the second. Nevertheless, the decision is defensible[1] as an attempt to provide compensation against the unlawful invasion of people's rights. In so far as it extends liability beyond what causal criteria would suggest, it will be relevant to ask how far plaintiff is compensated from collateral sources, which should go to reduce the first tortfeasor's liability. But it is not unknown for a legal system to treat certain wrongdoers as guarantors.[2] The precise mechanism by which the court ensures, in the case of two solvent tortfeasors, that plaintiff recovers the whole of his loss and that the apportionment between the tortfeasors is fairly made, has been explored with some precision in Canada[3] and Australia.[4]

Since the second wrongdoer cannot be held to have caused harm which had already occurred,[5] the alternative to holding the first wrongdoer liable, if plaintiff is not to be left without recourse in such cases, is to hold the second wrongdoer liable for having deprived the

97 [1970] AC 467.
98 [1970] AC 467, 496.
99 [1970] AC 467, 492.
1 *Stene & Lakeman Construction* v. *Evans* (1958) 11 DLR 2d 187; 14 DLR 2d 73; *Long* v. *Thiessen* (1968) 65 WWR 577; *Hicks* v. *Cooper* (1973) 41 DLR 3d 454 (damages to be assessed as on day before second accident).
2 Below, pp. 321 f.
3 *Penner* v. *Mitchell* [1978] 5 WWR 328 (Alta.).
4 *Nicholson* v. *Walker* (1979) 21 *SASR* 481.
5 *Performance Cars* v. *Abraham* [1962] 1 QB 33 (tortfeasor not liable for cost of respray of car already in need of a respray before he damaged it).

victim of his remedy against the first.[6] So far as causal connection is concerned there is no objection to so holding,[7] but the head of damage is not one which is normally recognized. Nevertheless, if the victim is unable to recover from the first wrongdoer, there is much to be said for allowing him to proceed against the second on this basis. In *Baker* v. *Willoughby*, however, the House of Lords was not disposed to admit this head of damage;[8] and in that case the wrong-doer was in any event untraceable and presumably not worth suing. If the later injury or disability is non-tortious, these considerations do not apply; plaintiff must put up with the vicissitudes of life. So, not surprisingly, when in *Jobling* v. *Associated Dairies*[9] the House of Lords was confronted with a case of this latter sort, it had doubts about the reasoning in *Baker* v. *Willoughby*. Defendant's breach of statutory duty caused plaintiff a back injury, thereby reducing his earning power. Three years later he was found to be suffering from a condition of the spinal cord that would have disabled him in any event. The House denied recovery for loss of earnings in respect of the period after the spinal condition manifested itself. This seems correct.[10] Defendant did not cause the loss of earnings after this period, and there is no reason of policy why he should be made to guarantee the victim against ill health. It should not matter whether the ill health disables plaintiff or obliges him to go into hospital before the trial[11] or is likely to do so later.[12] The onus of proving that the later disabling event was non-tortious should, in our view, lie on the first tortfeasor.[13]

Overtaken cause has been much discussed in Germany, but the decisions do not fall into a clear pattern.[14]

[6] Street, 'Supervening Events and the Quantum of Damages', (1962) 78 *LQR* 70.

[7] Strachan, 'The Scope and Application of the "but for" Causal Test', (1970) *MLR* 386, 393.

[8] [1970] AC 467.

[9] [1981] 2 All ER 752 (HL); cf. *Leschke* v. *Jeffs* [1955] QWN 67 (subsequent imprisonment); *Hodgson* v. *General Electricity* [1978] 2 Ll. R. 210 (subsequent unconnected heart condition). Cf. *The Carslogie* [1952] AC 292. Ideally (see Lord Wilberforce, [1981] 2 All ER 752, at p. 755; T. Hervey, (1981) 97 *LQR* 210) the effect of the second injury on collateral, including social security benefits, should be before the court in order to fix accurately the quantum of loss attributable to the non-tortious cause; but this does not affect the general principle.

[10] *Traian* v. *Ware* [1957] VR 200, 208; *Penner* v. *Mitchell* [1978] 5 WWR 328 (Alta.) applying *Andrews* v. *Grand & Toy Alta Ltd.* [1978] 1 WWR 577, 83 DLR 3d 452. Cf. McGregor, 'Variations on an Enigma: Successive Causes of Personal Injury', (1970) 33 *MLR* 378.

[11] The contrary was held in *Harwood* v. *Wyken Colliery* [1913] 2 KB 158 and supported by Lord Reid in *Baker* v. *Willoughby* [1970] AC 467, 494 but rejected in *Jobling* v. *Associated Dairies* [1981] 2 All ER 752, 768.

[12] *Penner* v. *Mitchell* [1978] 5 WWR 328, 332

[13] Cf. *Kingston* v. *Chicago R. Co.* (1927) 191 Wis. 610, 211 NW 913.

[14] *NJW* 6. ii (1953), 977 (defendant had plaintiff put in concentration camp in 1944 thus causing loss of earnings as factory manager: no recovery for period after 1945 when allies dismissed all such managers). *RG Seuff.* A 71, no. 87 (defendant partially

Cases may occur which fall, in a sense, halfway between the situation in which the victim is successively affected by the acts of two persons and the one in which he is simultaneously affected by the simultaneous acts of two persons. This will be the case when two persons act at different times but the victim's body is physically affected by both acts simultaneously, as when a man standing in the path of a falling boulder dislodged by one man is shot by another just as the boulder reaches him.

IV. ALTERNATIVE CAUSES

'Alternative cause' describes the situation when defendant's wrongful act is sufficient in combination with other conditions to produce the harm but, even had he acted lawfully, the same or similar harm would have been produced either through the wrongful act of some third person or without it. The difference between an alternative and an additional cause is that an alternative cause is hypothetical; the act or event to which it refers did not in fact occur. In contrast, an additional overtaken cause is not hypothetical, though it does not in the circumstances produce its normal effects, or not all of them. Despite this difference, many of the same issues which arise in regard to overtaken causes also surface when alternative causes are in question. In particular, it may make a difference whether the alternative cause would have been a wrongful act and whether it would have deprived plaintiff of economic opportunities of which he claims that the wrongdoer has deprived him. In the case of a hypothetical alternative cause the generally accepted view is that defendant's wrongful or criminal act has caused the harm, for which the wrongdoer is therefore criminally or civilly responsible, despite the existence of a set of alternative conditions sufficient to produce the same harm.[15]

Thus, to draw illustrations from some German criminal cases where the point has been considered, when accused had procured the detention of certain Jews in concentration camps it was no defence on a charge of unlawful deprivation of freedom to prove that, had accused not done this, other persons would have procured their detention.[16] Nor would it, on a homicide charge, reduce the offence to that of being an accessory for accused to show that, had

incapacitated plaintiff; another later assaulted him causing total incapacity: no recovery for loss of earnings after date of assault). *RG Seuff.* A 77, no. 68 (defendant stole object from plaintiff's house which was later burned, so that object would have been lost in any case: no reduction of damages—this may be regarded as closely analogous to alternative causation).

[15] Glanville Williams, *Joint Torts*, p. 240 n. 11. Above, pp. 124–5.
[16] *BGHSt* 2 (1951), 20.

he not committed a certain crime, another member of the gang would have done so.[17] A similar result would obviously be reached in civil law if *A* assaulted *B* or converted *B*'s goods and then relied on the defence that, had he not done so, *C*, acting independently, would have done the same.[18]

But not all cases are as simple as these. In particular, two complexities stand out. First, the existence of an alternative cause may sometimes lead to the conclusion that plaintiff has not suffered an infringement of the right for which he claims compensation. Secondly, it may be difficult to distinguish between cases in which there are alternative causes of harm and those in which the unlawful aspect of defendant's conduct is irrelevant.

The first point is not concerned with any causal principle but with the purposes of criminal and civil law respectively. In criminal law the wrong is not primarily the infringement of someone else's right to life, bodily safety, or goods but rather the interference with some state of affairs (the life of another, his possession of goods) contrary to the public interest. In larceny, for instance, it would be futile for accused to argue that the prosecutor had no right to the goods stolen because they had since been lawfully expropriated by the State. But in civil law the position is different. Compensation is there given for the infringement of some right and, where economic loss is concerned, plaintiff only establishes the right to compensation when he shows that, in the absence of wrongful acts on the part of the defendant or anyone else, he would have enjoyed the relevant economic advantage.[19]

An example may make this clear. In *Douglas, Burt & Buchanan Co.* v. *Texas & Pacific R. Co.*[20] defendants unlawfully maintained a bridge which obstructed the waterway and delayed plaintiff's barge, so that he suffered financial loss. But a lawfully[21] maintained bridge farther along the waterway would in any case have obstructed the barge, so causing the same delay. The Louisiana court held that no damages were recoverable for the loss attributable to the delay. Here the unlawfully maintained bridge undoubtedly caused the delay of the barge, and this remains true even if another bridge would in

---

[17] *BGHSt* 2 (1951), 20, 24. Cf. Mayer, *Strafrecht*, p. 133: no defence to quack on charge of negligent killing by administering harmful treatment to show that deceased would otherwise have consulted another quack who would have prescribed the same or worse treatment.

[18] Neumann–Duesburg [1953] *JZ*, p. 171.

[19] *The York* [1929] P. 178. Cf. *Smith* v. *Cawdle Fen Commissioners* [1938] 4 All ER 64, 71 (man killed on Monday who would have been hanged on Wednesday).

[20] (1922) 150 La. 1083, 91 So. 503; Green, *Proximate Cause*, pp. 168–70. Cf. *Cole* v. *Shell Petroleum* (1939) 149 Kan. 25, 86 P. 2d 740.

[21] The decision would be different if the second bridge was also unlawfully maintained. See below, p. 251.

any case have caused a similar delay. But it does not follow that
defendant's bridge caused the financial loss to plaintiff, for one can
only properly speak of plaintiff suffering financial loss if he would,
apart from defendant's act, have been able to exploit certain economic
opportunities. On the facts of the Louisiana case he could not do
so. Note that, even in civil law, this reasoning only applies to cases
where compensation is paid because plaintiff has been deprived of
economic opportunities. It would be quite irrelevant to compensation for, for example, pain and suffering: if A has negligently
caused B pain and suffering the fact that, if A had not done so, C
would have caused B greater pain does not in any way show that A
has not caused B pain and suffering, and, if C's act would have been
wrongful, A cannot insist that the fact that he has saved B from it
should be taken into account in assessing damages, in view of the fact
that the legal system aims to protect B against *all* wrongful invasions
of his interests. But if the alternative pain would not have been wrongfully caused, there is an argument for taking it into account. Thus, it
has been held in an American case that a tortfeasor who caused plaintiff a miscarriage was entitled to have the jury take account of the fact
that he had saved plaintiff the pangs of childbirth.[22]

The Romans were aware of the existence of this problem in the
field of compensation. Suppose defendant in breach of contract
places plaintiff's goods on the wrong ship and the ship and goods
are lost on the voyage. Labeo asserts that the owner can recover the
value of the goods.[23] Paul, however, argues that plaintiff cannot sue
if both the right and the wrong ship perish during the voyage.[24]
Windscheid agrees that defendant should not be liable for the value
of the goods.[25] Here defendant by his breach of contract has indeed
caused the destruction of the goods but he has not deprived plaintiff
of any economic advantage which he would otherwise have enjoyed.
Hence plaintiff cannot recover, except perhaps in one situation. If
defendant has wrongfully deprived plaintiff of an economic opportunity of which, in the alternative, another would *wrongfully* have
deprived him he should be liable to pay compensation, because,
it may be said, plaintiff has a right to any economic advantage
which he would enjoy apart from wrongful acts on the part of
anyone: hence Paul (or a later hand) in the *Digest* text cited[26] says
that no compensation is payable provided that both ships perished

[22] *Hawkins* v. *Front-Street Cable R. Co.* (1898) 3 Wash. 592, 28 Pac. 1021. *Contra:*
Morris v. *St. Paul City R. Co.* (1908) 105 Minn. 276, 117 NW 500 ('too remote,
speculative and uncertain' when plaintiff only pregnant two months): p. 502.
[23] *D.* 14. 2. 10. 1.
[24] Ibid.
[25] *Lehrbuch des Pandektenrechts*, s. 258 (2).
[26] *D.* 14. 2. 10. 1.

without fraud or fault on the part of their respective masters. For, clearly, if the master of the right ship was at fault in allowing it to be lost, plaintiff's goods would in any case have been lost by someone's wrongful act and he is entitled, in that situation, to claim that he has been wrongfully deprived of an economic opportunity.

The second difficulty is to distinguish genuine cases of alternative causation from cases where the wrongful aspect of defendant's act is causally irrelevant. When an unlicensed driver drives carefully but is involved in an accident, we say that the wrongful aspect of his conduct, not having a licence, was causally irrelevant.[27] How do we know this? We have to consider in what respects, if any, the other conditions present would have been altered had defendant had a licence.[28] Since defendant drove carefully, having a licence would have made no relevant difference to the course of events. Hence not having a licence is causally irrelevant. On similar reasoning it has been held, in German criminal law, that a chemist was not liable for negligent killing by renewing a phosphorus prescription without consulting the doctor, since the doctor would probably have continued the phosphorus treatment,[29] if consulted. So, too, the owner of a factory was not liable for negligently killing certain employees who died of anthrax when the statutory precautions which he did not take would probably not have eliminated the anthrax bacilli.[30] No doubt there is room for argument as to what should here count as a relevant difference in the causal process. Suppose it could be proved that the precautions would have eliminated some of the bacilli which entered the bodies of the deceased workers. The matter is clearly one of degree, allowing the court some discretion.[31] If compliance with the law would merely have eliminated some of the bacilli, leaving enough to kill, the law would not inquire, even if it were possible to determine, whether numerically the same bacilli would have entered the victims' bodies at precisely the same time. Generally speaking, perhaps, if lawful conduct would have resulted in a qualitatively similar process, very close in time and space to the

27 At any rate this is the preferable view. Above, pp. 210–11.
28 This is what the Germans call the procedure of 'substitution' in contrast with the procedure of 'elimination'. After much controversy the former was decisively upheld in *RGSt* 63 (1930), 392. (Accused rode bicycle without light; deceased collided with another unlighted cyclist and was killed: trial court held wrong in denying causal connection. It ought to have asked whether, if accused had had a light, deceased would have seen the other cyclist. Accused was acquitted of negligent killing on another ground).
29 *RGSt* 15 (1886), 151.
30 *RGSt* 63 (1929), 211.
31 Becht and Miller, op. cit., pp. 28, 31, 187, who advocate 'equating' injuries, i.e. treating them as identical and denying causal connection, when not to do so would intuitively lead to a wrong conclusion.

actual course of events, this will be enough to show that the wrongful conduct was not the 'cause'.[32] Conversely, if compliance with the law would have substituted a causal process either qualitatively different or differing in more than insignificant spatial or temporal respects, defendant or accused would properly be held to have caused the harm in question and should be liable subject to the point about compensation for loss of economic opportunities mentioned above. But when a doctor negligently administered cocaine instead of novocaine and the patient died, a German court held that it was a good defence on a criminal charge of negligent killing that the novocaine would probably have caused death.[33] The causal processes associated with the operation of the two drugs being presumably qualitatively different, this decision cannot, on strict causal principles, be supported.

One final consideration needs to be borne in mind. A court is likely to require some evidence that compliance with the law would have led to substantially the same harm before it will leave the issue to the jury.[34]

In such anomalous cases there are weighty considerations in favour of decisions either way. Perhaps, in general, liability is likely to be affirmed where criminal responsibility is based on the idea of causing harm, and to be denied where the notion of 'increasing the risk' is taken as the basis of responsibility. The idea of 'causing harm' involves close attention to the precise manner of the upshot, whereas the risk theory does not.

[32] *Goldblatt* v. *Tabacco* (1949) 299 NY 663, 87 NE 2d 58 (car parked two feet over line was projected another fifty feet and so killed decedent; wrongful parking not proximate cause of death): *Tennessee Trailways* v. *Ervin* (1969) SE 2d 733 (bus going at reasonable 65 rather than 73 m.p.h. would not have avoided accident); *Utzinger* v. *U.S.* (1970) 423 F. 2d 485 (if no projecting rails, speedboat would have run into tree and suffered comparable harm).

[33] *HRR* 1930, no. 2034 (RG).

[34] *Berry* v. *Borough of Sugar Notch* (1899) 43 Atl. 240 (Pa.); but equally the jury must have some evidence to support a finding that it would not: *Texas & Pacific R.* v. *McCleary* (1967) 418 SW 2d 494.

IX

FORESEEABILITY AND RISK

IN this and the next chapter we discuss various proposed substitutes for causal tests for limiting responsibility. Broadly speaking, these may be grouped under the rubric 'policy', but the principal form of the claim that policy dominates this branch of the law consists in an appeal to foreseeability or risk as the exclusive or at least the main test. The appeal to foreseeability or risk differs from some other policy theories in that it proposes a general and apparently factual test, and does not leave the decision to the choice of the judge or to special arbitrary rules of law.[1] But whereas the test of foreseeability is usually thought to be particularly appropriate to the civil law of negligence, that of risk is thought to apply to the law of tort generally. Since the risk doctrine turns out, on its most plausible interpretation, to be a generalized version of the foreseeability doctrine, we postpone the consideration of it to the end of the chapter and proceed to deal first with the notion of foreseeability.

A reading of many cases on 'proximate cause' or 'remoteness of damage' leaves on the mind a strong impression of the number and variety of references to foreseeability to be found in judgments, even when they professedly treat of causal problems. As Edgerton says,[2] 'Except only the defendant's intention to produce a given result, no other consideration has affected our feeling that it is or is not just to hold him for the result so much as its foreseeability.' These references are to be found not merely in the context of negligence, where they are to be expected, but also in contexts where foresight is apparently out of place. For instance an insurer cannot recover for damage to the property insured because, it has been said, the harm to him is unforeseeable.[3] Again, references to foresight are to be found in the context of strict liability.[4]

It is not surprising to find that lawyers often stress the importance of foreseeability in relation to problems of responsibility, for even outside the law the fact that harm was or was not foreseeable is frequently an important factor in blaming or excusing people for its occurrence. A mother who administers a strong drug to a crying

[1] Above, pp. 97–8.
[2] 'Legal Cause', (1924) 72 *U. Pa. LR* 211, 352; Harper and James, p. 1134.
[3] *Sinram* v. *Pennsylvania R. Co.* (1932) 61 F. 2d 767.
[4] *Madsen* v. *East Jordan Irrigation Co.* (1942) 101 Utah 552, 125 P. 2d 794.

child will be blamed for the harmful consequences if she knew or ought to have foreseen that such consequences were likely to follow and excused if she could not be expected to foresee this. A father who consents to the marriage of his daughter to a man who later treats her with cruelty will be blamed if he knew or ought to have known of the man's character and so have foreseen the consequences, excused if he had no reason to suspect the truth. In the first case we would naturally say that the mother had caused the harm, in the second that the father had merely made it possible by giving his consent; but in both the foreseeability of the harm, together with the fact that the parent could have avoided it, determines our moral judgment. Here the notion of foreseeability seems to represent a wider principle of responsibility than that of either causing harm or of providing opportunities for others to do harm.

Given the obvious importance of the notion of foreseeability, the problem that presents itself in the civil law of negligence is not whether foreseeability has a place in the law but precisely what its place is. The narrow view, formerly accepted in England, is that the foreseeability of harm is relevant to whether defendant was negligent but not to the extent of his responsibility once negligence is shown. This view draws a sharp line between culpability and compensation. The wider view, advocated by writers such as Goodhart[5] in England and Fleming James[6] in America, and on the face of it adopted by the Privy Council in *The Wagon Mound* (*No. 1*),[7] is that the foreseeability of harm is relevant also to the extent of a negligent defendant's responsibility. On this view no sharp line can be drawn between culpability and compensation; the questions whether defendant was negligent and whether he is responsible for the harm that follows are determined by the same test. On the narrow view, the extent of defendant's responsibility depends mainly on whether the harm for which recovery is sought was caused by his wrongful act and is of a type which is within the scope of the rule violated, while on the wider view the only causal question to be determined is whether defendant's negligent act was a necessary condition of the harm.

The wider view of the place of foreseeability in the law of negligence may be formulated thus: a defendant is responsible for and only for such harm as he could reasonably have foreseen and prevented. This principle in turn has two aspects, one limiting responsibility to something less than the harm which the negligent act would on common-sense principles be said to have caused, the other

5 *Essays in Jurisprudence & the Common Law*, chaps. 6 and 7; *Cambridge Legal Essays*, pp. 101–21; (1930) 39 *Yale LJ* 449.
6 'Legal Cause', (1951) 60 *Yale LJ* 761.
7 [1961] AC 388.

extending it beyond such harm. The limiting doctrine is that a defendant is not liable for unforeseeable harm even if, on the commonsense principles set out in Chapter VI, he caused it; the extending doctrine is that he is liable for foreseeable harm of which his act is a necessary condition even if, on common-sense causal principles, he did not cause it. Such, then, is the doctrine of foreseeability in its widest and simplest form. There is, however, a variant of the second aspect of the doctrine which, as has been said, extends responsibility to foreseeable harm even if not caused by the negligent act. This variant takes account of the possibility that harm of a foreseeable sort may come about by unforeseeable means, viz. through the conjunction with the negligent act of some coexisting condition or subsequent event which is itself unforeseeable.[8] The variant view is that a negligent defendant is liable for foreseeable harm only if the manner of its occurrence is also foreseeable.

In our exposition of the wide foreseeability doctrine we have treated foreseeability as representing a criterion for assessing the extent of a negligent defendant's responsibility which is to be substituted for the causal notions expounded in Chapter VI. It is true that this is not the only way of interpreting the doctrine. It may also be thought of as propounding a special legal meaning of causation different from the common-sense meaning;[9] or, again, it may be, in its limiting aspect, propounded not as an alternative but as a supplement to causal criteria.[10] Thus, it may be said that a negligent defendant should be responsible only for such harm as is both foreseeable and, on common-sense principles, caused by his negligent act. In order, however, to assess the merits of the widely held doctrine of foreseeability, we prefer to treat the doctrine as putting forward the notion of foreseeability not as an interpretation of or a supplement to that of causation but as an alternative.

Before we undertake a detailed examination of the wide foreseeability doctrine it is as well to deal with an objection to it which has been put forward with some insistence by Clarence Morris and which, if sustained, would be fatal to the doctrine. The objection is that it is merely arbitrary to call harm 'foreseeable' or 'unforeseeable' since in one sense everything is foreseeable, in another sense

---

[8] 'Foreseeable results of unforeseeable causes': Prosser, *Torts*, p. 280.

[9] Thus in some American states, e.g. Texas, the proximate cause issue is taken to consist of two elements, *sine qua non* and foreseeability.

[10] This is how the Privy Council decision in *The Wagon Mound (No. 1)* [1961] AC 388 has in practice been interpreted: *McKew* v. *Holland, Hannen & Cubitts* [1969] 3 All ER 1621 (HL); *Chapman* v. *Hearse* (1961) 106 *CLR* 112, 122 ('no occasion to consider reasonable foreseeability on the part of the particular wrongdoer unless and until it appears that the negligent act or omission alleged has, in fact, caused the damage complained of').

nothing.[11] 'The consequences of negligence are almost invariably surprises.'[12] All depends on the detail with which the harm is described. In *Hines* v. *Morrow*,[13] the facts of which were mentioned in Chapter IV,[14] plaintiff described his claim by saying that he 'slipped into this hole, created by defendant's negligence and was injured in attempting to extricate himself'. This would appear reasonably foreseeable, given the disrepair of the highway; but if one adopts the defendant's point of view and emphasizes that the injury was the breaking of plaintiff's sound leg by the stretching of the rope while his wooden leg was stuck in the mud, this hardly appears foreseeable. Must we conclude, with Clarence Morris,[15] that the notion of foreseeability is arbitrary, because it is impossible to settle how the harm should be described?

No description of an occurrence is uniquely correct. When a vase is broken, a description of the harm, given to show its full extent or cost ('the breaking of a Ming vase'), will differ from a description in terms of what could ordinarily have been foreseen ('the breaking of a vase'); but this does not make the latter arbitrary. *A* violently sets down a vase on a table and breaks it. To show that the harm, under the description 'the breaking of a vase', was foreseeable, it would suffice to point out certain facts known to *A*: that it was made of china, that the table was hard, and the force great. Here we implicitly appeal to the same broad generalizations as we would cite to show that the act was negligent, e.g. that an object of a certain consistency breaks when it strikes a hard surface with a certain force. These, with the particular facts known to *A*, enabled him to foresee harm under the description 'breaking of a vase', though not under the highly specific descriptions which might be given afterwards. The fact that *A* could not know that the vase he might break was a valuable one would not render its breaking unforeseeable. Nor will it affect *A*'s liability for the full value, for there is certainly no rule of law that the full value can only be recovered if it was known that the thing likely to be damaged would be of that value.

It is usually agreed that 'it is not necessary to show that this particular accident and this particular damage were probable; it is sufficient if the accident is of a class that might well be anticipated as one of the reasonable and probable results of the wrongful act'.[16] This view, though undoubtedly law, does not in itself provide any

[11] Prosser, *Torts*, p. 267; Macintosh and Scoble, *Negligence in Delict*, p. 72.
[12] *Clifford* v. *Denver, S.P, & Pacific R. Co.* (1886) 9 Colo. 333, 12 P. 219, 221.
[13] (1921) 236 SW 183 (Tex. Civ. App.); Prosser, *Selected Topics*, p. 218; Green, *Proximate Cause*, p. 22. Above, p. 95.
[14] See also p. 295.
[15] (1952-3) 101 *U. Pa. LR* 189, 196-8.
[16] *Haynes* v. *Harwood* [1935] 1 KB 146, 156 *per* Greer LJ; Pollock (1922) 38 *LQR* 165, 167.

means of determining the class of harm or accident which must be foreseeable; but that class can be determined by reference to the generalizations which one would have recourse to in describing conduct as negligent. Thus if the negligent act is firing a revolver, the harm is foreseeable if it is to things within the apparent range of the revolver, made of a material apparently permeable to bullets. On the other hand, if the shot punctures an inkpot which discharges ink on plaintiff's linen, the harm to the linen is not foreseeable (unless the presence of the inkpot within range was itself known to defendant) because the generalization about ink staining neighbouring objects when it is able to flow freely would not have been cited in support of the judgment that the person firing the revolver had acted negligently.

The objection that it is merely arbitrary to describe harm as foreseeable or unforeseeable must therefore be rejected, though our discussion has brought out at least one important limitation on the doctrine that the harm to be recoverable must be foreseeable, viz. that there will always be some details of the recoverable harm which are not foreseeable.

Conversely, the fact that harm described by reference to certain details is not foreseeable does not render the harm, more broadly described, unforeseeable. It is sufficient to stress that, to avoid fallacies, the first question to ask is not 'Was this harm foreseeable?' but 'Under what specific description which fits this harm has experience taught us to anticipate harm?' If we have learned from experience to expect a 'rainstorm' on seeing dark clouds, then the rainstorm was foreseeable even if, when it occurs, it has other characteristics (e.g. lasted two hours, covered an area of 40 sq. miles) which we could not foresee but which might appear, *ex post facto*, in a more specific description of it. Conversely, if we have learned to anticipate a *rainstorm* we cannot be said to have foreseen a hailstorm because it shares the same generic description, i.e. 'storm'. It is important to distinguish between the foresight, chance, or probability (i) that there would be an event A, which was also in fact a B (that there would be a rainstorm which in fact lasted two hours), and (ii) that there would be an event which was both A and B (that there would be a rainstorm lasting two hours). So with 'harm': if we have learned from experience that a violent blow may smash a glass this is foreseeable even if we cannot foresee the precise form in which it splinters. Conversely, the fact that this and some freakish further occurrence are alike 'harm to property' does not make the freak foreseeable.

We now go on to consider in more detail the wide foreseeability doctrine in its two aspects—limiting and extending responsibility by comparison with causal criteria.

I. THE DOCTRINE THAT ONLY FORESEEABLE HARM IS RECOVERABLE

That, in an action for negligence, only foreseeable harm is recoverable, is a doctrine which possesses many attractions, real or apparent, in particular those of consistency, simplicity, and fairness.[17] The doctrine appears consistent because it uses the same notions to determine the existence and extent of responsibility; simple because it eliminates the need for a difficult inquiry as to the causal relevance of the wrongful features of defendant's act, and fair because it protects a defendant from the danger of having to pay enormous sums in damages for harm which he could not have bargained for in advance. We consider these points separately.

Consistency. Holdsworth put forward the view that it is more logical to base liability for the consequences of a negligent act on the same grounds as liability itself. 'If we are basing liability upon a negligent act, and if negligence consists in a failure to foresee results which ought reasonably to have been foreseen, it would seem that the negligent person ought only to be made liable to the extent to which he ought to have foreseen those results.'[18]

To this it has been objected that there is no necessary reason why the ground for assessing damages should be the same as that used in fixing liability.[19] Once liability has been established the problem before the court is that of distributing the loss between the party in default and the innocent party. A strong argument against Holdsworth's view may be drawn from the law of intentional harms. It is generally agreed that when a defendant is liable because he has intentionally done harm, his liability is not restricted to the harm intended. Thus in *Wyant* v. *Crouse*[20] defendant wrongfully broke into plaintiff's shop, thereby committing an intentional trespass, and started a fire in his forge. He was not negligent in his management of the fire but, after he left, it spread in an unexplained way and set fire to the building, which was burned down. For this harm defendant was held liable, though he did not intend and was not negligent with regard to the spread of the fire. Similarly in *Vandenburgh* v. *Truax*[21] defendant frightened a boy (thereby committing an

[17] Goodhart (1952) 68 *LQR* 514, 533; Williams (1961) 77 *LQR* 179, 190; Seavey (1938-9) 52 *Harv. LR* 372, 386; Fleming (1961) 39 *Can. BR* 489, 522.
[18] *HEL* viii. 463. Cf. Pollock (1922) 38 *LQR* 165. Ihering put forward a similar view fifty years earlier, but the *BGB* did not adopt it.
[19] Lord Porter in (1935) 5 *Cam. LJ* 176, 177. Cf. Windscheid, *Lehrbuch des Pandektenrechts*, s. 258 (2) n. 14: 'Man verwechsle übrigens nicht das Ob der Verhaftung mit dem Umfang der Verhaftung.'
[20] (1901) 127 Mich. 158, 86 NW 527.
[21] (1847) 4 Denio. NY 464. Goodhart in 'Liability and Compensation', (1960) 76 *LQR* 567, 574 explains these decisions on the ground that the burning and loss of wine were foreseeable. Even if this was the case (and it is not the reason given), it would not show that the extent of liability is governed by the same criteria as its existence.

intentional assault) who, in his panic, ran into plaintiff's shop and overturned a cask of wine. For the loss of the wine defendant was held liable, though he did not intend it. It therefore seems that the existence and extent of liability are not necessarily governed by the same criteria.

A special, rather complex form of the argument from consistency is based on the alleged 'relativity' of negligence. It is argued against holding a negligent defendant liable for unforeseeable consequences that negligence is 'relative' only to the foreseeable consequences and that what are ordinarily called 'unforeseeable consequences' cannot properly be described as consequences of the negligent act. This raises the question of what is meant by saying that 'negligence is relative'. Here one must distinguish the tort of negligence from the concept of negligence or carelessness, for the claim that negligence is essentially relative means different things in each case. Applied to the tort of negligence the claim means only that legal rules limit the damage recoverable. Even if the law of negligence were simply that a negligent defendant is responsible for the harm caused by his act, this would still leave open the question whether *all* harm so caused is recoverable. In fact there are special principles excluding certain types of harm. Thus, plaintiff cannot normally recover in tort for a negligent invasion of his contractual interests;[22] he can recover for financial loss in the absence of physical harm[23] only in rather special conditions of 'proximity' when the relation between plaintiff and defendant is analogous to a contractual one.[24] None of this justifies the statement that the tort of negligence is 'relative' to the type of harm or the manner in which it occurs in any other sense than that it shows, what is obvious enough, that the scope of the tort is limited by specific rules.

Negligence itself, as opposed to the tort, consists in a failure to observe a certain standard of care. What particular precautions are necessary to comply with the standard depends on the circumstances and so, in this sense, negligence is indeed relative to the circumstances. As Cardozo CJ said in *Palsgraf*,[25] 'We are told that one who drives at reckless speed through a crowded city street is guilty of a negligent act and therefore of a wrongful one, irrespective of the consequences. Negligent the act is, and wrongful in the sense that it is unsocial, but wrongful and unsocial in relation to other travelers

22 *British Industrial Plastics* v. *Ferguson* (1938) 160 LT 95; *Cattle* v. *Stockton Water-works Co.* (1875) LR 10 QB 453; *Sinram* v. *Pennsylvania R. Co.* (1932) 61 F. 2d 767; *Weller* v. *Foot & Mouth Disease Institute* [1966] 1 QB 569.
23 *Spartan Steel Alloys* v. *Martin* [1973] 1 QB 27.
24 *Hedley Byrne* v. *Heller* [1964] AC 465; *Junior Books* v. *Veitchi* [1982] 3 All ER 201 (HL).
25 (1928) 248 NY 339, 162 NE 99.

only because the eye of vigilance perceives the risk of damage. If the same act were to be committed on a speedway or a race course it would lose its wrongful quality.'[26] This, however, is hardly relevant to the problem of the extent of a negligent defendant's responsibility.

But supporters of the foreseeability doctrine sometimes appeal to yet another sense of the relativity of negligence. Because the chance of a certain type of harm is the reason for designating an act negligent, they argue, the act is negligent only in relation to that type of harm. Goodhart further argues that consequences cannot 'flow from negligence' but only from an act, viz. certain bodily movements, so that it becomes improper to speak of harm as the consequence of a defendant's negligence or negligent act:[27] all one can properly say is that the harm was the consequence of his act, which was negligent in relation to certain foreseeable consequences. Neither of these assertions leads to the conclusion that it is designed to support. Even if it is true that an act is negligent in relation to certain consequences, this does not show that there is an impropriety in speaking of the consequences of a negligent act. If we cannot speak of the consequences of a negligent act, neither can we speak of the consequences of an intentional or voluntary act; and to add, as Goodhart does, that 'If negligence depends upon the consequences, then clearly the consequences cannot depend upon the negligence'[28] scarcely strengthens the point. This aphorism turns on an ambiguity. In the first phrase 'depends' means 'presupposes'. The description of conduct as negligent presupposes the likelihood of harm if that conduct takes place. In the second phrase 'depend' means 'be caused by'. Rewriting the sentence it only says 'If to call conduct negligent presupposes the likelihood of harm, the harm which actually occurs cannot be caused by the negligent conduct', which is a *non sequitur*. Because negligence presupposes the likelihood of certain harm it does not follow either that the responsibility of a negligent defendant must be limited to harm of that sort or that other harm cannot be the consequence of a negligent act. There remains the argument that considerations of policy nevertheless make such a restriction desirable.[29]

Simplicity.[30] Although there may be no logically compelling reason to restrict liability for a negligent act to foreseeable consequences, it remains true that, at least in one respect, the limitation to foreseeable harm gives a simpler rule than the limitation to harm caused by the

[26] (1928) 162 NE 100.
[27] *Essays in Jurisprudence and the Common Law*, p. 114.
[28] Op. cit., p. 114.
[29] Cf. Fleming, *Torts*, pp. 195-6.
[30] For contrasting views see Pollock (1922) 38 *LQR* 165, 167; Holdsworth, *HEL* viii. 464; and, most convincingly, Prosser, *Selected Topics*, pp. 215-21.

negligent act. This is because the limitation to foreseeable harm in many cases makes it possible to dispense with an inquiry whether all the wrongful aspects of the act were causally relevant.

This point is most easily brought out by the cases, considered in Chapter VIII, where there is alleged to be contributory negligence on plaintiff's part in driving without the statutory licence or registration.[31] Instead of embarking on the difficult inquiry whether the wrongful feature of plaintiff's act was a *sine qua non*, in the relevant sense, of the accident we can, by adopting the foreseeability doctrine, merely ask whether it was reasonably foreseeable that plaintiff, an unlicensed driver, would be involved in an accident. The answer would then depend on whether he in fact drove carelessly. The same reasoning applies when the act is not that of plaintiff but defendant. If defendant's negligence consists in setting in motion on the floor of his factory an unguarded fan[32] and plaintiff, working in the factory, contracts pneumonia owing to a chill caused by the fan we can, on the foreseeability doctrine, dispense with an inquiry into the causal relevance of all the wrongful features of the act and at once conclude that, since increase in air circulation was not the risk which made it negligent to set the unguarded fan in motion, defendant is not responsible for plaintiff's chill. In this way foreseeability provides a short cut to a conclusion to which the use of causal tests would also lead but by a longer route. Of course the question is not just one of contrasting techniques for reaching the same conclusion. The foreseeability doctrine will lead to a denial of liability when unforeseeable harm comes about owing to the coexistence of unforeseen circumstances; for instance it leads to the conclusion that in *Re Polemis*[33] defendant should not have been held liable for the destruction of the ship. Such a restriction cannot be justified merely because it provides a simpler solution, if the solution is unfair or inconvenient,[34] but the relative simplicity of the doctrine is undeniably attractive.

But the most important claim to simplicity of the foreseeability doctrine as a limitation of responsibility is not its simplification of the problems of *sine qua non* but its apparent success in bringing culpability and compensation within a single formula. It is by this that the doctrine in the last resort stands or falls and we shall see that in fact it falls, for the claim we have stated rests on an ambiguous use of 'foreseeable'. To understand this we must examine what is meant by 'reasonable foresight' in the law of negligence. When it is said that a defendant must take reasonable care to avoid harm which

---

31 pp. 209–10.
32 *Thurogood* v. *van den Berghs* [1951] 2 KB 537.
33 [1921] 3 KB 560.
34 Below, pp. 267 f.

he ought reasonably to foresee, it might at first sight seem that it is
his duty to take precautions if and only if the probability of harm,
on the basis of the available information, reaches a certain minimum.
This would be a complete misconception of the law of negligence,
for the existence of a duty to take precautions depends not merely
on the probability of harm but on many other factors. As Learned
Hand J. aptly said of the duty of a barge owner to have a custodian
on board in case it should break loose from its moorings, 'the owner's
duty . . . to provide against resulting injuries is a function of three
variables: (1) the probability that she will break away; (2) the gravity
of the resulting injury if she does; (3) the burden of adequate precautions'.[35] Often we have no moral or legal duty to prevent foreseeable harm because the harm is not sufficiently likely or not likely
to be more than trivial,[36] or the advantage that would have to be
given up in order to take precautions is too great. There are occasions
when a surgeon is justified in performing an operation from which
death is almost certain to result; on others he would be grossly
negligent in running even a very small risk of the patient's death. A
considerable risk is involved in crossing the streets of Oxford, but
life would come to a standstill if we did not sometimes run such
risks. Our moral and legal judgments of the actions of others depend,
not on the foreseeability of harm considered in isolation, but always
on foresight in relation to a practical decision; foresight of harm
such that in all the circumstances a reasonable man would adopt or
refrain from a particular course of action. Reasonable foresight, in
relation to culpability, is therefore a practical notion and we may
term the harm, the risk of which is sufficient to influence the conduct
of a prudent man, 'foreseeable in the practical sense'.[37]

Now it is conceivable that a legal system might restrict the responsibility of a negligent defendant to harm which is foreseeable in
this sense, though even so there would be the reservation to be made
that the law could not require all the physical details and economic
consequences of the harm to be foreseeable. But such a restriction
would effect a radical change in the existing common law of negligence, for it would in effect make it impossible for plaintiff to
recover for harm the risk of which was not a reason for calling
defendant's act negligent, viz. for what may roughly be called ulterior
harm. There are many sorts of harm for which recovery is at present

[35] United States v. Carroll Towing Co. (1947) 159 F. 2d 169, 173. Cf. Joffe v.
Hoskins, 1941 AD 431, 451 (South Africa); Nova Mink v. T.C.A. [1951] 2 DLR 241,
254.
[36] e.g. a bee sting. Wasserman v. Union Govt., 1934 AD 228, 230, 231 (South Africa).
[37] This sound point is exaggerated by Harari, The Place of Negligence in the Law
of Torts (1962), who concludes (p. 99) that foreseeability is 'utterly irrelevant' to
liability in negligence.

allowed, the risk of which *could* not intelligibly figure among the
reasons for calling defendant's act negligent, and so *could* not be
practically foreseeable, because the estimation of the risk of their
occurrence already presupposes the existence of a dangerous situation which it would be negligent to create. For instance, estimating
the risk that plaintiff will be injured in attempting a rescue from a
given peril presupposes that defendant has by some negligent act
brought about a situation which endangers the safety of the person
to be rescued. Similarly the risk that plaintiff, injured by defendant's
negligent act, will not receive the proper treatment in hospital can
only be estimated on the footing that defendant by some negligent
act has *ex hypothesi* caused physical injury to him. It is true that, at
this later stage, harm to a rescuer or medical mistreatment may be
called 'foreseeable' in the light of the situation created by defendant's
negligent act, but here 'foreseeable' or 'reasonably foreseeable' cannot mean foreseeable in the practical sense described above, but only
in the sense of 'not improbable' or 'not very unlikely' given the
situation created initially by the negligent act.

This is so because there is a logical absurdity in asking whether
the risk of further harm, arising from a harmful situation which a
reasonable man would not have created, would itself have deterred
a reasonable man from acting. To see its absurdity we must distinguish the case, with which it may be confused, where the same act
may be held negligent because of either of two independent risks: it
may be negligent to ride on the tow-bar of a lorry either because of
the risk of falling off or because of the risk of being hit from behind.
Here it is reasonable enough to ask of each risk separately whether
a reasonable man would have been deterred by it from standing on
the tow-bar. But where the risk of harm is created by a situation,
the risk of which occurring was itself enough to deter a reasonable
man, to ask whether he would be deterred by the further harm alone
is to put a question he cannot answer.[38] To press it would be to ask
the reasonable man first to imagine himself in a situation the risk of
which would have deterred him from acting, and then to tell us
whether in view of the further risk thus created he would have been
deterred. The second, theoretical sense of 'foreseeable' differs from
the practical sense of the word in two ways. First, the theoretical
foreseeability of ulterior harm need not be so great as of itself to be
sufficient to induce a reasonable man to take precautions. Thus, the
Restatement of Torts makes a defendant liable 'where there is a
realisable likelihood of [an intervening negligent act] but the likelihood is not enough in itself to make the actor's conduct negligent,

[38] For a forceful rejection of foreseeability as 'absolutely worthless' as a guide to
the jury in cases of ulterior harm see *Ehrgott* v. *Mayor of New York* (1884) 96 NY
App. 264.

the conduct being negligent because of other and greater risks which it entails',[39] and reaches a similar conclusion about liability for intervening acts which amount to intentional torts or crimes.[40]

Secondly, as was pointed out in Chapter VI, such notions of 'foreseeable', 'within the risk', 'probable', and the like always contain an implied reference to the information available. Obviously, what is unforeseeable to the defendant before he has done the negligent act may well become foreseeable at a later stage, after the initial harm has occurred, on the basis of the fuller information then available. Even if the practical and theoretical senses of 'foreseeable' were precisely the same, it would still not be true that a single criterion (foreseeability) was sufficient to determine both defendant's negligence and the extent of harm for which he was responsible, if his negligence on the one hand depended on the foreseeability of harm considered in advance, whereas the extent of his responsibility depended on the foreseeability of harm considered at a later stage, on the basis of different information.

It follows that advocates of the foreseeability doctrine (and the same criticism applies also to the risk doctrine) must either take the heroic step of denying responsibility for ulterior harm altogether (which has never seriously been suggested), or must abandon the claim that the foreseeability test enables the questions of culpability and compensation to be reduced to one. But, for the most part, courts and writers have simply failed to notice that 'foreseeable' was being used in two senses and have shifted unconsciously from the one to the other. Thus, it was said in a rescue case that 'everyone is bound to anticipate the results naturally following from his acts'.[41] This looks as if it meant that a motorist while driving should think not merely of the children whom he sees crossing the street, but of the adults who might dash out to rescue them, and of the surgeons who might operate on them negligently should they be run over and taken to hospital. As Bohlen[42] has said:

It is straining the idea of foreseeability past the breaking point to say that, when a defendant fails to inspect the brakes of his car, he should foresee that the brakes may fail to hold while a child is crossing the street, and that the plaintiff may be standing on the pavement at the precise instant of time when as a reasonable man he would regard it as possible to rescue the child with reasonable safety to himself. Yet to hold that the defendant in such a case is liable because he should have foreseen that the plaintiff

[39] s. 447, comment *a*.
[40] s. 448, comment *c*.
[41] *Illinois Central R. Co.* v. *Siler* (1907) 229 Ill. 390, 82 NE 362, 363. There are dozens of dicta to the same effect.
[42] Though Bohlen's main point is sound he is, perhaps, exaggerating the amount of detail which the defendant is required to foresee. Above, pp. 256-8.

would imperil himself to save the child requires the defendant to have had all this in mind. Such a use of the word 'foreseeable' is altogether different from that 'ordinary pre-vision to be looked for in a busy world' which Justice Cardozo has said is all that the law exacts in order that the actor may be free from negligence.[43]

A striking example of the confusion into which courts have been led, and the spurious use they make of the notion of defendant's duty to foresee harm which, in fact, only became a possibility after defendant had, by his negligence, caused the initial harm, is the decision in *In Re Guardian Casualty Co.*[44] In this case, through defendant's negligence, a taxi-cab was forced across the pavement and against the stone stoop of a house. About twenty minutes after the collision a policeman with other assistants was attempting to remove the taxi-cab from its position against the stoop, when, without negligence on the part of those doing the work, a stone which had been loosened by the impact of the cab fell on the pavement and struck deceased who was standing about 20 feet away. She died from her injuries. The court held not, as one might expect, that the acts of the policeman and helpers were reasonable acts done for the preservation of property[45] and so not such as, on causal principles, to relieve defendants of responsibility, but that 'the present defendants whose wrongful acts caused a vehicle to be projected across a sidewalk and against a building, with such force as to loosen parts of the structure, must have foreseen the necessity of removal of the vehicle from the sidewalk. They might reasonably have anticipated that the parts of the structure which were dislodged by the blow would fall into the highway. That a passing pedestrian might be injured when such an event took place in a city street, was also foreseeable.'[46]

One can only ask: *when* must defendants have foreseen the need to remove the vehicle and the danger from the loose stone?[47] Surely

---

[43] (1933–4) 47 *Harv. LR* 556, 557. For the use of foresight in rescue cases see *Haynes* v. *Harwood* [1935] KB 146, 163: 'It seems to me that if horses run away it must be quite obviously contemplated that people are likely to be knocked down. It must also, I think, be contemplated that persons will attempt to stop the horses and try to prevent injury to life and limb.' *Per* Maugham LJ. When must this be contemplated and what would be the point of contemplating it? See also *Hyett* v. *G.W.R.* [1948] 1 KB 345, 348; *Illinois Central R. Co.* v. *Siler* (1907) 229 Ill. 390, 82 NE 362; *Versic* v. *Conners* [1969] 1 NSWR 481 (foreseeable that after accident decedent would be jammed in gutter where his head would dam the rainwater so that he would drown). As to foresight of omissions to perform a duty see *Diehl* v. *Fidelity Philadelphia Trust Co.* (1946) 159 Pa. Super 513, 49 A. 2d 190.
[44] (1938) 253 App. Div. 360, 2 NYS 2d 232.
[45] Above, pp. 145–6.
[46] (1938) 2 NYS 2d 232, 234.
[47] The risk theory involves an exactly parallel shift from the risk (chance of harm) apparent before defendant acts to the risk after he acts or after the initial harm has occurred. Below, pp. 288–9.

only after the collision, when there was no longer any point in their foreseeing this, since it was too late to take effective action. Here the court uses the language of obligation, appropriate when practical foresight is in issue, in a context wholly divorced from it.

On the other hand sometimes courts take the practical test of foreseeability seriously and so unjustifiably deny liability for ulterior harm. A good example is *Mauney* v. *Gulf Refining Co.* In this case[48] the company negligently caused a fire to start at a filling station; a panic ensued in the town of Ripley, Mississippi, and people ran from the scene shouting that the tanks and the whole town would shortly blow up. A woman managing a café across the street rushed to get her two-year-old child, and in doing so fell over a misplaced chair and suffered a miscarriage. She sued the refining company and failed to recover, Griffith J. deciding the case on the ground that defendants could not have foreseen the precise accident. 'If the appellant didn't see a chair in her way in her own place of business it would impose an inadmissible burden upon appellees to say that they should have foreseen from across the street and through the walls of a building on another corner what appellant did not see right at her feet and in an immediate situation entirely familiar to her.'[49]

Here the court not merely insists on applying the practical test in order to determine the limit of responsibility but also requires such detailed prevision that, if similar criteria were generally followed, recovery for ulterior harm would hardly ever be allowed.[50]

The claim of the foreseeability doctrine to simplicity therefore turns out to be specious, except in so far as it eliminates certain problems when the description of the negligent act is complex.

Fairness. It is obvious that the application of causal principles, in the absence of some corrective, may make a defendant responsible for very large sums of damages, going far beyond what he could have contemplated or been prepared to meet in advance. The doctrines that coexisting circumstances, however extraordinary, such as the victim's eggshell skull, do not negative causal connection[51] and that normal subsequent events do not do so either[52] may, singly or in conjunction, 'impose a ruinous liability which no private fortune could meet and which is out of all proportion to the defendant's fault'.[53] To this the answer has been given that, if the liability is out

---

[48] (1942) 193 Miss. 421, 9 So. 2d 780 (Prosser, Wade, and Schwartz, p. 307).
[49] (1942) 9 So. 2d 780, 782.
[50] See also *Sinram* v. *Pennsylvania R. Co.* (1932) 61 F. 2d 767; *Woods* v. *Duncan* [1946] AC 401, 431 *per* Lord MacMillan; Prosser, *Selected Topics in the Law of Torts*, p. 218.
[51] Above, pp. 172 f.
[52] Above, pp. 162-3.
[53] Prosser, *Torts.* Cf. Jeremiah Smith, *Harvard Selected Essays on Torts*, pp. 649, 700, who points out that the fact that 'negligence' may not entail moral culpability is

of all proportion to the defendant's fault 'it can be no less out of proportion to the plaintiff's innocence'.[54]

The apparent unfairness of holding a defendant liable for a loss much greater than he could foresee to some extent disappears when we consider that a defendant is often negligent without suffering punishment or having to pay compensation. I may drive at an excessive speed a hundred times before the one occasion on which my speeding causes harm. The justice of holding me liable, should the harm on that one occasion turn out to be extraordinarily grave, must be judged in the light of the hundred other occasions on which, without deserving such luck, I have incurred no liability. There is therefore no necessary injustice in holding a negligent defendant liable for the harm he causes by his negligent act, a principle which has been expressed in the words of McLaughlin: 'The idea is that a man who "starts something" should be responsible for what he has started.'[55]

It is important not to exaggerate the gulf which divides those who take as a fundamental principle that a negligent defendant is responsible for the harm he has caused and those who start from the principle that a man is responsible only for foreseeable harm which he could reasonably prevent. The most fanatical adherent of the foreseeability doctrine would admit that a negligent defendant may be liable for harm even though its precise detail or extent was unforeseeable.[56] On the other hand, the most bigoted adherent of causal criteria would admit that it is a matter of legal policy to determine what sort of harm shall be recoverable in the law of negligence and that, in deciding this, attention should be paid to the frequency with which harm of a given type is observed to result from negligent conduct. As a matter of existing law, it is true that there are types of harm for which recovery is allowed only if they are brought about in a certain way, such as illness resulting from emotional shock, for which the law of negligence probably gives a remedy, in the absence of actual or threatened physical impact, only when the circumstances are such that a person of normally

only relevant in criminal law or when exemplary damages are in question. Bishop's argument against limiting liability to foreseeable harm (*New Criminal Law*, s. 327) that 'no man ever has a *right* to commit a *wrong* on any terms' would lead to the conclusion that there can be no limitation, causal or otherwise, on the liability of a person who has committed a wrongful act. The real question is whether the 'terms' should include compensation for the harm he causes by his wrongful act or should be limited to something less.

54 Prosser, *Selected Topics*, p. 217.
55 (1925–6) 39 *Harv. LR* 146, 164.
56 Above, pp. 256 ff.

phlegmatic disposition would be likely to be affected.[57] This means that the positive law of negligence acknowledges limitations both as regards the type of harm for which recovery is allowed and as regards the manner in which such harm is caused.

If the foreseeability doctrine were admitted, physical harm, for example, would be subdivided into types corresponding to the causal processes of which we take account when we foresee harm.[58] Thus, initial physical harm caused by mechanical, chemical, electrical, or psychological means might form separate categories, as harm caused by emotional shock does at present. The rule would be that, for each of these types of harm, plaintiff must show that defendant acted in a manner foreseeably likely to cause that type of harm. Indeed, though it would be going too far to say that these precise processes have been recognized as distinct for purposes of the law of negligence, the doctrine of *The Wagon Mound (No. 1)* has been applied almost exclusively in cases in which one of these types of process was foreseeable and another, which in fact occurred, not foreseeable.[59] No doubt a thoroughgoing application of the doctrine that there are distinct types of harm corresponding to distinct causal processes might involve certain alterations in pleading and procedure and in these respects would divide the tort of negligence into distinct torts[60] but it would not introduce a radically new principle into the law.

---

[57] *Bourhill* v. *Young* [1943] AC 92; *King* v. *Phillips* [1953] 1 QB 429; *Waube* v. *Warrington* (1935) 216 Wis. 603, 258 NW 497; *Cote* v. *Litawa* (1950) 96 NH 174, 71 A. 2d 792; *Resavage* v. *Davies* (1952) 199 Md. 479, 86 A. 2d 879; *Mulder* v. *South British Insurance Co.*, 1957 (2) SA 444 (W); *Amaya* v. *Home Ice Co.* (1963) 29 Cal. Rep. 33, 379 P. 513; *McLoughlin* v. *O'Brian* [1982] 2 All ER 298, 309 (HL).

[58] Fridman and Williams, 'The Atomic Theory of Negligence', (1971) 45 *Aust. LJ* 117.

[59] *Doughty* v. *Turner* [1964] 1 QB 518 (explosion instead of foreseeable splash); *Tremain* v. *Pyke* [1969] 3 All ER 1303 (*obiter*: transmission of disease by rat instead of foreseeable bites); *Rowe* v. *McCartney* [1976] 2 NSWLR 72 (defendant caused plaintiff slight injury and independent guilt feelings for having lent him car: guilt depression not of foreseeable type) but contrast *Hughes* v. *Lord Advocate* [1963] AC 837 (unpredictable explosion of lamp of same general type as foreseeable burning); *Bradford* v. *Robinson Rentals* [1967] 1 All ER 267 (frostbite of same general type as cold and chilblains); *Draper* v. *Hodder* [1972] 2 QB 556 (puppies biting child similar to bowling him over); *Vacwell Engineering* v. *B.D.H. Chemicals* [1971] 1 QB 88 (violent instead of foreseeable small explosion, cf. *Republic of France* v. *U.S.A.* (1961) 290 F. 2d 395 (defendants who failed to prevent smoking liable for foreseeable fire but not for disastrous explosion)); *Crankshaw* v. *Piedmont Driving Club* (1967) 115 Ga. App. 820, 156 SE 2d 208 (foreseeable that bad shrimp would make customer ill but not that someone would trip over her vomit).

Unusual consequences of proper medical treatment for an injury inflicted by defendant are taken to be of a foreseeable type: *Richards* v. *State of Victoria* [1969] VR 136; *Adelaide Chemical & Fertilizer* v. *Carlyle* (1940) 64 CLR 514; *Beavis* v. *Apthorpe* [1963] NSWR 1176; but contra: *Alston* v. *Marine & Trade Insurance*, 1964 (4) SA 112 (W) note, Honoré (1964) 81 *SALJ* 410 (interaction of drug properly administered and cheese produced stroke).

[60] See *King* v. *Phillips* [1953] 1 QB 429.

The advantage of this subdivision is that it would meet the objections of those who object to liability in a *Polemis-* or *Palsgraf*-like situation, when the causal processes which in fact occur are of a radically different type from those reasonably to be expected in advance: fire or explosion instead of mechanical impact. Furthermore, the proposal would limit responsibility in a more rational way than the present techniques of 'duty of care' and 'unforeseeable plaintiff', to which we turn later.[61] But the problem of ulterior harm would remain unsolved. There would be no recovery for such harm, which would in general be excluded as unforeseeable.

This difficulty has led to another variant of the foreseeability test, the 'threshold tort' doctrine. This, as stated by Enneccerus for German law,[62] lays down that whereas foreseeability of the initial harm is a necessary element in establishing liability for wrongs not actionable without proof of damage, once liability is established plaintiff need not show that the further harm suffered by him was foreseeable by the defendant. But this variant of the foreseeability doctrine amounts almost to a capitulation, because the limits of defendant's responsibility must be established by causal criteria. It would not even relieve defendant of responsibility in the *Polemis* situation, because the initial harm caused by the impact of the plank on the cargo was foreseeable and this would be a sufficient threshold tort to make defendant responsible for the ulterior loss of the ship. Causal criteria would be used to determine all but the first stage in responsibility. It is hardly surprising that this variant has not found favour since it offers no substitute, in terms of foresight, for causal doctrines.

Yet another variant is the so-called 'hindsight' test, which is intended to overcome the difficulty that, if the criterion of foreseeability is applied, a victim will not recover for harm to which an unknown and unusual circumstance, such as his abnormal susceptibility, contributes. The test may be stated in the words of the Oklahoma court in 1937, though the theory is to be found, so far as Anglo-American law is concerned, at least as early as Shearman and Redfield's work on Negligence[63] and in German law in Rümelin's version of adequate causation.[64]

According to the court the defendant is liable for 'all the consequences which a prudent and experienced man, fully acquainted with all the facts and circumstances which in fact exist, whether they could have been ascertained by reasonable diligence or not, would

---

61 Below, pp. 271–3.
62 *Lehrbuch des bürgerlichen Rechts*, ii. 69.
63 Shearman and Redfield (1898) s. 28.
64 'Theorie der adäquaten Verursachung vom Standpunkt der Nachträglichen Prognose', *Archiv für die civilistische Praxis*, vol. xc, pp. 171, 217 ff. Below, pp. 482–3.

have thought at the time of the negligent act as reasonably possible to follow, if they had been suggested to his mind'.[65] The advantage of this theory is that it allows recovery despite the fact that abnormal coexisting circumstances have contributed to the harm, and to that extent fits the decisions better than the other versions of the foreseeability theory. But it does this at the cost of permitting recovery for all harm of which defendant's act was a necessary condition even if brought about by a subsequent abnormal or coincidental occurrence. For from the point of view of one acquainted with *all* the circumstances existing at the time of the negligent act, few events that subsequently occur would appear unlikely.[66] Hence the 'hindsight' test would lead to almost unlimited responsibility.

The attempt to give effect to the apparently fair doctrine that a defendant should only be responsible for foreseeable harm leads to such complexity that some courts which have felt the need for limiting defendant's responsibility have adopted a quite different technique. This consists in denying recovery to all except a plaintiff whose person or property was foreseeably in danger at the time when defendant did the wrongful act: this is sometimes expressed by saying that no duty of care is owed to an unforeseeable plaintiff. This rule can be reduced to two elements: (i) the person or property of plaintiff must be within the 'apparent range' of defendant's act; (ii) there must have been some evidence available to defendant that there was a person or thing in the position in which plaintiff or his property was in fact situated. These requirements, though both concerned with space and time, are logically different. The question of apparent range is a general one: how far is a revolver shot likely, as a matter of common experience, to reach? The question of plaintiff's position is particular and can be formulated only when the harm has been done, and it is known how it was done. We can then ask whether it was likely that a person would be at the place required for defendant's act to cause harm at the time in question.

(i) *Apparent range.* If this part of the doctrine of the 'unforeseeable plaintiff' is adopted plaintiff will be unable to recover if he was located outside the 'area of potential danger':[67] e.g. if he was behind a tram some 50 feet from the point where defendant collided with another vehicle[68] or was behind a bus in a position of apparent safety when he was struck by the body of a pedestrian projected by

---

[65] *Butts* v. *Anthis* (1937) 181 Okla. 276, 73 P. 2d 843; *Leposki* v. *Railway Express Agency* (1962) 297 F. 2d 849; *Dellwo* v. *Pearson* (1961) 107 NW 2d 859 (Minn.) ('negligence is tested by foresight, but proximate cause is determined by hindsight'). For a slightly different formulation see *Restatement of Torts*, s. 433 (b).

[66] Prosser, p. 268.

[67] *Bourhill* v. *Young* [1943] AC 92, 98, *per* Lord Thankerton. For some of the difficulties involved in this notion see *Nova Mink* v. *T.C.A.* [1951] 2 DLR 241, 264.

[68] *Bourhill* v. *Young* [1943] AC 92.

defendant's negligently driven car.[69] But the majority of decisions in America firmly reject this limitation,[70] as does the old English case of *Smith* v. *L.S.W.R.*,[71] so that the authority of *Palsgraf*[72] in its favour cannot, as a matter of positive law, be called decisive. The reasoning behind the suggested rule is perhaps that, if the reason for calling harm foreseeable is that defendant's act is likely to set in motion causal processes which are likely to affect persons or things within a certain range, defendant should not be responsible if they extend beyond that range. Such a limitation is perhaps simpler to administer than some of those considered earlier but its justice is not self-evident. No one would suggest that a defendant should be relieved of responsibility because the effect of his dangerous act lasts longer than he expected, e.g. that the slight injury inflicted on plaintiff keeps him in hospital for a month rather than a day. Why should a different principle apply to the effects of defendant's act in space?

(ii) The second aspect of the doctrine of the 'unforeseeable plaintiff' is that a plaintiff, even within the apparent range of defendant's act, cannot recover if defendant had no reason to suspect his presence in the place where he was affected. Two South African decisions well illustrate this point. When defendant was negligent in backing a lorry against a door he was held not liable to plaintiff who, unknown to defendant, was working on a ladder behind the door.[73] When deceased was behind a horse standing in the middle of the road it was held that his widow could recover from defendant who negligently drove too close to the horse but did not see deceased; a majority of three judges to two decided that he ought to have suspected the presence of a person behind the horse.[74] Once again, there are decisions taking the contrary view[75] and the justice of the proposed rule is not self-evident. The requirement of a 'duty of care owed to plaintiff' seems to be based on the analogy of a contractual duty and to require, in effect, that to be able to sue in tort, the plaintiff must have been identifiable beforehand. Surely the analogy is a false one: duties in tort are imposed in order to protect the

---

[69] *Dahlstrom* v. *Shrum* (1951) 368 Pa. 423, 84 Atl. 2d 289; *Wood* v. *Pennsylvania R. Co.* (1896) 177 Pa. 306, 35 Atl. 699, 55 Am. St. Rep. 728. Cf. for property the New York fire rule: *Ryan* v. *New York Central R. Co.* (1886) 35 NY 210, 91 Am. Dec. 49.

[70] *Alabama R. Co.* v. *Chapman* (1886) 80 Ala. 615, 2 So. 738; *Wolfe* v. *Checker Taxi Co.* (1938) 299 Mass. 225, 12 NE 2d 849; *Kommerstad* v. *Great Northern R. Co.* (1913) 120 Minn. 376, 139 NW 713; *Robinson* v. *Standard Oil Co.* (1929) 89 Ind. App. 167, 166 NE 160.

[71] (1870) LR 6 CP 14 (spread of fire). Cf. *Atchison, Topeka & Santa Fe R. Co.* v. *Stanford* (1874) 12 Kan. 354; *Jeffrey* v. *Copeland Flour Mills* [1923] 4 DLR 1140.

[72] *Palsgraf* v. *Long Island R. Co.* (1928) 248 NY 339, 162 NE 89, 59 ALR 1253.

[73] *Workmen's Compensation Commissioner* v. *De Villiers*, 1949 (1) SA 474 (C).

[74] *Cowan* v. *Ballam*, 1945 AD 81.

[75] *Hill* v. *Winsor* (1875) 118 Mass. 251; *Barker* v. *Philadelphia* (1955) 134 F. Supp. 231; *Railway Express Agency* v. *Brabham* (1952) 62 So. 2d 713 (Fla.); *Law* v. *Visser* [1961] QSR 46.

persons and property of members of society generally, not only of those members whose presence within range defendant had reason to suspect in advance.

Summary. It may be convenient to summarize the arguments for and against the principle that, in the law of negligence, no recovery should be allowed for unforeseeable harm. As a matter of principle the main objection to it is that, if 'foreseeable' is interpreted in the practical sense, the principle would unduly restrict liability by preventing recovery for ulterior harm. So far as initial harm is concerned there is more to be said for the restriction, though it turns out to be somewhat complex in practice. Liability in negligence has and must have its limits but it is not clear that foreseeability is an appropriate notion for settling them.

Is the doctrine that only foreseeable harm is recoverable part of existing law? Certainly there were dicta of English judges in its favour,[76] but until 1961 these were outweighed by contrary expressions of opinion.[77] In that year the Privy Council, in *The Wagon Mound (No. 1)*,[78] adopted the doctrine and rejected the contrary opinions. In that famous case defendant's negligent spillage of furnace oil was (on a finding of fact based on restricted evidence)[79] foreseeably likely only to foul plaintiff's wharf. In fact the oil caught fire and destroyed the wharf. The Privy Council held that the fire damage was not recoverable, since it was not of the type that could reasonably have been foreseen by defendant. But in reaching this conclusion Lord Simonds embraced the principle that the criteria of culpability and compensation are the same,[80] namely, the foreseeability of the 'particular' harm. He sought thereby to simplify the law and to eliminate the need for an investigation of repulsive and obscure causal issues.[81] He did so without reference to the arguments to the contrary deployed in the first edition of this book.

The decision might, on a literal interpretation, have made a radical change in the law of tort, or at least of negligence. But it soon became clear that, while it would be accepted as authoritative in Britain and

[76] Pollock CB in *Rigby* v. *Hewitt* (1850) 5 Ex. 240, 155 ER 103, and *Greenland* v. *Chaplin* (1850) 5 Ex. 243, 155 ER 104. See also *Cory* v. *France, Fenwick & Co.* [1911] 1 KB 114, 122; *Woods* v. *Duncan* [1946] AC 401, 442; *Bourhill* v. *Young* [1943] AC 93, 101. The only actual decision in its favour in England was *Sharp* v. *Powell* (1872) LR 7 CP 253.

[77] e.g. Street, *Foundations of Legal Liability*, i. 90, 111–16 (tort); Beven, *Negligence*, 1. 92; *Restatement of Torts*, s. 435; Porter (1935) 5 *Cam. LJ* 176; McLaughlin (1925–6) 39 *Harv. LR* 149, 163; Green, *Rationale of Proximate Cause*, pp. 65, 88, 120.

[78] [1961] AC 388.

[79] In a later case brought by the owners of ships moored at the wharf and destroyed in the same fire, the fire damage was held to be foreseeable: *The Wagon Mound (No. 2)* [1967] 1 AC 617.

[80] [1961] AC 388, 423, 425.

[81] [1961] AC 388, 419 'scholastic theories of causation with their repulsive and barely intelligible jargon'.

the Commonwealth,[82] it would be taken to decide only the narrower point that the harm for which recovery was sought must be of a foreseeable type. Even this narrower rule has been accepted subject to an important restriction, namely that circumstances coexisting with the negligent act do not negative causal connection; in particular, a tortfeasor continues to take his victim as he finds him, no matter what his condition or susceptibility or how extraordinary its consequences.[83] This application of the common-sense causal notions explained in Chapter VI can be artificially reconciled with the narrower *Wagon Mound* rule by saying that, if some injury to the person of the victim by impact is foreseeable, any actual injury to him is of a foreseeable type, though perhaps much greater in extent than was anticipated. But so to argue is mere window dressing.[84] The truth is that this aspect of common-sense causal discourse has survived the *Wagon Mound*.

So far as the wider rule, equating culpability with compensation, is concerned, its drawbacks soon became evident. Taken literally, it would, for the reasons explained earlier,[85] have excluded compensation for ulterior harm. In the same year as *The Wagon Mound* was decided, Dixon CJ in the High Court of Australia grappled with the difficulty. In *Chapman* v. *Hearse*[86] defendant had negligently caused a road accident. A doctor stopped and sought to help those injured. Soon after he did so a following car, negligently driven, struck and killed him. Could defendant be held responsible for the doctor's death? It was held that he could. The notion of reasonable foreseeability was not to be applied as it would be in considering whether defendant was negligent in the first place. Whether the sequence of

---

[82] It was not followed in *Shuhlan* v. *Peterson, Howell & Heather* (1966) 57 DLR 2d 491 (Sask.) (car repair taking abnormally long owing to strike), but the courts which purport to follow it would have reached the same conclusion: see next note.

[83] *Smith* v. *Leech Brain* [1962] 2 QB 405 (minor burn turning to cancer); *McKillen* v. *Barclay Curle* [1965] SLT 19 (dormant lesion); *Malcolm* v. *Broadhurst* [1970] 3 All ER 508 (irritability after accident due to 'eggshell personality'); *Sayers* v. *Perrin* [1966] QSR 89 (polio virus); *Robinson* v. *Post Office* [1974] 1 WLR 1176 (CA) (allergy); *Warren* v. *Scruttons* [1962] 1 Ll. LR 497 (finger-prick affecting eye); *Wilson* v. *Birt* (1963) (2) SA 508 (epilepsy); *Negretto* v. *Sayers* [1963] SASR 313 (predisposition to mental disorder); *Hole* v. *Hocking* [1962] SASR 128 (minor burn causing brain haemorrhage); *Regush* v. *Inglis* (1962) 38 WWR. 245; *Purkess* v. *Crittenden* (1965) 114 CLR 164, 171–2; *Wintringham* v. *Rae* (1966) 55 DLR 2d 108 (reaction to injection); *Turley* v. *Saffin* (1975) 10 SASR 463; *Murphy* v. *McCarthy* (1974) 9 SASR 424.; *Burke* v. *Paul* [1967] IR 277; *Stephenson* v. *Waite Tileman* [1973] 1 NZLR 152 (immaterial whether wound linked with incapacity, via virus and brain damage or compensation neurosis); *Richards* v. *State of Victoria* [1969] VR 136; Linden, 'Down with Foreseeability', (1969) 47 *Can. BR* 545; *contra Blaikie* v. *British Transport* [1961] SC 44 (coronary from over-exertion in coping with defective boiler 'unforeseeable', hence no recovery).

[84] Though supported by Rowe, 'Demise of the Thin Skull Rule', (1977) 40 *MLR* 377.

[85] Above, pp. 263 f.

[86] [1961] SASR 51; 106 CLR 112.

events was reasonably foreseeable had to be decided in the light of the situation following the accident. Could it be said to be foreseeable at that stage that following traffic would injure those giving aid to the victims of the first accident? It must be shown that at that stage the sequence of events was foreseeable in the sense of 'by no means unlikely',[87] if plaintiff was to recover for the ulterior harm. The court therefore adopted, for ulterior harm, what we have termed the theoretical rather than the practical test of foreseeability.[88] It follows that, despite the use of the word 'foreseeable' at both stages, the criteria of culpability and compensation remain different after *The Wagon Mound*, as they were before it. Ulterior harm remains recoverable if, in the situation which develops after the initial harm, it is foreseeable in the theoretical sense, provided, as we shall see in the next section, that recovery is not excluded by some factor negativing causal connection.

The equation of culpability and compensation has not, therefore, been accepted by the courts.[89] So far as the present theme—that only foreseeable harm is recoverable—is concerned, the main effect of *The Wagon Mound*, in contrast with the previous rule of *Re Polemis*, has been to exclude compensation when a freakish turn of events occurs, which involves a very unexpected type of causal process.[90]

II. THE DOCTRINE THAT ALL FORESEEABLE HARM IS RECOVERABLE

We pass now to the second or enlarging branch of the doctrine of foreseeability, viz. that a negligent defendant is liable for all foreseeable harm of which his act was a necessary condition. 'As a general principle the defendant will be liable for all the foreseeable consequences of his act.'[91] Here 'consequences' might refer to harm causally connected, on the principles expounded in Chapter VI, with the negligent act, but, in order to assess the notion of foreseeability as a substitute for causation, we take 'consequences' as referring to all harm of which defendant's act was a necessary condition. Hence if the foreseeable harm comes about through the subsequent

[87] (1961) 106 CLR 112.
[88] Above, pp. 263 f.
[89] Joseph C. Smith, 'The Limits of Tort Liability in Canada: Remoteness, Foreseeability and Proximate Cause' in Linden, *Studies in Canadian Tort Law* (1968), pp. 88, 97.
[90] The hope expressed in 1961 that 'no definite meaning will be attached to it [foreseeability] by the courts. In this way the substance of the existing law can be retained, though under a new label, except in a few freakish cases' has been fulfilled: Honoré (1961) 39 *Can. BR* 267, 272.
[91] Salmond, *Torts* (12th edn.), p. 731, but there are qualifications in the 17th edn., pp. 512–13.

intervention of a free voluntary act or of an abnormal or coincidental event, which would on causal principles negative responsibility, defendant is still, on the doctrine here discussed, responsible for the harm.

There can be no question that, as the law stands at the moment, the doctrine now under discussion, though not invoked in all or even the majority of cases where on causal principles recovery would be disallowed, is nevertheless often applied by the courts. In Chapter VII we set out and classified under the heading 'Occasioning Harm',[92] a number of types of case in which courts have held a defendant liable for harm in actions for negligence despite the subsequent intervention of a voluntary act or coincidence, often on the ground that the harm which occurred was of the very sort the likelihood of which made defendant's conduct negligent.[93] These cases are, in fact, applications of the foreseeability or risk doctrine and its supporters may well argue that, if the enlarging doctrine is not wholly accepted at present, it ought to be and perhaps in future will be; or they may say that, with suitable modifications, it can be made to fit the decisions. We consider these points in turn.

Arguments of principle. The considerations of consistency, simplicity, and justice which were urged in favour of the doctrine of foreseeability in its restrictive aspect may also be urged in favour of the enlarging aspect of the doctrine. The unconvincing argument from consistency need not be dealt with again,[94] but the argument from simplicity has greater force here than in relation to the restrictive aspect of the foreseeability doctrine. If the law were that a negligent defendant was responsible for all foreseeable harm of which his act was a necessary condition it would be unnecessary to attend further to the manner of the upshot. Hence the court would avoid the complications of a causal inquiry at this stage of the case, though these complications would reappear later when the problem of ulterior harm was faced. Such simplification would be so great an advantage that, unless injustice to defendant results, it would be difficult to resist its acceptance.

The justice or fairness of the rule is therefore the decisive consideration. The factor which presents most difficulty is that the rule would allow recovery even in cases where the harm would not result from defendant's act but for the voluntary intervention of a third party. If the possibility of such intervention was sufficient to make the act negligent, it would of course be fair to hold defendant responsible and it would make no difference that the foreseeable harm

92 Above, pp. 194 f.
93 Above, pp. 195, 197–8.
94 Above, pp. 259 f.

must in this case be defined in such a way, e.g. 'theft', as to incorporate a reference to the intervention. Even, however, if the risk
of such intervention is not one of the things which made defendant's
act negligent, there is much to be said in favour of holding him
responsible if the ulterior harm was foreseeable. Take the simple case
where defendant negligently leaves a hole in the road unguarded. The
risk which makes this act negligent is that someone may fall in. As
the law stands, defendant is responsible, in accordance with strict
causal principles, if a third party accidentally or negligently jostles
plaintiff so that he falls into the hole but not if the third party
deliberately or recklessly throws him in.[95] But, if such deliberate acts
are foreseeable, perhaps because the area is one in which violence
and aggression are prevalent, why should it make a difference that
the risk of aggression was not what made it negligent to leave the
hole unguarded in the first place? Is it not that much worse to leave
a hole unguarded in an area in which violence is prevalent?

It used to be argued that the law's function was merely to provide
a plaintiff with one wrongdoer to sue; hence, if the third person
acted negligently or intentionally, the defendant who had first been
negligent was relieved of responsibility and plaintiff was left to sue
the third person. This was the 'last wrongdoer' principle,[96] but it has
long since been abandoned[97] because, among other objections, the
second wrongdoer may be insolvent or outside the jurisdiction or
immune from suit and a legal system cannot reasonably restrict a
plaintiff in this way. It did not, in any case, coincide with causal
criteria for limiting responsibility, for on causal principles a merely
negligent intervening act does not relieve defendant from responsibility, while on the 'last wrongdoer' principle it would do so.

Once the last wrongdoer principle is discarded it may be thought
that no rational distinction can be based on the different ways in
which foreseeable harm may occur. Ought not the character of the
intervening act to be relevant only to the intervening actor's responsibility? These important arguments may well be destined to
triumph in the end, though one should not underestimate the
strength of our intuitive conviction that a wrongdoer is entitled to
shift responsibility to a subsequent voluntary agent.

The variant view. At the moment, many lawyers and ordinary men
regard it as unfair to hold a wrongdoer responsible when some
independent person has deliberately exploited the situation created
by the wrongdoer, unless of course the chance of such exploitation
was what made the act wrongful. Hence, the doctrine that a defendant is responsible for all foreseeable harm of which his negligent

---

[95] Above, p. 137.
[96] Eldredge, p. 209. Fleming James, 'Legal Cause', (1951) 60 *Yale LJ* 761, 806.
[97] Its repudiation is implicit in *Illidge* v. *Goodwin* (1831) 5 CLP 190, 172 ER 934.

act is a necessary condition has not usually been advocated by courts or writers in its full rigour. Lawyers usually have confined themselves to the variant proposition that a defendant is responsible for such foreseeable harm if the manner of its occurrence was foreseeable: in particular if any intervening act necessary to its production was foreseeable.[98] Here 'foreseeable' is used in two senses, practical and theoretical. The end harm must be foreseeable in the practical sense, viz. the sort of harm the chance of which made the act negligent. The manner of occurrence of the intervening act or event must be 'foreseeable' in the theoretical sense that, given the negligent act or some consequence of it, its occurrence must not have been too improbable. This variant view therefore comes very close in one respect to the causal principle according to which abnormal or co-incidental subsequent events negative causal connection. Indeed, when dealing with that principle, we stated that the word 'un-foreseeable' might be used instead of 'abnormal' provided that it is understood in its theoretical sense. But the coincidence with causal principles is not complete, for on the modified foreseeability principle, a foreseeable but voluntary intervention would not relieve defendant from liability, while on causal principles defendant could shift responsibility to the subsequent voluntary agent. Prosser states the above principle as follows: 'The defendant ordinarily will not be relieved of liability by an intervening cause which could reasonably have been foreseen, nor by one which is a normal incident of the risk created.'[99]

Of intervening acts in particular Hamilton LJ said, 'No doubt each intervener is a *causa sine qua non*, but unless the intervention is a fresh, independent cause, the person guilty of the original neg-ligence will still be the effective cause, if he ought reasonably to have anticipated such interventions and to have foreseen that if they occurred the result would be that his negligence would lead to mis-chief.'[1] This view has been repeated by other judges[2] and has the

98 Salmond, *Torts*, p. 515; Prosser, *Torts*, p. 272. *Rulane Gas Co.* v. *Montgomery Ward & Co.* (1949) 56 SE 2d 689; (1950-1) 49 *Mich. LR* 288-90 (seller of defective gas water-heater not liable when repairman struck match and caused explosion, killing purchaser).

99 *Torts*, p. 266. The word 'ordinarily' was added in the 2nd edn.; cf. 4th edn., pp. 272, 276. 'Normal incident in the risk created' means: not unlikely in the light of defendant's act or its admitted consequences.

1 *Latham* v. *Johnson* [1913] 1 KB 398, 413. It later appeared that Lord Sumner did not extend this to intervening voluntary actions. *Weld-Blundell* v. *Stephens* [1920] AC 956, 986. Below, p. 280.

2 *Davies* v. *Liverpool Corporation* [1949] 2 All ER 175, 177 *per* Denning LJ; *Joffe* v. *Hoskins*, 1941 AD 431, 456 *per* Centlivres CJ; *Shearer* v. *Harland & Wolff* [1947] NI 102, 107 *per* MacDermott J. See also *Northwestern Utilities* v. *London Guarantee & Accident Co.* [1936] AC 108; *Foster* v. *Moss & Dell*, 1927 EDL 208; *Pietersburg Municipality* v. *Rautenbach*, 1917 TPD 252; *Lane* v. *Atlantic Works* (1872) 111 Mass. 136, 139.

support of the *Restatement of Torts*, which makes it clear, as do the
decisions cited, that the principle extends beyond interventions which
are foreseeable in the practical sense to those which are 'not highly
improbable' in the theoretical sense. Section 447 of the *Restatement*
makes a negligent defendant liable despite the intervening act of a
third person if

(*a*) the actor at the time of his negligent conduct should have realised
that a third person might so act, or

(*b*) a reasonable man knowing the situation existing *when the act of the
third person*[3] was done would not regard it as highly extraordinary that the
person had so acted, or

(*c*) the intervening act is a normal response to a situation created by the
actor's conduct and the manner in which it is done is not extraordinarily
negligent.[4]

Section 448 of the *Restatement* also holds a negligent actor liable
when the third person commits an intentional tort or crime, provided
that 'the actor at the time of his negligent conduct realized or should
have realized the likelihood that [a situation affording an opportunity for such tort or crime] might be created [thereby] and that a
third person might avail himself of the opportunity to commit such
a tort or crime'.[5]

Comments 447 (*a*) and 448 (*c*) state that the risk of negligent or
voluntary intervention need not have been what made defendant's
conduct negligent and this, taken in conjunction with 447 (*b*) in
particular, shows that the theoretical sense of 'foreseeable' is the one
appropriate to this rule. There is, indeed, a difference of opinion
about the time at which the probability of the intervention is to be
assessed, McLaughlin[6] supporting the time of defendant's act (which
would be appropriate if practical foreseeability were under discussion), Seavey[7] the time immediately after defendant's wrongful act or
the initial impact, Bohlen[8] and the *Restatement* the time immediately
before the wrongful intervention takes place. The latter view is the
one appropriate to the assessment of whether, on causal principles,
an intervening event is abnormal or a coincidence, provided it is
remembered that the person then judging the situation must be

[3] Our italics.
[4] This principle can be traced as early as the balloon case: *Guille* v. *Swan* (1822) 19
Johns NY 381, 383. 'Now if his descent . . . would ordinarily and naturally draw a
crowd . . . all this he ought to have foreseen and must be responsible for.'
[5] The caveat to this section leaves open the actor's liability if he should have realized
this had he been present when the tempting situated was created.
[6] (1925-6) 39 *Harv. LR* 170-2, 182-3. Inconsistent with cases such as *Sundquist* v.
Madison R. Co. (1928) 197 Wis. 83, 221 NW 392. Above, p. 177.
[7] Expounding the risk theory: (1942-3) 56 *Harv. LR* 72, 91.
[8] (1934) 47 *Harv. LR* 556, 557. *Restatement*, ss. 447 (*b*), 448 *caveat*.

credited only with the knowledge available to the ordinary man.[9] When, however, the intervening act is voluntary and is done with the deliberate intention of causing harm, it is at least doubtful, on the cases, whether the fact that the intervention was foreseeable is sufficient to render the wrongdoer liable for the ultimate harm.

The development of the law in the last century appears at first sight to afford support for the foresight theory on this point. A hundred years ago the law of negligence was relatively undeveloped. Then, even when a defendant had committed a wrong, he was not in general bound to guard against its exploitation by others. The most striking illustration of this was the rule of defamation that a defendant was not responsible for the foreseeable but unintended repetition of a slander.[10] This still holds in the case of defamation; on strict causal principles a distinction should be drawn between the repetition of a slander by a person who knows of its untruth or whose reaction in repeating it is not in accordance with human nature, but attributable to some idiosyncrasy,[11] and by one who believes it, and so is not fully informed, and whose repetition of it is natural in the circumstances.[12] However, though the doctrine was expressly based on causal grounds these distinctions were not drawn. As the New York court said, 'The special damages in such a case are not a natural, legal consequence of the first speaking of the words, but of the wrongful act of repeating them, and would not have occurred but for the repetition; and the party who repeats them is alone liable for damages.'[13]

In *Weld-Blundell* v. *Stephens*,[14] an action for breach of contract, Lord Sumner appeared to generalize the slander rule.

> In general [he said] . . . even though *A* is in fault, he is not responsible for injury to *C* which *B*, a stranger to him, deliberately chooses to do. Though *A* may have given the occasion for *B*'s mischievous activity, *B* then becomes a new and independent cause. . . . That a jury can finally make *A* liable for *B*'s acts merely because they think it was antecedently probable that *B* would act as he did apart from *A*'s authority or intention seems to me to be contrary to principle and unsupported by authority.[15]

As a statement of causal principles this would have been un-exceptionable had it been made clear that for *B*'s act to prevent

9 Above, pp. 165–6.
10 *Ward* v. *Weeks* (1830) 7 Bing. 211, 131 ER 81; *Terwilliger* v. *Wands* (1858) 17 NY 54.
11 Cf. *Lynch* v. *Knight* (1861) 9 HLC 577, 592, 111 ER 854 *per* Lord Campbell.
12 *Lynch* v. *Knight*, above, at p. 600 *per* Lord Wensleydale.
13 *Terwilliger* v. *Wands*, 17 NY 54, 57 *per* Strong J. 'The damage must be the legal and natural consequence of the words spoken.' *Vicars* v. *Wilcocks* (1806) 8 East 1, 3, 103 ER 244–245, *per* Lord Ellenborough.
14 [1920] AC 956.
15 *Weld-Blundell* v. *Stephens* [1920] AC 956, 986, 988.

causal connection it must have been voluntary[16] in the full sense, not done in ignorance of the truth; but Lord Sumner overlooked the possibility that *A* might be liable for *B*'s act on the non-causal ground that he had wrongfully exposed *C* to a risk of harm from *B*'s act. So, on the facts of *Weld-Blundell* v. *Stephens* the House of Lords ought, in the opinion of many lawyers, to have held that defendant's partner, who left the libellous letter lying in the third party's office, had a contractual duty to guard against its publication by the third party to the persons libelled.

But in this century the scope of the law of negligence has greatly widened. Duties have been imposed to guard against not merely the voluntary but even in certain circumstances the criminal acts of others.[17] Examples could be multiplied. They have led many lawyers to accept the view that voluntary but foreseeable interventions do not negative responsibility. But this is an exaggeration, even for the law of negligence. Thus, though there are at least two decisions which impose on a defendant who, by his negligence, has caused a collision with plaintiff or with plaintiff's vehicle, a duty to guard against the theft of his property at the scene of the collision, if he is disabled from looking after it himself,[18] this has not yet won general acceptance in Anglo-American law.[19] There is no general duty to guard against the foreseeable voluntary or criminal interventions of others. Thus, when the defendant wrongfully disturbed sheep which were being driven along a public road, he was held not responsible for the act of the shepherds who then left the sheep, which strayed and were impounded.[20]

The doctrine that foreseeable interventions do not prevent causal connection, mixed with the older doctrine, has often led courts to describe voluntary interventions as 'unforeseeable' whether they are in fact likely or not.[21] Only thus, some courts and writers have thought, could defendant's exemption from liability be justified.

For instance, in *Carter* v. *Towne*[22] plaintiff was a boy of eight to whom defendant sold gunpowder in breach of statute. The boy took

[16] As was emphasized by Tindal CJ in *Ward* v. *Weeks* (1830) 7 Bing 211, 215, who said that the repetition was 'the voluntary act of a free agent, over whom the defendant had no control'.

[17] Above, pp. 193 ff. *Stansbie* v. *Troman* [1948] 2 KB 48; *Hines* v. *Garrett* (1921) 131 Va. 125, 108 SE 690.

[18] *Brauer* v. *New York Central Railway* (1918) 91 NJL 190, 103 Atl. 166; *Patten* v. *Silberschein* (1936) 3 WWR 169, 51 BCR 133.

[19] *Duce* v. *Rourke* [1951] 1 WWR 305 (NS).

[20] *Anderson* v. *Van der Merwe*, 1921 CPD 343.

[21] This has been called a 'curious tribute to virtue'. Labatt (1897) 33 *Can. LJ* 713, 719.

[22] (1870) 103 Mass. 507. Cf. *McKinnon* v. *de Groseilliers* [1946] OWN 110 ('unforeseeable' that third party would remove plaintiff from defendant's hotel during a 'rough house').

the powder home and his aunt put it in a cupboard which was accessible to him. With his mother's knowledge he played with the powder and was hurt in an explosion. The court held that defendant was not liable for the boy's injuries, the acts of the aunt and the mother negativing causal connection. Harper classes their acts under the heading 'unforeseeable interventions',[23] yet the act of an over-indulgent mother or aunt can hardly be called highly improbable.

Again, in *Schmidt* v. *United States*[24] the government was negligent in leaving live shells on its land. Schmidt, a government contractor's employee, removed them to his home; his children played with them and were killed in an explosion. The court denied liability, saying: 'It is generally held that the original wrongdoer was not bound to anticipate that an adult of ordinary intelligence and understanding would commit a trespass and remove property to which he had no right, and that therefore his wrongful act was not within the range of reasonable expectation.' Yet there must be few indeed who would not remove derelict government property if they had the opportunity.[25] The act of a wife who goes off with another man while her husband is on war service is 'attributable not to war service but to the wife's personality and conduct' although it is surely not unlikely that she will do so.[26]

The voluntary acts of the adults in the *Carter*[27] and *Schmidt*[28] cases were, perhaps, not foreseeable in advance to the extent that the likelihood of them should have influenced defendant's conduct, but they were certainly theoretically foreseeable in the sense of being fairly likely given defendant's act.

What these decisions perhaps illustrate is that courts often adhere to the causal doctrine that a voluntary intervention, even if foreseeable, may exclude defendant's liability, but do this in a disguised form by calling such events 'unforeseeable'. So voluntary interventions come to be called 'unforeseeable', whether they are really improbable or not.

Rejecting the doctrine that a negligent defendant is liable for all foreseeable harm of which his act was a necessary condition, Lord Reid put the arguments against the use of 'foreseeable' to determine

23 *Torts*, s. 128.
24 (1950) 179 F. 2d 724. The dissent of Murrah CJ takes the view that the removal of the shell was 'commonplace' and 'within the range of apprehension' and that the father was not an 'intentional wrongdoer'.
25 Cf. *Watson* v. *Kentucky & Indiana Bridge Co.* (1910) 137 Ky. 619, 126 SW 146 (unforeseeable that intervening actor would deliberately set fire to petrol); *Scheffer* v. *Railroad Co.* (1881) 105 US 249, 26 Ed. 1070 (unforeseeable that victim of train accident would become mentally diseased and commit suicide).
26 *W.* v. *Minister of Pensions* [1946] 2 All ER 501; *Minister of Pensions* v. *Chennell* [1947] KB 250, 256.
27 *Carter* v. *Towne* (1870) 103 Mass. 507.
28 *Schmidt* v. *United States* (1950) 179 F. 2d 724.

the extent of liability in this context very forcibly. The case[29] was one in which defendant by his fault injured plaintiff so that for a time plaintiff lost control of his left leg. He later went down a flight of stairs which had no handrail, without using a stick or calling for his wife or brother-in-law, who were available, to help. His left leg gave way and he then jumped and broke his right ankle. It was held that the injury to the right ankle was not the consequence of the original negligence. Lord Reid pointed out that a negligent defendant is not liable for every consequence which a reasonable man could foresee. 'It only leads to trouble . . . if one tries to graft on to the concept of foreseeability some rule of law to the effect that a wrong-doer is not bound to foresee something which in fact he could quite readily foresee.'[30] It was not at all unlikely or unforeseeable that an active man suffering from the disability from which plaintiff suffered would take an unreasonable risk. But, having done so, he could not hold defendant liable for the consequences.

The House of Lords has therefore made it clear that, despite *The Wagon Mound (No. 1)*,[31] liability for ulterior harm does not simply depend on the harm being foreseeable, even in the theoretical sense of 'not unlikely'. To recover for such harm plaintiff must show a causal connection with defendant's wrongful conduct; and this is done, not just by proving that without the wrongdoing the harm would not have occurred, but by satisfying the court that no subsequent necessary condition of the harm was of the sort which negatives causal connection as plaintiff's unreasonable descent of the stairs did here. But other courts take the doctrine seriously, and hold that a negligent defendant is liable for ulterior harm when the intervention of a third person which contributes to the harm is 'foreseeable' in the sense of 'not unlikely given the initial wrong'. Thus in *Balido* v. *Improved Machinery*[32] defendants manufactured an unsafe moulding press. They later warned plaintiff's employers of its defects and offered to install safety devices but the employers continued to use the defective moulds and, years later, plaintiff's hand was crushed. The California court held that it was a jury question whether the neglect of the warning was 'foreseeable'. Here the continued use by plaintiff's employers of the press over a period

---

[29] *McKew* v. *Holland, Hannen & Cubitts* [1969] 3 All ER 1621 (HL); [1970] SC (HL) 20. Though the principle is clear the facts suggest that an apportionment of damages for the second injury might have been appropriate.

[30] [1969] 3 All ER 1621; cf. *Lamb* v. *Camden Borough Council* [1981] 2 All ER 408 (defendant wrongfully caused plaintiff's house to flood so that tenants left and squatters entered; not liable for squatter damage, though plainly 'likely'); *AG for Ontario* v. *Crompton* (1976) 74 DLR 3d 345, 349.

[31] [1961] AC 388. Regrets are expressed by Millner, '*Novus actus interveniens*: the Present Effect of *The Wagon Mound*', (1971) 22 *NILQ* 168, 182.

[32] (1973) 105 Cal. Rep. 890, 898-9.

of years could well be regarded as voluntary or reckless conduct which, on causal criteria, would negative responsibility.

A last point to note about the variant doctrine that a negligent defendant is liable for foreseeable harm only if the manner of its occurrence was not improbable is that the proviso is not a point essentially connected with the law of negligence. If it is rational in negligence to require that harm should occur in a fairly likely way, so is it in other torts.

Our examination of the enlarging aspect of the foreseeability doctrine may be thus summarized: (i) Over much of the field of negligence courts continue to apply the causal notions by which subsequent voluntary conduct and abnormal events cut short responsibility, but they often use the language of foreseeability in doing so—language which is appropriate to the intervention of abnormal or coincidental events but less so to voluntary or unreasonable interventions. (ii) Over a wide area, however, courts hold a defendant responsible notwithstanding such interventions if the likelihood of their occurrence was sufficient to make his act negligent. In assimilating the provision of such opportunities for harm to causal connection the courts have kept close to common non-legal notions. But they have gone further. (iii) Over a smaller but growing part of the field courts discard causal criteria and apply the theory that if the harm is of a foreseeable type and would not have occurred but for defendant's negligence he is responsible, whatever the manner of its occurrence or the nature of the intervening acts or events. To some extent, therefore, the law is in transition from a stage at which liability was based almost exclusively on negligently causing harm to one in which it is based not merely on causing harm but also on exposing others to a risk of harm by providing other persons or things with the opportunity of doing harm. Probably the future will see a considerable extension of the latter form of liability.

III. THE RISK THEORY

The preceding discussion makes it possible to deal with the risk theory quite shortly. This theory, of which Seavey was for a long time the protagonist,[33] has secured the allegiance of many theorists.[34] They do not, however, all adhere to it in a form from which clear conclusions can be drawn in particular instances. One can indeed distinguish a looser from a more stringent form of the risk

[33] 'Mr. Justice Cardozo and the Law of Torts', (1938-9) 52 *Harv. LR* 372; 'Principles of Torts', (1942-3) 56 *Harv. LR* 72; *Cases on Torts*, chap. 4, s. B.
[34] Keeton, *Legal Cause in the Law of Torts* (1963); Glanville Williams, 'The Risk Principle', (1961) 77 *LQR* 179.

theory. In its looser form it invites the judge to consider, when responsibility for harm is in dispute, on which of the parties the risk of that harm should fall. Should it lie on the victim or should it be transferred to the wrongdoer? This way of putting the matter is intended to keep alive the sense that even the best settled principles of responsibility (e.g. that a tortfeasor takes his victim as he finds him) are open to challenge. But, unless the answer is to be supplied by intuition, we need to define the extent of risk that we have in mind and to find principles of allocation which are generally acceptable. As regards the first requirement, it must be noted that the statement that the risk lies on the wrongdoer is unspecific and needs filling out. Do we mean that he bears the risk of the harm he *causes* by his wrongful conduct (even if unforeseeable), or that of the harm he *occasions* (of which his conduct is a *sine qua non*), or that he is, as it were, to *insure* plaintiff against harm which need not be either caused or occasioned by his conduct? Any one of these can be described as placing the risk on the wrongdoer, but they rest on different principles of responsibility. In order to decide what extent of risk should be placed on each party to the litigation principles to guide the allocation of risk are needed. It is a defect of much theorizing about risk that theorists often assert that the risk should be placed on one or other party without explaining what extent of risk they have in mind and on what principle the allocation they recommend is to be made. There are indeed principles which might serve as a guide. Some would recommend a search for the most economically efficient allocation of risks. Whether it is possible to determine what this is without reference to social and political values is debatable, and surely beyond the competence of courts. Nor, if such a programme were adopted, would it dispense with the need to solve causal problems of the sort which now arise in insurance law: to which of two risks of harm (e.g. fire damage or explosion) is a given loss to be attributed as its 'proximate cause' or 'efficient cause'.[35]

Those who follow the risk theory in this loose form need not, of course, commit themselves to any general principles of risk allocation. Indeed, they include writers such as Leon Green,[36] whose views are analysed in the next chapter. He believes that the many factors which influence an informed sense of judgment in the individual case, and which cannot be reduced to any formula, can nevertheless be appropriately conjured up by asking on whom the risk of loss ought to fall. This formulation may be expected to focus attention on the scope of defendant's duty and of the rule violated; this in

[35] e.g. Karin Kurtz-Eckhardt, *Causa proxima und wesentliche Bedingung* (Bamberg, 1977).
[36] 'The Causal Relation Issue in Negligence Law', (1961) 60 *Mich. LR* 543, 567, criticizing the first edition of this book.

turn may throw light on the range of risks which the rule is intended to guard against.[37] The merits and defects of this approach, too, are discussed in the next chapter.

There is, however, a more stringent form of the risk theory, closer to the views of Seavey, of which Foster has given a lucid exposition,[38] to which we are indebted. In this tighter version the risk theory is simply a generalization of the foreseeability doctrine. According to that doctrine, the limits of responsibility in the law of negligence should depend on the foreseeability of the harm that occurs, because the existence of negligence is itself determined by the foreseeability of harm of a certain type. The risk theory generalizes the notion that liability should extend but also be restricted to those types of harm the chance or risk of which formed *the* reason or *a* reason for the imposition of liability.[39] On this view the foreseeability theory is merely one application of the more general principle: and whenever in the preceding pages we have used the expression 'foreseeable' and 'unforeseeable' in the practical sense we might equally well have written 'within the risk' or 'outside the risk'. The risk theory, however, applies not merely to negligence but also to strict liability; harm is, in this context, said to be within the risk if it is of the sort the chance of which led to the imposition of strict liability.

Hence if defendant is under a strict liability, e.g. owing to the conduct of blasting operations on his land,[40] the theory demands that recovery be allowed only if the harm is 'within the risk' not of a particular blasting operation but of blasting in general; and here what is meant is that the harm should 'result from that blasting',[41] i.e. must be of a kind which commonly results from blasting, e.g. damage by flying debris or concussion, since these are the risks or dangers inherent in blasting. As in the case of the foresight theory one arrives here at the appropriate formulation of the risk by asking what is the reason for imposing strict liability for blasting. The answer will contain a reference to certain generalizations about explosions which will serve to give an appropriate formulation.

Like the foreseeability theory the risk theory has a restrictive and an extensive aspect. The restrictive aspect confines recovery to harm 'within the risk' and the classic statement of this point is Cardozo CJ's judgment in *Palsgraf*,[42] where he bases the principle on the alleged relativity of negligence, using arguments which have been

37 Fleming, *Torts*, pp. 202–3.
38 'The Risk Theory and Proximate Cause', (1953) 32 *Neb. LR* 72.
39 *Palsgraf* v. *Long Island R. Co.* (1928) 248 NY 339, 162 NE 99. On the various senses in which negligence is said to be 'relative' see above, pp. 259–60.
40 *Whitman Hotel Corporation* v. *Elliott & Watrous Engineering Co.* (1951) 137 Conn. 562, 79 A. 2d 591.
41 Ibid.
42 *Palsgraf* v. *Long Island R. Co.* (1928) 248 NY 339, 162 NE 99.

criticized above.[43] There is no need to repeat the arguments against this view, for all that has been urged against the restrictive aspect of the foreseeability doctrine applies with equal force to the risk theory. In particular, the doctrine will not fit torts of intentional wrongdoing, such as intentional assaults and trespasses and it leads to the denial of recovery for ulterior harm.

The other, extensive, aspect of the risk theory amounts to dispensing with causal tests when the harm that occurs is within the risk which led to the imposition of liability. In such cases defendant, it is urged, should be liable for harm 'within the risk' even if he does not cause it. Provided his act was a necessary condition of such harm no further inquiry is necessary. Thus in *Freirichs* v. *Eastern Nebraska Public Power District*[44] defendants ran a power line over a field. They were assumed to have been negligent in not sufficiently guarding the line. Deceased was electrocuted while engaged in laying a pipe through the field when a fellow worker negligently ran into the lower wire of the power line. The Nebraska court decided on appeal that defendants' negligence was not the 'proximate cause' of the death, since the negligence of the fellow employee was not foreseeable. If we assume that the decision was justified on causal grounds because the employee's conduct was reckless or extraordinarily negligent the facts show the contrast with the risk theory, for, on that theory, defendants should have been liable since their negligence was a *sine qua non* of the harm and the harm was of the sort (electrocution) which made it negligent not to guard the wires.

Again, according to the usually accepted interpretation of the *Rylands* v. *Fletcher*[45] rule a defendant who has on his land something noxious which escapes on to his neighbour's land is not liable if a third person intentionally caused the accumulation[46] or escape[47] or if it was caused by an act of God.[48] By the risk theory a defendant should be liable, even in these cases, since the escape of the noxious thing is the risk which leads to the imposition of strict liability.[49] If defendant keeps an animal which is to his knowledge dangerous to mankind and it harms plaintiff he is, on one view, which accords with the risk theory, liable for the harm even if a third person has provided the opportunity for the animal to do harm or even incited it.[50]

[43] pp. 260-1.
[44] (1951) 154 Neb. 777, 49 NW 2d 619.
[45] (1866) LR 1 Ex. 265; (1868) LR 3 HL 330.
[46] *Box* v. *Jubb* (1879) 4 Ex. D. 76.
[47] *Rickards* v. *Lothian* [1913] AC 263.
[48] *Nichols* v. *Marsland* (1876) LR 2 Ex. D. 1.
[49] Goodhart (1951) 4 *Current Legal Problems* 177, 178-84.
[50] Animals Act (England) 1971, s. 5, adopting *Baker* v. *Snell* [1908] 2 KB 825; Fleming, *Torts*, p. 349.

The *Restatement of Torts* states the law of 'absolute liability' in the form that the possessor of a dangerous animal is liable for the harm it does to others, irrespective of the unforeseeable intervention of human beings, animals or forces of nature,[51] and one who engages in an ultrahazardous activity is similarly liable for harm even if it would not have occurred but for such interventions.[52] Yet causal criteria are not here excluded but merely relegated to a later stage, for the harm done by the animal must 'result from' the 'dangerous propensities abnormal to its class'[53] or must 'result from a dangerous propensity that is characteristic of wild animals of the particular class'[54] and one who carries on an ultrahazardous activity is liable for the harm 'resulting' from the 'abnormally dangerous activity' though this is 'limited to the kind of harm, the possibility of which makes the activity abnormally dangerous.'[55] Ordinary causal principles reappear in order to determine the extent of liability for ulterior harm.

In order to provide for the recovery of ulterior harm, Seavey put forward the view that harm should be treated as 'within the risk' if, immediately after the initial impact, it would have appeared to one knowing the facts as not improbable that it should occur.[56] This is designed to allow recovery of ulterior harm in some cases and so bring the risk theory into conformity with the decisions,[57] but it involves abandoning the rationale of the theory. Improper medical treatment may appear not improbable given that defendant has negligently injured plaintiff in a road accident, but the possibility of improper medical treatment is not what makes defendant's conduct negligent.

Seavey's view, and the similar formulation of the *Restatement*, involve a shift similar to that noticed in the foresight theory, where practical foresight is displaced by theoretical foresight, when this is necessary to make the theory compatible with the cases and with ordinary notions of justice. The sense in which a mistake in medical treatment is 'within the risk' of a broken arm is not the same as the sense in which running a pedestrian down is 'within the risk' of negligent driving. Improper medical treatment is 'within the risk'

[51] s. 510.
[52] s. 522.
[53] s. 509.
[54] s. 507.
[55] s. 519.
[56] (1942) 56 *Harv. LR* 72, 91. Cf. Glanville Williams (1961) 77 *LQR* 179, 184 (as regards extent of liability, damage to be irrecoverable must be 'positively unforeseeable'; but, on the risk theory, why?)
[57] e.g. *Galbreath* v. *Engineering Construction Corp.* (1971) 273 NE 2d 121 (defendants exploding dynamite liable to plaintiff injured in gas escape, though gas escape was not the 'same risk').

inasmuch as it is *not improbable* given that plaintiff's arm is broken; there is a considerable chance of such treatment. But running a pedestrian down is an instance of the danger, viz. collision, which makes it negligent to drive too fast, and so 'within the risk' in a stronger sense than that of merely being not unlikely.

The attractiveness of the risk, as of the foresight theory, is twofold. First there is the claim that the criteria used in determining the extent of liability are the same considerations which lead to the rule of law imposing liability. Once this identity is abandoned, in order to meet the difficulty of ulterior harm, as it must be if the theory is to bear any relation to the facts, it is preferable to abandon the ambiguous notion of risk and frankly recognize that causal principles are indispensable, at least in the sphere of ulterior harm.

The second attraction of the risk theory is its simplicity in its extensive aspect; like the foreseeability doctrine, it is partly law already and may come to be law increasingly in future. Courts may be more inclined to give effect to it in the context of strict liability than in that of negligence. But, as yet, causal tests are more often and more widely employed.

One attempt to eliminate the conflict between the risk theory and causal tests is that of Keeton, who is a supporter of the risk theory. His views are discussed in the Preface.[58] It suffices to note here that at least one American case decides that a defendant may be liable for harm caused by his violation of a regulation even though the harm was not 'within the risk' which made it wrongful to commit the violation. In *Kernan* v. *American Dredging Co.*[59] defendant's tug carried a kerosene lamp not more than 3 feet above the water, in breach of a regulation which required a lamp to be carried not less than 8 feet above the water, in order it was assumed to aid navigation and prevent collisions. The lamp caught light when the tug entered petroleum-laden waters and an explosion resulted. Here, though the explosion was not within the risk which made it wrongful to violate the regulation, it was held to have been caused by defendant's breach of it, for which he was held liable.

We began the chapter by asking how far causal limitations on the extent of a tortfeasor's responsibility had been or should be replaced by tests based on whether the harm is foreseeable or 'within the risk'. Our survey shows that different answers must be given as regards the restrictive and extensive aspects of these doctrines. As a technique for limiting responsibility the notions of foresight and risk are inadequate because, if taken seriously, they exclude recovery for ulterior harm. If recovery for ulterior harm is allowed this can be

[58] Above, pp. lxii–lxv.
[59] (1958) 355 US 426.

achieved only by the use of 'foreseeable' and 'within the risk' in a theoretical sense which involves abandoning the simplicity of the original doctrines and reintroducing causal criteria in a disguised terminology. But as a technique for extending responsibility the notions of foreseeability and risk can be supported both in principle and, to some extent, from the cases. The principle that liability in tort may be based on wrongfully exposing others to the risk of harm does not, of course, mean that it is not also based on wrongfully causing harm to others. The former principle supplements but does not supplant the latter: for causal criteria will always be needed at the second stage, when ulterior harm is in question.

X

THE SENSE OF JUDGMENT AND MORAL BLAME

MUCH the most important notions that have been put forward as substitutes for causal limitations on responsibility in tort are those of foreseeability and risk considered in the last chapter. But there are other types of policy theory which deserve notice. Some writers share with the supporters of the foreseeability and risk theories the view that that concept of cause itself contains no element of use to the law except that of necessary condition (*sine qua non*), but have departed further from traditional ideas. They insist that the decisions of courts on the extent of a wrongdoer's liability are not and should not be reached by the application of *any* general principles[1] but by the exercise of the sense of judgment, unhampered by legal rules, on the facts of each case. In their view reference to general principles is a perhaps salutary part of judicial ritual but their recital can solve no problems. Instead it should be recognized that the judge, though he may weigh an indefinite number of considerations each with some bearing on the question, decides more or less intuitively what the extent of a wrongdoer's responsibility is to be. His sense of what is just or fitting may be relied on to guide him to a decision acceptable to society, or at any rate no worse than that which he would reach if he relied on the 'word schemes' which pose as definitions of 'proximate cause'. Such views have been put forward in most detail by Leon Green in his books *Rationale of Proximate Cause*[2] and *Judge and Jury*[3] and in subsequent articles. These have been influential in America and their influence has increased with the passage of time.[4]

Other writers, again, have seen in decisions on the limits of responsibility, traditionally couched in causal language, a direct application

[1] Edgerton, 'Legal Cause', (1924) 72 *U. Pa. LR* 211.
[2] 1927.
[3] 1930. Green's views, sympathetic to but dissenting from the main contentions of this book, are to be found in 'The Causal Relation Issue in Negligence Law', (1961) 60 *Mich. LR* 543; 'Foreseeability in Negligence Law', (1961) 61 *Col. LR* 1401; 'Duties, Risks, Causation Doctrines', (1962) 41 *Tex. LR* 42; '*The Wagon Mound No. 2*: Foreseeability Revised', (1967) *Utah LR* 197; cf. R. Cooke, 'Remoteness of Damage and Judicial Discretion', (1978) *Cam. LJ* 288; Dias, 'Trouble on Oiled Waters', (1967) *Cam. LJ* 62.
[4] They are endorsed by Fleming, *Torts*, 1st edn., p. 195, and partially by Prosser, 'Palsgraf Revisited', (1953-4) 52 *Mich. LR* 1, 32; *Selected Topics*, pp. 191, 241.

to defendant's conduct of judgments of moral blame.[5] The appeal made by both these types of theory is to our candour: they invite us to admit that in this sphere above all, 'general propositions do not decide concrete cases', and to see how frequently decision turns on the tribunal's sense of what is fit, proper, or just—which is not only unformulated but unformulable in general terms.

If this is their strength, the weakness of such theories lies in their exaggeration of the insight they provide. It is one thing to recognize that general principles do not determine decision uniquely in all cases, and another to conclude that therefore they afford no control or guidance and are not really used at all. Preoccupation with the discretion exercised in the borderline case is not a good reason for assimilating all judgment to the exercise of discretion. A judge faced with the task of applying a rule excluding vehicles from a park may find himself puzzled when confronted with the borderline case of a toy motor-car electrically propelled. He may consult his sense of what is fit or proper, weigh various factors, and so reach the decision that it is a vehicle for purposes of the rule. Another judge by the same route may reach a contrary conclusion. Yet these facts do not or should not incline us to accept the doctrine that a vehicle means anything which a judge in the exercise of his sense of judgment decides to exclude from a park. The same is true, in principle, of the more fluid concepts of causation.

In the next two sections we consider some representative theories that have stressed the intuitive character of judgments of proximate cause and their dependence on judgments of moral blame. In the third section we describe briefly the various ways in which courts limit the scope of torts such as negligence out of considerations of policy which should, in our view, be distinguished from limitations on responsibility in individual cases arising from the law's use of the causal principles outlined in Chapter VI.

I. GREEN'S VIEW

Green's atomistic view of policy limitations has been described in general terms in Chapter IV and may best be set out in his own words. We will describe his views on actions in tort, but the same principles are applied by him *mutatis mutandis* to actions for breach of contract and criminal prosecutions.[6] Green says, 'Phrased in terms of requisites, a tort comprehends: (1) an interest protected (2) against the particular hazard encountered (3) by some rule of law (4) which

---

[5] P. J. Kelley, 'Causation and Justice: a Comment', (1978) *Wash. ULQ* 635, 636 (identifying causation with the initiation of physical sequences).
[6] *Rationale of Proximate Cause*, chaps. 2–3.

the defendant's conduct violated, (5) thereby causing (6) damages to the plaintiff.'[7]

Green's general view is that requirements (1) and (2) are of prime importance, though not enough attention has been given to them in the cases, while requirement (5) is of comparatively minor importance and is in all cases a pure question of fact, the simplest element of legal liability.[8]

It will be recalled from the survey in Chapter IV that causation is considered by Green to be a simple question of fact best expressed in the terminology of 'substantial factor'. This terminology was the invention of Jeremiah Smith,[9] who thought that it best expressed the genuine, factual problems of causation to be found in the law of tort. According to Green the notion of a 'substantial', 'material', or 'appreciable' factor provides a formula which 'cannot be reduced to any lower terms. It has no multiples.'[10] Green asserts that the factual question must be put to the jury without any detailed explanation of how it is to be answered because, being a pure question of fact, no explanation would be of assistance.

But from the examples given by Green one may deduce that the notion of 'substantial factor' is not merely intended to replace the question whether the wrongful act was a necessary condition of the harm, but also certain ill-defined wider questions. Thus, in his discussion of *Central of Georgia Ry.* v. *Price*,[11] Green says that the 'only manner in which a cause issue could have become predominant was by considering whether defendant's negligence, as a factor in comparison with the other operative factors, really contributed appreciably to the injury'. It will be recalled that, defendants having in breach of contract set down plaintiff at the wrong place, she was obliged to spend the night at a hotel where a lamp exploded in her face. The best ground for not holding defendant liable in that case for the injuries to the passenger is probably that the explosion of the lamp was a coincidence, it being extremely unlikely that a lamp would explode upon any given night.[12] This the court expressed by saying that the failure to put off plaintiff at her destination was not the proximate cause of the injury.

Conversely Green sometimes considers that conduct was a 'substantial factor' in producing the harm when on causal principles one

[7] *Rationale of Proximate Cause*, pp. 3–4.
[8] Ibid., p. 4.
[9] (1911–12) 25 *Harv. LR* 103, 223, 303, 309; *Harvard Selected Essays on Torts*, pp. 649, 711.
[10] Op. cit., p. 137. Presumably 'multiples' should be 'factors'. Cf. *Judge and Jury*, p. 190.
[11] (1898) 106 Ga. 176, 32 SE 77; *Proximate Cause*, p. 32.
[12] There is no rule of policy excluding recovery for personal injuries following a breach of contract of this sort, either in England or America. *Hobbs* v. *L.S.W.R.* (1875) LR 10 QB 111; *Ehrgott* v. *Mayor of New York* (1884) 96 NY App. 264.

would doubt whether the wrongful aspect of defendant's conduct was a causally relevant factor.[13] Thus he gives as an example the following case. 'Suppose P is hunting on Sunday. While P is walking down the road with his gun, the defendant negligently drives his car so as to run over P. Can the defendant cite P's violation of the Sunday law as a defence? Most courts would say No, on the ground, confused though it be, that the violation of the Sunday law had nothing to do with the result (was not a *proximate cause* of it).'[14]

Green's criticism of the language used by the courts in such cases is that 'the violation of the Sunday law was a substantial cause factor in every sense of that term, but the two rules, the one which P was violating and the one which the defendant violated had different purposes and imposed duties on different planes'.[15] It may be true that the duties had different purposes and this would be a sufficient basis for decision and the easiest way of disposing of the case. Nevertheless, once we are clear that the harm the law seeks to prevent is injury to human beings and not merely injury on a Sunday the hunting *on Sunday* is not a *sine qua non* of the injury in the relevant sense explained in Chapter V, so that the wrongful act, contrary to Green's view, is not causally connected with the harm.

It is not at all clear what the notion of 'substantial factor' means to Green and, indeed, since it is said by him to be incapable of analysis, presumably the jury must rely on intuition to apply it. Yet Green does not treat this issue (said by him to be relatively unimportant) as a 'policy' question. That description is reserved for the really important questions: whether plaintiff's interest is one protected by the law and whether it is protected against the particular hazard in question. Here it is important to remember that the word 'hazard', in Green's usage, may be translated 'loss, injury, peril, risk, risk of loss, &c.'[16] It would appear from this explanation that instead of speaking of 'an interest protected against the particular hazard encountered' we might equally well speak of an interest protected 'in the circumstances of the case', or 'against harm occurring in the way in which it in fact occurred'. The reference to 'hazard' does not import that the event which occurred must have been likely or foreseeable in advance, for Green rejects the notion that foreseeability is of much assistance in determining questions of responsibility for harm.[17] Hence we shall substitute for Green's

13 Above, p. 113.
14 *Judge and Jury*, pp. 234–5.
15 Ibid., p. 235.
16 *Proximate Cause*, p. 3.
17 Ibid., pp. 88, 120. In '*The Wagon Mound No. 2*: Foreseeability Revised', (1967) *Utah LR* 197 Green calls foreseeability a 'delightful and useful fiction, with no restrictions in itself' which, when linked with the fictitious reasonable man, 'serves in every case to call forth a fresh judgment'.

references to 'hazard' the question whether the plaintiff's interest is protected in the circumstances of the case, since this is less likely to lead to confusion with questions of likelihood or foreseeability. Green, in effect, refuses to distinguish between the question whether defendant owed a duty in the circumstances of the case or, in particular, whether he owed a duty to plaintiff, and the question of proximate cause, i.e. whether a third factor negatives causal connection between the wrongful act and the harm, except so far as this is done, in cases of coincidence, under the vague heading of 'substantial factor'.[18] He treats them equally as questions of policy and does not think that any broad distinctions can be drawn between the types of policy involved in answering the two questions. In Green's view, the court must always ask, after examining the detailed facts of a case, whether plaintiff's interest is protected in these circumstances. What Green's approach entails may be brought to light by looking at his treatment of the extraordinary Texas case of *Hines* v. *Morrow*,[19] where defendants, in breach of statutory duty, left a hole in the road. When plaintiff tried to help extricate a truck from the hole, his artificial leg was trapped and his sound leg broken. Plaintiff succeeded in respect of his broken leg although the defence argued that the consequence was unforeseeable and so not proximate. Green comments: 'This was not the issue. The only problem was whether this risk fell within the radius of the rule which the plaintiff relied on i.e. the defendant's duty to keep the crossing in proper repair.'[20]

Hines v. *Morrow* serves to bring out the main weakness in Green's position. If the court is to ask itself whether plaintiff's interest is protected upon facts so bizarre as those, it clearly will not help to inquire what was the legislative intent of those who drafted the statute which defendant violated. Rules of law are drawn up not with detailed facts in mind, but with a view to covering a wide variety of possible circumstances. Reference to legislative intent or the policy of those who made the rule might at most reveal that they intended to protect a plaintiff who suffered bodily injury, or, perhaps, who suffered bodily injury through mechanical impact. It would be fruitless to ask whether the rule was intended to protect a plaintiff with a wooden leg which stuck in a mud hole, and whose sound leg was broken through his vain attempts to extricate himself. A system of law which included rules as complex as would be needed to deal with the circumstances of *Hines* v. *Morrow* would be so cumbrous and unwieldy that it could neither be learned nor used in practice. This

18 Above, pp. 293–4.
19 (1921) 236 SW 183 (Texas Civil Appeals); above, pp. 95, 105, 257.
20 *Proximate Cause*, p. 22.

Green recognizes, for he says such problems will remain after we have done all we can to identify the purpose or intended scope of rules.

What then are the criteria for answering the question which is said by Green to be the real issue in cases such as *Hines* v. *Morrow*: Did the risk fall within the radius of the rule which defendant violated? Here he affords little guidance and indeed his case is that there is no guidance to be had. But his language is deceptive: for he speaks of '*the* radius of the rule' whereas he is entitled on his own view to speak only of the radius which the judge, in the exercise of his sense of judgment, may think proper to give it. It may be worth noting that on conventional causal principles the decision in *Hines* v. *Morrow* seems correct. No intervening event that could be called a co-incidence occurred and the acts of plaintiff and his friend in seeking to extricate the truck were neither reckless nor grossly negligent so as to negative causal connection.

The difference between Green's approach and one which holds that common-sense principles may be of use in such cases is not that the latter provides a code from which decisions may be deduced. It is rather that, apart from questions of social policy which may be used to determine the general scope of legal rules, such causal principles will emphasize certain features, constantly recurring in particular cases, which are in a sense policy neutral.

It may be thought that this criticism is unfair to Green. Does he really intend courts to ask themselves the detailed questions which, we have suggested, they would have to do if his theory were applied? We may find an answer by looking at Green's treatment of a famous Connecticut case, *Mahoney* v. *Beatman*.[21] Defendant was driving his car northwards on the wrong side of the road. Plaintiff was driving at an excessive speed southwards and was forced by defendant off the concrete on to the shoulder of the road. Nevertheless, defendant's car struck the hub of the left front wheel of plaintiff's car. Plaintiff's chauffeur lost control of the car and it swerved in a circle to the left and crashed into a tree and stone fence on the opposite side of the road. The trial court found that the speed of plaintiff's car, though unreasonable, did not contribute to the collision, but did materially hamper plaintiff's chauffeur in controlling the car after the collision. It therefore found that plaintiff was entitled to recover damages only for the initial impact, not, in view of his contributory negligence, for the subsequent collision with the tree and stone fence;[22] it therefore awarded nominal damages. On appeal it was held that plaintiff was

---

21 (1929) 110 Conn. 185, 147 Atl. 762; Green, *Judge and Jury*, chap. 7, '*Mahoney* v. *Beatman*: a Study in Proximate Cause'.
22 Apportionment not being provided for in Connecticut at that time.

entitled to recover full damages since defendant's negligence was a 'substantial factor' in producing the whole damage.

Green asserts that the trial court confused causal relation and responsibility. He says that plaintiff's unreasonable speed 'cannot be removed from the case without making a new one, which was not before the court'.[23] This is a reference to the trial court's view that plaintiff's speed was not a causally relevant factor in the collision. 'The trial judge doubtless meant that the plaintiff's unreasonable speed ought not to relieve the defendant of responsibility for the initial impact.'[24] Green therefore concludes that speed was a 'substantial cause' of the whole damage but that the case should be decided not on causal principles but by considering the scope of the rules forbidding speeding and enjoining cars to drive upon the right side of the road. 'The duty violated by the defendant was clearly for the protection of travellers using the other side of the road. He should therefore pay for the damage he caused the plaintiff unless the duty violated by the plaintiff—excessive speed—in some way limited the defendant's duty.'[25] On the other hand, plaintiff's duty not to speed, asserts Green, is not intended to cover the situation in which defendant drives on the wrong side of the road. 'Under his duty to the defendant not to speed, he was not required to take into account the risk that just as he was passing the defendant, the latter would turn on to the wrong side of the road.'[26] Thus 'the two duties have different scopes; they comprehend different risks. The violation of one cannot be set off as a defence to the violation of the other, even though both violations admittedly contributed to the same result.'[27]

We are not here[28] concerned to defend the decision either of the trial court or of the appeal court in *Mahoney* v. *Beatman* but merely to consider Green's proposed solution. It is clear that the answers proffered by Green cannot seriously be regarded as representing the intention of the legislators or judges who first laid down the rules in question. The rule forbidding speeding on the highway can hardly have been made with any particular violation of the rules of good driving by other motorists in mind. It was made, rather, with a view to preventing accidents and giving compensation for injuries suffered on the highway generally. Similarly the rule requiring a motorist to drive on one side of the road is presumably made with a view to preventing accidents generally rather than protecting a plaintiff in

---

[23] *Judge and Jury*, p. 231.
[24] Ibid.
[25] Ibid., p. 233.
[26] Ibid.
[27] Ibid., p. 234.
[28] But see above, p. 227.

some specific situation such as occurred in *Mahoney*'s case. The question whether plaintiff's interest is protected in the particular circumstances of a case such as *Mahoney* differs, therefore, from the question whether the harm he suffered was causally connected with defendant's act chiefly in that no definite criteria are available for answering it and that a decision one way or the other would be open only to one inconclusive form of criticism, viz. that it did not accord with the critic's sense of justice, or that of most men in the community. Green's approach would, in fact, give judges or suitably directed juries an unlimited power to determine the limits of responsibility as they wished.[29]

Green's confidence in asserting that the two duties 'have different scopes' disguises the fact that this is a matter for the determination of which there are no agreed criteria. The policy substitute for causation may also have its dogmatisms.

One interest of the *Mahoney* case is that the causal principles involved are fairly clear and are different from what Green supposes. Plaintiff's speeding was, as shown in Chapter V,[30] not causally connected with the initial impact. This is not to assert that the appeal court was necessarily wrong in *Mahoney* v. *Beatman* in applying the vague 'substantial factor' test in order to allow plaintiff to recover in a jurisdiction which did not permit apportionment in cases of contributory negligence. It may well be the lesser of two evils, in such cases, to ignore the fact that plaintiff's contributory negligence was a cause of the harm and allow a recovery on the ground that defendant's act was more dangerous than plaintiff's.[31]

It appears then, on a broad survey, that the atomistic type of policy expounded by Green is open to greater objections than the views of those who support the foreseeability and risk theories, which at least afford the judge or jury a general standard by which to test responsibility. The main objections are the immense complexity of the rules that would be required to put Green's views into practice; the fact that the number and variety of rules would render all prediction impossible; and the fact that, since there could in practice be no such wealth of rules, judges would have a large discretionary power. It is significant that Green himself admits that he can give no more precise test than to suggest that the court should ask itself whether plaintiff's interest is protected against the particular hazard encountered: one is reminded of Bentham's remark that we are given

[29] Cf. W. S. Malone, 'Ruminations on *Dixie Drive It Yourself* v. *American Beverage*', (1969–70) 30 *La. LR* 363. The case is reported at (1962) 137 So. 2d 298. It was an orthodox decision (presumption that if halted truck had put out signals they would have been seen; negligence of passing driver is not 'superseding cause'; purpose of signal requirement is to protect road users).

[30] pp. 121–2.

[31] Above, p. 225.

'the same thing dished up over again in the shape of a reason for itself'.[32]

It is probable that some, perhaps many, judges are influenced by their intuitions of what would be fair limits to place on responsibility in tort. But, so far as judges do proceed in this way, they are likely to apply intuitively those limitations on responsibility which are most deeply ingrained in the thought of ordinary men, viz. the causal limitations explained in Chapter VI. A careful reading of Green's books and articles leaves the impression that these are precisely the limitations that he himself would very often wish to apply.

II. MORAL BLAME

Certain varieties of policy theory differ from Green's in their emphasis on what is just or morally blameworthy and are inspired by the belief that the obscurities of proximate cause may be avoided if determinations of the extent of liability for wrongdoing which are at present discussed in causal terms are treated as judgments about the social utility or justice of exacting compensation or punishment.[33] The belief that answers to questions of remoteness can be found in such judgments has appeared even to some modern writers excessively naïve;[34] and it is true that few who have professed this belief have shown how in concrete cases social policy and justice would operate as satisfactory determinants of those questions.[35]

We consider in this section a variety of such theories to all of which the following general comments apply. Such theories float somewhat ambiguously between two contentions which need to be considered separately. The first is that what lawyers *mean* by the language of proximate cause is that justice or social policy requires compensation to be exacted from a wrongdoer whose wrongful act was a necessary condition of harm. The second is that, whatever lawyers or anyone else mean by cause, we have in the combination of necessary condition and judgment of what is just or useful all we need as an answer to the problems of remoteness commonly discussed in causal terms. The first contention therefore offers an analysis of the lawyer's concept of proximate cause: the second an allegedly rational or morally satisfying substitute for it. As in Green's case, the strength of such theses is the salutary light they throw on

---

[32] 'The policy theorists have done almost nothing, outside the foreseeability and risk theories, to show how their ideas could be applied in particular cases.' Morris (1952-3) 101 *U. Pa. LR* 189, 221-2.

[33] See Honoré, *IECL*, xi, chap. 7-101 to 7-104 ('The Equity Theory').

[34] Clarence Morris, above and (1949-50) 34 *Minn. LR* 185-209; *Studies in Torts* (1952), pp. 244, 270; Morris, *Torts*, pp. 207-10.

[35] The writings of Wechsler on criminal law are a notable exception.

those dark corners where the vagueness inherent in the concept of cause logically permits a decision either way and the decision is often reached by taking into account, among other things, moral or social considerations. The weakness of these theories is twofold. First, they make the mistake of identifying the whole meaning of causal language with those moral or social factors to which appeal is made in borderline cases. Secondly they fail to do justice to the conviction, deeply ingrained in the very moral notions they invoke, that one ground for holding it just to exact compensation or punish the wrongdoer is that he caused harm. How can this be so if, as these theories claim, to assert that one has caused harm presupposes, because it includes in its meaning, the conclusion that it is just to punish or exact compensation?

A forthright statement of one such theory is F. S. Cohen's view that 'what we actually do when we look for a legal cause is to pick out of this infinity of intersecting strands a useful point at which public pressure can be placed'.[36] In the absence of a detailed explanation of what is meant by 'useful point' and 'public pressure' it is difficult to criticize this statement, but it has plainly no plausibility as an account of what lawyers mean by causation. Surely for them a madman's act is the cause of a victim's death even if no public pressure on him or anyone can avert such occurrences. This pragmatic view of the meaning of cause suffers from the same vice as the similar theory suggested by Collingwood who was prepared heroically to accept the conclusion that it is logically impossible to speak of discovering the cause of a disease unless we can use our knowledge to cure it.

Viewed not as an analysis of the meaning of legal cause but as a recommendation that responsibility for harm should depend on whether 'public pressure' could usefully be exerted on the wrongdoer, the theory would have very strange results. It would only apply to human acts and offer no guidance when the question, as under statutory schemes of compensation or insurance contracts, is whether harm is to be attributed to a natural event (war service, marine perils) or to the act of an enemy beyond the reach of the law. Within the narrower sphere to which it could apply it would presumably lead to certain classes of act being designated the cause of certain types of harm, on the grounds that this class of act is often followed by the given type of harm and that experience has shown that the incidence of such harm is less when punishment or compensation is prescribed. So liability would depend on an estimate of

---

[36] 'Field Theory and Judicial Logic', (1949-50) 59 *Yale LJ* 238, 252; G. Calabresi, 'Concerning Cause and the Law of Torts', (1975-6) 43 *U. Ch. LR* 69, 106 (in law the term 'cause' is used 'always to identify those pressure points that are most amenable to the social goals we wish to accomplish').

the probability, presumably based on statistics, that this 'public pressure' would in some sense be 'useful' to society. In tort this would mean, on one interpretation of the expressions quoted, that a wrongdoer who deliberately inflicts harm would not be liable to compensate his victim if the prospect of liability was in general an ineffectual deterrent. Of course, one can avoid this conclusion by interpreting 'useful public pressure' as referring not to a successful deterrent but to the fact that compensation satisfies our sense that it is just for those who have caused harm to pay for it. This, however, would be to reintroduce the notion of cause and appeal to the ordinary sense of the word by which causing harm is a ground for responsibility, not to be identified with or derived from it.

Other writers have sought to apply the notion of *moral guilt* or *blameworthiness* in the analysis of the legal meaning of causation or as substitutes for it in deciding questions of responsibility. One such view rests on the simple principle that, if defendant's act is morally blameworthy and a necessary condition of harm to plaintiff, plaintiff is generally entitled to recover. Another rests on a wider principle that, in assessing responsibility, the degree of moral blameworthiness may properly be a controlling factor in deciding whether an actor is legally responsible for harm of which his act was a necessary condition.[37] Probably both theories are intended not merely to give an account of the actual behaviour of courts beneath the smokescreen of causal language but to offer rational bases for responsibility.

Esmein[38] distinguishes between 'material causation', by which he means the requirements that defendant's act must be a necessary condition of the harm, and 'moral causation'. The latter comprises the additional requirements that defendant's act should be both legally wrong and morally blameworthy. These three elements together establish a relationship which is necessary and usually sufficient for legal responsibility. Foreseeability may be required in order to establish that defendant has committed a given legal wrong, in which case foreseeability is made by law a defining element, but in determining the extent of liability as distinct from its existence under such rules foreseeability is irrelevant. Esmein explains this on the theory that the finding of initial fault entails moral blame and casts a stain[39] on defendant who is then viewed as an outcast from whom compensation may be exacted for all harm of which his conduct was a necessary condition.

Again, this theory has no plausibility as an account of what lawyers or ordinary men understand by causing harm, nor would it be

---

37 Merrills, 'Policy and Remoteness', (1973–4) 6 *Ottawa LR* 18.
38 Planiol, Ripert, and Esmein, *Droit civil français*, vi. 730.
39 'Souillure'.

tolerable as a method for assessing responsibility. In the former role
it fails because it allows no place for the use of causal language in
determining whether contingencies other than human acts are the
cause of harm, and because it distorts the relation of causation to
moral blame. One ground at least for saying that an act is blameworthy is that it has caused harm to others and, if this is so, the
latter statement cannot be included in the meaning of the former.
Moreover, we can distinguish the case where a man both intends
harm to another and does an act which is a necessary condition of
the harm from one where his act has caused the harm. A man who
strikes another down, intending to kill him, but inflicts only minor
wounds has not caused his death if the victim is struck by lightning
and killed at the place where he falls. Because our judgments of
moral responsibility are powerfully influenced by causation in a
sense different from Esmein's 'moral cause', the latter also fails as a
satisfactory basis for legal responsibility and a substitute for ordinary causal principles. A person who has acted in a morally blameworthy way is not necessarily held morally responsible for all harm
of which his act is a necessary condition and it is easy to imagine
cases where we could not wish legal responsibility to extend so far.
Some limitation is required even if, with the advocates of the risk or
foreseeability theories, we phrase it in terms of 'risk', 'hazard', or
'foreseeability' rather than causation.

Esmein is indeed aware that courts limit responsibility to something short of what his doctrine of 'moral causation', strictly taken,
would require. He seems prepared, for example, to accept the view
that there are categories of intervening events which are not merely
'rare' but 'extraordinary' and lie beyond the limits of responsibility
even though they would not have occurred without some wrongful
act of a morally blameworthy character.[40] He also discusses cases
where the intervention of a second actor is regarded by courts as
excluding the responsibility of the first wrongdoer. He suggests that
the basis of these decisions is that courts make a comparative estimate of the moral blame attaching to these acts and exculpate the
less blameworthy. But these exceptions, as they appear to be, to the
strict doctrine of 'moral causation' and 'souillure' are not worked
out in detail; if they were, it would appear that 'moral blame' is
accorded far less importance than Esmein thinks, and perhaps that
causal principles very similar to those we have discussed really underlie the moral terminology he uses.

The second view put forward is that of the sliding scale. This may
be expressed in the following words of Street:[41] 'We find this to be

40 'Souillure'.
41 *Foundations of Legal Liability*, i. 111.

true, that as the wrongful act which is alleged to have caused the damage increases in moral obliquity or in illegality, the legal eye reaches further and will declare damage to be proximate which in other connexions would be considered too remote.' 'The more reprehensible the conduct, the more readily will judges find a causal connexion between the conduct and the injury complained of.'[42]

As a statement of factors that among others actually influence the judgment of courts when faced with debatable questions of the extent of responsibility, the words quoted have much truth. A court may allow its estimate of the moral iniquity of a defendant's conduct to affect its decision on any matter and no form of words can prevent judge or jury being influenced in this way. But it is another matter to see in this tendency a principle for determining the extent of legal responsibility, and it is not clear how a workable principle could be fashioned on a graded estimate of the immorality of conduct. Is it that a court must extend liability to all harm of which defendant's act was a necessary condition, notwithstanding the manner of its occurrence, if satisfied that the act was of the worst kind of moral obliquity? Or for this result to follow must the evil conduct have been inspired by an intention to bring about the actual harm?

A statement of this theory has been made by Watermeyer CJ.[43] He asserts that there is a series of progressively less blameworthy states of mind, intention, recklessness, heedlessness, and inattention. The blame attaching to conduct does not wholly depend on the state of mind of the actor, however, but also on the likelihood of harm and the probable seriousness of the harm, should it occur. Taking these three factors into account it is 'possible to construct a roughly graduated scale of culpability ranging from an act intentionally done for the purpose of causing great harm to an act inadvertently done which is unlikely to cause harm at all or, at most, trivial harm'.[44] In civil law, at least, the decision on this view depends on relative culpability, not causation.

The relative culpability of defendant's conduct is certainly an important consideration when non-causal limitations on liability are in issue. Thus, the scope of the law of negligence, as we shall see in the next section, does not in general extend to compensating a plaintiff for loss occasioned by a negligent act if his own impecuniosity contributed to it.[45] This is not because the negligent act did not cause the loss. If plaintiff's lack of means existed at the time of the wrongful act it was as much an existing circumstance as if he had

---

[42] F. S. Cohen, 'Field Theory and Judicial Logic', (1950) 59 *Yale LJ* 238, 259.
[43] 'Causation and Legal Responsibility', (1941) 58 *SALJ* 232; (1945) 62 *SALJ* 126, *sub nom.* 'Aquarius'.
[44] (1945) 62 *SALJ* 126, 129.
[45] Above, pp. 175-6, below, pp. 305-6.

suffered from latent polio or an eggshell skull;[46] and so it did not negative causal connection between the wrongful act and the loss to which the lack of funds contributed. But the exclusion of such loss in the law of negligence, which reflects considerations of legal policy, will not necessarily be adhered to when the wrongful conduct complained of consists of something gravely reprehensible, such as deceit.[47] For in that case the considerations which in general make it desirable for plaintiffs to bear the losses which they suffer through shortage of funds do not apply. An innocent plaintiff may, not without reason, call on a morally reprehensible defendant to pay the whole of the loss he has caused.

It is also possible to see how such comparative estimates of the immorality of conduct may help in cases of contributory negligence[48] where the law does not admit apportionment or where the rule of comparative negligence is accepted, as it increasingly is in the USA.[49] Courts might adopt the simple principle that of two negligent tortfeasors the more morally culpable, as assessed by the threefold test, should be treated as solely responsible. Where apportionment is allowed, measurement on this scale might serve as its basis. But apart from this the theory would yield results quite without support in the present law. If it is interpreted as meaning that a tortfeasor who has done a wrongful act of the most serious degree of culpability, which is a necessary condition of harm, is responsible for all such harm, no third factor in the shape of a coincidence or the deliberate intervention of a third party will displace it. If A shoots at B intending to wound him but misses he has surely done something morally very wrong and committed an assault. If B in consequence decides to move to another house and is injured in a railway accident *en route A* would, on this view, be liable in tort for his injuries. Conversely if the initial wrongful act was inadvertently done and likely only to cause little harm the loss would presumably always lie where it fell.

These results may be found satisfactory by some but they are without support in existing law. The plausibility of a similar theory in criminal law is considered in Chapter XIV.

III. THE SCOPE OF THE LAW OF TORT

It would be unsatisfactory to leave our survey of the various types of policy, put forward as a substitute for causal principles in determining the limits of responsibility in tort, without giving some

[46] Above, pp. 172 ff.
[47] *Doyle* v. *Olby* [1969] 2 QB 158.
[48] Which was the purpose the author had specially in mind.
[49] Fleming, 'Comparative Negligence at Last', (1976) 64 *Cal. LR* 239.

account of the way in which, in our view, courts fix those limitations by which causal principles must be supplemented if a workable system of law is to be developed. We have been at pains to insist on the need to distinguish between causal limitations, such as those set out in Chapter VI, and limitations of the sort illustrated by the New York fire rules. Both the administration and the understanding of the law will be served by pressing this distinction rather than by their fusion in an omnibus rubric of 'proximate cause'. Yet, of course, courts must and do make use of what we have called 'scope rules'.[50] How are these arrived at?

It would seem that courts have been influenced, in settling these rules, partly by very general, partly by particular considerations. The general factors are seen at work most obviously in the common law of negligence. They include such general principles of policy as the desire not to multiply actions beyond need, not to impose a crushing liability on defendants, not to admit actions in spheres where the facts are peculiarly difficult to prove, and not to discourage individual initiative. Thus, one very broad limitation on the scope of the tort of negligence is the fact that the common law is not on the whole concerned to compensate for the economic[51] and psychological repercussions on B, C, and D of physical harm caused to A. When an item of capital is damaged or destroyed, and especially when the most important form of capital, human skill, is impaired, important side-effects often follow. A's injury means that B, C, and D, his family, employees, tradesmen, insurers, suffer financial loss, anxiety and inconvenience. Apart from some historical anomalies, like the master's action for loss of services, the common law gives no remedy to B, C, and D in such circumstances. To do so would be burdensome to defendant, expose him to a multiplicity of actions, and derogate from the sound general principle that everyone should look to his own financial and emotional salvation. We cannot effectively protect our bodies against hurt but we can in a measure line our pockets and fortify our minds against the fluctuations of fortune. To the extent that we cannot do so, it is thought better that the State should intervene directly with schemes of industrial insurance and social benefits, so that the limits of liability can be precisely fixed by statute or regulation, rather than that the courts, with their clumsy and inelastic methods, should undertake to provide a remedy.

Rather similar considerations are seen at work so far as the first person injured is concerned. Courts will, indeed, allow a plaintiff who has suffered physically through defendant's wrong to recover,

---

50 Honoré, *IECL*, xi, chap. 7-97 to 7-99.
51 *Anglo-Algerian S.S. Co.* v. *Houlder Line* [1908] 1 KB 659; *S.A. de Remorquage à Hélice* v. *Bennetts* [1911] 1 KB 243; *Petition of Kinsman Transit Co.* (1968) 388 F. 2d 821. *Contra: Hanna* v. *McKibben* [1940] NI 120.

up to a point, the consequent economic loss,[52] but they tend to stop short when plaintiff's lack of funds is a contributing factor.[53] Such general notions of social policy and expediency seem to lie at the root of the rules by which courts circumscribe the harm recoverable in the tort of negligence, rather than any feeling that certain forms of harm brought about in certain ways are 'unforeseeable' or 'beyond the risk' or that it is intuitively unjust or inexpedient to make defendant pay compensation for them.

Rather different considerations underlie the rules defining the scope of particular statutory, as opposed to common law, rules in the field of tort. When a legislature supplements the common law, as by an act for the fencing of dangerous machinery, it is reasonable to suppose that it intends to achieve some limited object, the prevention of or compensation for some fairly narrowly defined type of harm, and often to restrict recovery to a particular class of persons. Thus, in England such fencing legislation has been interpreted as intended to protect factory workers only and as confined to harm caused by contact with the machinery,[54] e.g. through a part of the body or clothing being caught in it, thus excluding harm caused when part of the machinery flies out and hits someone.

The most famous case on rules of this sort, and one which distinguishes clearly between such scope rules and causal limitations, is *Gorris* v. *Scott*,[55] discussed in Chapter IV.

Such cases present problems in statutory interpretation which are to be solved, like other such problems, by ascertaining either what the law-maker really intended to achieve or, in the absence of admissible evidence about this, what purpose it is reasonable to seek to achieve by rules of the sort in question. To answer such problems may indeed be difficult and will often involve judicial legislation; no general formula can help in their solution and, in this sphere, the statute-by-statute method is the only possible approach.

There are, then, broadly the above two forms of policy limitation which the courts apply, and rationally should continue to apply, in the law of tort, particularly in the common law of negligence and in actions for breach of statutory duty. Is there any case for presenting such limitations in causal language or treating them, together with the causal limitations outlined in Chapter VI, as if they formed a single issue which could be brought under one formula? Obviously there is none. The genuinely causal limitations present issues which,

---

[52] *The Anselma de Larrinaga* (1913) 29 TLR 587; *The Columbus* (1849) 3 W. Rob. 158, 166 ER 922; *The Racine* [1906] P. 273; *The Argentino* (1889) 14 AC 519; *Spartan Steel Alloys* v. *Martin* [1973] 1 QB 27.

[53] Above, pp. 175–6.

[54] *Kilgollan* v. *Cooke* [1956] 1 WLR 527; [1956] 2 All ER 294.

[55] (1874) LR 9 Ex. 125, above, p. 93; Green, *Rationale of Proximate Cause*, p. 25.

however vague the criteria for their solution, are to be solved by the use of common-sense notions or analogies to them[56] and are eminently suitable for submission to a properly instructed jury. The types of limitation considered in this chapter involve general considerations of social policy or statutory interpretation and are eminently unsuited for submission to a jury. The first type of issue concerns what happened on a given occasion, whether on a certain set of facts A's injury can properly be called the consequence of B's act. This is quite different from the question whether the type of harm suffered by A is of the sort for which the law will give compensation when caused by an act of the type that B has committed. Serious confusion has often resulted from the attempt to treat these issues as if they were one, and in so far as such phrases as 'proximate cause' and 'direct cause' have contributed to the confusion, lawyers might well abandon them in the interests of clarity and simply ask 'Was the harm to A caused by B's act?' and 'Is the harm which A suffered of the sort for which sound legal policy requires compensation to be paid when it is caused by acts such as B's?' Almost all policy theorists would, of course, agree that these two questions should, in a sense distinguishable from ours, be kept separate; but most of them would interpret the causal question as referring to something much narrower (e.g. *sine qua non* or 'substantial factor') than the general types of limitation expounded in Chapter VI. What we are really concerned to stress, therefore, is that there exist in the law of tort two radically different techniques for limiting responsibility, causal and non-causal, and that both these should have a place in any workable system of law.

[56] *Healy* v. *Hoy* (1911) 115 Minn. 321, 132 NW 208, endorsed by Prosser, *Torts*, p. 290.

XI

CAUSATION AND CONTRACT

EXPLICIT discussions of causation are much less prominent in books about contract than in books about tort. The reason for this is probably the following. In the first place the harm for which compensation is to be paid in the law of contract is usually economic rather than physical, and establishing 'causal connection' between a breach of contract and economic loss, though it often involves problems of the sort discussed in Chapter VI in connection with the law of tort, also involves a different relation, viz. that of failing to provide a person with opportunities for gain. Secondly, the causal or near-causal problems which arise in actions for breach of contract are often relatively simple in comparison with the difficulty of determining the scope of the duty to pay damages, so that attention has been concentrated on the latter, but often in a terminology (e.g. 'natural and probable consequence') which straddles both issues and so makes it difficult to see what type of limitation on liability is being discussed. Finally, liability in contract is more often based on the notion of risk than in tort: a defendant is then obliged to pay compensation for having, by a breach of contract, provided the occasion for harm, though he would not ordinarily be said to have caused it. The fact that liability to pay compensation for breach of contract is based on these disparate or only loosely connected types of relation between defendant's conduct and the harm suffered by plaintiff is a factor which has probably discouraged common law writers from generalizing about causal connection in this sphere.[1] It has not, however, had this effect on the Continent[2] and, even in England, it is worth noting that, though talk of 'remoteness of damage' tends to obscure the matter, a plaintiff claiming damages for breach of contract must prove two things. First, he must, unless the case is one in which defendant bears the whole risk of the loss in question, show that the loss was caused by defendant's breach of contract.[3]

[1] See, however, Corbin, *Contracts*, chap. 55, ss. 997 ff., who propounds a version of the foreseeability theory.

[2] Note the awkward attempt by Enneccerus-Lehmann, ii. 65, to fit contractual applications of the notion of risk into the framework of 'adequate cause'.

[3] *Monarch Steamship Co.* v. *Karlshamns Oljefabriker* [1949] AC 196, 225 (remoteness 'in the sense of causal connection'); *Quinn* v. *Burch Bros.* [1966] 2 QB 370; *Sykes* v. *Midland Bank* [1971] 1 QB 113; Chitty on *Contracts* (24th edn.), nos. 1564-9.

Secondly, he must show that the loss is within the scope of the
relevant rules of legal policy, whether these are general rules regarding foreseeable types of harm or the special rule of the law of
contract that recoverable loss must have been within the contemplation of the parties at the time of contracting.
We discuss these points in turn.

I. ECONOMIC LOSS

The typical causal problem in tort concerns a train of events
culminating in what is termed physical harm, e.g. the destruction or
impairment of physical things, or the death, suffering, or impairment
of the health of persons. By contrast, the typical investigation involving causal language in contract concerns the extent of economic
loss which a breach of contract may be said to have 'caused'. This
may not involve physical harm. The loss, as when defendant fails to
deliver a chattel intended for resale, may arise essentially from a
failure to provide a stipulated opportunity for gain. We may speak
of the act or omission which, in the setting of normal social and
economic institutions, constitutes a denial or frustration of economic
opportunities as 'economic harm'. The absence of the gain which
would have been realized had the stipulated opportunity been provided may be termed 'economic loss'.

Though the typical problem of 'remoteness' in contract concerns
the estimation of economic loss arising from a frustrated opportunity
for gain rather than the connection between a wrongful act and
subsequent physical[4] harm both types of problem in fact occur in
both branches of the law. This is so because in tort actions the
estimation of the consequences of physical harm in terms of money
may involve considerations similar to those which arise in actions
for breach of contract. Thus, in *The Liesbosch*,[5] the House of Lords
decided that the owners of a dredger wrongfully sunk by defendant's
act were entitled not merely to the market value of the lost ship but
to the expenses which they had (notionally) incurred in purchasing
a substitute and to compensation for the fact that a contract on
which the ship was employed was thereby rendered less profitable.
Conversely, negligence causing physical harm to someone is often
concurrently a breach of contract with that person, as in the case of
an employee who sues his employer for physical injury caused by

[4] Or economic: see (ii) below.
[5] [1933] AC. On damages for deprivation of economic opportunities in tort see
Oakley v. *Lyster* [1931] 1 KB 148 (conversion); *Bodley* v. *Reynolds* [1846] 8 QB 779,
115 ER 1066; *Williams* v. *Peel River Land Co.* (1886) 55 LT 689; *Phillips* v. *L.S.W.R.
Co.* (1879) 5 CPD 280; *Strand Electric* v. *Brisford Entertainments* [1952] 2 QB 246;
Cervo v. *Swinburn* [1939] NZLR 430.

the employer's failure to provide safe equipment, which is often a breach of the contract of employment as well as a tort.

But though all forms of compensation involve, as it were, translating harm into money, contract is the sphere where this is most prominent and where the harm is most often purely economic. There are three main types of case to be considered.

(i) In the simplest cases a physical thing is destroyed or damaged and the harm is converted into money by ascertaining its market value or the difference between the market value of the thing in its damaged and undamaged state. The same may apply when defendant fails to provide plaintiff with or deprives him of a physical thing.[6] We assume, without investigating the theory of value, that the ascertainment of the market value does not involve causal problems of difficulty: but it may be argued that in depriving plaintiff of a thing defendant has deprived him of an economic opportunity equivalent to the value of the thing, so that these cases are mostly a simple variety of those discussed in (iii) below.[7]

(ii) But the assessment is often not as simple as this even when the harm is the destruction of a physical thing, such as a ship. The law allows, within certain limits, recovery of pecuniary loss in the form of extra expense caused to plaintiff by the occurrence of the wrong,[8] where 'caused' imports the principles set out in Chapter VI.

When a seller, in breach of contract, delivers defective goods, a buyer may recover, in certain cases, pecuniary loss which he is obliged to incur in the situation thus created: e.g. damages payable on a subcontract,[9] or costs incurred in the unsuccessful defence of an action on a subcontract,[10] or in compensating those deceived by the breach or advertising a change of supplier in order to protect his business reputation.[11] Similar considerations apply when physical injury is caused to a human being: the law does not primarily seek to value a lost limb (though it does so in so far as the giving of damages for pain, suffering, and disability is regarded as an oblique way of assessing its value) but allows recovery of such items as medical expenses which plaintiff is 'forced' to incur because it is not

6 When there is no market the third method of assessment (below) is employed. *France* v. *Gaudet* (1870) LR 6 QB 199; *The Arpad* [1934] P. 189.
7 On the distinction between value and loss of profits see *Wilson* v. *Lancashire and Yorkshire R. Co.* (1861) 9 CB (NS) 632, 142 ER 248.
8 *Liesbosch Dredger* v. *Edison* [1933] AC 449. Cf. *Erie Gas Co.* v. *Carroll* [1911] AC 105; *British Westinghouse Electric Co.* v. *Underground Electric R. Co.* [1912] AC 673; *Schlesinger* v. *Mostyn* [1932] 1 KB 349; *Hamlin* v. *G.N.R. Co.* (1856) 1 H. & N. 408, 156 ER 1261; *Hinde* v. *Liddell* (1875) LR 10 QB 265.
9 *Grébert-Borgnis* v. *Nugent* (1885) 15 QBD 85.
10 *Hammond* v. *Bussey* (1887) 20 QBD 79; 57 LJKB 58. Cf. *Smith* v. *Compton* (1832) 3 B. & Ad. 407, 110 ER 146.
11 *Banco de Portugal* v. *Waterlow* [1932] AC 452; *Holden* v. *Bostock* (1902) 18 TLR 317.

reasonable[12] to expect him to leave his injuries untended. These various types of expense have been neatly labelled by the civilian writers *damnum emergens* (incidental expense).

It is true that causal criteria similar to those set out in Chapter VI are here applied. If a shipowner obtains an unnecessarily expensive replacement for the ship destroyed by defendant's wrong, or the victim of an accident caused by defendant's wrong incurs unnecessary medical expenses, or the buyer of goods of defective quality unnecessarily pays damages to the subpurchaser[13] his act may be regarded as voluntary and so as negativing causal connection between defendant's wrong and the economic loss.

The principles applied here are the same as those applied in the cases discussed in Chapter VI where a plaintiff, threatened by some danger created by defendant, is injured in defending himself or his property from it. The crucial question is whether the step taken was 'reasonable' in the emergency and so should be treated as not wholly voluntary.

(iii) A third type of case corresponds to the Continental *lucrum cessans* (loss of profit). Very often, especially in contract, the debtor's obligation, as has been mentioned, is in substance to provide the creditor with an opportunity for gain.[14] When defendant negligently destroys or damages plaintiff's ship plaintiff can recover loss of freight on the charterparty on which the ship was engaged;[15] when a seller fails to deliver the goods sold the buyer can sometimes recover loss of profit on a resale of the goods.[16] Here it is usual to say that the loss of freight or loss of profit has been 'caused' by the tort or breach of contract. The lost opportunity is translated into money with the help of the notion of economic man, maximizing his gains and minimizing his losses. The norm taken in order to decide what loss defendant has 'caused' is a plaintiff making the best he can of his opportunities; hence a plaintiff may, in a proper case, recover not merely the market value of his lost opportunity, where there is a market, but the loss of a special, peculiar,[17] or even unique opportunity of which defendant has deprived him. It is normally irrelevant to inquire whether plaintiff would have made use of his opportunities.

12 Above, pp. 156–7.
13 *Le Blanche* v. *L.N.W.R.* (1876) 1 CPD 286 (taking a special train).
14 This need not be, strictly speaking, a profit. *The Mediana* [1900] AC 113.
15 *The Kate* [1899] P. 165; *The Philadelphia* [1917] P. 101; *The Fortunity* [1961] 1 WLR 351.
16 *Patrick* v. *Russo-British Grain Export Co.* [1927] 2 KB 535. Cf. *Fletcher* v. *Tayleur* (1855) 17 CB 21, 139 ER 973; *Leavey* v. *Hirst* [1944] KB 24; *Pell* v. *Shearman* (1855) 10 Ex. 766, 156 ER 650; *Lancs. & Yorks. R. Co.* v. *Gidlow* (1875) LR 7 HL 517.
17 *Simpson* v. *L.N.W.R.* (1876) 1 QBD 274.

The relation between the act of one who, without necessarily causing physical harm, fails to provide another with an opportunity for gain and the loss suffered by the other may be called 'causal connection' in a wide sense and the loss may be called an 'economic effect'; but the relation between wrongful act and the loss differs in some respects from that between physical harm and the act said to cause it and also from the relationship between incidental expense and the wrongful act in cases of type (ii) above.

The notion of causing economic loss by failing to provide a stipulated opportunity for gain is the contrary of the notion of *providing an opportunity*, which, as shown in Chapter VII, is often the ground of responsibility in tort, and of *assisting*, which is a ground of criminal liability. It has obvious affinities with the notion of one person preventing another doing a specific act which he would otherwise have done. But it has complexities not present in that simple case, because here, in order to estimate loss, we must speculate not about a single act but about the hypothetical gains which fulfilment of the obligation would have enabled plaintiff to realize in the setting of certain economic institutions whose continued operation is assumed.

Hence we do not inquire into actual events but ask how much less plaintiff's wealth is, in consequence of defendant's act, than it might have been had he exploited to the maximum advantage the opportunities which he was entitled to be given. On the other hand, the present relation resembles ordinary cases of causing physical harm or *damnum emergens* (incidental expense) in that, in order to ascertain what opportunities plaintiff has lost, it is necessary to discover how far plaintiff's present economic situation is attributable to defendant's wrongful act. For this purpose any expense voluntarily incurred by plaintiff, though by reason of defendant's act, will not count as its consequence, and any loss suffered in part through plaintiff's failure to mitigate damages will be irrecoverable by virtue of a rule analogous to that by which, at common law, plaintiff's contributory negligence barred an action in tort.[18]

II. LIMITATIONS ON LIABILITY IN CONTRACT

The liability of one who breaks a contract for harm which the innocent party would not have suffered but for the breach must clearly be subject to some limits. The need for limitation is especially clear in regard to compensation for loss of stipulated economic opportunities, since the provision of opportunities for gain may have a snowball effect: opportunities breed further opportunities. The

[18] *British Westinghouse* v. *Underground Electric Railways* [1912] AC 673; Chitty on *Contract* (24th edn.), nos. 1592–601.

delivery of machinery at the right time may not merely enable existing contracts to be performed but may lead to more numerous and
profitable contracts in the future and may have important long term
economic 'consequences', none of which would have ensued had the
machinery not been delivered at the right time. So failure to deliver
at the right time may sometimes plausibly be regarded as depriving
the innocent party of large gains spread over a long period.

The problem considered in this section concerns the character of
the limitations on the extent of a wrongdoer's responsibility for
breach of contract. Are the same limitations applicable to all forms
of harm for which a party to a contract may claim compensation,
or are different types of limitation appropriate to different types of
harm? Are the contractual limitations, or some of them, similar to
the causal and non-causal limitations of which courts make use in
tort? The second question may be left till later, but the first admits
of at least a provisional answer. When compensation is claimed for
physical harm or incidental expense[19] causal limitations of the type
considered in Chapter VI are in point and are in fact used by courts;
for here defendant's responsibility depends on an assessment of the
relation between an earlier contingency (the breach) and a later
contingency (the physical harm or incidental expense) in the light of
a third factor such as the intervention of another. When, however,
compensation is claimed for loss of profits or other economic advantages the court is not concerned to assess the relation between
an earlier act and a later event in the light of some third factor. To
show that defendant has deprived plaintiff of a certain opportunity
for gain it is necessary to show that, in the absence of defendant's
breach of contract, plaintiff would have been able to exploit the
opportunity (e.g. that plaintiff would not have been prevented by a
government embargo from exporting the goods which defendant
failed to deliver). But, if this 'but for' relationship is proved, there
is no further 'causal' question whether the loss of the economic
opportunity was attributable to some third factor rather than to
defendant's breach of contract. It is true that the fact that plaintiff
has alternative opportunities for gain (e.g. by sale on the home
market) may be taken into account in assessing the value of the
opportunity he has lost. But, even so, it remains true that the non-
delivery of the goods is properly described as the cause of the lost
export opportunity.

Hence, so far as causal considerations are concerned, there is
a good prima-facie case for treating separately limitations on
responsibility in contract when the claim is for physical harm or

---

[19] Viz. *damnum emergens*: economic loss of type (ii), pp. 310–11 above.

incidental expense and when it is for loss of profit or other opportunities for gain. This is the course we follow.

(i) *Physical harm and incidental expense.* When a party to a contract claims damages against the other party for physical harm, the courts, as in tort, impose limits of two different sorts: the harm must, unless defendant has taken on himself the risk of it, be caused by his breach of contract, and it must be, as in tort, of a foreseeable type, i.e. not brought about by a radically different causal process from that which was foreseeable at the time of the breach of contract.[20] There is, in addition, in contract the further policy limitation that the loss for which recovery is sought must have been within the contemplation of the parties at the time of contracting. Finally, the parties may by stipulation limit or extend defendant's liability. These last two factors do not, of course, come into play unless there is a contractual relationship between the parties, and it is this that can make the fixing of the limits of recovery in an action for breach of contract more complicated than it is in tort and, if the various heads of limitation are not carefully kept apart, can lead to confusion.

The causal limitations are those with which we are familiar in tort. They apply equally to actions for breach of contract. Thus, when defendant in breach of contract failed to tuck in the flap of the hall carpet when removing another carpet for cleaning, plaintiff who tripped and was injured on the flap recovered for his injuries in an action for breach of contract,[21] but it seems hardly credible that he would have recovered had some member of his family deliberately pushed him on to the dangerous spot intending to injure him.

Again, in *Parsons* v. *Uttley Ingham*[22] defendants installed a hopper for storing pig food. They failed in breach of contract to provide proper ventilation, with the result that the food stored became mouldy and plaintiff's pigs contracted a rare disease and died. Defendants were held responsible for their death, which was caused by their breach of contract; and, though the particular disease was unexpected, some harm to the pigs could have been foreseen, so that the 'type' of harm was not unforeseeable. On such facts there is no relevant difference between the limits of recovery in contract and tort; but, of course, if defendants had been asked to install a hopper with proper ventilation so that it could be exhibited in an agricultural museum, and plaintiffs had instead used it for their pigs, this use would not have been within the contemplation of the parties at the time of contracting. Consequently the loss of the pigs would not have been recoverable in an action for breach of contract even if,

20 *Vacwell Engineering* v. *B.D.H. Chemicals* [1971] 1 QB 88.
21 *Kimber* v. *Willett* [1947] 1 All ER 361; cf. *McMahon* v. *Field* (1881) 7 QBD 591.
22 [1978] QB 791 (CA).

when they actually installed the hopper with the defective ventilator, defendants had then been informed of the intended use, so that they could at the time of the breach foresee some harm to the pigs. This hypothetical example brings out the importance of distinguishing causal issues in such cases on the one hand, and the two types of policy limitation ('foreseeability' of the type of harm at the time of breach, 'contemplation' of the loss at the time of contracting) on the other.

Problems about physical sequences of events, such as happened in the cases cited, are satisfactorily dealt with by reference to the principles applicable in tort; they are not elucidated by an appeal to the 'contemplation' of the parties of the 'usual course of events', though this is sometimes said to be the test. As Baron Martin pointed out, in a case in which a series of physical events was in question,[23] very often there is no 'usual course of things' in the event of a breach, and no contemplation of the breach which actually occurs.

In the case Martin B. was considering, a ship was wrongfully left outside a dock, where it was damaged in a storm. The problem was whether the damage was the consequence of the breach of contract or of plaintiff's voluntary act in not removing the ship to a place of greater safety. In cases of this sort, when defendant is under a contractual duty to look after a physical thing, he will be liable *if by his breach of contract he causes harm to the thing.* Such harm is *ex hypothesi* in the contemplation of the parties at the time of contracting, since the contract is a contract to look after the thing. In *Wilson* v. *Newport Dock Co.*[24] plaintiff failed precisely because the breach of contract was not shown to have caused the storm damage.

Causal issues of the sort discussed in Chapter VI can arise as regards both physical harm and incidental expense. Thus, it may be a question whether an event later than defendant's breach of contract which contributes to cause such expense is coincidental in character or not. In *Monarch Steamship Co.* v. *Karlshamns Oljefabriker*[25] defendants broke their contract to provide a seaworthy ship to carry the cargo endorsed to plaintiffs, so that instead of arriving in Sweden in July 1939 it came three months late and was diverted by the British Admiralty owing to the war, thereby causing extra expense to plaintiffs. It was held that this expense was recoverable from defendants. The outbreak of war was not a very unlikely event at that period, and did not negative causal connection between the breach of the contract and the added expense. Again, expense, occasioned by the breach of contract, which plaintiff incurs voluntarily

23 *Wilson* v. *Newport Dock Co.* (1866) LR 1 Ex. 177.
24 (1866) LR 1 Ex. 177.
25 [1949] AC 196. 'Remoteness of damage' of this sort is 'in truth a question of fact'. Ibid., p. 223.

or unreasonably will not be regarded as caused by the breach.[26] In contract, as in tort, coexisting circumstances do not negative causal connection. Thus, when defendants in breach of contract failed to unload plaintiff's ship and the ship unexpectedly settled on a hidden anchor during the period of delay, recovery for the consequent physical damage was allowed, though the presence of the anchor was probably unforeseeable.[27]

Apart from the limitations listed, the parties may by stipulation impose their own limitations. They may exceptionally agree that no damage shall be recoverable above a certain maximum, even if the breach causes a greater amount of harm. The general rule as to the extent of recoverable physical harm may also be varied, if the parties agree, by placing the risk of harm of a certain sort on one of them[28] so that, if it occurs, he shall be responsible even if he did not cause it.

(ii) *Failure to provide opportunities for gain.* For loss of this sort, any rational legal system, having regard to the fact that contractual obligations are voluntarily assumed, will in general limit recovery to what the parties contemplated at the time of contracting as likely, or at least not unlikely,[29] to occur in the event of a breach. There is controversy about how exactly to express the degree of likelihood required, but at least it is clear that, while something less than an even chance may be sufficient,[30] the 'remote possibility'[31] which, according to *The Wagon Mound (No. 2)*, will in an appropriate case justify a finding that harm was 'reasonably foreseeable' in tort law will not be enough. Any more extensive recovery for breach of contract would work hardship. If loss likely to occur at the time of breach but not at that of contracting was taken into account, defendant would be forced to pay compensation for items the possibility of which might have led him, had he known of them, not to conclude the contract or to limit his liability under it. Hence the gain for the loss of which the plaintiff can recover in an action for breach of contract must be not merely foreseeable but, in Lord Reid's phrase, 'easily foreseeable'.[32] Again, if the degree of likelihood of harm, often very slight,[33] which is enough to make physical harm

26 *Le Blanche* v. *L.N.W.R.* (1876) 1 CPD 286.
27 *Great Lakes S.S. Co.* v. *Maple Leaf Milling Co.* (1924) 41 TLR 21 (PC).
28 Below, p. 321.
29 *Koufos* v. *Czarnikow (The Heron II)* [1969] 1 AC 350, 383 (Lord Reid), 406 (Lord Morris).
30 *Koufos* v. *Czarnikow* [1969] 1 AC 350, 383.
31 *The Wagon Mound (No. 2)* [1967] 1 AC 617.
32 *Koufos* v. *Czarnikow* [1969] 1 AC 350, 383, 389.
33 Thus, in *The Wagon Mound (No. 2)* [1967] 1 AC 617, where ignition of the furnace oil was found to be only a 'remote possibility', the Privy Council held that it could nevertheless be regarded as a reasonably foreseeable consequence of defendants' conduct, so that when they negligently spilled the oil in the harbour they were liable for the resulting fire when it unexpectedly ignited.

foreseeable in the practical or theoretical senses discussed in Chapter IX, were also enough to render a contract-breaker liable to pay for loss of profit, a seller of goods who failed to deliver would seldom escape liability for the buyer's loss of profit on a resale, since a resale would hardly be very unlikely. This, of course, is not the law. The Sale of Goods Act, which is declaratory of the common law in this respect, expressly confines the damage 'directly and naturally resulting in the ordinary course of events'[34] from non-delivery, when there is an available market, to the difference between the market and contract prices. The award of damages for loss of profit on a resale is exceptional. Similar rules are applied as regards non-delivery or delayed delivery of goods carried by land or sea.[35]

In English law the rule or rules in *Hadley* v. *Baxendale*,[36] as interpreted in later cases, express the limits placed on recovery for loss of stipulated economic opportunities. The main rule states that

where two parties have made a contract which one of them has broken, the damages which the other party ought to receive in respect of such breach of contract should be such as may fairly and reasonably be considered either arising naturally, i.e. according to the usual course of things, from such breach of contract itself, or such as may reasonably be supposed to have been in the contemplation of both parties, at the time they made the contract, as the probable result of the breach of it.[37]

The main rule is regarded as having two branches, the first allowing recovery of what arises 'naturally' from the breach, the second of what the parties 'contemplated' as likely to arise from it. As interpreted in later cases, especially *Victoria Laundry* v. *Newman Industries*[38] and *Koufos* v. *Czarnikow (The Heron II)*,[39] it is clear that both branches of the rule depend on what the parties knew or should have known at the time of contracting, the second on what they actually knew, the first on what reasonable persons in their position would have contemplated as not unlikely to occur in the event of a breach.[40] 'In cases of breach of contract', says Asquith LJ, 'the aggrieved party is only entitled to recover such part of the loss actually resulting as was *at the time of the contract*[41] reasonably

34 Sale of Goods Act, 1979, s. 51(2).
35 *Rodocanachi* v. *Milburn* (1886) 18 QBD 67; *Koufos* v. *Czarnikow* [1969] 1 AC 350.
36 (1854) 9 Ex. 341, 354, 156 ER 145, 151.
37 Ibid.
38 [1949] 2 KB 528.
39 [1969] 1 AC 350.
40 The account given is oversimplified, as there is disagreement on how many rules or branches the above extract contains and what their respective scope is. This does not, however, affect our argument.
41 Cf. French Code civil, art. 1150: 'qu'on a pu prévoir lors du contrat'. *Emslie* v. *African Merchants*, 1908 EDL 82; *Pacific Overseas Corp.* v. *Watkins Browne* [1954] NZLR 459; *Rivers* v. *White* [1919] 2 WWR 189.

foreseeable as liable to result from the breach. What was at that time reasonably foreseeable depends on the knowledge then possessed by the parties or, at all events, by the party who later commits the breach.'[42] To be foreseeable the loss (or 'some factor without which it could not have occurred') must be a 'serious possibility'[43] or 'real danger';[44] it need not be the case that the breach must *necessarily* result in the loss in question.

The statement by Asquith LJ needs elucidation. It is desirable, in order to determine the degree of foreseeability required by the rules, to consider separately (i) the use which plaintiff would have made of the opportunity which defendant failed to provide; (ii) the amount of the profit which plaintiff would have made; (iii) the circumstances which in conjunction with the breach prevented plaintiff making a profit; (iv) the occurrence of events subsequent to the breach which in fact affected plaintiff's economic opportunities.

(i) In the absence of notice of a special use, damages for loss of profits are assessed on the basis of the *ordinary* use of the subject-matter in the majority of cases. Thus the hull of a boom derrick is ordinarily used as a coal store and a defendant who fails in breach of contract to deliver one on time will be liable for loss of profits on the basis of that use even if the use actually intended was quite different.[45] Similarly, in the absence of notice of a resale, the seller of goods is liable to the buyer for loss of profit on resale only when there is known to the parties to be at least an even chance of it:[46] 'to make a thing probable, it is enough, in my view, that there is an even chance of its happening'.[47] Here the 'contemplated' or 'foreseeable' use means the *probable* use, that which is as likely as not.

(ii) In contrast with recovery for physical harm, where the details of the harm need not, even according to adherents of the foreseeability theory, themselves be foreseeable, the amount of profit recoverable is, in the absence of actual notice of a specially profitable subcontract, restricted to the *ordinary* profit, viz. that which would be made in the majority of cases.[48] Here again the 'contemplated' or 'foreseeable' profit means the usual profit.

(iii) The breach is often not enough by itself to prevent plaintiff realizing a profit: the conjunction with it of other circumstances such

---

[42] [1949] 2 KB 528, 540.
[43] *Monarch S.S. Co.* v. *A/B Karlshamns Oljefabriker* [1949] AC 196, 233.
[44] Ibid.
[45] *Cory* v. *Thames Ironworks Co.* (1868) LR 3 QB 181.
[46] *Hall* v. *Pim* (1928) 139 LT 50; *Patrick* v. *Russo-British Grain Export Co.* [1927] 2 KB 535, 540.
[47] *Hall* v. *Pim* (1928) 139 LT 50, 53 *per* Lord Dunedin, who rejected the view that a still higher probability was required. Lord Shaw would have awarded damages even if there was a lower probability of resale: 139 LT 55.
[48] *Horne* v. *Midland R. Co.* (1873) LR 8 CP 131; *Victoria Laundry* v. *Newman* [1949] 2 KB 528.

as the absence of alternative tools, machinery, or sources of supply is needed. In *Hadley* v. *Baxendale* itself the 'foreseeability' of such circumstances was in issue. In that case defendants had agreed by contract to deliver a broken mill shaft to repairers but had in breach of contract unduly delayed in doing so, so that the mill was out of action for a longer period than it would otherwise have been. It was held that they were not liable for the loss of profits so incurred by the mill owners. This was placed upon the basis that they had no knowledge at the time of contracting that the stoppage would occur if they delayed the return of the shaft. Thus, Alderson B. said that defendants had no knowledge beyond the fact that the article to be carried was the broken shaft of a mill and that plaintiffs were the millers of that mill; they did not know that unreasonable delay on their part *would result*[49] in the loss since the millers *might have had*[50] another shaft or their machinery *might*[51] have been out of order for some other reason. Hence the loss of profits could not reasonably be considered to have been within the contemplation of both parties when they made the contract. It would not follow naturally from the breach of contract 'in the great multitude of cases of this sort'.[52]

It seems clear from these statements by the court that it did not consider that the stoppage of the mill was a *very unlikely* event but rather that though the delay did indeed deprive plaintiffs of an opportunity to earn profits, the loss of profits was not *so likely* that defendants could fairly be considered to have taken it into account in making the contract.[53] The wording of the judgment suggests that the likelihood of such circumstances coexisting with the breach must be considerable if plaintiffs are to recover for loss of profits: Lord Reid speaks of a 'very substantial degree of probability'.[54]

(iv) Sometimes a breach will only deprive a plaintiff of an opportunity for gain in conjunction with a later event. In *Otter* v. *Church*[55] solicitors mistakenly advised deceased in 1944 that he was absolutely entitled to property of which in fact he was tenant-in-tail. In 1945 deceased was killed in action without disentailing the property. It was held that the solicitors were liable to deceased (and so to his estate) for depriving him of the opportunity of increasing his

[49] Our italics.
[50] Our italics.
[51] Our italics.
[52] *Hadley* v. *Baxendale* (1854) 9 Ex. 341, 355-6.
[53] It is not necessary for plaintiff to show that defendant *undertook* to pay for the loss in question should it arise in consequence of his breach; there need not be a term of the contract to that effect: *Koufos* v. *Czarnikow* [1969] 1 AC 350, 421-2. Nevertheless, the basis of the rule is that in making a contract a reasonable person takes account of certain fairly likely risks and not of other more remote ones.
[54] *Koufos* v. *Czarnikow* [1969] 1 AC 350, 388.
[55] [1953] 1 All ER 168.

estate. Here it was probable, though not certain, that deceased would
have executed a disentailing deed had he known the truth: for him
to have done so would be 'foreseeable' as explained in (i) above.
The chance that deceased would be killed on active service was
'foreseeable' in another sense, viz. 'more than a remote possibility',
and this further contingency was necessary in order finally to deprive
him of the choice legally open to him. It is only in the context
of this fourth type of problem that 'foreseeability', in the sense of
the theoretical foreseeability relevant to determining whether an
intervening event is a coincidence, enters into the assessment of
damages for loss of profit. It is only in relation to this fourth type
of problem that foreseeability of the contingency might plausibly
be assessed on the information available at the time of breach.

The rules in *Hadley* v. *Baxendale* are rules of legal policy intended
to promote a fair balance between the contracting parties. They try
to ensure that a contracting party is not held liable for items of loss
of a sort that would not enter into his calculations when deciding
whether to make the contract or on what terms to make it. They are
of special importance in setting limits to the items of prospective
gain for the loss of which recovery can be had in an action for breach
of contract. Some confusion has arisen and still arises when they are
treated as if they also provided a solution to the causal problems
which must be dealt with when damages are claimed for physical
harm and incidental expense, or as if they could be equated with
the rule (expressed in *The Wagon Mound No. 1*) which protects a
wrongdoer from being made liable for freakish causal processes of
a type which, at the time of his wrongful act, he had no reason to
envisage.

Thus, some writers and judges have come to see an analogy between the rules limiting recovery for physical harm in tort and the
rules in *Hadley* v. *Baxendale*.[56] In truth the two are not comparable.
As we have seen above, the substantial degree of probability involved
in the application of *Hadley* v. *Baxendale* to cases of loss of profit is
different from and greater than that involved in determining whether
intervening events are so abnormal or coincidental as to negative
causal connection between an earlier act and later physical harm or
incidental expense. There is also some absurdity in the notion that
questions as diverse as these should be regulated by the same principle. Where compensation is sought from a defendant who has
failed to provide a stipulated opportunity for gain, liability must
necessarily be assessed by reference to hypothetical gains, and it is

56 Salmond, *Torts*, p. 516; Greer LJ in *Haynes* v. *Harwood* [1935] 1 KB 146, 156;
The Arpad [1934] P. 189, 216; *The Edison* [1932] P. 52, 70–1.

reasonable to limit these to gains which would be made in circumstances likely to occur or contemplated by the parties. Where, however, physical harm, etc., which would not have occurred without defendant's earlier wrongful act has actually occurred, the question whether liability should extend to it is more reasonably determined by considering not hypothetical events but the character of the intervening events and circumstances.

Yet it cannot be said that the distinction we have urged between these two types of problem is recognized in the cases; judges often pay lip-service at least to the idea that the rules in *Hadley* v. *Baxendale* provide a solution for all problems of the assessment of damages in contract. Lord Denning, on the other hand, has endorsed the distinction we make between physical harm and loss of economic opportunities and has justly observed that the attempt to treat them under a single umbrella is apt to issue in a 'sea of semantic exercises'.[57]

III. RISK IN CONTRACT

There are situations in contract in which a defendant, as we saw in Chapter VII, is liable for negligently providing the opportunity for another person or thing to cause harm to plaintiff.[58] But one who breaks a contractual obligation is often liable for thereby occasioning harm even if he has not been negligent in failing to guard against the type of human or natural intervention which occurs: this is sometimes true of a tortfeasor also.[59] In such cases it is said that the 'risk' of loss of a certain kind 'falls' on the party in breach, a phrase which normally means that that party is liable for loss of a certain kind, irrespective of the manner of its occurrence, if it would not have occurred but for the breach. Thus a seller of specific goods who fails to deliver on the date agreed must bear the risk of their destruction unless such destruction would[60] also have occurred had they been delivered on the due date. In effect this makes a defendant liable, in the terminology of our earlier chapters, for 'occasioning' as opposed to 'causing' harm in the strict sense. Often courts, by using the language of risk rather than that of causation, have implicitly marked this distinction. Thus, in *Lilley* v. *Doubleday*[61]

---

[57] *Parsons* v. *Ingham* [1978] QB 791, 802 (CA).
[58] *De la Bere* v. *Pearson* [1908] 1 KB 280; *Stansbie* v. *Troman* [1948] 2 KB 48.
[59] e.g. in detinue. *Ballett* v. *Mingay* [1943] KB 281.
[60] The Sale of Goods Act, 1979, s. 20(2), says that 'where delivery has been delayed through the fault of either buyer or seller the goods are at the risk of the party in fault as regards any loss which *might* not have occurred but for such loss'. The word 'might' is mysterious.
[61] (1881) 7 QBD 510, 511, Cf. *D.* 14. 2. 10. 1; 7. 1. 36. 2; *BGB*, s. 848.

Grove J. says, 'If a bailee elects to deal with the property entrusted
to him in a way not authorised by the bailor, he takes upon himself
the risks of so doing, except where the risk is independent of his acts
and inherent in the property iself.' This seems to be a way of saying
that if the goods perish and they would not have done so but for the
bailee's act, the bailee must pay their value: nothing is said about
the need for the wrongful dealing to be the cause of the loss.

Sometimes, however, courts use causal language in dealing with
problems of this sort and this has been a potent source both of
confusion and of scepticism about the objectivity of causal judgments; for sometimes the use of such language means that the court
is basing liability on causal connection (in the ordinary sense) whilst
at others the court is merely stating, in an obscure way, the principle
that defendant 'bears the risk'.

The former type of use of causal language is illustrated by the
Federal rule in the United States as to a common carrier's liability
for loss of goods. This lays down that the carrier is liable for loss
which would not have occurred but for his breach of contract in
delaying the goods, unless the loss occurs by an 'unforeseeable'
intervening event;[62] or unless it is due immediately to some cause
such as accidental fire involving no negligence on the part of the
carrier and within a valid exception in the bill of lading, but the
goods have been brought within the peril stipulated against (i.e. to
the place where they were destroyed at the time in question) by
negligent delay in transportation.[63]

In other jurisdictions liability is really based on the principle that
defendant bears the risk but the courts use causal terminology. For
instance, in *Bibb Broom Corn Co.* v. *Atchison, Topeka & Santa Fe
R. Co.*[64] defendants negligently failed to send forward plaintiff's corn
from Kansas City or to notify the railway company which ought to
have transported it. During the delay the corn remained in certain
rail yards where it was destroyed in a great flood. In holding that
defendants were liable despite the intervention of an act of God the
court concluded that 'defendants' neglect concurred and mingled
with the act of God'.[65] Hence, although defendants could not reasonably have anticipated or foreseen the flood, they should be held
responsible for it and 'should not be relieved by an application of
the abstract principles of the law of proximate cause'.[66] A similar

62 *Toledo & Ohio Central R. Co.* v. *Kibler Co.* (1918) 97 Ohio St. 262, 119 NE 733;
Memphis & C.R. Co. v. *Reeves* (1870) 77 US 176. In New York, *Michaels* v. *New
York Central R. Co.* (1864) 30 NY 564, 86 Am. Dec. 415 disallows the exception of
act of God.
63 The Massachusetts and Pennsylvania doctrine.
64 (1905) 94 Minn. 269, 102 NW 709.
65 (1905) 102 NW 709, 711.
66 This shows a partial recognition that the court was departing from ordinary
causal principles.

sentiment was expressed in the old case of *Davis* v. *Garrett*[67] in which
the court held defendants responsible for the loss of plaintiff's lime.
Defendants had contracted to carry the lime by barge to London
but made an unnecessary deviation during the course of which a
storm wetted the lime and, the barge catching fire, the lime was
totally destroyed. Despite the fact that loss from act of God was
specifically excepted in the contract of carriage the court held that
defendants must pay for the lime since 'no wrongdoer can be allowed
to apportion or qualify his own wrong'.[68] The tendency of this
reasoning is to assimilate cases in which an act of God or coincidence
intervenes to ordinary cases of concurrent causes.

However, there is a distinction between the two classes of case.
This is most clearly shown when there is an intervening event of an
extraordinary character or one which would in conjunction with
the defendant's wrongful act on ordinary principles amount to a
coincidence. The intervention of such an event prevents, on ordinary
causal principles, the original act from being treated as a concurrent
cause of the ultimate harm, while in cases in which there is an
intervening event of an abnormal sort but nevertheless not so extraordinary as to amount to an act of God or a coincidence, both the
wrongful act and the subsequent abnormal event may be treated as
concurrent causes of the ultimate harm. The reasoning in the cases
we have considered, however, obliterates this distinction. It is true
that no machinery exists in Anglo-American law for the apportionment of loss between a wrongful act of the defendant and a subsequent natural event. Even, however, in a system of law which does
make provision for such apportionment, as did French law in certain
circumstances,[69] the distinction between these two classes of case is
of importance.

Yet other courts, while not using causal language, fail to state
clearly the principle of risk upon which the decision is really based.
In the *Green-Wheeler*[70] case defendant was guilty of negligent delay
in forwarding plaintiff's goods and during the delay the goods were
destroyed by a flood which was so extraordinary as to constitute an
act of God: they would not have been so destroyed but for the
negligent delay. The court decided that defendant should be held
liable despite the intervention of an act of God because the negligent
delay increased the chance of the occurrence of a contingency such
as an unprecedented flood.

[67] (1830) 6 Bing. 716, 130 ER 1456.
[68] *Davis* v. *Garrett* (1830) 6 Bing. 716, 724, *per* Tindal CJ.
[69] *The Lamoricière*, Cass. 19. 6. 1951; *Dalloz A.* 1951, 717 (cyclone four-fifths
responsible for damage to ship). The decision is now discredited.
[70] *Green-Wheeler Shoe Co.* v. *Chicago, Rock Island & Pacific R. Co.* (1906) 130
Iowa 123, 106 NW 498. The court stressed that the action was for tort, not breach of
contract, but this is in fact irrelevant: see above, p. 315.

324 THE COMMON LAW

This reason is, however, not convincing. It is true that the chance of the goods being destroyed at a given place by an extraordinary flood is greater if the goods remain there for a longer period than is provided by the contract. But it is incorrect to say that the mere delay increases the chances of the goods being destroyed by such an extraordinary event unless the chance of an extraordinary event occurring at the place at which the goods are wrongfully detained is greater than it would be at the place to which they should have been dispatched. This, however, was not taken into account by the court which said, 'It is not sufficient for the carrier to say by way of excuse that, while a proper and diligent transportation of the goods would have kept them free from the peril by which they were in fact lost, it might have subjected them to some other peril just as great. He cannot speculate on mere possibilities.'[71] Clearly, it is impossible to conclude that defendant's act increased the risk of an extraordinary flood destroying the goods unless the court speculates on what the chances would have been had the goods been dispatched as they should have been. It seems that the court must have been thinking of the principles, set out in Chapter VI, by which a wrongdoer is relieved of liability by the subsequent intervention of an event of a coincidental sort or one the chance of which occurring was not increased by the wrongful act. But on the principle that the party in default bears the risk this reasoning is unnecessary: if defendant has provided the opportunity for the harm and the harm would not have occurred but for his act it is immaterial whether the chance of its occurrence was greater, equal, or less given the wrongful act.

The types of case we have considered present a choice between two principles, liability for causing harm[72] and liability for occasioning harm. Of these the latter is, in this context, preferable, because its application avoids a sometimes difficult inquiry into the coincidental or abnormal character of a subsequent event such as a flood or fire and because the carrier can easily insure the goods against loss. Unfortunately the respective merits of the principles have been canvassed as if the issue turned on the interpretation of phrases such as 'proximate cause', and the fact that different jurisdictions have reached different solutions has been hailed as if it showed that causal expressions have no definite meaning.

---

71 (1906) 106 NW 498, 500.
72 There are, of course, intermediate solutions by which defendant is relieved of liability by some intervening causes (e.g. act of God) and not others (coincidence).

XII

CRIMINAL LAW: CAUSING HARM

IN this and the next two chapters we deal with causation in criminal law and follow a course similar to that chosen for the law of tort. The present chapter deals with causing physical and economic harm; the next with interpersonal transactions such as causing, inducing, helping, or permitting others to do harm; the final chapter with possible substitutes for causation as a ground for responsibility which have appeared to some writers better adapted to the 'policy' or special purposes of criminal law.

It will be seen that, as in tort, so in criminal law courts have often limited responsibility by appealing to the causal distinctions embedded in ordinary thought, with their emphasis on voluntary interventions and abnormal or coincidental events as factors negativing responsibility. Indeed, the general course of decision in the two spheres is strikingly similar. Of course, one must bear in mind that in criminal law, as in tort, there are situations in which a defendant or accused person is liable not for harm caused by his own conduct but for the conduct of another. In criminal law these include the liability of those who aid or counsel a crime, of co-conspirators, and of those who execute a common criminal purpose. Apart from these instances, there are a few cases, as we shall see, in which ordinary causal limitations are disregarded and an accused person is made to bear the risk of harm which he occasions by his unlawful act. But, perhaps because the common law has never developed the notion of criminal negligence to the extent that continental codes have done, the risk theory, by which an actor is held responsible for occasioning harm by giving others the opportunity to do mischief, has not become as prominent in crime as in tort.[1] Thus, a leading writer on criminal law says[2] 'At the present time foreseeability is recognized as having no application to the issue of

---

[1] Instances of this sort of liability are not, however, unknown. Thus there may be manslaughter by negligence: *Palmer* v. *State* (1960) 164 Atl. 2d 467 (mother who could have removed 20-month baby from danger liable for not doing so with result that her lover beat and killed the child); *Story* v. *United States* (1926) 16 F. 2d 342 (permitting drunk to take wheel and drive so that deceased was killed). When suicide is a crime it may be homicide to furnish a person with the means to kill himself: *People* v. *Roberts* (1920) 211 Mich. 187, 178 NW 690; but when suicide is not a crime it is also not a crime to furnish the means of committing suicide, barring resort to violence or deception, unless aiding or soliciting suicide is itself made a crime: *Sanders* v. *State* (1908) 54 Tex. Cr. R. 101, 112 SW 68.

[2] Perkins, *Criminal Law*, p. 726.

proximate cause in criminal cases except those in which the harm results from intervening causes.'

We proceed now to deal with the causing of physical and economic harm and follow the method of exposition adopted in Chapter VI.

I. VOLUNTARY CONDUCT

The free, deliberate, and informed intervention of a second person, who intends to exploit the situation created by the first, but is not acting in concert with him,[3] is normally held to relieve the first actor of criminal responsibility. One must distinguish, however, the situation where the first actor's conduct was sufficient in the existing circumstances to bring about the harm (e.g. a mortal wound in the sense defined in Chapter VIII)[4] from that where it was not sufficient without the intervention of the second actor. We deal with the latter situation first.

Here most decisions relieve the first actor of responsibility. In *Smith* v. *State*[5] accused wrongfully wounded the victim; the doctor, in probing the wound, intentionally killed him. It was held that this intervention relieved defendant of responsibility for homicide. In *People* v. *Elder*[6] accused knocked the victim down. A bystander then independently kicked the victim so that he died. Accused was properly found not guilty of homicide in view of the bystander's intervention.

In *Hendrickson* v. *Commonwealth*[7] a husband had a violent argument with his wife, who ran out of the house; he then shut the door. She remained out in 18 inches of snow and was found dead the next day. The husband was convicted of manslaughter but a new trial was ordered on appeal, partly because there was no evidence that the husband prevented the wife's re-entering the house.[8] The significance of this evidence could only have been to show that her remaining outside for the night was her own voluntary act. In *State* v. *Preslar*[9] after a husband had beaten his wife she started, with her

3 In the first edition we added 'and intending to bring about the harm which in fact occurs or recklessly courting it'. For the reasons given above (pp. 136-7) this definition of voluntary conduct is too narrow. What is required is that the agent should reach a decision and act on it in circumstances in which his decision can be regarded as exploiting the situation created by defendant, even if his execution of the decision is defective in some way, for example owing to want of skill.
4 Above, p. 241.
5 (1888) 50 Ark. 545, 8 SW 941.   6 (1894) 100 Mich. 515, 59 NW 237.
7 (1887) 85 Ky. 281, 7 Am. St. R. 596. See also *R.* v. *Storey* [1931] NZLR 417.
8 Ibid., p. 599.
9 (1885) 48 NC 417; *Wilson* v. *State* (1893) 24 SW 409; *Scott* v. *State* (1917) 13 Okla. Cr. App. 225, 163 P. 553; *Blackburn* v. *State* (1872) 23 Ohio 146 (suicide). Cf. *R.* v. *Fretwell* (1862) L. & C. 161, 169 ER 1345; *People* v. *Fowler* (1918) 174 P. 892, 896 (Cal.); *R.* v. *Hilton* (1838) 2 Lew. 214, 168 ER 1132, where it is not clear whether the intervention was intended to do harm. In the *Wilson* and *Scott* cases it is stated or implied that the first actor would be guilty of homicide if his act 'materially contributed' to the death.

son, to walk to her father's house two miles off but when within 200 yards of the house lay down in the woods, saying that she did not wish to continue until the morning. She died of exposure but the husband was acquitted of homicide, since the wife had exposed herself in the woods without necessity and there were circumstances showing deliberation in her leaving home. The relevance of this could only have been to show that her acts of leaving home and exposing herself were fully voluntary. In *Carbo* v. *State*[10] defendant had by criminal negligence created a risk of explosion in a building. Deceased, a fireman, was warned of the danger and requested to stay out. He persisted in going in and was killed. It was held that his foolish act was a 'superseding cause'.

Again, in *R.* v. *Storey*,[11] the facts of which are given below, one witness gave evidence that, after the collision for which accused was responsible, deceased deliberately drove across the road to get to an open space where, the soil being loose, his car fell down the bank. According to Myers CJ causal connection between negligent driving and death would be negatived if two conditions were fulfilled: (i) deceased drove across the road voluntarily and was not forced across it as a result of the impact, and (ii) if crossing the road was not the reasonable and natural thing to do to take the car to a position of apparent safety and to ascertain the extent of the damage and discuss with accused responsibility for the collision.[12] Myers CJ's two conditions correspond to two aspects of unfree conduct which were distinguished in Chapter VI,[13] viz. brute physical impulsion and the pressure of danger to one's safety, rights, or interests. The phrase 'reasonable and natural thing to do' should, it is submitted, be taken as meaning 'reasonable with a view to avoiding further harm to the deceased and his car and to maintaining his legal rights'. If so, Myers CJ's reasoning is in substance that the intervention of a fully free actor would relieve accused of further responsibility.

Again, when accused boarded a train to rob and deceased, the fireman, went in front of them and was shot by a person resisting the robbery, it was held correct to direct the jury that, if the fireman placed himself in a position of danger voluntarily and not through fear of violence, they should acquit accused of homicide.[14]

By contrast, the Indiana court in *Stephenson* v. *State*,[15] discussed in Chapter IV,[16] by a majority of 3 to 2 declined to apply the principle

---

[10] (1908) 62 SE 140. [11] [1931] NZLR 417. Below, p. 346.
[12] [1931] NZLR 417, 443. [13] pp. 142–7.
[14] *State* v. *Taylor* (1900) 41 Tex. Cr. R. 564, 55 SW 961; *Taylor* v. *State* (1901) 63 SW 330; *Keaton* v. *State* (1900) 57 SW 1125 (Tex.).
[15] (1932) 205 Ind. 141, 179 NE 633; (1931–2) 45 *Harv. LR* 1261; (1932–3) 31 *Mich. LR* 659. Cf. *Wilson* v. *State* (1893) 24 SW 409 (Tex. Cr. App.) (accused hit deceased on head with rock; then another inflicted fatal knife wound: accused not guilty of homicide unless his blow 'materially contributed' to the death).
[16] Above, pp. 95, 99.

that a fully voluntary intervention relieves accused of further responsibility. Accused raped deceased in circumstances of great brutality, biting her all over the body. He then removed her to a hotel room where she took a large dose of bi-chloride of mercury. Accused refused to summon medical aid and imprisoned her for several hours before leaving her at her home. She died a month later partly of the effects of the chloride poisoning and partly from a breast wound inflicted by defendant which resulted in an abscess. Accused was convicted of murder and appealed on the ground that the taking of poison was the intervening act of a responsible actor, viz. a voluntary act. On appeal it was held that, even if deceased was fully responsible when she took the poison and was not compelled by fear to do so, the conviction could be sustained on the ground that the breast abscess, caused by accused's violent conduct, 'actively contributed' to the death.

The conviction might well be supported on the ground that accused deprived the victim of medical aid after she had taken the poison and that this deprivation, which reduced her chances of recovery, as shown by the medical evidence, was an act done with knowledge that the victim was likely to die:[17] or again that the girl, in her distracted state, was irresponsible. The actual reasoning adopted by the court is, however, open to the criticism that the voluntary act of taking poison happened after the breast wound and would be regarded, on ordinary causal principles which the court itself appears to recognize, as negativing causal connnection between wound and death. Of course it is natural to sympathize with the attempts of a court to find a way to convict a brutal criminal on a capital charge and not merely for a lesser offence. The doctrine that a person whose conduct excites moral disapproval may be punished for doing what he has not done is, however, a dangerous one and it was this doctrine that, in effect, the Indiana court was applying.

A more acceptable approach is that of the Southern Rhodesian court in *R. v. Nbakwa*.[18] On the asumption that suicide is not a crime in Roman-Dutch law,[19] so that accused could not be guilty as an accessory, the question was whether, on the following facts, he had committed murder as a principal. He had lost his daughter and accused his mother of killing her. His mother did not deny the charge but promised to commit suicide. Eight days later, his mother still not having committed suicide, he fetched a rope, tied a noose to the end and said to her: 'I have already fixed the rope. Get up and hang

17 But in fact the jury acquitted on the count alleging homicide by false imprisonment. Cf. *R. v. Huggins* (1730) 1 Barn. KB 358, 396, 94 ER 241, 267.
18 1956 (2) SA 557 (SR).
19 A different result follows if suicide is regarded as self-murder. *Commonwealth* v. *Bowen* (1816) 13 Mass. 356.

yourself', which she did.[20] The Southern Rhodesian court held that accused had not committed murder or attempted murder, since although he had persuaded his mother to kill herself, he had used neither physical compulsion nor threats.

The court was correct, it is submitted, in concluding that the accused had not 'caused' the death, though it is perhaps unhappy to call the act of deceased a *novus actus interveniens*.[21] The real question, as in *Stephenson*'s case,[22] was whether the provision, by an unlawful act, of a reason for another voluntarily to kill himself amounts to 'killing' that person or 'causing' his death. The solution most in accordance with common-sense principles is that it does not amount to 'causing' the death, considered as a physical event, because a voluntary act intervenes, nor to 'causing' deceased to take her own life, because no compulsion is used.[23]

When the first act is sufficient to cause the harm. In this situation the case for holding the first actor responsible despite the voluntary intervention of the second is naturally much stronger. The divergent authorities were discussed in Chapter VIII.[24] The point at issue is whether doing an act sufficient to produce harm, with the intention of producing it, should be regarded as a ground of responsibility for the harm even when the act cannot strictly be said to have caused it. The difficulty is that the intervention of a second actor with the same intention initiates a process which neutralizes that started by the first actor, though it culminates in the intended harm. There are certainly some contexts in the law where, unless the first actor is held responsible, the result will be unsatisfactory.[25]

Non-voluntary Conduct

Many of the same factors are taken into account in assessing whether the intervening actor's conduct is voluntary in the full sense as in civil law.

Physical compulsion. When the victim, assaulted by accused and dazed, staggered dizzily against an iron post and sustained injuries resulting in his death,[26] the dizzy staggering obviously did not negative causal connection between the assault and death and could indeed hardly be called an act.

20 1956 (2) SA 557, 558 (SR).
21 1956 (2) SA 557, 559 (SR).
22 (1932) 205 Ind. 141, 179 NE 633.
23 Above, p. 57.
24 Above, pp. 241-5.
25 Above, pp. 239 f.
26 *Conner* v. *State* (1937) 177 So. 46, 179 Miss. 795.

Self-preservation. An act done for the preservation of the victim's life or bodily safety is generally held not to negative causal connection in criminal law. Thus Stephen[27] says, 'If by actual violence or threats of violence [accused] causes[28] a person to do some act which causes his own death, such act being a mode of avoiding such violence or threats, which under the circumstances would appear natural to the person injured' an accused person is deemed to have committed homicide. This is amply supported by the cases. In *R. v. Pitts*[29] deceased had slipped or fallen into a river while attempting to escape from accused. It was held correct to direct the jury that, if accused struck deceased and deceased, under an apprehension of immediate violence from the circumstances by which he was surrounded, threw himself into the river and was drowned, accused was guilty of homicide, even though the act of deceased was not strictly 'necessary' but was a reasonable step in the circumstances.[30] But when it is safe to remain on board a wrecked ship and very imprudent to take to the water, and yet some of those on board choose to do so and are drowned, their action negatives causal connection between the criminal negligence of the captain which caused the wreck and their deaths.[31]

The same principle has been applied by an American court to the act of a victim who, in order to preserve her chastity, took a risk which led to her death. In that case accused persuaded the victim to get in his car and thereafter attempted to assault her. She immediately opened the door of the car and jumped. Her skull was fractured in the fall and she died. The court held that the deceased was placed in substantial apprehension of danger by defendant's criminal act in the circumstances then surrounding her. Consequently accused might be guilty of homicide despite the intervention of her act.[32]

27 Art. 262 (c).
28 This may refer either to the accused's intentionally inducing the victim by threats to do the act, e.g. by saying, 'Jump out of the window or I will shoot you', or to his doing an act which operates, though not so intended, as the victim's reason for doing a non-voluntary act, e.g. when the accused attempts to shoot the victim, who, to escape the attack, jumps out of the window. We are here concerned with the latter sense of 'causes'; for the former see below, pp. 366–73.
29 (1842) C. & M. 284, 174 ER 509.
30 Cf. *R. v. Grimes* (1894) 15 NSW 209; *R. v. Evans* (1812) Russell, *Crime*, i. 469; *Adams v. People* (1884) 109 Ill. 444, 50 Am. Rep. 617; *Letner v. State* (1927) 156 Tenn. 68, 299 SW 1049, 55 ALR 915; *State v. Shelledy* (1859) 8 Iowa 477; *R. v. Hickman* (1831) 5 C. & P. 151, 172 ER 917; *Hendrickson v. Commonwealth* (1887) 85 Ky. 281, 7 Am. St. Rep. 596; *R. v. Mjobe*, 1938 EDL 303; *R. v. Sikona* 1937 S. Rhodesia 54; *R. v. Halliday* (1889) 61 LTR 701; *R. v. Beech* (1912) 23 Cox CC 181; *R. v. Curley* (1909) 2 CAR 96; *Taylor v. State* (1900) 41 Tex. Cr. 564, 55 SW 961; *Patterson v. State* (1936) 184 SE 309; *State v. Benham* (1967) 23 Iowa 154; *Whiteside v. State* (1930) 29 SW 2d 399; *Morris v. State* (1895) 33 SW 539 (Tex.); *People v. Freeman* (1936) 60 P. 2d 333 (Cal.); *R. v. Donovan* (1850) 4 Cox. 399.
31 *US v. Warner* (1848) 4 McLean 463.
32 *People v. Goodman* (1943) 182 Misc. 585, 44 NYS 2d 715.

Again, when defendant, driving a car, grabbed the coat of his woman passenger and she jumped out of the car, thereby sustaining concussion and grazes, it was held that the jury might properly find him guilty of an assault occasioning actual bodily harm.[33] Only if the victim did something 'daft' could it be said that the injuries were occasioned by her voluntary act and hence 'too remote' a consequence of the original assault. Note that 'occasion' is here used as equivalent to 'cause'; it is not enough that the injury would not have occurred but for the assault, for that would be true even if the victim did something 'daft'. Even if the response takes the form not of an attempt to escape but of legitimate self-defence, the act done in self-defence does not negative causal connection. Thus, when defendant shot at armed police while using as a shield a pregnant girl, who was killed by shots fired by the police at him in self-defence, it was held that he might properly be convicted of manslaughter.[34]

The same legal result follows if the act done with a view to self-preservation is that of a third party. The most striking illustration, in criminal law, of this principle was the decision in *Commonwealth* v. *Moyer*[35] by the court of Pennsylvania, followed in the later case of *Commonwealth* v. *Almeida*.[36] In the *Moyer* case defendants were engaged in a robbery at a petrol station. During the course of it some firing took place and the owner of the petrol station used his revolver in self-defence. The attendant at the station was killed and it was alleged that the shot that killed him was fired by the owner of the station, not by accused. The jury were directed that accused could be convicted of murder if the bullet which killed deceased came from the revolver fired by the latter's employer in an attempt by him to frustrate the robbery. The Pennsylvania court held that this direction to the jury was correct, since the act of defending oneself is a primal human instinct and is also the right and duty of persons threatened with aggression.[37]

This decision was reached under the felony-murder doctrine, which lays down that when an act of violence done in the course of a felony such as robbery causes death, the doer is guilty of murder. It does not matter whether the felon intended to kill the victim or, indeed, anyone. If this doctrine was consistently applied, it seemed to follow a robber would be guilty of murder even if the victim was

---

[33] *R.* v. *Roberts* (1971) 56 CAR 75.
[34] *R.* v. *Pagett*, *The Times* 4.2.83 (approving the statement of the law in our 1st edn., pp. 296 f.).
[35] (1947) 357 Pa. 181, 53 Atl. 2d 736.
[36] (1949) 362 Pa. 596, 68 Atl. 2d 595, 12 ALR 2d 183; *Commonwealth* v. *Thomas* (1955) 382 Pa. 639, 117 Atl. 2d 204.
[37] *Contra: Commonwealth* v. *Moore* (1904) 26 Ky. LR 356, 88 SW 1085; *State* v. *Oxendine* (1924) 187 NC 658, 122 SE 568.

one of his accomplices[38] rather than, as in *Almeida*, an off-duty policeman, or if the fatal shot was fired by the police in their attempt to prevent the escape of the felons rather than by the victim of the robbery.[39] Indeed, if the victim of the fatal shot was the robber himself he could be said to have committed suicide. These conclusions, resulting from the combination of causal principles with the felony-murder doctrine, seemed so extreme that in *Commonwealth* v. *Redline*[40] the Pennsylvania court restricted them. It did so, however, on reasoning which cannot be supported. In the *Redline* case accused engaged in an armed robbery and the police, trying to catch them as they fled, shot one of their accomplices. They were charged with the murder of the accomplice. The court held that on these facts the jury were not entitled to find them guilty of murder, since the killing of the accomplice by the police was an instance of justifiable killing, whereas in *Almeida*, where on one view the police shot and killed an off-duty policeman, the killing was excusable. But, since the issue concerns the responsibility of the robbers and not that of the police, the distinction between justifiable and excusable killing by the latter is not relevant.[41] In *Commonwealth* v. *Meyers*[42] the court recognized this and therefore overruled its earlier decision in *Almeida*. In doing so, however, it did not reject the causal reasoning in the earlier cases. Instead it adopted the view that the necessary mental element was lacking and could not be circumvented, in the circumstances, by recourse to the felony-murder doctrine. If, on the other hand, a felon were to resort to violence or threats of violence, so that the threatened person or the police shot a bystander or co-felon in self-defence, the felon might be guilty of homicide if he acted with the appropriate mental attitude, viz. a wanton disregard for life.

On the other hand, when the act done in self-preservation is 'unreasonable' it negatives causal connection. Thus accused, a white soldier, entered a black railway coach at night and began to hit and kick the blacks. One of them jumped from the moving train and was killed; it was held, unplausibly, that, as accused was unarmed and deceased surrounded by his friends, his fear was not well grounded and there was no *nexus* between the conduct of accused and the death.[43]

---

[38] *Commonwealth* v. *Bolish* (1955) 381 Pa. 500, 113 Atl. 2d 464, 474-5 (killing of co-conspirator engaged in arson); *contra*: *People* v. *Ferlin* (1928) 203 Cal. 587, 265 P. 230.

[39] *Commonwealth* v. *Thomas* (1955) 382 Pa. 639, 117 Atl. 2d 204.

[40] (1958) 391 Pa. 486, 137 Atl. 2d 472; *People* v. *Washington* (1965) 402 P. 2d 130 (Cal.).

[41] Note 71 *Harv. LR* 1565-7.

[42] (1970) 438 Pa. 218, 261 Atl. 2d 550.

[43] *R.* v. *McEnery*, 1943 SR 158; *U.S.* v. *Warner* (1848) 4 McLean 463 (7 Cir.).

R. v. *Dowdle*[44] does not fit into the pattern described. There defendant with others was charged with committing a robbery in the course of which deceased, in trying to escape from them, accidentally tripped and fell down a flight of steps, sustaining fatal injuries. Williams J. directed the jury to consider 'Was this death an accident or was it the result of a push or violent blow?'[45] Accused was acquitted of homicide. The direction seems inept, since the fall might both be an accident and at the same time a consequence of the violence used by the robbers, which made it a matter of self-preservation to run away. The evidence that defendant had agreed with the others that violence might be used was, however weak.

Preservation of property. As in civil law, an act done to save property does not in general relieve a wrongdoer of responsibility. In *State* v. *Leopold*[46] accused was held rightly convicted of murder when he set fire to a building to collect the insurance and two sons of the tenant were burnt to death, even if the boys' father sent them into the burning building to recover property: the court described such an effort to recover property, whether by the father or children, as 'natural'. On the other hand, though the matter was not judicially determined, when the parents of Linda Auld ordered her (presumably unlawfully) to shoot her dog and, to avoid doing so, she shot herself, her parents' order was presumably not the cause of her death since to shoot herself was not a 'natural' way of protecting her dog.[47]

Avoiding detection. It is a question whether the act of a person who, in order to avoid detection or punishment, pursues a certain course of conduct, will be regarded as voluntary within the meaning of this principle. The question might have arisen but was not in fact considered by the Privy Council in *Meli* v. *R.*[48] In this case appellants took deceased to a hut where he was struck over the head with an instrument; then, believing him to be dead, they took him out and rolled him over a cliff in order to make the incident appear like an accident. The medical evidence was that the injuries received in the hut were not sufficient to cause death, which was due to exposure at the foot of the cliff. Accused argued upon appeal that the blows in the hut, though intended to kill, did not in fact cause death, while the act of rolling deceased over the cliff, though it caused death, was not motivated by an intention to kill.

The Privy Council held that it was impossible to divide the transaction in that way and that the blows and the rolling over the edge

44 (1900) 26 VLR 637; under the name *R.* v. *O'Shannessy* (1901) 7 Arg. LR 10.
45 *R.* v. *O'Shannessy* (1901) 7 Arg. LR 10.
46 (1929) 110 Conn. 55, 147 Atl. 118.
47 *New York Times* 7.2.68, cited by Kadish and Paulsen, *Criminal Law and its Process* (3rd edn. 1975), p. 371.
48 [1954] 1 WLR 228; cf. *R.* v. *Church* [1966] 1 QB 59.

of the cliff formed part of one transaction. If, however, the case had been one in which one of two persons not acting in concert struck deceased on the head and the other rolled him over the cliff, the court would have had to decide the causal problem involved. It is conceived that the intervention of the second party, since he labours under a mistake,[49] might not be held to negative causal connection. On the other hand if the act of rolling a body mistakenly thought to be a corpse over the edge of a cliff is regarded as reckless or grossly negligent this might relieve the first actor of responsibility for homicide.

In a German case[50] accused turned on the gas in his bedroom for an hour, intending to kill his wife, who was asleep. He went away and three hours later returned and turned on the gas a second time, believing his wife dead but intending to simulate an accident. The medical evidence showed that the wife died after the gas had been turned on the second time. The Supreme Court of the British Zone decided that the accused was guilty of murder (*Mord*) as his act on the first occasion contributed to his wife's ultimate death by weakening her condition. Here again, the second gassing might be treated as a non-voluntary intervention because accused laboured under a mistake.

Legal obligations. Similar principles apply to the act of a person performing his legal duty. In *Commonwealth* v. *Almeida*[51] accused with others was engaged in a robbery when the police came on the scene. Shots were exchanged and a policeman was killed. Accused was convicted of murder and it was held immaterial whether the fatal shot was fired by a policeman or a robber, since the police were acting in the performance of their duty and with a view to self-preservation. On the other hand in *Commonwealth* v. *Moore*[52] it was held that a rioter was not responsible for the death of a bystander shot by a soldier quelling the riot. The court pointed out that if the contrary were decided a rioter would be guilty of the murder of a fellow rioter shot in repelling the riot and would have committed suicide if he himself were shot. This unexpected conclusion follows, however, from the felony-murder doctrine, not from any mistake in applying the principle that an act done in execution of a legal duty does not negative causal connection.

49 Above, pp. 149–51. However, in *R.* v. *Khandu* (1890) ILR 15 (Bom.) 194 on similar facts accused was convicted of attempted murder only.
50 *OGHBZSt* 2 (1949), 285.
51 (1949) 362 Pa. 596; 68 Atl. 2d 595; 12 ALR 2d 183; for other aspects of this decision see above, pp. 331–2. Cf. *State* v. *Glover* (1932) 330 Mo. 709; 50 SW 2d 1049 (murder when fireman died fighting fire set by arson of accused).
52 (1904) 26 Ky. LR 356, 88 SW 1085. Cf. *Commonwealth* v. *Campbell* (1863) 89 Mass. 541, 83 Am. Dec. 105; *Butler* v. *People* (1888) 125 Ill. 641, 8 Am. St. R. 423.

Moral obligations. An act reasonably done to rescue the victim or render him medical assistance, even if the actor is not legally bound to help, ought not on principle to be regarded as relieving the actor who inflicted the original wound of responsibility for homicide, if death ensues from the attempt to rescue or the assistance given. *R.* v. *Wrigley*[53] seems to conflict with this proposition. Accused, in a fight, struck the victim's head on the ground; others laid the victim out on a stool, from which he fell and died. It being uncertain from the medical evidence whether the cause of death was accused's blow or the fall from the stool, the judge doubted whether there was evidence for the jury on a manslaughter charge and accused was acquitted. It would seem that there was at least a moral obligation on those who laid the victim on the stool to do what they could to render assistance. A different direction might well be given today.

Accident. When an intervening act is not fully free, the fact that it is done in such a way that the actor accidentally or even negligently causes harm does not negative causal connection. For example, a mere accident occurring in the course of conduct reasonably designed for self-preservation from a danger created by defendant's negligence does not exclude liability for the resultant harm. In *R.* v. *Barker*[54] accused was charged with manslaughter. As the mate of a vessel he was drunk and navigated so unskilfully that it was stranded some distance from the shore. Passengers of their own accord put off in small boats and made for the shore but, without negligence on their part, the boats upset and a child was drowned. The New South Wales court held that defendant could rightly be convicted of the manslaughter of the child on the ground that his death was the 'direct and natural result' of defendant's conduct. In this case the passengers had acted reasonably with a view to their own self-preservation in setting off in the boats, and the upsetting of the boat, if an act at all, was accidental, not attributable to any negligence of the passengers.

Negligence. Nor in general does even a negligent act[55] done by one who is performing a duty or protecting his interests negative causal connection if done in response to the situation wrongfully created by defendant. It is different if the response is so 'unnatural' or

53 (1829) 1 Lew. 171, 168 ER 1001.
54 *Sydney Morning Herald* 15 and 17 Oct. 1852. Cf. *People* v. *Fowler* (1918) 178 Cal. 657, 174 P. 892; Sayre, p. 183; *Letner* v. *State* (1927) 156 Tenn. 68, 299 SW 1049; *Thornton* v. *State* (1899) 107 Ga. 683; 33 SE 673; *Norman* v. *U.S.* (1902) 20 DC App. 494; *R.* v. *Curley* (1909) 2 CAR 96, 109.
55 *R.* v. *Benge* (1865) 4 F. & F. 504, 176 ER 665; *Belk* v. *People* (1888) 125 Ill. 584, 17 NE 744. On rather similar facts accused was acquitted of manslaughter in *R.* v. *Ledger* (1862) 2 F. & F. 857 175 ER 1319; *R.* v. *Bennett* (1858) Bell 1 also treats an intervening negligent act as negativing responsibility in a case of constructive manslaughter.

'unreasonable' that causal connection is negatived on the ground of its abnormality. 'When a person inflicts a wound on another which is dangerous, or calculated to destroy life, the fact that the negligence, mistake, or lack of skill of an attending physician or surgeon contributes to the death affords no defence to a charge of homicide.'[56] Similar conclusions have, on the whole, been reached in England and the Commonwealth.

Unreflective acts. The decisions hold, as in civil law, that an act which is unreflective does not negative causal connection. In *R.* v. *Martin*[57] accused blocked the exit to a theatre with an iron bar and then by way of a joke shouted 'Fire'. A panic occurred and during the stampede some members of the theatre audience were wounded when they ran into the iron bar. It was held that accused could be convicted of maliciously wounding the victims of his joke, the panic not relieving him of responsibility. Again in *Conner* v. *State*,[58] when a third person instinctively pushed the victim, who was dazed by accused's assault, to 'straighten him up', this did not negative causal connection between the assault and the subsequent injury to the victim.[59]

The same has been held when the defendant provoked the reaction. In *Wise* v. *Dunning*[60] a Protestant preacher made provocative speeches to which the Catholics of Liverpool retaliated by committing breaches of the peace. When the preacher proposed to hold further meetings the magistrates bound him over to keep the peace. It was held that their action in doing so was justified, partly upon the ground that the breaches of the peace on the previous occasion were the consequence of his provocative speeches, for, though the retaliation by the Catholics was unlawful, it was 'natural' in the circumstances.

Acts of persons under a disability. In criminal as in civil law the intervening act of a child, insane person, or one who is incapacitated through drink or illness, does not in general negative causal connection.

This is most obvious in the case of children. In *R.* v. *Michael*,[61] intending the death of her child, accused bought a bottle of laudanum and handed it to a woman named Stevens with instructions to give the child a teaspoonful every night. Stevens, who had charge of the child, did not do this but left the bottle on the mantleshelf where

56 8 ALR 516. But see below, pp. 352-62, where cases of medical mistreatment, etc., are examined in more detail.
57 (1882) 8 QBD 54.
58 (1937) 177 So. 46, 179 Miss. 795; *R.* v. *Gonya*, 1919 EDL 62.
59 *People* v. *Cobler* (1934) 37 P. 2d 869 (victim unsteady and fell on iron smoking-stand); *Cunningham* v. *People* (1902) 63 NE 517 (Ill.).
60 [1902] 1 KB 167.
61 (1840) 9 C. & P. 356, 173 ER 867.

another child, aged five, found it and gave it to accused's child who drank the contents and died. This was held to be murder since the administration of the poison by an 'unconscious agent' was equivalent to administration by the accused herself. This reasoning is unsatisfactory, since the child was not in any sense an agent, conscious or unconscious, of the mother, who intended Stevens alone to give the poison to the child; but the decision may be justified on the ground that, in our terminology, the act of the child of five did not negative causal connection between the accused's act and the death.

Again in *R. v. Low*[62] accused, an engineer, was convicted of manslaughter. His duty was to manage a steam engine used for raising miners to the surface. On the day in question he deserted his post, leaving the engine in charge of an ignorant boy who, before accused went away, declared himself to be utterly incompetent to manage it. In consequence of the boy's incompetence one of the miners was thrown down the shaft and killed. This was held to be the consequence of defendant's negligence.

Insane persons. That the intervening acts of insane persons do not normally negative causal connection in criminal law is supported by *Johnson v. Alabama*.[63] There is was held that when accused interfered in order to help his insane parent, whom officers were attempting to arrest, and freed his parent's hands thereby enabling him to kill one of the officers, accused was guilty of homicide. The reason given was: 'The person who unlawfully sets the means of death in motion . . . is the guilty cause of the death at the time and place at which his unlawful act produces its fatal result.'

Mental stress in illness. In *State v. Angelina*[64] accused was alleged to have inflicted a mortal wound[65] on deceased. A minute or two later deceased shot himself in the head inflicting a wound not necessarily fatal,[66] and about twenty minutes later died. The jury were instructed that if accused inflicted a mortal wound on deceased who thereafter died, the accused was guilty of murder, provided the shot fired by him 'really contributed either mediately or immediately' to the death, even though they might believe from the evidence that deceased would have died from other causes, or would not have died from the shot fired by the accused had not other causes operated with it.

It was held that this was a misdirection since the true principle is that if, after a mortal blow or wound is inflicted by one person,

62 (1850) 3 C. & K. 123, 173 ER 489.
63 (1905) 142 Ala. 70, 38 So. 182. Cf. (1708) Kelyng 53, 176 ER 221.
64 (1913) 73 W. Va. 146, 80 SE 141. Above, p. 243. .
65 Viz. one very likely to cause death on this occasion given the victim's constitution and the likelihood of medical assistance. Above, p. 241-2.
66 Viz. if the victim had not already been wounded.

THE COMMON LAW

another independent responsible agent in no way connected in causal relation with the first, intervenes and wrongfully inflicts another injury, the 'proximate cause' of the homicide, the latter and not the former is guilty of murder. If, on the other hand, the act of deceased was not that of an intervening responsible agent, but the act of one rendered irresponsible by the wound inflicted by accused and the 'natural result' of that wound, then accused would be guilty of murder since his act would have been 'the causing cause of the immediate death of deceased'.[67] The distinction turns on whether the intervening act is that of a person who is responsible for his actions and who acts voluntarily or that of a person who, through mental stress resulting from illness or injury, is incapable of a free and deliberate choice.

In this case the original wound was sufficient to cause death; but it is surmised that the same principle would apply if the original wound were not 'mortal'.

An act done in delirium will not negative causal connection.[68]

Earned benefits. The principle that the cause of a benefit earned by a person's own effort is that effort and not any other factor[69] is applied in criminal law to the case where the opportunity to earn is obtained by a false pretence on the part of accused. If accused by a false pretence is enabled to place a bet on a horse which subsequently wins and the bookmaker pays the winnings[70] or accused by a false pretence is enabled to enter for a race which he then wins, thereby obtaining the prize money,[71] courts treat his own efforts or skill as the cause of obtaining the money to the exclusion of the false pretence.

Thus, in *R.* v. *Clucas*[72] the accused induced bookmakers to bet with them by representing that they were commission agents acting on behalf of a number of workmen who were placing small bets on horses, whereas in fact they were making bets in considerable sums of money on their own account. Some of these bets proved to be winning bets and in respect of them they received money from the bookmakers. The Court of Criminal Appeal held that they could not be convicted of obtaining this money by the false pretence that they were acting on behalf of a number of workmen since 'the effective cause which led the bookmaker to pay the money was the fact that these men had backed a winning horse'. Consequently it

---

[67] *State* v. *Angelina* (1913) 73 W. Va. 146, 80 SE 141, 143, *per* Miller J.

[68] *McKane* v. *Capital Hill Quarry* (1926) 134 Atl. 640 (Vt.); *State* v. *Rounds* (1932) 160 Atl. 249, 253 (Vt.).

[69] Above, pp. 141, 160-2.

[70] *R.* v. *Clucas* [1949] 2 KB 226.

[71] *R.* v. *Dickenson* (Roscoe, *Crim. Evid.* (13th edn.), p. 408; *The Times* 25.7.1879; Russell, *Crime*, ii. 1407).

[72] [1949] 2 KB 226.

was immaterial that the false pretence might have been a 'contributing cause'.[73] Again, in *R. v. Lewis*[74] Rowlatt J. held that a schoolmistress could not be convicted of obtaining her month's salary by false pretences, though she obtained her appointment as a teacher by a false representation that she possessed a teacher's certificate, since 'the salary was paid because of the services not because of the falsehood'. In this case, too, the false pretence merely created an opportunity for defendant to earn the money. In *R. v. Larner*[75] accused entered a swimming race by presenting a forged letter from the secretary of a club. He was given 20 inches start in consequence and won the race, thereby obtaining a prize. It was held that as the start was so small the obtaining of the prize was 'too remote' a consequence of his false pretence. The point of the decision is, clearly, that the real cause of his winning was his own skill.

On the other hand, when accused by his false pretence obtains some advantage other than an opportunity to practise his skill, and without this further advantage he would not have gained the benefit in question, the court will treat the benefit as gained partly by his work or skill and partly by the false pretence; this is enough to secure a conviction for false pretences. In *R. v. Button*[76] accused sent to the secretary of an athletic meeting a statement in the name of Sims, another athlete, containing a record of Sims's performances, which were undistinguished. Accused, who was a good runner, impersonated Sims and was given a favourable handicap for the race, which he won. He did not obtain the prize since he was discovered before he could apply for it. It was held, nevertheless, that he could be convicted of an attempt to obtain the prize by false pretences, on the ground that had the prize money been paid over to him this would have been the consequence of his false pretence, since 'it was also owing, in part at least, to the false pretences, for by means of the false pretences he obtained a longer start than he would have had if his true name and performances had been known'.[77] So, in *R. v. Dickinson*[78] accused, a professional, represented himself as an amateur, entered a race for amateurs and was allowed a start. He won the race and was convicted, like Button, of attempting to obtain the prize by false pretences.

[73] [1949] 2 KB 226, 230. 'Contributing cause' is not a happy expression with which to describe an act which merely created an opportunity for gain.
[74] Somerset Assizes, Jan. 1922; quoted by Turner and Armitage, *Cases on Criminal Law*, p. 343 n.
[75] (1880) 14 Cox 497.
[76] [1900] 2 QB 597.
[77] [1900] 2 QB 600 *per* Mathew J.
[78] Roscoe, *Criminal Evidence* (13th edn.), p. 408; Russell, *Crime*, ii. 1407; *The Times* 25.7.1879.

Turner[79] suggests that in such cases accused might always be convicted of obtaining money by false pretences, since the payment made by the organizer of the race is made in consequence of an implied representation that accused has won the race fairly and honestly. This, however, raises a question of fact. Sometimes the mind of the person paying the money may be influenced by an express or implied representation to this effect, but in most cases he is satisfied with the knowledge that accused has won the race. In the Australian case of *R.* v. *Lambassi*[80] accused entered for a race and submitted a false list of performances. After he had won a heat and before the final he signed a document declaring that the list was correct. He won the final and was paid the prize money. It was held that he could be convicted of obtaining the prize money by false pretences, though he had not obtained a favourable handicap by submitting the false list of performances, since the secretary of the club who paid the prize money stated that he would not have paid it but for the written declaration, and the court held that it was unnecessary to show that the money was paid *solely* in consequence of the prisoner's fraud. It was immaterial that the 'chain of causation' was different from what the accused expected.[81] On the special facts of this case it seems that the payer was influenced by the false statement of performances.

II. ABNORMALITY

As in Chapter VI we consider this topic under the three headings of physical states and events, the behaviour of animals, and non-voluntary human conduct.

Physical States and Events

The basic principle is that a physical state or event, even if subsequent to the act of defendant, does not negative causal connection if it is normal or usual in the context. Nor does even an abnormal circumstance coexisting at the time of defendant's wrongful conduct. The first part of the principle is illustrated by *Hendrickson* v. *Commonwealth*.[82] In that case the Kentucky court held that if a husband drove his poorly dressed wife from their home into the snow and she died of exposure, the jury might find the husband guilty of

79 Russell, *Crime*, ii. 1408; *Kenny's Outlines*, p. 286.
80 [1927] Vic. LR 349; 49 *Aust. LT* 23; 33 Arg. LR 298.
81 Ibid., *per* McArthur J.
82 (1887) 85 Ky. 281, 7 Am. St. Rep. 596. Cf. *R.* v. *Martin* (1868) 11 Cox CC 136; *People* v. *Keshner* (1953), s. 304 NY 968, 110 NE 2d 892; *Bradley* v. *Queen* (1957) 6 DLR 2d 385.

manslaughter provided that it was not the wife's voluntary act to remain outside. The continued cold weather obviously would not negative causal connection between the husband's act and the wife's death, nor can the normal operation of the tides on a man left unconscious on the seashore be regarded as negativing causal connection;[83] though there might be cases in which the extraordinary operation of natural forces would exclude it.[84] This principle might appear to conflict with the decision in *R.* v. *Gill*.[85] In that case accused was indicted for 'throwing down skins into a man's yard' by which another man's 'eye was beat out'. On the evidence it appeared that defendant threw the skin down but 'the wind took the skin and blew it out of the way' and in that way the prosecutor's eye was damaged. Defendants were acquitted. This case cannot be cited to establish any clear principle since no reason is given for the decision, but it is of interest because Beale used it as a prime example of his mechanical theory of causation, by which an act 'exhausts its causal efficacy' when the 'active force' comes to rest[86] in a position of apparent safety. This theory takes as its basis the principle that, when the defendant has set in motion a series of events, he remains responsible until such time as the events so set in motion have come to rest in a passive state. Thereafter he is not responsible if an 'independent active force' intervenes and harm is thereby caused. The facts of *Gill*'s case suggest the mechanical analogies which Beale developed into an elaborate system. The decision no doubt turned on the distinction between damage 'directly' and 'indirectly' done for purposes of the civil action of trespass and the crimes of assault and battery. Whatever the proper distinction may be for that purpose, it does not seem that the cessation of a series of mechanical events, and the fact that for the moment no further physical movement is occurring, have any decisive importance for our common-sense judgments of causation. Thus, on facts such as those of *Gill*'s case it would appear proper to draw a distinction between the occurrence of a normal wind and the occurrence of an abnormal wind or hurricane, the former not being sufficient to negative causal connection while the latter might well be held to do so. This is the view, it is submitted, which would be taken by a modern court.

Coincidences. In criminal as in civil law a conjunction of events amounting to a coincidence is held to negative causal connection. In

[83] *R.* v. *Hallett* [1969] SASR 141.
[84] Ibid., p. 150.
[85] (1719) 1 Strange 190. Cf. *Amies* v. *Stevens* (1718) 1 Strange 127.
[86] *Selected Essays on the Law of Torts*, pp. 730, 748.

342 THE COMMON LAW

Bush v. *Commonwealth*[87] deceased was assaulted by accused and received a wound, not necessarily mortal; she was then taken to hospital where she caught scarlet fever from a nurse and died. The court held that accused was not guilty of homicide for 'when there is a supervening cause, not naturally intervening by reason of the wound, the death is by visitation of providence, and not from the act of the party inflicting the wound. . . . If the death was not connected with the wound in the regular chain of causes and consequences, there ought not to be any responsibility.' Here the reference to something not in the 'regular' chain of causes and consequences is perhaps an obscure way of referring to a coincidence.

As the above cases and others cited in the preceding section show, the death must, in order that accused may be convicted, be a consequence, on ordinary causal principles, of the act done by accused[88] It is not enough that the act was a necessary condition of the death. If this is so, Seavey is wrong in stating that if a kidnapper is carefully driving a car in which the person kidnapped is a passenger, and a collision occurs in which the passenger is killed, the kidnapper may be under the felony-murder doctrine guilty of murder, kidnapping being a felony.[89] The collision would be a mere coincidence, not a consequence of the kidnapping. A similar restriction is presumably to be placed on the misdemeanour-manslaughter and transferred malice doctrines.[90]

Coexisting circumstances. As long ago as Hale it was thought that 'if a man be struck of some such disease which possibly by course of nature would end his life in half a year and another gives him a wound or hurt which hastens his end by irritating and provoking the disease to operate more violently or speedily, this hastening of his death sooner than it would have been is homicide or murder.'[91]

A modern version of this is given by Stephen, who says that 'a person is deemed to have committed homicide, although his act is not the immediate or not the sole cause of death, if by any act he hastens the death of a person suffering under any disease or injury which apart from such act would have caused death.'[92]

[87] (1880) 78 Ky. 268; *Livingston* v. *Commonwealth* (1857) 14 Gratt (55 Va.) 592; *Quinn* v. *State* (1914) 106 Miss. 844, 64 So. 738; *Lewis* v. *Commonwealth* (1897) 42 SW 1127 (Ky.).
[88] *People* v. *Arzon* (1978) 401 NYS 2d 156 (by starting fire defendant caused fireman to put himself in position where he was vulnerable to an independent fire, which killed him; held, there was evidence of causal connection between defendant's act and the death of the fireman); cf. above, pp. 168-70.
[89] (1938) 52 *Harv. LR* 372, 386. But, as Seavey says, the kidnapper is not civilly liable!
[90] Glanville Williams, *Criminal Law*, pp. 106-7, suggests restrictions based on foreseeability.
[91] Hale, *PC* i. 428.
[92] *Digest*, art. 262 (d).

An existing illness or susceptibility of the victim does not negative causal connection. In *R.* v. *Fletcher*[93] accused struck deceased who at the time was so ill that she could not possibly have lived more than six weeks if she had not been struck. In consequence deceased died earlier than she would otherwise have done. Accused was held to have committed homicide. Again, in *Commonwealth* v. *Giacomazza*[94] deceased was suffering from arterio-sclerosis and coronary thrombosis when accused shot him. The hospital record described the subsequent death as due to these two conditions and gunshot wounds inflicted by the accused. It was held to be a question for the jury whether causal connection between the shooting and the death was made out. 'If a person inflicts a wound with a deadly weapon in such a manner as to put life in jeopardy, and death follows as a consequence of this felonious and wicked act, it does not alter its nature or diminish its criminality to prove that other causes co-operated in producing the fatal result.'[95]

Similarly, in *Levy* v. *The King*[96] accused inflicted stab wounds on deceased who was suffering from latent syphilis of the liver and consequently, when treated with penicillin and sulfa-drugs, was unable to resist the effect of the drugs and died. It was held that provided the treatment was reasonable accused might rightly be convicted of murder and the jury might find that the stabbing of accused was the 'effective cause' of the death.[97] So, in *State* v. *Frazier*[98] appellant struck deceased on the jaw with his fist. A slight laceration on the inside of deceased's mouth resulted. Deceased was,

---

[93] (1841) Russell, *Crime*, p. 472; *State* v. *Matthews* (1886) 38 La. Ann. 795; *People* v. *Ah Fat* (1874) 48 Cal. 61; *Rogers* v. *State* (1894) 60 Ark. 76, 29 SW 894; *R.* v. *Martin* (1832) 5 C. & P. 128, 172 ER 907; *R.* v. *Ryall* (1843) 7 JP 116.

[94] (1942) 311 Mass. 456, 42 NE 2d 506.

[95] *Commonwealth* v. *Hackett* (1861) 84 Mass. 136, 142. Cf. *State* v. *Block* (1913) 87 Conn. 573 (deceased suffering from alcoholism); *Baker* v. *State* (1892) 30 Fla. 41. 11 So. 492; *State* v. *Scates* (1858) 50 NC 409; *Bradley* v. *Queen* (1957) 6 DLR 2d 385; *Griffin* v. *State* (1899) 50 SW 366 (Tex.); *R.* v. *Cheesman* (1836) 7 C. & P. 455; *Hollywood* v. *State* (1911) 120 P. 471 (Wyo.); *R.* v. *Martyr* [1962] QSR 398; *contra*: *R.* v. *Johnson* (1827) 1 Lew. CC 164 (drunkenness). If deceased's state of health is very delicate there may be a doubt whether it was defendant's act which precipitated the death: *Fine* v. *State* (1952) 246 2d 70 (very high blood pressure, minor assault).

[96] (1949) 51 WALR 29; *R.* v. *Makali*, 1950 (1) SA 340 (N) (heart disease).

[97] Cf. *R.* v. *Dyson* [1908] 2 KB 454, where deceased was suffering from meningitis when wounded by accused on the occasion in question. In this case the meningitis was the consequence of a previous wrongful act on the part of accused but the previous act had occurred more than a year before the death of the deceased and consequently no charge of homicide could be founded upon it.

[98] (1936) 339 Mo. 966, 98 SW 2d 707. Cf. *Ex. p. Heigho* (1910) 18 Idaho 566, 110 P. 1029, in which again deceased was suffering from a heart disease when accused engaged in a violent fight which frightened deceased so that she died. It was held that there might be cases in which a charge of homicide could be sustained when the death was caused by fright and therefore it should be left to the jury to determine whether the act of the accused was the 'direct and actual' cause of the death of the woman: p. 1032.

unknown to accused, a haemophiliac, and the laceration produced a haemorrhage lasting ten days and ending in his death. The Missouri court held that it was no defence that the blow struck would ordinarily not have been dangerous to life and that accused did not know that deceased was a haemophiliac. Consequently appellant was rightly convicted of manslaughter.[99] Several cases have emphasized that it is immaterial as regards causal connection, though of course relevant to *mens rea*, whether accused knew of or could foresee the susceptibility.[1]

Slight acceleration of death. The foregoing principle is well established and applies over a wide area, but there is some difficulty in applying it to the special case where the victim is dying from a wound or illness and his death is only slightly accelerated by an act of accused which would not be sufficient to kill a person in a normal state of health. Quite apart from the law on the subject, such an act would be described as 'accelerating' rather than 'causing' death, for causal language has to be modified to fit such cases of additional causation. Some support for the vague common-sense distinction between accelerating and causing death may be found in *R. v. Adams*,[2] where Devlin J. directed the jury in a case of this kind that 'if life were cut short by weeks or months it was just as much murder as if it were cut short by years . . . '. But 'that does not mean that a doctor who is aiding the sick and the dying has to calculate in minutes or even in hours and perhaps not in days or weeks the effect upon a patient's life of the medicines which he administers or else be in peril on a charge of murder. If, for example, because the doctor has done something, death occurs at eleven o'clock instead of twelve o'clock or even on Monday instead of Tuesday, no people of common sense would say, "Oh, the doctor caused her death" '; so that if the doctor gave the proper treatment 'the fact that accidentally it would have shortened life did not make any grounds for convicting him of murder'. It cannot be said that any precise doctrine can be drawn from this case since, while stating that a doctor was in no different position from an ordinary person, Devlin J. also suggests that the fact that accused was administering a drug to relieve

99 Cf. *R. v. Hayward* (1908) 21 Cox 692, a case of death caused through fright in which the accused was found guilty of manslaughter of his wife and it was held to be immaterial that she was suffering from a persistent thymus gland, which contributed to her death, whether or not the accused knew of this abnormal state of health. *People v. Studer* (1922) 211 P. 233, 59 Cal. App. 547 (mother ejected from home by accused dies of brain haemorrhage: conviction for manslaughter upheld).

1 *Nelson v. State* (1938) 198 SE 305, 58 Ga. App. 243; *Wells v. State* (1933) 167 SE 709, 710, 46 Ga. App. 412; *R. v. Cheesman* (1836) 7 C. & P. 455; *State v. Frazier* (1936) 98 SW 2d 707; *Commonwealth v. Fox* (1856) 73 Mass. 585, 587.

2 *The Times* 9.4.1957; Glanville Williams, *The Sanctity of Life and the Criminal Law*, p. 289; Smith and Hogan, *Criminal Law*, p. 271.

suffering and might not know for certain what would be its effect
should be taken into account on a charge of murder. Certainly a
general principle that 'accelerating' death cannot be a basis of liability for homicide would run counter to existing law and would be
a dangerous doctrine. The correct principle must surely be that a
doctor has a duty not merely to prolong life but, when that proves
no longer possible, to continue to relieve a patient's suffering. It is
therefore permissible for him, when the patient is doomed to die
shortly, to administer pain-killing drugs with his consent, even if they
slightly shorten life. It does not follow that it would be permissible, as
opposed to understandable, for someone without such a duty to do
the same. In general, it is important to cleave to the principle that
the slightest acceleration of death, e.g. by shooting a man strapped
in the electric chair, is homicide.[3]

Glanville Williams cites *R.* v. *Macdonald*[4] for the proposition that
a pre-existing disease may be held to be the cause of death to the
exclusion of accused's later act which accelerated death. There the
victim's death from tuberculosis was probably accelerated by a
wound from the shot fired by accused, who was acquitted of murder.
The case is ill reported and, if the principle involved is indeed what
Glanville Williams suggests, it runs counter to many decisions cited
above; it can hardly be said to turn, as he implies, on the fact that
the charge was murder. Probably the point is really one of evidence;
the prosecution must prove beyond a reasonable doubt that death
was indeed accelerated by the act of accused.

The question whether a slight acceleration of death amounts to
homicide is also raised in relation to patients who have suffered what
is called 'brain stem death', when by artificial stimulus the bodily
functions of blood circulation and respiration continue, though the
controlling mechanism of the brain has irreversibly ceased to function. In that case it may be said that a doctor who discontinues life
support (e.g. after removing an organ required for transplant) has
discontinued support to a person already dead, so that his act cannot
amount to homicide. On that view, if it was accused who inflicted
on the patient the injuries which resulted in brain stem death, the
later intervention of the doctor can afford no defence on a charge of
homicide. It cannot negative causal connection between the act of
accused and the patient's death because the patient is already dead

---

[3] *R.* v. *Dyson* [1908] 2 KB 454, 457; *Commonwealth* v. *Bowen* (1816) 13 Mass. 356,
360 ('no period of human life which is not precious as a season of repentance').
[4] (1844) 8 JP 138. He also cites *Livingston* v. *Commonwealth* (1857) 14 Gratt. (55
Va.) 592, 602 which was a case concerning the intervention of a later coincidental
event, viz. catching a disease independent of the wound (peritonitis).

when the doctor terminates the life support system.[5] Whether it should be a crime of some sort for an unauthorized person to terminate the life support of an 'irreversible' is debatable. Such an act should not be regarded as homicide, since a body which cannot regain the exercise of its directive functions is effectively dead. It would be different if the patient, though in a coma, had not suffered brain stem death, since there is always a possibility in such a case that an individual may recover the control of his directive functions.

Other types of circumstance. It is not easy to find examples in criminal law in which courts have considered abnormal circumstances other than those relating to the bodily condition of the victim. One example may be drawn from French law. On a charge of negligent wounding it was held that accused, in charge of a vicious dog, was guilty of this crime when the dog bit the victim who was wearing a dirty pair of trousers, so that his wound became more seriously infected that it would otherwise have been and he died of tetanus infection.[6]

The effect on causal connection of an abnormal physical condition of the place where the victim was located was considered in a New Zealand case already discussed.[7] Accused was charged with manslaughter and with the statutory crime of causing death by negligent driving. In attempting to cut in he had collided with another car which then travelled diagonally across the road and fell down a bank, the occupants being killed. He sought to give evidence in defence that the deceased driver was guilty of contributory negligence in that his car was in a defective state, and that there was loose earth at the place where the car fell over the bank. Myers CJ refused to admit the evidence and directed the jury to convict if accused by negligent driving caused the collision and if deceased would not have died but for his negligence. The full bench of the New Zealand court, including Myers CJ, later held that the exclusion of the evidence and the direction to the jury were incorrect, since, though contributory

5 In *R.* v. *Malcherek, R.* v. *Steel* [1981] 2 All ER 422 the point arose but was not decided, on the ground that, on a conventional view of death as occurring only when breathing and heart-beat also stop, the injuries inflicted by defendants were then still a 'continuing, operating and indeed substantial cause' of the death (p. 428). The doctors who discontinued the life support were acting conscientiously in doing so, so that, even if another doctor might have adopted a different course, they could not be said to have acted in such an unreasonable or grossly negligent way as to negative causal connection (ibid., p. 429); cf. *R.* v. *Kitching* [1976] 6 WWR 697, 715; *R.* v. *Finlayson* [1978] SLT 60.
6 Cass. Crim. 18.11.1927; *Sirey* 1928.1.192. *Mayes* v. *People* (1883) 106 Ill. 306 (victim carrying oil lamp; oil caught fire when accused threw glass at her, burning her to death; accused guilty of murder). *Commonwealth* v. *McAfee* (1971) 108 Mass. 458 (victim stumbled against chair); *Rigsby* v. *State* (1910) 91 NE 925 (Ind.) (medical care not available).
7 *R.* v. *Storey* [1931] NZLR 417. Above, p. 327.

negligence is no defence in criminal law, accused may show that the
negligence of deceased was the 'sole cause' of death.[8] The defects in
the car, whether pre-existing or 'caused or accentuated by the impact',[9] and the looseness of the soil would not, in the view of Myers
CJ, negative causal connection but the conduct of deceased would
do so if voluntary and not the 'reasonable and natural' thing to do
in the circumstances.[10] The court was therefore prepared to treat the
victim's physical location as a coexisting circumstance which the
wrongdoer took at his peril.

Causal independence. A physical event which is itself the consequence, on ordinary causal principles, of accused's conduct, no
voluntary act or abnormal circumstance having intervened, does
not, of course, negative causal connection though the 'chain' may
be 'long', i.e. there may be a series of events each connected to the
preceding event as consequence to necessary condition. In *Williams*
v. *United States*[11] the accused struck the victim with a lighted lamp
which fell to the floor and broke, setting fire to a rug; thereafter in
the scuffle the fire spread to the victim's clothes and he suffered burns
from which he died. A conviction for homicide was sustained. A
simpler instance is when a wound inflicted by defendant causes a
disease which in turn causes death.[12]

Animal Behaviour

A distinction is drawn, it will be remembered, between the independent behaviour of animals and animal behaviour which is a
reaction or response to the wrongdoer's act.[13]

As regards independent behaviour the principle ordinarily
adopted is that the normal interventions of animals do not negative
causal connection, but an intervention which is extraordinary in
itself or in conjunction with the defendant's wrongful act or some
admitted consequence of that act, so as to amount to a coincidence,
relieves accused of responsibility.

In *R.* v. *Halloway*[14] Halloway was indicted for murdering Payne.
He tied Payne to a horse's tail. It appears that the horse thereupon
set off, probably being startled by the sound of blows, and drew
Payne along the ground three furlongs, breaking his shoulder,

8 [1931] NZLR 417, 448.
9 [1931] NZLR 417, 444.
10 [1931] NZLR 417, 443.
11 (1927) 20 F. 2d 269, 57 App. DC 253.
12 *Powell* v. *State* (1882) 13 Tex. Cr. R. 244, 254; *Lochamy* v. *State* (1921) 152 Ga.
235, 109 SE 497; *State* v. *Harmon* (1915) 92 Atl. 853 (Del.); *People* v. *Kane* (1915)
107 NE 655 (NY); *State* v. *Rounds* (1932) 160 Atl. 249, 252 (Vt.).
13 Above, p. 181.
14 (1628) Cro. Car. 131, 79 ER 715.

'where-of he instantly died'. Halloway was found guilty of murder, the sudden alarm of the horse not being regarded as an extraordinary intervening event.[15]

It has not been possible to find an example in the cases of the independent behaviour of an animal amounting to a coincidence. A set of facts on which the problem might arise would be the following. Accused meets his victim in the street and, intending to kill him, strikes him a blow with his fist so that he totters backwards. Just then a dog dashes past so that the victim trips and falls, fracturing his skull, and ultimately dies from the fracture. It is thought that accused would not be guilty of murder since it was very unlikely that just at the moment when the victim was staggering a dog would dash past. Here the animal's behaviour would, in conjunction with the blow, amount to a coincidence.

If the animal behaviour is a reaction or response to the wrongful act its effect on responsibility depends on whether it is 'natural', i.e. in accordance with the nature of that kind of animal.

Natural animal behaviour has been held not to negative causal connection in criminal law. In the *Harlot*'s case[16] accused was delivered of a child which she laid away in an orchard and covered with leaves. A kite struck at it with its claws and the child in consequence soon died. She was convicted of murder, the reason given by the court being that the will is equivalent to the deed. A more modern view of the facts would be that the attack by the kite was in accordance with the nature of the animal and consequently not such as to negative causal connection.

In determining what is in accordance with an animal's nature the circumstances of the case may be taken into account. In *R.* v. *Hickman*[17] accused struck deceased with a small stick and deceased rode away along the road. Accused rode after him and, on deceased spurring his horse, the horse winced and threw him, with fatal consequences. One count of the indictment alleged that deceased, from a well-grounded apprehension of further attack, spurred on his horse whereby it became frightened and threw him, inflicting a mortal wound. The court held that the count was sufficiently proved since the death was clearly caused by the frightening of the horse. This may be accounted for on the ground that the fright of the horse and its consequent throwing of the deceased was natural behaviour on the horse's part in the circumstances of the case, while the spurring

15 This version of the facts of the case is based principally upon the account in 1 Wm. Jones 198, 82 ER 105. An alternative version is that the horse was ridden away by accused.
16 (1560) Crompton's *Justices*, p. 24; Turner and Armitage, p. 109.
17 (1831) 5 C. & P. 151, 172 ER 917.

of the horse did not negative causal connection as it was a reasonable measure of self-preservation.

On the other hand, behaviour which is unnatural for the species of animal concerned has been held, in criminal as in civil law, to negative causal connection. In *People* v. *Rockwell*,[18] when accused knocked a man down with his fist and thereupon a horse jumped on him or kicked him, inflicting injuries from which he died, defendant was not guilty of homicide. Here the act of the horse was presumably not in accordance with the nature of a horse, a concept which, as we have seen, is strongly influenced not merely by the idea of what is usual for the species but also by our notions of proper behaviour for the animal in question.[19]

Non-voluntary but Abnormal Human Conduct

Human conduct, like animal behaviour, may either be independent or dependent, in the sense of being a reaction or response to defendant's wrongful act.

As regards independent human conduct the broad principle is that, if it is normal, it does not negative causal connection[20] but if extraordinary or such as in conjunction with the wrongful act to amount to a coincidence, it does.

Coincidences. Though no very clear examples of this category are found in the cases, the following is possibly an instance. In *R.* v. *Horsey*[21] accused was indicted for the murder of a person unknown. He set fire to a stack of straw in an enclosure. While the fire was burning deceased was seen in the flames and his body was afterwards found in the enclosure. Bramwell B. directed the jury that a man is not answerable 'except for the natural and probable result of his own act; and therefore, if you should not be satisfied that the deceased was in the enclosure at the time when the prisoner set fire to the stack but came in afterwards, then as his own act intervened between the death and the act of the prisoner his death could not be the natural result of the prisoner's act'. The jury returned a verdict of 'not guilty'. Bramwell B.'s dictum appears rather too broadly stated, since a distinction ought presumably to be drawn between an intervening act which amounts to a coincidence and an intervening act which is normal or likely in the circumstances. It seems clear, however, from the facts of the case that the court had in mind that the entry of deceased, if it occurred after the prisoner had set fire to the stack, could only have been a voluntary act or coincidence.

[18] (1878) 39 Mich. 503 (Waite, *Cases*, p. 221).
[19] Above, p. 181–2.
[20] *People* v. *Fowler* (1918) 178 Cal. 657, 174 P. 892; *People* v. *Kibbe* (1974) 321 NE 2d 773 (victim, left helpless at side of road, struck by truck and killed).
[21] (1862) 3 F. & F. 287, 176 ER 129.

Again, in *R.* v. *Stripp*[22] accused was acquitted, on appeal, of culpable homicide. He was driving a car and took a bend on the wrong side of the road. Deceased, who was drunk, was riding a bicycle in the opposite direction and at the last moment swerved into the path of accused so that there was a head-on collision. The reason for the decision was that 'It cannot be said that the negligence of the driver of the vehicle was the proximate cause of the disaster'. Here the reasoning of the court appears to have been that, though contributory negligence is not a defence to a charge of homicide, the action of the deceased was so foolhardy as to negative causal connection between the negligent driving of the accused and the death of the cyclist.[23] In such cases the conduct which negatives causal connection may be regarded as so abnormal as to be a coincidence.

Dependent conduct. The broad principle, as in tort, is that a reckless or grossly negligent reaction negatives causal connection. The most important cases in this connection concern medical negligence and the failure of a wounded or injured person to seek treatment or to follow medical advice. These we discuss separately in section IV of this chapter. But the principle is not confined to such cases. Thus, in *Commonwealth* v. *Root*,[24] two men agreed to race their cars in excess of the speed limit on the highway. One of them, trying to pass the other when a truck was approaching from the opposite direction, swerved across the dividing line of the highway and into the path of the oncoming truck. In the ensuing crash he was killed. The court held that the agreement of the other man to race with deceased could not be regarded as the proximate cause in criminal law of the death of deceased. The wider doctrines of causation currently applied in tort law should not be extended to criminal law. From the point of view of our analysis the decision is to be justified on the following grounds. Despite the unlawful agreement to race, the swerve of deceased into the path of the truck was a reckless act which on common-sense criteria would negative causal connection with the ensuing death. In tort law, however, there are some decisions which extend liability by making defendant, on facts such as these, liable for *encouraging* his partner's recklessness,[25] while on the other hand the fact that deceased agreed to the dangerous course of action may debar his estate or dependants from recovering from the other in a civil action. But these doctrines have no place in criminal law, in which it is not normally enough merely to prove that accused

22 1940 EDL 29.
23 Perhaps the court was influenced by the analogy of the last clear chance rule. Above, pp. 219–25.
24 (1961) 403 Pa. 571, 170 Atl. 2d 310; *contra: Jacobs* v. *State* (1966) 184 So. 2d 711, 716, 717.
25 e.g. *Stapley* v. *Gypsum Mines* [1952] AC 663 (above, pp. 215–16), where the encouragement of reckless conduct appears to be treated as a reason for imposing liability.

occasioned the harm; he must have 'caused' it in the strict sense. Although, therefore, the meaning of 'cause' in this central sense is not different in criminal and civil law, the grounds of responsibility are sometimes wider in civil law.

III. CONTRIBUTORY CAUSES

In criminal as in civil law causal connection may exist between a wrongful act and harm despite the existence of contributory causes.[26] Thus, Wharton says,[27] 'one whose wrongful act hastens or accelerates[28] the death of another or contributes to its cause is guilty of homicide though other causes co-operate'. The 'other causes' include circumstances besides the wrongful act which might be cited as the causal explanation of the harm, or part of it, and also other acts lawful or unlawful of which the harm is a consequence. The first may be illustrated with reference to cases on the abnormal susceptibility of the victim,[29] the second from the facts of *R. v. Benge*.[30] A foreman negligently allowed rails to be taken up. An engine-driver negligently failed to keep a proper look-out and an accident occurred in which deceased was killed. It was held that the foreman might be guilty of homicide despite the driver's negligence. A particular application of the notion of contributory causes is to the situation in which two or more attack a victim who dies of the combined effect of the wounds so inflicted. Provided that the assaults form part of a single incident it is usually held that each caused the victim's death if the death would not have occurred at the time it did but for the wound in question.[31] It is only when there is a separation in time between attacks that the later may be held to negative causal connection with the earlier.

An example of death resulting from the combined effect of a lawful and an unlawful act is *People v. Brown*,[32] where accused fired one shot in self-defence which wounded deceased and another when the danger was past. It was held correct to direct the jury that he was guilty of homicide if the second shot contributed to the death.

Has the *de minimis* maxim any application in criminal law? There

26 See above, p. 205.
27 Wharton, *Homicide*, s. 27.
28 See, however, pp. 344-6.
29 *Commonwealth* v. *Giacomazza* (1942) 311 Mass. 456, 42 NE 2d 506. Above, pp. 342-3.
30 (1865) 4 F. & F. 504, 176 ER 665; *Schulz* v. *State* (1911) 130 NW 972 (Neb.); *People* v. *Clark* (1951) 235 P. 2d 56 (Cal.).
31 *State* v. *Francis* (1928) 149 SE 348, 364 (SC); *State* v. *Luster* (1935) 182 SE 427, 431 (SC).
32 (1923) 216 P. 411 (Cal.); *Rogers* v. *State* (1894) 29 SW 894; *State* v. *Rounds* (1932) 160 Atl. 249, 253.

352 THE COMMON LAW

are those who assert that it has.[33] In general this seems dubious. The slightest shortening of life, for example, is homicide.[34] It is wrong to direct a jury that if a defendant is less than a fifth to blame for the harm that has occurred he is not guilty.[35] But when a defendant makes an insignificant contribution to a combined causal process, e.g. by throwing a piece of paper on a raging fire or by administering a slight scratch to a man bleeding to death, his contribution may no doubt be disregarded.

When the concurrent cause is the contributory negligence of the victim, civil law allows this to be pleaded as a complete or partial defence, while in criminal law contributory negligence is no defence[36] though the victim's reckless or grossly negligent behaviour or his voluntary decision to court death or injury may negative causal connection, on ordinary principles, between accused's act and the harm.[37] But this does not mean that different principles of causation are applied in civil and criminal law, merely that different legal results follow from the application of the principle of contributory negligence only in the civil law.

IV. DOCTOR'S OR VICTIM'S NEGLIGENCE

It is convenient to discuss in a separate section a group of cases of some importance in the law of homicide where a wrongful act of accused, such as an assault or wounding, is followed by improper medical treatment, want of proper care by the victim, or refusal on his part to undergo the proper or recommended treatment. The question to be decided is in what circumstances these intervening factors relieve the original wrongdoer of responsibility for the victim's death. The types of case mentioned may be classified into three groups.

In the first the original wound is not of a character sufficient to kill the victim without the maltreatment, nor is the latter sufficient to kill without the original wound. The problem here is whether the factors which have been held to negative responsibility in civil law, such as gross negligence[38] subsequent to the initial wrong, are also

33 Perkins, *Criminal Law*, p. 695.
34 Above, pp. 344-6.
35 *R.* v. *Hennigan* [1971] 3 All ER 133.
36 *R.* v. *Swindall and Osborne* (1846) 2 C. & K. 230 175 ER 95; *R.* v. *Storey* [1931] NZLR 417; *R.* v. *Hutchinson* (1864) 9 Cox 555, 557; *R.* v. *Jones* (1870) 11 Cox 544; *R.* v. *Dant* (1865) L. & C. 567, 169 ER 1517; *R.* v. *O'Reilly Builders (Pty.) Ltd.*, 1946 NPD 392; *State* v. *Custer* (1929) 129 Kan. 381, 282 P. 1071, 67 ALR 909; *R.* v. *Longbottom* (1849) 3 Cox 439; *R.* v. *Walker* (1824) 1 C. & P. 320, 171 ER 1213. Contra: *R.* v. *Birchall* (1866) 4 F. & F. 1087, 176 ER 918; *Graives* v. *State* (1937) 172 So.716 (Fla.); *Embry* v. *Commonwealth* (1930) 32 SW 2d 979.
37 *Prince* v. *State* (1919) 12 Ohio. App. 347; *R.* v. *Bunney* [1894] 6 *Queensland LJ* 80, 82; *Commonwealth* v. *Root* (1961) 403 Pa. 571, 170 Atl. 2d 310.
38 Above, pp. 152, 184.

held to do so in criminal law, or whether different tests may operate, more or less favourable to accused. In the second group of cases the original wrongdoer's conduct was of a kind sufficient, in the existing circumstances, despite with the medical aid normally to be expected, to cause death, though subsequent negligence by doctor or victim may have accelerated death. Here the original wound is said to be 'mortal' in the second of the three senses distinguished in Chapter VIII,[39] or at least 'dangerous'. Where this is the case, some authorities hold that subsequent negligence does not relieve accused of liability for homicide even though the negligence was so 'gross' or extraordinary as to have that effect had the original wound not been mortal. They sometimes base this conclusion on the ground, which is common to the first and second groups of cases, that the wrongful act of accused 'contributed' to the death, since the subsequent negligence would not have resulted in death apart from the initial wound or injury. Despite this common feature, the second group of cases is marked off linguistically from the first; for it is natural to say of them that the first act 'caused' death while the later negligence merely 'accelerated' it. In a third group of cases the subsequent negligence of doctor or patient would have been sufficient, apart from the original wound, to cause death though the occasion for treatment would not have arisen but for the attack; here the court is inclined to hold that the subsequent conduct prevents the original wrongdoer being convicted of homicide, at least if he did not inflict a 'mortal' wound.[40] In such cases the subsequent negligent conduct inflicts a 'mortal' injury not merely in the second sense but in the first, viz. by doing something which would be sufficient to kill a person of normal constitution, e.g. administering a fatal dose of a drug. If negligence of this sort follows the infliction of a 'mortal' wound the case is one of additional causation as described in Chapter VIII.[41]

Improper Medical Treatment

On this subject reference is often made to the discussion by Hale. Hale says: (1) If a person gives another a wound, which might by skilful treatment be cured and it is not, it is a case of homicide. (2) If a person inflicts a non-mortal wound and the victim dies from treatment, 'if it can clearly appear that this medicine and not the wound was the cause of his death, it seems it is not homicide; but

[39] The three senses are: (i) of a type sufficient to kill a normal person; (ii) very likely to kill *this* victim given the circumstances, including the likelihood of medical aid; (iii) in fact causing this victim's death. Above, pp. 241–2.
[40] Cf. *Walker* v. *State* (1902) 116 Ga. 537, 42 SE 787.
[41] pp. 235–49.

then it must appear clearly and certainly to be so'. (3) If a person receives a wound not in itself mortal and fever or gangrene sets in because of improper medical treatment or want of treatment, and death ensues, it is homicide. 'For that wound, though it were not the immediate cause of his death, yet it was the mediate cause thereof, and the fever or gangrene was the immediate cause of his death, yet the wound was the cause of the gangrene or fever and so, consequently, is *causa causati*.'[42]

A more modern version of the law on this subject is given by Stephen, who says,

A person is deemed to have committed homicide . . . (a) if he inflicts a bodily injury on another which occasions surgical or medical treatment, which causes death. In these cases it is immaterial whether the treatment was proper or mistaken, if it was employed in good faith and with common knowledge and skill, but the person inflicting the injury is not deemed to have caused the death if the treatment which was its immediate cause was not employed in good faith, or was employed without common knowledge or skill.[43]

We may gather from these two quotations that some doubt surrounds the effect of improper medical treatment on the responsibility of the accused person. Hale appears to draw a distinction between the case in which death ensues because of want of medical treatment and the case in which it ensues because 'the medicine and not the wound' is the cause of death. This might mean that the improper medical treatment negatives causal connection only when the victim would have died from the effect of the treatment when he did, irrespective of the fact that he had previously been wounded by the accused person, the case falling under the third group distinguished above. It is difficult to see how else we may interpret Hale's statement that it is not homicide if the 'medicine and not the wound' was the cause of death. On the other hand, Stephen appears to allow that treatment lacking in common knowledge and skill, though not sufficient to produce death without the previously inflicted wound, may negative causal connection. There may therefore have been a development of legal opinion in this respect during the last two and a half centuries.

If we turn to the cases we find that Stephen's opinion that improper or mistaken treatment employed in good faith and with common knowledge or skill does not negative causal connection is

42 Hale, *PC* i. 428. The reference is to the frequently cited maxim *causa causae est causa causati*.
43 *Digest of the Criminal Law*, art. 262: cf. Israel, Criminal Code Ordinance, s. 219(a).

in general followed. Thus in *R.* v. *McIntyre*[44] accused administered
a blow to the victim. This rendered a restorative necessary and in
taking the restorative the victim choked and died. The jury were
directed that if they found that the brandy went down the wrong
way and so caused her death they might find accused guilty of
homicide. Again, in *R.* v. *Pym*[45] accused wounded the victim in
a duel. Competent surgeons performed an operation which they
regarded as necessary but which was in fact unnecessary. The victim
died and it was held that evidence of the fact that the operation
was unnecessary was inadmissible. In *R.* v. *Forrest*[46] the victim was
wounded through the culpable negligence of accused and taken to
hospital where he contracted blood poisoning and died, the ward in
which he was treated being insufficiently ventilated. The wounds
would not in the absence of blood poisoning have caused death. The
accused was held guilty of manslaughter since the treatment given
had been 'in good faith with common knowledge and skill'.

But in *R.* v. *Jordan*[47] the Court of Criminal Appeal allowed an
appeal on the following facts. Accused inflicted a severe wound on
the victim, stabbing him in the stomach. He died shortly afterwards
of pneumonia and accused was convicted of murder. On appeal
medical evidence was given that the cause of death was the continued
administration of terramycin, after it had become known that the
patient was intolerant of it, and, since this evidence might have
influenced the verdict on the issue of causal connection, the conviction was quashed. This is in accordance with Stephen's view, on
the assumption that the mistake made amounted to lack of common
knowledge or skill.

The standard set by Stephen of 'common knowledge or skill'
appears to require proof of something more than ordinary negligence
in order that one who inflicts a wound may be relieved of liability
for homicide. As Perkins points out, improper medical treatment is
unfortunately entirely too frequent in human experience for it to be

[44] (1847) 2 Cox 379; *R.* v. *Burgess & McKenzie* [1928] 2 DLR 694; *Levy* v. *R.* (1949) 51 WALR 29.
[45] (1846) 1 Cox 339; *R.* v. *Davis* (1883) 15 Cox 174; *R.* v. *Evans & Gardiner (No. 2)* [1976] VR 523, 531; *People* v. *Paulson* (1967) 225 NE 2d 424; *State* v. *Edgerton* (1896) 69 NW 280 (Iowa); *Downing* v. *State* (1901) 39 SE 927 (Ga.); *State* v. *Pell* (1909) 119 NW 154, 158 (Iowa); *State* v. *Tomassi* (1950) 75 Atl. 2d 67 (Conn.); *State* v. *Little* (1961) 358 P. 2d 120 (Wash.); *Commonwealth* v. *Eisenhower* (1897) 37 Atl. 2d 521 (Pa.).
[46] (1886) 20 *South Australia LR* 78.
[47] [1956] *Crim. LR* 700; Glanville Williams, *Causation in Homicide,* [1957] *Crim. LR* 429, 510; A. V. Lansdown, 'Causation in Homicide', (1960) 77 SALJ 427, 'Again Causation in Homicide', (1962) 79 SALJ 137. Similar rulings: *R.* v. *Clark* (1842) 6 JP 138; *R.* v. *McIntyre* (1847) 2 Cox 379 (direction to jury). *Coffman* v. *Commonwealth* (1873) 73 Ky. 495; *R.* v. *Markuss* (1864) 4 F. & F. 356, 176 ER 598, 599. On this point *R.* v. *Pym* (1846) 1 Cox 339 must be regarded as overruled.

considered abnormal in the sense of extraordinary.[48] Perhaps 'gross' negligence best expresses Stephen's idea, though it cannot be said that the English decisions have echoed these words. A decision of the military appeal court, however, adopts the common-sense causal test by posing the question whether the original wound was still 'operating' at the time of death or was merely the 'setting' for another 'overwhelming' cause which made the first no more than 'part of the history'.[49] Most of the American authorities require at least gross negligence[50] to negative causal connection and the American view is in accordance with the standard accepted in the law of tort.[51] Of course, if the physician acts in bad faith or is intoxicated or if the victim consults a quack this will negative causal connection with the subsequent harm.[52]

Though Stephen does not distinguish between cases where the original wound was mortal and those where it was not, some cases do so.[53] In *Bush* v. *Commonwealth*[54] where the original wound was not mortal, it was said that the unskilful treatment does not relieve an accused person who has given a mortal wound of responsibility but may do so when the wound was not mortal. In *People* v. *Cook*[55] accused inflicted a dangerous wound on the victim but the death was immediately occasioned by an overdose of morphine. The jury were instructed that only if the wound was not in itself mortal and death was caused *solely* by the morphine must they acquit.[56] The direction was upheld on appeal since if the original wound were mortal 'grossly erroneous medical treatment' would not relieve from responsibility as 'there is no chance for the injured person to recover, and therefore the reason which permits the showing of death from medical treatment does not exist'. One American case extends this to the situation in which accused inflicts a dangerous, though not mortal wound, and the victim is negligently treated by the surgeon. If the victim dies accused is on this view guilty of homicide provided

[48] Perkins, *Criminal Law*, pp. 716-17.
[49] *R.* v. *Smith* [1959] 2 QB 35.
[50] *Parsons* v. *State* (1852) 21 Ala. 300; *McDaniel* v. *State* (1884) 76 Ala. 1; *Tibbs* v. *Commonwealth* (1910) 138 Ky. 558, 128 SW 871; *People* v. *Townsend* (1921) 214 Mich. 267, 269, 183 NW 177, 181. This is statutory in Texas: *McMillan* v. *State* (1910) 126 SW 875.
[51] Above, pp. 152, 184.
[52] Perkins, *Criminal Law*, p. 719.
[53] *R.* v. *McIntyre* (1847) 2 Cox 379. This distinction is not adverted to in *R.* v. *Jordan* [1956] *Crim. LR* 700 and, with the increasing perfection of surgery and medicine, wounds of a sort which would formerly have been mortal may be so no longer.
[54] (1880) 78 Ky. 268; *Hall* v. *State* (1928) 159 NE 420, 426 (Ind.).
[55] (1878) 39 Mich. 236.
[56] This must mean 'if the morphine was sufficient to kill apart from the prior wound'.

that the original wound 'contributed' to the death, viz. the medical negligence would not have killed apart from the first wound.[57]

The result of these cases seems to be as follows. Where, as in England, the distinction between mortal wounds and others is not insisted on, subsequent negligent treatment if lacking in 'common knowledge or skill' may relieve accused of further liability even if it is not of a character sufficient without the wound to cause death and *a fortiori* if it is. Where the distinction is drawn, if the original wound is mortal no subsequent negligence relieves accused of responsibility for homicide. If it is not mortal though 'dangerous' some authorities allow subsequent negligence to relieve only if it is of a character sufficient to have killed the victim independently of the wound.

It may be asked how far the criminal law on the subject of improper medical treatment differs from the civil law in these cases. If Stephen's statement concerning lack of common knowledge and skill is taken as correct and as laying down that only gross negligence in treatment will negative causal connection, it follows that the same standard is accepted in civil and criminal law. The Texas Penal Code lays down that 'if such injury [inflicted by accused] be the cause of death, without its appearing that there has been any gross neglect or manifestly improper treatment of the person injured, it is homicide'.[58] This, if it correctly states the common law,[59] appears very similar to the generally accepted principle of civil law that only an extraordinary medical mistake negatives causal connection.[60] The Texas law may, however, go further than common law decisions in allowing gross medical mistreatment to relieve accused of liability for homicide even when the wound inflicted was mortal. At most, therefore, the distinction between criminal and civil law in this area is that in criminal law as opposed to civil law it *may* be sufficient for homicide that accused did something which would have caused the victim's death in the absence of medical treament, even though it was in fact gross mistreatment which caused the death.

Want of proper care by victim. A second group of difficulties is concerned with the failure of the victim to take proper care of his injuries. On this, it will be remembered, Hale's view was that the

[57] *State* v. *Snider* (1918) 81 W. Va. 522, 94 SE 981. The same result is prescribed when the wound is 'dangerous' by New Zealand Crimes Act 1961, s. 166; Canadian Criminal Code.

[58] Texas Penal Code Ann., art. 1202. 'If the deceased is negligent in caring for himself after receiving injury, or if his physicians or others so grossly mistreat him as to cause his death, then the defendant is not responsible, under the law of this state, for the death of the deceased.' *Noble* v. *State* (1908) 54 Tex. Cr. 436, 113 SW 281, 283.

[59] Which is denied by G.C.T. in 31 *Mich. LR* 659, 679 n.: but see Wharton, *Criminal Law*, i. 257, 261.

[60] *Purchase* v. *Seelye* (1918) 231 Mass. 434, 121 NE 413, 8 ALR 503. *Restatement of Torts*, s. 457.

358   THE COMMON LAW

'unruly conduct of the patient' is no defence to a charge of homicide.[61] Stephen says, 'If [accused] inflicts a bodily injury on another, which would not have caused death if the injured person had submitted to proper surgical or medical treatment, or had observed proper precautions as to his mode of living',[62] accused is deemed to have committed homicide if death ensues. This was the view adopted in *R. v. Wall*[63] where accused, the governor of a prison, illegally flogged the victim who, however, in defiance of orders but in accordance with the general practice in the military hospital to which he was taken, drank spirits to excess after the flogging, a fact which contributed to his early death. It was held that the death was nevertheless the consequence of the illegal flogging. Courts are reluctant to allow that a failure on the part of the victim to observe proper precautions for his own health negatives causal connection or even that it may have hastened death. In *Levy*[64] the facts of which have already been noted, the victim left hospital against the advice of his doctors for a period of four hours while undergoing treatment. The court held that there was no evidence that his absence contributed to his death or affected his chances of recovery. On the other hand, it was held in an American case that the failure of the victim to observe proper precautions might negative causal connection. In this case[65] accused, who was drunk, was resisting arrest with some violence. The victim took hold of him to assist in the arrest, though he (the victim) knew that he had a serious heart disease and had remarked a few hours previously that he was feeling ill. Accused did not strike deceased, who shortly afterwards died; the medical evidence was that his death was due to dilation of the heart, accelerated by the physical exercise and excitement of taking part in the arrest.

The court gave two reasons for holding that accused was not guilty of manslaughter on these facts. The first was that when death eventuates without a blow or direct physical injury it is said to be caused by the wrongful act only if it is the 'probable and natural consequence' of the unlawful act of the accused. The second was that deceased's 'intervening act in rolling and tumbling in pain on the court house yard, instead of lying quiet and still, was probably as much responsible for his ensuing death as was the initial excitement

---

[61] *R. v. Rew* (1662) Kelyng 26, 84 ER 1066. Cf. *R. v. Reading* (1661) 1 Keb. 17, 83 ER 704.
[62] Art. 262 (*b*).
[63] (1802) 28 St. Tr. 51.
[64] *Levy v. R.* (1949) 51 WALR 29 (above, p. 342). Cf. *Bowles v. State* (1877) 58 Ala. 335 (riding over rough road and eating sweet potatoes contrary to doctor's orders does not negative causal connection between shooting and death); *Pyles v. State* (1954) 78 So. 813, 815; *State v. Johnson* (1934) 36 Del. 341, 175 Atl. 669.
[65] *Hubbard v. Commonwealth* (1947) 304 Ky. 818, 202 SW 2d 634.

caused by the conduct of the accused'.[66] This suggests that the neglect of proper precautions may on occasion amount to a factor negativing causal connection. Perhaps a distinction should be drawn between extraordinary neglect on the victim's part to attend to his wounds[67] or to follow the prescribed treatment and mere ordinary negligence which in a civil case would amount to contributory negligence or failure to mitigate the harm. If this view were adopted, gross neglect on the victim's part, like gross neglect on the part of the doctor, would negative causal connection in both civil and criminal law, at least if the original injury were not mortal. If it was mortal, there is American authority to suggest that the courts will be reluctant to permit a criminal jury to decide that any degree of want of care on the part of the victim will relieve defendant of responsibility for homicide. On Stephen's still stricter view, even gross negligence, recklessness, or perhaps suicide by failure to attend to wounds will not exonerate the wounder from criminal liability for killing, whether the wound was mortal or not. Stephen's view is plainly a departure from the causal principles adopted in this connection in tort law, and can only be upheld on a certain view of penal policy. This view would place on the wrongdoer the risk of death which would not have occurred but for the wounding, even though in general risk liability has but little place in criminal law.

Refusal of treatment. A third problem concerns the refusal of the victim to undergo treatment. The views of Stephen on this were set out above.[68] Clearly the solution of this problem must be on lines similar to the cases where accused fails to take precautions for his own recovery. In *R. v. Holland*[69] accused waylaid the victim and assaulted him, severely cutting one of his fingers. The surgeon advised the victim to have his finger amputated, telling him that unless it were amputated his life would be in great danger; but the victim refused to allow amputation. An infection set in which ultimately caused death. Nevertheless the jury were held to have been properly directed that the death was the consequence of the original assault by accused, who was found guilty of murder. It might appear that this is inconsistent with certain decisions in civil law and more particularly with the doctrine, developed by the courts in their interpretation of the Workmen's Compensation Acts, that the unreasonable refusal of the victim of an industrial accident to undergo proper medical treatment bars his claim for compensation under

[66] *Hubbard* v. *Commonwealth* above, *per* Stanley, Commissioner.
[67] *R. v. Flynn* (1868) 16 WR 319 (CCR Ir.).
[68] pp. 358.
[69] (1841) 2 Moo. and R. 351; *R. v. Mubila*, 1956 (1) SA 31 (SR); *Franklin v. State* (1899) 51 SW 951.

that Act.[70] This doctrine was characterized by Lord Wright as a piece of judicial legislation:[71] 'I find it not very logical to say that the workman's refusal breaks the chain of causality between the accident and the incapacity. On the contrary, *effects* of the accident still remain.' But the view that, if incapacity is 'due to' the workman's unreasonable refusal to undergo an operation, it does not 'result'[72] from the original accident appears quite consistent with causal principles; for if a workman refuses treatment from some defect of moral courage or because he is content to put up with the disablement[73] his conduct amounts either to voluntarily allowing the disablement to continue or to behaviour so 'unreasonable' or 'unnatural' as to negative causal connection with it. Of course, the matter is one of degree and it would be in accordance with the spirit of the statute not to be overexacting in considering whether the workman's conduct was unreasonable.[74] Lord Wright's view illustrates the need to distinguish between 'results' and 'effects', for the *effects* of the injury *on* the workman, viz. the changes it produced in his body, do indeed continue despite his unreasonable refusal to undergo an operation; but *results* carry different limitations from *effects* and where, as here, 'result' is used, this may prevent the disability being attributed to the original injury.

This doctrine of civil law is not necessarily inconsistent with modern criminal law, for it must be remembered that since the decision in *Holland*,[75] medical science has advanced greatly and a refusal to undergo an operation which may have appeared obstinate but not unreasonable or reckless in 1841 might at the present day be treated by the courts in a different light.

R. v. *Blaue*[76] appears, however, to reject the idea of an evolution in this regard since 1841. In that case accused inflicted four serious stab wounds on deceased, one of which pierced her lung. Deceased was a Jehovah's witness and for that reason refused a blood transfusion, though she knew that without it she would die, as she did. The jury were directed on these facts to find causation proved, and

70 *Warncken* v. *Moreland & Son* [1909] 1 KB 184, 189; *Cant* v. *Fife Coal Co.* [1921] SC (HL) 15; *Fyfe* v. *Fife Coal Co.* [1927] SC (HL) 103; *Steele* v. *Robert George* [1942] AC 497; *Matters* v. *Baker* [1951] SASR 91. *McAuley* v. *London Transport* [1957] 2 Ll. LR 500.

71 *Steele* v. *Robert George* [1942] AC 497, 503. Our italics. *Rothwell* v. *Caverswall Stone Co.* [1944] 2 All ER 350, 355.

72 Workmen's Compensation Act, 1925, s. 9(1).

73 *Steele* v. *Robert George* [1942] AC 497, 499, *per* Simon LC.

74 Perhaps this was Lord Wright's substantial point for he goes on to point out that the operation may not be successful and that the workman's physical or mental idiosyncrasies should be taken into account (sc. in judging whether his conduct was reasonable).

75 (1841) 2 Moo. and R. 351.

76 [1975] 3 All ER 446 (CA).

the direction was upheld on appeal. The appeal court pointed out that the physical cause of death was the bleeding, which was in turn caused by the stab wound, not by any decision of deceased. By what standard, the court asked, could the law judge whether her decision to refuse a blood transfusion was unreasonable? It was the policy of the law that those who use violence on others must take their victims as they find them. It seems to us that the decision in this case is correct but the reasoning unsatisfactory. The fact that the physical process started by accused (bleeding) continued up to the moment of death is not conclusive. What if the victim had called for a blood transfusion and the doctor had refused to administer one, saying that he preferred to play a round of golf, so that the victim died? In that case, too, the bleeding would have continued until death but death would surely have been caused by the doctor's callousness, not the original wound.

Again we can decide whether the victim's refusal of treatment is reasonable without deciding whether any particular religious belief is a rational one. The question is not whether it is reasonable, as in this case, to believe that blood transfusion is wrong, but whether a person whose life is in danger can reasonably be expected to abandon a firmly held religious belief. The answer must surely be no. An element of legal policy certainly enters into such a judgment; in a society which attached little value to conscience a different judgment might be reached. But the question to be decided is whether the decision to refuse treatment is not merely deliberate and informed (as it clearly was in the *Blaue* case) but also a free one. In view of the high value attached in our society to matters of conscience, the victim, though free to accept any belief she wished, is not thereafter free to abandon her chosen belief merely because she finds herself in a situation in which her life may otherwise be in danger. So it was not her free act to refuse a transfusion.

This is the most satisfactory ground on which to justify the *Blaue* decision. To point to the victim's belief as something which the wrongdoer must 'take as he finds it', like a tendency to bleed, is less satisfactory. It suggests that her belief is a psychological quirk. The court's argument would be appropriate, on the other hand, in a case where mental derangement on the victim's part led her to refuse treatment.

Despite *R. v. Blaue*, therefore, there remains a case for the proposition that an unreasonable refusal of treatment may negative causal connection between the infliction of a wound and the death which the treatment would have prevented. And, clearly, the law should be the same as regards the victim's gross neglect to attend to his wounds and his unreasonable refusal of treatment. On the other hand, it is clear that the idea that one who deliberately wounds another takes on himself the risk of death from that wound, whatever the reason for the failure to treat it properly, has an attraction which may be only partly penal in origin. It seems to draw, in addition, on the primitive idea that an omission to treat or cure, like the failure to turn off a tap, cannot be called a cause of the death or flooding in the same sense as the infliction of the wound or the original turning on of the tap.[77]

Our survey of the place of doctor's and victim's negligence in the law of homicide, where differences of policy between civil and criminal law might be expected to make themselves felt, yields a meagre harvest.

(i) On Stephen's view, which has some modern support, there is no difference between civil and criminal law as regards the effect of medical negligence: in each case gross negligence ('want of common knowledge or skill') is required to negative responsibility for death.

(ii) If Stephen's view is accepted there is a clear difference between civil and criminal law so far as the victim's failure to attend to his wounds or undergo medical treatment is concerned. But is is questionable how far the older authorities on this point are still good law.

(iii) Where the original wound is 'mortal' or even merely 'dangerous' there is a tendency in the American cases not to allow subsequent negligence on the part of either doctor or victim to negative liability for homicide. This tendency is not, however, necessarily confined to criminal law; a similar notion was seen at work in Chapter VII in civil law, where there is an increasing tendency to impose on a wrongdoer liability for harm occasioned by his conduct even if it comes about through a voluntary intervention or some abnormal conjunction of events.[78] The areas in which civil law has imposed risk liability of this sort are not, of course, the same as in criminal law. Intervening medical malpractice is not, for example, one of them. What this shows is not that the notion of cause has different meanings in civil and criminal law but that the cases in which responsibility is imposed for occasioning as opposed to causing harm depend on the legal policy appropriate to the particular branch of the law.

---

[77] That there is no fundamental difference between acts and omission in this regard is pointed out in *R. v. Evans & Gardiner (No. 2)* [1976] VR 517, 528.
[78] Above, pp. 194–204.

XIII

CRIMINAL LAW: CAUSING, INDUCING, PERMITTING, HELPING OTHERS TO ACT

THIS chapter deals with the place in the criminal law of those relationships which we have termed interpersonal transactions. These are relevant whenever causing, inducing, helping, encouraging, or permitting others to act is a sufficient ground for criminal responsibility, even though the statutory or common law rule under which the liability arises is not expressly formulated in these terms.

It is convenient to deal separately in criminal law with those cases where the person who induces or permits or helps another to do harm is regarded as the principal offender and those where he is regarded as a mere participant in the wrong committed by another.

The first group includes those cases where accused is liable as a principal offender for causing harm through an innocent or irresponsible agent, and the numerous statutory offences which forbid a person to 'cause', 'suffer', 'permit', or 'allow' another to do some specified act. In the second group we deal with the various sorts of participation in crimes committed by others.

I. THE PRINCIPAL OFFENDER

Inducing Another to do Harm

Homicide. Criminal prohibitions, common law or statutory, are normally formulated as forbidding some act such as 'killing' or 'causing death'. The problem considered here is to what extent such forms of expression cover the act of an accused person who brings about death, etc. by inducing another to act in a certain way. Of course the central case of homicide which satisfies the definition of 'causing death' is one where death is brought about without the intervention of another person, e.g. by shooting. Here the 'causal connection' traceable from the act to the harm is of the simplest kind, like that between two physical events. But it is also clear that when offences are defined either by simple verbs (like 'killing') or in causal terms ('causing death') the required causal connection exists in certain cases where the harm is brought about by the act of another, viz. where it can be said that accused caused the second act.

This is the case only when accused intends the intervening actor to do what he does and the intervening actor's conduct is not wholly voluntary. Hence, a person may be guilty of homicide by inducing another to kill or to do an act dangerous to life which in fact results in death, if the means used amount to coercion, deceit, or the exercise of authority; but not if mere persuasion of an adult responsible person is employed, of if accused's conduct operates, without his intending it, as a reason for the other's act. In a similar way, where suicide is not a crime, a defendant will be liable for homicide by causing a person to commit suicide only when he purposely does so by force, duress, or deception.[1]

It would therefore be homicide to induce another to jump out of a high window by threats of force, if the jump resulted in death, or to induce another by a lie to take a path in a fog leading over the edge of a cliff,[2] or to order an inferior to do a specifically dangerous act, in the absence of justification, which results in the inferior's or another's death, or for a husband to hit his wife and tell her to jump in the river, knowing she cannot swim, so that when she does as he says she drowns.[3] In *U.S.* v. *Freeman*[4] the master of a ship ordered a seaman in weak health to go aloft; the seaman complied, fell, and was drowned. It was held that the jury might rightly convict the master of manslaughter. On the other hand merely to advise another to kill himself would not make accused the principal offender on a charge of murder if the advice was taken; hence, where suicide is not a crime, the giving of such advice will not entail liability for homicide either as principal or as participant.[5] 'If, however, as in England, where suicide is not a crime, statute creates an offence of aiding, abetting, counselling, or procuring the suicide of another, the person who advises another to commit suicide may be liable for that offence.'[6]

Deception. In the crime of obtaining the ownership, possession, or control of property by deception[7] it is implied by the use of the word 'obtains' that the victim must have been induced by the pretence to part with his property. Here, though the act of the victim is not voluntary in the full sense, he does at least intend to transfer the

---

1 American Model Penal Code, s. 210. 5.
2 Glanville Williams, [1957] Crim. LR 519.
3 *State* v. *Myers* (1951) 7 NJ 465, 81 Atl. 2d 710.
4 (1827) 4 Mason 505.
5 *R.* v. *Nbakwa*, 1956 (2) SA 557 (SR). Above, pp. 328–9.
6 Suicide Act 1961, s. 2.
7 Theft Act 1968, s. 15.

ownership of the thing in question; if the means used were not false statements but threats of force the crime would be larceny by intimidation.

In order to constitute an obtaining by deception accused must in the first place have induced the prosecutor to believe what he said. For instance, a person cannot be convicted of obtaining property by deception if the prosecutor knew the truth of the alleged deception. 'It is abundantly clear that a person cannot be convicted of the offence of obtaining goods or money by false pretences[8] unless the mind of the prosecutor has been misled by the false pretence, and he has been induced to part with his property thereby.'[9]

The principle may be illustrated from *R. v. Mills*.[10] Accused was employed to cut chaff at 2*d*. per fan. He stated that he had cut sixty-three fans. The prosecutor, his employer, knew that this statement was untrue because he had seen accused add eighteen fans of cut chaff to the heap, but he paid for the sixty-three fans nevertheless. The court held that accused could not be convicted of obtaining payment for the extra eighteen fans by false pretences. In such a case the victim has, of course, made the payment voluntarily, but that is not the essential point. The prosecution fails because the false pretence did not induce a mistake.

In the second place the false belief must be at least part[11] of the reason for making the payment. If the victim believes the statement but is not influenced by it in making the payment accused has not obtained the money by deception. Whether the deception acted on the mind of the person to whom it was addressed should in the ordinary way be proved by direct evidence, i.e. by asking him his reason for parting with the property.[12] If there is no direct evidence it is sometimes possible to infer that the reason for doing so could only have been the deception,[13] but where there is another possible explanation, indirect evidence is not sufficient.[14] The principle that it is sufficient for liability to show that the payment was made because of the false representation may, however, be qualified in special

[8] The crime of obtaining property by false pretences was the forerunner of the modern crime of obtaining property by deception. So far as causal connection is concerned, the same principles apply.

[9] *R. v. Light* (1915) 11 CAR 111, 113 *per* Rowlatt J. The court in this case went on to decide that this principle does not apply to an attempt to obtain money by false pretences. Cf. *R. v. Roebuck* (1856) 7 Cox CC 126; *R. v. Hensler* (1870) 11 Cox 570; *R. v. Dale* (1836) 7 C. & P. 352; *R. v. Bulmer* (1864) 9 Cox CC 492; *R. v. MacDonald* (1947) 88 Can. CC 358, 19 MPR 237 (NS). Contrast *R. v. Finch* (1908) 72 JP 102; *R. v. Burton* (1886) 16 Cox CC 62; *R. v. Perera* [1907] VR 240.

[10] (1857) Dears and B. 205; 26 LJMC 79.

[11] Not necessarily the whole. *R. v. English* (1872) 12 Cox CC 171; *R. v. Lince* (1873) 12 Cox CC 451.

[12] *R. v. Laverty* [1970] 3 All ER 432, 433.

[13] *R. v. Sullivan* (1945) 30 CAR 132.

[14] *R. v. Laverty* [1970] 3 All ER 432.

cases where the party deceived had a duty to scrutinize the representation made to him and to reach an independent conclusion. These conditions are perhaps not satisfied in the case of an official or tribunal which reaches decisions according to a routine. Thus in *R. v. Cooke*[15] the registrar of the borough of Nottingham was charged with obtaining money from the Treasury by a false return of fees due. He objected that the commissioners of the Treasury were acting in a quasi-judicial role in deciding whether to pay the fees. Coleridge J. dismissed this argument, saying 'The return and minute are mere procedure and matter of regulation'.

The question whether one who knowingly gives false evidence at a murder trial with intent to procure the conviction and execution of the accused is guilty of murder, if he succeeds, might appear to involve this point. It has been inferred from the discontinuance of proceedings in the case of *Macdaniel*[16] and the failure to prosecute Titus Oates for murder that no such charge would lie; the argument has been used that the cause of death is the acceptance of the perjured evidence by the jury. But neither the jury nor the judge exercises a discretion and their verdict and sentence cannot properly be likened to the decision of the manager of a mental asylum to retain an inmate in custody, which was held in civil law to negative causal connection because it is not really the finding of a fact but the exercise of an independent discretion.[17]

'*Causing*' *others to act: miscellaneous statutory offences.* The verb 'to cause' is sometimes met in civil law but much more frequently in statutes creating criminal offences. The question to be discussed is whether any useful guidance can be given about the interpretation of 'to cause' in such contexts. There is, of course, a danger in generalizations about statutory interpretation which attempt to derive uniform principles from a variety of statutes enacted at different times with different objects in view. It must be remembered therefore that the principles of interpretation we are here suggesting are not intended to be rigid. They are open, no doubt, to modification in the light of the circumstances in which the statute was enacted or the purposes which it had in view.

Dr J. Ll. J. Edwards in his valuable work '*Mens Rea*' *in Statutory Offences*[18] has dealt in some detail with the interpretation of 'causing' in criminal statutes.[19] His point of view, however, is somewhat different from our own, for he has concentrated upon the extent to

15 (1852) 1 F. & F. 64, 175 ER 627.
16 (1755) 19 St. Tr. 746, 810–14; 1 Leach 44.
17 *Harnett* v. *Bond* [1924] 2 KB 517; [1925] AC 669. Above, pp. 159–60. For a discussion of cases where, despite the false pretence, accused is alleged to have earned the money by his own skill or effort see above, pp. 338–40.
18 1955.
19 Edwards, op. cit., chap. 6.

which the doctrine of *mens rea*, and particularly the requirement that accused shall have known all the elements of the offence alleged to have been committed, is implied by the use by the legislature of the verb 'to cause'. It may be that this concentration upon the element of *mens rea* tends to obscure the existence of other problems of interpretation. Thus, in every criminal offence, apart from cases of strict liability, the prosecution must prove not merely the existence of *mens rea* but also that accused did the act (in this case 'causing' another to do something) forbidden by law. Our procedure will therefore involve a separate treatment of these two elements, with a particular emphasis upon that type of *actus reus* which consists in 'causing' another to do an act.

Edwards's main conclusions about 'causing' are two. In the first place he distinguishes between an alleged sense of 'causing' which is synonymous with instigation in the sense of commanding, counselling, or procuring[20] the commission by a principal offender of a crime and a sense in which it has an independent meaning. It would appear, however, that 'causing' cannot ever be identified with 'counselling', 'commanding', and 'procuring' by an instigator, since the notion of 'causing' another to act implies that the act of the person 'caused' to behave in a particular way is less than fully voluntary;[21] whereas the notions of 'counselling' and 'procuring' are consistent, as is shown below,[22] with the act of the principal being fully voluntary. The correct proposition would be, rather, that 'causing' a person to act refers to a species of the genus 'inducing' or 'instigating', viz. to those cases where accused makes use of threats, lies, or authority to induce the second actor to act in a particular way and that 'counselling' is another species.

Edwards's second main doctrine is that the element of knowledge is implied when the legislature uses the word 'causing' and that therefore, despite some cases which might appear to the contrary, it is a principle of interpretation that, when the legislature makes responsibility dependent upon the accused having 'caused' something, the prosecution must normally show that the accused knew of the elements of the offence. 'A person shall be deemed to have caused or encouraged the unlawful carnal knowledge of a girl under sixteen years if he has knowingly allowed the girl to consort with any prostitute.'[23] 'Here in the clearest possible terms', says Edwards, 'is an acknowledgment by the legislature that guilty knowledge is

20 Below, p. 380.
21 *R.* v. *Wilson* (1856) 26 LJMC 18, is against this view. Edwards also mentions 'encouraging', which is slightly different.
22 pp. 380 ff.
23 Children Act, 1908, s. 17(2).

the minimum requirement of such an offence based on "causing".'[24] However, the enactment quoted does not lead to the conclusion which Edwards draws from it, since it refers merely to a case in which the legislature *deems* accused to have caused or encouraged something. This might rather be used as an argument that, had the legislature not so deemed, 'knowingly allowing' by itself would not have been sufficient to support a charge of 'causing' the unlawful carnal knowledge mentioned in the section: still less does it show that knowledge is a *necessary* element in 'causing' another to do an act.

Edwards, in developing his doctrine, does not distinguish between causing others to act and causing harm to occur, but to understand the case law on 'causing' it is necessary to bear two preliminary points in mind. First, the question whether *A caused* some act to be done is not the same as the question whether some act of *A* was the cause of something happening. Important differences exist, as explained in Chapter II, between cases of causing persons to act by providing motives or reasons, and cases of causing things to happen. In particular, an element of intention (intending the other to act in a specified way) is essential if one person is to be said to 'cause' another to act but not when he is said to cause some event to happen. This is, however, not an independent legal requirement of a certain state of mind in the accused person, but part of the meaning of 'causing' in the sense of providing a reason for the non-voluntary act of another.

When 'causing' is forbidden. We now consider separately those statutes in which accused is forbidden to cause a certain act and those in which he is enjoined to cause it. As to the first, it is convenient to consider in turn the elements of *mens rea* and *actus reus* (or state of affairs forbidden by law).[25] A full discussion of the required mental element would be outside our scope, but it is not clear that knowledge on the part of accused of all the elements of the forbidden state of affairs is essential in order that he may be said unlawfully to have caused it. Edwards himself cites some examples of this:[26] thus, the legislature has used the phrases 'knowingly causes or procures',[27] 'wilfully causing or knowingly suffering',[28] 'knowingly or wilfully causes or procures',[29] 'negligently causes'.[30] These examples suggest that there may be cases of 'causing' things to happen or persons to

---

24 Edwards, op. cit., p. 147. Cf. pp. 137, 143.
25 *Actus reus, Tatbestand*; we know of no convenient English phrase for this notion: perhaps 'proscribed state of affairs' is the best.
26 Op. cit., p. 142.
27 Ready Money Football Betting Act, 1920, s. 1.
28 Thames Conservancy Act, 1932, s. 123.
29 Midwives Act, 1951, s. 15(4).
30 Water Act, 1945, sch. 3, pt. 13, cl. 64(1).

act which are consistent with accused's not knowing all the elements of the offence. It seems clear that in cases of causing things to happen, at least, Edwards's doctrine is wrong. For instance, in *Moses* v. *Midland Railway*[31] the court had to consider an Act which penalizes every person who 'causes to flow' into any waters containing salmon any poisonous matter.[32] In construing this section Avory J. said that it was not necessary to show that accused had intentionally caused the flow to take place since this was a case of absolute prohibition, but it would be a defence to show that the accused did not know of *and* could not reasonably have prevented the escape. Hence he would have been prepared to convict a defendant under this section although he did not know of the escape of the poisonous matter, provided he could have prevented it. In *Alphacell* v. *Woodward*[33] the House of Lords, emphasizing that 'to cause' must be given a common-sense meaning, adopted a similar view. There defendants conducted polluted water to a settling tank which communicated with the river. If the pumps worked properly the water was recycled, but they did not, and the polluted water entered the river. It was held that defendants had caused the water to enter the river, though they did not intend this nor did they know of its entry. They had designed the scheme and operated it by conducting the water to the tanks. This was not like a previous case[34] in which defendants stored fuel oil near a river but the oil entered the river only because some unknown person opened a valve. Here there was no such intervening act of a third party or of God. A statute of this sort therefore imposes strict liability for causing harm, which is excluded if it can be shown that harm was caused not by defendant's conduct but something else which negatives causal connection.[35]

Whether the same is true of causing others to act is by no means clear; here Edwards's doctrine is more plausible. Yet in *Lewis*[36] accused was convicted of 'causing poison to be taken' when he left sugar containing corrosive sublimate for a Mrs Daws, but the shopkeeper with whom she left it delivered it by mistake to Mrs Davis, who took it and became ill. Here accused did not know the identity of the person to whom the poison was mistakenly delivered. Again, in an Australian case,[37] accused was convicted of contravening a by-law that 'no person shall cause to be sold . . . adulterated,

---

[31] (1915) 113 LTR 451.
[32] Salmon Fisheries Act, 1861, s. 5. A case of causing something to happen, not of causing another to act.
[33] [1972] AC 824.
[34] *Impress (Worcester)* v. *Rees* [1971] 2 All ER 357.
[35] Preface, pp. xliv–xlv.
[36] (1833) 6 C. & P. 161.
[37] *Shakespeare* v. *Taylor* (1890) 24 South Australia LR 51.

unwholesome or diluted milk' when he knew nothing of the adultera-
tion of the milk by his servant.

Prima facie Edwards's doctrine that the use of the word 'cause' in
statutes implies that accused must have intended or known of all the
elements of the offence is in accordance with the natural meaning of
the word so far as causing others to act is concerned. Thus, one
would not, perhaps, outside the law, be said to have made a person
drive without a licence if one merely ordered him to drive thinking
that he had a licence when in fact he had not. But it is not clear that
the law requires such detailed knowledge; indeed its approach to
these problems may be similar to that employed when the question
is whether a person accused of a statutory offence can be convicted
if he lacked knowledge of some elements defining the offence.[38]

'Causing' and omissions. If we now turn to consider the *actus reus*
or forbidden state of affairs we find that it has often been stated that
to 'cause' another to act implies a positive act on the part of accused
and that the difference between 'causing' and 'permitting' another's
act lies precisely in the distinction between act and omission.

It is, however, very doubtful whether the proposed distinction is
valid. It seems that an omission might, though rarely, be held to
'cause another' to act. Suppose *A* threatens that unless *B* or *C* reveals
a certain secret he will shoot *D*. *B* remains silent; *C* then reveals the
secret. *B*'s silence (an omission to speak) might well be said to have
'caused' *C* to speak.[39] This suggests that in those rare cases where
an omission can be regarded as putting pressure on another to act
an omission might properly be said to 'cause' the other's action. If
this is correct the difference between 'causing' and 'permitting' is not
that between act and omission but between compelling another to
act and leaving him free to choose while withdrawing an obstacle
should he make a certain choice.

There are, however, some decisions which suggest a distinction
between acts and omissions. Thus,[40] one of two brothers purchased
a van but took out an insurance policy in the name of the other
brother. While driving the van he killed a person, whose widow sued
on the ground that the brother in whose name the policy stood had
'caused or permitted' the owner of the van to drive without an
insurance policy. The court held that the brother in whose name the
policy stood had not caused the driving, since all he had done was to
stand by with knowledge that his brother was making an inaccurate
statement.[41] McKinnon LJ said that defendant might be said to have

---

[38] e.g. *R.* v. *Prince* (1875) LR 2 CCR 154.
[39] We are indebted to the late professor Sir Rupert Cross for this example. Cf.
James v. *Smee* [1955] 1 QB 78, 97 *per* Slade J. dissenting.
[40] *Goodbarne* v. *Buck* [1940] 1 KB 771. A civil case.
[41] Road Traffic Act, 1930, s. 35(1). On the 'permitting' point see below, p. 377.

assisted or permitted the false statements to be made but could not be said to have caused the driving. In *Korten* v. *West Sussex C.C.*[42] it was held that the accused, managing director of a firm, could not be held to have 'caused' an invoice sent out by the servant of the firm to be false, when he had taken no active part in the matter, but might be convicted of having 'permitted' this to occur.[43] This is also the view taken by Edwards who, in discussing the case of *Hardcastle* v *Bielby*,[44] draws attention to the distinction between 'causing' a heap of stones to be laid upon the highway and 'allowing' it to remain there at night, to the danger of a person passing thereon. The first, it was held, requires proof that the stones were laid by the authority of the accused: 'the laying of the stones must be proved to have been the act of the surveyor'.[45] On the other hand, allowing the stones to remain would require no positive act.

It should be noted that the case may be one of causing others to act though the relevant verb is in the passive voice. The statute may, for instance, say that the accused shall not 'cause matter to be printed'.[46] This, however, must be interpreted as a case of causing others to act, since it is impossible for matter to be printed except through human agency.

Where criminal responsibility depends on 'causing' others to act[47] there are three elements which the prosecution must prove. First, the act of accused must be a part of the reason for the act of the person 'caused' to behave in a particular way.[48] Secondly, accused is only held to have caused another to act if he makes use of threats, lies, or the exercise of authority and thereby induces the second to act. Numerous dicta call attention to this view. Thus, Lord Goddard CJ has said of a statutory provision forbidding a person to 'cause' another to use a motor vehicle on a road in a defective condition, '"causes" involves a person who has authority to do so ordering or directing another person to use [the vehicle]'.[49] Hence, a garage proprietor who had returned a motor vehicle to a customer in a defective condition was acquitted under this section since he had no authority over the customer, who was ignorant of the defect. Similarly, in the interpretation of the insurance provisions of the Road

---

[42] (1903) 88 LTR 466.
[43] See also *McLeod* v. *Buchanan* [1940] 2 All ER 179; *Moses* v. *Midland Railway* (1915) 113 LTR 451; *R.* v. *Chainey* [1914] 1 KB 137; *Rushton* v. *Martin* [1952] WN 258.
[44] [1892] 1 QB 709.
[45] Ibid., p. 712, *per* Collins J.
[46] Copyright Act, 1842, s. 15.
[47] *Contra* in cases of causing things to happen. *Kirkheaton Local Board* v. *Ainley* [1892] 2 QB 274; *Butterworth* v. *West Riding of Yorkshire Rivers Board* [1909] AC 45, 53.
[48] Above, p. 54.
[49] *Shave* v. *Rosner* [1954] 2 QB 113, 116.

372   THE COMMON LAW

Traffic Act, it has been held that a person who is not the owner of a
car and has no right of control over it cannot be said to have 'caused'
another to use the car without an insurance policy being in force.[50]
Again, it has been decided that when a publisher employed defendants to print a book containing passages which infringed plaintiff's
copyright, and defendants were later released by the publisher from
their contract, so that the remainder of the printing, including the
offending passages, was done elsewhere, defendants could not be
held to have 'printed' the offending matter nor to have 'caused' it to
be printed by agreeing to the release. Once they had been released
from their contract they had no control over the printing.[51]

It is sufficient that accused had legal control over the intermediary.
In one case, when a husband had covenanted to be liable for acts to
be done by him or for such as he should 'cause or procure to be
done' the court held that the covenant applied only to the acts of
persons who were bound to obey his order, like trustees for him.[52]
'To cause the user involves some express or positive mandate from
the person causing to the other person, or some authority from the
former to the latter arising in the circumstances of the case'.[53] In this
way Lord Wright summarized the interpretation of the word 'causes'
for purposes of motor insurance under the Road Traffic Act.

Occasionally, however, an accused person has been held to have
caused another to act without having authority or control over the
intermediary or using threats or lies. In R. v. Wilson[54] accused was
charged with 'causing' a noxious thing to be taken by a woman with
intent to procure a miscarriage.[55] She gave mercury to the woman
and advised her to take half of it in a glass of gin, which she did,
thereby making herself very ill. It was held that accused could be
convicted under this section, despite the argument of her counsel
that as she had merely been advising the woman she could not be
said to have 'caused' her to take the mercury. Pollock CB said, 'We
are all of opinion that this was a "causing to be taken" within the
statute and that the conviction is right.'[56] This decision is at variance
with the ordinarily understood meaning of 'to cause', which is not
consistent with the mere giving of advice unaccompanied by threats,
lies, or commands. Perhaps the court thought there was an element
of deceit in the conduct of accused. In another case it was held that

50 *Goodbarne* v. *Buck* [1940] 1 KB 771.
51 *Kelly's Directories* v. *Gavin & Lloyds* [1901] 2 Ch. 63. See also *Hardcastle* v.
Bielby [1892] 1 QB 709; Edwards, op. cit., p. 146.
52 *Re de Ros' Trust* (1885) 31 Ch. D. 81, distinguishing *Young* v. *Smith* (1865) LR 1
Eq. 180.
53 *McLeod* v. *Buchanan* [1940] 2 All ER 179 (HL).
54 (1856) 26 LJMC 18.
55 (1837) 7 Wm. IV and 1 Vic., c. 85, s. 6.
56 *R.* v. *Wilson*, above, at p. 19.

accused could be convicted of 'causing' poison to be taken by her mistress when she put arsenic in the coffee and told her mistress that she had prepared the coffee for her.[57] Here again, there was an element of deceit in the conduct of accused, though the lie (that the coffee was fit to drink) was merely implicit.

This requirement of the use of authority, coercion, or deceit implies that the act of the intermediary must not be fully voluntary, if accused is to be convicted, and it is indeed this which distinguishes 'causing' from other cases of inducing such as advising, persuading, etc., though the decision in *R* v. *Wilson*[58] is to the contrary.

Thirdly, it must in general be the purpose or intention of accused that the intervening actor should act as he did. However, one must not assume that a full knowledge of every element of the proscribed state of affairs must be proved by the prosecution. Thus, the court might decide that the owner of a car was guilty of 'causing' a motor vehicle to be used on a road in a defective condition if he instructed his son to use the car upon his, the owner's, business, although neither knew of the defective condition of the car. Whether this construction would be correct depends, as in all cases of the interpretation of criminal statutes, upon what elements the court considers so important that knowledge of them must be proved, as compared with subsidiary elements of which knowledge need not be proved though they are part of the proscribed state of affairs. In the supposed case it may well be that the legislature requires the prosecution to show that accused intended his son to use the car upon the road but dispenses with proof of knowledge that the car was in a defective condition.

When 'causing' is enjoined. We now consider briefly the interpretation of those statutes which enjoin the subject to cause a given state of affairs or action. An example may be taken from the case of *Stiles* v. *Galinski*,[59] which concerned a by-law imposing on landlords a duty to 'cause every area, the interior surface of every ceiling . . . to be thoroughly lime-washed' and 'cause every part of the premises to be cleansed'.

The notion of 'failing to cause' another to act is logically different from that of causing another to act and none of the three elements distinguished in relation to the latter need necessarily apply to it. Accordingly it seems that such enactments are prima facie to be interpreted in the sense that knowledge is not an essential element of responsibility and mistake is no defence. Presumably, however, such statutes imply that accused must be able to produce the state

---

[57] *R.* v. *Harley* (1830) 4 C. & P. 369.
[58] (1856) 26 LJMC 18.
[59] [1904] 1 KB 615.

374 THE COMMON LAW

of affairs designated, so that compliance must be within his power. When a statute requires a person to cause another to do an act it is implied that accused has some authority or control over the other. Thus, college statutes frequently provide that the head of the college shall 'cause the officers of the college to perform their duties'. This would be inappropriate if the head of the college was not in a position of authority. It would further appear that an injunction to cause another to act would be satisfied if the other did the act at the request of accused, whether or not he acted voluntarily. This may constitute a distinction between the interpretation of the word 'causes' in a statute which forbids and one which enjoins.

Occasioning harmful or unlawful acts

Because the law of criminal negligence has not been fully developed in the common law world, except in relation to statutory offences such as causing death by dangerous driving[60] criminal responsibility has seldom been based on the fact that accused provided others with opportunities for doing harm. Some cases of this sort might come within the law of homicide, as when a schoolteacher, parent, or childminder intentionally or by recklessness or gross negligence provides the opportunity for another to kill a child committed to his or her charge.[61]

Apart from such rare cases the problem of liability for occasioning harm has arisen in the law of unlawful assembly. This crime is committed, among other ways, by three or more persons who assemble together in such a way as to 'cause' a breach of the peace. In *Beatty* v. *Gillbanks*[62] accused were bound over to keep the peace on the ground of having unlawfully assembled to the disturbance of the public peace. They were members of the Salvation Army and their parades were frequently opposed by a rival organization calling itself the 'Skeleton Army'. It was held that the parades and processions of the Salvation Army were not provocative but that the Skeleton Army without justification attacked them and breaches of the peace ensued. The court held that accused could not be found guilty of unlawful assembly on those facts, since although 'everyone must be taken to intend the natural consequences of his own acts' the evidence showed that the disturbances were *caused* by other people antagonistic to the Salvation Army and that no acts of violence were

60 Road Traffic Act, 1960, s. 1.
61 In a German case a husband, knowing that his wife had threatened to kill their child, deserted her without informing the authorities of the danger. His wife then killed the child. He was held rightly convicted of negligent killing, the wrongful and negligent act being not the desertion in itself but the failure to inform the authorities. *BGH St* 7 (1954), 268.
62 (1892) 9 QBD 308.

committed by the accused. Hence the conviction of the accused must be quashed for if it were upheld 'a man may be convicted for doing a lawful act, if he knows that his doing it may *cause* another to do an unlawful act'.[63]

It will be noticed that Field J. is inconsistent in his use of the word 'cause'. In the earlier part of his judgment he states that the disturbances were caused by the Skeleton Army while in the later passage he appears to contemplate that the accused by doing a lawful act caused the Skeleton Army to produce the disturbances. In the second passage 'tempt' would have been more apt than 'cause'.

Upon common-sense principles the court was correct in concluding that the Salvation Army could not strictly be said to have 'caused' the disturbances, since they did not provoke the Skeleton Army. But on the other hand they provided by their parades an occasion and temptation for the Skeleton Army to commit breaches of the peace and they knew from previous occasions that such breaches of the peace were likely to occur. The real problem was therefore whether the law of unlawful assembly is aimed not merely against those who *cause* breaches of the peace but also against those who do an act which, to their knowledge but without their intending it, tempts others to break the peace and in that way *occasions* breaches of the peace.

Perhaps the law of unlawful assembly extends as far as this, for doubt has been thrown on *Beatty* v. *Gillbanks*. In *Wise* v. *Dunning*[64] the point did not really arise, since upon the facts of that case accused had acted in a provocative way and the reaction of the Catholics who resorted to breaches of the peace could not be regarded as fully voluntary. Hence accused might properly be said to have 'caused' the disturbance in the strict sense of the word.[65] However, in *Wise* v. *Dunning* Darling J. said, 'If there be a conflict between [*Beatty* v. *Gillbands* and *R.* v. *Justices of Londonderry*][66] I prefer the law as it is laid down in *R.* v. *Justices of Londonderry*', where it was held that a magistrate was justified in binding a person over to keep the peace if there was evidence to warrant the apprehension that there was likely to be a breach of the peace if the person bound over were allowed to do what he proposed to do. Perhaps it is enough, to secure a conviction for unlawful assembly, to show that accused occasioned a breach of the peace.

The later case of *Duncan* v. *Jones*[67] turns upon the crime of obstructing the police in the performance of their duty. One of the

63 (1892) 9 QBD, p. 314, *per* Field J. Our italics.
64 [1902] 1 KB 167. Above, p. 336.
65 Above, p. 149.
66 (1891) 28 LR Ir. 440.
67 [1936] 1 KB 218.

duties of a policeman is to prevent breaches of the peace which he reasonably apprehends, and one reason for apprehending a breach of the peace is that the person whose conduct is in question has previously caused a breach of the peace. In this case Mrs Duncan had a year previous to the events in question held a meeting opposite to an unemployment centre and had made speeches of such a character that a disturbance at the centre ensued. It was held that the police were justified in forbidding her to hold another meeting at the same place since they reasonably apprehended a breach of the peace should she do so. In so deciding Lord Hewart CJ said: 'The case which we have before us indicates clearly a causal connection between the [previous meeting] and the disturbance which occurred after it—that the disturbance was not only *post* the meeting but was also *propter* the meeting'.[68] This might mean either that Mrs Duncan had by threats, provocation, or some such means caused the previous disturbance in the sense that the reaction to her speeches was not wholly voluntary or, on the other hand, that she had merely occasioned it by providing a temptation or excuse for the previous disturbances or, thirdly, that she had induced by argument, advice, or incitement a disturbance which was nevertheless the voluntary reaction of those participating. Probably even the second of these relations would be sufficient so far as the crime of obstructing the police in the execution of their duty is concerned.

This branch of the law illustrates the need carefully to distinguish the different possible types of relation between the conduct of one person and the act of another done 'in consequence of' or 'because of' that conduct.

'Permitting', 'suffering', and 'allowing' harmful acts[69]

We do not deal in detail with the interpretation of these words in statutory offences but merely outline the respects in which their interpretation differs from that of the word 'causes'.

'Permitting', 'suffering', and 'allowing' will be treated as if they were equivalent expressions[70] though in fact they differ in certain respects, for to permit something implies that one has the legal right to prevent it while to allow may imply merely a physical power to prevent. 'Permitting' may be summarily defined as failing to prevent what one could prevent. Statutes frequently use both one or more of these words and 'causes' either conjunctively or disjunctively.

---

68 [1936] 1 KB 218, 223.
69 Edwards, op. cit., chaps. 4, 5, 7.
70 Edwards, op. cit., pp. 125, 162; *Somerset* v. *Wade* [1894] 1 QB 574, 576 *per* Mathew J.; *Ferguson* v. *Weaving* [1951] 1 KB 814, 820.

A person may be convicted of permitting an offence whether or not he possesses *mens rea* in the sense of knowing of all the constituents of the offence. In this respect no distinction is drawn between causing and permitting an offence. In *Korten v. West Sussex C.C.*[71] it was held that the managing director of a chemical company was rightly convicted of 'permitting a false invoice'[72] when he allowed an invoice to be sent out stating that a fertilizer contained 38 per cent phosphates, though he did not know that this statement was false: the notion of 'permitting' would, however, presumably entail the minimum knowledge that the letter was to be sent and the power to stop it. Thus, in *Hardcastle v. Bielby*,[73] the facts of which have been mentioned above,[74] it was held that accused had not allowed stones to remain upon the highway since he had no knowledge that they were there and 'it would be monstrous to hold that a man may be fined under the statute because an accident has happened, which it was impossible for him to prevent'.[75]

Finally, there must be present in such cases the element of control, viz. ability to prevent what accused fails to prevent. This was strongly emphasized in the case of *Goodbarne v. Buck*, already cited,[76] but it is not necessary to show that specific authority was given by the accused to the intermediary.[77] Permitting has been said to be 'a lesser and vaguer term' than causing, and 'may denote an express permission, general or particular, as distinguished from a mandate'. Hence a father who knowingly allowed his daughter to sleep in the same room with a man might be held to have permitted the unlawful carnal knowledge of a girl under the age of sixteen and even to have 'encouraged' it.[78] In this context the word 'encourages' may be taken as slightly stronger than the word 'permits' or 'allows': it implies approval of the permitted course of action.

II. PARTICIPATION IN CRIME

So far we have considered cases where one who 'causes' or 'permits' another to act in certain ways is liable as a principal offender either because the offence of which he is guilty is defined explicitly

[71] (1903) 72 LJKB 514. Cf. *Laird v. Dobell* [1906] 1 KB 131.
[72] Fertilizers and Feeding Stuffs Act, 1893, s. 3(1)(*b*).
[73] [1892] 1 QB 709.
[74] p. 371.
[75] *Hardcastle v. Bielby*, above, at p. 713, *per* Collins J. The reasoning is unsatisfactory, since accused might know that the stones were on the highway and yet be unable to move them.
[76] [1940] 1 KB 771; *Rochford R.D.C. v. Port of London Authority* [1914] 2 KB 916, 922-3.
[77] *McLeod v. Buchanan* [1940] 2 All ER 179, 187 *per* Lord Wright.
[78] *R. v. Ralphs* (1913) 9 CAR 86; Children Act, 1908, s. 17(1); Children Act, 1908 (Amendment Act), 1910, s. 1.

by reference to 'causing' or 'permitting' others to act in certain ways, or because his use of innocent or irresponsible persons amounts to doing something, such as killing, or causing some harm proscribed by law. We now consider cases in which a person other than the principal offender is held liable as a participant for instigating or helping the principal offender to bring about the proscribed state of affairs. Participants may conveniently be classified into those who induce the principal offender to act and those who help, facilitate, or permit his act. For the former type of criminal responsibility Stephen uses the word 'instigation'. This is apt to cover those who 'counsel or procure' an offence.[79] On the other hand, 'instigation' is inappropriate to describe the conduct of one who aids or abets the commission of an offence. There is therefore a broad distinction between those participants who instigate a crime and those who merely assist in it. Lord Goddard said,[80] in relation to what used to be called misdemeanours, that 'aid and abet' describes the position a participant who is present and takes part in the principal offence, while 'counsel and procure' describes the position of one who is not present but is an accessory before the fact.[81] Usually a participant in a crime is charged with 'aiding, counselling and procuring' the principal crime and the prosecution will then succeed if one of these is proved.

Nowadays those who aid, counsel, or procure offences are liable in English law to be tried, indicted, and punished as principal offenders.[82] Hence the only practical importance of the distinctions we are investigating is that the prosecution must prove that the participant's conduct fell within one of the categories mentioned. If the indictment mentions only one form of participation it may be a question whether a conviction is proper if the accused has been guilty of another form. The distinctions have, however, greater practical importance in some common law jurisdictions other than England and in continental law similar distinctions are to be found. In German law the *Anstifter*[83] (instigator) is more severely treated than the *Gehilfe*[84] (helper). In the French code there is no difference in punishment but those who instigate (*provoquer*)[85] the crime are distinguished from those who procure the means for or assist it. The Italian code in certain circumstances imposes a special punishment on those who instigate (*determinare, instigare*)[86] others to commit a crime.

---

[79] Accessories and Abettors Act, 1861, s. 8.
[80] *Ferguson* v. *Weaving* [1951] 1 KB 814, 818.
[81] This overlooks the possible cases of persons who assist but are not present when the offence is committed and those who are present counselling but do not assist.
[82] Accessories and Abettors Act, 1861, ss. 1, 8.
[83] *StGB*, s. 48.
[84] *StGB*, s. 49.
[85] Code pénal, art. 60.
[86] Codicè penale, arts. 111, 115.

Instigation refers primarily to the case when the principal decides to commit the crime because the participant has done or said something to make the crime appear a desirable course of action in the principal's eyes. In some such cases, where the participant uses threats or lies, he may be said to have 'caused' the principal to act.[87]

Assistance refers primarily to the case when the principal decides independently to commit the offence but the participant provides the means or opportunity.

Instigation. In cases of instigation properly so called, viz. 'counselling' or 'procuring', accused must be shown to have provided a reason for the principal to commit the criminal act. It is not necessary here to repeat the analysis of this notion, which has been discussed elsewhere.[88]

In relation to the word 'counsels' it is a question whether accused is responsible if he *persuades* the principal, not by using threats or bribes but by pointing out the advantages of the proposed course of action, or again if, without attempting to persuade the principal, he gives him *advice* in a take-it-or-leave-it way. The alleged participant might say to the principal: 'Do steal that food, since your family is starving and morality enjoins theft in preference to starvation' or 'Make up your own mind; but many wise men have thought that it was better to steal than to starve.' In neither case has accused appealed to the principal's fear or cupidity; but in the first he intends the principal to follow his advice while in the second he is indifferent.

Many legal systems have refused to admit mere advice as a sufficient ground of liability. In the Roman law of theft mere counsel did not make a defendant liable as an accessory.[89] In German law an accused person is guilty of instigation if he induces another to commit a crime by gift, promise, threat, abuse of authority or power, intentionally inducing or promoting a mistake, or by other means.[90] The context suggests that the 'other means' must involve an appeal to fear or cupidity consisting in more than the mere adducing of existing reasons for a given act. In French law a person is punishable as an accomplice if he has instigated a crime by gift, promise, threat, abuse of authority or power, or by blameworthy manoeuvres or tricks, or has given instructions for its commission.[91] Here, clearly, the accomplice must either have appealed to these motives or have

---

[87] In *R.* v. *Bourne* (1952) 36 CAR 125, accused was held to have caused his wife to have carnal knowledge of a dog by inducing her to submit to this by threats of violence and so to be liable to conviction as a participant (principal in the second degree on accessory) in bestiality, the wife's act being unlawful though perhaps not punishable, in that she could successfully have pleaded coercion.

[88] Above, pp. 53–7.

[89] Justinian, *Inst.* 4. 1. 11.

[90] *StGB* 48 (*Anstifter*).

[91] Code pénal, art. 60.

been at least in a position of *de facto* authority. The English law is otherwise. The word 'counsels' seems appropriate to the giving of mere disinterested advice.

Leading English writers assume that persuasion without threats or bribes suffices to make an accused person an accessory if the principal commits the offence.[92] Even the giving of disinterested advice without an attempt to persuade may perhaps come within the expression 'counsels'. Though this would not naturally be described as counselling or advising an offence it would be a case of tendering advice about a proposed offence.

According to Stephen,[93] Iago could be convicted as an accessory to Desdemona's murder only because he said to Othello: 'Do it not with poison, strangle her in her bed.'[94] This is counsel rather than command.

It seems that advice can be reduced to three forms: (i) advising another to do something, (ii) advising another how to do something, (iii) advising another about a proposed course of action. The first form clearly would be sufficient to render accused liable as an accessory or for aiding and abetting but there is a possible doubt about the second and more doubt about the third.

The word 'procures' would appear not to include some forms of 'counselling', since 'procures' seems equivalent to 'induces' where the person inducing intends the principal to act as he does and provides a reason on which he acts. Stephen, who took a narrow view of the scope of instigation, thought it would not be murder for *A* to tell *B* of facts, e.g. that *C* had seduced *B*'s wife, which operated as a motive for *B* to murder *C*, since 'It would be an abuse of language to say that *A* had killed *C*, though no doubt he has been the remote cause of *C*'s death.[95] But if the causal relation required between accessory and principal offence were that implied by the word 'kills' there would be no need to distinguish principals in the first degree in murder from accessories.

The 'remote' relation of providing a reason for another's act may be enough for the law of instigation. In Stephen's case, *A* has merely drawn *B*'s attention to existing facts and has given no advice to *B*, but if *A* intends that *B* should kill *C* a court might regard *A*'s act as amounting to a form of instigation. If *A* fabricates the story *B* is not a fully voluntary actor and *A* may be said to have 'caused' *B* to kill *C*.

In cases of instigation the principal offender's act may be fully voluntary. If the instigator proceeds by offering an inducement, such

92 Turner, *Outlines*, p. 88; Glanville Williams, *Criminal Law*, s. 57.
93 *HCL* iii. 8.
94 *Othello*, IV. i. 210.
95 HCL iii. 8.

CRIMINAL LAW: CAUSING, ETC., OTHERS TO ACT

CRIMINAL LAW: CAUSING, ETC., OTHERS TO ACT   381

as a gift or the promise of a reward, or by advising the principal to do the act, this is plainly consistent with the fully voluntary character of the principal offender's act. The conclusion will be the same if the instigator, without offering an inducement or reward, plays on the principal's feelings as by taunting him with cowardice. On the other hand, if the instigator's means of persuasion include threats, coercion or the issuing of commands to an inferior, this will normally justify the conclusion that the act of the principal, whether or not such as to exempt him from criminal liability, was not fully voluntary within the narrow meaning we have given to the term.[96] If the act of the principal offender is not fully voluntary then the instigation will amount to a *causing* of the principal offender to commit the crime in one sense of that word. In other cases it will not strictly be correct to say that the instigator has *caused* the principal to act as he does; but the principal offender's act may, in a sense, be described as the *consequence* of the instigation. The required sense is that in which, whenever one person acts because another has done or said something with the intention of providing a reason for the act, the act of the principal may be described as a consequence of the conduct of the other person.

In general an instigator is responsible for the act of the principal offender only if the principal offender has acted in the way in which the instigator intends him to act. However, some difficulties arise when the principal offender departs from the agreed plan. Stephen's view on this point was that 'when a person instigates another to commit a crime and the person so instigated commits a different crime the instigator is not an accessory before the fact to the crime so committed',[97] but 'if a person instigates another to commit a crime and the person so instigated commits a crime different from the one which he was instigated to commit, but *likely to be caused by* such instigation, the instigator is an accessory before the fact'.[98] In Italian law,[99] when the crime committed is different from that intended by one of the participants he remains responsible for it if the result is the *consequence* (*conseguenza*) of his act or omission.

The basis of the legal rules by which a departure from the agreed plan sometimes relieves an instigator from liability is obscure. Three main theories have been propounded:

(i) The first is that the instigator is liable provided that he as well as the principal had the necessary *mens rea* for the completed offence.

[96] It does not follow from the fact that duress may be successfully pleaded by accused that the party exercising the duress is not an accomplice. *R.* v. *Bourne* (1952) 36 CAR 125. Above, p. 379 n. 87.

[97] *Digest*, art. 22.

[98] Stephen, op. cit., art. 20. Our italics.

[99] Codicè penale, art. 116.

On this theory, if *A* gives *B* poison to kill *C* but *B*, without the authority or knowledge of *A*, kills *C* by shooting, *A* is liable as an accessory before the fact to the murder of *C* since he intended that *C* should be killed, and thereby satisfied the mental requirement of the law of murder. This solution is supported by Stephen.[1] Indeed, on this principle, even if *B*, without *A*'s authority, instead of poisoning *C*, poisons or shoots *D*, *A* is an accessory before the fact to the murder of *D*, for here too *A* intends to kill a human being and, by the doctrine of transferred malice, an intention to kill one person may support a charge of murder when another has been killed in consequence.[2]

Authority on the subject is difficult to find. On principle it may be argued that the law should not attend to a mere numerical difference in the victim and that, on any theory of punishment, such a divergence between the agreed plan and the crime committed should be neglected. The same argument may be put forward when the instigator intends that the victim should be killed in one way but the principal, departing from the agreed plan, chooses to kill in another way. On the other hand, it may be argued, on the analogy of agency in civil law, that a deliberate departure from the agreed plan to which, to the knowledge of the principal, the instigator would not have agreed, should relieve the instigator of criminal responsibility.

If this first theory is adopted the instigator can never be responsible when the principal commits a different crime from that agreed, in the sense of one requiring a different form of *mens rea*.

(ii) A second view is that the instigator is relieved of liability only when the act of the principal is unlikely.[3] This would lead to the conclusion that the instigator may be liable even though the principal commits a crime different from that agreed, provided that the crime committed would be a likely consequence of the instigation. It would relieve the instigator of liability if the principal committed a crime falling into the legal category agreed but in a way unlikely to ensue from the instigation.

Some support for this may be found in the cases. In *R* v. *Longone*[4] accused was charged as an accessory before the fact to a murder. He had given *A* poison to kill his, *A*'s, wife. *A* put the poison in the water of the hut usually occupied by his wife; to the knowledge (probably) of *A* but unknown to accused, the hut was occupied that night by another person who drank the water and died. Accused's conviction as an accessory to murder was quashed on appeal. Watermeyer JA upheld the appeal of accused on the ground that he was

1 Art. 19; Foster, *Crown Cases*, pp. 369, 370.
2 Williams, *Criminal Law*, p. 101.
3 Stephen, arts. 19 and 20, combines the first and second theories.
4 1938 AD 532.

'criminally responsible for the direct consequences of [his unlawful act in giving the poison to the principal] and within limits for its indirect consequences', viz. such steps on the part of the principal as the instigator ought reasonably to have foreseen but not for unforeseeable acts. Again, in *R.* v. *Radalyski*[5] the instigator induced the principal to procure the abortion of the victim. During the operation the victim's death occurred, probably because the principal placed her hand over the victim's mouth to stifle her screams. It was held that the instigator could properly be convicted of murder on these facts since he was responsible for the 'ordinary consequences' of his act of persuading the principal to procure the abortion.

These cases may equally well be explained upon the ground that in *Radalyski* as opposed to *Longone* there was no decision on the part of the principal to embark on a course of action to which the instigator had not agreed.

(iii) Hence it may be worth considering a third view, viz. whether the principles applied to relieve the instigator from liability, when the principal departs from the agreed plan, may not better be explained as turning on principles analogous to those on which the responsibility of one who provides another with an opportunity to do harm is limited, viz. when the second actor reaches an independent decision.[6] Some cases, indeed, seem to go further and even when there is no deliberate change of plan on the principal's part, exonerate the instigator if the principal knows that the agreed plan has miscarried and endangered someone other than the intended victim but fails to take steps which he could in order to save him.

The notion that such a failure to intervene when a plan miscarries relieves the instigator of liability may be supported by referring to the facts of the old case of *R.* v. *Saunders and Archer*.[7] In that case the instigator advised the principal to murder his, the principal's, wife by giving her a poisoned apple. The principal did so but the wife gave the apple, uneaten, to her child. The principal, though he loved the child, did not dare to reveal that the apple was poisoned and the child ate it and died. The principal was held guilty of the murder of the child but the instigator was acquitted as an accessory before the fact owing to the intervention of the sequence of events not contemplated by him. This may be supported, for modern law, on the ground that the act of the principal in not revealing the fact that the apple was poisoned when he became aware of the changed situation, amounted to a new independent decision relieving the instigator of liability. Similarly, upon another interpretation of the

5 (1899) 24 VLR 687, 5 Arg. LR 51.
6 Above, pp. 203–4.
7 (1578) Plowden 473.

facts of *R. v. Longone*[8] Tindall and de Wet JJ A concluded that
the accessory's appeal must succeed since, after the principal had
discovered that his wife was not sleeping in the hut but the victim
was, he took no steps to throw away the poisoned water. The ground
of decision adopted by these judges is in accordance with *R. v.
Saunders and Archer*[9] and appears acceptable, unless the view is
taken that the silence of the principal in the changed circumstances
is not a fully voluntary act since to speak would expose him to a
charge of attempted murder. This was the view apparently taken by
another of the judges in *Longone's*[10] case. De Villiers JA (dissenting)
was of the opinion that accused would not have been responsible
had the principal decided for his own purposes to murder a different
victim, but that mere failure to warn the victim after discovery that
he and not the wife was sleeping in the hut did not have the effect of
relieving the instigator from liability.

If a voluntary change of plan relieves from liability, conversely
the fact that the principal makes a mistake or accidentally produces
a result other than that intended, cannot relieve the instigator of
liability provided that the crime is of the same legal category as that
agreed. Hence if accused describes one victim to the principal and
the principal attacks and kills another victim whom he mistakes for
the one described, the instigator is guilty as an accessory before the
fact to the murder of the victim killed by mistake.[11] The same result
follows if accused has instigated the principal to rob a victim and in
the course of the robbery the victim resists and is accidentally killed.
Under the felony-murder doctrine (no longer law in England) the
defence of accident is not available to the principal offender when
he has caused death in the execution of a robbery; neither will it be
to the accessory.[12]

In *R. v. Shikuri*[13] the owner of a lorry was charged with culpable
homicide. He had sat next to his servant who was, with his authority,
driving the lorry at an excessive speed. The servant, through faulty
steering, struck a car which he was attempting to overtake and
swerved across the road, thereby striking another car and killing the
driver. It was held that on this evidence accused could not be convicted of culpable homicide since he had given no implied authority
to the servant to steer negligently. Here again, it may be that the
independent decision of the servant was the decisive factor relieving
accused of liability as an accessory.

8 1938 AD 532 (South Africa). Above, p. 382.
9 (1578) Plowden 473.
10 1938 AD 532.
11 Foster, op. cit., p. 370.
12 Stephen, *Digest of Criminal Law*, art. 20, examples.
13 1939 AD 225.

Assistance. Cases of *assistance* are usually described by the use of the word 'aid'. The usual case is intentionally providing the means or opportunity for the principal's act.[14] If the principal commits a burglary while the person accused of aiding and abetting holds a ladder for him, or lends him a car for the purpose,[15] or sells someone Croton oil and at the purchaser's request drops it in a piece of candy knowing that the purchaser intends a practical joke, with the result that the person who eats the candy suffers injury,[16] it is clear that the accessory can be found guilty without its being shown that his assistance was the 'cause' of the principal's act in the sense of providing a reason for it, or indeed in any sense of 'cause'. For the accessory is liable, presumably, even if the completed crime would have been possible without the assistance in question, e.g. if the principal could have found another ladder.

But if the proffered assistance is ineffective and the accused has not been guilty of some other form of participation, such as giving encouragement, he should strictly be guilty of no more than an attempt to aid and abet. An example is found in a German case where accused looked for matches in order to assist a friend to set fire to a heap of straw in which W. was asleep. He failed to find any, but his friend found one and set fire to the straw, seriously injuring W. The accused was acquitted of giving assistance (*Beihilfe*) since the fire would equally have occurred without his efforts.[17] Encouragement was not alleged. But German law insists on 'causal connection' in every case of assistance in the minimal sense that the assistance must have been a 'condition' of the completion of the crime, which means that use must have been made of the help offered. It may be an open question in English law whether an unsuccessful effort to find a ladder in order that the principal might commit a burglary would entail responsibility.

The provision of an opportunity can be illustrated from *R. v. De Marny*.[18] Accused edited a paper in which were inserted advertisements of books which, as he knew, were obscene. He was convicted of aiding and abetting the publication of obscene matter. 'The result of the insertion of the advertisements in the defendant's paper was to give information as to where these things could be obtained to persons who, but for the advertisements, would or might never have known of their existence and, therefore, it is not going

[14] Williams, op. cit., pp. 190 ff.

[15] *R. v. Bullock* [1957] 1 WLR 1; [1955] 1 All ER 15. Cf. *R. v. Price* (1858) 8 Cox 96; *R. v. Baker* (1909) 28 NZLR 536 (sending letter explaining how to open a safe is 'counselling').

[16] *State v. Monroe* (1897) 121 NC 677, 28 SE 547 (defendant was charged with assault and battery as a principal).

[17] *RGSt* 26 (1895), 351.

[18] [1907] 1 KB 388.

too far to say that the publication was directly brought about by the act of the defendant.'

Encouragement, as distinct from provision of means or opportunity, may amount to 'aiding'. An accused person may be convicted for aiding on the ground that his presence at the time when the principal committed the crime was an encouragement for him to do so.[19] Thus in *R.* v. *Coney*[20] accused watched an unlawful fight but there was no evidence that they took any part in the management of the fight or that they said or did anything. The court held that they could not be found guilty of aiding and abetting the prize fighters on these facts, since nothing they had done could be construed as an encouragement to fight or to continue fighting. On the other hand in *Wilcox* v. *Jeffrey*[21] accused, knowing that an American saxophone player was forbidden to perform by an order under the Aliens Act, attended a performance by the saxophonist and gave it enthusiastic publicity in his magazine. It was held that his presence at the concert, on the facts of the case, amounted to an encouragement of the American to contravene the order and that consequently he could be convicted of aiding and abetting the contravention. Such cases differ from instigation in that it need not be shown, in order to establish encouragement, that the principal decided to commit the crime because of the encouragement; but perhaps it is necessary that the act of encouragement should be known to the principal. Encouragement may sometimes operate as a reason for the principal to persist in a decision already reached; in that case it is like instigation in providing a reason for (persisting in) a course of action.

Independent assistance. Assistance may be independent, i.e. there may be no communication between principal and accessory. As a separate ground of criminal responsibility this may be illustrated by an imaginary example given by Schreiner JA in *R.* v. *Mtembu.*[22] In the example one person attacks the victim and the other independently persuades the victim to leave his weapon at home. Here, clearly, it is not necessary to show that the accused who persuaded the victim to go unarmed 'caused' the other murderer to make the attack or even that he could have prevented his doing so; but he must have known that the other intended to attack the victim. In an Alabama case accused, knowing that the principal intended to kill the victim, independently sent a telegram in order to prevent a

---

19 Continental writers usually construe encouragement as 'psychological assistance'.

20 (1882) 8 QBD 534. Contrast *R.* v. *Murphy* (1833) 6 C. & P. 103, and see as to duels *R.* v. *Young* (1838) 8 C. & P. 644; *R.* v. *Cuddy* [1842] 1 C. & K. 210.

21 [1951] 1 All ER 464.

22 1950 (1) SA 670, 678 (AD).

warning reaching him. The victim was killed and accused was held to have abetted the murder.[23]

This differs from the ordinary case of assistance in that there is no agreement between principal and accessory. Assistance need not operate through the mind of the principal; instigation must. Again, it seems unnecessary to prove that the assistance was a *sine qua non* of success.[24]

Two doubtful cases, not falling within instigation or assistance, deserve mention. What is in fact mere *approval* has in one case been treated as a ground of liability as an accessory. In *Howell* v. *Doyle*[25] accused were convicted of counselling or encouraging the commission of an offence under the Australian Crimes Act, section 5, even though the principal offence was not committed by reason of the counselling or encouraging but for other reasons.[26] The offence in this case was the continuing one of boycott hindrance. It is doubtful whether *approval* is a separate ground of liability but if it is obviously the prosecution need not show 'causal connection', of however tenuous a sort, between the act of accused and the criminal conduct of the principal offender.

Hawkins said that evincing an express liking, approbation, or consent to another's felonious design would, if the felony is committed, make a person an accessory.[27] This, though restricted to a prior approval may be too strict. No doubt allowing someone to borrow a car for purposes of a burglary may amount both to 'approval' and to 'assistance'; but merely to say, on hearing that *X* intended to burgle *Y*, 'That is a good idea' might be encouragement if communicated to the burglar but otherwise would, despite Hawkins, possibly be no offence.

It is generally thought that *ratification* plays little part in criminal law, but Schreiner JA has suggested that it may sometimes do so. In *R.* v. *Mgxwiti*[28] he took the view that accused might be found guilty of murder if he joined in an attack on the deceased which led to her death, even if he did so after she had been mortally wounded and without doing anything which contributed to or hastened her death. He was prepared, to this limited extent, to adopt in criminal law the principle that by joining in the attack the accused ratified the previous attacks on the part of other persons. The other judges did not find it necessary to deal with this point. In so far as the principle of

[23] *State* v. *Tully* (1894) 102 Ala. 25, 13 So. 722 (Michael and Wechsler, p. 699).
[24] Williams, op. cit., p. 184.
[25] [1952] Victoria LR 128; (1952) 59 Arg. LR 337.
[26] 'The absence of a causal connection between the counselling alleged and the commission of the principal offence is immaterial.' (1952) 59 Arg. LR 337, 342, *per* Herring CJ.
[27] *PC* ii, chap. 29, s. 16.
[28] 1954 (1) SA 370 (AD).

ratification is accepted, there is clearly no reason to show a causal connection in any sense between the act of accused and the harm.

This summary survey of the various forms of participation in crime shows that to speak of 'causal connection' as a universal element in criminal liability may be misleading. To do so may conceal the variety of different relationships on which responsibility depends. Only when an instigator uses threats, lies, or authority to induce the principal to commit a crime can he reasonably be said to 'cause' the principal so to act. In other cases of instigation, e.g. by bribes or the giving of disinterested advice, the principal may be said to act in consequence of the instigator's conduct, so that there is a different variety of 'causal connection'. When the participant merely assists he neither 'causes' the principal to act nor does the latter act 'in consequence' of his assistance. Probably the assistance need not even be a *sine qua non* of success, for the difference between 'helping' and 'trying to help' is better explained as a distinction between providing a means which is in fact used and trying unsuccessfully to provide such a means or providing a possible means which is not used. Still, the provision of a means which is in fact used by another to carry out his plan, like the provision of an opportunity which is in fact exploited by another, may in a broad sense be said to give rise to a causal relationship. A person who supplies a burglar with a ladder which the latter uses to break in would be said to have contributed to the success of the break-in. And if someone failed to provide a ladder as promised or removed the burglar's ladder knowing he intended to use it, so that the burglar was unable to find a means of entry, the failure of the break-in could properly be called a consequence of the failure to provide, or of the removal of, the means of entry.

XIV

CAUSATION AND THE PRINCIPLES OF PUNISHMENT

In tort, as we saw in Chapter VII, the courts frequently hold a wrongdoer liable for eventual harm, even if this would not have materialized had not a voluntary intervention of some third person or some extraordinary natural event combined with the wrongdoer's action to produce it. In such cases many writers have seen at work a general principle that, if the prospect of such harm occurring is a sufficient reason for holding the wrongdoer's act negligent, or, in cases of strict liability, for the imposition of that form of liability, then responsibility should extend to all such harm. The attractions of such a general principle are great. It is relatively simple and seems consistent; it finds the key to problems of 'remoteness' in the same factors that are relevant in the classification of the initiating act as wrongful; and it appears to relieve the courts of the need to scrutinize the precise manner in which harm actually eventuates in particular cases. So attractive has the principle seemed as a simplification of the old confused doctrines of *novus actus* and 'superseding cause' that it is often put forward not merely as a justification for *extending* liability beyond the limits apparently imposed by the older causal principle but also as justification for *restricting* a tortfeasor's responsibility to harm 'within the risk'. We have argued that this principle is open to the objection that it fails to cater for many species of ultimate harm which under the present law are recoverable in tort, and in our view, justly so.[1]

Writers on criminal law in common law countries, unlike their Continental colleagues, tend to steer clear of theory. Of course they recognize that in criminal as in civil law wrongful conduct must be shown to be causally relevant to, and so generally speaking a *sine qua non* of, the proscribed harm.[2] They tend to add to this that the conduct must be a 'substantial factor' in bringing about the harm.[3] This formula is partly designed to exclude liability on the part of a defendant who has made an insignificant contribution to a causal

---

[1] Above, pp. 289–90.
[2] *R. v. Dalloway* (1847) 2 Cox 273.
[3] Perkins, *Criminal Law*, p. 696 (serves to emphasize common sense and rule out purely theoretical abstractions); Smith and Hogan, *Criminal Law*, pp. 271, 274; *R. v. Benge* (1865) 4 F. & F. 504.

390 THE COMMON LAW

process.[4] In addition, it is sometimes used in a way which suggests that an appeal is being made to the common-sense criteria by which certain factors are marked off as negativing causal connection between a wrongful act and harm which would not have occurred without it.[5] To this the decisions cited in the previous two chapters are testimony. But, at least *de lege ferenda*, some writers on criminal law have felt the attraction of the risk theory or something similar to it as a way out of the perplexities thrust upon courts by legal rules which define offences in causal terms. Here prima facie the prospects of a simple general theory seem brighter than in tort; for the element of 'ulterior harm' which obstructed it in tort is scarcely relevant in crime, and the general requirement of *mens rea* in crime seems to offer the possibility of fashioning intelligible principles of limitation in its terms.

It is sometimes boldly asserted that the limitation of *mens rea* renders unnecessary any principle of causation other than the *sine qua non* rule in criminal law. Thus Turner[6] says, 'It is . . . reasonable to say that an event is caused by one of [the necessary conditions] if it would not have happened without that factor' and that the requirement of *mens rea* was introduced in order to obviate the hardship which might have arisen from an unrestricted application of this principle. 'Under the modern conception of *mens rea* no hardship can result from any fine drawn investigation of causes, since the more remote the cause the greater the difficulty of proving that the accused person intended or realised what the effect of it would be.'[7] To the same effect is Enneccerus[8] who also considers that the requirement of fault[9] renders unnecessary in criminal law any limiting principle beyond that of the equivalence of causes and conditions.[10]

The arguments of these writers do not, however, cater for the complexity of the criminal law in its present form. In the first place there are many contexts in criminal law in which *mens rea*, in the sense of intention to produce the harm proscribed by the law, or recklessness in relation to such harm, is not an essential element. This is true not only in many statutory crimes but also where doctrines of

---

4 Above, pp. 351–2.
5 *R*. v. *Hallett* [1969] SASR 141, following *R*. v. *Bristow* [1960] SASR 210; *R*. v. *Smith* [1989] 2 QB 35.
6 *Kenny's Outlines of Criminal Law*, p. 20. For a detailed criticism see Honoré, *Die Kausalitätslehre im anglo-amerikanischen Recht im Vergleich zum deutschen Recht* (1957), 69 Z. Strafrechtswissenschaft 95, some parts of which require to be modified; G. Williams, 'Causation in Homicide', (1957) *Crim. LR* 429; Y. Schachar, 'Causation, *mens rea* and Negligence in Homicide Offences', (1977) 3 *Tel Aviv St. L.* p. 84.
7 Turner, op. cit., pp. 20–1.
8 Op. cit. ii. 61.
9 *Schuld, faute, colpevolezza* (i.e. intention or negligence).
10 Below, pp. 444–5.

constructive crime (felony-murder or misdemeanour-manslaughter) are retained and, so far as vicarious responsibility is concerned, in such common law crimes as libel and public nuisance.[11] Apart from this objection it is not at present the law that an accused person is guilty of a crime merely because his act was a necessary condition of the harm proscribed by law and he intended, when he acted, to produce that harm or was reckless whether he produced it. This would entail liability although the harm occurred owing to the intervention of a voluntary actor or was attributable to a coincidence.

If accused gave the victim a blow intending to kill him, and the victim was struck by a falling tree on the way to hospital and killed, Turner's simple doctrine might make him liable on a charge of murder. Similarly if accused struck the victim a blow intending to kill him and the victim while in hospital was killed owing to the act of a nurse who took pity upon him and intentionally gave him an overdose of morphine, again, on the simple doctrine, accused would be responsible. But on the decisions accused would escape liability in such cases because his act was not the cause of the death.[12]

It is plain that something more elaborate than the simple combination of *mens rea* and *sine qua non* is required in a substitute for or analysis of 'proximate cause' that caters for the complexity of the facts and accords with the main trends of decision. Two positions of this sort have been worked out in some detail by American jurists and we consider these in the next two sections.

I. CAUSATION AND IMPUTATION

Jerome Hall in his *Principles of Criminal Law*[13] distinguishes causation from imputation. The former consists of the notion of *sine qua non* and also what he calls 'physical causation', viz. that a cause must instantiate a recurrent physical sequence. These elements are, however, said by Hall to be inadequate to constitute the relation (imputability) between proscribed harm and human action or omission which the law requires for criminal liability. For this there must be two further elements, (*a*) the actor must believe that his conduct will bring about the proscribed harm; this is called 'perception of the end-means relationship'; and (*b*) there must be no rule of social policy excluding responsibility and so 'influencing the meaning of "cause" in adjudication'.

[11] Williams, *Criminal Law*, pp. 276-7, denies that liability for these common law crimes is or was strict in other respects, but see Smith and Hogan, *Criminal Law*, p. 78.
[12] Above, pp. 326-9.
[13] *Principles of Criminal Law*, p. 256 (references are to the first edition, 1947). Cf. Legros, *L'Elément moral dans les infractions*, chap. ii.

Hall's view is, then, that in criminal law the prosecution has to show that the act of accused was a *sine qua non* of the occurrence of the harm and that in addition the harm was imputable to him in the sense explained. 'In torts, the tendency is to lay the total damage "caused in fact" at the door of any harm doer, especially if he intended to commit any tort, with little concern for the foreseeability of what actually happened. But in penal law, with distinctive objectives and sanctions, defensible on moral grounds, there usually is and always should be a sharp differentiation of causation from imputation for intentional or reckless harm doing. *Sine qua non* is too crude a notion to be employed there.[14]

The requirement that the cause must instantiate a recurrent physical sequence is not explained in detail by Hall and is little stressed; it seems only to mean that any purely physical connection between accused's act and the harm shall exemplify known physicochemical laws. Subject to some doubt on this point, Hall's doctrine appears to be that accused, to satisfy the requirements of imputability, must not merely have intended the consequence which occurred or been reckless in relation to it, according to the type of *mens rea* required, but must have believed that his conduct was the appropriate means towards it. Thus Hall speaks of 'intentional or reckless action or inaction with reference to the *foreseen* harm'[15] and refers to perception of the means-end relationship. This is to introduce an additional requirement beyond the *sine qua non* rule and the principle that accused must have intended or been reckless with reference to the harm. There are therefore on this view not two but three requirements that must be satisfied before we could say that accused has in a legal sense caused the harm in question.

Even this addition fails to meet the problem when the actor takes steps which he believes to be appropriate means but which are in fact inadequate and the harm eventuates either through the intervention of another person or from some coincidence as in the cases cited above.[16] Here all Hall's requirements are complied with but the sequence of events is different from what the actor expected. To avoid the conclusion that accused is liable in such cases a further stipulation is necessary, viz. that the means adopted must in fact be adequate and not merely a factor without which the harm would not have occurred. But 'in fact adequate' only means that the result is brought about without the intervention of occurrences held to negative causal connection. This, however, is to adopt (so far as intervening events are concerned) common-sense principles of the type explained in Chapter XII.

14 Hall, *Principles*, pp. 258-9.
15 Op. cit., p. 259.
16 pp. 326-9, 341-2.

Quite different objections arise in cases of strict or near strict liability. These are doctrines which Hall holds objectionable and false to the spirit of the criminal law. We are not of course concerned to defend them, but, as long as they form part of the law, the causal connection between act and harm required for responsibility in such cases cannot be explicated along Hall's lines and yet cannot without absurdity or injustice be reduced to merely the *sine qua non* relation. Thus, it is a generally accepted doctrine of Anglo-American criminal law that death caused by an act, or at any rate an act of violence, done in the commission of a felony, at any rate a felony of violence, amounts to murder.[17] It is also generally held that death caused by an act, or at any rate an act of violence, done in the course of the commission of a misdemeanour[18] such as assault, amounts to manslaughter. A further generally accepted rule is that death caused by an act intended to kill is murder even though the actual victim is not the person whom accused intended to kill. Under any or all of these doctrines an accused person may, as Hall recognizes, be guilty although he could not have foreseen the harm that occurred, or at any rate could not have foreseen the way in which it occurred. Thus Hall disapproves of the decision in *State* v. *Frazier*[19] by which a defendant who slapped a haemophiliac in the face was held guilty of manslaughter when the haemophiliac unexpectedly died, although accused did not know that he suffered from this disease. The disapproval may be justified, but so long as the law retains these doctrines some account of the relationship between act and harm sufficient for responsibility is required which does not depend on accused's knowledge or belief.

Hall's definition of legal imputability in terms of the elements so far described is not apparently designed to cover those cases where, although proscribed harm would not have occurred without accused's act, the conduct of other persons (as distinguished from natural events) is also involved in the production of the harm. To deal with these cases Hall invokes a 'corollary' of the fundamental principle that if certain harms are proscribed in criminal law their imputation to a particular person or persons is rested ultimately on voluntary conduct. This 'corollary' is the principle that 'no one is responsible for what others with whom he is not allied do or bring about'.[20] He discusses this principle in relation to the exceptional case

[17] Abolished for England by the Homicide Act, 1957, s. 1.
[18] In England the felony/misdemeanour distinction was abolished by the Criminal Law Act 1967, s. 1. The rule as to constructive manslaughter is now stated in the form that death must be caused by an unlawful act which subjects another to the risk of some harm to the person: *R.* v. *Church* [1966] 1 QB 59; *R.* v. *Creamer* [1966] 1 QB 72, 82.
[19] (1936) 339 Mo. 966, 98 SW2d 707. Above, pp. 343-4; Hall, op. cit., p. 260.
[20] Op. cit., p. 261.

of *People* v. *Lewis*[21] (discussed above as an example of additional causation)[22] where after accused had dealt the victim a 'mortal' wound the latter cut his own throat. He considers that the question of accused's liability depends on whether the act of the victim in cutting his throat was the voluntary act of a responsible agent (and so an 'independent intervening cause') or whether it was done, in Hall's words, because he 'had become insane or, because of excruciating pain, his suicide had been merely an automatic reaction'. It is also clear that Hall considers that this principle, making the responsibility of accused depend on the voluntary or non-voluntary character of intervening acts, is general, not confined to anomalous cases like *People* v. *Lewis*.

This acknowledgement of the crucial importance of voluntary action seems to us correct. If elaborated it would result, so far as causal problems are generated by intervening human acts, in the principles expounded in the first section of Chapter XII. What is required of course is a discussion of the variety of ways in which an action may be less than fully voluntary: insanity and 'automatic reactions' are only two of these. Moreover in any full treatment the notion of one person causing another to act needs elucidation. Hall writes as if this presented no difficulties.

Finally Hall's treatment falters over the idea of *sine qua non*. Initially he considers this to be part, though a subordinate one, of 'legal causation' or 'imputability', but in discussing cases where two wrongdoers simultaneously do an act sufficient to kill their victim he finds no difficulty in the view that both are responsible. His explanation is that the act of each is a 'sufficient force'. This requires further explanation on the lines discussed in Chapter VIII.[23]

II. THE DRAFT AMERICAN MODEL PENAL CODE

The most lucid, comprehensive, and successful attempt to simplify problems of 'proximate cause' in the criminal law is that contained in the draft Model Penal Code prepared by the American Law Institute.[24] This is notable for its explicit confrontation of many of the difficulties neglected by other theories but, in considering the attractions of the general formulae proposed by the Code (which are set out below), two things should be borne in mind. First, this attempt to cut loose from the obscurities, and complexities of the

[21] (1899) 124, Cal. 551, 57 P. 470.
[22] Above, p. 243–4.
[23] pp. 235–6.
[24] The American Law Institute, Model Penal Code, Draft 1962, s. 2.03, 2.06 and Reporter's Comments on s. 2.03 at pp. 132–5 of Tentative Draft 4. The Reporter is Professor Wechsler of Columbia University.

'encrusted precedents' of 'proximate cause' is part of a proposed Code which at certain points abandons established legal doctrines (such as that of constructive homicide) where these are considered irrational or unjust by modern standards. Accordingly the admirably brief solution offered for the special problem of causation is something *de lege ferenda*; though on the assumption that other reforming parts of the Code were adopted so that, for example, neither constructive crime nor strict liability needed consideration, the divergence from current law attributable solely to the Code's proposals in relation to causal problems would probably be slight.

Secondly, to be fully understood these proposals must be seen in relation to a general doctrine concering the rationale (or rather the multiple rationalia) of criminal punishment.[25] The relevance of the general doctrine is this. When problems of 'proximate cause' have most vexed the criminal law it has generally been the case that though accused's action was a *sine qua non* of the proscribed harm, this has come about in a manner very different from that contemplated or from that which might have been expected. At any rate in cases of intentional harm[26] accused will in any case be liable for some offence such as attempt and the solution of the problem of causation will only determine the severity of punishment. Thus, a man intending to kill his wife shoots at her, but misses or only slightly wounds her; to escape him she leaves home but is killed in a railway accident in the train in which she travels. In such an extreme case most people would not only refuse to say that the man had caused his wife's death but would recoil at the prospect of punishing him with the same severity as that reserved for murder. In most jurisdictions he will be guilty of the lesser crimes of attempted murder or wounding with intent to kill.

Yet the rationale of this apparently firm distinction is far from obvious. It raises the general question; on what 'theory' of punishment is it reasonable to punish attempts less severely than completed crimes? On a retributive theory as it is usually understood, i.e. the principle that the severity of punishment is to be measured by the wickedness of the criminal (supposing this to be ascertainable by human judges) the attempt and the completed crime inspired by the same intention should be punished alike. On a deterrent theory the rationale of the differential severity of punishments is complex. First,

[25] This is elaborated in Michael and Wechsler's 'Criminal Law and Its Administration' and in Wechsler and Michael, 'A Rationale of the Law of Homicide', (1937) 37 *Col. LR* 701, 1261.

[26] So far as cases of harm arising from negligent conduct are concerned the issue of guilt or innocence will often turn on whether his act has caused the harm. This is so under existing Anglo-American law; it might arguably be different under a well-considered penal code.

one crime if unchecked may cause greater harm than another, and hence on general utilitarian grounds greater severity may be used in its repression than in the repression of the less harmful crime. Secondly, the temptation to commit one sort of crime may be greater than another and hence a more severe penalty is needed to deter. Thirdly, the commission of one crime may be a sign of a more dangerous character in the criminal needing longer sentence for incapacitation or reform. These are independent justifications for different penalties; for it is not necessarily or even generally true that the greater the harm, the greater also is the temptation. There is, however, nothing in these elements of the deterrent theory to require or explain a distinction between the punishment of a completed crime and an attempt; they cannot be differentiated either in respect of the harm they are likely to cause, if unchecked, or by the strength of the temptation to commit them or their testimony to the dangerous character of the criminal.

At this point Wechsler and Michael appeal to considerations wider than the deterrent theory and point to the fact that a completed crime awakens more social resentment than an attempt; however dubious its rationality in this respect, common-sense justice would be outraged if the attempt were punished as severely. Popular discrimination for the purpose of punishment between attempts and completed crimes may rest on a sense that, among other things, punishment should be proportionate to the harm actually done, or possibly on some appreciation of the Benthamite principle that lesser penalties should be used where this will not weaken the deterrent force of the law (the principle of 'frugality' in punishment). Wechsler and Michael discuss these alternatives, but add that even if popular discrimination here rests on acceptance of retaliation as a measure of punishment 'the legislator or judge who takes account of the state of public sentiment as a means to avoiding nullification does not thereby embrace the popular theory'.[27]

On general utilitarian grounds, and if the operation of the courts is not to be nullified, this refusal to punish criminals for what they try to do as severely as for completed crimes must be respected. To respect it will not weaken the deterrent force of the law's threat since the criminal who embarks on a crime contemplates success and will not be less deterred if he knows that the punishment in the event of failure will be less than if he succeeds.[28] The same considerations apply to the case where accused fails to achieve his objective in the

[27] (1937) 37 *Col. LR* 1261, 1295 n. 80.
[28] Wechsler and Michael concede, however, that whenever (as in treason and some homicides) the probability of conviction is greater in the event of failure than in the event of success the threat of an equally severe penalty for attempts may increase the deterrent efficacy of the law. Ibid., 1295 n. 81.

manner contemplated but owing to some coincidence or to the act of another the intended harm is brought about. Here the connection between the accused's act and the harm is that he intended it and it would not have occurred without his act; but here too the plain man's sense of justice refuses to identify what he has done with a crime successfully completed in the manner contemplated. The upshot seems too extraordinary or too dependent on another's volition to be the 'doing' of the accused. To this obstinate sense of a difference the law should defer by treating less severely the anomalous case and it may do so normally without diminishing its deterrent force.

Viewed thus, problems of proximate cause assume a different form; for, 'when concepts of "proximate causation" disassociate the actor's conduct and a result of which it was but-for cause the reason always inheres in the judgment that the actor's culpability with reference to the result, i.e. his purpose, knowledge, recklessness, or negligence was such that it would be unjust to permit the result to influence his liability or the gravity of the offence of which he is convicted'.[29] How abnormal, coincidental, or unexpected the manner of upshot must be to require a different penalty in deference to the sense of justice is not susceptible of precise definition. This must be a matter for the jury to determine and the problem of 'proximate cause' on this view of the matter is essentially that of devising a clear formulation of the issue to which the jury should attend. Section 2.03 of the Code provides alternative formulations of this issue as an integral part of the following general definition of causal relationship.

Causal Relationship Between Conduct and Result; Divergence Between Result Designed or Contemplated and Actual Result or Between Probable and Actual Result[30]

(1) Conduct is the cause of a result when:

(*a*) it is an antecedent but for which the result in question would not have occurred; and

(*b*) the relationship between the conduct and result satisfies any additional causal requirements plainly imposed by law.

(2) When purposely or knowingly causing a particular result is a material element of an offense, the element is not established if the actual result is not within the purpose or the contemplation of the actor unless:

(*a*) . . .

(*b*) the actual result involves the same kind of injury or harm as that designed or contemplated and is not too remote or accidental in its occurrence to have a just bearing on the actor's liability or on the gravity of his offense.

[29] Model Penal Code, Tentative Draft 4, p. 132.
[30] Op. cit., Proposed Official Draft 1962, s. 2.03. Copyright. Reprinted here with the permission of the American Law Institute.

(3) When recklessly or negligently causing a particular result is a material element of an offense, the element is not established if the actual result is not whithin the risk of which the actor is aware, or in the case of negligence, of which he should be aware unless:

(*a*) . . .

(*b*) the actual result involves the same kind of injury or harm as the probable result and is not too remote or accidental in its occurrence to have a just bearing on the actor's liability or on the gravity of his offense.

The gist of these provisions is that though an act is the cause of any harm which would not have occurred without it, an actor shall not be treated as having knowingly caused it if it occurred in a manner different from that contemplated, or as having recklessly or negligently caused it, if it was not within the risk of which he was or should have been aware, unless (in addition to all other requirements) a further condition is satisfied. This is that the actual manner of occurrence is not too remote or accidental to have a just bearing on his liability or the gravity of his offence.

The attractions of this scheme are obvious. But though some of our criticisms may be met by use of another section of the code,[31] or by amendment with which it would still be superior to previous attempts to deal with 'proximate cause' it is open to one major criticism: it does not provide *specifically*[32] for those cases where causal problems arise because, although the accused did not intend it, another human action besides accused's is involved in the production of the proscribed harm. These are treated merely as one kind of case where harm may or may not be 'too remote or accidental' in its manner of occurrence. This is surely a weakness in a scheme which is designed to reproduce, and to allow the jury to express, the convictions of common sense that, even if harm would not have occurred without the act of accused, it is still necessary to distinguish, for purposes of punishment, one manner of upshot from another. For whatever else may be vague or disputable about common sense in regard to causation and responsibility, it is surely clear that the *primary* case where it is reluctant to treat a person as having caused harm which would not have occurred without his act is that where another voluntary human action has intervened. This has powerfully influenced the law and the language of decision. Indeed, a modification of the Model Penal Code which has been proposed in California,

31 Art. 2, s. 2.06.
32 At first sight the language of the scheme ('too remote or accidental') seems apt only to refer to physical events but the Reporter's comments show that it is intended to cover intervening human acts: 'Here the draft makes no attempt to catalogue the possibilities, to deal with intervening or concurrent causes *natural or human*, unexpected physical conditions, distinctions between the infliction of mortal and non-mortal wounds. it deals only with the ultimate criterion by which such possibilities ought to be judged.' Op. cit., p. 133.

and adopted in New Jersey and two other states, takes account of the possibility that the result may be too 'dependent on another's volitional act' to have a just bearing on the defendant's liability or the gravity of his offence.[33] To discard the criterion of voluntary intervention in favour of the tests proposed in the Model Penal Code may produce the following difficulties:

(i) If the cases discussed in Chapter XII, where a voluntary intervention of another was held to negative accused's responsibility,[34] are compared with the cases in the same chapter where accused was not relieved because, although the harm would not have happened without another's act, this was an act done in an emergency or under mistake or in the reasonable defence of threatened interests,[35] it is surely evident that the appropriate question to consider, in relation to intervening acts, is whether they were deliberate, fully voluntary actions. This is not only the natural question to ask but, in spite of the fringe of vagueness surrounding the types of behaviour accepted as not wholly voluntary, is also fairly easy to answer with guidance from the general trend of decision. To discuss these cases of human interventions in terms of what is or is not 'too remote or accidental' will often force the jury to think in quite unfamiliar terms, unless the reference to harms which are 'too remote' is taken to import the common-sense causal distinctions which are traditionally put to the jury under the rubric 'proximate cause'. Thus if, as in *Hendrickson* v. *Commonwealth*,[36] a husband's violence drives a wife out into the cold where she dies of exposure, the question whether she deliberately exposed herself or did this in a state of panic or frenzy, or because she could not find shelter, are intelligible determinants of responsibility. On the other hand it is surely confusing to ask whether what she did was 'too accidental' for it was in no way accidental. If the alternative formulation put forward in earlier drafts of the Model Penal Code is taken ('Was her death from exposure rendered substantially more probable?') the possibility of assessing differently the increased probability from different points of view or at different stages may generate confusion. Whether or not the woman deliberately exposed herself it might be plausibly said that accused had no reason when he attacked her to think that her death from exposure was rendered more probable; the same question considered in the light of the circumstances after the attack might be answered differently.

[33] California Joint Legislative Committee for Revision of the Penal Code, Penal Code Revision Project, Tentative Draft no. 2, 1968; NJ Code of Criminal Justice, NJ Stat. Ann. tit. 2C, s. 2C: 2–3; Del. Code Ann. tit. 11 702–216; Hawaii Rev. Stat., ss. 702–215 (2) and 702–216 (2).
[34] pp. 326–9.
[35] pp. 329–38.
[36] (1887) 85 Ky. 281, 7 Am. St. R. 596. Above, p. 326.

(ii) Cases such as *State* v. *Angelina*,[37] where accused inflicted a 'mortal' wound and the victim 'accelerated' his death by shooting himself, give rise to perplexities on any theory of causation. But apart from the difficulty of applying to such cases of 'additional causation' the simple notion of the 'but-for' relation which the scheme uses, no place is provided for a distinction which surely must be weighed however such anomalous cases are decided. If the victim's suicide was the act of one maddened by pain or despair, the case for holding accused liable is obviously stronger than if it was a deliberate act, done, for example, to shield accused from a charge of homicide. Yet on the tests proposed in the scheme it might be impossible to discriminate in this way: neither outcome was accidental in any sense and the victim's suicide is so strange an outcome of a murderous attack that whether it was done deliberately or on an insane impulse the increase of probability due to the attack must be either negligible or identical or both.

(iii) The above considerations apply with special force to cases of manslaughter arising from careless driving such as *R.* v. *Storey*.[38] There deceased, after the collision, drove his car to the side of the road where the soil was loose and was killed when his car fell down a bank. On the footing that deceased's action was a reasonable step to take in the predicament in which he was placed, this would rank as a not fully voluntary act and accused's careless driving would be held the cause of the death. Again this issue seems a simpler and more natural one than the question whether the sequence of events was too remote or accidental to have a just bearing on his liability.

It must, however, now be noted that certain cases of this sort may fall under a later section (2.06) the material parts of which are as follows.

Liability for the Conduct of Another: Complicity

(1) A person is guilty of an offense if it is committed by his own conduct or by the conduct of another person for whom he is legally accountable, or both.

(2) A person is legally accountable for the conduct of another person when:

(*a*) acting with the kind of culpability that is sufficient for the commission of the offense, he caused an innocent or irresponsible person to engage in such conduct;

'Causing a person to engage in conduct', as used here, is not limited to cases where the accused intends another to act. As the

37 (1913) 73 W. Va. 146, 80 SE 141. Above, pp. 243 and 337–8.
38 [1931] NZLR 417. Above, pp. 327, 346.

Reporter makes clear[39] a motorist who recklessly runs down a pedestrian who dies under an emergency operation carefully performed will be liable for manslaughter under this section. For in the 'but-for' sense here given to 'causing'[40] he will have caused the surgeon to act as he did.

How far does this wide provision meet the criticims made above of the scheme in section 2.03? Plainly it will in many cases be similar to a provision that human interventions which are not fully voluntary or reckless, shall not negative causal connection between the accused's act and harm. For often the act of an innocent or irresponsible person which would not have been done but for the act of the accused, will be done by one who is mad, under a mistake, or acts under a duty or in the reasonable defence of his interests in some emergency. There will then be no need to submit such acts, if they were intended by the accused or within the risk, to the awkward criteria of section 2.03. Yet these will not always be avoidable for the following reasons.

I. A criminal or tortious act is presumably not that of an innocent person. If therefore we suppose the surgeon in the motorist's case to have operated negligently or recklessly, or deliberately to have killed the pedestrian, the motorist could not be liable under this section for causing the surgeon so to act. All such cases would fall for consideration under section 2.03 as cases of causing *death*, where the manner of occurrence diverges from that contemplated or within the risk. Appraisal under the criteria 'not too remote or accidental', which we suggest may be inappropriate or confusing, will then be necessary.

II. Even when intervening acts fall prima facie within section 2.06 because they are innocent (e.g. a deliberate suicide where this is not a criminal offence) or irresponsible (e.g. the suicide of one maddened by pain) appraisal of such acts under the criteria of section 2.03 may still be necessary. *A* shoots and slightly wounds *B* who thereupon cuts his throat and dies. If, as may well be, it is found that *B* would not have committed suicide but for *A*'s attack, but this was not intended by *A* or so likely an outcome as to be within the risk, this will not dispose of the question whether *A* recklessly caused *B* to commit suicide. For the definition of 'recklessly causing a result' contained in section 2.03 will be applicable to 'causing another to

---

[39] Op. cit., Tentative Draft 1, p. 17. Other examples given are (1) A man recklessly leaves his car keys with an irresponsible known to have a penchant for mad driving: he is accountable for homicide due to such driving if the irresponsible uses the car in that way; (2) An aggressor provokes his victim to fire in reasonable self-defence: he is guilty of manslaughter, at least if a bystander is hit.
[40] The Reporter says in such cases 'liability rests on causing behavior of another even though they are not always thought of in this way': op. cit., p. 18.

engage in conduct' in this section; and since there is divergence between the actual result (B's suicide) and what was intended or within the risk (B's death from A's shot), this and all such cases of divergence falling within section 2.06, will also have to be appraised by the criteria of section 2.03.

In general the tests proposed in the Model Code for dealing with cases where accused's conduct would not have resulted in harm without the presence of extraordinary or coincidental events other than human actions, correspond with the criteria which we have discussed under the heading of Abnormality in Chapter XII.[41] What is 'too accidental' will in general be what is coincidental or highly unlikely and vice versa. In one respect, however, the scheme would change the law possibly for the better; as we have explained, highly abnormal conditions of things or persons existing at the time these are affected by a wrongdoer's act are in general not held to negative causal connection between the act and harm though this would not have occurred without the abnormal condition. In almost all legal systems such existing conditions are treated differently from extraordinary events intervening subsequently to the wrongful act. The draft scheme, however, draws no such distinction and it would seem that if, as in the cases discussed in Chapter XII,[42] a person succumbed to an attempt to kill him only because he suffered from some rare disease unknown to his assailant, it might be argued that accused neither knew nor should have known that his conduct would render the actual manner of death more probable. Of course the fact that the draft Code of which the scheme is a part eliminates the misdemeanour-manslaughter as well as the felony-murder doctrine makes this point of less importance de lege ferenda; but it would still represent a change in the law in a case where accused, intending to kill, inflicts a minor wound which results in death only because of the victim's unusual condition.

It should be noticed that the code paragraph 'treats but-for cause as the causality relationship that normally should be regarded as sufficient'.[43] Without certain qualifications this will give rise to difficulties where each of two wrongdoers independently inflict, either in succession or simultaneously, wounds sufficient to kill a normal man, and generally wherever 'additional causation' in any of the forms discussed in Chapter VIII is present.[44] In all such cases it will be true

[41] pp. 340 ff.
[42] pp. 342–4.
[43] Op. cit., s. 2.03, p. 1 (a), 3, p. 216 and reporter's comments Tentative Draft, p. 133. The notion that but-for causation is sufficient is rejected in People v. Warner-Lambert (1980) 414 NE 2d 660 (defendants, who created explosion hazards after warning of danger, not liable for deaths in explosion in absence of evidence of cause of explosion).
[44] pp. 235–49.

that if one or other wrongdoer had complied with the law the harm done would nevertheless have occurred. The same is true of one who accelerates the death of one dying from a previously inflicted wound. *Strict liability.* The Code (s. 2.05) assumes that the only connection required between act and harm where liability is strict is that the harm would not have occurred without the act. Yet surely the elimination of *mens rea* as an element in liability does not mean that the accused is to be liable for harm, even if it only occurred through the conjunction of his act with the deliberate act of some independent person or with some quite extraordinary event.[45] The plain man's protest would be that in such cases the accused 'did not do it', even though the harm would not have occurred without what he did.

III. THE SCOPE OF CRIMINAL LIABILITY

Any system may limit or extend criminal responsibility out of deference to considerations other than those causal principles which concern the character of intervening acts or events. Criminal law has, like the rest of the law, its special scope rules giving effect to a variety of 'policies', and the judgments of courts will often be powerfully influenced in reaching a decision on any aspect of responsibility by their moral estimate of the character of a prisoner or the viciousness of his conduct. But, we think, nothing is gained by fusing these considerations of policy or expressions of moral judgment with the causal elements in responsibility.

The requirement that if accused is to be guilty of murder the victim's death must supervene within one year and a day from his infliction of the wound[46] should be recognized for what it is—as a special limitation on the scope of the law of homicide.[47] The same is true of many broader and vaguer limitations of the scope of legal rules, such as the following.

In *R.* v. *Pocock*[48] the defendant negligently failed to maintain a highway in good condition; deceased suffered injury and died through an accident attributable to the defective state of repair of the highway. The court decided that accused was not guilty of manslaughter; perhaps because, as Green suggests, death caused by

[45] Constructive homicide, the English equivalent of the felony-murder and misdemeanour-manslaughter doctrines, was not so interpreted in English law (*R.* v. *Horsey* (1862) 3 F. & F. 287, 176 ER 129 and above, pp. 349–50; also *R.* v. *Towers* (1874) 12 Cox C. C. 530). It seems clear that strict liability is not to be so interpreted either; at least where causing physical harm is involved.
[46] *R.* v. *Dyson* [1908] 2 KB 454; *State* v. *Dailey* (1922) 134 NE 481 (Ind.).
[47] Thus, it has been abandoned in Pennsylvania: *Commonwealth* v. *Ladd* (1960) 166 Atl. 2d 501; cf. *People* v. *Brengard* (1934) 191 NE 850 (NY).
[48] (1851) 5 Cox 172.

an act of this type is not within the scope of the law of manslaughter.[49] On the other hand Green treats in the same way, as depending on policy, a case such as *Taylor*[50] in which deceased was so threatened by a group of bandits on a train that he moved to a place of danger where he was shot by those resisting the bandits and was killed. Here, surely, the problem was whether the act of deceased in moving to the dangerous place was a purely voluntary act so as to negative causal connection between the felony in which accused was engaged and the death of the victim.

Again, it has been said that there is a special rule of criminal law by which accused cannot be held guilty of homicide unless there was some physical impact upon the victim. Thus Stephen says[51] that there is no responsibility 'when the death is caused without any definite bodily injury to the person killed; but this does not extend to the case of a person whose death is caused not by any one bodily injury but by repeated acts affecting the body which collectively caused death though no one of them by itself would have caused death'. Stephen is here referring, in particular, to the question whether death caused by emotional shock falls within the scope of the law of homicide or not, a·question on which there are differing decisions.[52] But it is significant that Stephen himself places this supposed limitation under the rubric 'when causing death does not amount to homicide', so that he treats this as a case in which death is caused by the act of accused but the law does not hold him responsible. It is doubtful whether the weight of modern authority favours the rule tentatively expressed by Stephen.

A third limitation, based really upon the scope of the law of homicide, not upon any causal consideration, is the supposed rule, also mentioned by Stephen,[53] that a defendant is not guilty of homicide 'when death is caused by false testimony given in a court of justice'. Stephen also places this limitation under the class of cases in which causing death does not amount to homicide. There is not in fact any clear decision that murder by perjury is impossible;[54] but in *R. v. Macdaniel*[55] proceedings were discontinued when, the

49 Cf. *R.* v. *Murton* (1862) 3 F. & F. 492, 176 ER 221, 225.

50 *State* v. *Taylor* (1900) 41 Tex. Cr. R. 564, 55 SW 961. Green, *Proximate Cause*, p. 60. Appellant, one of the bandits, was found guilty of murder.

51 *Digest*, art. 263 (*b*).

52 For liability: *R.* v. *Towers* (1874) 12 Cox 530; *R.* v. *Hayward* (1908) 21 Cox 692; *R.* v. *Dugal* (1878) 4 Quebec LR 350; Treitel (1954) 70 *LQR* 168. Against liability on the facts: *Commonwealth* v *Couch* (1908) 106 SW 830, 32 Ky. LR 638 (Waite, Cases, p. 219).

53 Art. 263 (*c*).

54 Provision for homicide by perjury is made by statute in Nevada: NRS (Nev.) 199, 160 (1967); California (Ann. Cal. Pen. Cod. s. 128); Tasmania, Criminal Code s. 153(6) (when there is a conspiracy of two or more).

55 (1755) 19 St. Tr. 746, 810–14; 1 Leach 44; Foster (1746) 131–2.

question having been reserved for the consideration of the judges, the Attorney-General refused to argue that Macdaniel was guilty of murder although he had given false testimony in a court on the basis of which deceased was convicted and hanged. The point was never decided and the Attorney-General's refusal to argue it has been attributed by some to a desire not to discourage informants from giving evidence in murder trials. Even if the supposed rule is to be accepted it is best interpreted in Stephen's sense not as a special rule of causation but as a limitation of policy.[56]

It is, we think, important to distinguish such scope rules peculiar to the criminal law from principles of causation in order that the differences between causation in criminal and civil law should not be exaggerated.

Belief in the existence of special principles of causation in criminal law is not supported by the fact that the scope of the law of homicide may not extend, in the view of some, to death caused by nervous shock or by the giving of evidence at a trial, whilst in civil law the causing of death or loss in these ways sometimes undoubtedly entails liability.[57] On the other hand, as has been noted, there are rare instances in criminal law in which liability is based on the notion that a person who creates a grave risk or certainty of harm is liable for the harm so occasioned however it comes about.[58] Considerations of criminal policy determine the imposition of risk liability in these cases; and the incidence of such liability naturally differs from the incidence of risk liability in civil law, where the arguments of policy are different. The notion of occasioning harm differs, of course, from that of causing harm in the strict sense.[59] But, in so far as it is employed, it is the same notion in criminal and civil law.

[56] Smith and Hogan, *Criminal Law*, p. 284 cite analogies such as the protection of witnesses from actions for defamation: *Watson* v. *McEwen* [1905] AC 480; cf. *Marrinan* v. *Vibart* [1963] 1 QB 528.

[57] *Hambrook* v. *Stokes* [1925] 1 KB 141. Law Reform (Miscellaneous Provisions) Act (New South Wales) 1944, s. 4.

[58] Above, pp. 350, 357, 359, 361–2.

[59] Above, pp. 186, 194–204, 374–6.

XV

EVIDENCE AND PROCEDURE

IN this chapter we deal with certain questions of evidence and procedure as they touch those issues which may, in the broadest sense
be termed 'causal'. How are such issues settled? What is involved in
proving the presence of 'causal connection' between a wrongful act
and harm? Here some of the difficulties arise because of the variety
of types of causal connection, others from the ambiguities of the
expression 'burden of proof', which is used in the formulation of a
wide range of issues, procedural and evidentiary, others again from
the interplay of questions of proof and principles of legal policy.

I. EVIDENCE ON CAUSAL ISSUES

How causal connection is to be proved is not a question to which
writers on evidence have devoted much attention. Wigmore is, of
course, an exception. The second volume of his treatise contains a
detailed analysis of the topic. This is a valuable pioneering effort but
it would not be profitable to attempt to criticize Wigmore's arguments in detail because they fail to take account of certain important distinctions which we have expounded elsewhere in this
book. The first is the distinction between particular causal statements
on the one hand and, on the other, (a) those causal apophthegms
which summarize in a form convenient for use in everyday life what
experience has shown often to be the cause or consequence of an
event of a given type, and (b) highly specific generalizations specifying a cause and concomitant conditions believed to be invariably
followed by a consequence of a given type, such as Mill thought
were implied by and required for the defence of particular causal
statements. Instead of recognizing these distinctions Wigmore
wavers uncertainly between a Mill-like view of causation[1] and the
view that causal statements are reducible to statements of probability. Thus, he insists that causal processes are identified by Mill's
principles of inductive logic and says that 'stated in its broadest form
the notion of cause and effect is merely that of invariable sequence',
yet immediately afterwards advances the inconsistent view that 'an

[1] *Treatise on Evidence* (3rd edn.), s. 446.

assertion of causation means usually only an assertion of high probability or strong tendency'.[2]

For criticisms of Mill's view we refer the reader to Chapter I[3] and for a refutation of the view which identifies causal and probability statements to our discussion of the continental theory of 'adequate cause' in Chapter XVI.[4] If our arguments are accepted it is necessary to attempt a fresh classification of the causal issues which require to be proved by evidence.

It should be noted that not all causal issues can be settled by evidence. The determination, on causal principles, of the limits of responsibility in a case where the sequence of events is sufficiently established does not depend on adducing further evidence but on characterizing the upshot in terms of necessarily vague categories such as 'voluntary conduct' or 'coincidence'. This is, indeed, the element of truth behind the too crude modern dichotomy of causal issues into those of cause-in-fact and cause-in-law. Evidence is relevant to the determination of two other types of causal problem, viz. what may be termed the explanatory and the hypothetical. The first arises when it is not clear how certain harm came about or for what reasons a person did a certain act. The second arises when a court, in order to determine whether a wrongful act was in the appropriate sense a necessary condition of the harm, inquires whether compliance with the law would have averted the harm.[5]

The latter is the form of inquiry in which courts are most commonly involved when the issue is whether an omission to take precautions required by law was the cause of harm on a particular occasion. Both types of inquiry may, of course, be made in the same case. If the issue is whether an employer's failure to disinfect brushes caused his employee to contract anthrax the court will have to determine, first, whether the anthrax bacilli which infected the employee came from the brushes in the factory and, secondly, whether the precautions enjoined by law would have killed those very bacilli or enough of them to avert the illness. It is, however, convenient to deal separately with explanatory and hypothetical inquiries.

2 Ibid., s. 446
3 p. 22.
4 pp. 467 ff.
5 Lawyers speak as if counter-factual conditional statements such as 'if he had complied with the law the harm would not have occurred' can be true or false, though the evidence may make it difficult to determine which. Mackie, *Cement*, 54, on the other hand, holds that such statements cannot be true or false but only 'acceptable or unacceptable'. They may, however, be 'well or poorly supported' by inductive evidence; and the relation between such evidence and the 'acceptability' of a counter-factual statement is like that which lawyers take to hold between the evidence and the truth of such a statement.

Evidence in Explanatory Inquiries

An explanatory inquiry of a (broadly) causal character may concern either physical events or human acts. In the first, the court seeks to discover the cause or causes of the event; in the second it seeks rather the reason or reasons for the act.

Physical events. Three types of issue may arise in this connection: (i) it may occasionally be necessary for one party to establish the possibility of the occurrence of a particular causal process: thus, a plaintiff in a tort action may have to show that a blow on a person's skin can cause cancer,[6] viz. that causal connection between the two is possible either because at least one instance is known to have occurred previously or because this possibility is consistent with known laws or principles; (ii) often the issue is: which of two or more possible causal processes was instantiated on a given occasion. Thus, the court may have to decide whether sickness was caused by inhaling poisonous gas or eating infected food; whether a fire in a field was caused by lightning or by a smouldering cigarette end or by a magnifying glass; (iii) thirdly, though the causal process is known its author may be uncertain. We may know that sickness was caused by poisonous gas but be ignorant who or what allowed the gas to escape from the pipe. The third type of issue presents no special problems of evidence but the first two do.

(i) Very often expert evidence will settle whether an *A* can cause a *B*. A doctor may give evidence that a blow on the skin can cause cancer.[7] Such evidence, coupled with the fact that on this occasion an *A* was followed by a *B*, does not in itself prove that this *A* caused this *B*.[8] The probable truth of such a singular causal statement, e.g. that *this* blow caused *this* cancer, may be established in different ways by evidence:

(*a*) That a certain proportion of cases of cancer are caused by blows and that there is no evidence of the presence of other possible causes of cancer on this occasion. The higher the proportion of cancers known to be caused by blows the more convincing is the evidence.

(*b*) That a high proportion of blows of this sort cause cancer. This state of affairs is compatible with a very small proportion of cases of cancer being caused by blows.

(*c*) That, although medical science has not established with certainty that a blow ever causes cancer, a high proportion of blows

---

6 *Kramer Service Inc.* v. *Wilkins* (1939) 184 Miss. 483, 186 So. 625; Prosser, Wade, and Schwartz, p. 286.

7 *Tubemakers of Australia* v. *Fernandez* (1976) 10 ALR 503 (blow on head can cause Dupuytren's contracture though only about one case in twenty has traumatic origin).   8 *Blackstock* v. *Foster* (1958) SR (NSW) 341.

have been followed by cancer or a high proportion of cancers preceded by blows. Here it is possible, but unlikely, that the correlation between cancers and blows is a mere coincidence.

Note that the determination of such causal issues will not be affected if the point of view of medical science is that blows never 'cause' cancer but only accelerate or precipitate it.[9] That point of view will affect the assessment of damages in a civil case, since it will show, if correct, that the victim had a predisposition to cancer. But it does not throw doubt on the proposition that, from the point of view of a legal inquiry into responsibility, a wrongful act such as the blow may properly be treated as the cause of the cancer which, in the existing circumstances, including the predisposition, it precipitates.

The first method of establishing causal connection in a particular case may be illustrated by *Barkway* v. *South Wales Transport Co. Ltd*.[10] In this case the tyre of a bus burst, causing the bus to overturn and roll down a bank. It was proved that the burst was the result of the disintegration of the plies in the outer cover of the tyre, caused in turn by an impact fracture of the plies. Such a fracture occurs rarely but is nearly always caused by an exceptionally severe blow against the tyre. There was no direct evidence that such a blow had occurred but the House of Lords concluded that it must have occurred, and since defendants had no proper system for reporting blows, the disaster was the consequence of their negligence. The plaintiff here succeeds because most instances of harm of this sort are caused in this way.

The second type of argument might be appropriate when plaintiff seeks to show that defendant's act caused her to suffer nervous shock; the fact that a high proportion of experiences of the type she suffered cause shock would be strong evidence of causal connection between the experience and the shock on this occasion.

The third type of argument may be illustrated by *Roe* v. *Minister of Health*.[11] There McNair J. had to decide whether the injection of phenol into a patient's theca had caused paralysis. In deciding that it had, he proceeded by analogy with known physical laws.

None of the medical witnesses had consciously ever seen the results of injecting phenol into the human theca. Accordingly, the arguments for and against this view had necessarily to be based largely on deductive[12] reasoning from the observed effects of phenol in other circumstances and the known effects of other toxic substances on the contents of the theca itself . . . I have come to the conclusion that the phenol theory is sufficiently established

9 Cf. *Enge* v. *Trevise* (1960) 26 DLR 2d 529.
10 [1950] 1 All ER 392 (HL).
11 [1954] 2 QB 66.
12 Such reasoning by analogy is not, strictly speaking, deductive.

for it to form the basis of a finding by the court that the injuries were in fact caused by the injection of phenol with the nupercaine.[13]

If causal connection cannot be established in any of these ways, recent decisions show that plaintiff may nevertheless sometimes succeed if he can show that defendant's wrongful conduct made a 'material contribution' to the disease or injury. The doctrine of material contribution applies to conditions (e.g. silicosis, dermatitis) which are known often to be caused by prolonged exposure to some agent (e.g. dust) but where the effect of any particular period of exposure is hard to gauge. Thus, in *McGhee* v. *National Coal Board*[14] the House of Lords held that defendants' failure to provide washing facilities for an employee who worked in brick dust, and who later developed dermatitis, had 'materially contributed' to the disease, for which they were therefore liable, though other causes of the dermatitis could not, in the existing state of medical knowledge, be ruled out. Defendants had prolonged plaintiff's exposure to the dust and so increased the risk that he would contract dermatitis, as he in fact did. If defendants were not held liable they could in the present state of medical knowledge break their duty with impunity. In the limited class of cases in which the defendant contributes to or fails to counteract a process which has a cumulative effect, the House of Lords was therefore prepared to dispense with proof of causal connection. It remains open in principle for defendant to show that the disease was contracted from some other source, but in practice it may often, as in this case, be impossible to do so.

(ii) *Choosing between two or more causes.* When the actual cause of an occurrence is unknown, in the sense that there is not sufficient evidence to show in detail what happened on the occasion in question, a court must often decide between two or more possible causes of harm. It will then look for evidence of the characteristically different processes by which different causes produce their effects. Thus, it may be that a certain sort of dermatitis caused by brick dust is typically found on the back of the hand, as in this instance.[15] If this evidence is not available the court may decide that the cause of the harm has not been established and hence the party on whom the persuasive burden rests has not made out his case.

In *Alling* v. *Northwestern Bell Telephone Co.*[16] when decedent was killed by lightning in his house, the court declined to infer that the lightning had entered the house through a piece of uninsulated wire

13 *Roe* v. *Minister of Health* [1954] 2 QB 66, 70.
14 [1972] 3 All ER 1008 (HL); *Bonnington Castings* v. *Wardlaw* [1956] AC 613; Weinrib, 'A Step Forward in Factual Causation', (1975) 38 *Mod. LR* 518.
15 *Gardiner* v. *Motherwell Machinery* [1961] 1 WLR 1424 (HL).
16 (1923) 156 Minn. 60, 194 NW 313.

left by defendant extending through the wall; for there were several possible ways in which the lightning might have entered and there was nothing to show that it had come through the wire rather than in another way.

Medical men are often asked to say which of two or more possible causes accounted for a given disease or death. A doctor may, for example, testify that leukaemia, which appeared a few days after an accident, was probably caused by the accident or on the contrary that it was probably unconnected with it.[17] If there is a conflict of evidence, the jury or trier of fact will have to make up its or his mind on the causal issue and in doing so to take account of the incidence of the burden of proof and of the standard of proof appropriate to the litigation. It is not for the expert to give evidence that the standard of proof is satisfied.[18]

Human acts. When it is sought to explain a human act by discovering the reasons for it the actor's evidence of his reasons, if correctly remembered and honestly stated, is of great weight and his statement of his reasons is therefore always admissible, though not conclusive, evidence on such an issue.[19] In the absence of such evidence other conduct on the part of the actor may throw light on his reasons, or the court may be able to reach a conclusion on the basis of ordinary knowledge about the usual reasons for acting in a particular way.

Evidence in Hypothetical Inquiries

Causal issues often involve a hypothetical inquiry into the question whether compliance with the law by defendant or accused would have averted the harm which occurred. Compliance with the law is of course not always a straightforward notion. When what is alleged against defendant is a neglect of duty, the first step in investigating causal connection is to ask what the course of events would have been had defendant fulfilled his duty;[20] and, as we shall see, more than a minimal compliance may be notionally required of him, since a reasonable man does not necessarily confine himself to doing the minimum.[21] If what is alleged is the violation of a conditional prohibition (e.g. by driving without a licence), we must ask what

[17] *Commissioner for Government Transport* v. *Adamcik* (1961) 106 CLR 292; *R.* v. *White* [1910] 2 KB 124.
[18] *Dahl* v. *Grice* [1981] VR 513.
[19] Above, p. 56.
[20] *Thomas* v. *Baltimore & Ohio R. Co.* (1973) 310 Atl. 2d 186 (Md.); *Maindonald* v. *Aero Club* [1935] NZLR 371; *Cole* v. *Shell Petroleum* (1939) 149 Kan. 25, 86 P. 2d 740; *City of Piqua* v. *Morris* (1918) 98 Ohio St. 42, 120 NE 300; *Waugh* v. *Suburban Club Ginger Ale* (1948) 167 F. 2d 758; *Woods* v. *Davidson* [1930] NI 61 (HL).
[21] Below, p. 412 n. 25.

hypothetically would have happened if he had driven with a licence, not if he had not driven at all.[22] Though the latter would equally have been a compliance with the law, and indeed represents the course which defendant, not having a licence, ought to have followed, the law does not prohibit driving, but only doing so without a licence. The imagined situation is here intended to resemble the actual one as closely as possible save that its unlawful features are eliminated. Again, if what is alleged against defendant or accused is simply a positive act of wrongdoing like shooting, it will be necessary, in order to establish that the act was a causally relevant condition,[23] to ask the hypothetical question whether in its absence the remaining conditions would together have been sufficient to bring about the harm which ensued.[24] But whereas when positive misconduct is alleged the hypothetical inquiry is relatively straightforward, neglect of duty and the violation of conditional prohibitions pose a number of difficulties from an empirical point of view, of which four deserve mention:

(i) If defendant could have complied with the law in more than one way, should it be assumed that he would have complied with it in the cheapest way, to the minimum extent, or in the most effective way? In *Corn* v. *Weir's Glass*[25] Devlin J. said that court should inquire how the particular employer was likely to have complied with the regulation requiring a handrail on the assumption that, as a prudent employer, he would seek to give the best protection he could to his employee. Since defendant has admittedly neglected his duty, any reference to what he would have done had he been minded to fulfil it seems out of place. The test should rather be: what would a reasonable person in his position have done to comply with the law? Hence, if the question is whether defendant's speeding contributed to plaintiff's injuries the matter can properly be tested on the hypothesis that defendant drove at a reasonable speed, not just marginally within the speed limit.[26]

(ii) When a precaution is designed to provide against harm of a certain type and, in its absence, harm of that type occurs, it may be very difficult to say, even when a sequence of physical events is in

22 See Preface, p. lx.
23 Above, pp. 114–22.
24 Becht and Miller, *The Test of Factual Causation*, pp. 171 ff., 185–6, argue that in the case of strict liability causal connection is to be established with defendant's 'conduct' (i.e. his positive act) but in the case of negligence with the 'negligent segment of his conduct'. In the latter case a 'parallel series' (i.e. estimation of the course of events had defendant performed his duty) must be constructed, but they think this is seldom necessary in the case of positive acts. This mirrors to some extent the distinctions drawn above, but does not rest on any clear principle.
25 [1960] 2 All ER 300 (CA).
26 *Biggers* v. *Continental Bus* (1959) 157 Tex. 351, 303 SW 2d 359. Becht and Miller, p. 202 opt for the 'highest safe speed'. This seems correct.

question, whether the precaution would have averted the harm. In the absence of reliable evidence about the hypothetical course of events, a court is naturally inclined to give effect to the policy enjoining the precaution by assuming, unless there is evidence to the contrary, that the precaution would have averted the harm. In such cases a court is not inquiring purely into what would have happened in a certain event, but at least partly seeking to encourage acceptable standards of behaviour.

(iii) When human reactions are in question a difficulty often arises from the fact that we can seldom say with assurance how a person would have reacted to a situation which did not in fact occur.[27] Here in the absence of reliable evidence, (and the person in question may not be sure what his reaction would have been), we are obliged to use, for purposes of the inquiry, a notion of a standard, 'reasonable' person bent on avoiding harm—the analogue in this context of the 'economic man' who is used to assess damages for loss of profit.[28] It is usually thought that the court should make use of the standard harm-averting man only when there is no reliable evidence of how the person in question would have reacted;[29] but, even so, in many cases the hypothetical inquiries involved in the decision of causal issues are not purely concerned with asking, 'What would have happened had X complied with the law?' but rather, 'What would have happened had everyone concerned done his best to avert harm?' —which is in some ways nearer, 'What ought to have happened?' than, 'What would have happened?'

Since such hypothetical questions are often, in the absence of reliable evidence, not strictly decided on the balance of probabilities (in civil issues) it is correct to say that there is often a presumption that those concerned would have done their best to avert harm. Such presumptions introduce an element of legal policy even into decisions on that element in causal issues ('cause-in-fact') which modern writers like to distinguish, as purely factual, from the policy-laden decisions on 'proximate cause'. This has been pointed out, with some exaggeration, by Wex Malone,[30] whose views, despite the criticisms of Becht and Miller,[31] contain a kernel of truth.

[27] To some extent this is true of animal reactions. Thus, it is not obvious that a railway whistle means nothing to a cow, though that was decided in *Holman* v. *Chicago, R.I. & P.R. Co.* (1876) 62 Mo. 562.

[28] Above, pp. 311–12.

[29] *McWilliams* v. *Arrol* [1962] 1 WLR 295 (HL); *Wigley* v. *British Vinegars* [1964] AC 307; *Duyvellshaff* v. *Cathcart* (1973) 47 ALJR 410.

[30] 'Ruminations on Cause-in-fact', (1956–7) 9 *Stan. LR* 60; Klemme, 'The Enterprise Liability Theory of Torts', (1976) 47 *U. Colo. LR* 153, 163–4; Thode, 'The Indefensible Use of the Hypothetical Case to Determine Cause in Fact', (1968) 46 *Tex. LR* 423; (1968) 47 *Tex. LR* 1344; *contra*: J. A. Henderson, 'A Defense of the Use of the Hypothetical Case to Resolve the Causation Issue', (1968) 47 *Tex. LR* 183.

[31] Becht and Miller, pp. 24, 173–4.

(iv) When the hypothetical inquiry involves several contingencies it naturally becomes more difficult to calculate what would have occurred had the law been obeyed. A court will be reluctant to conclude that compliance with the law would have averted harm or produced a benefit if the hypothetical happy outcome depends on several unknown contingencies.

We deal with these last three difficulties in turn.

(a) *Precautions designed to avert harm of a type which occurs.* In actions for breach of statutory duty the English Court of Appeal in *Vyner* v. *Waldenburg*[32] appeared to suggest that, if plaintiff proved the breach and injury to himself and the breach could have caused the injury (viz. was of the sort which either has on at least one occasion caused such an injury or might in accordance with known causal laws do so), and if the injury was also of the sort which the statute was designed to prevent, defendant had the burden of showing that the precaution would not have averted the injury. After running for ten years this doctrine was condemned by the House of Lords in *Bonnington Castings* v. *Wardlaw*,[33] where it was reaffirmed that an employee injured in a factory must in an action against his employer for breach of statutory duty 'prove his case by the ordinary standard of proof in civil actions: he must make it appear at least that, on a balance of probabilities, the breach of duty caused or materially contributed to his injury'.[34] On the facts plaintiff was held to have proved his case.

In English law, therefore, considerations of policy do not dictate a presumption that a statutory precaution would have averted harm of the type it was designed to avert; plaintiff must show that, in the particular instance on which he relies, the precaution would more probably than not have done so. In America divergent approaches are to be found in the cases; many courts make use of presumptions similar to that adopted by the English Court of Appeal in *Vyner* v. *Waldenberg*.[35] According to Malone, matters of policy and estimates of factual likelihood have become hopelessly intervolved.[36]

(b) *Human reactions.* So far as human reactions are concerned there is perhaps a distinction to be drawn between the breach of a duty of care, designed to protect plaintiff against harm, and the breach of a duty of disclosure, designed to enable plaintiff to make an informed choice. When defendant fails in a duty of the first sort,

32 [1946] KB 50.
33 [1956] AC 613; *Barnett* v. *Chelsea Hospital* [1968] 1 All ER 1068.
34 *Bonnington Castings* v. *Wardlaw* [1956] AC 613, 620, *per* Lord Reid; *Power* v. *Snowy Mountains Authority* [1957] SR (NSW) 9; *Corn* v. *Weir's Glass* [1960] 1 WLR 577; *Hall* v. *Fairfield Engineering* [1964] SLT (HL) 97; Fleming, *Torts*, 181.
35 [1946] KB 50.
36 (1956–7) 9 *Stan. LR* 60, 72.

and there is no clear evidence how plaintiff or others would have reacted had defendant fulfilled his duty, several courts make use of a presumption that he would have done his best to avert harm. Thus in *Zinnel* v. *U.S. Shipping Board*[37] defendants failed to provide a guard rope on their ship and plaintiff's intestate was washed overboard. Though it was uncertain whether deceased would have seized the rope had there been one, the court concluded that causal connection was proved having regard to the fact that one of the purposes of having such a rope was that it could be seized by those in danger of being washed overboard.[38] Sometimes the decisions give the impression that the hypothetical occurrence of a reaction may be established by something less than a balance of probabilities.

It seems that sometimes in considering hypothetical reactions the court addresses itself not so much to finding the most probable reaction as to discovering what would have occurred had the person concerned acted reasonably: it assumes that he would have so acted. One reason for this may be that 'a hypothetical inquiry as to what *A* would have said if *B* had said something other than what he did say'[39] or what *A* would have done if *B* had done something else is unsatisfactory because usually a matter of speculation. In *Williams* v. *Sykes & Harrison*[40] the question was whether there was a causal connection between defendant's failure to guard some machinery and an injury suffered by plaintiff when he tried to clean the machinery in a 'hopelessly dangerous' manner. The court decided that causal connection was established since the presence of a guard *might* have deterred[41] plaintiff from acting as he did by reminding him of the danger. Perhaps this argument would no longer be upheld, since it is now clear that the correct legal test, at least in England, is not what plaintiff as a reasonable man should have done but what on the evidence he probably would have done.[42] When, however, there is no evidence that he would have refused to use the equipment intended for his safety, the House of Lords has endorsed the view that an inference of causal connection may be drawn;[43] and it is natural that sympathy for the plaintiff should lead courts to be reluctant to infer that precautions intended to avert harm would

[37] (1925) 10 F. 2d 47 (2 Gr.). Cf. below, p. 458.
[38] Cf. *Rovegno* v. *San Jose Knights of Columbus Hall* (1930) 108 Cal. App. 591, 291 P. 848 (absence of lifeguard).
[39] *Jones* v. *Williams* (1857) 24 Beav. 47, 62; *Re Alms Corn Charity* [1901] 2 Ch. 750, 762; *Underwood* v. *Bank of Liverpool* [1924] 1 KB 775, 789.
[40] [1955] 1 WLR 1180.
[41] Ibid., p. 1191 *per* Hodson LJ; p. 1193 *per* Morris LJ; p. 1188 *per* Singleton LJ.
[42] Above, p. 414 n. 33.
[43] *Ross* v. *Portland Cement* [1964] 1 WLR 768, 775 (HL); *O'Donnell* v. *M'Kenzie* [1967] SC (HL) 63.

have been ineffective,[44] even though the burden of persuasion on the issue of causal connection is firmly placed by *Bonnington*[45] on the plaintiff.

Earlier, a view still more favourable to the injured workman had been advanced. In *Roberts* v. *Dorman Long & Co. Ltd.* Lord Goddard said that if a person is under a duty to provide safety belts or other appliances and fails to do so he cannot be heard to say: 'Even if I had done so they would not have been worn.'[46] This would, taken literally, estop defendant from disputing the existence of causal connection between breach and harm, provided that the appliance would, if used, have averted it. The other members of the Court of Appeal did not go as far as this, nor does the analogy cited by Lord Goddard from cases where there is a duty to inquire: for it has merely been decided that when loss is said to be the consequence of failure to make an inquiry it is 'impossible, beforehand, to come to the conclusion that a false answer would have been given, which would have precluded the necessity of further inquiry'.[47] Lord Goddard's doctrine is inconsistent with the decision of the House of Lords in *Bonnington Castings* v. *Wardlaw*,[48] which applies not merely to physical sequences of events but to human reactions.

When, therefore, there is convincing evidence of how the person in question would have reacted this ought, on any reasonable view, to be acted on, and in some cases such evidence has been accepted. When an hotel keeper failed to provide a proper fire escape and a guest was burned to death, recovery was excluded when it was shown that the guest had locked himself in his room, was heard beating on the door and made no attempt to escape by jumping on to an adjoining roof, as others did:[49] he would not have used the fire escape had there been one.

Furthermore if the greatest efforts on the part of all concerned would probably not have averted the harm causal connection is not made out. In *New York Central Co.* v. *Grimstad*[50] decedent's wife alleged that her husband was drowned through defendant's negligent

---

[44] *Smith* v. *Auckland Hospital* [1965] NZLR 191 (CA finding that plaintiff would not have agreed to operation had he been warned there was a slight risk); *Baguley* v. *Babcock* [1962] SR (NSW) 286 (boy of 16 rather than 15 would have been able to handle machinery without danger!); *Gardner* v. *National Bulk Carriers* (1962) 310 F. 2d 284 (failure to turn back after several hours and search for seaman overboard).

[45] *Bonnington Castings* v. *Wardlaw* [1956] AC 613.

[46] [1953] 1 WLR 942, 946.

[47] *Jones* v. *Williams* (1857) 24 Beav. 47, 62; *Re Alms Corn Charity* [1901] 2 Ch. 750, 762; *Underwood* v. *Bank of Liverpool* [1924] 1 KB 775, 789.

[48] [1956] AC 613.

[49] *Weeks* v. *McNulty* (1898) 101 Tenn. 495, 70 Am. St. Rep. 693. *Jackson* v. *Vokins & Co.* [1957] 2 Ll. LR 451; *Nolan* v. *Dental Manufacturing Co. Ltd.* [1958] 2 All ER 449.

[50] (1920) 264 F. 334; *Blacka* v. *James* (1964) 205 Va. 646, 139 SE 2d 47.

failure to equip their barge with a lifebuoy. He fell overboard and was seen struggling in the sea but disappeared almost immediately. The court concluded that there would have been no time to use the buoy had it existed: hence causal connection was not established. Somewhat different considerations apply to the breach by defendant of a duty of diagnosis[51] or disclosure, for example the duty of a doctor to disclose to a patient the risks of the treatment he recommends. Here, if the treatment turns out unsuccessful, the patient will be sorely tempted to say that, had he been told of the risks, he would not have chosen to undergo it; and, in contrast with the case of safety equipment, there is not likely to be independent evidence of his probable reaction had defendant disclosed the dangers. Hence it is not surprising that some courts[52] have adopted an objective test[53] and asked what the reaction of an average or reasonable patient would have been. To the determination of this issue the patient's testimony is relevant but not decisive. The adoption of such a standard in malpractice cases can be interpreted as a method of protecting doctors against unwarranted claims, but can equally be seen as a *pis aller* resorted to because direct evidence of the patient's probable reaction is unlikely to be reliable.

(c) *Several contingencies.* It is more difficult to prove a connection which depends on several hypothetical contingencies than one which depends on few. When defendants were late in delivering four gallons of whiskey plaintiff's lumberjacks would not go into the water, his raft was constructed late and missed the rains which would have taken it to market in time for a profitable sale, but plaintiff failed to recover the loss of profit from defendant.

The fact that the whiskey was not sent may have caused the hands not to go into the water, but it is a far cry between constructing the raft at Thomas and marketing the product at Wilmington. The whiskey may have arrived and still the raft remain unconstructed. The raft may have been constructed and loaded and still never reach Wilmington. It requires quite a stretch of the imagination to conceive that had the four gallons of corn whiskey arrived at Thomas, the raft would have been properly constructed, loaded and

---

[51] *Pieck* v. *Medical Protective Co.* (1974) 64 Wis. 574, 219 NW 2d 242 (not proved that plaintiff would have had abortion if pregnancy had been diagnosed in time).

[52] *Canterbury* v. *Spence* (1972) 464 F. 2d 772; *Reibl* v. *Hughes* (1980) 114 DLR 3d 1; Picard, 'Patients, Doctors and the Supreme Court of Canada', (1981) *Oxf. JLS* 441. A variant suggested in *White* v. *Turner* (1981) 15 CCLT 81 (Ont.) is that the patient must show both that he would have refused the treatment and that a prudent patient in his position would have done so. Other courts adopt a subjective test: *Sykes* v. *Midland Bank* [1971] 1 QB 113 (CA).

[53] A similar issue arises in wrongful birth and wrongful life cases when the court has to determine whether, if suitably informed, a mother would have terminated a pregnancy: *Becker* v. *Schwartz* (1978) 46 NYS 2d 401, 386 NE 2d 985; T. K. Foutz, (1979–80) 54 *Tul. LR* 480.

safely conducted over a heavy freshet to Wilmington and the merchandise duly and profitably marketed. Whiskey is very potential at times, but it cannot be relied upon to produce such beneficent results as are claimed for it in this case.[54]

Similar facts. In order to reach a conclusion in a hypothetical inquiry a court may admit evidence of cases similar to the one under consideration.[55]

The difficulties noted in connection with hypothetical inquiries have led some observers[56] to suggest that, in fairness to plaintiffs, they should be entitled to recover damages proportioned to the likelihood that, if defendant had complied with the law, the harm to them would have been averted or minimized. Thus, if a plaintiff whose bones have not reunited can show a 40 per cent chance that, if the doctor had set them properly, they would have united, he should recover 40 per cent of his consequent disability.[57] Just as there are decisions which impose liability on a defendant for exposing plaintiff to a substantial risk of the harm that in fact occurs,[58] so there might be liability for depriving plaintiff of a chance of recovery. This would be to treat plaintiff's chance of recovery as something like a lottery ticket of which defendant deprived him.

*Combination of Explanatory and Hypothetical Inquiries:
Res ipsa loquitur*

Sometimes only a partial explanation of how harm occurred is available, in the sense that no connection with any act of defendant or his servants is established; nevertheless the court is prepared to conclude that, whatever the cause, its mischievous operation could have been prevented by reasonable care on defendant's part. Plaintiff is struck on the head by a bag of flour falling from a warehouse; who or what projected it is unknown but, as a reasonably competent warehouse owner is usually able to prevent bags falling from its windows, the court may conclude that defendant's negligence was the cause of the damage—a compendious way of saying that, whatever the full causal explanation, due care could have averted the

54 *Newsome* v. *Western Union Telegraph Co.* (1910) 69 SE 10 153 NC 153.
55 *Metropolitan Asylum District* v. *Hill* (1882) 47 LT 29 (HL).
56 e.g. Green (1961) 60 *Mich. LR* 543, 558; Atiyah, *Accidents, Compensation and the Law* (1970), p. 125.
57 The contrary was decided in *Kuhn* v. *Banker* (1938) 133 Ohio St. 304, 13 NE 2d 242; cf. *McWilliams* v. *Arrol* [1962] 1 All ER 623; *Barnett* v. *Chelsea Hospital* [1968] 1 All ER 1068; *Sykes* v. *Midland Bank* [1971] 1 QB 113, 129. For an argument in favour see W. H. Pedrick, 'Causation, the "Who Done It" Issue and Arno Becht', (1978) *Wash. ULR* 645.
58 Above, p. 410.

harm. The court is here combining an explanatory and a hypothetical inquiry.

It is usually in cases of this sort that the maxim *res ipsa loquitur*[59] is prayed in aid. Of course the maxim may also be cited when the evidence points to a particular act of negligence by defendant as the cause of harm, and no one can admire the absurd procedural rule that when there is only a specific allegation of negligence or specific evidence has been led, *res ipsa loquitur* cannot apply.[60] The reasoning on which *res ipsa loquitur* is based is usually, however, stated to be the argument that if the harm is of a sort that does not normally occur unless defendant has been negligent then his negligence is probably the cause of the harm.[61]

The form of the argument makes it clear that those writers are correct who have asserted that *res ipsa loquitur* represents no separate principle of the law of evidence.[62] Hence it is not surprising that no satisfactory line can be drawn between *res ipsa loquitur* cases and those where it does not apply.[63] In practice its main use is when the proponent has proved that harm has been caused by the movement of an inanimate object, and the desired inference is that this movement was caused by the negligence of the person in control of the object at the time. But this is only the most prominent of the situations in which the most probable inference is that the defendant has been negligent. If plaintiff sits down in a chair in defendant's shop and it collapses, injuring him, the natural inference is that the collapse was the consequence of defendant's negligence. To decide the contrary on the ground that the use and control of the chair were in plaintiff is to disregard common sense.[64]

It is said that *res ipsa loquitur* does not apply if the cause of the harm is known.[65] This is a dark saying. The application of the principle nearly always presupposes that some part of the causal process is known, but what is lacking is evidence of its connection with defendant's act or omission. When the fact of control is used to justify the inference that defendant's negligence was responsible

---

[59] Fleming, *Torts*, pp. 302 f.

[60] Prosser, *Selected Topics*, p. 346. The contrary has been held in *Anchor Products* v. *Hedges* (1966) 115 CLR 493; *Voice* v. *Union S.S. Co.* [1953] NZLR 176; *Neal* v. *Eaton Co.* [1933] 3 DLR 306.

[61] *Scott* v. *London & St. Katherine Docks Co.* (1865) 3 H. & C. 596, 601 *per* Erle CJ; *Mahon* v. *Osborne* [1939] 2 KB 14, 21.

[62] Prosser, *Selected Topics*, p. 311; Fleming, *Torts*, p. 302.

[63] An unsatisfactory formulation of the conditions for *res ipsa loquitur* by Wigmore (1st edn. iv, s. 209) has led some courts to neglect convincing evidence which did not fall within his formulation, e.g. because the thing was not in defendant's exclusive control.

[64] *Kilgore* v. *Shepard Co.* (1932) 52 RI 151, 158 Atl. 720. Contrast *Parker* v. *Miller* (1926) 42 TLR 408.

[65] *Barkway* v. *South Wales Transport Co. Ltd.* (1950) 1 All ER 392. Above, p. 409.

it must of course be shown that the thing in his control in fact caused the harm. In a sense, therefore, the cause of the harm must be known before the maxim can apply. Probably the limitation only means that there is no room for an inference that some unspecified act of negligence caused the harm when it is proved that a particular act of defendant did so, or that some other person's act was responsible. But this is too obvious to need stating.

In the *Barkway* case, once it was shown that the cause of the burst tyre was the disintegration of the plies, and that this in turn was caused by a heavy blow, it became clear that defendant's negligence was the cause of the disaster because reasonable care on their part would have revealed the occurrence of the blow. Hence resort to the maxim *res ipsa loquitur* was unnecessary.

Wigmore said that when *res ipsa loquitur* is to be applied 'the injurious occurrence must have happened irrespective of any voluntary action at the time by the party injured'.[66] It is unfortunate that this should be stated as a condition precedent. Sometimes the evidence points either to no negligence or to plaintiff's own negligence, e.g. if all that is known is that he fell down in a tram.[67] On the other hand the natural inference may be that both plaintiff and defendant were negligent and it is arguable that this is true of the ordinary highway collision where the only evidence is the fact of the collision, e.g. if both drivers are dead.[68] In a jurisdiction in which contributory negligence is a complete bar, this inference leads to judgment for defendant, but when apportionment is allowed, it is submitted that a court should apportion if it appears more likely than not that the harm was caused by the negligence of both parties.[69] It is very different when natural inference is that either plaintiff or defendant has negligently caused the harm but not both, or that only one of several co-defendants has done so. Here, if it is not more likely than not that one is responsible, the plaintiff in a civil action has not discharged the burden of proof and if he succeeds in such a situation it is because of a special rule shifting the persuasive burden of proof.[70]

Hence if regard is had to the type of inference underlying *res ipsa loquitur* there is no reason to require plaintiff to eliminate his own conduct as a cause before appealing to the maxim.[71] Wigmore speaks of plaintiff's 'voluntary conduct'. Of course if the evidence shows

---

66 3rd edn., s. 2509.
67 *Rystinski* v. *Central California Traction Co.* (1917) 175 Cal. 336, 165 P. 952.
68 *Baker* v. *Market Harborough Industrial Co-operative Society Ltd.* [1953] 1 WLR 1472.
69 Prosser, *Selected Topics*, pp. 338–9.
70 Below, p. 425.
71 Prosser, however, accepts this requirement. *Selected Topics*, p. 339.

that he acted voluntarily in our narrow sense, e.g. if he threw himself under the wheels of a car, no further explanation of the harm is needed. But why should plaintiff in the ordinary case negative his own responsibility before appealing to the fact that, as harm of this sort is usually caused by negligence, it probably was so caused on this occasion?

II. PROCEDURAL EFFECT OF EVIDENCE ADDUCED

Great confusion surrounds the terminology used in discussing the procedural effect of evidence given by the parties.[72] When we speak of the burden of proof being on one party or shifting to the other we may mean one of two types of 'burden' which correspond to two different problems that may arise in a case. The first is the problem whether an issue of fact should be submitted to the trier of fact as one on which he must form a judgment or whether, in view of the conclusive character of the evidence or its lack, only one view is possible. The second is a problem which arises only when it is decided that there is evidence on which the trier of fact is entitled to form a view. The judge must then direct the jury or direct himself, if he is sitting without a jury, on the question which side has the task of persuading the tribunal of fact on the issue in question.

The first sense of 'burden of proof', which is relevant to the first of these problems, is the burden of adducing enough evidence to prevent the issue being withdrawn from or not put to the jury or a directed verdict given. Thus, in a civil case in which the plaintiff alleges negligence, the issue of negligence will not be put to the jury unless evidence has been adduced on which they can reasonably find that defendant was negligent. Again, on a charge of homicide, the issue of provocation will not be put to the jury unless evidence has been adduced by accused or elicited from the prosecution witnesses on which they might reasonably find in favour of accused on that issue. This 'evidentiary' burden does not shift but, on any given issue, it may or may not have been discharged; for, at a given stage, either there is sufficient evidence for the issue to go before the jury, or it is for one of the parties to adduce such evidence.

A different though closely related type of 'burden' is the burden of proof in the sense of the need to persuade the tribunal of fact of the truth of a proposition with the appropriate degree of cogency. This is the only 'burden of proof' which need be mentioned to a jury since, *ex hypothesi*, if the burden of adducing evidence is not satisfied the case is withdrawn from or not put before the jury or a directed

[72] Cross, *Evidence*, p. 86.

verdict is given. On whom, then, does the burden of proving causal connection lie? It is for the plaintiff or prosecution in most cases to persuade the tribunal of fact of the existence of causal connection between wrongful act and harm. It is theoretically possible and, according to one view, sometimes actually the case in civil law that, when plaintiff has given evidence of special cogency, the burden of persuasion then shifts to defendant who is bound affirmatively to prove the absence of causal connection, with the appropriate degree of cogency, viz. on a balance of probabilities.

The two types of burden may most easily be distinguished thus: when A has the evidentiary burden, B is entitled to have the issue withdrawn from or not put before the tribunal of fact or a directed verdict given unless A discharges it: when A has the burden of persuasion B is entitled to succeed unless the evidence is sufficiently cogent to persuade the tribunal of fact on a balance of probabilities or beyond a reasonable doubt as the case may be of the truth of A's contention. In the case of a persuasive burden there will be, corresponding to the burden on A, a presumption in favour of B.

Many writers also use the expression 'burden of proof' to characterize the position, e.g. on a criminal charge when, the prosecution having adduced evidence on which the jury could convict, accused is in jeopardy unless he adduces evidence throwing doubt on the case for the prosecution. Such writers also speak of this as an evidential burden, though clearly it should be distinguished from the sense of evidential burden explained above, since failure to discharge the burden in this third sense does not result in the exclusion of any issue from the jury. The same writers also use the word 'presumption' in a corresponding sense. It may be questioned whether it is necessary to employ 'burden of proof' and 'presumption' in this sense in order to describe the judicial process. Would it not suffice to say that accused or defendant runs a risk that the issue will be decided against him unless he throws doubt on the evidence so far adduced? The risk may, of course, be a great one in a case where a reasonable man would come to a conclusion adverse to him, and in such a case he runs the risk that the judge's direction will clearly indicate the conclusion to which he thinks the jury ought to come.

The burden of adducing evidence of causal connection normally rests on plaintiff at the beginning of a civil case. Occasionally causal connection between defendant's conduct and the harm may be admitted on the pleadings. In the ordinary case the burden rests on plaintiff until he has adduced enough evidence to prevent the issue being withdrawn from the jury, and a verdict entered for defendant at the close of plaintiff's case on the ground that there is no evidence of causal connection.[73] Thereafter neither party has a burden of adducing evidence, though defendant may be in jeopardy unless he presents further evidence which throws doubt on plaintiff's case. This will be the position if such matters as *novus actus interveniens* or the loss attributable to a pre-existing condition of the plaintiff are treated as part of the single causal issue which is already before the jury. If however, such matters are treated as raising separate issues, the 'evidentiary' burden in relation to them will be on the defendant. Thus, the evidentiary burden of showing that plaintiff suffered from a disability or susceptibility before he was injured by defendant's wrong, so that, though causal connection is not negatived, damages should be reduced on that account, rests on defendant.[74] How much evidence he must adduce is another matter; it does not affect the incidence of the burden.

The burden of persuading the court or jury of the existence of causal connection rests on the plaintiff or prosecutor at the beginning of a case. If in a civil case the plaintiff claims damages for several items of harm, he must show that each is causally connected with defendant's wrongful conduct.[75] In a criminal case, at least in English law, it never shifts. In civil law it sometimes does so. 'Shifting' means that defendant must prove the contradictory of plaintiff's contention. We now examine some of the exceptional cases in which the burden of adducing evidence or of persuading the tribunal of fact is said in the appropriate sense to 'shift'. Usually the court does not state what type of burden it has in mind.

(i) The California court has decided that, when two defendants acting independently have each been proved negligent and harm has occurred which is clearly the consequence of the negligence of only one of them, but the evidence does not establish which, 'a requirement that the burden of proof [of causal connection] be shifted to defendants becomes manifest'.[76] This means that the persuasive burden is shifted; defendant must prove that his act was not the cause of the harm.

In *Summers* v. *Tice*[77] both defendants negligently fired at the same time at a quail and plaintiff was struck in the eye by a shot from one of the guns, it being impossible to establish which. A judgment against both defendants was upheld.

[73] *Deutsch* v. *Connecticut Co.* (1923) 98 Conn. 482, 119 Atl. 891.
[74] *Watts* v. *Rake* (1960) 108 CLR 158; *Sayers* v. *Perrin* [1966] QLR 89.
[75] *Edwards* v. *Hourigan* [1968] QR 202; *Negretto* v. *Sayers* [1963] SASR 313.
[76] *Summers* v. *Tice* (1948) 33 Cal. 2d 80, 199 P. 2d 1, 4, *per* Carter J.
[77] Approved in *Cook* v. *Lewis* [1952] 1 DLR 1, 18, *per* Cartwright J.

We must distinguish the case where defendants are acting in concert[78] and one has clearly caused the harm; here the other is responsible not for having caused the harm but on the special ground
that he engaged in a common venture with the first.[79]

The principle involved seems reasonable when both or all the
defendants against whom it operates are shown to have been at fault
on the occasion in question, and the doubt merely concerns which
of them caused the harm. For it is fairer that the burden of identification be borne by the wrongdoers rather than their victim when it
is their multiplicity alone which precludes the latter from identifying
the responsible culprit.[80] In *Sindell* v. *Abbott Laboratories*,[81] however,
the California court extended the principle to a case in which defendants were not shown to have been at fault but only to have had
a substantial share in the market for the sale of the product which
injured plaintiffs. Children whose mothers during pregnancy had
taken a certain drug, not then known to be dangerous, later developed cancerous growths as a result. Though they could not show
which firms had manufactured the particular samples of the drug
taken by their mothers, it was held that they could recover, on the
basis of strict products liability, against those firms which individually or together had at that time a substantial share of the
California market in the drug. Though it remains open in theory for
a firm to show that its product did not cause the harm in the individual case, in practice it could not do so. Hence in effect the court
dispenses with the need to prove fault and causal connection and
instead treats the manufacturers of the drug as collectively insuring,
in proportion to the market share of each, those who suffer harm
after using the drug. As Richardson J. points out in his dissent,[82] this
is a radical departure from traditional conceptions of tort law, with
their emphasis on the matching of plaintiffs and defendants.

(ii) A variant of the last view, supported by Rand J. in the Supreme
Court of Canada, is that the burden is shifted if plaintiff shows that
defendant was negligent and that either he or another has caused
the harm and defendant 'by confusing his act with environmental
conditions . . . has in effect destroyed the victim's power of proof'.[83]
This probably also refers to a persuasive burden.

[78] *Oliver* v. *Miles* (1926) 144 Mis. 852, 110 So. 666, 50 ALR 357.
[79] Above, p. 325.
[80] Fleming, *Torts*, p. 301.
[81] (1980) 163 Cal. Rep. 132, 607 P. 2d 924; cf. *Bichler* v. *Eli Lilly* (1981) 436 NYS
2d 625; (1980) 94 *Harv. LR* 668.
[82] *Sindell* v. *Abbott Laboratories* (1980) 607 P. 2d 924, 939.
[83] *Cook* v. *Lewis* [1952] 1 DLR 1, 4; *Woodward* v. *Begbie* [1962] Ont. R. 60, 31
DLR 2d 22; cf. *Saint-Pierre* v. *McCarthy* [1957] QR 421; *Gardiner* v. *National Bank
Carriers* (1962) 310 F. 2d 284; *Haft* v. *Lone Palm Hotel* (1970) 478 P. 2d 465 (lifeguard
if present at pool might have been able to establish how deceased drowned); *contra*:
Matthews v. *McLaren* (1969) 4 DLR 3d 557, 566 and see E. R. Alexander (1972) 22
U. Toro. LJ 98; E. J. Weinrib (1975) 38 *MLR* 518, 525.

But the argument is in any case a weak one,[84] since it is no wrong to another to make it difficult for him to prove a case and, if such a category of wrongdoing were to be introduced, it would constitute an arbitrary form of strict liability, since defendant could often not know in advance whether his conduct was likely in the outcome to present difficulties of proof to a potential victim.

(iii) When the evidence makes it more likely than not that one or other of two defendants has been guilty of negligence causing the harm but does not make it clear which, the California court has again ruled that the (persuasive) burden is on each defendant to disprove negligence and causal connection between his own conduct and the harm.

In *Ybarra* v. *Spangard* [85] plaintiff suffered a shoulder injury during an operation for appendicitis. He joined as defendants the diagnostician, surgeon, anaesthetist, owner of the hospital, and two nurses. One or more of them was clearly responsible and it was held that their control of the things which might have harmed plaintiff 'places upon them the burden of initial explanation', a phrase which may mean either that a persuasive burden rests on each of them or perhaps merely that they are in jeopardy on the issues of negligence and causal connection.

Whether the burden is shifted on such facts has not been decided in English law, but Denning LJ has by different reasoning reached a view similar to that of the California court,[86] while McNair J. was of the opposite opinion.[87]

(iv) These last cases raise the question whether *res ipsa loquitur* in general shifts the persuasive burden of proof. There are certainly statements by courts and writers suggesting that the burden of persuasion shifts,[88] but a closer examination often raises a doubt whether the burden of persuasion is really meant or whether the effect is merely that defendant is in jeopardy since there is evidence on which the trier of fact may and indeed reasonably ought to find against him on the issues of negligence and causal connection.

Our earlier discussion of *res ipsa loquitur* made it clear that the maxim is merely a form of the argument that a particular sort of

[84] B. Hogan, '*Cook* v. *Lewis* Re-examined', (1961) 24 *MLR* 331.
[85] (1944) 25 Cal. 2d 486, 154 P. 2d 687.
[86] *Roe* v. *Minister of Health* [1954] 2 QB 66, 82.
[87] [1954] 2 QB 66; cf. *Nesterczuk* v. *Mortimore* (1965) 115 CLR 140; *Maher-Smith* v. *Gaw* [1969] VR 371; *Hillyer* v. *St. Bart's Hospital* [1909] 2 KB 820, 827; *Macdonald* v. *Pottinger* [1953] NZLR 196.
[88] Phipson, *Evidence* (12th edn. 1976), s. 116. Best, *Evidence*, 12th edn., p. 285 (not mentioning *res ipsa loquitur* but citing *Byrne* v. *Boadle* (1863) 2 H. & C. 722); *Scott* v. *London & St. Katherine Docks Co.* (1865) 3 H. & C. 596, 600 *per* Blackburn J. 'Is not the fact of the accident evidence to call upon the defendants to prove that there was no negligence?'

contingency probably caused harm because, more often than not, harm of that sort is so caused. One view of its procedural effect is that it merely exposes defendant to the risk of a finding of negligence causally connnected with the harm to plaintiff if he fails to throw doubt on or explain away plaintiff's evidence.

Although it has occasionally been decided in England that a defendant in a *res ipsa loquitur* case has the persuasive burden[89] of disproving negligence and causal connection, Prosser's explanation of these decisions may well be historically correct;[90] sometimes the relation between the parties is such, as when plaintiff is being carried by defendant for reward,[91] that the burden of disproving negligence and causal connection is a matter of law placed on defendant from the beginning. Dicta of some English judges[92] that *res ipsa loquitur* shifts the 'burden of proof' may mean either that defendant is in jeopardy unless he adduces evidence throwing doubt on plaintiff's case, or that he must prove the absence of negligence to be more likely than not:[93] the latter view now apparently prevails,[94] no doubt because, with the disuse of jury trials in civil cases, a permissible inference tends to be treated as a mandatory one. On the other hand in countries in which juries are still common, the former view is often preferred.[95]

(v) The (persuasive) burden of proving contributory negligence is on defendant; so is the burden of proving unreasonable failure on plaintiff's part to avoid the consequences of wrong.[96] These issues of course involve proof of causal connection between the plaintiff's conduct and the harm.

In some instances other than the foregoing it has been said that a presumption of causal connection arises. This expression may either mean that the persuasive burden rests on the party against whom the presumption operates or that that party is in jeopardy on the

[89] *Angus* v. *London, Tilbury & Southend R. Co.* (1906) 22 TLR 222.
[90] *Selected Topics*, p. 305.
[91] *Christie* v. *Griggs* (1809) 2 Camp. 79; 170 ER 1088; cf. *Travers & Sons Ltd.* v. *Cooper* [1915] 1 KB 73 (bailment of goods).
[92] Lords Simon and Simonds in *Woods* v. *Duncan* [1946] AC 401, 419, 439. In this case Lieut. Woods was held to have proved that he was not negligent. Cf. *Heywood* v. *A.G.*, [1956] NZLR, 668, 680. *Moore* v. *Fox* [1956] 1 QB 612. *Barkway* v. *South Wales Transport Co.* [1948] 2 All ER 460.
[93] *Ballard* v. *North British R. Co.* [1923] SC (HL) 43, 54; *The Kite* [1933] P. 154; *The Mulbera* [1937] P. 82. *Rolland Paper Co.* v. *C.N.R.* (1957) 11 DLR 2d 754.
[94] *Barkway* v. *South Wales Transport Co.* [1948] 2 All ER 460. *Moore* v. *Fox* [1956] 1 QB 612; *Henderson* v. *Jenkins* [1970] AC 282; *Ludgate* v. *Lovett* [1969] 1 WLR 1016. The reason is that, the evidence being undisputed, it cannot properly be disbelieved.
[95] *Nominal Defendant* v. *Haslbauer* (1967) 117 CLR 448; *Government Insurance* v. *Fredrichberg* (1968) 118 CLR 403; *Temple* v. *Terrace Co.* (1966) 57 DLR 2d 631; *Rolland Paper* v. *C.N.R.* (1958) 13 DLR 2d 662; *Hawke's Bay Motor* v. *Russell* [1972] NZLR 542.
[96] *Wakelin* v. *L.S.W.R.* (1886) 12 App. Cas. 41, 47; Williams, *Joint Torts*, p. 387; *Caswell* v. *Powell Duffryn Collieries* [1940] AC 152, 172, 183; *Hercules Textile Mills* v. *K. & H. Textile Engineers* [1955] VLR 310.

issue in question unless he throws doubt on the existing evidence in favour of his opponent. These we now discuss.

(vi) The Illinois court has held that on a charge of homicide 'when the State has shown the existence, through the act of the accused, of a sufficient cause of death, the death is presumed to have resulted from such act, unless it appears that death was caused by a supervening act disconnected from any act of the defendant'.[97] This presumption, if it merely means that the jury are entitled to and reasonably might find adversely to accused unless the prosecution evidence is subsequently shaken or explained away, seems reasonable, even on a criminal charge, if the act proved was sufficient to cause the harm and defendant's contention is merely that some other cause accelerated the harm. But if treated as throwing a persuasive burden on accused it is inconsistent, for English law, with the principle underlying the decision in *Woolmington* v. *D.P.P.*[98] According to this the persuasive burden is not shifted even when the prosecution adduces strong and unchallenged evidence on a particular issue.[99]

(vii) It is said that in Admiralty law, when a ship damaged in a collision is subsequently lost, there is a presumption that the loss was occasioned by the collision.[1]

(viii) When a defendant alleges an alternative cause, viz. that if he had complied with the law plaintiff would have suffered the same or substantially similar harm, that issue will be left to the jury only if there is some evidence to support the allegation.[2]

(ix) According to Glanville Williams, who distinguishes between 'scientific' and 'legal' cause, the former corresponding roughly to our 'necessary condition', 'once the causal nexus is scientifically established between the defendant's act and the plaintiff's damage, the presumption should be that no event has interposed to make the damage too remote in law. The burden of rebutting this presumption would then rest on the defendant.'[3] This view, of course, stems from the author's general theory of causation: if accepted it would have far-reaching consequences. Thus, suppose in an action under the Fatal Accidents Acts it is proved that *B* negligently injured *A*, and that *A* was taken to hospital, given an anaesthetic, and died under the anaesthetic. On Williams's view, his dependants need only show that but for injury he would not have been given the anaesthetic; they need not show that the anaesthetic was a reasonable one to

---

[97] *People* v. *Meyers* (1946), 392 Ill. 355, 64 NE 2d 531, 533.
[98] [1935] AC 462.
[99] 'Malice' in that case; but the principle is of general application.
[1] *The San Onofre* [1922] P. 243, 251, *per* Scrutton LJ; *The City of Lincoln* (1889) 15 PD 15.
[2] *Berry* v. *Borough of Sugar Notch* (1899) 43 Atl. 240 (Pa.).
[3] *Joint Torts*, p. 242.

428 THE COMMON LAW

give. This would, it is submitted, change the present law in a way which could only be justified in those cases in which courts were prepared to base liability on the risk theory and where the consequence of which defendant's act was the 'scientific cause' fell within the risk. If, on the other hand, Williams means only that the issue of whether the giving of the anaesthetic negatived causal connection will not be put to the jury or considered by the trier of fact unless there is some evidence to suggest that it may have been unreasonable to administer it, his view is free from objection.[4]

III. THE DIVISION OF FUNCTION BETWEEN JUDGE AND JURY

We have made no attempt to suggest in detail how causal issues should be allocated between judge and jury in those jurisdictions in which trials are commonly conducted before juries. To do so would require a close acquaintance with procedural issues in those jurisdictions. But in outline if the views advocated in this book are accepted the division of function which would be appropriate is clear. All those issues which are on our analysis genuinely causal should be submitted to the jury or trier of fact provided there is some evidence before it or him which could form the basis of a finding. In criminal law, for example, it is for the jury to say whether in a case of homicide death was caused by the conduct of the defendant. We should have thought this too plain for argument were it not that Smith and Hogan maintain that 'whether a particular act which is a *sine qua non* of an alleged *actus reus* is also a cause of it is a question of law'.[5] This seems contrary to the authorities[6] and also wrong in principle.

Of course, the facts may be so plain on this as on any other issue that the judge in England is entitled to direct the jury what finding they should arrive at.[7] But this is merely to say that there must be some evidence on which a finding can be based, and whether such evidence exists is admittedly a question of law for the court.

---

[4] *Simpson* v. *Standard Telephone & Cables* [1940] 1 KB 342, 350. Cf. *Caswell* v. *Powell Duffryn Collieries* [1940] AC 152, 169, 171; *Dominion Natural Gas Co.* v. *Collins* [1909] AC 640; *Steele* v. *Robert George* [1942] AC 497; Lalou, *Traité pratique de la responsabilité civile*, p. 718.

[5] Smith and Hogan, *Criminal Law*, p. 272.

[6] *Brennan* v. *R.* (1936) 55 CLR 253; *R.* v. *Jordan* (1957) 40 CAR 152; *R.* v. *Blaue* [1975] 3 All ER 446, 450 ('the issue of the cause of death in a trial for either murder or manslaughter is one of fact for the jury to decide'); *R.* v. *Cato* [1976] 1 All ER 260, 264; *Palmer* v. *State* (1960) 164 Atl. 2d 467 (Md.); *R.* v. *Evans & Gardiner (No. 2)* [1976] VR 517, 531 (pointing out that in *R.* v. *Jordan* (1957) 40 CAR 152 the Court of Appeal wrongly usurped the function of the jury on this point); *R.* v. *Pagett. The Times* 4.2.1983.

[7] *R.* v. *Blaue* [1975] 3 All ER 446.

So far as civil actions are concerned, in jurisdictions in which they are tried by jury the questions of fact to be submitted to them will in a proper case include whether the wrongful conduct of defendant or defined state of affairs was a causally relevant condition of the harm and also whether some other contingency (voluntary conduct or abnormality) negatives causal connection between conduct and harm.

The first issue can often, though not always, be put as a 'but for' question. Would the harm have occurred if defendant had not driven negligently, or stored a dangerous substance on his land or failed to provide a proper guard? In answering it the jury will often have to make up its mind what the course of events would have been had defendant complied with the law, but that, too, raises a question of fact of a (recondite) sort.[8]

The second question is often put, in current practice, by asking whether there was a continuous and unbroken sequence of events leading up to the harm, or whether there was a superseding or new intervening cause which interrupted the chain of events. A simple form of words is probably preferable. *Was the harm the consequence of defendant's wrongful conduct or was something else the cause of the harm to the exclusion of defendant's conduct?* If it is necessary to enlarge on what the something else might be, why not refer to the broad criteria analysed in this book? For example, was the later treatment given by Dr *X* so extraordinary that it can be regarded as the sole cause of the harm? Was what happened subsequently just a coincidence? Did *Y* decide to intervene, knowing of the dangerous situation, freely and without being under any duty to do so? Did *Z* try to exploit the situation by stealing from the unconscious man? It is quite easy to find a form of words which avoids jargon, scholastic or modern, and which a jury can understand and apply. It seems unnecessary and undesirable to qualify the notion of cause with adjectives ('proximate' or the like) or to decorate it with metaphors, in order to make it comprehensible to a jury.[9] The attempt to do so is more likely to confuse than to instruct a jury.

On the other hand, the problems of legal policy involved in determining the proper scope of statutory or common law rules, the types of damage for which the law provides a remedy, and the appropriate allocation of risks in different branches of the law, so far as they come within the function of courts, fall more naturally to the judge than to the jury. They raise questions of law, not fact. If the risk and policy theorists are right in thinking that the issues of 'proximate cause' are exclusively issues of policy, they should surely

[8] Above, p. 407 n. 5.
[9] *Fitzgerald* v. *Penn* (1954) 91 CLR 268, 276-8.

be decided by judges alone.[10] In consequence, our view, which is also the traditional view, and the one which conforms better with the existing practice, is that there should be a division of function between judge and jury.

Once the policy issues (in our sense) have been decided in favour of the plaintiff, assuming that they are so decided, the causal issues, whether they concern, in current terminology, 'but for' causation, superseding cause or *novus actus interveniens*, should go to the tribunal of fact, but in simplified language. This conclusion as to the appropriate division of function between the tribunal of law and the tribunal of fact is an important practical consequence of the difference between our views and those of the modern risk and policy theorists.

10 But this is not the conclusion drawn by, for example, Prosser, *Torts*, s. 45.

PART III

THE CONTINENTAL THEORIES

XVI

INDIVIDUALIZING THEORIES
AND THEORY OF CONDITIONS
(*BEDINGUNGSTHEORIE*)

IN this and the next chapter we examine some of the more prominent
theories of causation propounded on the Continent. The interest of
doing so, from the point of view of the student of the common law,
may lie in learning how the causal problems with which he is familiar
appear to lawyers who do not share his empirical outlook and who
view legal concepts against the background of systematic philosophy. In order to emphasize the difference of approach we touch
only lightly on the views of those, such as the French writers, who
distrust systems and tolerate inconsistencies,[1] and concentrate instead on the German language writers who have invented and sys-
tematized the main theories.[2] Their work has been elaborated by
writers in other European countries and in Latin America and accepted by the courts in many of these countries. On the other hand
we have attempted to make the theories more intelligible by citing
freely from the decisions of the courts which purport to apply them.
Most of the theories were designed to meet the problems of criminal law in the first place and, accordingly, the reader will find a
greater emphasis on these problems and on the decisions of criminal
courts than we would expect in a discussion of causation in the
common law.

[1] Joly, 'Vers un critère juridique du rapport de causalité au sens de l'article 1384
alinéa 1er du code civil', *Rev. trim. dr. civ.* (1942), 257 at p. 273 ('we should renounce
these foreign importations'). The account in Honoré, *IECL*, xi, chap. 7 is based on
the classifications adopted by French writers and, for the 'direct cause' theory, see
ibid. 7–1 ff.
[2] 'Le problème causal en matière de responsabilité était fait pour séduire l'esprit
des juristes d'Allemagne.' Marty, *Rev. trim. dr. civ.* (1939), pp. 685, 689.

The expression 'theories of causation' is used because the writers with whom we are dealing did not until recently regard an inquiry into causal principles as in principle different from an attempt to construct a scientific theory. In our view this approach is mistaken; the 'theories' are in fact conceptual, not empirical investigations. But the use of the word is inveterate, and it would distort the views of Continental writers to present them as if they purported to give an analysis of the meaning or use of 'cause' in the law.

Unlike the Anglo-American writers who have made piecemeal contributions to the study of causation, Continental jurists have not hesitated to apply to the law philosophical doctrines of considerable complexity.[3] Indeed some German writers have sought to identify the legal notion of cause either with Kant's doctrine, embodied in the statement that 'everything which occurs presupposes some other thing upon which it follows in accordance with a rule',[4] or with Mill's doctrine of a cause as a complex of conditions invariably followed by a given type of consequence. Von Kries on the other hand constructed on the basis of a philosophical theory about the nature of probability a theory of causation[5] specially adapted for use by lawyers. Other writers have distinguished the legal and philosophical notions of cause and have pointed, in particular, to the fact that the law is not primarily concerned with explanation[6] but rather with fixing the limits of responsibility; yet even those writers who refuse to identify the legal and philosophical notions of cause are influenced by systematic philosophy to a greater extent than are Anglo-American writers.

One corollary of this is that the Continental writers are reluctant to admit that common sense or the ordinary use of causal expressions outside the law is a reliable guide for the lawyer.[7] To this von Kries and the adequacy theorists form a partial exception, for they considered that the causal judgments of the ordinary man confusedly reflected the fact that the alleged cause had or had not 'increased

---

[3] This applies primarily to those writing in German and to a lesser extent to those writing in Italian, Spanish and Dutch. The French contributions, on the other hand, are decidedly empirical, perhaps more so than the English. See Marty, 'La relation de cause à effet comme condition de la responsabilité civile', *Rev. trim. dr. civ.* (1939), at p. 700.

[4] Leonhard, *Die Kausalität als Erklärung durch Ergänzung*, pp. 26, 31; Liepmann 'Zur Lehre von der adäquaten Verursachung', *Golddammers Archiv*, 52, 326; *Einleitung in das Strafrecht* (1900), p. 50.

[5] Viz. the 'adequate cause' theory: see below, pp. 467–78.

[6] Tarnowski, *Die systematische Bedeutung der adäquaten Kausalität*, p. 70; Radbruch, *Die Lehre von der adäquaten Verursachung*, p. 325. But Radbruch inconsistently adds that the law gives psychological explanations of physical events while science gives physical explanations of psychological events.

[7] Nagler, *Leipziger Kommentar zum Strafgesetzbuch*, i. 24; Tarnowski, pp. 60, 64.

the objective probability' of the consequence.[8] A second corollary is that, despite the profusion of different 'causal' expressions to be found in the codes,[9] the older writers on the whole treated 'causal connection' as a uniform and unvarying element in legal responsibility.[10]

Generalizing and Individualizing Theories

The fundamental distinction recognized by Continental theorists is between those theories which recognize that every particular causal statement is implicitly general, in the sense that its truth is dependent on the truth of some general statement of regularities, and those theories which do not recognize this. Theories of the first kind are known as '*generalizing* theories'; those of the second kind as '*individualizing* theories'. To readers who are influenced by Hume's and Mill's analyses of causation an individualizing theory which completely divorces the notion of causation from causal generalizations or laws may seem strange; literally taken, such theories seem to insist that there is a quality of 'being a cause' or 'being causally efficacious' which inheres in or belongs to particular acts or events and perhaps also to omissions, so that, just as a blow may have the quality or attribute of being heavy, so it may have the quality or attribute of being a cause or being causally efficient. On this view the causal quality or efficacy of a particular action or event is primary, not a feature derived from the fact that it is an instance of a kind of event believed to be regularly or generally connected with an event of some other kind. There is, however, still some merit in these theories as a reminder that the claim that the whole meaning of causal connection is to be found in the notion of regular sequence is mistaken.[11] We have seen that the circumstances of individual cases have much to do with the distinction between causes and mere conditions.[12]

[8] Below, p. 467. Rümelin, 'Die Verwendung der Kausalbegriffe im Straf- und Zivilrecht', *AcP* 90, pp. 171, 190.

[9] e.g. German: *StGB*, s. 211 (tötet), s. 222 (den Tod verursacht), s. 263 (dadurch beschädigt), s. 26 (bestimmt hat), *BGB*, s. 287 (während des Verzugs durch Zufall eintretende Unmöglichkeit); French: Code pénal, art. 319 (quiconque aura commis un homicide ou en aura été la cause), art. 309 (s'il est résulté), ibid. (auront été suivies), ibid. (l'ont occasionnée); Spanish: list compiled by L. Jiménez de Asúa from Latin American Penal Codes: (causar, producir, provocar, procurar, verificar, ocasionar, originar, acarrear, crear, dar motivo (causa, ocasión, lugar), hacer surgir, resultar, tener por resultado, sobrevenir, derivar, proceder, ocurrir, a consecuencia de, por efecto de, sequido de), *Tratado de Derecho Penal* (2nd edn. 1958) iii. 589–91.

[10] Köstlin, *Neue Revision der Grundbegriffe des Kriminalrechts*, p. 455; von Buri, *Die Kausalität und ihre strafrechtlichen Beziehungen*, p. 11; Enneccerus-Lehmann, ii. 62 nn. 3–4.

[11] Indeed, Mackie, *Cement*, p. 121 argues that 'it is only in a very tenuous sense that any singular causal statements are implicitly general', though he does not base this on any view that being a cause is a quality of events or an intrinsic attribute.

[12] Above, p. 33.

As their name suggests, the generalizing theories insist that, if a particular act or event is a cause of something, its status as a cause is derived from the fact that it is of a kind believed to be generally connected with an event of some other kind.

The individualizing theories themselves divide into two main types: the first of these, 'necessity' theories,[13] insist not only that 'being a cause' is an intrinsic attribute of particular events, but that if an event is genuinely a cause it *necessarily* produces its effect because of its own nature, because 'it is what it is in itself'.[14] A 'mortal' wound[15] is a cause of death *necessarily*; for if it did not cause death, it would not be a mortal wound. Perhaps the only plausibility which this theory has is due to its failure to distinguish between two senses of the dangerous word 'necessity'. The meaning of 'mortal' may be so defined that as a matter of logic nothing shall count as a mortal wound if death does not result; but this incorporation of a causal relation into the meaning of a general expression does not show the causal relation to be a necessary one or more than an instance of a regular sequence.

The second type of individualizing theory is the 'efficiency' theory.[16] This also insists that the relationship between a particular cause and its effect is not derived from their status as instances of a regularity, but differs from the necessity theory in allowing that events may possess causal efficacy in varying degrees or proportions. A cause, to be a cause, must, as a particular act or event, be efficient; but the concurrence of several factors may be required to contribute the 'causal energy' needed for the production of an effect. This strange terminology, like the English metaphors of varying causal 'potency' which are its counterparts, is an attempt to analyse the concept of causation in terms of the most familiar case: that of a moving thing causing another to move. Like all such extensions of a single case to the whole field, it fails mainly because it provides no criteria for determining the existence of the property of causal efficiency or the measurement of its varying degrees.

Between the individualizing and generalizing theories we must place the Continental variant of the doctrine of the equivalence of conditions, the 'theory of conditions'.[17] Some have adopted this doctrine in the form that any necessary condition is entitled to be called a cause; others in the form that the word 'cause' is reserved

13 Honoré, *IECL*, xi. 7-60 to 7-66.
14 For an English version of this theory see H. W. B. Joseph, *An Introduction to Logic*, p. 408, and for a criticism, A. J. Ayer, *Foundations of Empirical Knowledge*, pp. 201-2.
15 On this expression see also above, pp. 241-2.
16 Honoré, *IECL*, xi. 7-67 to 7-70.
17 *Bedingungstheorie, Äquivalenztheorie.*

for the totality of all necessary conditions. It might well be thought that this theory should be classed with the generalizing theories on the ground that a condition X can only be shown to be a necessary condition of an occurrence Y by appeal to general laws showing that Y never occurs without X. But most German theorists have thought that the classification of a condition as necessary can be made, without recourse to known generalizations,[18] by an appeal to the imagination.[19] The generalizing theories, of which the most important is the 'adequate cause' or adequacy theory, make contact with modern ideas of probability. According to a version of the adequate cause theory, which is widely received by civil courts on the Continent, a contingency is for legal purposes a cause of harm if it increases the probability of the occurrence of harm of that sort.[20] The generalizing theories accord with the principles we have extracted from common sense in their insistence both on the essential connection in the central case between particular causal statements and certain generalizations and on the importance of the contrast between normal and abnormal conditions.

Lastly there is one curious strand in German philosophical thought in connection with human action that demands attention. Most thinkers rigidly adhere to the view that in considering whether a human actor has caused harm only the actor's physical movements may be regarded as relevant, not his state of mind: once it is found that such movements were the cause of harm the question whether the act was deliberate, mistaken, or accidental is relevant only to the question of fault or *mens rea*. 'The disposition of the will can add nothing to and take nothing from the existence of the act and its causal property.'[21] This view is a reflection of the sharp distinction made by Kant between imputation (*Zurechnung*) and causation,[22] and is based on the identification of causation with physical processes.

Sometimes this identification is expressed in the aphorism 'Kausalität ist blind, Finalität sehend'. Emphasis on this identification

[18] An outstanding example is von Kries. The fact that a reference to general laws is necessary in order to establish that an event was a necessary condition of another event is recognized by Engisch, *Die Kausalität als Merkmal der strafrechtlichen Tatbestände* (1931), p. 18.

[19] i.e. whether we can imagine Y without X. See below, pp. 443 f. Mackie, *Cement*, p. 60 distinguishes a 'primitive' way of supporting singular causal sequences which relies on imagination from a 'sophisticated' one which makes use of general propositions.

[20] For a detailed exposition and criticism see below, pp. 471, 485-8.

[21] *RGSt* 19 (1888), 141, 146. Jescheck, 'Anstiftung usw.' (1956) 71 *SchwZSt* 225, 226.

[22] 'Zurechnung (imputatio) in moralischer Bedeutung ist das Urteil, wodurch iemand als Urheber (causa libera) einer Handlung, die alsdann Tat (factum) heißt und unter Gesetzen steht, angesehen wird.' *Rechtslehre, Einleitung*, p. 29. Cf. *Prolegomena*, pp. 114-19; Antoliséi, *Il Rapporto di Causalità in Diritto Penale*, p. 180.

prevents some German writers from recognizing that in causal inquiries it is sometimes illuminating to cite voluntary conduct, sometimes conduct which is less than fully voluntary and sometimes mere physical movements as the cause of an event.[23] Much depends on the context. In some contexts physical movements described as such are appropriately cited as the cause of harm; a doctor may cite a sudden movement as the cause of a heart attack. In other contexts the search for an explanation, quite apart from considerations of fault, may make an answer in terms of some person's deliberate act the appropriate answer to the question what was the cause of the harm; e.g. the deliberate act of the deceased in swallowing poison, as opposed to his mistakenly swallowing poison administered by another.

We proceed, after a historical introduction, to analyse in detail the two most important theories, the theory of conditions and the adequacy theory.

I. INDIVIDUALIZING THEORIES OF CAUSATION

Causation has been intensively discussed by Continental lawyers for the last 150 years. Whereas in the Anglo-American world one could, before 1959, when the first edition of this book was published, point only to Leon Green's *Rationale of Proximate Cause* as a comprehensive study of the subject, on the Continent dozens of books have been published dealing solely or substantially with causation, and numerous theories and variants of theories have been propounded. Some observers have thought that this torrent of speculation and systematization has produced only a welter of fruitless and confusing abstractions[24] and that the problem would be better left to the unfettered discretion of the judge.[25] Nevertheless, the German courts and, to a varying extent, the courts of other European countries, have adopted and adhered to one of the main theories: most criminal courts adopt the theory of conditions while civil courts adopt the adequacy or some similar theory.

'Necessary' Causes

At the beginning of the nineteenth century lawyers generally took the view that a cause in law meant a 'necessary' cause in the sense that, given the alleged cause, the alleged consequence necessarily

23 This range of possible cases was perhaps overlooked by Lord Sumner in *Samuel v. Dumas* [1924] AC 431, 462, where he decided that the cause of the scuttling of a ship was not the voluntary act of the master and crew who scuttled it but the entry of the sea-water. The majority of the House of Lords thought otherwise.
24 Berner, *Lehrbuch des deutschen Strafrechts* (1898), p. 116.
25 Dernburg, *Bürgerliches Recht* (1899), II. i. 65.

followed[26] by virtue of an intrinsic property of the alleged cause. This was applied particularly to the law of homicide and a distinction was drawn between mortal and non-mortal wounds.[27] If the accused gave a mortal wound and the victim died he had caused death in the legal sense but not if he gave a non-mortal wound and the victim died through the concurrence of gangrene, unskilful treatment, or some other intervening factor.

This view was unduly favourable to the accused and depended on the notion that lethality was an attribute inherent in some wounds and not others. It was criticized by Stübel,[28] with whose works the scientific discussion of causation in the legal sphere really began. Stübel and later Köstlin[29] pointed out that human experience did not provide any examples of 'necessary' causes and the law did not, in order to establish causal connection, require that the act under consideration should have been 'necessary or even sufficient, predominant, or indispensable in the circumstances'.[30] On the contrary each act presupposes, in order to achieve its effect, a number of external circumstances and conditions as subsidiary causes; only the sum of all subjective and objective conditions can together be considered as the cause of the effect in the sense of being indispensable[31] in the circumstances.

According to Stübel the contrast between 'necessary' and 'accidental' or 'coincidental'[32] had no place in the law, whilst Köstlin wished to retain a distinction between what was coincidental in itself and coincidental only from the standpoint of the actor (i.e. unforeseen).[33] These writers were feeling their way towards certain distinctions which have been made explicit in more recent discussion.[34] On the one hand, even if a set of conditions of a certain kind were always followed by a given consequence this would not justify the conclusion that the conditions 'necessarily' produce the consequence by virtue of a special causal property. Secondly, it is very seldom possible to assert that a certain consequence always follows upon a *single* earlier condition. Clearly it does not in cases of 'intellectual origination'[35] or psychological influence; when one person

[26] Above, p. 434.
[27] In Spain this distinction continued to determine responsibility until late in the nineteenth century. See A. H. Ferrer, *La relación de causalidad en la teoria del delito.*
[28] *Über den Tatbestand der Verbrechen, die Urheber derselben, etc.* (1803).
[29] C. R. Köstlin, *Neue Revision der Grundbegriffe des Kriminalrechts* (1843), p. 453.
[30] Ibid.
[31] But this is a muddle, for though the totality of all such conditions may have been together sufficient to produce the consequence one cannot conclude that the totality was indispensable in the circumstances, since there may have been another such set present on the same occasion. Above, pp. 112, 122-5.
[32] *Zufällig.*
[33] Köstlin, p. 455.
[34] F. Leonhard, *Die Kausalität als Erklärung durch Ergänzung* (1946), p. 4.
[35] Köstlin, p. 455.

is influenced by the promptings, suggestions, or threats of another it is by no means always true that he would always be influenced by the same threat, etc., in the same way. Similarly, in relation to natural events, a revolver shot in the shoulder may cause death on a particular occasion although such a shot is not *always* followed by death. The example of a mortal wound might seem to be to the contrary, but a wound is called 'mortal' (in one sense of the word)[36] only because it is nearly certain that counteracting conditions which would avert death will be absent. In general, the most that can be asserted of a single condition is that it is *frequently* followed by a given event.[37]

When the concept of a single condition, *necessarily* followed by a particular consequence, fell into discredit, legal science did not at once transfer its allegiance to the notion of a condition frequently or usually followed by a particular consequence. Instead a number of individualizing theories developed.[38] These are of the sort with which Anglo-American lawyers are familiar.

'Efficient' and Similar Causes[39]

The most important, perhaps, is the theory which treats as the cause of an event the *efficient* or the *most efficient* condition.[40] This theory is generally termed metaphysical[41] since it is said to have its roots in the Aristotelian concept of an efficient cause[42] or source of motion, and perhaps it is not unfair to add, is incapable of translation into literal terms, or at any rate into non-mechanical terms. The chief exponent of this theory was Birkmeyer,[43] who argued that a certain quantity of energy attached to each condition of an event and that by 'cause' the law meant that condition to which the greatest quantity attached and which therefore made the greatest contribution to the result. In the event of equally great contributions made by two or more acts each might be regarded as a cause and so punishable. But the quantity of energy could not be exactly measured and 'the judge in determining the causal quality of a concrete event may decide in accordance with his full and unfettered discretion'.[44]

36 For other senses see above, pp. 241-2.
37 Leonhard, op. cit., pp. 27-31.
38 Above, p. 433.
39 Above, p. 433.
40 *Wirksamste Bedingung, condition génératrice.*
41 E. S. K. Engisch, *Die Kausalität als Merkmal der strafrechtlichen Tatbestände* (1931), p. 28.
42 *Stößende Ursache, causa efficiente*: Aristotle, *Metaphysics*, 1. 3. 11.
43 *Ursachenbegriff und Kausalzusammenhang im Strafrecht*, Rektoratsrede, Rostock (1885). See also R. Horn, *Kausalbegriff*, p. 66; Thyren, *Abhandlungen aus dem Strafrecht*, vol. i.
44 Birkmeyer, op. cit., p. 18; von Buri, *Die Kausalität* (1873), p. 9.

This theory had obvious metaphysical attractions while seeming to escape some of the difficulties of the necessity theory. It also claimed support from introspection, since it is asserted that we know from our own experience that some conditions are 'more efficient' than others and from that can infer, by the use of sympathy and understanding, that the experience of others is the same.[45] Children and primitive people, it is argued, naturally explain events in terms of substances and attribute greater or less force or activity to different substances, animate or inanimate.[46]

Of von Buri's criticisms of Birkmeyer two are of particular importance and may be said to have led to the defeat of the individualizing school. The first is that, on Birkmeyer's own admission, no precise criteria can be given for the distinction between efficient and non-efficient causes and the decision must therefore be left to the discretion of the judge.[47] Birkmeyer gives some examples of efficient causes but does not further justify their characterization as such; he treats their efficiency as self-evident.

Secondly, so far as the notion of efficiency can be literally applied, it is not clear, argues von Buri, that the law does accept this criterion. For instance, in a case of participation in crime the principal may have pulled the trigger while the accessory stood by motionless keeping watch; yet accessory and principal are both held to have caused the state of affairs which is proscribed by the criminal law (*Tatbestand*);[48] the 'relative intensity with which their will has been expressed'[49] and so the relative 'efficiency' of their acts is taken into account only for purposes of punishment. To accommodate such cases Birkmeyer was obliged to distinguish between 'causing' and 'providing the occasion'[50] or 'influencing',[51] for he held, consistently with his general theory, that a free human decision could not be caused.[52] These points are indeed well taken and important,[53] but his theory suffered in German eyes from its failure, as compared with von Buri's, to provide a unified theory of causation for the criminal law.

---

[45] Engisch, op. cit., p. 28. For an English version of this theory see A. C. Ewing, 'A Defence of Causality', *Proc. Aristoc. Soc.* 33 (1932-3), 91.

[46] Leonhard, op. cit., pp. 9–11.

[47] M. von Buri, *Die Kausalität und ihre strafrechtlichen Beziehungen* (1885), pp. 7–9.

[48] *Actus reus* is sometimes used in similar though not identical sense. Thus Turner defines *actus reus* as 'such result of human conduct as the law seeks to prevent' (*Kenny's Outlines*, p. 13).

[49] Von Buri, op. cit., pp. 4–5.

[50] *Veranlassung.*

[51] *Beeinflussung.*

[52] Von Buri, op. cit., p. 10.

[53] Above, pp. 42, 51 ff.

Birkmeyer further held that an efficient cause may be interrupted in its operation, as when a mortally wounded man is struck by lightning, but failed to give a clear elucidation of the notion of interruption. In view of these defects and criticisms the notion of an efficient cause was eclipsed by the theory of conditions. In Germany it has not been resuscitated, though in Italian civil law[54] it is still preferred by some to the adequacy theory and its terminology makes an occasional reappearance when a writer or judge is momentarily caught off his guard.

Birkmeyer's theory is in fact not without its merits. A more literal account of the notion of the comparative efficiency of different conditions of the same event could be given in terms of the more or less dangerous character of the various conditions, and one factor in determining this would be the greater or lesser frequency with which they would be followed by harm of a defined sort.[55] In theory at least numerical values could be assigned to represent the frequency of the harm occurring given each condition, and the condition most frequently followed by harm would often be selected as the most dangerous and so as the cause. However, such a reconstructed theory of efficient causes would cease to be an individualizing theory,[56] since what is likely to happen can be ascertained only by reference to what happens or would happen on an average if a large number of examples were taken with a known basic condition in common, other conditions remaining unknown in advance in each particular case. But a theory based on likelihood encounters in turn a number of serious objections which we consider later in connection with the adequacy theory.

Many nineteenth-century writers besides Birkmeyer adhered to one of the individualizing theories, most of which are variants of his. They held that the cause of an event was that condition which could be described as the principal or most 'active' condition,[57] or as sufficient in itself to produce the event,[58] or, refining Birkmeyer's mechanics, the condition which is decisive in the sense of 'tilting the balance between forces in a state of equilibrium',[59] or of 'changing the direction of events'[60] or releasing 'potential energy' and supplying

[54] Teucro Brasiello, *Codice Civile, Libro delle Obbligazioni, Commentario* (1949), iii. 234.
[55] Another factor would be the seriousness of the harm which followed a given condition.
[56] Above, p. 433.
[57] Titmann, Cf. Trendelenburg, *Logische Untersuchungen* (3rd edn.), ii. 184–5 (*tätigste Bedingung*).
[58] Feuerbach, Grolman. At this point the necessity and efficiency theories are indistinguishable.
[59] Binding, *Normen* (1872), i. 113; ii. 472 (*Obergewichtstheorie*).
[60] Wachenfeld.

a driving force.[61] There is a striking similarity between such metaphors and those used by Anglo-American lawyers. The natural tendency of such theories is to select the event nearest in time to the alleged consequence as its cause. This view was adopted by Ortmann with the qualification that the cause must be the act of a free agent other than the injured party, 'free' being taken in a wide sense as compatible with negligent or accidental conduct.[62] The efficiency theory, however, has been altogether rejected, except in such specialized branches of the law as marine or industrial insurance where the question of the cause of a loss or the scope of an occupational risk arises. Such exceptions have been explained on the ground that in marine and industrial insurance the law is mainly concerned with responsibility for the consequences of natural events rather than of human conduct. The concept of efficiency, it is held, can be applied to natural events, perhaps because things have a measurable motion even if it must be rejected for human conduct. Heavy seas have a greater causal 'value' than ordinary waves; but human conduct may upset their relative values, e.g. by blowing a hole in the hull of the ship so that ordinary waves become more 'efficient' than they would otherwise be.[63]

Given the difficulties of the notion of efficiency, the modern tendency is rather to speak of the 'essential condition' (*wesentliche Bedingung*) as the cause in those contexts, such as insurance and strict liability, in which the question is whether the harm is attributable to broadly described conditions (marine perils, war risks, the operation of a vehicle). Even here, however, there are divergent opinions. Lindenmaier would use the notion of adequacy even in these contexts and accept that there might be more than one adequate cause of the harm.[64] Deutsch would accept the phrase 'essential condition' but take it to represent a technique for determining the scope of the branch of the law in question (*Schutzbereich*).[65] Kraemer advocates the use of the notion of essential condition in public law.[66] In a case, however, in the Bundesgerichtshof in which the public authority required a patient to take an inoculation which, though the risk involved was very slight, proved harmful in the outcome, it was held that the inoculation was the adequate cause of the harm.[67] This is

[61] Kohler, *Goltdammers Archiv*, 51. 327, 336 (*Kraftauslösende Bedingung*).
[62] Ortmann, *Goltdammers Archiv*, 23. 268; 24. 94.
[63] H. Mayer, *Strafrecht: Allgemeiner Teil* (1953), 137.
[64] F. Lindenmaier, 'Adäquate Ursache und nächste Ursache', *ZgesHRrecht und Konkursr.* 113 (1950), 207.
[65] E. Deutsch and Ch. von Bar, 'Schutzbereich und wesentliche Bedingung im Versicherungsrecht und Haftungsrecht', *MDR* (1979), 536.
[66] H.-J. Kraemer, 'Die Kausalität im öffentlichen Recht', *NJW* 1965, 182.
[67] *BGHZ* 18 (1955), 286; *NJW* 1955, 1876.

really an instance of liability for an imposed sacrifice.[68] The public authority requires the individual to sacrifice his interests, if need be, to those of the public as a whole, and the public should therefore properly bear the risk of the harm which the sacrifice may entail.

Even if we take into account the continued fondness of the French civil courts for the expression *cause génératrice*,[69] it must be recognized that in the twentieth century the individualizing theories have suffered a decline.[70] This is in marked contrast with the continued popularity of the metaphors of 'potency', etc., with Anglo-American courts and, to a lesser extent, writers. Though some German writers regard the individualizing theories as more in accordance with common sense than other views and so in principle the only correctly conceived theories,[71] the vague character of common-sense judgments of causation and the obscure metaphors involved in the individualizing theories themselves have stood in the way of their acceptance. Hence those who, like Nagler, wish to revive the individualizing point of view introduce nowadays a different criterion of cause—viz. that only such conditions of an event as are socially reprehensible are in the legal sense causes;[72] thus only those road users who have contravened traffic regulations or customs can be regarded as having in law caused a road accident.

II. RISE OF THE THEORY OF CONDITIONS (*BEDINGUNGSTHEORIE*)

The germ of the theory of conditions is perhaps contained in the notion *versari in re illicita*[73] applied in many systems of criminal law in the past and in quite modern times by the Spanish Supreme Court.[74] One who takes part in an illegal activity is responsible for all harm which would not have occurred but for his participation. But in its modern form the theory was first expounded by the Austrian writer Glaser.[75]

[68] Deutsch, *Haftungsrecht*, 1 (1976), pp. 139, 394.
[69] Planiol-Ripert-Esmein, *Traité pratique de droit civil français* (1952), vi, arts. 541-2; Suprema Corte (It.) 21. 3. 1952 (*causalità efficiente*).
[70] However, some Marxist writers say that each condition plays a defined part in bringing about a given consequence, the part of some being greater than that of others. Otherwise one would have to treat the peace-loving efforts of democratic peoples and the hysterical war-mongering of western imperialists as equally important conditions of a future war. J. Lekschas, *Die Kausalität bei der verbrecherischen Handlung* (1952), p. 43.
[71] Nagler, *Leipziger Kommentar zum Strafgesetzbuch* (1954), i. 23.
[72] Ibid., p. 24.
[73] 'Versanti in re illicita imputantur omnia quae sequuntur ex delicto . . . tenetur etiam pro casu.'
[74] A. H. Ferrer, *La relación de causalidad en teoría del delito*, chap. 1.
[75] *Abhandlungen aus dem österreichischen Strafrechte* (1858), i. 298.

If one attempts wholly to eliminate in thought[76] the alleged author [of the act] from the sum of the events in question and it then appears that nevertheless the sequence of intermediate causes remains the same, it is clear that the act and its consequence cannot be referred to him . . . but if it appears that, once the person in question is eliminated in thought from the scene, the consequences cannot come about, or that they can come about only in a completely different way, then one is fully justified in attributing the consequence to him and explaining it as the effect of his activity.[77]

This is a way of expressing the idea that every *sine qua non* or necessary condition of an event is its cause. We leave for later consideration the sense in which 'condition' is here to be understood and note merely that it is characteristic of the Continental theory of conditions to decide whether a condition is a *sine qua non* by a process of elimination in thought (*hinwegdenken*) or assimilation (*hinzudenken*). The Continental formulation suggests that the existence of causal connection depends on the imaginative power of the judge; this difficulty is avoided by the usual Anglo-American formulation, 'Would compliance with the law have averted the harm?'

Shortly after Glaser in Austria, von Buri in Germany adopted a similar view.[78] His arguments were strongly influenced by the mechanical analogies favoured by the supporters of the theory of efficient cause. It is in general impossible to distinguish the different *parts* of a consequence,[79] he argued; if three thieves each take 1,000 marks from a chest containing 3,000 marks, the loss is divisible but usually, for instance if three persons attack and kill a fourth, the harm is indivisible.[80] Hence we cannot say that the act of each has caused a part of the harm. Can we say that each has caused the whole harm? Von Buri takes the analogy of a mill. Suppose that a certain quantity of water is required to turn the mill-wheel and that one mill-pond provided four-fifths of this quantity, another one-fifth, it would nevertheless be correct to say that the water from each mill-pond was the cause of the wheel turning since each was equally necessary and neither would produce any effect without the other.

To Birkmeyer's objection that, if each condition is ineffective without the others, only the sum of all the conditions can be the cause of

---

[76] *Wegdenken, hinwegdenken.*

[77] Glaser, op. cit. Note the similarity between this formulation and the account of 'parallel series' given by Becht and Miller (though only for omissions), above, Preface pp. lix–lxi; and Mackie's account of 'possible worlds', *Cement*, pp. 52 ff., 57 ff., 265–6.

[78] *Teilname und Begünstigung* (1860); *Abhandlungen* (1862); *Goltdammers Archiv* (1863), pts. 11, 12 (1866), p. 612; *Gerichtssaal* (1870), p. 4; *Die Causalität* (1873); *Blätter für Rechtspflege* (1876), p. 193; *Zeitschrift für die gesammte Strafrechtswissenschaft* (1882), p. 233; *Die Kausalität und ihre strafrechtlichen Beziehungen* (1885).

[79] *Die Kausalität und ihre strafrechtlichen Beziehungen*, p. 1.

[80] Above, pp. 225–6.

an event,[81] von Buri gave no convincing reply. Indeed no satisfactory answer to this objection can be given unless appeal is made to the common-sense contrast of cause and condition which lies outside the scope of such theories. Thus Tarnowski, who is aware of the difficulty, states the theory of conditions as follows: 'The theory of conditions takes as its starting-point the proposition that all conditions of a consequence, which cannot be eliminated in thought without eliminating the consequence also, are equivalent and *therefore*[82] each single one of these necessary conditions can be regarded as a cause of the consequence.' The '*therefore*' hardly serves to conceal the *non sequitur*. The only arguments adduced to support this reasoning are that the legal concept of cause is not necessarily the same as the philosophical concept and that each condition is sufficient to produce the consequence provided that the other conditions are also present; each condition may be regarded as completing the set. But no reasons are given for borrowing some parts of the philosophical (i.e. Mill's) theory and omitting others.

Von Buri does not refer to Mill's writings. However, the theory of conditions soon became associated with Mill's name. Von Bar, a contemporary of von Buri, who held à different theory of causation, cites a long extract from Mill's *Logic*[83] dealing with the equivalence of conditions.[84] When the theory of conditions came to be accepted by Continental criminal courts and writers, it was justified by the adoption of parts of Mill's philosophy rather than by von Buri's notion of the equal efficiency of conditions.[85]

The German Reichsgericht in its criminal division accepted the theory of conditions from the start. In a case decided in 1880 accused left a wine bottle containing a solution of arsenic on the window-sill and left the house, though she should have foreseen that her husband, addicted to drink, might taste it, which he did, with fatal consequences. She was convicted of negligent killing,[86] despite the intervening carelessness of the husband, since, 'without her act of putting in position and leaving the bottle of poison, the husband of the accused would not have been killed, hence the occurrence of the whole consequence was conditioned by this conduct on her part and therefore her conduct was fully *causal*'.[87] German criminal courts including the Bundesgerichtshof have with almost unbroken con-

81 Op. cit.; Gerichtssaal, xxxvii. 257, 261.
82 Our italics.
83 J. S. Mill, *Logic*, p. 217.
84 L. von Bar, *Die Lehre vom Kausalzusammenhange im Rechte, besonders im Strafrechte* (1871), pp. 6–7.
85 The Marxist writer Lekschas thinks that there is a sound core in the notion of a *sine qua non* but that the credit for discovering it belongs to Hobbes, *Principles of Philosophy* ix, s. 101. J. Lekschas, *Die Kausalität bei der verbrecherischen Handlung* (1952), pp. 24–5.
86 *Fahrlässige Tötung* (*StGB*, s. 222).
87 *RGSt* 1 (1880), 373, 374.

sistency adhered to this theory ever since and it has been adopted by the criminal courts of most other European countries, though the very extensive liability which would otherwise follow from it has been limited by theories of fault or *mens rea* and unlawfulness. Of the German writers who followed von Buri the most prominent exponents of the theory of conditions are von Liszt, Radbruch, Dohna, von Lilienthal, and Beling. The most recent writers on criminal law are, however, not nearly as whole-hearted in its support as the courts, for the theory of conditions makes causation an element of minor importance in criminal liability, reducing it to the issue of what American writers term 'cause-in-fact', with the result that matters which, from a common-sense viewpoint, turn on causation, have to be considered under another rubric, such as fault (*mens rea*) or unlawfulness. Hence even those writers who support the theory of conditions tend to introduce elements of the adequacy theory in some other part of the theory of criminal responsibility, or, like Antolisèi, to modify it by admitting exceptions, e.g. that if exceptional or very rare events have contributed to bring about the consequence the connection between act and consequence is merely 'occasional', not causal.[88]

In civil law the theory of conditions has had very little success, courts preferring on the whole to make use of the adequacy theory or of the metaphors associated with the individualizing theories. Nevertheless, some notable writers[89] have advocated it for civil law in view of its apparent simplicity and the ease with which it can be applied. It can further be argued in its favour that it reduces causation to a pure question of fact and is the only theory which avoids confusion with the requirement of fault.[90] It does, however, lead to a very complex theory of fault or unlawfulness,[91] designed to obviate the extension of responsibility beyond due limits.

III. THE NOTION OF A CONDITION

We now deal in greater detail with the theory of conditions. There is a part of this theory which is common to it and the adequacy theory, viz. the analysis of the notion of a condition. Radbruch says that the theory of adequate cause starts from the same point as von

[88] F. Antolisèi, *Il rapporto di causalità nel diritto penale* (1934), p. 193. 'Causal' and 'occasional' connection are, according to Antolisèi, two species of the genus 'conditional' connection.
[89] J. C. de Wet, 'Opmerkings oor die vraagstuk van veroorsaking', (1941) 5 *Tydskrif vir Hedendaagse Romeins-Hollandse Reg*, p. 126; '"Estoppel by Representation"*in die Suid-Afrikaanse Reg*', p. 18; *Strafreg*, p. 22.
[90] De Wet does not admit that the notion of a *causa sine qua non* amounts to a theory of causation, since, he says, if causation is a pure question of fact there can be no theory of causation. 'Opmerkings', p. 133. Above, pp. 432–3.
[91] Zevenbergen, '*Over het vraagstuk der Causaliteit in art. 1401 BWB*' Meijers, WPNR, 3442, p. 553 n. 10.

Buri's theory, viz. the notion of a collective cause (or complex set of conditions) and the equivalence of all conditions.[92] Perhaps this is an overstatement, but at least the adequacy theory requires that every cause must first be a necessary condition of the consequence; it then accepts the equivalence of conditions in the sense that the only ground for distinguishing between them is derived from estimates of probability drawn from general statements of probabilities.

We consider first in what sense the theory of conditions understands 'a condition' and next what it says about equivalence.

We treat the notion of a condition under the following headings: (i) sets of conditions; (ii) the difficulty about omissions; (iii) the generalization (description) of the consequence; (iv) the generalization of the condition; (v) the procedure of elimination and substitution; (vi) additional and alternative causation; (vii) interpersonal transactions; (viii) proof in hypothetical inquiries.

(i) *Sets of conditions.* As we have seen, the conduct of the actor is usually stated to be a condition of a consequence, 'if once it is eliminated in thought, the consequence at once falls away'.[93] The procedure of elimination, however, presupposes that the condition being investigated may be a member of a complex set of conditions or collective cause.[94] Does such a set contain a limited or unlimited number of members? Sometimes it is suggested that the number is limited and the complete set theoretically enumerable; thus Grispigni objects to the view that exceptional conditions exclude liability because, he says, there is always *some* unforeseeable or exceptional condition of an event, but it may not amount to more than one-hundredth part of the causal complex.[95] This can meaningfully be said only if a complete count of the conditions is possible. But most writers agree that the conditions of an event are unlimited, at least if the negative conditions are included. The notion of the sum of the conditions of an event 'leads to infinity'.[96] For instance, it is a condition of the spread of a fire which could have been extinguished that *A* did not put it out, *B* did not put it out, etc., for an indefinite series of persons; hence it is impossible to state the whole set of conditions in a particular case.[97] This, however, is not really fatal to the procedure of elimination or to the notion of a necessary condition[98] since it is in many cases possible to state a limited number

92 Radbruch, p. 333.
93 *RGSt* 66 (1932), 181, 184. Above, p. 443.
94 *Gesamtursache.* Köstlin, p. 453. Leonhard, op. cit., p. 5.
95 Grispigni, 'Il nesso causale nel diritto penale', *Riv. it. dir. pen.* 13 (1935), 3, 14–15.
96 Von Bar, p. 8.
97 Nagler, op. cit., p. 18 n. 3.
98 Engisch, however, op. cit., p. 20, makes the point that the notion of necessary condition is derivative from that of causal law or generalization and hence wishes to substitute the notion of 'condition in accordance with a (causal) law' for 'necessary condition'.

of positive conditions of an event which suffice to produce it in the absence of counteracting conditions,[99] and causal laws or natural laws do usually contain just such specifications of the positive conditions of events.[1] The absence of counteracting conditions may be treated for practical purposes as a single negative condition, and there is no need for the unattainable complete enumeration.

(ii) *The difficulty about omissions.*[2] This difficulty has been felt more acutely in Continental than in Anglo-American law. The objections to treating an omission as a cause apply equally to treating it as a condition; hence they are dealt with here. It is said of omissions that they (*a*) are nothing[3] and (*b*) are not movements.

If omissions are nothing, there seems no reason why they should figure even theoretically among the conditions of an event; it would actually be superfluous and pointless to mention them, for nothing would thereby be added to what is already known of the event. But in fact it is in many circumstances not pointless to mention an omission among the conditions of an event, for instance to mention that *X*, who was suffering from a disease of which he died, failed to consult a doctor. The explanation of this is that we sometimes know how to prevent a harmful occurrence though we may not know how it is caused. The theory that descriptions of conduct which do not involve movements[4] are nothing, coupled with the obvious fact that there is sometimes point in drawing attention to omissions, has led to heroic attempts to demonstrate that omissions are 'really' something, i.e. positive acts. To this end it has been said that omissions, though they have no existence in the physical world, exert a psychological influence.[5] It is true that sometimes, for instance, silence gives consent. If a husband keeps silent when his wife declares her intention to kill their child his omission to speak may exert a psychological influence and so encourage her to act. But this is not always true, even when human conduct is in question: a warder's omission to guard a mental patient, so that he escapes and does harm, does not exert a psychological influence on the patient, but merely provides him with an opportunity.[6] Still less does my omission to turn off a tap exert a psychological influence on the water which then floods my neighbour's property.

[99] Von Bar, op. cit., p. 11.
[1] Engisch, op. cit., p. 21.
[2] Honoré, *IECL*, xi. 7-24 to 7-28.
[3] Enneccerus-Lehmann, ii. 70, 'Ein Nichtgeschehen kann nicht wirken, ein Nichts kann keine Folgen haben'. The author thinks that under certain circumstances an omission may be *treated* by the law as equivalent to a positive act, though it is not really so. Antolisèi, chap. 5.
[4] J. Bennett, 'Morality and Consequences 1: Killing and letting Die', *Tanner Lectures* 2 (1981), 47 f. develops a theory of 'positive and negative instrumentality' in this connection.
[5] Geyer, *Grundriß zu Vorlesungen über gemeines deutsches Strafrecht.*
[6] *RGSt* (1882), 332.

Another argument for assimilating omissions to positive acts is that a positive act precedes or accompanies the omission and it is this which is really the condition or cause of the event. Partly this merely reflects the familiar theory that a duty to act can only be based on a preceding act of the person subject to the duty, e.g. a doctor has a duty to attend a patient only if he has undertaken to do so, never merely because the patient needs attention; but this is inconsistent with positive law[7] and with ordinary usage. Another form of the same argument is that omissions to perform a duty, with which the law is mainly concerned, are themselves the consequences of positive acts, i.e. of the act of repressing the actor's inclination to perform the duty or of 'driving the possibility of having the inclination underground' so that it never, so to speak, comes to the surface.[8] This presupposes that consciousness of the duty is an essential condition of breach of duty, a doctrine which receives some support from legal writers[9] but would not account for those instances in ordinary usage where we speak of inadvertent omissions, e.g. when someone has failed to turn up at a meeting because he has forgotten the date of it. However, von Buri was prepared to cater for such cases of inadvertent omission on the theory that the positive act involved was busying oneself at the relevant time with other ideas and thereby preventing the consciousness of duty from obtruding itself.[10] But even if it is conceded that there always are some such psychological conditions of an omission they are not usually treated as acts: on the contrary they are contrasted with acts. Further, it is not the psychological antecedent which common sense or law treats as significant, but the omission to perform the duty, which may have many and varying psychological antecedents.

Another attempt to view omissions as 'really' positive asserts that an omission is equivalent to the removal of an obstacle to the occurrence of a consequence;[11] such removal is itself positive. An 'obstacle' primarily refers to a factor which is known or assumed to be present and which would prevent a purpose from being achieved. If a warder fails to guard a mental patient, who then commits suicide, the warder's omission is indeed equivalent to the removal of an obstacle in the way of the patient's purposes; but an employer's failure to guard dangerous machinery is not naturally described as

---

[7] e.g. the crimes of *omission de porter secours* and *unterlassene Hilfeleistung*. Code pénal, art. 63; *StGB*, s. 330 c. Similarly the duty of support often depends on family relationships, not on prior undertakings or acts: children must support parents though they have not begotten them and have not promised to support them.

[8] Von Buri, p. 15.

[9] It is usually held that consciousness of unlawfulness (*Unrechtsbewusstsein*) is part of the notion of fault. Mezger-Blei, *Strafrecht* (14th edn. 1970), i, 164.

[10] Op. cit., p. 16.

[11] Nagler, op. cit., p. 38.

the removal of an obstacle to the workman's injury, since the workman does not intend to injure himself.

A related view is that an omission does not set causal laws in motion but removes an obstacle to their operation.[12] Not rescuing a drowning man removes an obstacle to the operation of the physical and physiological laws involved in drowning. The arguments we have just considered also apply to the use of 'obstacle' here. But partly this view reflects the belief that, since causal principles are usually stated in positive terms, they cannot incorporate negative descriptions, so that the apparently negative conditions must be shown to be 'really' positive. This is obviously a *non sequitur*.

Nevertheless, Continental writers have continued to feel a difficulty about the causal status of omissions, and underlying this feeling is a genuine distinction between two types of knowledge, viz. knowledge of what will, in normal circumstances, produce a given result and knowledge of what will, in normal circumstances, prevent it. There is indeed a contrast between causing by intervening and by not preventing.[13] The cases in which an omission is said to be a cause are mostly those in which the law requires precautions to be taken to prevent harm.

The argument that causation always involves movement has attracted some writers.[14] The objections to it were noted in Chapter II.[15]

(iii) *Generalization (description) of the consequence.* The Continental writers speak of the generalization rather than of the description of a consequence. The problems which, under this name, have vexed Continental theorists arise from the fact that any particular may be classified under a number of different descriptions of different levels of specificity. Only the context can determine which is appropriate for legal purposes. These problems have been the more acute because some writers appear to entertain the notion that there is in principle an ideal complete description of every event, which for the purposes of the law undergoes abstraction. The complete description is called the 'concrete description'.

Of what must a wrongful act be shown to be a necessary condition?[16] If we ask this in a case of homicide, we are first inclined to answer 'death', for homicide is unlawfully causing death; but if all men are

---

[12] Engisch, pp. 27–8. An alternative view is that causation is not an essential element in crimes of omission but is replaced by a different relation, i.e. 'not preventing'; Honoré, *IECL*, xi. 7–23.

[13] J. Bennett, above, p. 447 n. 4.

[14] *Alle Verursachung ist Bewegung*. Krückmann, op. cit.; *Jherings Jahrbuch* 55, 25.

[15] pp. 29–31.

[16] Honoré, *IECL*, xi. 7–39. Unless otherwise stated this means necessary in the sense of the theory of conditions, i.e. such that in its absence the consequence would not have occurred.

mortal, no act can be a necessary condition of a man's death. Hence
'death' is too wide.[17] Suppose then we say that the act must be a
condition of the particular death in all its details.[18] This at once
appears too narrow, for if A when killed by B is wearing a coat sold
him by C, C's act in selling him the coat is a necessary condition of
A's death while wearing this coat; and his wearing this coat is one
of the 'details' of his death.[19] Hence the writers make various
attempts to steer a course between these two extremes.

Traeger's test[20] was whether without the wrongful act the consequence would have been different from the point of view of legal
appraisal. Bodily injury and death are two legally different categories; hence the act of the accused may be a condition of death,
according to Traeger's view, even if the deceased person would in
any case have been wounded. Suppose, however, that B is attempting
to wound C when A shouts. C turns towards A and so is wounded
in the side, not in the back as he would otherwise have been. Is A's
shout a necessary condition of C's wound? The legal category would
be the same without his shout. Traeger is in a difficulty, which he
solves arbitrarily by making a distinction between the case where A
intended a warning and where he intended to distract C's attention.
He maintains that the shout is not a condition of the wound in the
first case but is in the second, there being a special doctrine of
the law relating to accessories that the slightest difference in the
consequence is sufficient to make an act of assistance a condition
and so to support a charge of aiding and abetting.

Traeger also maintained that large differences in the time of death,
wounding, etc., or in the seriousness of a wound, were significant
and entered into the description of the consequence, while small ones
were neglected. But law and common sense agree that it is possible
to kill a man who is certain to die very shortly:[21] a mortally wounded
man may be murdered. To deal with cases of additional causation,[22]
as when two men simultaneously shoot and kill a third, Traeger
introduced the argument that the consequence would not be the
same without the act of one of the attackers, since death from one
mortal wound is not the same as death from two mortal wounds;

[17] Tarnowski, op. cit., p. 39.
[18] Von Liszt-Schmidt, *Lehrbuch des deutschen Strafrechts*, p. 157: 'What is of significance is not whether B would have died without the expression of A's will but
whether he would have died on this day, in this way, and under these circumstances.'
[19] Engisch, op. cit., p. 9, gives a similar example: A paints a vase, B throws it on
the ground and breaks it: A's act is a necessary condition of the fact that a painted vase
was broken. For the distinction between conditions *sine qua non* merely incidentally
connected with the harm and causally relevant factors see above, pp. 115-21.
[20] *Der Kausalbegriff im Straf- und Zivilrecht*, p. 46.
[21] Tarnowski, op. cit., p. 41.
[22] Below, pp. 455-7.

but this is to adopt arbitarily, for a limited purpose, the view that a consequence must be described 'concretely' in all its details.

Radbruch argued that we must distinguish characteristics of the conseqence which interest us from those which do not.[23] Only the interesting factors form part of the description of the consequence. Tarnowski's view is comparable; he asserts that the description depends on the nature and circumstances of the crime and that no general formula for all crimes is possible.[24] The question remains whether some closer guide to the interesting or relevant factors can be given.

M. L. Müller,[25] reacting against Traeger's view, proposed a 'concrete' description of the consequence, at least so far as details of time and place are concerned; but he nevertheless regarded the fact that a broken vase was painted or the victim of a murder was wearing a particular coat as irrelevant. The legal category was relevant, he maintained, to the description of the condition, not of the consequence. The Reichsgericht appeared to adopt his view in a case in which the accused was convicted of arson when he had set fire to part of a house already on fire;[26] it then appeared to adopt a different view in a case in which a doctor who administered cocaine instead of novocaine as an anaesthetic was acquitted of negligent killing, since the novocaine would probably also have led to death.[27]

None of these views is satisfactory since the difficulties spring from the fundamental defects of necessary condition as a test of causation. In general, the appropriate description of harm will be the description implied in the relevant legal rule (e.g. death). The fact that the harm may also be described in further detail ('in a red coat', 'on a Monday') is only of importance because a reference to some of this detail will be required to show that a particular unique instance of the legally proscribed harm has occurred. The fact that acts such as selling a red coat to the victim will be necessary conditions of the harm thus described is irrelevant.[28] Moreover, in cases of additional and alternative causes the test of necessary condition must break down altogether and must be replaced by that of generally sufficient conditions.

Further, a theory of how consequences should be described for legal purposes may be made to embody special legal doctrines. Thus Hartmann[29] thinks that the 'way' in which the consequence occurs

[23] Op. cit., p. 82.
[24] Op. cit., p. 39.
[25] *Die Bedeutung des Kausalzusammenhangs im Straf- und Schadenersatzrecht* (1912), p. 10.
[26] *RGSt* 22 (1892), 325.
[27] *HRR* 1930, no. 2034 (RG); H. Mayer, op. cit., p. 134. Above, p. 251.
[28] This point is neglected in discussions of relevance in the law of evidence.
[29] *Das Kausalproblem im Strafrecht* (1900), p. 77.

should be incorporated into its description: when a rail accident occurs because the signalman was drugged we should speak of the consequence not as a 'rail accident' but of a 'rail accident occurring because a signalman was drugged'; this ensures that the drugging of the signalman counts as a necessary condition of the accident and excludes the argument that it was not a condition because the signalman was also handcuffed independently of the drugging. But even if 'way' could be sufficiently defined[30] Hartmann's view would be no more than an attempt to base responsibility on whether the actor's conduct made a difference to the 'way' in which the consequence occurs. This restriction on responsibility requires to be justified and in fact few lawyers would wish to treat differently the case where A shoots B as he is falling from a precipice, so ensuring that B dies in a different way, shooting instead of impact, and where A shoots B on whom C has already inflicted a fatal shot, so that B dies in the same way. In any case, references to the manner of occurrence such as 'accident occurring *because* a signalman was drugged' involve a knowledge of causal processes which depends on common-sense principles.

Except where the special features of events which, like death, are certain to occur at some time create difficulties, the German puzzles will be avoided by using not the notion of necessary condition, but that of a condition which is generally sufficient, with others, to produce the harm, described in terms of the relevant legal rule.[31] This description may require some further qualification in the following type of case. Suppose a man would with normal medical treatment die of a disease in five years' time. Dr A treats him so unskilfully that he dies in two years' time; or Dr B treats him so skilfully that he lives for ten years. The treatment by each doctor is sufficient, with other conditions, to produce the patient's death, though after differing intervals of time: yet we are not at all inclined to call B's treatment a condition of the patient's death. This is because, when a consequence is described as 'death', it is normally implied that it occurred before the time it would normally have been expected on the information available when the alleged cause occurred. Causing a person's death normally involves shortening his expected span of life. The patient's death would with normal treatment have been expected in five years' time. Hence A's treatment is causally connected with his death. B's treatment would be causally connected with the prolongation of his life. The law would surely adopt this implication of the ordinary usage of terms like 'death'. Accordingly it is appropriate to adopt the description 'death' which

30 It could only be defined by reference to causal processes.
31 Above, pp. 111–12.

is expressed or implied in the relevant rule of law but to interpret it as follows: 'death' means any dying before the deceased, given his constitution, would normally have died; 'bodily injury' prima facie means any bodily injury, since persons do not in the normal course of things suffer bodily injury; the destruction of property means its destruction before it would normally disintegrate. There is a distinction between killing and prolonging life, reducing the extent of a wound and making it worse, damaging an object and repairing it. Sometimes the law may express or imply a more detailed description; killing a Norman was once a more serious crime than just killing. But usually a rule which refers to causing death will be *pro tanto* satisfied by proof of any instance of death occurring before it would normally occur. The details of the killing are only relevant in showing that the facts of the case present an instance of the state of affairs proscribed by the law.

(iv) *Generalization of the condition.* This presents serious difficulties for the adequacy theory but less for the theory of conditions. We can accept Müller's conclusion that the condition must be described in accordance with legal categories: e.g. 'false pretences or the perversion or suppression of the truth';[32] the prosecutor or plaintiff must prove an instance of what is described, and for this purpose must adduce details, e.g. that *A* falsely told *B* on such-and-such a date at such-and-such a place that he had a suitcase full of banknotes.

(v) *The procedure of elimination and substitution.* As will be remembered, Glaser first proposed and von Buri adopted the procedure of hypothetical elimination in order to test whether an act or omission was a necessary condition of a consequence.[33] The two main problems that arise for them in this connection are whether the act or omission is simply eliminated or whether another is substituted for it,[34] and whether there is a difference between acts and omissions in this respect.

It is simplest to take the case of omissions first. Suppose accused was riding a bicycle without a light; the court wishes to determine whether this was a condition of a collision. Obviously it can do so only by asking whether a collision would have occurred if the other conditions had been similar but accused's bicycle had had a light. The elimination of the condition, according to the terminology of the German courts, involves the substitution of the act which accused

[32] *StGB*, s. 263.
[33] Above, pp. 442–3.
[34] Apparently 'elimination with substitution' is the supposition that the actor was in a position to which the law violated by him applied and that he complied with it (e.g. by driving with a licence). 'Simple elimination' is the supposition that he was not in a situation to which the law applies (e.g. not driving) and that the situation remained in all other respects unchanged (e.g. no one else drove).

omitted. Thus in one case[35] accused and his brother were riding bicycles without lights at night; the deceased coming in the opposite direction collided with the brother and was killed. Accused was charged with negligent killing and the prosecution argued that, had the accused had a light, the deceased would have been able to see his brother's bicycle. The trial court held that there was no causal connection between the failure to have a light and the death, because it eliminated accused from the scene altogether, and concluded that the accident would still have occurred. On appeal it was pointed out that the true inquiry was what would have occurred had the accused been present with a lighted bicycle.[36] The procedure of 'eliminating' an omission entails supplying what was omitted, and hence the 'substitution' of the duty omitted.[37]

Probably the best solvents of scepticism on this point are the licence cases. In German and French law it has been held that to drive a car without a licence or employ a worker without an identity card is not necessarily the cause of a road or industrial accident in which the car or worker is involved while so driven or employed.[38] Whether it is depends on whether the driver, if he had had a licence, would have driven more skilfully and thereby avoided the accident; similarly for the permit case. It seems clear that a conclusion can be reached only by going beyond simple elimination of the condition and supposing, e.g., that the actor was driving and complied with the law by having a licence which he had obtained by complying with the required conditions, e.g. attaining the appropriate standard of proficiency in driving.

However, the Reichsgericht before the war in certain cases purported to adopt a procedure of elimination without substitution.[39] This was to avoid denying liability in cases of alternative causation,[40] e.g. when if A had not shot B, C would have done so at the same place and time. Since the war it has been recognized that substitution is necessary. But the recognition has come in an unsatisfactory way, because it too has occurred in cases[41] of alternative causation which are anomalous.

[35] *RGSt* 63 (1930), 392.
[36] Accused was acquitted on the ground that he owed no duty to light his bicycle for the benefit of the deceased. Above, p. 252 n. 28.
[37] For an account of the method of constructing counterfactual hypotheses in such contexts ('parallel series') see Preface, pp. lix–lxi.
[38] For French law see Civ. 20. 10. 1932 (driver without licence not liable to pedestrian run over if he was driving properly); Cass. Soc. 7.5.1943; *Sirey* 1943. I. 106; *Dalloz A*. 1943. 51 (employer not responsible for industrial accident to foreign worker unlawfully employed without identity card). Anglo-American law is similar: above, p. 211.
[39] *RGZ* 141 (1933), 365.
[40] Above, pp. 249–53; Honoré, *IECL*, xi. 7-126 to 7-129.
[41] e.g. *NJW* 6 (II) (1953), 977.

The procedure of simple elimination seems at first sight more satisfactory when the alleged cause is a positive act. If accused shot deceased with a revolver it seems necessary only to notice that, if accused's shot is eliminated, deceased's death is eliminated also. But this is an illusion. When an unlawful positive act is eliminated, the conduct which consists in refraining from that act in accordance with the law is substituted for it. In all cases, whether positive acts or omissions are in question, we must ask what difference it would have made had accused or defendant acted lawfully, but the circumstances otherwise remained the same.[42] It is only when the hypothetical lawful conduct would have prompted another to act unlawfully that the procedure of substitution may sometimes give a result which is intuitively unsatisfactory. But this is because it is an overriding purpose of the legal system to prevent the unlawful invasion of rights and legally protected interests. Thus, if it is the case that, had accused not unlawfully shot deceased, someone else would have done so, it is likely in most cases that the hypothetical outcome would have been different in point of time, place, or manner of upshot in more than some minimal respect. But, even if it would not, liability will be imposed, in order to give effect to the overriding purpose mentioned.

(vi) *Additional and alternative causation.* It is unnecessary to repeat the definitions of these terms, which were set out in Chapter VIII.[43] What we have termed 'additional' causation is often called 'cumulative' by Continental writers.

It is agreed that in cases of additional causation, as where A and B simultaneously shoot C in a fatal part of the body, both should be legally responsible for the death; but this seems inconsistent with the theory of conditions if elimination or substitution is taken as the test of whether an act is a condition. Some half-hearted attempts have been made to circumvent or obviate the difficulty. Enneccerus[44] mentions the fiction that the consequence occurs twice, the fact that the law is primarily concerned with fixing responsibility, and the argument that each act is a necessary condition *for itself*. Tarnowski[45] argues that, in the case of simultaneous shots by A and B, we cannot say that the victim's death would have occurred in the absence of A's shot, since this presupposes that B's shot is a necessary condition of the death; this turns on an ambiguity in the expression 'necessary condition'. What is presupposed is that B's shot is sufficient, with other circumstances, to produce death; not that no other similarly sufficient condition was present on this occasion. Tarnowski also

[42] Preface, p. lx; above, pp. 411–13.
[43] pp. 204, 234, 241.
[44] Op. cit. ii. 69.
[45] Op. cit., p. 46.

argues that the 'class' of lethal shots must be eliminated,[46] and presents this as a theory of how conditions should be described, but this would only demonstrate that some lethal shot was necessary, not that any particular member of the class was.

None of the arguments adduced to reconcile the theory of conditions with the need to impose liability on both actors in cases of additional (including overtaking)[47] causation seems convincing. The notion of a necessary condition requires to be supplemented by that of a sufficient condition.

So far as overtaking causation is concerned, there are divergent views. One group of writers thinks that an overtaking cause should be taken into account as regards mediate, but not immediate harm.[48] Another opinion draws the line between positive harm and *lucrum cessans*.[49] Only as regards loss of gain or profit would overtaking causes count. A third opinion is that the decision to regard or disregard them is one of policy and depends on the purpose of the rule violated.[50] A fourth view, which, however, merely displaces the problem without solving it, is that it concerns the assessment of damages.[51] We have discussed these matters more fully in Chapter VII.[52] We agree with the second opinion in that we consider that an overtaking cause should be taken into account when compensation is claimed for loss of future profits, earnings, or other advantages. This is, however, subject to the rider that, if the overtaking cause is itself an unlawful invasion of the victim's rights, the policy of protecting the victim against such unlawful invasions has precedence over purely causal criteria.[53] Hence in such cases compensation is claimable from the first wrongdoer even for the period after the overtaking cause operated or would have operated.

Alternative causation presents analogous difficulties for the theory of conditions. Some of the German cases have been discussed above.[54] An issue, not discussed there, which has featured prominently in German writing and decision, has been that of procedural irregularity. It sometimes happens that an accused or defendant does in an irregular way something which he would have been entitled to

[46] Op. cit., p. 47.
[47] Above, pp. 244–7.
[48] Neuner, 'Interesse und Vermögenschaden', *AcP* 133 (1932), 277; Larenz, 'Präventionsprinzip und Ausgleichsprinzip im Schadenersatzrecht', *NJW* 1959, 865; Hermann Lange, 'Zum Problem der überholenden Kausalität', *AcP* 152 (1952), 153.
[49] H. Niederländer, 'Schadenersatz bei hypothetischen Schadensereignissen', *AcP* 153 (1954), 41.
[50] E. von Caemmerer, *Das Problem der überholenden Kausalität* (1962).
[51] Zeuner, 'Zum Problem der überholenden Kausalität', *AcP* 157 (1958–9), 441.
[52] Above, pp. 245–9.
[53] Only to this extent can one accept W. Rother, 'Adäquanztheorie und Schadenverursachung durch mehrere', *NJW* 1965, 177.
[54] Above, pp. 247, 250–1.

do in a regular way. For example, he strikes without notice when he would have been entitled to strike after a period of notice. If a long shut-down then ensues, can the employer claim to have suffered a loss of production, as a result of the absence of notice, for the whole period, or is he confined to the relatively short period of notice prescribed?

On purely causal grounds it seems at first sight that the loss that would have been caused had the correct procedure been followed cannot be recovered. Is it not the case that, had the accused or defendant exercised his rights as a lawful and reasonable man, the same harm would in whole or in part have ensued? There is, however, a complication. In these cases it is not a legal requirement that the defendant *should* exercise his rights according to the lawful procedure. He need not exercise them at all. The potential striker or union may, instead of giving the required notice of a strike, refrain from striking. Even if it is very likely that he would have struck in any case, the object of the procedural requirement may be to afford an opportunity for negotiation to take place and for the parties to have second thoughts.[55] In any instance in which a procedural requirement is directed towards the possibility that someone will change his mind and reach a different decision, it would nullify that requirement to hold that the loss which could have been inflicted by following the proper procedure was irrecoverable. Hence, on grounds which were in part causal but mainly a matter of legal policy it was decided in the *Metal Workers* case[56] that the union which struck without notice was liable for the whole loss suffered by the employer, not merely for the loss for the period of required notice. The union might have changed its mind. Negotiations might have taken place. Even if it was likely that the strike would in any case have occurred, the object of the law was to provide an opportunity for second thoughts.[57]

(vii) *Interpersonal transactions.* Continental writers usually designate interpersonal transactions by the unsuitable phrase 'psychological causation'—unsuitable because it more naturally applies to causal processes which operate 'through the mind' analogously with physical processes, e.g. hypnotism.[58]

[55] Deutsch, *Haftungsrecht*, 1 (1976), 175.
[56] *BAG* 6, 321.
[57] H. Wittman, 'Die Berufung auf rechtmässiges Alternativverhalten', *NJW* 1971, 549 wrongly, in our view, treats the notice to be given by an employee as *merely* meant to give an employer time to find a replacement. But he rightly insists that, if that were the case, the cost of readvertising the post would not be recoverable against an employee who left without notice; cf. *BGHZ* 20 (1956), 275; *NJW* 1956, 1027 (municipality demolishes house without observing correct procedure).
[58] Above, p. 58.

When one person provides the reason or part of the reason for another to act it is often but not always the case that the latter would not have acted as he did but for the act of the former.[59] When accused was charged with obtaining a premium of 600 marks by false pretences the prosecution failed since the widow who had paid the money in order to obtain a loan of a larger amount admitted that she would have done so even had she known that accused was lending on his own account and not on behalf of an imaginary *H*.[60] This admission was taken to mean that the false statement was no part of her reason for paying the money. But when accused falsely told certain guards that deceased had killed several inmates of concentration camps, and one of the guards then shot deceased dead, it was held that accused was rightly convicted of instigating the guard to commit malicious wounding with fatal consequences even if the guard had already decided to beat up deceased and would have done so without being prompted by accused.[61] The cases are distinguishable only if we assume that the guard, unlike the widow, was influenced by the false statements at least to the extent that his determination to do violence to the deceased was thereby reinforced. The court in the second case did not appear to notice that its decision was inconsistent with the theory of conditions as normally interpreted.

(viii) *Proof in hypothetical inquiries.* Whether an act is a condition of a given consequence involves consideration of what would have happened upon a hypothetical set of facts.[62] According to the German cases the hypothetical event and so the status of the act as a condition must be established with certainty or with a probability bordering on certainty. It was held to be error in the trial court to convict accused when the evidence merely showed that the harm, an outbreak of fire, *could* or *might* have been excluded by taking certain precautions.[63] There is often a doubt what the reaction of a human being would have been in hypothetical circumstances; since we do not command evidence that human conduct is completely determined such questions can never be answered with more than a high degree of probability. When the question was whether a doctor, if consulted, would have continued a certain treatment the fact that the treatment was medically appropriate and that there was no reason for him to discontinue it was held sufficient to permit the court to conclude with a probability bordering on certainty that he would have continued it.[64]

59 Above, pp. 55, 192–4.
60 *RGSt* 1 (1879), 48.
61 *BGHSt* (1952), 223.
62 Above, pp. 411–14.
63 *RGSt* 75 (1940), 50; *BGHSt* 11 (1958), 1.
64 *RGSt* 15 (1886), 151.

IV. THE IDENTIFICATION OF CAUSES AND CONDITIONS

The identification of causes and conditions required by the theory of conditions creates certain difficulties for the criminal courts which adopt the theory of conditions. We have seen how they are sometimes embarrassed by the fact that an act which from a common-sense point of view is the cause of harm would not, upon a literal interpretation of the theory of conditions, count as a condition.[65] We may now ask how the courts deal with the converse difficulties which arise when harm which from a common-sense point of view would not count as caused by an act is treated by the theory, owing to the identification of causes and conditions, as a consequence in law.

The identification leads to liability in cases of coexisting conditions such as the susceptibility of the victim,[66] of contributory negligence,[67] and of the concurrent negligence of a third party.[68] This is acceptable unless the negligence is gross or unnatural. The awkward cases, in which the theory of conditions appears too strict, are cases of voluntary interventions and intervening abnormal or coincidental acts or events, including grossly negligent acts.

Voluntary interventions. It was once thought that voluntary interventions could be regarded as a statutory exception to the theory of conditions in view of the provisions dealing with aiding and abetting crimes, which would be superfluous if the theory of conditions were literally applied.[69] Frank argued that there was an implied prohibition[70] on inquiry into the causes of voluntary acts. From this it is deduced that there is no liability for negligent instigation or assistance of the principal offender or for instigation of or assistance in committing suicide, where suicide is not a crime.[71] However, the courts have reached the conclusion that this statutory exception, if it exists at all, does not extend beyond instigation, assistance, and perhaps suicide.[72] The main reason for this conclusion is that Frank's

---

[65] Above, pp. 455–7.

[66] *RGSt* 5 (1881), 29; 27 (1895), 93; 54 (1920), 349. Maurach, op. cit., p. 157. The Bundesgerichtshof affirmed this course of decisions in *BGHSt* 1 (1951), 332; the classical case is that of the haemophiliac. *RGSt* 54 (1920), 349 above. For similar Spanish decisions see Ferrer, p. 354.

[67] *RGSt* 1 (1880), 373; 6 (1882), 249; 22 (1891), 173; 5 (1881), 202; 57 (1923), 393. An example is where the occupier of a house set on fire by the accused returned to recover property and was burned to death. *RGSt* 5 (1881), 202.

[68] *RGSt* 57 (1922), 148; 67 (1931), 12; 34 (1901), 91; 7 (1882), 111; 66 (1932), 181; *BGHSt* 4 (1953), 360.

[69] *StGB*, ss. 48, 49.

[70] *Regressverbot* or *Rückgriffverbot*.

[71] Engisch, p. 82. Cf. above, p. 364.

[72] *RGSt* 64 (1930), 316; 64 (1930), 370.

view would make it impossible for accused to be found guilty of
crimes of negligence when he had neglected a duty to guard against
the voluntary act of another. Thus a seller was convicted of negligent
export of forbidden goods when he sent them to a person living near
the frontier without inquiring whether they were intended for export,
though from the circumstances it appeared probable that they were.
[73] Again a husband was convicted of negligently killing his child
when he deserted the household without informing relatives or the
police, although his wife had frequently threatened to kill herself
and the child, which she did.[74]

In consequence of these and other decisions on negligence many
authors have adopted the view that cases of the intervention of free
and voluntary acts form no exception to the theory of conditions.[75]
However, this cannot be taken as finally settled. The main argument
in favour of their view is that words such as 'kills' or 'killing' are
presumably used in the same sense by the legislature in creating the
crimes of intentional killing and negligent killing; so whatever causal
relation is implied by the one is implied also by the other. The theory
of conditions, it is asserted, provides an account of the only relation
which would hold in both classes of case. On the other hand the
description of the deserting husband's act as 'negligently killing his
child' seems somewhat artificial and it may be that the law is in such
cases extending the meaning of words such as 'kills', 'wounds', and
'burns' for reasons of policy; so that the relation of 'providing an
opportunity for killing' or 'not preventing killing', which would more
naturally be used to describe the conduct of accused, may not be the
same as the causal relation implied by the use of 'kills', etc., in
ordinary speech or in other contexts of the law.

The Italian penal code expressly makes this distinction, for after
providing that no one is guilty of a crime unless the harmful or
dangerous event which forms part of the crime is the consequence
of his act, it goes on to say that failing to prevent an event, in the
case of one who has a legal duty to prevent it, is equivalent to
causing it.[76]

German courts have on other occasions appeared to recognize that
voluntary intervening conduct negatives causal connection between
condition and consequence. In a case where three persons not acting
in concert attacked and killed a fourth, the court said that when
one person has given a mortal wound he can be convicted only of

[73] *RGSt* 58 (1924), 366.
[74] *BGHSt* 7 (1954), 268.
[75] Nagler, op. cit., p. 19; Maurach, *Deutsches Strafrecht* (4th edn. 1971), *Allg. Teil*,
pp. 207–10.
[76] Codice Penale, art. 40: 'non impedire un evento, che si ha l'obbligo giuridico di
impedire, equivale a cagionarlo'.

attempted homicide if the death is subsequently accelerated by the independent act of another.[77] But on the facts it was held open to the jury to find that two of the three were guilty of intentional homicide since the act of the second did not accelerate the death. This decision appears to recognize that the intervention of a voluntary actor negatives causal connection; but this is inconsistent with the theory of conditions.[78]

German military courts also recognize the importance of a voluntary intervention from the point of view of causal connection. An NCO was charged with 'disobedience whereby danger of serious prejudice [to military discipline] was brought about'. He had collected and sold empty cartridge cases and applied the proceeds for purchasing equipment for his men. It was held that if the disobedience consisted in the sale of the cartridge cases and the prejudice arose from the application of the proceeds the accused could not be convicted because the sale and application were not causally connected.[79] The reason why there was no causal connection is clearly that, although the sale was a *sine qua non* of the application of the proceeds, a voluntary decision intervened.

In Germany the status of a voluntary intervention from the point of view of the theory of conditions must therefore be regarded as undecided. In Spain, where the theory of conditions is taken by the courts as the starting-point, an exception is made when there is the 'express and deliberate fault of the victim'[80] or the 'voluntary act of a third person'.[81] This, according to Ferrer, cannot be explained on any causal theory but only by the fact that the law is concerned not with causation but with responsibility, which is a teleological problem.[82] In Italy the legislature has enacted that the concurrence of pre-existing, simultaneous or subsequent causes, even if independent of the act or omission of accused, does not exclude causal connection between the act or omission and the result, but subject to the proviso that subsequent causes exclude causal connection when they are *sufficient by themselves* to determine the result.[83] Many writers have pointed out that the proviso cannot be interpreted literally; but it appears to leave room for some mitigation of the awkward results of the theory of conditions. Subsequent voluntary conduct might be regarded as within the proviso.

[77] *RGSt* 19 (1888), 141.
[78] The decision appears in any event to contravene the theory of conditions since the same consequence would have occurred without the intervention of the second actor. On additional causation see pp. 455-7.
[79] *RMG* 10 (1906), 40. Cf. *RMG* 18, 58; 20, 237.
[80] S. 6.2.1923. A. H. Ferrer, p. 360.
[81] S. 30.9.1909. Ferrer, p. 360.
[82] Ferrer, p. 376.
[83] Codice penale, art. 41.

Abnormal intervening events and acts. The courts have met the difficulty of reconciling the theory of conditions with the requirements of common sense in cases of coincidence and extraordinary intervening events or acts in various ways. In one case the Bundesgerichtshof stated that while reaffirming its adherence to the theory of conditions, it was unnecessary to decide what the position would be as regards causal connection if a victim wounded by the accused was struck and killed by lightning in the place where he was immobilized by the wounding, or if he was killed in an accident while on the way to consult the doctor.[84] The more usual approach, however, is to deal with the difficulty under the heading of fault. Two cases may be contrasted. In one accused drove a lorry in the early morning with an unlighted trailer. He was stopped by the police and then ordered to drive to the nearest petrol station, the policeman intending to follow behind him in a car and so protect him from collision from the rear. However, before the police car was in position another lorry collided with the unlighted trailer from the rear and the driver was killed. Accused was convicted of negligent killing because his omission to light the trailer was a necessary condition of the death and he was negligent (in relation to the death) because the course of events was not unforeseeable or beyond all probability.[85]

In another case, however, accused, who was drunk, was wheeling his bicycle home at night when he fell in the road. A passing motorist stopped and removed him to the side of the road. As the motorist was returning to his car another motorist driving negligently from behind collided with the first motorist's car and killed his wife. Accused was acquitted of negligent killing since, though his act was causally connected with the death according to the theory of conditions, he was not negligent because the combination of the attempt at rescue and the negligence of the second motorist made the course of events unforeseeable, though neither was unforeseeable by itself.[86]

This shows how the awkward effects of the theory of conditions may be mitigated by the use of a doctrine that negligence is relative to the course of events, as in other cases it is by the notion of the purpose of the rule violated (*Normzweck*).[87] By an application of common-sense principles of causation the same conclusion might well have been reached but for different reasons. In the first case the fact that a collision occurred with an unlighted vehicle just at the moment before the police vehicle was in position would not, perhaps,

[84] *BGHSt* 1 (1951), 332, 334.
[85] *BGHSt* 4 (1953), 360.
[86] *BGHSt* 3 (1952), 62.
[87] Above, p. 454 n. 36.

be regarded as a coincidence negativing causal connection, since there is, even during a short period of time, an appreciable likelihood that an unlighted vehicle on a road will be struck by another from behind in conditions of poor visibility. On the other hand, the likelihood that a lighted vehicle which has stopped at the side of the road for a short period will be struck from behind, as in the second case, is so small that the occurrence might reasonably be regarded as a coincidence; and the court's language indicates that it was the combination or coincidence of the two events which it regarded as the decisive factor.

The German writers themselves have made a number of objections to the application of the theory of conditions in criminal law. First, it departs from ordinary usage, as we have repeatedly emphasized, and hence on this ground Beling, for example, who had first accepted the theory, later rejected it. Secondly, it leads to what is regarded as too extensive responsibility in some classes of case. One of these is the eggshell skull or haemophiliac type of case; it is thought too harsh to hold an accused person liable for harm of which the pre-existing susceptibility of the victim is a concurrent cause. The adequacy theory, which is preferred in this respect, is only a part cure for the mischief, because it relieves an actor from liability not when there is an abnormal auxiliary condition but when the act does not significantly raise the probability of the harm. On this basis accused is not guilty of homicide if he has given a very light blow; but if he has given a fairly heavy blow which has resulted in death because the victim was a haemophiliac, he is liable. Common-sense principles do not, of course, afford a remedy for this difficulty, since they draw a distinction between pre-existing conditions of the victim and subsequent abnormal events.

Another objectionable class of case is felt to be that of crimes aggravated by their consequences,[88] such as malicious wounding with fatal consequences. This may seem strange to an Anglo-American lawyer, who is used to the felony-murder doctrine, which may make accused liable for the full crime of murder in circumstances where there is no initial crime as serious as malicious wounding. But in Germany the injustice has been felt to be such that the legislature has intervened by adding an extra requirement of fault or *mens rea* in such cases, viz. that the ultimate harm must have been at least negligently brought about;[89] this enables the court to consider not only whether the ultimate harm was foreseeable by the accused at the time of his act but also whether the actual course of events has

[88] *Erfolgsqualifizierte Delikte*, viz. cases where an act already punishable is more severely punished if it has certain consequences. These were modified by the Act of 4 Aug. 1953 which requires at least negligence in relation to the further consequences.
[89] *StGB*, s. 56.

been 'outside all experience',[90] and hence to relieve him from liability in the event of a coincidence.

The cases least catered for by any of the possible correctives to the theory of conditions are those in which accused does an act intended to produce the harm but the harm occurs through the intervention of a subsequent voluntary act or abnormal event or act: for example, *A* wounds *B* intending to kill him and *B* is on his way to consult a doctor when he is deliberately killed by *C* or struck by a falling tree, neither of which would have occurred but for the original wounding, since *B* would not otherwise have been at that place. The theory of conditions does not provide a satisfactory solution of this difficulty and in practice, as we have seen, common-sense causal limitations are introduced in a disguised form as part of the theory of fault.

As we shall see in the next chapter, something similar is true not only of the theory of conditions which is the prevalent doctine in German criminal law, but also of the theory of adequate cause which has long been dominant in civil law. There too common-sense causal limitations are introduced in order to correct the deficiencies of the theory.

[90] On the relativity of negligence see above, pp. 260-1.

XVII

THE GENERALIZING THEORIES: ADEQUATE CAUSE

THE theory of conditions, described in the last chapter, has been accepted by the criminal courts of Germany and several other countries for the last hundred years. Not all writers, however, even in the field of criminal law, have been satisfied with it and in civil law it has failed to gain the allegiance of the courts, which have felt that it would lead to an undue extension of civil liability. Instead, civil courts have turned to the so-called generalizing theories[1] for guidance; of these the most successful and multiform has been the *adequate cause* or *adequacy theory*.[2] The choice of term is sometimes significant, since 'adequacy' is preferred to 'adequate cause' by those who see the theory as wholly or partly concerned to set non-causal limits to civil responsibility rather than to elucidate the meaning of causal connection in civil law.

The generalizing theories differ from the individualizing theories in that, though they also concentrate on the selection of one from among a set of conditions of an event as its cause, they select a particular condition as the cause of an event because it is of a kind which is connected with such events by a generalization or statement of regular sequence. Most individualizing writers, on the other hand, were satisfied to select a condition as the cause of an event if it 'contributed' more of the 'energy' needed to 'produce' the event on a particular occasion than any other condition. The generalizing writers, however, are not satisfied by the demonstration that if an identical set of conditions is assembled on another occasion then, at least when natural occurrences are involved, an event of the same kind will follow, and that in this sense every condition of an event is *generally* connected with it. They seek rather a general connection between a condition and a subsequent event in the sense of a relation which will hold good although the condition is combined with a varying set of other conditions. So 'general' here primarily means 'not confined to a determinate *set* of conditions'.

---

[1] See above, p. 433.
[2] *Theorie der adäquaten Verursachung; Adäquanztheorie.*

Von Bar was the forerunner of the generalizing school. He took as his starting-point the theory of conditions as expounded by Glaser[3] but denied Glaser's conclusion that every condition is entitled to be called a cause. 'Every cause of an event', says von Bar, 'must necessarily be a condition but it is incorrect to call every condition a cause.'[4] The selection of causes is relative to the purpose of the inquiry; when a stone is dropped gravitation is the cause of its fall for the scientist, the act of letting it go for the lawyer or moralist. Our notion of cause, he asserts, is derived from our experience as children that our body regularly obeys our will and that, by exploiting a knowledge of regular sequences practical purposes can be achieved. But all such regular sequences, including statements of natural laws, presuppose the existence of auxiliary conditions which are regarded as being *regularly* present and the absence of counteracting conditions, which are regarded as exceptional.[5] These regular or normal conditions are not causes; on the contrary, their existence is presupposed by any causal statement. A cause is a condition which *departs* from the ordinary or regular course of events. 'A man is in the legal sense the cause of an occurrence to the extent that he may be regarded as the condition by virtue of which what would be otherwise regarded as the regular course of events in human experience is altered.'[6] On the other hand, one must not identify 'being the cause of an event' with doing an act which foreseeably will be followed by that event. Thus, a doctor undertaking a dangerous but necessary operation, which in fact results in the patient's death, foresees death but is not, according to von Bar, the cause of it.[7]

The example of the dangerous operation illustrates one of the weaknesses in von Bar's exposition: his failure to distinguish clearly between the requisites of fault, unlawfulness and causal connection.[8] The doctor's act in performing the dangerous operation would, unless he failed to use due care, be necessary and so not unlawful. Hence he would not be legally responsible even if his act were causally connected with the patient's death.

However, von Bar's emphasis on the importance of the 'regular course of events'[9] in causal contexts marked an important advance,

3 Von Bar, op. cit., p. 4. Above, pp. 442-4.
4 Von Bar, loc. cit.
5 Op. cit., pp. 9-11.
6 Ibid., p. 11.
7 Ibid., p. 14.
8 Now said by some Anglo-American lawyers to be a virtue. *Roe* v. *Minister of Health* [1954] 2 QB 66, 84, *per* Denning LJ.
9 'Cours habituel des choses'. P. Bouzat and J. Pinatel, *Traité de droit pénal et de criminologie* (2nd edn. 1970), i. 266 n. 1.

for the notion of the 'normal course of events' is indeed fundamental in the analysis of causation.

I. RISE OF THE ADEQUATE CAUSE THEORY

The theory of adequate cause appeared to offer both a justification for and a more precise formulation of von Bar's reference to the 'regular course of events'. It was the Freiburg physiologist von Kries who first advanced this theory in the 1880s.[10] Von Kries was interested in the mathematical theory of probability and also in the statistical aspects of sociology[11] and considered that the notion of probability could be applied to the law also. Objective probability[12] (*Möglichkeit*), he argued, must be distinguished from subjective probability (*Wahrscheinlichkeit*), for objective probability is a relationship between events independent of our knowledge.

Von Kries appears to use 'objective' to make at least three different points:

(i) that a statement of the relative frequencies[13] of classes of events is independent of our knowledge or expectation. Thus if a die shaped as a regular cube is thrown a large number of times it is found that a six turns up approximately one-sixth of the total number of throws; hence the relative frequency of sixes to throws is about one-sixth. On the basis of a knowledge of this frequency one might assert that the probability of a particular throw being a six was about one-sixth; this would be to apply to a particular case a statement of regular frequencies and so to apply an objective relation between classes of events in making a particular probability statement. One important sort of particular probability statement is indeed a statement applying relative frequencies in this way and von Kries's point is therefore of importance; but this is not the only way in which the probability of a particular occurrence is estimated.[14]

[10] J. von Kries, *Die Prinzipien der Wahrscheinlichkeitsrechnung* (1886); *Über den Begriff der objektiven Möglichkeit und einiger Anwendungen desselben* (1888); *Über die Begriffe der Wahrscheinlichkeit und Möglichkeit und ihre Bedeutung im Strafrechte* (1889)—*ZStW* ix. 528. Antolisèi, op. cit., p. 117 advanced its Germanic origin as a reason for rejecting the adequate cause theory. Grispigni ('Il nesso causale nel diritto penale', (1935) *Rivista italiana di diritto penale* 13. 31) replied that the theory of conditions was also of German origin and that the adequate cause theory had been adumbrated by the Italians Romagnosi and Carrara (*Programma* 1, s. 1093).

[11] Lexis, *Zur Theorie der Massenerscheinungen in der menschlichen Gesellschaft* (Freiburg, 1877).

[12] The natural translation of this word is 'possibility' and *possibilité* was the word used by Laplace for probability in an objective sense; so also Cournot, *Exposition de la théorie des chances et des probabilités*, from whom von Kries drew his distinction. Kneale, *Probability and Induction*, p. 170. But the use of the term 'possibility' in this sense would be a source of confusion for the lawyer and we have therefore preferred 'objective probability'.

[13] See Kneale, op. cit., p. 152.

[14] Below, p. 469.

It is important to realize that frequency generalizations, though 'objective', are relative to the class of events chosen for comparison and to the description of the class. Thus, though one might loosely speak of the 'frequency of deaths from tuberculosis', in order to estimate probabilities we must know the frequency as a proportion of some other class, e.g. deaths from all causes in Great Britain in a given year. This proportion will clearly not be the same as the relative frequency of deaths from tuberculosis to the total number of persons in Great Britain in a given year. There is nothing in the statement that the relative frequency of ordinary throws of a die and sixes is about one-sixth inconsistent with the possibility that a machine might be constructed which would always or nearly always throw a six. The relative frequency of *throws with the machine* and sixes would differ from the relative frequency of ordinary throws and sixes. Hence while statements of relative frequency are true, whatever our knowledge and expectation, statements applying such frequencies alone to determine the probability of a particular event are always based on incomplete information, since the person making the estimate knows only that there has been or will be an event of one class and is using the relative frequencies to determine the probability that this also was or will be an event of another class. If the person making the estimate knew more about the circumstances he would not need to rely merely on the relative frequencies of the two classes of events.

Von Kries's point is a good one; but the difficulty of ascertaining relative frequencies and of settling the description of the classes of events between which the frequencies hold is very great. Questions of description we leave for later consideration.[15]

(ii) Von Kries further treated statements of relative frequency as themselves merely the sign of more fundamental relations between classes of events; it is these more fundamental relations that are described by him as relations of objective probability. Thus, the objective probability, he says, of a regular die turning up a six is exactly one-sixth and the observed frequencies, which are not, of course, exactly one in six are merely signs of this. This part of his theory is open to criticism in so far as it assumes the existence of relations between classes of events which are real but not derived from observation. But for purposes of the legal theory of causation we may neglect this part of von Kries's theory and argue as if he was merely concerned with relative frequencies. We therefore speak henceforth of the (objective) probability of B given A as if this were derived merely from the relative frequency of events of class A and class B.

15 Below, pp. 479 ff.

(iii) Von Kries also argued that statements of probability were 'objective' in the sense of not being based on a *mistaken* estimate of the frequencies, such as might be made by a person asked to estimate the probability of a die turning up a six who did not realize that the die was loaded. But this is a trivial point; a person making any estimate may be mistaken about the facts on which he bases it. Von Kries's substantial point is that statements of relative frequencies are objective in sense (i). It is important, however, to realize that when we say that a particular event *B* is more or less probable given another event *A* we are not always merely applying our knowledge of the relative frequencies of events of classes *A* and *B*. We may instead be drawing a tentative conclusion from a generalization for which the evidence is inconclusive, as when we say that *X* who is suffering from a certain disease will probably become blind, because there is strong but not conclusive evidence for the generalization that everyone who suffers from the disease becomes blind. Common to both these instances is the fact that a particular probability statement is made on the basis of incomplete knowledge; but the knowledge may be incomplete either because the best generalization available is a statement of frequencies or because the evidence, either for a particular fact or for a universal generalization, is inconclusive. Particular probability statements may be called 'objective' in von Kries's sense so far as they merely apply frequency generalizations.

Von Kries applies the concept of objective probability as a constituent element of causal statements in the following way. A given contingency will be the *adequate cause* of harm if and only if it satisfies two conditions: (i) it must be a *sine qua non* of the harm, (ii) it must have 'increased the objective probability' of the harm by a significant amount.[16] The idea of increasing objective probability may perhaps be made clear by the following example: a certain proportion of human beings suffer from tuberculosis; from this is inferred the objective probability of a human being's suffering from tuberculosis. A higher proportion of miners suffer from tuberculosis and the objective probability of a miner's so suffering is correspondingly greater. Hence a man's becoming a miner is said to increase the probability of his catching tuberculosis and, if he would not have caught it but for becoming a miner, to be the adequate cause of his catching the disease.[17] The bare relationship signified by *sine qua non* or necessary condition is treated by von Kries as a causal relationship distinguished from adequate cause as 'non-adequate' or

---

[16] The word *begünstigen* is used for 'to increase the objective probability'; its opposite is *gleichgültig sein* or *indifferent sein*.

[17] Von Kries, *Über die Begriffe der Wahrscheinlichkeit und Möglichkeit*, above, p. 467 n. 10.

'coincidental':[18] this non-adequate relation can be established, says von Kries, by attending solely to the particular case without applying generalizations.[19]

Von Kries further claims that the results reached by applying his notion of adequacy are very similar to those which a layman, and still more a lawyer with a trained sense of justice,[20] would reach by appealing to the teachings of experience and the regular course of events, and offers his theory as a rational reconstruction of these more intuitive notions. Indeed the adequacy theory itself is sometimes stated not in the strict form given above but in the loose form that a condition is the adequate cause of a consequence if it has a tendency, according to human experience and in the ordinary course of events, to be followed by a consequence of that sort.[21]

The results obtained by the two approaches will indeed often converge. Thus becoming a miner is the adequate cause of catching tuberculosis because of the substantially greater frequency with which miners catch it than human beings as a whole. It is also true that the conditions which together with being a man, etc., suffice to produce tuberculosis, e.g. prolonged exposure to coal dust, are such as miners are frequently exposed to. Such conditions may be called normal for miners. Hence it will often be true that, when a condition has increased the objective probability of a consequence, the consequence will be found to have occurred in the ordinary course of events without the intervention of any abnormal contingency. There will, however, be a divergence if a consequence of the class of which there is a greater probability occurs, but only owing to the intervention of an abnormal contingency, e.g. a man takes a job as a miner in a certain town where he meets and marries a girl from whom he contracts tuberculosis. Here becoming a miner is the adequate cause of catching the disease but the disease has not occurred in the ordinary course of events (for a miner).

Von Kries gives as an example of non-adequate causation the case of a coachman who in breach of duty falls asleep so that the coach deviates from the agreed route; during the course of the deviation the passenger is struck by lightning, which he would not have been on the correct route.[22] Here 'falling asleep' as opposed to 'keeping

---

18 *Zufälliger Erfolg.*
19 In this he was in our view mistaken, *pace* Mackie, *Cement*, pp. 77 f., 121, since generalizations are needed in order to establish the existence of the relationship of necessary condition.
20 *Gebildetes Rechtsgefühl.* The difference between a trained and untrained sense of justice von Kries saw in the supposed fact that the untrained layman makes causal judgments without appealing to generalizations while the trained lawyer makes use of generalizations of probability for this purpose.
21 Enneccerus-Lehmann, ii. 63.
22 Op. cit., p. 532.

awake' does not significantly increase the probability of 'passenger being struck by lightning'.[23] The chances of being struck by lightning are in fact small whether the coachman is asleep or awake, and if the passenger is in fact struck by lightning this will ordinarily be described as something out of the ordinary course of events, and the fact that lightning struck at that particular spot will be treated from a common-sense point of view as a coincidence. Here a divergence between the two methods of approach is avoided only because the lightning is incorporated in the description of the consequence.

Hence, though there is not a complete correspondence between von Kries's theory and von Bar's appeal to the normal course of events, there is often a convergence. Von Kries indeed thinks that the use of the notion of the normal course of events points in the right direction and he admits that his stricter notion of increased probability cannot be applied with mathematical accuracy; there is no clear line between adequate and non-adequate causes.[24]

Von Kries does not explain whether by increasing the risk to a significant extent he is referring to an act which increases the risk considerably or to one which increases it to a considerable risk. This may be important in practice. Suppose that there is a rare disease, peculiar to bakers. The risk of a non-baker contracting the disease is nil and therefore A's act in becoming a baker increases the risk of it infinitely in relation to what it was for A previously. But becoming a baker does not entail any considerable risk of contracting the disease and therefore on a second possible interpretation A's act is not the adequate cause of contracting the disease. The second interpretation is more consistent with von Kries's general position.

Von Kries's work appeared to show that the promptings of common sense were scientifically reputable and his work was soon accepted and developed by those who felt the theory of conditions to be artificial and only tolerated it because of its supposed philosophical repute. The first to do this was a criminal law writer, Merkel.[25] Others soon followed suit; among the best known are Helmer,[26] Rümelin,[27] Leipmann,[28] and above all Traeger.[29] According to Traeger, for a condition to be the adequate cause of harm it must

[23] This illustrates how much turns on the description of the class of consequences. If the description were 'passenger being killed' falling asleep would increase the probability of it.

[24] Op. cit., p. 533.

[25] A. Merkel, *Lehrbuch des deutschen Strafrechts* (1899), p. 99.

[26] *Über den Begriff der fahrlässigen Täterschaft* (Straßburger Dissertation, 1895).

[27] *Der Zufall im Recht* (1896), p. 44; *Die Verwendung der Kausalbegriffe im Straf- und Zivilrecht* (1900).

[28] *Einleitung in das Strafrecht* (1900), p. 67.

[29] *Der Kausalbegriff im Straf- und Zivilrecht* (1904). This is the work on causation most frequently cited in German civil courts.

have raised the objective probability of the harm to a not inconsiderable extent, taking account of (1) all those circumstances which a very perceptive observer would have noticed at the time the condition was set, and (2) circumstances actually then known to the person who sets the condition. In reaching a conclusion regard is to be had to all laws and teachings of experience known at the time of judgment. The civil senate of the Reichsgericht accepted the adequate cause theory in 1898[30] and it and the civil senate of the Bundesgerichtshof have followed it since; it has also been accepted by the civil courts of Austria and Switzerland and to a varying extent of other Continental countries.[31]

Some have thought that von Kries's appeal to probability in solving causal problems could be justified by the growing importance of statistical laws in science and by the fact that in quantum theory it appears impossible in principle to formulate them otherwise.[32] Hence some have maintained that it has now ceased to be even a theoretical ideal of science to discover causal laws in the sense of statements of conditions which are invariably followed by a given event without exception.[33] Other scientists maintain the contrary, and whichever group is right, the causal principles to which we appeal in everyday life, if particular causal statements are challenged, are not thereby invalidated,[34] though it is proper to point out that their supposedly invariable character depends on consequences and conditions being somewhat roughly described. The law is satisfied, in deciding whether the negligence of a motorist caused a collision with another vehicle, with a description of the positions of the two vehicles which would not be accurate enough for the purposes of particle physics.

Von Kries's claim that the conclusions of the adequacy theory would largely coincide with those reached by a 'trained sense of justice', however, met with opposition. Tarnowski argued that 'a trained sense of justice' was too vague and uncertain a notion to vindicate the adequate cause theory.[35] For not merely does the ordinary man's sense of justice leave him in uncertainty in borderline cases but, even when it leads to a clear decision, no one can say whether the decision is based on fault, causation, or some other

30 *RGZ* 42, 291 (breach of contract in storing goods susceptible to damp on ground not cause of damage to them by flood).
31 Its application is discussed by Peczenik, *Causes and Damages*, pp. 153–282, especially for Scandinavia; Vanquickenborne, *Oorzakelijkheid*, pp. 250–329, especially for Belgium and the Netherlands; Honoré, *IECL*, xi. 7-80 to 7-90 (general survey).
32 W. Heisenberg, *Das Naturbild der heutigen Physik*, p. 27. This view, rather than the contrary opinion of Einstein, now commands assent amongst most physicists.
33 H. Kelsen, *Vergeltung und Kausalität* (1941), pp. 256–76.
34 Leonhard, op. cit., p. 85.
35 H. Tarnowski, *Die systematische Bedeutung der adäquaten Kausalität für den Aufbau des Verbrechensbegriffs* (1927), p. 15.

element in responsibility. These criticisms led not to the abandonment of the notion of adequacy but to its derivation from a new
principle. Tarnowski, Grispigni, and others argued that both civil
and criminal law involve normative judgments. The law decides that
a person should or should not have done a given act at a given time.
But, it is argued, such a judgment is only rational so far as the person
in question had at that time[36] the possibility of influencing the actual
course of events. Hence the normative judgment cannot extend to
an event of which the actor did not increase the probability though
his act was a necessary condition of it.[37] The relation of adequacy is
therefore a presupposition of any normative judgment.

According to Tarnowski adequacy belongs to the factual, not the
normative part of the legal process. According to Grispigni, it belongs to the normative part, and the notion of cause is to be understood in the law in a normative sense.[38] Otherwise Grispigni's
argument is very similar. The object of many norms is to forbid
conduct because of its tendency to produce certain consequences
known usually to follow from it.[39] Hence we must look to the
moment when the law's threat operates or should operate on the
mind of the actor. If the consequence was probable given the act, if
the act was 'capable' of producing it, the norm forbids the act in
relation to that consequence, otherwise not.[40]

These views presuppose that the law's 'normative judgment' relates not merely to whether defendant or accused should have done
the original act but to the whole *Tatbestand* consisting of act, conditional connection, and consequence. This seems inconsistent with
the wording of Continental codes which appear, like Anglo-
American statutes, to forbid certain acts because of their tendency,
in general, to produce harm, but not conditionally upon there being
a specific probability in a particular case that the harm will occur.
There appears to be in the works of Tarnowski and Grispigni a
confusion between the rationale and the content of a norm forbidding certain conduct. The reason for the imposition of a norm
does not always settle the limits of its operation.

There are several possible cases in which the law may hold a
person responsible for the consequences of his conduct although,
in a certain sense, the conduct did not significantly increase the
probability of the harm. In the first place the law may forbid conduct

---

[36] It is a further question, on which different views are held, whether the actor must
have realized that he could by his conduct increase the probability of the harm.
[37] Tarnowski, op. cit., p. 339, no. 3. But why cannot an actor influence the course
of events by failing to decrease the probability of harm?
[38] Op. cit., p. 17.
[39] Above, pp. 469–70.
[40] Grispigni, op. cit., pp. 18–20.

because, although the amount by which the conduct would increase or fail to decrease the risk of harm occurring is very small, the harm if it did occur would be very great. Thus an employer may have a special duty to provide goggles for a one-eyed mechanic because, though his doing so would not greatly decrease the risk of blindness, which was small in any event, the possible harm is very serious.[41] Secondly the law may hold a person responsible for harm which is a consequence of his conduct although such conduct does not in general significantly increase the risk of such harm. The legislator may have miscalculated the probabilities. Finally, the act may, upon the description adopted by the legislator, significantly increase the risk of harm although in the light of the information available to the actor it does not do so. Thus 'administering poison' may be made a crime because of its tendency to injure health and life; yet on the information available to X, who gave Y poison, the risk may have been negligible, because X knew that Y regularly took an antidote. Suppose that on this occasion Y forgot to take the antidote and unexpectedly died. There seems no reason why X's conduct should not form the subject of a normative judgment; because the law may simply have forbidden the administration of poison, irrespective of whether on the information available to the actor on a given occasion the conduct would significantly increase the risk of harm.

This modern justification by Grispigni of the concept of adequacy means that adequacy is not necessarily now regarded as a theory of causation. The change has been marked by the fact that while the older generation spoke of the 'adequate cause' theory, recent writers speak of the 'adequacy' theory.[42]

After the Second World War the courts of the Federal Republic reinterpreted the notion of adequacy in such a way as to make it at least in part a vehicle for setting fair limits to responsibility and also showed an increasing awareness of the importance of determining the scope of the legal rule under consideration. In doing so they sometimes expressed themselves in terms to which many modern American writers would assent. Thus, in the important *Edelweiss* decision in 1951[43] the Bundesgerichtshof affirmed the traditional adequacy doctrine in the formulation adopted by Traeger[44] but then went on to explain that the formula need not be rigidly adhered to. 'Only if courts remain conscious of the fact that the question is not really one of causation but of the fixing of the limits within which

---

41 *Paris* v. *Stepney B.C.* [1951] AC 367.

42 *Adäquanztheorie.* But Nagler refused to adopt the new form, regarding it as a philological barbarity.

43 *BGHZ* 3 (1951), 261.

44 Above, pp. 471–2.

the author of a condition can fairly be made liable for its consequences, viz. basically one concerning a positive presupposition of liability, can they avoid schematizing the adequate cause formula and guarantee correct results.' Through defendant's negligence the *Edelweiss* had jammed in a canal and there was evidence of subsequent mistakes on the part of professional persons in charge of the canal, of an unexpectedly sudden rise in the water level, and of a failure of electric current. But for these contingencies the *Edelweiss* would not have sunk. The trial court 'ought to have examined whether the conjunction of these numerous conditions, partly set by incompetent persons and partly, perhaps, merely fortuitous, did not lie outside the normal range of experience',[45] since a wrongdoer is not responsible for the intervention of incompetent persons acting in a wholly unusual and inappropriate way. The court probably did not intend to replace the precise doctrine of adequate cause by a vague appeal to the fair limits of responsibility. Otherwise there would have been no point in repeating Traeger's careful formula for calculating the probability of the type of harm which occurred. The facts of the case call to mind the common-sense principles by which grossly negligent intervening acts or coincidental events can negative responsibility. It may therefore not be too fanciful to see in the Bundesgerichtshof's decision an invitation to judges to treat adequacy as a guide, sometimes imperfect, to the application of those common-sense principles.

A different interpretation, however, is suggested by an important decision of the same court twenty-one years later.[46] Here the defendant caused a road accident. The cars involved were left blocking the highway for fifteen minutes before the police arrived. Impatient oncoming drivers circumvented the stationary cars and damaged the pavement, which belonged to the municipality. The court held the defendant not liable for the cost of repairing the pavement. His conduct was indeed the adequate cause of the damage, but it merely provided the 'occasion' for the detour made by the oncoming drivers, who had acted 'of their own free will' and had not been 'provoked' by defendant's conduct. Nor could it be said that defendant had left his car blocking the highway for an unreasonably long time.

This case clearly recognizes that factors other than adequacy set limits to civil liability. The court explains its decision by holding that the impatient drivers alone, not the defendant, were 'master of the situation'.[47]

[45] *BGHZ* 3 (1951), 261, 267.
[46] *BGHZ* 58 (1972), 162.
[47] *BGHZ* 58, 167 ('Herr des schadenstiftenden Geschehens'). E. Deutsch, 'Regressverbot und Unterbrechung des Haftungszusammenhangs im Zivilrecht', *JZ* 1972, 551, explains the decisions in terms of a restriction on the scope of the norm violated, but adopts the idea that the free intervention of a third party excludes liability; cf. LG Düsseldorf, *NJW* 55, 103 (the 'grass verge' case).

There is therefore some evidence that in the post-war period the Bundesgerichtshof has been willing to modify or supplement the adequacy theory on grounds connected, in its terminology, with 'fairness' or 'mastery of the situation' but which could be more simply explained in the light of the common-sense principles we have expounded. Some writers have indeed spoken of the 'decline and fall' of adequacy[48] or of adequacy as an 'empty formula'.[49] Neither the courts' decisions nor their language justifies so dramatic a description of the situation. But it is significant that, in addition to the developments so far mentioned, the German courts have given increasing attention to the idea that liability can be limited by reference to the purpose of the rule violated (*Normzweck*) since each rule has its appropriate scope (*Schutzbereich*).

This was a theme that, following Rabel,[50] von Caemmerer eloquently restated in his inaugural address in 1956.[51] In a passage which has affinities with modern American writing he said that the notion of cause is really that of *sine qua non*. Any further questions are 'merely concerned with the purpose and scope of the rule imposing liability. The question of the limits of liability is to be solved by deploying the meaning and range of the particular rule, not by applying general causal formulae.'[52] Soon afterwards, in 1958, the Bundesgerichtshof adopted this approach in a case in which the husband of defendant had caused a road accident in which plaintiff was injured. Plaintiff was prosecuted for careless wounding of defendant's husband (who later died) and fined. On appeal, however, he was acquitted. He then sued defendant for the costs he had incurred in the criminal proceedings. He failed, since none of the rights listed in the relevant section of the German civil code[53] had been violated. But the Bundesgerichtshof made the point that 'none of the mischiefs which the law was meant to prevent has materialized'. Thus it adopted the language of *Schutzbereich*. The court pointed out that while the economic consequences of physical injury, such as medical expenses and loss of earnings, fall within the scope of the duty not to inflict bodily injury on others, the cost of defending oneself on a criminal charge is not within the ambit of the duty.

---

48 Heinrich Lange, 'Herrschaft und Verfall der Lehre vom adäquaten Kausalzusammenhang. Versuch einer Ehrenrettung', *Festgabe K. Oftinger* (1969), p. 321, attempts a rehabilitation but at the expense of admitting several exceptions.
49 G. Berbert, 'Die Leerformel der Adäquanz', *AcP* 169 (1969), 421.
50 E. Rabel, 'Die Grundzüge des Rechts der unerlaubten Handlungen', *Deutsche Ref. Int. Kong. Rechtsvergl. 1932.*
51 Von Caemmerer, *Das Problem des Kausalzusammenhangs im Privatrecht* (1956); cf. *Das Problem der überholenden Kausalität im Schadenersatzrecht* (1962).
52 *BGHZ* 27 (1958), 137.
53 *BGB* s. 823 (1).

In the 1958 case the prosecution costs were not, of course, consequent upon the physical injury to plaintiff.[54] But even harm which is genuinely a consequence of defendant's conduct may be outside the scope of his liability. Thus, defendant injured plaintiff in a road accident and as a result plaintiff was examined in hospital, so that a condition (arteriosclerosis) was discovered which would not otherwise have come to light so soon. As a result, plaintiff was dismissed from his employment for being unfit to work. It was held that he could not recover from defendant his loss of earnings through being dismissed.[55] The discovery might be the 'adequate' consequence of the accident, but each person must bear for himself the risk that his physical or mental defects may be, from his point of view, prematurely uncovered. In this type of case the notion of *Normzweck* overlaps with the idea that there are certain risks which the legal system expects each of us to bear for himself (*Lebensrisiken*) and not to transfer to others except by insurance. One of these is the risk that the truth about oneself will emerge. The losses arising from these risks could be said to be outside the scope of the legal system as a whole, rather than of any particular norm.[56]

Some German writers have thought that the *Normzweck* concept, together with the notion that certain risks are to be borne by the victim in any event, could replace adequacy as a limiting factor in civil liability.[57] But this is to claim too much. The 'scope of rule' concept is a useful supplement to that of adequacy[58] in a limited range of cases, but it is a distinct notion, independent of probability.[59] It is useful when we can deduce that the rule violated has a clear and limited purpose, or where the interest affected (e.g. in the truth remaining hidden) is not worthy of protection.[60] Where this is not the case, to rely on the scope of the rule is to overestimate the imagination of the legislator[61] and in effect to entrust the decision to the unfettered discretion of the judge.[62] Why should the vague

[54] J. G. Wolf, *Der Normzweck im Deliktrecht* (1962), p. 14.
[55] *BGH* 7 June 1968; *JZ* 1969, 702.
[56] J. Esser and E. Schmidt, *Schuldrecht* (5th edn. 1976), p. 173, hold that the *Normzweck* should reflect a 'socially justified division of risks'.
[57] J. G. Wolf, *Der Normzweck im Deliktrecht* (1962), p. 5; E. A. Kramer, 'Schutzgesetze und adäquate Kausalität', *JZ* 1976, 338, thinks that the two often coincide. U. Huber, 'Normzwecktheorie und Adäquanztheorie', *JZ* 1969, 677, holds that there is no room for adequacy besides the scope of the norm and the notion of the victim's 'sphere of risk' (*Gefahrbereich*).
[58] Rümelin, *AcP* 90 (1900), 305; H. Stoll, *Kausalzusammenhang und Normzweck im Deliktrecht* (1968), p. 6.
[59] Deutsch, *Haftungsrecht* (1976), p. 151.
[60] E. Deutsch, 'Begrenzung der Haftung aus abstrakter Gefährdung wegen fehlender adäquater Kausalität', *JZ* 1966, 556.
[61] H. Stoll, *RabelsZ* 27 (1962-3), 553, 557.
[62] As did Hermann Lange, *Deutscher Juristentag Tübingen*, 43 (1960); but see now Hermann Lange, 'Adäquanztheorie, Rechtswidrigkeit, Schutzzwecklehre und selbständige Zurechnungsmomente', *JZ* 1976, 198.

generalities of the adequacy theory be replaced by a still more incalculable notion, the *asylum ignorantiae* of judicial decision?[63]

In summarizing the post-war developments in civil liability it would be fair to say that German courts have come to employ at least three distinct types of limitation. The first is adequacy which, though modified in some degree, has not been entirely supplanted. There is indeed a case for excluding liability for highly improbable consequences. Secondly, there are common-sense causal limitations of the sort expounded in this book. Thirdly, there are the currently popular limitations derived from the scope of the rule violated or the type of loss suffered. We welcome the way in which German law has shed the monistic idea that all the appropriate limitations on civil responsibility can usefully be reduced to a single formula. It represents a trend that fully accords with our own views of the way in which the law should develop. It may be worth noting in this connection that the new Netherlands civil code expressly excludes liability for harm which does not fall within the scope of the norm violated.[64]

II. DETAILED APPLICATION OF THE ADEQUACY THEORY

We have already considered the historical development of the adequacy theory.[65] Its details may be approached through a discussion of a famous case.[66] The owner of two lighters sued a contractor for breach of contract by which the lighters were to be towed from Cuxhaven to Nordenham on 28 October 1909, on which day the weather was fine. The contractor began to tow on the 28th but despite the owner's objections returned to port. The weather forecast for the 29th was favourable and the lighters were towed on that day but during the voyage a storm broke out and they suffered severe damage. On appeal it was held that the delay by the contractor was the adequate cause of the damage. The court said that the damage need not be foreseeable; it was sufficient that the 'objective probability of a consequence of the sort that occurred was generally increased or favoured' by the breach. On the facts the delay had increased the risk of loss since, at the end of October, it is more likely that the weather will hold for a journey of six hours begun in good weather than it will hold on the following day, even if the weather forecast is favourable.[67]

63 Schickedanz, 'Schutzzwecklehre und Adäquanzlehre', *NJW* 1971, 916.
64 Art. 6. 3. 1. 2.
65 Above, pp. 467 ff.
66 *RGZ* 81 (1913), 359. Cf. *RGZ* 105, (1922), 264 (shooting by policeman the adequate cause of death in hospital from influenza during epidemic).
67 *RGZ* 81 (1913), 363.

The court also discussed the case from the standpoint of the common-sense or loose notion of the 'natural course of events'. It held that the consequence need not follow in accordance with a rule but that it must not occur only through the intervention of a contingency 'contrary to the natural course of events',[68] which could equally well have occurred without the breach of contract: a collision of the lighters with a steamer on the 29th, which would not have occurred in fact on the 28th since the steamer in question would then have been out of range, would have been such a contingency. But the storm was not unusual for the time of year.[69]

We deal first with the adequacy theory as strictly formulated and consider in turn: (i) the generalization (description) of the consequence; (ii) the generalization (description) of the condition; (iii) amount of the increase in probability required; (iv) alteration of risk; (v) calculation of probability; (vi) difficult cases; (vii) relation of the adequacy theory to the 'normal course of events'.

(i) *Generalization of the consequence.* The problem of the 'generalization' of the consequence, in the adequacy theory, is that of describing the class of events whose probability must be shown to have been significantly increased by the wrongful act. It is clear that the so-called concrete description of the consequence in 'all its details' advocated by some for the description of the consequence in order to ascertain whether an act is a condition,[70] cannot be applied here; the description must be 'abstract'.

The adequacy theory is concerned with the relation of probability between the condition and the ultimate consequence, not between the condition and any third factor which contributes to produce the ultimate harm.[71] But the probability of the occurrence of the third factor can be made indirectly relevant to the adequacy of the condition by incorporating the third factor in the description of the ultimate consequence. If defendant gravely wounds the victim and leaves him under a tree where he is struck by lightning and killed, the wounding may be adequate if the harm is described as 'death' but possibly not if it is described as 'death by lightning'. The incorporation, in the description of the consequence, of such a third factor enables the adequacy theory to reach almost the same conclusions as would be reached by applying the common-sense

---

[68] The contingency here is not the storm but the conjunction of the storm and the exposure of the ship to it while at sea.

[69] *RGZ* 81 (1913), 362. Cf. above, pp. 168–70.

[70] Above, p. 450.

[71] Radbruch, op. cit., p. 339; von Kries, op. cit., p. 532; Enneccerus–Lehmann, op. cit., p. 63. This is often expressed by asking whether the condition has a general tendency to bring about harm of the same kind as that which has occurred.

principle that an intervening coincidental event negatives causal connection,[72] for if the conjunction of a wrongful act and an intervening contingency is very unlikely, the wrongful act will not often have significantly increased the risk of a conjunction of the intervening contingency and the ultimate harm. It is very unlikely that a tree will be struck by lightning just at the moment that accused has left his wounded victim beneath it; it will also in general be true that the act of accused in leaving his victim under the tree has not significantly increased the risk of the victim's being killed by lightning. Hence there is a tendency among the theorists of adequate cause to incorporate in the description of the consequence such third factors as will enable the results of applying the theory to accord with common-sense judgments about coincidences.

Thus Radbruch says that while strictly it is only the ultimate consequence whose adequacy falls to be determined one should also, in fixing the description of the consequence, take account of the 'most important points of transition from the bodily movement to the final consequence', according to their class description.[73] Another solution is to require, in addition to adequacy, 'typical causal sequence' at least when the case concerns a crime aggravated by its consequences.[74] A third is to require, in addition to adequacy, that the probability relationship should not be unsuited to explaining the configuration of events, in view of later contingencies not imputable to the actor.[75] Von Kries himself states the adequacy theory at times in a form which is inconsistent with the requirement that it is only the ultimate harm for which the condition must be adequate. Thus he says that the problem is whether 'the connection . . . with the consequence is a generalized one or merely a particularity of the case in question, whether the factor (the conduct in question) . . . is generally apt, or possesses a tendency, to bring about a consequence of that sort, or whether it has merely occasioned it accidentally'.[76] His contrast between having a tendency to bring about a consequence and bringing it about accidentally can only be sustained if those factors which might lead one to say that the consequence had followed accidentally or by a coincidence are incorporated in the description of the consequence.

But this would make the notion of increased probabilities quite unworkable. For even if we can settle what are the 'important' third factors which must be incorporated into the description of the

72 Above, pp. 164–7.
73 Radbruch, op. cit., p. 339.
74 Helmer, op. cit., p. 49.
75 Liepmann, op. cit.
76 *Vierteljahrsschrift für wissenschaftliche Philosophie*, 12 (1888), 179, 200–1. Accidentally = *in zufälliger Weise*.

consequence the same difficulties of description are met again in describing these factors.[77] If 'death' must be replaced by 'death by lightning', why not 'death by forked lightning'? Where will the process of extending the description stop? It could not logically stop short of including every factor relevant to the probability of the ultimate harm. The court will then be asking questions such as whether a light blow on the head significantly increases the risk of death under an anaesthetic for an alcoholic who has suffered gunshot wounds in the war—the sort of question for answering which there are likely to be no statistics and which is too complicated for common sense to estimate. The estimates of probability which the adequacy theory requires are practicable only if the description of the consequences remains fairly general. The only rule of description consistent with positive law is to adopt the description expressed or implied in the codes, 'death', 'bodily injury', etc., but subject to the proviso mentioned in our discussion of the notion of a condition, that this means 'death before it would normally occur', etc.[78] But this would at once reveal the divergence between the adequacy theory and common-sense judgments of causal connection.

(ii) *Generalization of the condition.* Obviously whether the wrongful act increases the risk of the harm depends on its description. Thus, 'giving a man a light blow on the head' may not significantly increase the risk of death but 'giving a man with a weak heart a light blow on the head' might do so. One's first inclination is to favour a description of the act restricted to the terms of statute: i.e. if the statute forbids 'wounding' to describe the act of an accused as 'wounding X'. But clearly the adequacy theorists need to distinguish between wounds of different degrees of seriousness, some adequate for their consequences, others not. Again, is one to stop short of an inclusion of all those factors which are relevant to the probability of a consequence of the class in question? If so, the reference to the weak heart of the victim must be incorporated in the description of the act, whether it was known or ascertainable at the time or not. Again, should we incorporate in the description of the act a reference to its relations with then future events, for example, speak of 'leaving a wounded victim under a tree about to be struck by lightning'? Most writers have felt the need to draw a line between a description restricted to the words of the rule of law in question and one which incorporates every feature of the act relevant to the probability of the consequence.

The problem of what facts should be incorporated in the description of the wrongful act for purposes of the adequacy theory is

[77] Parallel difficulties in Anglo-American law are discussed above at pp. 165-6, 256-8.

[78] Above, pp. 452-3.

called by the writers the problem of ontological consideration, to distinguish it from the problem of what knowledge of laws or generalizations the person calculating probabilities is to be credited with (nomological considerations). The latter problem is discussed under (v) below.[79]

Wundt[80] held that only conditions existing at the time of the act should be incorporated in the description of the act. Radbruch objected that even if the conditions 'operated' later their causes existed earlier; from the point of view of determinism, they have been certain to 'operate' from eternity and, in any case, the notion of conditions 'operating' or 'intervening' is metaphysical; there is no particular moment at which the conditions other than the one in question 'receive it as a comrade in arms'.[81]

Von Kries's doctrine was that the act must be described in the light of what the actor knew at the time of his act; if he was misinformed, this should be taken into account. Thus, if accused set fire to what he mistakenly believed to be an empty house, the proper description of his act, for purposes of the adequacy theory, is 'setting fire to a house'; of course we cannot say 'setting fire to an empty house' for this would be a false description of his act. Others, such as Traeger,[82] thought this too narrow and included in the description of the act those factors of which either the actor or an experienced man[83] or the most prudent[84] man, at the time of the act, should have known; Rümelin went further and included 'what was or has become known otherwise, for example, circumstances existing at the time of the wrongful act which have been discovered through the subsequent course of events'.[85] Rümelin's view involves a 'retrospective forecast',[86] or the use of 'hindsight'. Rümelin does not allow for the incorporation of future events, but if Radbruch's criticism of the distinction between existing conditions and future events is accepted, the description of the act would indirectly cover subsequent events and it would be rare indeed that it was not adequate for the consequence.

Rümelin attempted to meet this difficulty by an exception to his principle, viz. that, if the wrongful act merely brought the injured party to the place and at the time of a later event, then conditions existing at the time of the wrongful act are not incorporated in the description of the act if they were not known to or ascertainable by

[79] pp. 488-90.
[80] *Logik*, i. 2, 342.
[81] Radbruch, op. cit., p. 344.
[82] Op. cit., pp. 159 ff. Affirmed in *BGHZ* 3 (1951), 261, 266.
[83] Allfeld, Kriegsmann v. Rohland, Köhler.
[84] Von Hippel.
[85] *Kausalbegriffe*, p. 19. *AcP* 90, pp. 188, 216, 220, 260.
[86] *Nachträgliche Prognose*.

the actor at the time.[87] This view reflects indirectly the principle that when the causally relevant feature of defendant's conduct is that he has displaced the victim in place or time, and the victim or his property is harmed at the substitute place or time, defendant is not held to have caused the harm unless the chance of the occurrence of the harmful event at the substitute place or time is greater than it was at the original place or time.[88]

Rümelin's view has not met with general acceptance[89] and the prevalent opinion is that of Engisch[90] that the description should incorporate only circumstances known or knowable at the time of acting: it was at one time disputed whether this meant known or knowable to the actor[91] or, as Traeger says,[92] to a 'most prudent man' who is 'the actor himself freed from the defects which hamper his powers of perception in any direction'. Thus, if the actor gave the victim a slight shove at the edge of a cliff and the victim fell over the cliff and was killed, von Kries's view would have been that for purposes of deciding whether the shove significantly increased the probability of death, the act should be described as 'giving a slight shove on the edge of a cliff' only if the actor knew that he was standing on the edge of a cliff. Traeger would say that it must be so described if the most prudent of men would have realized this—as he might not if the events occurred in a thick fog; Rümelin's view was that the act should be so described, even though the most prudent of men would not have discovered the proximity of the cliff at the time. Traeger's view has now been endorsed by the Bundesgerichtshof.[93]

Strictly speaking, the Traeger principle of description should be stated in the negative, viz. that circumstances not known or knowable either to the actor or a most prudent man are excluded from the description. This caters for the possibility that the actor knows some circumstance which a very prudent man would not know. In this case what he knows should be taken into account in settling the description of his conduct.[94]

Apart from the description of the condition and consequence, a third problem of the same sort must be solved in order to apply the adequacy theory. This concerns the description of the initial class

[87] Op. cit., p. 130.
[88] Above, pp. 122, 168–70.
[89] In *BGHZ* 3 (1951), 261, 266 it was held too wide.
[90] Op. cit., p. 55.
[91] This was von Kries's view.
[92] Op. cit., p. 159: *einsichtigster Mensch.*
[93] *BGHZ* 3 (1951), 261, 266: the increased probability of the consequence must be judged in the light of 'alle zur Zeit des Eintritts der Begebenheit dem optimalen Beobachter erkennbaren Umstände'.
[94] H. Mayer, op. cit., p. 137.

with which it is sought to compare the wrongful act; for the adequacy theory involves a comparison of the probability of the harm but for the act and given the act. This is not necessarily the same as a comparison of the probabilities before and after the act. Thus if the wrongful act consists in dispatching goods by the wrong aeroplane, this might well increase the risk of their destruction relatively to their not being dispatched at all, but not relatively to their being dispatched by the right plane, if the wrong plane was as safe as the right one. In this instance it is easy to make the right substitution, since it is clear what compliance with the law would have involved, and so to arrive at a description of the class of events with which comparison is sought. However, the same problems of the detail of description remain to be answered in this case too; thus, if the right plane had a leaking fuel tank, ought this to be included in a description of what compliance with the law would have involved, and if so should this be done in any event or only if the actor or a most prudent man would have noticed it?

For purposes of the adequacy theory the only general guide of value to the description of the wrongful act is the fact that, for causal purposes and for the calculation of relative frequencies, there is always an implied contrast which will often help toward an appropriate description of both; and in a legal context this contrast is usually between the actual wrongful conduct of defendant and his conduct hypothetically altered to the minimum extent needed to make it lawful and reasonable.

On the problem of the degree of detail of description required there is no agreement among the Continental writers. This is not surprising, for the problems are perplexing. In our discussion of the notion of a coincidence we pointed out that to make sense of this notion, the third intervening factor must be described as it would be by persons without special knowledge of the situation. This is more satisfactory than to make the description depend on the knowledge of the actor or of an 'optimal observer'.

The adequacy theorists are agreed that any special knowledge possessed by the actor must be incorporated in the description of the act[95] but disagree whether this is an illogical exception to the adequacy theory. Thus H. Mayer asserts that imputability, not objective probability, is the test of causation, since otherwise the actor's special knowledge of extraordinary circumstances could not be taken into account, since this is 'nothing in the events themselves'.[96] However, this is to misunderstand the adequacy theory, for the probability of harm is no less 'objective' for being relative to the description

[95] Affirmed in *BGHZ* 3 (1951), 261, 267.
[96] Op. cit., p. 137.

of the condition.[97] There is, of course, a general justification for incorporating circumstances known to the actor in the description of an act, for the actor may be presumed to be exploiting them for his own purposes.

There is a great exaggeration of this truth about description in Antolisèi's doctrine of the 'sole human cause'. Antolisèi maintains that not only must all external factors, whether really instrumental or not, taken into account by the actor be regarded as imputable to him[98] but also 'all the elements without distinction which he can employ for this purpose: in other words all the external factors which man can dominate'.[99] By this method the conclusion is reached that the act in question is often the *sole* cause of the harm, since all the other factors have been incorporated in it.[1] But causal problems are difficult enough without gratuitously introducing a fiction that the actor is exploiting or dominating circumstances of which he is in fact unaware.

(iii) *How great an increase in probability is required?* Von Kries, it will be remembered, held that the cause of an event in law was that condition which *significantly* increased the probability of the event. Not all subsequent theorists are agreed on this. Thus Tarnowski maintains that the *slightest* increase in probability is sufficient to make a condition an adequate cause.[2] His objection is partly to the vagueness of a 'significant' or 'considerable' increase.[3] This is part of his general objection to the application of common-sense distinctions in the law. He also complains, with a considerable measure of truth, that there is a confusion in many writings between the increase in the probability of harm attributable to the wrongful act and the resultant probability.[4]

Tarnowski's difficulty is the objection that if the slightest increase in probability makes a condition an adequate cause there will be few conditions which are not adequate. But the objection should not be overstated, for though there must have been some probability of the harmful consequence given the condition in question[5] this may have been less than the probability would have been without the condition. If one man snatches another from a lion's den there is no doubt some probability even outside the den that the man will be

[97] Above, p. 468.
[98] *Il rapporto di causalità nel diritto penale*, p. 186.
[99] Ibid., p. 188.
[1] Antolisèi adopts not the adequacy theory but the theory of conditions, subject to certain exceptions.
[2] Op. cit., pp. 177-8, 218-27.
[3] 'Berechenbar'—Liepmann, *Einleitung in das Strafrecht* (1902), p. 72. 'Beacht-lich'—von Bar, *Gesetz und Schuld* (1907), p. 106.
[4] Op. cit., pp. 218, 222.
[5] H. Mayer, op. cit., p. 137.

eaten by a lion but the act of snatching him from the den has certainly not increased the probability of this. If it is said that, since the harm has occurred, there must have been a very great probability of its happening at the time of the wrongful act in the particular case, this may be true on a description of the act which incorporates all the circumstances now known to have existed at the time, as in Rümelin's view, but may be quite untrue in relation to the ordinary man's or even the most prudent man's description.[6]

Even if a necessary condition does not always increase the risk of the harm that has occurred, it is argued that it does so in cases in which no one would think a causal connection established. Von Kries gives the example of a railway accident caused by the fault of the defendant or accused; the victim is obliged by the accident to spend some time in a town where he would not otherwise have stayed, and he there catches typhus. Von Kries says that the risk of catching typhus is increased by the accident but that the accident is not the adequate cause of catching typhus. Tarnowski argues that in the absence of detailed knowledge about different places along the railway line, the probability of catching typhus is taken to be the same at the victim's original destination as at the place where he caught typhus; hence the accident has not increased the risk of catching typhus, and is, even on Tarnowski's view, non-adequate.[7] Of course, all depends on the description of the wrongful act which caused the accident; normally this would not be described as occurring near a place where a typhus epidemic was raging[8] and hence Tarnowski's exegesis of this case seems preferable to von Kries's.

Von Kries gives another example of a condition which increases the risk of the harm but in his view not significantly. If accused leaves open the door of his house this slightly increases the risk that someone will enter and kill an occupant; but no one would say that accused had caused the death. Tarnowski replies that though the probability is increased by leaving the door open it is a question depending on the positive law of participation in crime whether the free and intentional intervention of a third person is inconsistent with liability.[9] This suggests that the theory often diverges from common-sense views of causation. Going for a walk is not the cause of being run over in a road accident, though it increases the probability of this happening.[10] Even a considerable increase of risk may be

6 Above, p. 482.
7 Op. cit., p. 220.
8 But suppose that a 'most prudent man' would know of the epidemic in that place? This casts doubts on the utility of introducing, in order to settle the description, a 'most perceptive man' bent on incorporating every detail he can.
9 Op. cit., p. 222.
10 Leonhard, op. cit., p. 32.

consistent with facts in which no one other than a blind adherent of the adequacy theory would hold the condition to be the cause of the harm; climbing up a mountain considerably increases the risk of falling down a mountain[11] but would not ordinarily be called its cause. The only plausible version of the adequacy theory is, indeed, that which requires that the act in question should increase the risk of the harm to a considerable or significant risk. No numerical value can be given to this; but the harm need not be more likely than not.[12] It seems too much even to demand that the resultant probability should be such that the consequence is 'typical', i.e. frequently instantiated,[13] for if a revolver shot is aimed at someone at a great distance the probability of the victim's being hit may be very small, yet if he is hit the person aiming the revolver has undoubtedly caused the wound or death.

This last example perhaps serves to bring out the weakness in the whole attempt to represent causal judgments as depending on estimates of increased probabilities or risks; for the common sense of the matter is that firing a revolver is the cause of injury if and only if the shot hits the victim, irrespective of the probability at the time of the firing that the victim would be hit. The probabilities depend on the competence of the marksman, the range, the type of revolver, the strength of the wind, and many other factors; but causal judgments do not, at least directly; for the probabilities are relevant to them only in that they affect our weighing of the evidence. The improbability of the event may make us disinclined to believe that it *was* a consequence of the act in question. We may doubt whether the victim really was wounded by the shot which the accused fired, and be inclined to believe that some other shot *caused* the wound. But *if* we assert that defendant's shot caused the wound we must be prepared to support our assertion with something more than foreseeability. We would trace the causal connection with the aid of generalizations, no doubt loosely formulated, about ignition, the movements of bodies and the bodily tissues of human beings, and would attempt to distinguish cases in which the consequence did not follow the shot.

Of course, if causal connection is established at all, the events must be explicable in retrospect and there must therefore be *some* description of the condition which involves a certainty or very high probability of the harm occurring. But this consideration should not be allowed to obliterate the distinction between statements of causal

---

[11] Ibid., p. 33. Whether it is a universally necessary condition of falling down depends on whether there are other ways of getting up a mountain than climbing up it.
[12] Antolisèi, op. cit., p. 187.
[13] Kriegsmann, *Gerichtssaal*, 68 (1906), 143, 148.

THE CONTINENTAL THEORIES

connection and statements of probability; for the use of the latter is to argue from one event to the other on the basis of limited knowledge, not to argue from one to another in the light of 'complete' knowledge. With the recognition of this distinction must disappear the whole claim to elucidate causal judgments with the help of the notion of increased probability, or indeed of probability at all.

(iv) *Changing the risk*. According to a version of the adequacy theory favoured by Enneccerus[14] a condition may be the adequate cause of an event, without increasing the risk of it, if it has *changed* the risk of it. 'Changing the risk' here means that, though the probability of the harm may not be greater than before, the factors other than the wrongful act which, in conjunction with it, will suffice to produce the harm, and which may be present, are different. Thus the seller who without urgent reason disregards the buyer's instructions as to delivery, by sending the goods by a different route, is responsible for the destruction of the goods on that route. This is intended to support Enneccerus's thesis that even when the law places the risk of loss on one of the parties, liability depends on the establishment of causal connection between a breach of contract or tort and the loss.[15] But the words of the sections to which he refers are against this construction, for two of the three sections expressly state that the defendant is liable for loss even though it occurs through accident or coincidence in such cases.[16] Enneccerus says that although change of risk is sufficient to make a condition the adequate cause of an event, the condition is not an adequate cause if it is entirely indifferent or immaterial from the point of view of the event; an example of this is sending goods by one of two alternative rail routes from Frankfurt to Berlin. It is not easy to see why the risk is not changed in this case, for though the main possibility of harm to the goods may still be from, let us say, derailment, there is a difference between derailment on one line and on another. It is indeed difficult to imagine any condition of an event which does not 'change the risk' of it. Enneccerus's view can logically only lead back to the theory of conditions.

(v) *The calculation of the probabilities*. The matters here dealt with are the laws or principles available, the time at which the judgment of probability is to be made and the person making it.

The generalizations on the basis of which judgments of probability are to be made in order to apply the adequacy theory are discussed

[14] Op. cit., ii. 64.
[15] *BGB*, s. 287 (debtor in default liable for supervening impossibility); s. 447 (seller failing to obey buyer's instructions as to delivery); s. 848 (defendant wrongfully detaining plaintiff's goods).
[16] 'Durch Zufall eintretende Unmöglichkeit' (*BGB*, s. 287); 'Haftung für Zufall bei Entziehung einer Sache' (*BGB*, s. 848).

by the writers under the rubric 'nomological considerations'.[17] The view which clearly accords with von Kries's theory is that the estimate of probabilities should be based on the best available evidence; this includes all the known generalizations about the frequencies of the relevant classes. Thus the Reichsgericht said that adequacy must be judged from the standpoint of one who has at his disposal all the experience and knowledge of mankind,[18] and Engisch speaks of 'maximum knowledge of laws'.[19] The generalizations are not confined to the teachings of everyday experience but include those known only to experts. The Bundesgerichtshof has said that all experience available at the date of judgment should be taken into account.[20]

However, some writers consider that only those generalizations known at the time of the wrongful act should be taken into account, not those discovered later.[21] The reason given is the familiar one that for purposes of a normative judgment no attention should be paid to matters which could not have been taken into account by the actor.[22] But this also applies to expert knowledge of laws discovered before the act, which the actor did not know or could not discover. Rümelin therefore argued that all laws which were not available to ordinary human experience should be excluded and expert knowledge should be admitted for purposes of calculation only if an average expert would know them; for example, medical laws so far as an average doctor would know them.[23]

But these views strike at the roots of the adequacy theory, for they destroy its claim to base causal judgments on 'objective relations', which would require use of the best evidence of the relative frequencies available at the time of judgment, and not mistaken estimates of them which would have been made by a person with defective knowledge of natural laws. Hence to place typhus germs in one's wife's food was said not to be the adequate cause of her death when the bacillary theory of disease was not well established.[24] Surely this is an affront to the common-sense standards of judgment which the adequacy theory purports to respect, for a lawyer would ordinarily say that in such a case the husband's act was the cause of the death but that the element of fault or *mens rea* was lacking.

17 Above, p. 482.
18 'Das gesamte deutsche Recht', p. 734. *RGZ* 81 (1913), 359, 360.
19 Op. cit., p. 57: *nomologisches Höchstwissen*.
20 *BGHZ* 3 (1951), 261, 267.
21 Engisch, loc. cit.
22 Above.
23 *Kausalbegriffe*, pp. 19–21. He was prepared to apply this even when the actor knew of laws which formed no part of ordinary human experience. Radbruch, op. cit., p. 368.
24 'Das gesamte deutsche Recht', p. 734.

There has also been discussion of the person who is notionally to make the judgment of probability. According to Rümelin the judge, representing the average man, must estimate probabilities from his own knowledge of natural laws and his own experience, whereas Thon[25] considers that the judgment of a normal man should be taken. These are but further ways of restricting the evidence of the probabilities to be taken into account.

The only view really compatible with the adequacy theory is that all laws and all experiences should be used to make the best possible estimate of the probabilities; if a more accurate estimate is possible at the time of judgment than at the time of the wrongful act, so much the better. In the terminology of the German writers, ontological restrictions, which affect the description of the wrongful act, can be admitted but nomological restrictions cannot.

(vi) *Difficult cases.* In this section we consider a number of cases which create real or apparent difficulty for the adequacy theory.

When the law places the risk of a defined loss on one of the parties[26] the adequacy theory cannot, despite Enneccerus's contrary view,[27] be applied without distortion. It should instead be accepted that in such cases the wrongful conduct need only occasion the harm and that it is sufficient, therefore, to establish that the conduct was a *sine qua non* of its occurrence.

The relation of the adequacy theory to intervening events, whether normal or amounting, in conjunction with the wrongful act, to co-incidences, may create awkwardness. If accused gives the victim a slight wound and the wounded person is involved in a road accident on the way to the doctor, von Kries says that it is unjust to hold accused responsible for a crime aggravated by its consequences, such as malicious wounding with fatal consequences, and that the adequacy theory avoids this injustice.[28] In this case the light wound may not have significantly increased the risk of death and there is an intervening coincidence, so that the same result is achieved whether the adequacy theory or common-sense principles are applied. But if accused gives the victim a heavy blow which, however, does not immediately kill him and the victim is involved in a fatal accident on the way to the doctor, the adequacy theory requires that the death should be treated as the consequence of the blow, unless the consequence is described as being 'death in a road accident'

25 Op. cit., pp. 10-11. Similarly, Grispigni, op. cit., p. 26.
26 Enneccerus-Lehmann, op. cit., 217. Swiss Code of Obligations, ss. 103, 306 (borrower not using in accordance with contract).
27 Op. cit. ii. 62 n.
28 Von Kries, *Über den Begriff der objektiven Möglichkeit*, p. 125. Tarnowski, op. cit., p. 57. The injustice is mitigated by the requirement of enhanced *mens rea* introduced in 1959.

rather than simply 'death'. But this recourse to more detailed description is arbitrary. The notion of coincidence offers a more rational explanation of the denial of liability.[29] A problem of this sort arose in a case in which the defendant had undertaken to keep the plaintiff's goods 'absolutely dry'. He left them, however, at ground level in open sheds. A dam burst and the goods were flooded. The plaintiff claimed damages and alleged that the goods should have been stored on the first floor where they would have been safe. Here it would apppear that the storage on the ground increased the risk of damage to the goods but the damage was caused by an act of God or coincidence, i.e. the bursting of the dam. The Reichsgericht held that the storage on the ground floor was wrongful, since there was a danger of humidity at ground level, but that the loss was not caused by the wrong.[30] The reason given was metaphorically expressed; the damage did not 'lie in the direction' of the obligation and the causal relation was 'broken' by an event amounting to *force majeure*. The decision, though supposed to be an application of the adequacy theory, appears easier to reconcile with common-sense causal principles than with the adequacy theory.

We have already set out the facts of a famous decision of the German courts in the case of the Cuxhaven lighters.[31] Here the court concluded that the delay of one day in the towing significantly increased the risk of damage to the ships. The case resembles the *Monarch*[32] case in English law, where it was held, though not in very clear language, that the outbreak of war and consequent diversion of the plaintiff's ship were not factors which negatived causal connection between the wrongful delay caused by the defendants and the expenses incurred because of the ship's diversion. The *Monarch* can be justified on common-sense principles since the outbreak of war was much more likely when the ship arrived than when she should have arrived; and the Cuxhaven case could, perhaps, also be justified on the ground that the storm was much more likely on the 29th of October than on the 28th. On these facts the increase in the risk of the ultimate harm, which makes the condition adequate, and the increase in the likelihood of the intervening event, which is required for responsibility in common law systems, concur.

In other cases the wrongful act may not significantly increase the risk of harm but the harm may nevertheless occur without the intervention of an act of God or coincidence. Thus to give a man a slight scratch on the finger may not significantly increase the risk of death but nevertheless the finger might become infected; amputation

---

[29] Antolisèi, op. cit., p. 197 n. 1. Köstlin, op. cit., p. 461. Above, pp. 164–7.
[30] *RGZ* 42 (1898), 291.
[31] *RGZ* 81 (1913), 359. Above, pp. 478–9.
[32] *Monarch S.S. Co. v. A/B Karlshamns Oljefabriker* [1949] AC 196. Above, p. 169.

might be necessary; the anaesthetist might be slightly careless and give the victim an overdose from which he died. It might be impossible to point to an intervening event which amounted to a coincidence and hence, from a common-sense point of view, the death might be treated as the consequence of the scratch although the scratch was not adequate for it. This is particularly likely when it is natural to describe the events in terms of a 'chain'—i.e. a series each connected to the preceeding event as necessary condition to consequence. Some may feel that common-sense principles lead to injustice here; but the elements of fault or *mens rea* are intended to remedy any possible injustice.

Maurach propounds a difficult case.[33] Suppose that A and B each independently and without the knowledge of the other put half a lethal dose of poison in C's glass; C drinks the contents and dies. By the theory of conditions both A and B have caused C's death; by the adequacy theory neither has, since half a lethal dose does not significantly increase the risk of death. From a common-sense point of view the problem is to decide whether for each actor the fact that the other places a similar dose in the glass is to be treated as an intervening coincidental event or a circumstance of the act. One answer might be that the person, whether A or B, who first put in poison has not caused C's death; since the act of the second was a coincidence negativing causal connection; but the doctrine that an abnormal condition of the person or thing affected existing at the time of the act does not negative causal connection might be extended to make the second actor liable.[34]

The difficulties of the adequacy theory in dealing with intervening coincidental events are also felt in dealing with unnatural or unreasonable reaction of animals or men. Thus, if A wounds B by a heavy blow and B is treated for his wound by a doctor in a way contrary to the most elementary rules of medicine, so that B dies, A's act is by the strict adequacy theory the cause of B's death; but the Reichsgericht made an exception to this when the doctor 'contrary to all medical rules and experience is guilty of a gross failure to take into account the elementary requirements of reasonable and reliable medical procedure';[35] in this case the further harm is not adequately caused by the original injury.[36] This illustrates the Protean character

33 Op. cit., p. 162 (*b*).
34 This solution may be criticized and defended on the grounds explained above at pp. 179–80.
35 *RGZ* 102, 230. The case concerned an action against a doctor for the injury done to the patient when, through his failure to make a proper diagnosis, the patient went to hospital where he received further unskilful, but not outrageously unskilful, treatment. Recovery was allowed for the harm consequent upon the hospital mistreatment. Cf. *BGHZ* 3 (1951), 261, 268. Von Caemmerer, op. cit., p. 18.
36 German courts have applied the same principle to the mistakes of professional lawyers. *RGZ* 140 (1933), 1, 9.

of the adequacy theory, for this result can only be reached by defining the harm as 'injury caused by gross medical mistakes'. Even so, it does not follow that, because such gross mistakes are happily rare, defendant's act did not appreciably increase the chances that one would occur. The increase in the risk may be great though the resultant probability is small; there is a standing danger of confusion, in the adequacy theory, between the notion of a substantial increase of the risk and that of increasing the risk to a substantial one. In any case it appears that the adequacy theory is once again surreptitiously borrowing from common-sense causal principles.

Voluntary interventions may also be a source of difficulty for the adequacy theory. In one case[37] the security police wrongfully arrested deceased and while he was being transported under arrest he was, it seems, deliberately shot by a member of the force. It was argued that the defendant, who procured the arrest, was vicariously responsible for the act of arrest but not for the shooting. Hence plaintiff, widow of the deceased, argued that the shooting was the consequence of the arrest. The court rejected this argument, stating the adequacy theory in the form that conduct is only the adequate cause of an event if it has a tendency in the light of experience to bring about a consequence of the kind in question.[38] It decided that the arrest was not the adequate cause of the shooting; only the conduct of the security officers who shot deceased could be considered its cause.[39] This last observation is from a common-sense point of view correct but can hardly be derived from the adequacy theory. It is arguable that the arrest of someone during a time of civil disturbance does significantly increase the risk of his being shot, for example, while he or others are resisting arrest or while attempts at rescue are made; so that on the adequacy theory the decision should have been otherwise. If it is answered that arrest does not increase appreciably the risk of voluntary shooting, this, whether true or not, depends once more on the incorporation into the description of the consequence of a feature which is relevant to common-sense causal judgments.[40]

There is much the same divergence between the adequacy theory and common-sense principles in the case of voluntary interventions

---

[37] *RGZ* 106 (1922), 14. Cf. *JW* 1912, 459: *RGZ* 50 (1902), 219 (rescue not voluntary because done under legal or moral duty).

[38] *RGZ* 106 (1922), 15.

[39] A French court decided that when defendant was responsible for *X*'s death he was liable to *X*'s heirs for damage to *X*'s business consequent upon their having quarrelled after his death. Req. 18. 12. 1933. Gaz. Pal. 1934. 1. 395. This seems a harsh decision.

[40] The decision in *RGZ* 135 (1932), 144, 154, holding defendant vicariously liable for the negligence of an employee in failing to guard a car, so that an unlicensed mechanic drove it away and injured the plaintiff, turns on the existence of a duty to guard against the voluntary act of the mechanic.

as for coincidences. The consequence may be of the same general
kind of which the wrongful act increased the risk, yet may come
about through a voluntary intervention. Thus accused may give the
victim a heavy blow and leave him at the side of the road where a
passing stranger murders him. On the other hand the wrongful act
may not significantly increase the risk of the consequence, which
may nevertheless occur through the concurrence of non-voluntary
acts of others. Thus, the accused may give the victim a light blow
which, owing to the victim's susceptibility, knocks him out so that
he lies in the road where he is accidentally run over by a passing car,
and killed. Here the death is the consequence of the light blow on
common-sense principles[41] but not on the adequacy theory.

(vii) *Relation of adequacy to the 'normal course of events'*. It remains to note that the courts which apply the adequacy theory for
the most part shift freely from asserting that causal connection exists
because the act significantly increased the risk of the harm to asserting that it exists because the harm occurred in the normal course
of events and in accordance with human experience.[42] In cases of
pre-existing susceptibility of the victim the test of increased risk is
more likely to lead to responsibility being affirmed than that of the
normal course of events. Thus it has been held that when a horse hit
a man on the head and he suffered damage to his health the previous
morbid nervous predisposition did not affect causal connection.[43] A
similar result was reached when a man suffering from heart disease
was unexpectedly killed through rough handling by a police officer.[44]
The notion of increased risk is also used to explain why recovery
is often allowed for neurosis following bodily injury to the plaintiff,[45]
or a child of the plaintiff.[46] On the other hand when the court
wished to deny recovery to the owner of a mink farm for his loss
when, owing to the noise of the defendant's aircraft, the mother
mink killed their young, it gave as a reason that under normal
circumstances harm of this sort does not follow such noise and
vibration,[47] thus making use not of the notion of increased risk but
of that of the normal course of events and using a narrow description
of the consequences.

In this way the courts preserve a certain flexibility of approach
and are able to achieve results which on the whole are acceptable to

[41] Cf. *People* v. *Fowler* (1918) 178 Cal. 657, 174 Pac. 892.
[42] e.g. *RGZ* 69 (1908), 57, 59.
[43] *JW* 1906, 739, no. 7 (*RGZ*).
[44] *RGZ* 91, 347; Cf. *RGZ* 75, 19 (nervous disorder aggravated by legal proceedings—recovery allowed).
[45] *RGZ* 159, 257.
[46] *RGZ* 133, 272.
[47] *RGZ* 158, 38. A similar decision was reached in *Madsen* v. *East Jordan Irrigation
Co.* (1942) 101 Utah 552, 125 Pac. 2d 794 on the ground that the reaction of the
mother mink was unforeseeable: cf. *Nova Mink* v. *T.C.A.* [1951] 2 DLR 241.

common sense by applying at times the notion of increased risk, at others that of normality. But this proves only that the adequacy theory is tolerable provided it is supplemented by common-sense tests of causal connection and by the notion of the scope of the legal rule (*Normbereich*) whenever it would otherwise give inconvenient results.

III. LIMITATION OF RESPONSIBILITY BY REFERENCE TO COMMON-SENSE CAUSAL PRINCIPLES

In the nineteenth century, Köstlin[48] was one of the few writers who stressed the importance in the law of a characterization of those factors which negative causal connection. However, several writers and courts have attributed some importance to the breaking[49] or interruption[50] of causal connection or to the intervention of a new causal sequence.[51] Thus Ferrer[52] sums up the decisions of the Spanish supreme court in criminal cases as follows: 'This investigation leads us to the result that the objective nexus of production is negatived only when there has intervened later the wilful or gravely culpable act of a third person or the intentional or grossly negligent act of the victim.' On the other hand the Spanish courts hold that the pre-existing susceptibility of the victim does not negative causal connection,[53] as when he has suffered previous injuries.[54] The negativing factors are called 'extraneous accidents'[55] and one may assume that they would include acts of God and coincidences though there do not seem to be any clear criminal law decisions on this point. In much more metaphorical language, the Spanish supreme court in civil cases has recommended to inferior tribunals in solving causal problems to attend to the purpose of the rule of law in question and continued: 'or even, what is less difficult, it will be sufficient for the court to direct its course of action towards the evaluation of those conditions or circumstances which common sense in each case may mark as indicative of responsibility, within the infinite chain of causes and effects'.[56]

[48] Op. cit., p. 453.
[49] *Unterbrechung.*
[50] *Interruzione.*
[51] *Kausalreihe.*
[52] Op. cit., p. 363.
[53] Ferrer, op. cit., p. 354.
[54] Decision of 11.6.1934.
[55] *Accidentes extraños.*
[56] Decision of 25.1.1933. Romero and Jiménez, *Diccionario de Derecho Privado*, ii. 3425.

The Reichsgericht and several German writers[57] at one time appeared to take the view that a new 'causal sequence' negatives causal connection. The Reichsgericht did this in certain cases of procedural fraud[58] at a time when the court was not bound to accept the uncontradicted evidence of a party to civil proceedings. In several prosecutions for the giving of fraudulent evidence in civil proceedings resulting in damage to the victim, the Reichsgericht held that the acceptance by the court of the evidence was an independent causal sequence which interrupted causal connection between the fraud and the damage to the party who lost the action. Here of course the court was deceived by the false evidence, so that its acceptance of the evidence was not fully voluntary.[59] Later, the rules of procedure having been changed, the Reichsgericht decided differently in a similar case while repeating that the 'causal sequence' doctrine would apply to a case in which the judge decided not on the evidence but on other grounds. But then the false evidence would not be a necessary condition of the harm.

The argument about 'interrupting' causal connection has mainly centred about voluntary acts. We discussed in connection with the theory of conditions Frank's notion of *Regressverbot*,[60] that it is forbidden to inquire into the causes of a voluntary act and so to go behind a voluntary act in the search for a cause. Enneccerus is inconsistent in his attitude to the notion of 'breaking causal connection' by voluntary acts; for as a theory of causation, he condemns the notion,[61] yet he asserts that causal connection is 'broken' when the immediate cause of a consequence is the 'independent act of a man resting on his own free decision',[62] though he makes certain reservations which, however, only amount to a preference for a narrow sense of 'voluntary' such as we ourselves propose. How this is reconciled with the adequacy theory or the theory of conditions remains obscure. In one case defendant's predecessor fraudulently misrepresented the earnings of a firm during the previous year and induced plaintiff thereby to purchase a business jointly with *X*. *X* defrauded the plaintiff in the management of the business and fled abroad. An action to claim compensation for the damage suffered through *X*'s fraud failed, for though the fraudulent misrepresentation was a necessary condition of the loss the connection was held

---

[57] Nagler, op. cit., p. 19, no. 10. Maurach, op. cit., p. 165. These writers still adhere to this view but do not explain what a new causal sequence is, except that Nagler says that the main case is the independent decision of another person.

[58] *RGSt* 1, 227; 2, 91; 5, 321; etc.

[59] *RGSt* 67 (1934), 44.

[60] Above, p. 459.

[61] Op. cit., p. 64 n. 3.

[62] Op. cit., p. 67.

so 'remote' that it could not reasonably be taken into account.[63] No reference was made in the Reichsgericht to the voluntary character of the intervening act.

But, as we saw when discussing the trend of decisions by the Bundesgerichtshof,[64] it does pay attention to the grossly unreasonable or purely voluntary and self-interested character of intervening acts. These it regards as relieving the defendant of further responsibility. It seems, therefore, that, even if the language employed is unclear (the person who intervenes freely is 'master of the situation'; defendant's conduct is then 'completely meaningless' so far as the ultimate harm is concerned), causal principles are being applied. These are in effect the common-sense principles we have outlined which, long obscured by the ascendancy of the adequacy theory, now play their part, along with other techniques, in fixing the bounds of civil liability. Causal connection between conduct and harm, as traditionally understood, therefore remains a basic element in liability. 'It provides the framework of responsibility for one's actions.'[65]

---

[63] *RGZ* 78 (1912), 270: 'Ein so entfernter Zusammenhang'.

[64] Above, pp. 475-6.

[65] E. Deutsch, *Haftungsrecht*, 1 (1976), p. 135: 'Er gibt das Gerippe des Einstehens für eigenes Tun'.

LIST OF PRINCIPAL WORKS CITED

E. R. ALEXANDER, Note, (1972) 22 *U. Toro. LJ* 98.

AMERICAN LAW INSTITUTE, Model Penal Code. Proposed Official Draft, 1963.

—— *Restatement of the Law Second. Torts 2d*, 4 vols. and (Appendix) 5 vols. (St. Paul, Minn., 1965-79).

G. E. M. ANSCOMBE, *Intention* (Oxford, 1957).

F. ANTOLISÈI, *Il Rapporto di Causalità nel Diritto Penale* (Padua, 1934).

AQUARIUS (WATERMEYER CJ), 'Causation and Legal Responsibility', (1941) 58 *SALJ* 232; (1945) 62 *SALJ* 126.

ARISTOTLE, *Metaphysics*.

—— *Nicomachean Ethics*.

P. S. ATIYAH, *Accidents, Compensation and the Law* (3rd edn. London, 1980).

A. J. AYER, *Foundations of Empirical Knowledge* (London, 1940).

G. AZZALI, *Contributo alla Teoria della Causalità nel Diritto Penale* (Milan, 1954).

A. D. BASS and M. WRIGHT, 'An Objective Study of the Whiplash Victim and the Compensation Syndrome', (1964-5) 6 *Man. LJ* 333.

H. BATTIFOL, (1961). *Arch. Ph. Dr.* p. 253 (review).

J. H. BEALE, 'The Proximate Consequences of an Act', (1920) 33 *Harv. LR* 633.

T. L. BEAUCHAMP and A. ROSENBERG, *Hume and the Problem of Causation*. (New York, 1981).

A. C. BECHT and F. W. MILLER, *The Test of Factual Causation in Negligence and Strict Liability* (St. Louis, Miss., 1961).

D. C. BENNETT, (1961-2) 3 *Melb. ULR* 93 (review).

J. BENTHAM, *Theory of Fictions* (ed. C. K. Ogden, 1932).

G. BERBERT, 'Die Leerformel der Adäquanz', *AcP* 169 (1969), 421.

BERNER, *Lehrbuch des deutschen Strafrechts* (1898).

W. M. BEST, *Evidence* (12th edn. London, 1922).

T. BEVEN, *Negligence* (4th edn. London, 1928).

BINDING, *Normen* (1872).

BIRKMEYER, *Ursachenbegriff und Kausalzusammenhang im Strafrecht* (Rektoratsrede, Rostock, 1885).

P. Q. R. BOBERG, (1961) 78 *SALJ* 120 (review).

F. BOHLEN, Review of Harper, *Torts*, (1933-4) 47 *Harv. LR* 556.

—— *Studies in the Law of Torts* (Indianapolis, 1926).

J. BORGO, 'Causal Paradigms in Tort Law', (1979) 8 *J. Leg. Stud.* 419.

P. BOUZAT and J. PINATEL, *Traité de droit pénal et de criminologie* (2nd edn. Paris, 1970).

SPENCER BOWER, *Actionable Misrepresentation* (2nd edn. 1927).

R. B. BRAITHWAITE, *The Nature of Scientific Explanation* (Cambridge, 1953).

A. W. BRASIELLO, *Codice Civile, Libro delle Obbligazioni*. Vol. III: *Commentario, Dei fatti illeciti* (Florence, 1948).

M. S. BRODIN, 'The Standard of Causation in the Mixed-Motive Title VII Action: a Social Policy Perspective', (1982) *Col. LR* 292.

J. P. BROWN, 'Towards an Economic Theory of Liability', (1973) 2 *J. Leg. Stud.* 323.

G. CALABRESI, 'Concerning Cause and the Law of Torts', (1975) 43 *U. Ch. LR* 105.

CAMBRIDGE *Legal Essays* (Cambridge, 1926).

C. E. CARPENTER, 'Workable Rules for Determining Proximate Cause', (1932) 20 *Calif. LR* 229, 396, 471.

CHARMONT, *Les transformations du droit civil* (Paris, 1912).

R. D. CHILDRES, (1960-1) 32 *Miss. LR* 222 (review).

CHITTY on *Contract* (24th edn. London, 1977).

R. H. COASE, 'The Problem of Social Cost', (1960) 3 *J. Law Econ.* 1.

F. S. COHEN, 'Field Theory and Judicial Logic', (1950) 59 *Yale LJ* 238, 251-6.

R. H. COLE, 'Windfall and Probability: a Study of "Cause" in Negligence Law', (1964) 52 *Cal. LR* 459, 764.

R. G. COLLINGWOOD, *An Essay on Metaphysics* (1940).

R. COOKE, 'Remoteness of Damage and Judicial Discretion', (1978) *Cam. LJ* 288.

L. K. COOPERIDER, (1960) 58 *Mich. LR* 951 (review).

A. L. CORBIN, *Contracts* (St. Paul, 1950, 1963).

COURNOT, *Exposition de la théorie des chances et des probabilités* (1843).

J. H. COUTTS, (1960) 23 *MLR* 708 (review).

RUPERT CROSS, *Evidence* (5th edn. London, 1979).

D. DAVIDSON, 'Actions, Reasons and Causes', *J. Phil.* 60 (1963), 685.

M. DAVIES, 'The Road from Morocco: *Polemis* from *Donoghue* to No-Fault', (1982) 45 *MLR* 534.

DERNBURG, *Bürgerliches Recht* (1899).

E. DEUTSCH, 'Begrenzung der Haftung aus abstrakter Gefährdung wegen fehlender adäquater Kausalität', *JZ* 1966, 556.

—— 'Regressverbot und Unterbrechung des Haftungszusammenhangs im Zivilrecht', *JZ* 1972, 551.

—— *Haftungsrecht*, 1 (Cologne, 1976).

—— and CH. VON BAR, 'Schutzbereich und wesentliche Bedingung im Versicherungsrecht und Haftungsrecht', *MDR* (1979), 536.

J. C. DE WET, 'Estoppel by Representation' *in die Suid-Afrikaanse Reg* (Leiden, 1938).

—— 'Opmerkings oor die vraagstuk van veroorsaking', (1941) 5 *Tyd. Hed. Rom-Holl. Reg* 126.

—— and H. L. SWANEPOEL, *Strafreg* (Durban, 1949).

—— (1962) *Act. Jur. (SA)* 139 (review).

R. W. M. DIAS, 'Remoteness of Liability and Legal Policy', (1962) *Cam. LJ* 178.

—— 'Trouble on Oiled Waters', (1967) *Cam LJ* 62.

W. DRAY, *Laws and Explanation in History* (Oxford, 1957).

500   LIST OF PRINCIPAL WORKS CITED

T. A. EATON, 'Causation in Constitutional Torts', (1981–2) 67 *Iowa LR* 443.

H. W. EDGERTON, 'Legal Cause', (1924) 72 *U. Pa. LR* 211, 352.

J. LL. J. EDWARDS, *Mens Rea in Statutory Offences* (London, 1955).

A. A. EHRENZWEIG, *Negligence without Fault* (Berkeley, 1951).

LAURENCE H. ELDREDGE, *Modern Tort Problems* (Philadelphia, 1941).

K. ENGISCH, *Die Kausalität als Merkmal der strafrechtlichen Tatbestände* (1931).

L. ENGLARD, 'The System Builders: a Critical Appraisal of Modern Tort Theory', (1980) 9 *J. Leg. Stud.* 27.

L. ENNECCERUS-H. LEHMANN, *Lehrbuch des bürgerlichen Rechts* (15th edn. Tübingen, 1958). Vol. II: *Recht der Schuldverhältnisse*.

R. A. EPSTEIN, 'A Theory of Strict Liability', (1973) 2 *J. Leg. Stud.* 151.

—— 'Defenses and Subsequent Pleas in a Scheme of Strict Liability', (1974) 3 *J. Leg. Stud.* 165.

—— 'Intentional Harms', (1975) 4 *J. Leg. Stud.* 391.

—— 'Nuisance Law: Corrective Justice and its Utilitarian Constraints', (1979) 8 *J. Leg. Stud.* 49.

—— 'Causation and Corrective Justice: a Reply to Two Critics', (1979) 8 *J. Leg. Stud.* 477.

P. ESMEIN, *Cours de droit civil approfondi*.

J. ESSER and E. SCHMIDT, *Schuldrecht* (5th edn. 1976).

A. H. FERRER, *La relación de causalidad en la teoría del delito* (Madrid, 1948).

J. G. FLEMING, 'The Passing of Polemis', (1961) 39 *Can. BR* 489.

—— 'Collateral Benefits', *IECL* vol. xi (1971), chap. 11.

—— 'Comparative Negligence at Last', (1976) 64 *Cal. LR* 239.

—— *The Law of Torts* (5th edn. Sydney, 1977).

G. P. FLETCHER, 'Fairness and Utility in Tort Theory', (1972) 85 *Harv. LR* 537.

FOSTER, 'The Risk Theory and Proximate Cause', (1953) *Nebraska LR* 72.

M. A. FRANKLIN, 'Tort Liability for Hepatitis: an Analysis and Appraisal', (1972) 24 *Stan. LR* 439.

G. H. L. FRIDMAN and J. S. WILLIAMS, 'The Atomic Theory of Negligence', (1971) 45 *Aust. LJ* 117.

P. GARDINER, *The Nature of Historical Explanation*.

D. GASKING, 'Causation and Recipes', *Mind*, 94 (1955), 479.

GEYER, *Grundriß zu Vorlesungen über gemeines deutsches Strafrecht*.

GLASER, *Abhandlungen aus dem österreichischen Strafrechte* (1858).

A. L. GOODHART, *Essays in Jurisprudence and the Common Law* (Cambridge, 1931).

—— 'Liability and Compensation', (1960) 76 *LQR* 567.

—— 'Obituary: Re Polemis', (1961) 77 *LQR* 175.

S. GOROVITS, 'Causal Judgments and Causal Explanation', *J. Phil.* 62 (1965).

LEON GREEN, *Judge and Jury* (Kansas City, 1930).

—— *Rationale of Proximate Cause* (Kansas City, 1927).

—— 'The Causal Relation Issue in Negligence Law', (1961) 60 *Mich. LR* 543.

LEON GREEN, 'Foreseeability in Negligence Law', (1961) 61 *Col. LR* 1401.
—— 'Duties, Risks, Causation Doctrines', (1962) 41 *Tex. LR.*
—— '*The Wagon Mound No. 2*: Foreseeability Revised', (1967) *Utah LR* 197.
C. O. GREGORY, 'Proximate Cause in Negligence: a Retreat from Rationalisation', (1938) 6 *U. Ch. LR* 36.
F. GRISPIGNI, 'Il nesso causale nel diritto penale', *Riv. it. dir. pen.* 13 (1935), 3.
SIR M. HALE, *Pleas of the Crown* (London, 1736).
J. HALL, *Cases and Readings on Criminal Law and Procedure* (1st edn. Indianapolis, 1949).
—— *General Principles of Criminal Law* (Indianapolis, 1947).
HALSBURY'S *Laws of England* (4th edn. London, 1973–).
ROGER HANCOCK, (1960–1) 6 *Nat. LF* 143 (review).
A. HARARI, *The Place of Negligence in the Law of Torts* (Sydney, 1962).
F. V. HARPER and FLEMING JAMES, Jr., *The Law of Torts* (Boston, 1956).
H. L. A. HART, 'Varieties of Responsibility', (1967) 83 *LQR* 346.
—— and A. M. HONORÉ, 'Causation in the Law', (1956), 72 *LQR* 58, 260, 398.
HARTMANN, *Das Kausalproblem im Strafrecht* (1900).
HARVARD *Selected Essays on the Law of Torts* (Cambridge, Mass., 1942).
HELMER, *Über den Begriff der fahrlässigen Täterschaft* (1895).
J. A. HENDERSON, 'A Defense of the Use of the Hypothetical Case to Resolve the Causation Issue', (1968) 47 *Tex. LR* 183.
A. HESS, *Über Kausalzusammenhang und unkörperliche Denksubstrate* (1895).
T. Hobbes, *Elements of Philosophy* (London, 1656).
T. B. HOGAN, '*Cook v. Lewis* Re-examined', (1961) 24 *MLR* 331.
SIR W. HOLDSWORTH, *History of English Law* (London, 1903–56).
C. J. HOLLOWAY, *Language and Intelligence* (London, 1951).
A. M. (= TONY) HONORÉ, 'Die Kausalitätslehre im anglo-amerikanischen Recht im Vergleich zum deutschen Recht', *ZStrW* 69 (1957), 95.
—— 'The Right to be Careless at Others' Risk', (1961) 39 *Can. BR* 267.
—— Note on *Alston v. Marine Insurance*, (1964) 81 *SALJ* 410.
—— 'Causation and Remoteness of Damage', *IECL* vol. xi (1971), chap. 7.
U. HUBER, 'Normzwecktheorie und Adäquanztheorie', *JZ* 1969, 677.
D. HUME, *Inquiries concerning the Human Understanding* (Selby-Bigge edn. Oxford, 1946).
FLEMING JAMES and R. F. PERRY, 'Legal Cause', (1951) 60 *Yale LJ* 761.
HANS-HEINRICH JESCHECK, 'Anstiftung, Gehilfenschaft und Mittäterschaft', *SchwZSt* 71 (1956), 225.
L. JIMÉNEZ DE ASÚA, *Tratado de Derecho Penal* (Buenos Aires, 1950).
A. JOLY, 'Vers un critère juridique du rapport de causalité au sens de l'article 1384 alinéa 1er du code civil', *Rev. trim. dr. civ.* (1942), 257.
H. W. B. JOSEPH, *An Introduction to Logic* (2nd edn. Oxford, 1916).
S. H. KADISH and M. G. PAULSEN, *Criminal Law and its Process: Cases and Materials* (3rd edn. 1975).

I. KANT, *Grundlegung zur Metaphysik der Sitten* (Leipzig, 1838).
—— *Prolegomena zu einer jeden künftigen Metaphysik* (Leipzig, 1838).
R. E. KEETON, *Legal Cause in the Law of Torts* (Columbus, Ohio, 1963).
P. J. KELLEY, 'Causation and Justice: a Comment', (1978) *Wash. ULQ* 635.
H. KELSEN, *Vergeltung und Kausalität* (The Hague, 1941).
C. S. KENNY, *Outlines of Criminal Law* (19th edn. by J. W. C. Turner, Cambridge, 1966).
J. H. KING, 'Causation, Valuation and Chance in Personal Injury Torts Involving Pre-existing Conditions and Future Consequences', (1981) 90 *Yale LJ* 1353.
H. C. KLEMME, 'The Enterprise Liability Theory of Torts', (1976) 47 *U. Colo. LR* 153.
W. C. KNEALE, *Probability and Induction* (Oxford, 1949).
KÖSTLIN, *Neue Revision der Grundbegriffe des Kriminalrechts* (1843).
H.-J. KRAEMER, 'Die Kausalität im öffentlichen Recht', *NJW* 1965, 182.
E. A. KRAMER, 'Schutzgesetze und adäquate Kausalität', *JZ* 1976, 338.
KRÜCKMANN, 'Verschuldensaufrechnung, Gefährdungsaufrechnung, und Deliktfähigkeit', *Jherings Jahrbuch*, 55, 25.
K. KURTZ-ECKHARDT, *Causa proxima und wesentliche Bedingung* (Bamberg, 1977).
LABATT, 'Rationale of Causation in Actions of Tort', (1897) 33 *Can LJ* 507.
O. LAHTINEN, (1963) 49 *ARSP* 368 (review).
H. LALOU, *Traité pratique de la responsabilité civile* (14th edn. Paris, 1949).
W. A. LANDES and R. A. POSNER, 'Joint and Multiple Tortfeasors: an Economic Analysis', (1980) 9 *J. Leg. Stud.* 517.
HEINRICH LANGE, 'Herrschaft und Verfall der Lehre vom adäquaten Kausalzusammenhang', *AcP* 156 (1957), 114.
—— 'Herrschaft und Verfall der Lehre vom adäquaten Kausalzusammenhang. Versuch einer Ehrenrettung', *Festgabe K. Oftinger* (1969), 321.
HERMANN LANGE, 'Zum Problem der überholenden Kausalität, *AcP* 152 (1952), 153.
—— 'Adäquanztheorie, Rechtswidrigkeit, Schutzzwecklehre und selbständige Zurechnungsmomente', *JZ* 1976, 198.
A. V. LANSDOWN, 'Causation in Homicide', (1960) 77 *SALJ* 427.
—— 'Again Causation in Homicide', (1962) 79 *SALJ* 137.
K. LARENZ, 'Präventionsprinzip und Ausgleichsprinzip im Schadenersatzrecht', *NJW* 1959, 865.
F. H. LAWSON, *Negligence in the Civil Law* (Oxford, 1950).
R. H. LEFLAR, (1961) 75 *Harv. LR* 1691 (review of Becht and Miller, above).
H. LEGROS, *L'Élément moral dans les infractions* (Paris, 1954).
LEIPZIGER *Kommentar zum Strafgesetzbuch* (1954).
J. LEKSCHAS, *Die Kausalität bei der verbrecherischen Handlung* (1952).
LEONHARD, *Die Kausalität als Erklärung durch Ergänzung* (1946).
A. LEVITT, 'Cause, Legal Cause and Proximate Cause', (1922) 21 *Mich. LR* 34.
LEXIS, *Zur Theorie der Massenerscheinungen in der menschlichen Gesellschaft* (1877).

LIEPMANN, *Einleitung in das Strafrecht* (1900).

—— 'Zur Lehre von der adäquaten Verursachung', *Goltdammers Archiv*, 52, 326.

A. M. LINDEN, 'Down with Foreseeability', (1969) 47 *Can. BR* 545.

F. LINDENMAIER, 'Adäquate Ursache und nächste Ursache', *ZgesHR* 113 (1950), 207.

L. E. Loeb, 'Causal Theories and Causal Overdetermination', *J. Phil.* 71 (1974), 525.

H. LUNTZ, D. HAMBLY, and R. HAYES, *Torts: Cases and Commentary* (Sydney, 1980).

C. T. MCCORMICK, *Handbook on the Law of Damages* (St. Paul, 1935).

R. G. MCELROY, *Impossibility of Performance*, ed. Glanville Williams (Cambridge, 1941).

H. MCGREGOR, 'Variations on an Enigma: Successive Causes of Personal Injury', (1970) 33 *MLR* 378.

—— *The Law of Damages* (London, 1980).

J. C. MACINTOSH and C. NORMAN-SCOBLE, *Negligence in Delict* (3rd edn. Cape Town, 1948).

J. MACKIE, *The Cement of the Universe* (Oxford, 1974).

J. A. MCLAUGHLIN, 'Proximate Cause', (1925-6) 39 *Harv. LR* 149.

W. S. MALONE, 'Ruminations on Cause-in-fact', (1956-7) 9 *Stan. LR* 60.

—— 'Ruminations on *Dixie Drive It Yourself* v. *American Beverage*', (1969-70) 30 *La. LR* 363.

J. H. MANSFIELD, 'Hart and Honoré: Causation in the Law', (1963-4) 17 *Vanderbilt LR* 487.

G. MARTY, 'La Relation de cause à effet comme condition de la responsabilité civile', *Rev. trim. dr. civ.* (1939), 685.

D. L. MATHIESON, 'The Detonator Case', (1961) *NZLR* 261.

R. MAURACH, *Deutsches Strafrecht* (4th edn. 1971).

H. MAYER, *Strafrecht*. Allgemeiner Teil (1953).

H. and L. MAZEAUD and A. TUNC, *Traité théorique et pratique de la responsabilité civile*, i (6th edn. Paris, 1965), ii, iii (5th edn. Paris, 1958).

A. MERKEL, *Lehrbuch des deutschen Strafrechts* (1899).

J. G. MERRILLS, 'Policy and Remoteness', (1973-4) 6 *Ottawa LR* 18.

M. MEYERS, 'Problems in the Application of Duty-Risk Analysis to Jury Trials in Louisiana', (1979) 39 *La. LR* 1079.

E. MEZGER-BLEI, *Strafrecht* (14th edn. 1970).

J. MICHAEL and H. WECHSLER, *Criminal Law and its Administration*.

J. S. MILL, *A System of Logic Ratiocinative and Inductive* (8th edn. London, 1886).

M. A. MILLNER, '*Novus actus interveniens*: the Present Effect of *The Wagon Mound*', (1971) 22 *NILQ* 168.

J. MOORMAN, *Verhandelingen over de Misdaden* (Arnhem, 1764).

CLARENCE MORRIS, *Studies in Torts* (1952).

—— *Torts* (Brooklyn, 1953).

—— 'Duty, Negligence and Causation', (1952) 101 *U. Pa. LR* 189.

—— 'On the Teaching of Legal Cause', (1939) 39 *Col. LR* 1087.

—— 'Proximate Cause in Minnesota', (1950) 34 *Minn. LR* 186.

M. L. MÜLLER, *Die Bedeutung des Kausalzusammenhangs im Straf- und Schadenersatzrecht* (1912).

R. NEUNER, 'Interesse und Vermögenschaden', *AcP* 133 (1932), 277.

J. NGUYEN THANK NHA, 'L'Influence des prédispositions de la victime sur l'obligation à réparation du défendeur à l'action en responsabilité', *Rev. trim. dr. civ.* 74 (1976), 1.

H. NIEDERLÄNDER, 'Schadenersatz bei hypothetischen Schadensereignissen', *AcP* 153 (1954), 41.

G. D. NOKES, (1960) 9 *ICLQ* 353 (review).

P. NOWELL SMITH, 'Are Historical Events Unique?' *Proc. Aristot. Soc.* 57 (1957), 107.

D. PAYNE, 'Reduction of Damages for Contributory Negligence', (1955) 18 *MLR* 344.

A. PECZENIK, *Causes and Damages* (Lund, 1979).

W. H. PEDRICK, (1964) 58 *NWULR* 853 (review).

—— 'Causation, the "Who Done It" Issue and Arno Becht', (1978) *Wash. ULQ* 645.

R. M. PERKINS, *Criminal Law* (2nd edn. Mineola, NY1969).

J. J. PHILLIPS, 'Reflections on Factual Causation', (1978) *Wash. ULQ* 661.

S. L. PHIPSON, *Evidence* (12th edn. London, 1976).

E. PICARD, 'Patients, Doctors and the Supreme Court of Canada', (1981) *Oxf. JLS* 441.

PLANIOL-RIPERT-ESMEIN, *Traité pratique de droit civil français* (1952).

SIR F. POLLOCK, 'Liability for Consequences', (1922) 38 *LQR* 165.

LORD PORTER, 'The Measure of Damages in Contract and Tort', (1935) 5 *Cam. LJ* 176.

R. A. POSNER, 'A Theory of Negligence', (1972) 1 *J. Leg. Stud.* 29.

—— 'Strict Liability', (1973) 2 *J. Leg. Stud.* 215.

—— 'Epstein's Tort Theory: a Critique', (1979) 8 *J. Leg. Stud.* 457.

—— 'The Concept of Corrective Justice in Recent Theories of Tort Law', (1981) 10 *J. Leg. Stud.* 187.

POTHIER, *Traité des obligations* (10th edn. Paris, 1861).

W. L. PROSSER, 'Palsgraf Revisited', (1953–4) 52 *Mich. LR* 1.

—— *Selected Topics on the Law of Torts* (Ann Arbor, Mich., 1953).

—— *Handbook of the Law of Torts* (4th edn. St. Paul, Minn., 1971).

—— J. W. WADE, and V. E. SCHWARTZ, *Cases and Materials on Torts* (6th edn. Mineola, NY, 1976).

E. RABEL, 'Die Grundzüge des Rechts der unerlaubten Handlungen', *Deutsche Ref. Int. Kong. Rechtsvergl. 1932.*

RADBRUCH, *Die Lehre von der adäquaten Verursachung* (Berlin, 1902).

RAMASWAMY IYER, *Torts* (5th edn. Calcutta, 1957).

S. RANIERI, *La causalità nel diritto penale* (1936).

S. RAUHAUSER, 'The Duty-Risk Experience in Louisiana Tort Law', (1977) 23 *Loyola LR* 523.

M. J. RIZZO, 'A Theory of Economic Loss in the Law of Tort', (1982) 11 *J. Leg. Stud.* 281.

—— and F. S. ARNOLD, 'Causal Apportionment in the Law of Torts: an Economic Theory', (1980) 80 *Col. LR* 1399.

H. Roscoe, *Criminal Evidence* (16th edn. London, 1952).

W. Rother, 'Adäquanztheorie und Schadenverursachung durch mehrere', *NJW* 1965, 177.

P. J. Rowe, 'Demise of the Thin Skull Rule', (1977) 40 *MLR* 377.

Rümelin, 'Die Verwendung der Causalbegriffe im Straf- und Civilrecht', *Acp* 90, 171.

—— *Der Zufall im Recht* (1896).

Sir W. D. Russell, *Crime* (10th edn. London, 1950).

Sir J. Salmond and R. F. V. Heuston, *The Law of Torts* (18th edn. by R. F. V. Heuston and R. S. Chambers, London, 1981).

Y. Schachar, 'Causation, Mens Rea and Negligence in Homicide Offences', (1977) 3 *Tel Aviv St. L. L.* 84.

E. Schickedanz, Schutzzwecklehre und Adäquanzlehre', *NJW* 1971, 916.

W. Seavey, 'Mr. Justice Cardozo and the Law of Torts', (1938-9) 52 *Harv. LR* 372.

—— 'Principles of Torts', (1942-3) 56 *Harv. LR* 72.

—— P. Keeton, and R. E. Keeton, *Cases on Torts* (St. Paul, 1957).

Shavell, 'An Analysis of Causation and the Scope of Liability in the Law of Torts', (1980) 9 *J. Leg. Stud.* 463.

Shearman and Redfield, *The Law of Negligence* (1898).

M. Siniscalco, *Riv. it. dir. proc. pen.* 3 (1962), 501 (review).

Jeremiah Smith, 'Legal Cause in Actions of Tort', (1911) 25 *Harv. LR* 103, 223, 303.

John C. Smith and B. Hogan, *Criminal Law* (4th edn. London, 1978).

Joseph C. Smith, 'The Limits of Tort Liability in Canada: Remoteness, Foreseeability and Proximate Cause', in A. M. Linden (ed.), *Studies in Canadian Tort Law* (1968), 88.

Young B. Smith and William L. Prosser, *Cases and Materials on Torts* (Brooklyn, NY, 1952).

Sir J. F. Stephen, *Digest of the Criminal Law* (9th edn. London, 1950).

H. Stoll, *RabelsZ* 27 (1962-3), 553 (review).

—— *Kausalzusammenhang und Normzweck im Deliktrecht* (Tübingen, 1968).

D. M. A. Strachan, 'The Scope and Application of the 'But For' Causal Test', (1970) 33 *MLR* 386.

Harry Street, *The Law of Torts* (6th edn. London, 1976).

T. A. Street, *Foundations of Legal Liability* (Northport, NY, 1906).

Stübel, *Über den Tatbestand der Verbrechen, die Urheber derselben, usw.* (1803).

G. C. T. 'Causal Relation between Defendant's Unlawful Act and the Death', (1932-3) 31 *Mich. LR* 659.

H. Tarnowski, *Die systematische Bedeutung der adäquaten Kausalitäts-theorie für den Aufbau des Verbrechensbegriffs* (Leipzig, 1927).

E. W. Thode, 'The Indefensible Use of the Hypothetical Case to Determine Cause in Fact', (1968) 46 *Tex. LR* 423, 47 *Tex. LR* 1344.

—— 'Tort Analysis: Duty-Risk v.Proximate Cause', (1977) *Utah LR* 1.

Traeger, *Der Kausalbegriff im Straf- und Zivilrecht* (1904).

Trendelenburg, *Logische Untersuchungen* (3rd edn.).

506   LIST OF PRINCIPAL WORKS CITED

A. TUNC, Note on Paris 18.4.1955, *Dalloz A.* 1956.2, 354.

J. W. CECIL TURNER, *Kenny's Outlines of Criminal Law* (16th edn. Cambridge, 1952).

—— and A. Ll. Armitage *Cases on Criminal Law* (Cambridge, 1953).

M. VANQUICKENBORNE, *De Oorzakelijkheid in het Recht van de Burgerlijke Aansprakelijkheid* (Gent, 1971).

L. VON BAR, *Die Lehre vom Kausalzusammenhange im Rechte, besonders im Strafrechte* (1871).

VON BURI, *Abhandlungen* (1862).

—— *Die Kausalität* (1873).

—— *Die Kausalität und ihre strafrechtlichen Beziehungen* (1885).

—— *Teilname und Begünstigung* (1860).

E. VON CAEMMERER, *Das Problem des Kausalzusammenhangs im Privatrecht* (Freiburg im Br., 1956).

—— *Das Problem der überholenden Kausalität im Schadenersatzrecht* (Karlsruhe, 1962).

J. VON KRIES, *Über den Begriff der objektiven Möglichkeit und einiger Anwendungen desselben* (1888).

—— *Über die Begriffe der Wahrscheinlichkeit und Möglichkeit und ihre Bedeutung im Strafrechte* (1889).

—— *Die Prinzipien der Wahrscheinlichkeitsrechnung* (1886).

VON LISZT-SCHMIDT, *Lehrbuch des deutschen Strafrechts* (26th edn. 1932).

J. W. WADE, W. K. CRAWFORD, and J. L. RYDER, 'Comparative Fault in Tennessee Tort Actions: Past, Present and Future', (1975) 41 *Tenn. LR* 423.

U. WAGNER, 'Successive Causes and the Quantum of Damages in Personal Injury Cases', (1972) 10 *Osgoode Hall LJ* 369.

WAITE, *Cases on Criminal Law and Procedure* (Chicago, 1937).

G. J. WARNOCK, 'Every Event has a Cause', *Logic and Language*, Series II, pp. 95, 103–4.

H. WECHSLER and J. MICHAEL, 'A Rationale of the Law of Homicide', (1937) 37 *Col. LR* 701, 1261.

E. J. WEINRIB, 'A Step Forward in Factual Causation', (1975) 38 *MLR* 518.

F. WHARTON, *Criminal Law* (12th edn. Rochester, NY, 1932).

MORTON WHITE, (1960) 60 *Col. LR* 1058 (review).

J. H. WIGMORE, *Treatise on Evidence* (3rd edn. Boston, 1940).

D. B. WILLIAMS, 'Compensationitis: Real v. Imaginary', (1977) 127 *New LJ* 757.

GLANVILLE WILLIAMS, 'Causation in Homicide', (1957) *Crim. LR* 429, 510.

—— 'The Two Negligent Servants', (1954) 17 *Mod. LR* 66.

—— *Joint Torts and Contributory Negligence* (London, 1951).

—— *The Sanctity of Life and the Criminal Law* (London, 1958).

—— 'Causation in the Law', (1961) *Cam. LJ* 62.

—— 'The risk principle', (1961) 77 *LQR* 179.

B. WINDSCHEID, *Lehrbuch des Pandektenrechts* (9th edn. Frankfurt am Main, 1906).

SIR PERCY H. WINFIELD, *A Textbook of The Law of Tort* (6th edn. by T. Ellis Lewis, London, 1954).

H. WITTMAN, 'Die Berufung auf rechtmässiges Alternativverhalten', *NJW* 1971, 549.

J. G. WOLF, *Der Normzweck im Deliktrecht* (Göttingen, 1962).

C. A. WRIGHT and M. LINDEN, *Canadian Tort Law* (7th edn. Toronto, 1980).

LORD WRIGHT, 'Notes on Causation and Responsibility in English Law', (1955) *Cam. LJ* 163.

A. ZEUNER, 'Zum Problem der überholenden Kausalität', *AcP* 157 (1958-9), 441.

INDEX

Metaphors, 1, 14–15, 30, 73–4, 97, 442, 482, 495
Metaphysics, 439
Michael, J., 395 n., 396 n.
Mill, J. S., 12–25, 29–34, 39, 44–51, 60, 62, 69, 111–12, 406–7, 444
Miller J., 338
Minimalism, xxxiv–xxxv, lxvii–lxxiii
Mink, 494
Misdemeanour-manslaughter doctrine, 391, 393
Misrepresentation, 192–4, 338–40
Mistake, 149–51, 184–5, 353–7
Mitigation of damages, 230, 313, 359–60
Moorman, J., 244
Moral blame, 62–83, 232–4, 291–2, 299–304, 328
'Moral causation', 301–2
Moral obligation, 147–8, 217, 335
— responsibility, lxxviii–lxxix
Morris, Clarence, 94 n., 98 n., 107 n., 108 n., 256–7, 299 n.
Morris LJ, 189 n., 415 n.
Mortal wound, 241–2, 352–3, 356–7, 400, 437, 460–1
Müller, M. L., 451, 453
Multiple causation, 19, 87, 122–8, 135; see also Additional causes; Concurrent causes
Murrah CJ, 282 n.
Myers CJ, 327, 346

Nagler, J., 442, 446 n., 496 n.
'Natural and probable' consequences, 358
'Natural and probable result', 192
Natural consequences, 146, 148, 280 n.
— reactions, 148, 183–4, 327, 330, 333
'Natural result', 335, 338
'Naturally arising', 317
— resulting', 87 n.
Nature of animal, 181–2
'Necessary', meanings of, 112–13
Necessary act, 330
— condition, see Sine qua non
Necessity theory, 436–8
Negative conditions, 2–3, 30, 37–8, 50–1, 139–41
Negligence, 64, 118 n., 152–3, 182–5, 194–203, 259–90, 325, 335–6, 352–62, 374, 395 n., 444, 459–60; see also Contributory negligence
Nervous disposition, 173–4, 274 n.
— shock, 269, 404

Neurosis, 178
Neutralizing causes, 124, 206–7, 239–45
'Nomological considerations', 482, 488–9
Non-voluntary acts, 142–62, 177–8, 191, 310–11, 329–38, 364–6, 400
Normal conditions, 31, 33–41, 62, 466
'Normal course of events', 466, 470
'Normal response', 278
Normative judgments, 473
Normzweck, 1, 103, 476–7
Not causing others to act, 373–4
Not preventing the acts of others, 140, 449, 460
Not providing opportunities, 3, 311–12, 316–21
Not providing reasons, 3
Nova causa interveniens, 134 n.
Novus actus interveniens, xlv, 5, 73, 134 n.
Nowell Smith, P., 9 n.
Nuisance, 229, 231

Objective probability, 467–70, 484
Obligations, 147–8, 217, 334–5
Occasioning harm, xlv–xlvii, 26, 186, 194–204, 276, 374–6
Omissions, 2–3, 30, 37–8, 50–1, 59, 127–8, 139–41, 370–1, 407, 411–18, 447–9
'Ontological considerations', 482, 490
Operation, 158–9, 173, 184
'Operative' cause, 73, 97
Opportunities, 2, 43, 59–61, 80–2, 126, 158–9, 194–200, 312, 383, 385
Opportunity, last, 219–25
Ordering others to act, 51, 364, 371–3
Ordinary language, 1–3, 26–59, 432–3, 463
Ortmann, 441
Outlaw, 211
Overdetermination, xxxix–xlii, 122–5, 235–49, 402–3, 455–6
Overtaking cause, 179–81, 237, 245–9, 455–6
'Owing to', 87

Pain and suffering, 226, 244, 251
Panic, 148–9, 177, 336
Paradigms, lxxiv–lxxvi
Parke B., 213
Paul, 251
Pensions, 161
Perjury, 160, 404–5